2/22/12
#85.00

ARCHITECTURAL LIGHTING DESIGN
THIRD EDITION

GARY STEFFY, LC, FIALD, IES, Hon. Aff. AIAMI

JOHN WILEY & SONS, INC.

Cover

The images on the cover illustrate the essence of lighting—choreographing patterns of light and dark on surfaces and objects to make environments eminently livable and workable. Fom left to right: Chapel of the Word, Marywood Health Center, Grand Rapids, Michigan, ©Gene Meadows; JW Marriott, Grand Rapids, Michigan, ©Kevin Beswick; Cathedral of the Most Holy Blessed Sacrament in Detroit, Michigan, ©Gene Meadows; and JW Marriott, Grand Rapids, Michigan, ©Kevin Beswick. Back cover top three images ©Kevin Beswick and bottom image ©Gene Meadows.

Chapter Banner Thumbnails

The images in the chapter banners are credited on pages iv and v (the acronym GSLD is Gary Steffy Lighting Design).

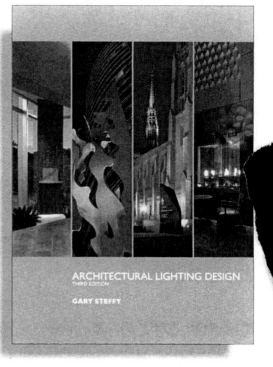

Limit of Liability/Disclaimer of Warranty

While the publisher and the author have used their best efforts in preparing this book, they make no representations or warranties with respect to the accuracy or completeness of the contents of this book and specifically disclaim any implied warranties of merchantability or fitness for a particular purpose. No warranty may be created or extended by sales representatives or written sales materials. The advice and strategies contained herein may not be suitable for your situation. You should consult with a professional where appropriate. Neither the publisher nor the author shall be liable for any loss of profit or any other commercial damages, including but not limited to special, incidental, consequential, or other damages.

For general information about our other products and services, please contact our Customer Care Department within the United States at (800) 762-2974, outside the United States at (317) 572-3993 or fax (317) 572-4002.

Wiley also publishes its books in a variety of electronic formats. Some content that appears in print may not be available in electronic books. For more information about Wiley products, visit our web site at www.wiley.com.

Copyrights and Trademarks

It is acknowledged by the author and publisher that all service marks, trademarks, and copyrighted images/graphics appear in this book for editorial purposes only and to the benefit of the service mark, trademark, or copyright owner, with no intention of infringing on that service mark, trademark, or copyright. Nothing in this book should be construed to imply that respective service mark, trademark, or copyright holder endorses or sponsors this book or any of its contents.

This book was set in GillSans Light by Gary Steffy. This book is printed on acid-free paper. ∞

Library of Congress Cataloging-in-Publication Data

Steffy, Gary R.
    Architectural lighting design / Gary R. Steffy. —3rd ed.
        p. cm.
    Includes bibliographical references and index.
    ISBN 978-0-470-11249-6 (cloth)
    1. Lighting, Architectural and decorative. I. Title

TH7703 .S78 2008
621.32—dc22   2008007355

Printed in the United States of America
10 9 8 7 6 5 4 3

Contents

Contents

Preface

©Kevin Beswick

This third edition could have been a mash-up of lighting techniques, technologies, energy efficiencies and standards, and sustainability. After all, it seems that's how it has been for the last half decade as constituencies make and stake claims on our environment with score sheets and carbon tallies and, in some instances, unintentionally trampling the everyday space-users' rights. Instead, ALD/3e takes lighting to the next level. With an uncompromised, indeed expanded outline of lighting design aspects to be addressed if our built settings are to wring the most out of their very existence. The kinds of light sources (electric and daylight), strategies, luminaires, and techniques to achieve those design aspects while minimizing the havoc on Earth's environment are clearly presented.

The breadth, depth, and timeliness of ALD/3e's content makes this *the* reference resource for anyone making decisions with regard to lighting. For students and first-time designers, background and clear discussion and direction on lighting design factors, criteria, and resolutions are offered. For experienced practitioners, design and strategy checklists offer unfettered yet quick reviews. Daylighting and electric lamp information cuts to the chase on the latest strategies, technologies, and design issues relevant to today's practice requirements. Anyone interested in standard incandescent lamps, T12 fluorescent lamps, mercury vapor, high pressure sodium, and low pressure sodium lamps or decorating-with-light strategies will be disappointed here. So, too, will those looking for an easy formulaic way to achieve nothing more than LEED points, which can short-circuit sustainability with living and working settings that offer little comfort and utility for long-term use for their specific clients' needs. ALD/3e is for those who want to do lighting right on many counts and understand the underlying principles.

Lighting can transform settings and users. It can transcend time. In an ironic twist, this design medium targeted as an energy "sink" can, itself, render all other systems and related expenditures either moot or superbly effective. It is even more important today to properly light, express, and enliven that dark granite wall that took so much effort to remove from the Earth, properly dress, transport, and install on site—what a waste, indeed, to allow it to sit there darkly and contribute to another vapid, uninteresting space. Perhaps more egalitarian, isn't it ever more important to properly light the offices housing our most costly resource—people—in furnished, finished space that itself embodies significant amounts of energy used in its creation, transportion, and installation? To spend resources on construction, furnishings, finishes, and people only to marginalize the lighting is the ultimate slap to sustainability.

As both a practicing lighting designer and an educator (with stints at Michigan State University, The Pennsylvania State University, Wayne State University, and the University of Michigan) and guest lectures at Louisiana Tech, University of Kansas, University of Colorado, and Ball State University among others, I believe I bring a valuable and holistic perspective to lighting design. The first and second editions were fun to write and both brought fresh knowledge to my own practice and to that of others. Feedback on the readability of those editions was very positive. Some universities adopted the last edition as a class text, which was gratifying. However, changes in technology and attitude about design since 2002 have left much of the lamp, ballast, and luminaire discussions dated. LEDs, while still not the panacea extolled nearly a decade ago, are finding utility—as both eye candy and functional lighting (as we discovered and implemented in a significant way on a hospitality project in 2007 where I was recently

Solution Hint
The solution icon has been added to readily identify specific practices for better lighting.
Image ©Stockxpert

Highlighter
The highlighter icon has been added to readily identify key aspects.
Image ©Stockxpert

photographed [see adjoining photo—more imagery throughout the text on this project and many others]). More importantly, practical experience in daylighting convinced me that a sea change in architectural design practice is necessary if daylighting is ever to be a significant contributor, at least in the States. The daylighting chapter has been materially altered to express the challenges and offer insights on meeting those challenges. Similarly, on lighting controls, a change in accepted practice must be near if we are to reign in our excesses in power use and replacement cycles.

Acknowledgments

Thanks to my editor at John Wiley & Sons, Inc., Margaret Cummins, and her assistant, Lauren Poplawski, for their encouragement, insights, and expedient production. I am grateful to the late Professor John Flynn for his devotion to lighting and architectural engineering during his tenure at Penn State. Thanks also to Steve Squillace, David DiLaura, and Mark Rea. Steve was my boss and mentor at Smith, Hinchman & Grylls in Detroit in the late 1970s and early 1980s. David DiLaura, now Professor Emeritus at the University of Colorado, was (and still is) the provocateur—asking the tough questions about the vagaries of lighting design. Dr. Mark Rea, now with the Lighting Research Center at Rensselaer, and others, including Howard Brandston, were even more direct (shall I say pushy?) provocateurs. All of these folks helped to push my level of interest and professionalism in lighting, and for that I thank them immensely.

Mrs. John Flynn was instrumental in fulfilling my efforts to present some of Professor Flynn's work here in Chapter 7. Mrs. Flynn has kept much of John's work intact and available for review and, in this case, publication so that others may learn from his endeavors in the subjective aspects of lighting. Thank you, Iris.

Reviewers over the last decade have been especially helpful in this rewrite effort. All are insightfully direct. Breaking apart the long and laborious material on programming and criteria now results in Chapters 4, 5, 6, 7, and 8. Developing and diagramming lighting layouts and controls is now better addressed with improved graphics and expanded topics in Chapters 12, 13, and 14. However, repetitious dialogue remains to hit various key points again and again. Every day in practice, we see too many folks willing to sacrifice energy efficiency and/or sustainability aspects for an easy design or initial cost payoff. We also see folks "designing" just enough to garner LEED points, but without going the distance to maximize efficiencies or so shortsighted to yield lousy designs.

Thanks to Gary Woodall for help in artwork development. Thank you, Laura (my wife), for letting me write away in quiet. Thanks to the manufacturers and especially the photographers for their gracious permission to use their respective artwork throughout. Of course, thanks to clients for the opportunity to practice lighting design.

Finally, where would I be without production and copy editors and proofreaders? Thanks very much to Amy Zarkos for her thorough effort. Thanks, too, to Amy Handy and Shannon Egan.

Practice and enjoy good lighting. Without it we have no environments worthy of the expense, trouble, and environmental havoc—however small that may be— that their creation and operation incur.

Gary Steffy, LC, FIALD, IES, Hon. Aff. AIAMI
President
Gary Steffy Lighting Design Inc.
Ann Arbor, Michigan
grs@gsld.net

D iving right into a discussion on **light** and lighting will inevitably result in references to terms and techniques unfamiliar to the reader. However, learning terminology out of context in a lengthy glossary format is uninspiring. So, throughout this text, terms and phrases in boldface type are defined in sidebars for quick reference while freeing the text of verbose definitions.

Lighting has direct and indirect effects on health and well-being. For example, glare can result in poor ergonomics (as people adjust to avoid the glare). Visibility of tasks and therefore accuracy and/or speed and/or volume of work can be hampered with poor lighting. The lighting design must address these and other physiological and psychological issues.

Lighting affects Earth's resources. However, energy savings are a fallacy if lighting yields user dissatisfaction, lower productivity, higher turnover, or reduced senses of safety and security. Efficient, comfortable, useful, attractive lighting is achievable. Automated controls (on both a room-by-room basis and on a whole-building basis) can reduce energy consumption. Using Earth's resources wisely is smart practice. Minimizing the amount of material pulled from Earth and minimizing the spent material put back into the Earth should be de rigueur. Employing lighting technologies that maximize system life and efficiency and judiciously using light are recommended for enhanced **sustainability**. The lighting design must address efficiency and sustainability.

Costs, at least in America, are heavily scrutinized—many times without proper context to the purpose of the project at hand. Environments are constructed to help people live and work in an efficient and comfortable manner. These environments should be long lasting. An office environment's lighting infrastructure, should have a lifespan of at least 20 years. The relative costs of owning and operating a typical office building over 20 years, including the workers' salaries and benefits, are shown in Figure 1.1. A snapshot of typical annual operating costs is shown in Figure 1.2. Sacrificing long-term function and operation for initial cost or expedience is a waste of resources. The lighting design must address the long-term aspects of user satisfaction, comfort, and productivity.

light
Visible radiation. Energy or electromagnetic waves operating at a frequency that stimulates photoreceptors in the eye. But think of our response to light as an "aftereffect." We see what happens after electromagnetic waves react to or interact with surfaces, objects, and materials. This reflected and/or transmitted light comprises our visual scene.

sustainability
The concept of meeting the needs of the present without compromising the ability of future generations to meet their needs[1] (a variety of definitions are in use; however, this is most succinct). Arguably, the entire concept of lighting as we know it today is not sustainable forever, but with conscious design and operational decisions, it can be more sustainable than its current form—in other words, we can extend or sustain our activities longer into the future than if we make no attempt toward sustainable design. For example, recycling (capturing and reusing) the minute amounts of mercury in fluorescent and metal halide lamps will sustain manufacturing of those lamps without seeking new sources of mercury *and simultaneously* avoid landfill contamination.

Figure 1.1

Based on a 20-year cycle, this pie chart illustrates relative costs of workers and facilities in the US. Initial costs include construction and financing. Operating costs include maintenance and energy costs. People costs include salaries and benefits. Based on information from IBM.[2]

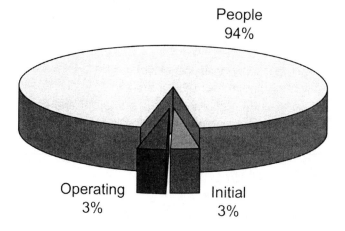

People
94%

Operating
3%

Initial
3%

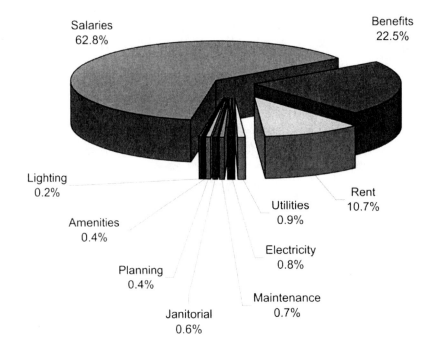

Figure 1.2

Based on Department of Labor data (2000), Building Owners and Managers Association data (2000), and International Facility Management Association data (1997), this pie chart represents a breakdown of common office building costs on an annual basis.[3]

Salaries
62.8%

Benefits
22.5%

Lighting
0.2%

Amenities
0.4%

Planning
0.4%

Janitorial
0.6%

Utilities
0.9%

Electricity
0.8%

Maintenance
0.7%

Rent
10.7%

quad
A US Customary unit of energy equal to 293 billion kilowatt hours (kwh).

architectural lighting design
Lighting design dealing with more permanent applications associated with architecture and landscape architecture. Unlike the more trnasitory applications of theater lighting, concert lighting, tradeshow exhibit lighting, and the like. Throughout this text, architectural lighting design and architectural lighting designer (or lighting design, lighting designer, and designer respectively) refer to the act of or the individual involved in the act of designing lighting for permanent architecture and/or landscape architecture.

In the United States, close to US$10 billion per year of lighting hardware is sold.[4] Lighting consumes nearly 22 percent or 8.25 **quad**s of the electrical energy produced each year, or roughly 2.4 trillion kilowatt hours.[5] This results in expenditures approaching US$60 billion per year on electricity for lighting, not to mention the attendant charges for electricity to run air conditioners to cool some of that load. More significantly, however, some of these lighting expenditures propel the working Americans who earn combined salaries of US$6.2 trillion.[6] These folks use about 65 percent of the lighting energy or US$39 billion to produce goods and services worth in excess of US$10.9 trillion per year—that is, lighting energy costs are less than 0.4 percent of the costs of the goods and services produced.[7] The remainder of the lighting energy is used in residential and outdoor settings. The lighting design challenge: leverage lighting expenditures to get the most out of the built environment in a more sustainable fashion—more productive, comfortable, functional, and efficient living and work environments.

Architectural lighting design (aka lighting design, see Figure 1.3) introduced as a program of calculation, code compliance, and rote layout and energy procedures would be uninspiring and misleading. So, too, if it were introduced solely as a decorative art. Lighting is a science *and* an art. While many of the issues introduced here are grounded in science, much of the practical application discussed here is grounded in the art of lighting design. So you will get a good dose of the author's perspective of what constitutes good lighting design practice—a perspective that has evolved and changed since the writing of the first edition nearly twenty years ago. Other lighting designers may practice differently—with different emphasis on different lighting criteria, on different lighting techniques, on different physiological

and/or psychological aspects, and on different cultural aspects. Indeed, this is what makes lighting more an art and less a science.

Other lighting design branches include automotive, television/studio, theater, exhibit/display, and concert. Some designers work in more than one branch, crossing from theater and/or concert to architectural, for example. This book deals with lighting design intended for permanent architectural applications, such as commercial (offices), institutional (healthcare, educational, and libraries, etc.), hospitality (restaurants, clubs, lounges, and hotels, etc.), governmental (government centers and courthouses, etc.), research (laboratories), and industrial. Residential and retail applications are also considered a part of architectural lighting design and are included here. However, these two applications rely heavily on theatrical techniques.

In the 125-plus years since the introduction of a commercially viable incandescent lamp, and no doubt accelerated with the commercial introduction of the fluorescent lamp 70 years ago, shortcuts and rules of thumb solely addressing **illuminance** or **power budget**s have evolved to shape lighting "design" in an effort to make lighting a rote procedure to save time (for the designers, engineers, distributors, manufacturers, and contractors). Today, energy legislation and light trespass and light pollution ordinances are the excuses du jour for the sad lighting that is implemented every day in most every application. This book will help the reader realize pitfalls of such limited design efforts and explore the amazing potential that light (and, therefore, lighting) has on human comfort, productivity, visual "fabric" and architectural enhancement, and quality of life.

The reference to "lighting designer" or "designer" throughout this text is to the individual or group responsible for the design, layout, and specification of the lighting to achieve various lighting effects (qualities) and quantities on any given project. Lighting designers may have formal titles, such as architect, interior designer, electrical engineer, or lighting designer. On most projects worldwide, the architect, the interior designer, and/or the electrical engineer design the lighting. Sometimes contractors and distributors design lighting.

Figure 1.3

Architectural lighting design addresses needs of the occupants while responding to the architectural aesthetic and/or the mechanics of the architecture.
Image ©Gene Meadows

illuminance
The quantity of light falling on a given surface. Although important, illuminance is much too often the only criterion used to design a lighting solution. This is poor practice. US Customary: footcandles or fc. SI: lux or lx. 10.76 lx = 1 fc.

power budget
A code limit on the amount of total watts used for lighting a room or building. US Customary: watts per square foot or W/sf or W/ft². SI: W/m². Exactly 10.76 W/m² = 1 W/ft².

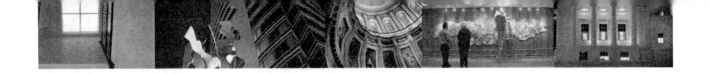

soft (art) issues
Those aspects of lighting design that are not well grounded in scientific research, but based on anecdotal evidence (experience) and, perhaps, limited formal study(ies) and are believed to contribute to the success/failure of any given lighting design.

hard (science) issues
Those aspects of lighting design that are reasonably well grounded in scientific research and/or industry consensus as contributing to the success/failure of any given lighting design. Specific criteria targets can be established and then solutions derived via calculations to show compliance with criteria.

physiological
Pertaining to the human body's physical response. Lighting initiates vision through muscular, chemical, and neurological actions.

So, like its predecessors, this edition of *Architectural Lighting Design* is based on the author's lighting design experiences. Many of the issues covered here are "soft"—that is, anecdotal evidence suggests that their consideration is worthwhile, but you are likely to find that your own knowledge of these **soft issues** will grow and perhaps change with your design experiences. This growing experience base will then help to further enhance and shape your own design approach. Such refinement will continue as long as your design career continues if you are to remain a competitive, innovative designer.

Certainly, **hard issues** are addressed here, too. These include more engineering/scientific issues for which bodies of both empirical and anecdotal evidence exist. The successful lighting designer balances the soft and hard issues on every project. For residential projects, for example, soft issues are typically more important. Yet, for commercial projects, hard issues are typically more important. Nevertheless, tempering the hard issues with soft issues in commercial projects will generally lead to better work environments.

It is because of these soft and hard issues that lighting is often cited as both an art and a science. Lighting involves space, volume, form, texture, color, image (e.g., corporate image), and people—most of all, people. Lighting is both a **physiological** and **psychological** inducer. Above all else, regardless of the corporate image or the designer's ego, light (and, therefore, lighting) must be about the people who are to use the space. Our task should be development of solutions that enhance people activities.

1.1 Conventions

psychological
For purposes here, pertaining to the human mind's emotional or subjective response. In other words, the brain's reaction to physiological actions brought on by light. Light and color are believed to influence people's psychological reactions and influence their preferences for various architectural and/or landscape settings.

luminaire
The entire assembly of hardware components, including lamp(s), ballast(s), transformer(s), driver(s), lens(es), reflector(s), socket(s), wiring and wiring connections, housing, etc., that result in a complete, operational (once installed and "hooked up") lighting assembly (aka, light fixture).

Metrication has been accomplished throughout the world except in a few countries, the United States being the proverbial tail wagging the dog. Unfortunately, and increasingly, this requires a proficiency in both Système Internationale (SI) units and US Customary (aka English, American, or inch-pound) units. Table 1.1 outlines the more pertinent lighting metrics and respective units. Although both US Customary and SI units are referenced throughout the text, for precise, hard conversions, use Table 1.1. In this text, US Customary units are reported and intended to be exact. Metric conversions may be rounded slightly. It is never wise, therefore, to speak of quantitative lighting criteria without attaching the intended unit of measure. For example, when one discusses the average illuminance in a parking lot, a responsible reference is to 5 lux. If one were to simply indicate that the lot illuminance is 5, the party hearing the information may, depending on his/her country of origin and educational background, mistake such a reference as 5 footcandles (which is about ten times the intensity of 5 lux and outrageously high for most parking lots).

Experience with any metric is important to understanding its significance and to appreciating degrees of variability and absolute quantities. In other words, look for opportunities to measure distance and to measure illuminance and luminance during educational exercises. This will allow greater ease of use of these metrics in a design career and will encourage greater rapport with the other design professionals on a project team and with peers.

more online @
physics.nist.gov/cuu/Units/index.html
www.convertworld.com/en/
www.unitconversion.org/

Architectural Lighting Design

Conventions Table 1.1

Metric	US Customary	Système Internationale (SI)	Conversion (US to SI)
Illuminance	footcandle (fc)	lux (lx)	multiply fc by 10.76
Length	inches (in)	millimeters (mm) [used for lighting hardware dimensions]	multiply inches by 25.4
	feet (ft)	meters (m) [used for architectural dimensions]	multiply feet by 0.3
Luminance	candelas per square foot (cd/ft^2)	candelas per square meter (cd/m^2)	multiply cd/ft^2 by 10.76
Energy	kilowatt hours (KWH)	kilowatt hours (KWH)	NA
Power	watts (W)	watts (W)	NA
Power budget	watts per square foot (W/ft^2)	watts per square meter (W/m^2)	multiply W/ft^2 by 10.76
Thermal temperature[a]	°F	°C	°C = (°F - 32) * 0.6
Color temperature[b]	K	K	NA

[a] Used in architectural engineering as the metric for ambient or surface temperatures in the built environment.
[b] Used in lighting as the temperature metric of heat necessary to achieve visible radiation from "black body radiators" such as a hunk of iron.

So, the problem for the lighting designer is not first and foremost a fashion problem—not an issue of selecting the most stylish current **luminaire**. It is not primarily a problem of picking the most efficacious (see **efficacy** sidebar) **lamp** or the cheapest luminaire. And it is not primarily a problem of addressing the politically correct issues of the day. The problem is about vision—helping end users to see comfortably and effectively. Seeing tasks well and offering sufficient comfort and pleasantness that people stay long enough to perform the task(s) expected of them in a reasonable timeframe is the charge to be fulfilled by lighting designers. Not necessarily "work," but living situations, such as reading the newspaper, shopping, strolling a downtown street with friends, enjoying a **son et lumière**, etc. Without light and/or the use of our eyes, we have neither visual architecture nor visual interior design. Engineering principles and artistic principles must be used together to address the physiological and psychological needs of the viewers—the people using the environments. Chapter 2 offers a more detailed discussion on the problem that lies ahead for any lighting designer on every project. Then the remainder of the text is devoted to helping the designer establish a systematic approach for solving the problem on each project. This is an approach to identify issues and techniques for resolution, a framework for developing solution options, and a method for specifying the solution and following it through construction. Think about a lighting design approach this way. Three projects with identical uses, but three different clients need lighting design work. Depending on how each client prioritizes issues, the lighting design will and should be different. In one, emphasis might be on first cost. In another, emphasis might be on worker comfort/productivity. In the third,

1.2 Problem: Vision

efficacy
The effectiveness of a lamp in producing light (**lumens**) relative to the power (watts) required to operate the lamp. Expressed as **lumens** per watt (LPW).

lumens
A measure of the amount of light emitted by a light source (lamp, sky, or sun) or falling onto a surface regardless of directionality.

lamp
The device producing the visible energy (light). Light bulb is the more colloquial reference.

son et lumière
French for "sound and light show." Sometimes may refer to just a light show or a light and water show. Typically involves carefully sequenced light, sound, and/or water effects.

emphasis might be on sustainability. It is highly unlikely that the same lighting equipment laid out in the same way will meet these and other varying goals of all three projects while also meeting the users' physiological and psychological issues. The designer has to reserve the vision issues as foremost in any situation—otherwise what's the point of doing any construction project or expending any amount of energy, regardless how miserly? Of course, this will, at times, conflict with the client's stated goals. Part of the design assignment, then, is to develop a lighting program, a lighting design, and a "sales pitch" to advance a lighting design appropriate for the users.

1.3 Industry

control
The electrical device(s) or mechanism(s) responsible for controlling the operation of the lighting in an environment. Could be simple toggle switches for on/off control, occupancy sensors, or programmable time machines that provide an elaborate son et lumière. Not to be confused with **optical control**.

optical control
A reference to the method(s) used to control the intensity and distribution of light. Typically involving refractors (lensing), reflector(s), and/or louvers.

packaging
A reference to the method(s) sometimes used by lighting manufacturers' representatives, distributors, and/or contractors whereby they attempt to package all of the lighting equipment required on a project into a single bid or quotation from a limited number of manufacturers. This typically means the rep and/or distributor and/or contractor substitute an inferior product for the specified product. Sometimes the client saves money, but gets poor value since the lighting equipment is not equal to the specified equipment. Sometimes the client saves very little or no money with a much greater profit margin for the rep, distributor, and/or contractor. The client still gets poor value.

Lighting is about a US$10 billion dollar (annually) industry in the United States alone. It wasn't too long ago that anyone with a tin-bending operation in a basement or garage could and did manufacture luminaires. As material and labor costs increased, though, and as code and industry standards demanded safer, better-performing products, it became necessary to mass produce luminaires. And industry consolidation occurred. Decades ago, there were many lamp and **control**s manufacturers as well. Similarly, as production costs rose and standards were instituted and/or became sufficiently rigorous, consolidation occurred.

This consolidation has typically meant more choices of fewer styles of equipment. Worse, however, this consolidation has meant a greater increase in **packaging** of lighting equipment during both the specification and/or the purchase of lighting equipment for any given project. More on this in Chapter 14.

At this writing, General Electric (GE), Osram Sylvania, and Philips are the dominant lamp manufacturers (in the United States and globally). In the US, luminaire conglomerates are Acuity Brands, Cooper Industries, Hubbell, and Philips. Acuity includes Holophane, Hydrel, Lithonia, and Peerless. Cooper includes Halo, Metalux, Neoray, RSA, and Shaper. Hubbell includes Columbia, Kim, Kurt Versen, Prescolite, and Sterner. Philips includes Alkco, Ardee, Color Kinetics, Day-Brite, Gardco, Lam, Lightolier (luminaires and controls), and Nessen. Of course, there are many, many relatively small lighting manufacturers with excellent reputations and products. A reasonable listing is online at lighting-inc.com.

Controls range from simple on/off toggle switches to automated timeclocks to whole building systems that can literally address each individual luminaire within the building. Some luminaire vendors also make lighting controls. Other controls vendors include Leviton, Lutron, and Pass & Seymour.

```
more online @
nema.org/econ/data/prod/lighting/
www.aboutlightingcontrols.org/
www.acuitybrands.com/
www.cooperlighting.com/
www.genlyte.com/
www.hubbelllighting.com/
www.lighting-inc.com/searchman.html (listing service)
```

Worldwide, several organizations have taken the lead in the form of professional, technical, and trade associations, including **CIBSE, IALD, IESNA,** and **PLDA.** The International Commission on Illumination (CIE or Commission Internationale de l'Eclairage) is the global organization on lighting technical matters. Constituent organizations of the CIE include many of the world's leading lighting organizations. The IESNA is the North American organization on lighting technical matters. Several such illuminating engineering groups are in place around the globe.

The IALD is an international professional society—engaged in activities promoting the profession of independent lighting design and promoting a corresponding code of ethical practice. This means practitioners operate in a mode independent from manufacturers, distributors, sales representatives, and electrical installers where conflicts of interest are likely. The IALD has about 550 members. The Professional Lighting Designers Association (PLDA) is advancing the interests of those in the various lighting professions in Europe. PLDA has a membership base of about 100.

The Rocky Mountain Institute (RMI) is a nonprofit organization promoting energy **conservation** and Earth sustainability. Although individual memberships are not available, individual and corporate donations are used to partially fund the organization's efforts. RMI is not a standards-setting body, but does help drive a continued interest in popular and scientific circles in energy effective use of Earth's resources.

While all of the aforementioned organizations have the singular goal of maintaining or improving the human condition, there are certainly disputed means to that end. The designer needs to be familiar with the premises and/or criteria espoused by each organization, whether it be of technical, aesthetic, individual-level, societal-level, and/or ethical importance, and then help the client assimilate these criteria into priorities that best address client needs without sacrificing longer-term global needs.

Industry trade organizations also exist and contribute significantly to the transfer of information and/or the development of guidelines related to their specific mission. For example, the National Electrical Contractors Association (NECA) has a series of documents on the installation of lighting equipment for various applications, some of which have been approved as **ANSI** standards. The National Electrical Manufacturers Association (NEMA) develops technical standards, lobbies governmental agencies, and collects and disseminates industry data.

```
more online @
www.ansi.org
www.cibse.org/
www.cie.co.at/cie/
www.pld-a.org/
www.iald.org/
www.ieij.or.jp/english/ (Japan)
www.iesanz.org/ (Australia/New Zealand)
www.iesna.org/ (North America)
www.iessa.org.za/ (South Africa)
www.ile.org.uk/ (UK)
```

1.4 Organizations

CIBSE
Chartered Institution of Building Services Engineers (Society of Light and Lighting).

IALD
International Association of Lighting Designers is a professional association devoted to the interests of independent lighting consultants.

IESNA
Illuminating Engineering Society of North America is the technical organization associated with lighting engineering and practice.

PLDA
Professional Lighting Designers Association (formerly European Lighting Designers Association) is devoted to the interests of independent lighting consultants.

conservation
Preserving and renewing, when possible, human and natural resources. The use, protection, and improvement of natural resources according to principles that will ensure their highest economic or social benefits.[8]

ANSI
American National Standards Institute serves as administrator and coordinator of private sector voluntary standardization efforts in the US. Documents may be submitted only by organizations meeting ANSI's accreditation standards. This assures due process is followed, that the document has been reviewed and revised in an open forum and meets consensus opinion. ASHRAE, IESNA, NECA, and NEMA are accredited by ANSI.

1.5 Codes/Standards

In the United States, lighting equipment for nearly all applications must comply with the National Electrical Code (NEC). As such, most lighting equipment must comply with Underwriters Laboratories (UL) standards. The NEC is intended to address the hazards of shock and fire by providing a scientifically based consensus electrical code. UL standards establish safety requirements and parameters for testing of same for all kinds of products, including lighting and lighting-related components. Several nationally recognized testing labs (NRTLs) in the United States offer testing, listing, and labeling services for lighting equipment, including UL, ETL (ETL SEMKO), and CSAUS (Canadian Standards Association for US). Products tested successfully can exhibit the respective lab's labels. In Canada the CSA offers standards similar to those UL espouses. The European Union relies on the *Conformité Européenne* (CE) standards for safety, health, and environmental protection. Lighting products meeting these standards bear the CE label. Designers need to specify equipment meeting standards in respective jurisdictions.

The International Electrotechnical Commission (IEC) prepares and publishes international standards for electrical and electronic technologies. The International Code Council (ICC) prepares building codes, including the International Building Code (IBC) adopted by many US state governments and the International Energy Conservation Code (IECC).

ASHRAE
American Society of Heating, Refrigerating and Air-conditioning Engineers is the technical organization associated with mechanical (heating, ventilating, and air conditioning) engineering and practice.

In the United States, all states now have some form of energy code, as mandated by the 2005 Energy Policy Act (EPAct). The latest energy standard, **ASHRAE/IESNA 90.1-2004**, closely parallels the California Energy Commission's Title 24.6 code and is a code requirement in many states. These codes are intended to limit the electrical energy consumed by lighting and, thereby, limit fossil fuel consumption and subsequent pollutants from producing electricity.

EPA
The United States Environmental Protection Agency.

Lamp disposal has been brought to the fore as both a health (toxicity) issue and as a sustainability issue (the "churn" of expending Earth's resources and subsequent disposal of spent material). The **EPA** now requires that all lamps not meeting the toxicity characteristic leachate program (TCLP) be considered universal waste. In general, lamps that do not pass the EPA's TCLP need to be disposed in accordance with specific state or federal requirements or, preferably, recycled. Typically, for larger corporate sites for example, this means bulk quantities of lamps failing the TCLP must be disposed as a hazardous waste if not recycled, which is preferable. Where lamps are TCLP-compliant, then they may be disposed in landfills. However, recycling is still encouraged. Further, some states require that even TCLP-compliant lamps be disposed similarly to hazardous waste if not recycled.

Other regulations exist regarding lighting installations. Some municipalities now have local ordinances on parking lot, street, and area lighting (typically establishing

minimum requirements or maximum requirements or both), **light pollution**, and/ or **light trespass**. The conundrum for the designer is helping the client establish priorities—safety, security, and commerce for nighttime users or the strong tug of a now-popular politically correct movement to view more stars in the urban night sky.

```
more online @
www.almr.org/ (recycling)
www.ashrae.org/
www.bcap-energy.org/ (energy codes)
www.cemarking.net/
www.csa.ca/
www.cibse.org/
www.darksky.org/
www.energy.ca.gov/title24/index.html
www.energycodes.gov/
www.iccsafe.org/index.html (building codes)
www.iec.ch/
www.intertek-etlsemko.com/portal/page/cust_portal/ITK_PGR
www.iesna.org/
www.lamprecycle.org/
www.nema.org/stds/lamps-env.cfm#download
www.nfpa.org/
www.ul.com/welcome.html
```

light pollution
Overlighting that directly (through mis-aiming or poor luminaire design) or indirectly (reflected from ground planes or building surfaces) scatters in the night air to create a "haze of light" through which astronomy is difficult.

light trespass
Light from one property falling onto another property or glare visible from a neighboring or receiving property and that causes a nuisance to users of the receiving property.

1.6 Certification

Architects, engineers, and, more recently, interior designers in the building construction industry have been traditionally seen as the parties responsible for upholding life safety standards. As such, these individuals are required to hold licenses by states in which they practice (at this writing, not all states require licensing or registration of interior designers). As part of defining a means of egress, lighting is a life safety building issue. As a complete building system, however, lighting has not been a serious component in the licensing of the design professionals. Indeed, lighting has been relegated status as a building commodity by some—as long as a minimal base standard of lighting is installed, folks living and working in the building will be well satisfied, or so the thought goes. However, in recent years, lighting efficiency has increasingly taken the brunt of the building energy codification. Lighting plays a prominent role in the sustainability story. Installation and maintenance of lighting plays a larger role in the application of energy efficient technologies on an ongoing basis. So, as society has demanded more from less with respect to lighting energy, a need arose to certify those people involved in all phases of lighting. Since 1990, an effort has been underway to develop industry-wide certification for the lighting professions—lighting designers (including architects, engineers, interior designers, and lighting consultants), lighting installers, lighting maintenance, lighting manufacturers, and the like. Thanks to seed funding from the IALD, significant program funding from the US EPA, support from the **DOE**, and major support from the IESNA, there now exists a certification body for lighting: National Council on Qualifications for the Lighting Professions (NCQLP). Based on educational background, career experience, and tested-standing, folks involved in lighting can be certified. Certification is then maintained on a three-year basis with **CEU**s or retesting.

This certification strengthens the common ties among the lighting disciplines or professions. If the designer is sufficiently engaged in specifying up-to-date technologies in a way that offers comfortable, productive, and aesthetically pleasing environments

DOE
The United States Department of Energy.

CEU
Continuing education units (CEUs) are credits awarded to designers who attend seminars, lectures, courses, tradeshows, and other events that are accredited by respective professional associations. CEUs help ensure one's knowledge on a particular topic or specialty is kept current. For example, to maintain one's NCQLP lighting certification (LC) status, a certain number of CEUs are required every three years.

in an energy-efficient way, then manufacturing and product distribution, installation, and maintenance personnel should be sufficiently competent to develop, make, sell, install, and maintain the lighting accordingly. Otherwise, much is lost in lighting system integrity and ultimately in user comfort and productivity. Further, energy savings and environmental progress are limited if not forfeited.

This certification is voluntary. It is anticipated that building developers, facility managers, local, state, and federal governmental building agencies will eventually require that lighting design, manufacturing and distribution, installation, and maintenance functions are performed by NCQLP-certified (denoted by LC for Lighting Certified) professionals. Some universities' lighting programs are deemed sufficiently rigorous to allow graduates to sit for the exam a year early.

Another more recent certification—Leadership in Energy and Environmental Design (LEED)—is of the building itself. Here, in an effort to encourage sustainable design, buildings are awarded points for various energy efficiency and environmentally sustainable strategies successfully employed. Enough points garners certification.

more online @
www.ncqlp.org/
www.usgbc.org/

1.7 Education

Lighting education has advanced considerably in the past 20 years. While there are yet no degreed undergraduate lighting programs, there are several Master's programs and a doctoral program in lighting. Further, many undergraduate design programs offer lighting design classes. A search online yields the most current options.

Because no formal degreed undergraduate programs in lighting exist, many lighting designers have educational backgrounds in related fields. Theater, electrical engineering, architecture, interior design, and architectural engineering are some typical degrees and/or careers leading to lighting design. Various universities have excellent lighting courses within the human ecology, architecture, fine arts, home economics, or engineering schools. Usually, though, one or two lighting courses are the extent of a student's exposure to lighting. With just these few classes and a passion for lighting, however, a career in lighting is practical and possible. Some schools offer additional independent study in lighting. For the student looking for more formal education in lighting, a Master's degree in lighting from a respected program is suggested. Perhaps a measure of the amount of student interest generated at any given lighting program is evident through IESNA student chapters and/or IALD student membership. Schools with IESNA student chapters and/or several IALD student members identify strong and/or storied programs.

One way to expand one's knowledge about lighting is to more deliberately observe the surrounding environment. Observation is such an obvious tool, yet so seldom used to educational advantage. Every waking hour of every day we see built environments. Many are poorly lighted, and many people even comment about the poor state of the lighting, yet we continue to design dreadful solutions. We should be more observant, identifying what is successful, what is less successful, and what is unsuccessful. A working journal is one means of recording observations in both sketch and written word. A digital camera (without the use of flash) also offers a reasonable record of existing environments. Here, however, written record

Observation Journal

Twice each week, study the lighting of interior spaces and capture the look in sketch form. Use shade, shadow, highlight, and other techniques to illustrate the lighting. Include a several-sentence paragraph describing the lighting equipment, the resulting effect, whether or not you like the lighting, and why and if it is suitable for the function. EXTRA CREDIT: Obtain an **illuminance meter** and make illuminance measurements throughout the space Note these in the journal, indicating the location of the measurement, elevation above floor. Take precaution to avoid introducing body shadow(s) on the meter as this results in erroneous readings.

illuminance meter
A device used to measure illuminance (in fc or lx). Most typically available in digital readout.

needs to be made in a PDA or in the form of an oral recording on camera with the image. The journal is a preferable option for the designer interested in developing and/or maintaining hand-drawn graphic skills. These sketches can, with some experience, be completed in about an hour and help the observer understand how light "renders" surfaces and spaces and can lead to better visualization of proposed designs. Included with the sketch should be a short description of the environment, the tasks, the technical aspects of the lighting (including sky conditions for daylight situations), whether or not the lighting seems appropriate, and how it might be improved.

```
more online @
www.lighting-education-trust.org/
www.ncqlp.org/certification/intern.html
```

1.8 Continuing Ed

The need for continuing education in lighting is growing due to the continuing education requirements of registration and/or certification and the rapid changes in lighting technologies and codes. Several universities offer week-long seminars from time to time. The IESNA offers classes periodically through its section chapters and at its annual conference. The IESNA and the IALD offer seminars and workshops at the annual trade show LightFair. PLDA offers seminars at its annual show. Technical and application papers presented at the IESNA annual conference are also excellent means of maintaining current techniques and practice. CIBSE, ILE, (Institution of Lighting Engineers) and others also offer lighting seminars. In addition to LightFair, a host of lighting trade shows takes place annually or biannually around the globe. The lamp manufacturers, GE, Osram Sylvania, and Philips, have regularly scheduled seminar programs at their respective lighting education centers around the globe. Several luminaire manufacturers offer regular seminars. The Internet is likely to allow the offering of distant learning programs from many of these organizations and from universities. All of this activity may qualify for CEUs.

```
more online @
www.cibse.org/
www.cooperlighting.com/education/
www.gelighting.com/na/business_lighting/education_resources/conferences/
www.iald.org/
www.iesna.org/
http://www.ile.org.uk/
www.lightfair.com
www.lightingdesignlab.com/
www.lightolier.com/index.jsp?A=210
www.lithonia.com/Training/LightingCenter/index.asp
www.lrc.rpi.edu/resources/index.asp
www.nam.lighting.philips.com/us/lac/
www.sylvania.com/LearnLighting/LIGHTPOINT/
```

1.9 Publications

Staying abreast of current technologies and design styles takes more commitment than a week-long refresher course every few years. Many of the organizations cited in Section 1.4 publish newsletters, magazines, and/or journals devoted to lighting issues. A number of paid-circulation magazines have established broad appeal by addressing architectural lighting design in whole or in part on a monthly or bimonthly basis. *Architectural Lighting* offers articles and reviews for those involved

in designing and specifying architectural lighting. This magazine is available free to qualified industry members. *Architectural Record* publishes a special *Lighting* section on a periodic basis. *Lighting Design + Application* is the magazine the IESNA publishes monthly. Other periodicals include *Architectural SSL* (solid state lighting or LEDs), *Home Lighting*, and *Illuminotecnica Europe Light*. Some manufacturers, such as ERCO and Zumtobel/Staff, also publish magazines on a periodic basis.

Other lighting publications include research journals, newsletters, and papers (some presented in formal settings) by researchers and application specialists. The IESNA publishes the journal *LEUKOS* with peer-reviewed topical research and application papers. The CIBSE publishes *Lighting Research & Technology* quarterly, documenting research work and results. The Lighting Research Center (LRC) at Rensselaer Polytechnic Institute offers information by hard-copy subscription publications and by online content. Consider the United States' Lawrence Berkeley National Laboratory (LBL) repository. Here, papers are available on lighting technologies, controls techniques, and lighting applications.

```
more online @
www.architecturalssl.com/
www.archlighting.com/
archrecord.construction.com/
eetd.lbl.gov/
www.homelighting.com/
www.iesna.org/LDA/iesnalda.cfm
www.iesna.org/leukos/introduction.cfm
www.illuminotecnica.com/base_menu_uk.htm
www.ledsmagazine.com/
www.lighthouse.org/aboutus/newsletters/
www.lightsearch.com/resources/magazines/index.html
www.lrc.rpi.edu/searchpublications.asp
```

1.10 Internet

The Internet has revolutionized information exchange. Lighting and vision can be readily researched in a timely manner. Search engines should be used on a periodic basis to review such topics as architectural lighting, architectural lighting design, lighting design, lighting research, lamps, luminaires, building codes, energy codes, and vision. Even find current events in the lighting business.

```
more online @
www.edisonreport.net/
```

1.11 Endnotes

[1] DANTES Glossary, Sustainability (web page, October 23, 2006), http://www.dantes.info/Projectinformation/Glossary/Glossary.html. [Accessed July 9, 2007.]

[2] Steven Ternoey, et. al., *The Design of Energy-Responsive Commercial Buildings* (New York: John Wiley & Sons, 1985), p. 178.

[3] Light Right Consortium, The Benefits of Quality Lighting (web page, 2007), http://www.lightright.org/market/values.htm. [Accessed June 23, 2007.]

[4] NEMA, Domestic Shipment of Products within the Scope of NEMA's Lighting Systems Division (web page, 2007), http://www.nema.org/econ/data/prod/lighting/. [Accessed March 7, 2007.]

[5] DOE, Lighting Energy and Consumption (web page, 2007), http://www.eere.energy.gov/buildings/tech/lighting/. [Accessed May 19, 2007.]

[6] Infoplease, National Income by Type (web page, 2007), http://www.infoplease.com/ipa/A0104648.html, 2003 "Compensation of employees" data. [Accessed May 19, 2007.]

[7] Infoplease, Gross Domestic Product or Expenditure (web page, 2007), http://www.infoplease.com/ipa/A0104575.html, 2003 data. [Accessed May 19, 2007.]

[8] EPA, Terms of Environment: Glossary, Abbreviations and Acronyms (web page, October 2, 2006), http://www.epa.gov/OCEPAterms/cterms.html. [Accessed July 9, 2007.]

Lighting affects how people feel, react, and function in various settings. Lighting is a biology or physiology problem as well as a psychology problem. To develop a successful lighting plan for any situation, the designer must understand the problem as such. This is the most crucial step in any lighting design. How well are people expected to function? How comfortable are people expected to be while they function? What is/are the function(s)? How can lighting best help with functionality and simultaneously influence people's emotional or subjective reactions in a positive way? Who are these people, and how do they feel, react, and function in their present lighting situation(s)? There are too many people with too many experiences in too many functional settings who are our clients. A better understanding of them and their needs is necessary before an answer can be proposed to meet their specific needs in a given architectural and social setting.

Vision is an amazing sense. It has a detection range of a million to one (sunlight to moonlight). It perceives things as "bright" when fully adapted under full moonlight, and yet perceives things as "dark" when fully adapted in the midst of a ferocious thunderstorm. It can identify an apple as red or an orange as orange under most light sources (regardless of the light source color) and under most intensities. It can ignore all of this if it is not tuned to "observe." Vision is under the control of the observer. Lighting designers can enhance or limit vision. So, the lighting issues that will be discussed here revolve around physiological and psychological issues.

electromagnetic energy
Electromagnetic energy or radiation is emitted when atomic particles vibrate. The frequency of the vibration determines the kind of radiation emitted. High-frequency vibrations result in very short wavelength radiation, such as cosmic rays, gamma rays, and X-rays. Low-frequency vibrations result in long wavelength radiation, such as microwaves, radio waves, and sound waves. Moderate-frequency vibrations result in ultraviolet radiation, light, and infrared radiation. All of these varying wavelengths of radiation make up the electromagnetic spectrum. The metric for wavelengths is meters. Wavelengths of visible radiation are measured in billionths of a meter—10^{-9} meters or nanometers (nm). The shortest wavelengths of visible energy are about 380 nm (deep violet). The longest are about 770 nm (rich red).

The eye responds to differences in specific reflected and transmitted **electromagnetic energy** (which we call "light")—the eye sees **chromatic** and **luminance contrasts**. Figure 2.1 outlines the electromagnetic spectrum and highlights the range of radiation to which typical, healthy eyes are sensitive. Daylight, moonlight, flame, and electric light characteristics interact with a given setting (architectural, landscape architectural, or native natural), creating reflections and transmissions of various wavelengths of visible energy for people to behold. Lighting designers can manipulate these reflections and transmissions to advantage—that is the charge of the lighting design team.

Because we see light reflecting from or transmitting through materials, the surface characteristics of these materials are critically important to the color and amount of reflected or transmitted light. Indeed, a good interior design plan can be ruined by bad lighting. Alternatively, a good lighting design plan can be ruined by bad interior design. These maxims hold for architecture and landscape architecture. So, a team effort is, indeed, a necessity if there is any hope of getting the most out of the lighting and out of the interiors, the architecture, and/or the landscape architecture.

more online @
imagine.gsfc.nasa.gov/docs/science/know_l1/emspectrum.html
www.physicsclassroom.com/Class/light/U12L2a.html
physics.about.com/od/lightoptics/a/vislightspec.htm

2.1 Physiology

chromatic contrast
Color contrast or color difference between two or more colors. Perceived by a typical, healthy eye. For example, a sunflower viewed against its green leaves.

luminance contrast
Measured brightness difference between two or more elements or details in the viewed scene as perceived by a typical, healthy eye. For example, when one looks through a window, one sees the luminance contrast between an overcast sky and the wall adjacent to the window.

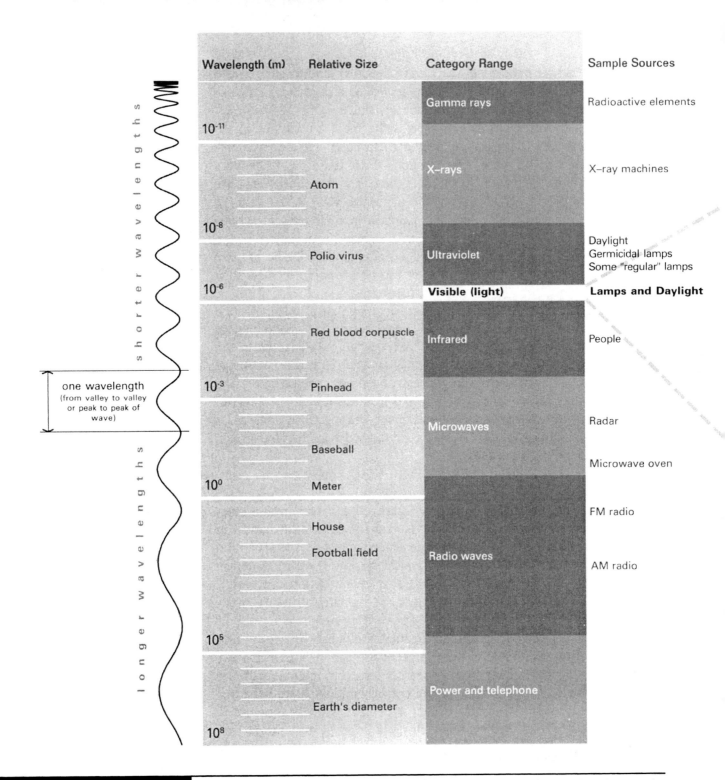

Wavelength (m)	Relative Size	Category Range	Sample Sources
		Gamma rays	Radioactive elements
10^{-11}		X–rays	X–ray machines
	Atom		
10^{-8}		Ultraviolet	Daylight Germicidal lamps Some "regular" lamps
	Polio virus		
10^{-6}		**Visible (light)**	**Lamps and Daylight**
	Red blood corpuscle	Infrared	People
10^{-3}	Pinhead		
		Microwaves	Radar
	Baseball		Microwave oven
10^{0}	Meter		FM radio
	House		
	Football field	Radio waves	AM radio
10^{5}			
		Power and telephone	
	Earth's diameter		
10^{8}			

shorter wavelengths

one wavelength
(from valley to valley
or peak to peak of
wave)

longer wavelengths

2.2 The Eye

The eye is diagrammed in Figure 2.2. The cornea is a protective sheath over the lens that also provides much of the refractive (focusing) power. The iris is a thin, colored membrane (thus, one's eye color) that constricts (dilates) the pupil (located in the center of the iris) to control the amount of entering light. This shutter-like adjustment works with photochemical changes in the eye's photoreceptors (rods and cones; discussed in depth under 2.3 Color Vision), resulting in

Architectural Lighting Design

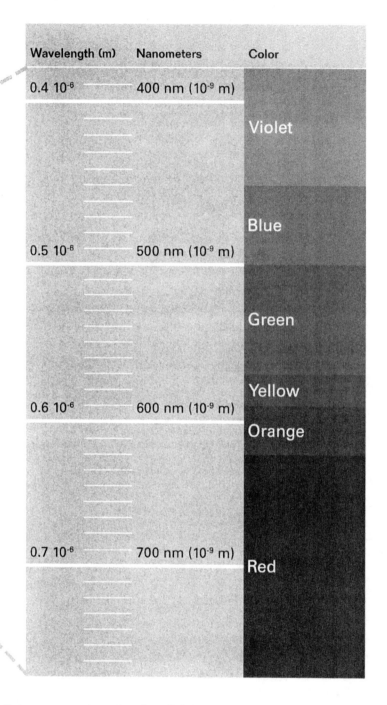

Wavelength (m)	Nanometers	Color
0.4 10⁻⁶	400 nm (10⁻⁹ m)	
		Violet
		Blue
0.5 10⁻⁶	500 nm (10⁻⁹ m)	
		Green
		Yellow
0.6 10⁻⁶	600 nm (10⁻⁹ m)	
		Orange
0.7 10⁻⁶	700 nm (10⁻⁹ m)	
		Red

Figure 2.1

The electromagnetic spectrum is diagrammatically represented here. A small but extremely significant portion is visible to humans. This is highlighted at 10⁻⁶ meters (**visible radiation [light]**) is typically reported in nanometers, or 10⁻⁹ meters—so 700 nm (deep red) is also 700 10⁻⁹ meters, or 0.7 10⁻⁶ meters, or 700 billionths of a meter). The speed with which these wavelengths travels (**speed of light**) is perceived as instantaneous. Resource: Electromagnetic Spectrum Chart, The Exploratorium (http://explo.stores.yahoo.net/emsmain.html).

visible radiation (light)

Colors of visible electromagnetic energy or visible radiation are not as neatly categorized as shown. The visible spectrum is a continuum of colored light—a rainbow. There is not great unanimity in the scientific community about the short wave cutoff on visible radiation. Some references cite 400 nm as the shortest visible energy, while other references cite 380 nm. On the long wave cutoff, some references cite 700 nm, while others cite 770 nm as the cutoff. This graph shows 380 to 770 nm. Also, color categories here are for simple reference. Each color category can be further refined (e.g., blue-green and green-blue). For purposes of lighting design, it is reasonable to simply assign colored light the mid-value wavelength within the range shown here. So, for example, yellow light is 580 nm, blue light is 470 nm, and so forth.

speed of light

Light travels at about 186,000 miles per second (300,000 km per second). This is much faster than the **speed of sound** and why thunder is so slow to follow a lightning strike.

speed of sound

Sound travels at about 750 miles per hour or 0.2 miles per second (1200 km per hour or 0.3 km per second).

what's known as adaptation (see 2.4 Adaptation). At the same time, this shutter-like action works in conjunction with muscles to shape the lens for optimal focusing of the entering light.

After passing through the pupil, light then enters the lens. This is a crystalline diaphragm that focuses incoming light onto an imaginary point just behind the lens. Here, the focused light (which constitutes the image) inverts for a final "projection" onto the retina. The process of the lens focusing an image onto the retina is known as accommodation (see 2.5 Accommodation).

One or several structural defects in the eye can cause objects or scenes to appear out of focus. If the cornea is a bit too round or the entire eyeball a bit too

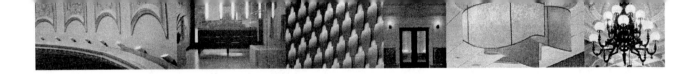

long, the focal length of objects/tasks is too short and objects actually are focused in front of the retina. This phenomenon is called **myopia**, or nearsightedness, as only nearer objects can be seen clearly.[1] If the cornea is a bit too flat or the entire eyeball a bit too short, then the focal length is too long and objects are focused behind the retina in a condition known as **hypermetropia** (or hyperopia), or farsightedness.[2]

myopia

Nearsightedness. A condition, common to nearly 30% of the US population, where the eyeball is a bit too long or the cornea is a bit too round. Images are focused short (in front) of the retina. Near objects/tasks are clearly accommodated (focused), while distant objects/tasks are somewhat out of focus.[1]

hypermetropia (or hyperopia)

Farsightedness. The eyeball is a bit too short or the cornea is a bit too flat. Images are focused long (behind) the retina. Far objects/tasks are clearly accommodated, while closer objects/tasks are somewhat out of focus.[2]

long, the focal length of objects/tasks is too short and objects actually are focused in front of the retina. This phenomenon is called **myopia**, or nearsightedness, as only nearer objects can be seen clearly.[1] If the cornea is a bit too flat or the entire eyeball a bit too short, then the focal length is too long and objects are focused behind the retina in a condition known as **hypermetropia** (or hyperopia), or farsightedness.[2]

Photoreceptors on the retina are activated by the focused light, and these, in turn, initiate signals or impulses through the optic nerve to the brain where image interpretation takes place. During relatively bright scenes, the cone photoreceptors are primarily active. Cones respond to higher luminance and detect color. These cells (of which there are about 4 million) are concentrated at the macula and are responsible for detail vision. Sharpest vision occurs in the fovea, which is located at the center of the macula. Rods (of which there are about 100 million) respond to lower brightness and do not detect color. Rods are absent in the fovea, but populate the rest of the retina and are, therefore, responsible for night vision. Since the cones populate the fovea exclusively, there can be no detailed vision in very low luminance (dim) situations. This explains why viewing of dim stars is accomplished with peripheral viewing and not by looking directly at a distant star or region of interest of the sky.

```
more online @
hyperphysics.phy-astr.gsu.edu/hbase/ligcon.html#c1
www.accessexcellence.com/AE/AEC/CC/vision_background.html
www.howstuffworks.com/eye.htm
www.kellogg.umich.edu/patientcare/conditions/index.html
www.nei.nih.gov/
www-staff.lboro.ac.uk/~huph/
www.tedmontgomery.com/the_eye/index.html
```

2.3 Color Vision

20/20 vision

The customary standard in the United States for "reference" vision. This does not constitute perfect vision. The first value (always "20") represents the distance in feet at which the individual in question views objects/tasks clearly; the second value represents the distance in feet at which an individual with "normal reference" sight would view those same objects/tasks clearly. For example, 20/100 vision in an eye means that the tested eye must be within 20 feet of a visual target to see it as well as a normal reference eye would see at 100 feet from the same visual target! The metric equivalent is 6/6 vision.[3]

Color vision takes place under relatively high brightness conditions. Such vision is known as photopic. Under these conditions, the best detail vision is possible. For typical healthy eyes, corrected if necessary to **20/20 vision**, blue-green light (images) projects precisely onto the fovea. Violet-blue light (images), however, focuses slightly in front of the fovea. Hence, in an attempt to focus these images, the lens of the eye becomes slightly less convex and, therefore, the violet-blue image(s) appears to be slightly farther away. Red light (images), on the other hand, focuses slightly behind the fovea. Here, the lens becomes slightly more convex and, therefore, the red images appear to be slightly closer to the observer. These phenomena are sometimes used to advantage in design efforts—warm colors tend to advance, while cool colors tend to recede.

Color vision deficiency (color blindness) is typically hereditary. The deficiency may be minor, in which case distinguishing between several shades of the same color is difficult. In some cases, however, one color cannot be distinguished from another. About 8 percent of men and 1 percent of women have some form of color deficiency. Red-green deficiency, the inability to distinguish red from green, is most common. Blue-yellow deficiency is less common. Complete color blindness (being able to distinguish colors only as shades of black, gray, and white) is quite rare.[4] Some color vision deficiency does occur with age. As the lens clouds,

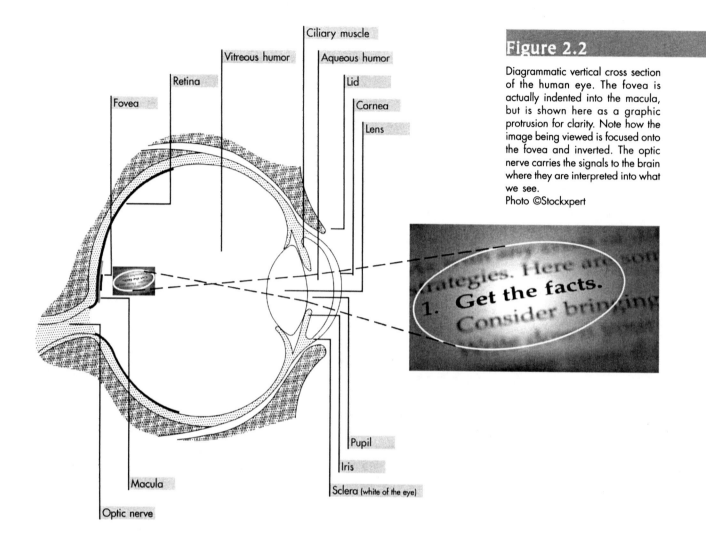

Figure 2.2

Diagrammatic vertical cross section of the human eye. The fovea is actually indented into the macula, but is shown here as a graphic protrusion for clarity. Note how the image being viewed is focused onto the fovea and inverted. The optic nerve carries the signals to the brain where they are interpreted into what we see.
Photo ©Stockxpert

there is less ability to distinguish color at lower light intensities and/or to distinguish between dark colors.[5] Generally, all colors are dulled, but blue is particularly muddied.

Color is not an inherent characteristic of surfaces. The color makeup of the light striking surfaces is as responsible for what color(s) healthy eyes see as the surface material itself. The upshot is this: the designer must carefully assess the light source(s) and the surface material(s) on projects to be assured that people see the intended color palette and that the most efficient use of light and color is achieved.

Color vision lessens with lower brightness settings. Mesopic vision refers to vision that occurs typically at dusk or dawn brightness settings, typified by environments lighted to perhaps 0.2 to 2 fc (2.2 to 22 lux). Here, both rods and cones are operating, but the detailed vision the cones offer is diminished by the relatively low brightnesses. Studies over the ten-year period from 1990 to 2000 offer strong evidence that mesopic vision is enhanced somewhat by light that is richer in the bluer portion of the visible spectrum. This enhancement is most dramatic, however, under scotopic vision.

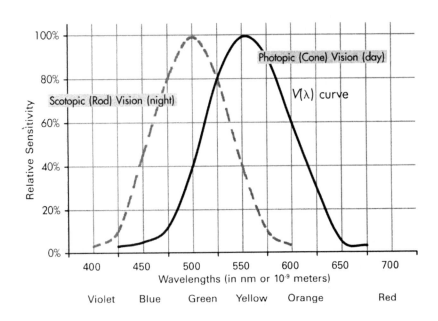

Figure 2.3

Eye sensitivity shifts depending on lighting conditions. The rods are most sensitive to the blue-green portion of the visible spectrum. So, in scotopic vision (low light or "night") conditions when rods are fully responsible for vision, blue-green light is most effective. The cones are most sensitive to the green-yellow portion of the visible spectrum. So, in photopic vision (high light or "day") conditions when cones are primarily responsible for vision, green-yellow light is most effective. The sensitivity curve shown for photopic vision is also known as the V(l) curve—the universally accepted vision response curve to light and used in the development and reporting of lamp photometric data.

visual acuity
Ability to clearly see objects and details.

Scotopic vision takes place under very low brightness settings, typified by environments lighted to less than 0.2 fc (2.2 lux—full moonlight might offer 0.5 lux[6]). In such settings, blue-rich electric light sources offer significant **visual acuity** enhancement to eyesight over more yellow sources. For nightlighting of pedestrian paths and around residential areas, this is an important consideration. Studies show that using blue-rich sources to have an effect similar to that of doubling or nearly tripling light intensities using more yellow sources—a significant finding for safety and security and for the conservation of our resources.[7, 8, 9] Figure 2.3 illustrates eye sensitivity under scotopic conditions and under photopic conditions. Recognize that because lamps rich in green light register as more efficient in standardized photometric tests. Beware of specifying the most efficient lamps available without first having assessed their color rendering and spectral power distribution (**SPD**) or, better yet, personally reviewing an operating lamp sample's effect on skin tones and color palettes.

```
more online @
  www.aoa.org/
  www.hazelwood.k12.mo.us/~grichert/optics/intro.html
  www.hhmi.org/senses/b110.html
  www.webmd.com/eye-health/eye-glossary
  www.99main.com/~charlief/Blindness.htm
```

2.4 Adaptation

Adaptation is a key process and one over which the lighting designer can have positive influence. Older eyes have longer adaptation periods than younger eyes because of the reduced elasticity of the iris and slowed photochemical process. The photochemical changes take place in the light-sensing cells of the retina. So, when sighted people move from bright spaces to dark spaces and vice versa, adaptation occurs. The brighter the bright space and the longer the exposure to the bright setting, then the more dramatic the adaptation process when moving to a dark setting. Likewise, the darker the dark space and the longer the exposure to the dark setting, then the more dramatic the adaptation process when

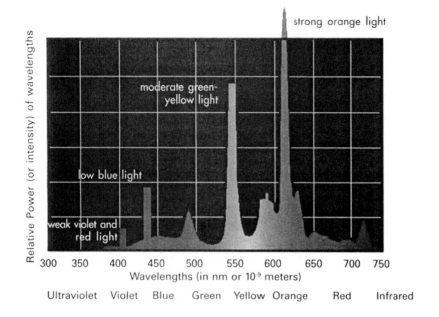

strong orange light

moderate green-yellow light

low blue light

weak violet and red light

Relative Power (or intensity) of wavelengths

300 350 400 450 500 550 600 650 700 750

Wavelengths (in nm or 10⁻⁹ meters)

Ultraviolet Violet Blue Green Yellow Orange Red Infrared

Figure 2.4

Spectral power distribution curve for GE's 830 fluorescent lamp. Note the strong spike of orange, a slightly weaker spike of yellow-green, and a weaker spike of blue. This is a triphosphor lamp—that is, a lamp composed of three phosphor layers. Each layer produces a specific color range of light (in this case, orange, yellow-green, and blue). The orange, yellow-green, and blue combine to make a relatively full spectrum white light. The greater strength of the orange results in a warm white light that renders skin tones quite well. Because of little violet and red light, violet and red materials will appear dulled.
Image courtesy of General Electric Company

moving to a bright setting. However, adapting from bright to dark typically takes more time than adapting from dark to bright. So, when designing interior space adjacencies or exterior site lighting immediately adjacent to ingress/egress to buildings, this adaptation should be considered. For example, people walking from the bright outdoors into a theater will experience relatively long adaptation periods, readily leading to tripping or disorientation. This effect from bright to dark is known as dark adaptation. Complete dark adaptation can take half an hour or longer. Because of this lag, and because of a momentary sense of blindness experienced when one first enters a darkened space, dark adaptation can be dangerous. This adaptation can be minimized by designing a space or series of spaces that act as both a time transition and a progressive dimness transition. Longer transition times and less harsh dimness transitions are appropriate for older users (typically over 40 years of age for purposes of vision/lighting issues).

Adapting from dark settings to bright settings may take just a few minutes. This is known as light adaptation. In extreme cases, say moving from dark theaters to daylit exteriors, some pain (typically referred to as glare) may be experienced as the eyes adapt.

Another form of adaptation is transient adaptation—experienced when the user is relatively stationary (so the overall environment is not changing as it does when walking from an outdoor setting at noon into a theater). As the user scans the scene, and if he/she is in a relatively dark zone but scanning to a bright luminaire or to an extraordinarily bright zone, then adaptation occurs. Adaptation also occurs with a converse situation—if the user is in a relatively bright zone but scanning to a dark zone, adaptation occurs. So, a person looking from a brightly lighted (read "overlit") parking lot into a nearby shrubbed area can experience this momentary or transient adaptation. Such a situation better allows muggers to hide. A more successful lighting solution may rely on a less bright parking area and some landscape lighting to keep the outlying or perimeter shrub area in some low level of brightness. So consistency or uniformity of brightness has a significant influence on adaptation

SPD

Spectral power distribution. A measure of the power or intensity of electromagnetic energy present in a given light source.[10] Typically reported in graph form showing the relative intensity of the various wavelengths of energy produced by a given light source (see Figure 2.4). Some light sources, like daylight on a sunny day, have a rather complete or full spectrum of visible energy (all colors of light are present to some degree). Other light sources, such as blacklights, have a very limited spectrum of light (mostly ultraviolet and deep violet electromagnetic energy is present in the SPD of blacklights). Recognize the implications, then, on how people perceive color. If a blacklight (rich in violet light) is aimed onto a red surface, the red surface will appear black since the red pigment is capable of reflecting only red light that strikes it, yet the blacklight only produces violet light. SPD is responsible, then, for how colors are rendered.

and people's abilities to see a complete scene comfortably. Consider for a moment the effect of moonlight on a rural setting. Although the light level is very low (and, therefore, the brightnesses are very low)—a full moon on a clear night might provide 0.5 lux (0.05 fc)—the uniform light allows individuals to distinguish objects and movement in the landscape. Indeed, with sufficient time to adapt to such low brightnesses, most people can read newspaper headlines!

Some research indicates that in low vision situations, the SPD of the light source(s) can improve perceptions of brightness.[11, 12] Light sources with a high component of blue (known as "blue-rich" or "bluer") have the effect of reducing the size of the pupil (as would happen in higher light intensity settings), thereby providing the sensation of greater brightness. This can be used to benefit in various applications. In the situation of housing for the elderly, light sources relatively richer in blue than typical residential lighting (e.g., using fluorescent lamps of a minimum of 3000K **color temperature** and preferably up to 5000K instead of incandescent lamps) might be used in architectural details (e.g., coves, electric "skylights," etc.) in an effort to enhance impressions of brightness. In the situation of an open office area that houses both computer-aided design (CAD) operators (demanding very low intensities) and clerical staff (using local task lights for work light, but not wanting the impression of a cave as a work setting), light sources very rich in blue (e.g., 5000K fluorescent lamps alone or even fitted with blue filter sleeves) might be used in an attempt to satisfy both sets of workers.

color temperature
Also known as correlated color temperature (CCT) because all color temperature ratings are based on a standard reference approximating daylight—hence, the color temperature is correlated to a reference light source. Color temperature is a measure of the whiteness of light produced by a given lamp with 0K as black (producing no light). A candle flame has a color temperature of about 2000K. A standard incandescent lamp has a color temperature of about 2700K, while the new, crisp white halogen lamps typically have a color temperature of about 3000K. See Figure 7.11.

2.5 Accommodation

Accommodation is the process of focusing on an object or task. The ciliary muscle contracts to adjust the shape of the lens. Because accommodation is a muscular activity, a constant focus on a single object or task is tiresome. Indeed, eye breaks are recommended from time to time during the course of a work day so that focusing is not limited to static viewing situations. On the other hand, continually changing focus from one object/task (that is near, for example) to another object/task (that is somewhat farther, for example) fatigues the ciliary muscle from too much operation. This constant accommodation (as might occur when one views from very close task work to more distant task work) can result in visual fatigue. Particularly problematic with folks working on tasks involving computers and hard copies—alternately viewing close computer monitor and slightly more distant paper documents. Here, for example, the paper task should be positioned at the same distance and on the same plane as those of the computer screen position.

2.6 Aging

Aging affects the eye several ways, any one of which can reduce the effectiveness of one's vision. Together, however, these age-related effects can have a debilitating effect on vision. It is important to remember that all body functions tend to slow with age. The process of adaptation slows. This leads to a potentially serious issue when moving from bright settings to dim or dark settings. Although some degree of adaptation takes place in the first ten minutes when moving from bright to dark settings, it may take 30 to 60 minutes for older eyes to fully adapt to very dark settings. The designer should minimize the degree of these changes by developing transition spaces and recognizing that surface finishes greatly affect adaptation luminances—an

all-white room lit to half a footcandle (about 5 lux) is a much easier transition than an all-black room lit to the same level. Further, potential obstacles should be avoided—such as steps or quick and/or abrupt grade or directional changes.

Accommodation also slows with age. Again, transitions from space-to-space or area-to-area should be gradual. Objects or tasks should be arranged so that accommodation is now limited. That is, the focal distances for the common and/or the more important visual items or tasks should be about the same. Hence, a designer might develop a sitting room in a home for an elderly client with the guests' chairs and/or sofa within a constant distance (diameter) from one another. Similarly, the television and favored objects and artwork might be kept within a constant distance from the likely preferred viewing position(s).

Presbyopia is an age-related phenomenon whereby the eye can no longer focus on near objects. The lens hardens and, hence, is less elastic as the eye ages. Focusing of near objects/tasks becomes more difficult. At the age of five, one has a near focus of perhaps 7 cm (about 3 in). By the age of 21, one has a near focus of perhaps 12 cm (about 5 in). By the age of 42, one has a near focus of about 25 cm (about 10 in). At the age of 46, near focus is about 32 cm (about 13 in), and that is considered a reasonable reading distance. But by the age of 55, near focus is now at arms' length reading distance, which is about 55 cm (about 22 in)—hence holding the newspaper this far away becomes a practical, if tiresome, necessity without corrective eyewear.[14, 15] Presbyopia does not affect accommodation of far objects/tasks.

As the lens ages, it can become somewhat cloudy and yellow. By the age of 60, it may take two to three times as much light for an individual to see tasks as he/she required at 20 years of age.[16, 17] A sufficiently cloudy, yellow lens is known as a **cataract**. As the lens clouds, images become less focused and more blurred. The yellowing combined with the clouding reduces the overall image/scene brightness. Increased sensitivity to glare may also result from the increased scattering of light. So, while increased light intensities are desirable to overcome the dullness imposed by the clouding and yellowing, the locations and directionality of the light sources used are important—they should be kept out of the main line of sight or should be used to produce relatively uniform brightness. In general, fewer, high-wattage luminaires should be avoided. Vision improvement with intraocular implant surgery by an **ophthalmologist** may be so exceptional that the energy ramifications may be significant compared to doubling or tripling light levels.

Constant exposure to ultraviolet (UV) radiation, cigarette smoke, and certain medications can lead to or accelerate cataract development.[13, 18] Heredity may also play a role. Diabetics tend to be more susceptible to cataracts. Some protective measures can be taken. In daylight situations, eyes should be shielded with sunglasses specifically designed to limit or eliminate UV radiation transmittance. In electric light situations, if eyes are likely to be exposed directly to nearby light sources for a period of time and/or light intensities are quite high, luminaires should be fitted with lensing that limits or eliminates UV radiation. Lensing for eyewear should be selected to limit or eliminate UV radiation transmittance.

more online @
www.aoanet.org/
www.lrc.rpi.edu/programs/lightHealth/AARP/pdf/AARPbook3.pdf
www.medem.com/MedLB/sub_detailb.cfm?parent_id=30&act=disp
www.nlm.nih.gov/medlineplus/cataract.html
webvision.med.utah.edu/light_dark.html

cataract
A clouding of the lens ultimately leading to hazy or blurred vision. Symptoms include: cloudy or filmy vision, increased glare sensitivity, halo around light sources when viewed directly, faded colors, poor night vision, multiple or double vision, and frequent changes in eyewear prescriptions.[13]

ophthalmologist
A physician specializing in the diagnosis and treatment of visual disorders and eye disease. Licensed to practice medicine and perform surgery—skills unavailable from an **optometrist**.

optometrist
A professional who examines eyes for defects and prescribes corrective lenses.

2.7 Astigmatism

Astigmatism is a refractive error caused by an irregularly shaped cornea. Normally, the cornea is essentially a portion of a sphere—with equal curvature in all directions. However, in some situations, the cornea is not quite spherical. As such, the cornea cannot then refract all of the light rays onto a single point or zone within the eye. Astigmatism is common and is not age related. It can be addressed with corrective lenses. Typical symptoms are blurred vision, headaches and visual fatigue (from the strain of attempting to focus), and/or squinting, eye discomfort, or irritation.[19, 20]

2.8 SAD

Seasonal affective disorder, SAD, affects perhaps 1 to 10 percent of the population, depending on which studies are referenced and in what region of the world the research was done. As its name indicates, SAD is a seasonal disorder attributed to the lack of light—either in duration and/or in intensity—during the winter months. It typically sets in between August and September and then ends the following March or April. Symptoms include lethargy, decreased concentration, and fatigue. Increased sleep, increased eating, and increased weight are common results of SAD. Studies show that between 60 and 90 percent of SAD patients can be treated successfully with light therapy. White light exceeding intensities of 250 fc (about 2500 lx) is necessary to have an impact. Most success appears to come from initial treatment consisting of 30 minutes of exposure to 1000 fc (about 10,000 lx) in the morning. Light treatments are often made with fluorescent light boxes. Ultraviolet radiation is filtered from the treatment lamps to minimize the side effects of those wavelengths. It is important to reiterate that light therapy is based on white light of sufficient intensity. Indeed, intensity is more important than the spectral power distribution of the light source—so-called full spectrum lamps show no appreciable benefit in treatment compared to standard fluorescent lamps. In any event, people suspected of having SAD should undertake light treatment only under the care of a physician and/or an opthalmologist.

more online @
www.fhs.mcmaster.ca/direct/depress/sad.html
www.websciences.org/sltbr/jama.htm
www.websciences.org/sltbr/pubinfo.htm#SAD
www.geocities.com/HotSprings/7061/sadhome.html

2.9 Circadian Rhythm

Circadian is of Latin origin and means "about a day." Circadian rhythm refers to the biological cycle of plants and animals. Research concludes that light absorption in the human eye sets and affects our circadian rhythms. As such, light therapy is seen as a method (if not the primary method) of adjusting circadian rhythms for jet-setters and night-shift workers. Doses of daylight or daylight-like intensities (thousands of lux) during the waking hours are important to setting or adjusting the circadian rhythm.[21] Similarly, the absence of light (total darkness) during the sleeping hours is important. Designs can accommodate both of these conditions. Special "light rooms" where shift workers can take a "day break" might be designed into those facilities where two or three shifts

Figure 2.5

Planning the location, distribution, and intensity of luminances help establish people's reactions. The success of lighting designs is more reliant on planning luminances than addressing illuminances (light levels). In this library, the juxtaposition of brighter background to dimmer foreground further distinguishes the uses.
Image ©Gene Meadows

are common, although this should be done only under consultation of specialized medical personnel. Residential settings (e.g., houses, apartments, hotels, etc.) can be designed with blackout shades (an absolute necessity for shift workers sleeping during daylight hours), as well as with carefully controlled exterior lighting at the minimum intensities of safety and security for the particular nighttime activity situation (to maximize the integrity of the normal sleeping period of darkness). If any nightlight whatsoever is required or desired, this should be very low level red light (an excellent application for **LED**s).

more online @
www.circadian.com/
www.jneurosci.org/cgi/reprint/21/16/6405.pdf
www.nsf.gov/news/news_summ.jsp?cntn_id=100858&org=NSF&from=news

LED
Light emitting diode is a solid state light source typically producing very specific wavelength(s). See Chapter 10 for more detailed discussion. *SOLUTION HINT: Red light is believed to limit the interruption of melatonin production during sleeping hours even if a quick trip to the restroom is necessary. Low-output red LEDs used in well-shielded or louvered steplights can be highly effective as nightlights.*

2.10 Psychology

Perceptions of lighted settings are the result of the brain's interpretation of physiological reactions to those lighted settings. These perceptions constitute the psychology of lighting and depend not only on the light intensities, patterns, and color, but also on the interpreter's previous experiences, culture, and mood. While many people might agree on the level of comfort; degree of attractiveness; spatial attributes, such as visual order, volume, simplicity; and the sense of personal space, such as intimate or public in a particular setting, these perceptions can vary mildly to wildly between people. Nor are these perceptions even held universally by all individuals. Hence, the psychology of light is less tangible with a less certain outcome than when encountered with the physiology of light. Nevertheless, a range of studies over the years does identify that lighting influences perceptions in a meaningful and somewhat predictable way.[22, 23] Flynn and colleagues concluded that the experience of lighted space is, at least to some extent, a shared experience.[24]

We like spaces that evoke a sense of pleasantness. Many people relate to the sense of spaciousness, relaxation, intimacy, apprehension, clarity, and so on. For sighted individuals, these responses are largely influenced by what they see. **Luminance**, then, is a significant factor in subjective responses. Luminance location (peripheral versus overhead) influences pleasantness, spaciousness, and relaxation. Luminance distribution (uniform versus nonuniform) influences spaciousness and relaxation. Luminance intensities (bright versus dim) influence visual clarity. This can be used to assist in the success of a lighting design. Figure 2.5 illustrates how luminance location, distribution, and intensities influence perceptions. In the foreground, relatively nonuniform (dappled downlighting and framing projectors), more peripheral and low luminances (achieved with compact fluorescent low wattage, low transmittance pendents) set the scene for a relaxed library youth area. In the background, uniform, overhead, and greater luminances (achieved with linear indirect fluorescent pendents) set the scene for visual clarity and a more spacious and purposeful library stack area and reading room. Later discussion in Chapter 7 expands on the psychological or subjective aspects of lighting.

People appear to have luminance and illuminance preferences for work settings. So light can be used to help direct attention to tasks and make the setting comfortable from a brightness perspective for long term work. The lighting designer has immense influence and, therefore, immense responsibility in addressing luminance and illuminance not only on behalf of people's anticipated/desired physiological response, but on behalf of people's subjective or psychological response. Indeed, it makes little sense to establish light levels that are considered appropriate for, say, reading, if people don't want to read in the resulting lighted setting. This is the ultimate waste of energy and earth resources.

more online @
irc.nrc-cnrc.gc.ca/pubs/bsi/92-5_e.html

luminance

The amount of light reflected from or transmitted through a material. Measured in candelas/ft² (candelas/m²). Perceived as **brightness** (see sidebar next page). Luminance is the product of illuminance and the surface of interest. Opaque materials will reflect illuminance—with dark surfaces reflecting a small amount and light surfaces reflecting a large amount. Translucent materials will both transmit and reflect illuminance—with dark materials transmitting a small amount and light surfaces transmitting a large amount. Luminance depends on illuminance and surface reflectance or transmittance properties. *SOLUTION HINT: Architectural (space) ighting is more efficient with matte, higher-reflecting ceiling and wall materials. However, if the light source is too efficient and the reflecting and transmitting surfaces too reflective and transmissive, overlighting and glare occur.*

Solution

2.11 Endnotes

[1] American Optometric Association, Vision Conditions: Myopia (web page, 2007), http://www.aoa.org/x4688.xml. [Accessed June 16, 2007.]
[2] American Optometric Association, Vision Conditions: Hyperopia (web page, 2007), http://www.aoa.org/x4696.xml. [Accessed June 16, 2007.]

[3] American Optometric Association, Vision Conditions: Visual Acuity: What is 20/20 Vision? (web page, 2007), http://www.aoa.org/x4695.xml. [Accessed June 16, 2007.]

[4] American Optometric Association, Vision Conditions: Color Deficiency (web page, 2007), http://www.aoa.org/x4702.xml. [Accessed June 16, 2007.]

[5] Prevent Blindness America, Color Blindness (web page, 2005), http://www.preventblindness.org/eye_problems/colorvision.html. [Accessed June 16, 2007.]

[6] Peter Boyce, Human Factors in Lighting 2nd Edition (London: Taylor & Francis, 2003), p. 9.

[7] Yunjian He, et. al., Evaluating Light Source Efficacy Under Mesopic Conditions Using Reaction Times, Conference Proceedings—1996 IESNA Annual Conference (New York: Illuminating Engineering Society of North America, 1996), 236–257.

[8] Alan L. Lewis, "Equating Light Sources for Visual Performance at Low Luminances," Journal of the Illuminating Engineering Society, 1998, no. 1: 80–84.

[9] Alan L. Lewis, "Visual Performance as a Function of Spectral Power Distribution of Light Sources at Luminances Used for General Outdoor Lighting," Journal of the Illuminating Engineering Society, 1999, no. 1: 37–42.

[10] Carl Rod Nave, Spectral Power Distribution (web page, 2007), http://hyperphysics.phy-astr.gsu.edu/hbase/vision/spd.html. [Accessed June 16, 2007.]

[11] S. M. Berman, "Energy Efficiency Consequences of Scotopic Sensitivity," Journal of the Illuminating Engineering Society, 1992, no. 1: 3–14.

[12] S. M. Berman, et. al., "Spectral Determinants of Steady-State Pupil Size with Full Field of View," Journal of the Illuminating Engineering Society, 1992, no. 2: 3–13.

[13] National Eye Institute/National Institutes of Health, Cataract (web page, 2007), http://www.nei.nih.gov/health/cataract/cataract_facts.asp. [Accessed June 16, 2007.]

[14] Peter Howarth, This is Peter Howarth's Teaching Home Page, Loughborough University, Presbyopia (web page, 2000), http://www-staff.lboro.ac.uk/~huph/presby.htm. [Accessed September 24, 2000.]

[15] T. M. Montgomery, Optometric Physician, Anatomy, Physiology and Pathology of the Human Eye: The Crystalline Lens (web page, 2007), http://www.tedmontgomery.com/the_eye/index.html. [Accessed June 16, 2007.]

[16] W. N. Charman, "Age, lens transmittance, and the possible effects of light on melatonin suppression," Ophthalmic and Physiological Optics, 2003, no. 2: 181–187.

[17] Mark S. Rea, ed, The IESNA Lighting Handbook: Reference and Application, Ninth Edition (New York: Illuminating Engineering Society of North America, 2000), p. 10–15.

[18] American Optometric Association, Eye Diseases: Cataract (web page, 2007), http://www.aoa.org/x4714.xml. [Accessed June 16, 2007.]

[19] U-M Kellogg Eye Center Department of Ophthalmology and Visual Sciences, Eye Conditions/Astigmatism (web page, 2007), http://www.kellogg.umich.edu/patientcare/conditions/astigmatism.html. [Accessed June 16, 2007.]

[20] Peter Howarth, This is Peter Howarth's Teaching Home Page, Loughborough University, Astigmatism (web page, 2003), http://www-staff.lboro.ac.uk/~huph/astig.htm. [Accessed June 16, 2007.]

[21] George C. Brainaird, et. al., "Action Spectrum for Melatonin Regulation in Humans: Evidence for a Novel Circadian Photoreceptor," The Journal of Neuroscience, August 15, 2001, 21(16): 6405–6412.

[22] Dale Tiller, Lighting Quality, National Research Council of Canada, http://irc.nrc-cnrc.gc.ca/pubs/bsi/92-5_e.html. [Accessed June 16, 2007.]

[23] Belinda Collins, Evaluation of Subjective Response to Lighting Distributions: A Literature Review/NISTIR 5119 (Gaithersburg, MD: National Institute of Standards and Technology, 1993).

[24] John E. Flynn, et. al., "Interim Study of Procedures for Investigating the Effect of Light on Impression and Behavior," Journal of the Illuminating Engineering Society, 1973, no. 3: 94.

brightness
The subjective sensation caused by luminance(s). Recognize that this "sensation" not only depends on the luminance of the object and on the eyes doing the viewing and on the viewer's experience and mood, but also on the surrounding or environmental luminance conditions. For example, a car headlight energized during the day is not at all bright. However, the same car headlight at dusk does indeed have some "good" brightness. At night, the headlight has sufficient brightness to be considered bothersome. On a rainy night, the headlight has such intense brightness as to be glary. But the luminance of the headlight remains constant during each of these situations. Luminaires seen against dark backgrounds are usually glary. *SOLUTION HINT: Use higher-reflecting wall and ceiling finishes or where darker finishes are present use lower-wattage lights recognizing brightness impressions and illuminances will suffer.*

2.12 References

Flynn, John E., Kremers, Jack A., Segil, Arthur W., and Steffy, Gary R. 1992. Architectural Interior Systems, 3rd ed. New York: Van Nostrand Reinhold.

Hedge, Alan. 2007. Vision and Light, DEA 350 Human Factors: Ambient Environment, Cornell University (web page, January 2007), http://ergo.human.cornell.edu/studentdownloads/DEA350pdfs/vision.pdf. [Accessed September 16, 2007.]

IESNA Lighting for the Aged and Partially Sighted Committee. 1998. Recommended Practice for Lighting and the Visual Environment for Senior Living. New York: Illuminating Engineering Society of North America.

Lam, William M. C., Ripman, Christopher H., ed. 1992. Perception and Lighting as Formgivers for Architecture. New York: Van Nostrand Reinhold.

Moyer, Janet Lennox. 2005. The Landscape Lighting Book, 2nd ed. New York: John Wiley & Sons, Inc.

Phillips, Derek. 1997. Lighting Historic Buildings. New York: McGraw-Hill.

Rea, Mark S., ed. and Thompson, Brian J., general ed. 1992. Selected Papers on Architectural Lighting. Bellingham, WA: SPIE Optical Engineering Press.

Rea, Mark S., ed. 2000. The IESNA Lighting Handbook: Reference & Application. New York: Illuminating Engineering Society of North America.

Rosenzweig, Mark R. 1999. "Vision: From Eye to Brain." In Biological Psychology: An Introduction to Behavioral, Cognitive, and Clinical Neuroscience, 2nd ed. Sunderland, MA: Sinauer Associates, Inc.

P erhaps obvious, but many times not clearly detailed, it must be understood what kind of project is to be undertaken; the extent of the work to be undertaken; the amount of compensation for time invested in the project according to some predetermined fee arrangement; and who or what group will represent the people who intend to use the planned space(s). Once such necessary formalities are dispensed, then lighting design can move forward.

The phases of lighting design typically parallel architectural design work and might include programming, design strategies, schematic (or preliminary) design, design development, contract documents, and construction administration. Figure 3.1 shows the linear progression of a project from start to finish. Depending on the size of the project and/or the schedule, some of these activities may be merged with one another or even eliminated altogether from the designer's scope. Typically, the larger the project, the longer the schedule, and/or the more and distinct the phases, the greater the time requirements to complete the project, and the greater the fees necessary. So before starting work, the designer must understand what the work encompasses.

3.1 Project Specifics

The size, extent, location, and type of the project and its schedule must be understood before getting underway. Certainly, an office on the floor of an industrial plant may, but not necessarily will, be different than an office in the executive suite of a Fortune 500 company. Indeed, either of these offices will likely be different from that of a dot-com skunk-works. Further, few clients are willing to pay identical fees to perform the same analysis on a 100 ft² (about 9 m²) office as might be expected on a 250,000 ft² (about 23,000 m²) office. Alternatively, few clients have reservations about adding a room here and there during a project's early schematic phase. This "scope creep" can easily balloon into a significant amount of work. Clearly understand and reiterate the extent of the project prior to commencement.

The area of the project is important. This will offer some sense of the likely variety of space types involved. Additionally, larger projects typically enjoy the benefits of economies of scale—greater quantities of lighting hardware generally result in a lower per-unit cost. Further, the size of the project will offer clues to the depth of problem solving involved. Larger projects tend to have larger teams involved and, thereby, require greater time commitments for meetings to review design options and systems' integration issues. Larger projects tend to offer bigger challenges on dealing with expansive floor plans and mitigating sameness throughout. Finally, larger projects challenge the designer on specification and maintenance standards—minimizing the numbers and types of lamps, luminaires, ballasts, and lighting control devices involved.

The number of different space types involved is important information. Here, the designer will have an early sense on the diversity of the people and tasks that will need to be accommodated.

Understanding the schedule is critical to the timing and the degree of performance by the designer for the various stages of the design effort. Extraordinarily fast schedules tend to limit the designer to assessing hardware on which data is readily available, and limit the designer to the number of design

Figure 3.1

In a typical project, the progression of work is not strictly linear as depicted here. That is, several iterations may occur within some steps or even between steps. For example, in the 3rd step, the pre-liminary design needs to respond to the architecture—so if the architecture is evolving while preliminary lighting design is underway, then the preliminary lighting design will need to change or evolve with the architecture. Some design, some review, some revision, some more design, and so on. There are also times when the project so significantly changes midway through design that the process needs to begin anew. For example, if the project size doubles during the 4th step, then it may be necessary to start anew with the 2nd step. The progression of work is also related to **project scope**.

project scope
Depending on project economics, the team makeup, the schedule, and/or the client's level and breadth of concern about lighting, the scope may include an entire project, just a few rooms or areas, and just a few steps (e.g., 2nd, 3rd, and 4th). At times, just one step (typically the 4th) is undertaken. Abbreviated versions of the 2nd and 3rd steps are then appended to the 4th step (programming and schematic designing are still a necessity, just not formally recognized as full-blown steps).

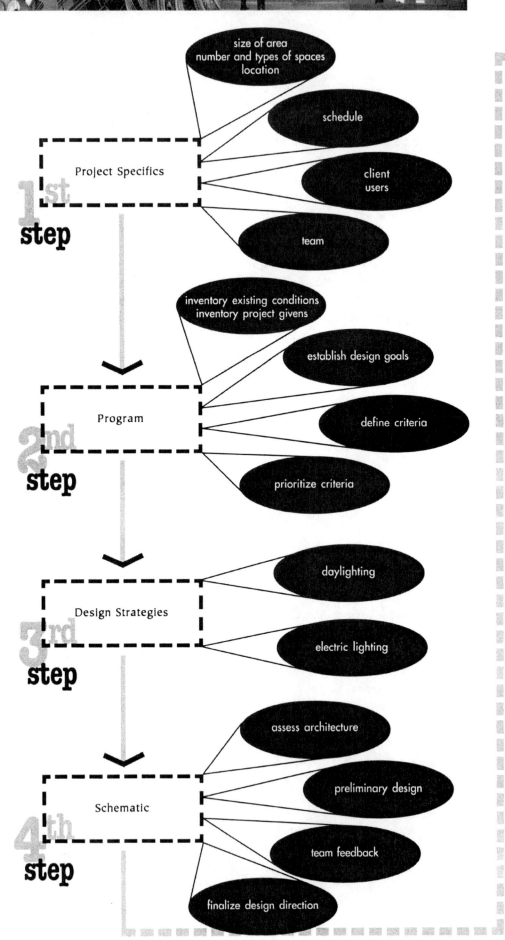

Architectural Lighting Design

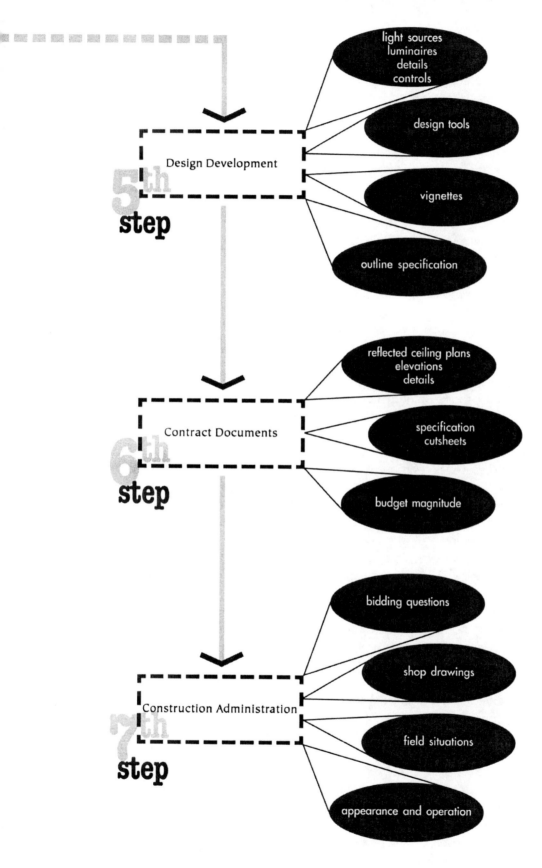

5th step

Design Development
- light sources
- luminaires
- details
- controls
- design tools
- vignettes
- outline specification

6th step

Contract Documents
- reflected ceiling plans
- elevations
- details
- specification
- cutsheets
- budget magnitude

7th step

Construction Administration
- bidding questions
- shop drawings
- field situations
- appearance and operation

scheme iterations that can be reviewed prior to settling on a preferred option. Knowing the client and having access to the client influence the success of any given lighting design. Inevitably, and most times unintentional, information filtration occurs with every communicating party on a project. With ever-increasing communication speeds and where more work is to be accomplished in less time, there is a tendency to edit out information for brevity's sake. Much gets lost in translation between the actual users, the client, the client's representative, the architect, the engineer, and so on. Many times, users, particularly on large projects, are not representing themselves during the project design process. Sometimes, the client (the individual representing the entity paying the design fees) is far removed from the actual users of the building. The lighting designer's client might be an architect, an engineer, a developer, a facility engineer, or a manager in the users' corporation, or the president or CEO of the users' corporation. The further removed from the users, the more care must be taken in interpreting lighting information provided by the client. Additionally, lighting decisions made by the client may not well represent the users' needs. For example, a developer may reject lighting options because they do not meet preconceived cost parameters, when, in fact, no lighting system at that cost point will meet the users' needs. Asking more pointed questions of the client and more carefully addressing programming may be necessary to better understand and address users' needs and convince the client of same.

On larger projects and those that are to be more successful, a team of design professionals is appropriate. Figure 3.2 outlines an organization chart of one possible team arrangement. This team is responsible for addressing the human (users) and the technical issues on the project. Additionally, and usually subliminally, the team must deal with ego(s). The team should then attempt to deal with these human, technical, and ego issues together. A team typically consists of a users' representative, an owner's representative, an architect, an electrical engineer, an interior designer, a mechanical (**HVAC**) engineer, a lighting designer, a fire-protection consultant, an acoustician, a landscape architect, a structural engineer, and a construction manager. Other possible team members may include a wayfinding consultant, a security consultant, and a code consultant. Depending on the scale and duration of the project, contractors play an important role on the team, reporting to the construction manager. Recognize that some of these team members may be one in the same. For example, an architect may elect to perform interior design, lighting design, fire protection, and acoustical services. Nevertheless, quite a few players are involved. Ignoring representatives of certain disciplines or attempting to work without their input may frustrate the design process and ultimately frustrate the owner, leading to unsatisfactory results. On the other hand, it is incumbent on all team members to share any specific requirements that they may have of other professionals on the team. For example, if the lighting designer has no knowledge that the HVAC engineer intends to return air through ceiling luminaires, then there is a great likelihood that the ceiling luminaires will not be specified with this air-return capability; indeed, there may not even be any ceiling-recessed luminaires planned for the project.

Fine examples of teamwork are often found on historic restoration projects. On these projects, additional team members, beyond those cited above, might include art conservator, materials and painting conservators, an historian, and, most importantly,

HVAC
Heating, ventilating, and air-conditioning. Used as a reference to the professional (HVAC engineer) and/or to the system (HVAC). Pronounced as H-V-A-C or as H-Vac.

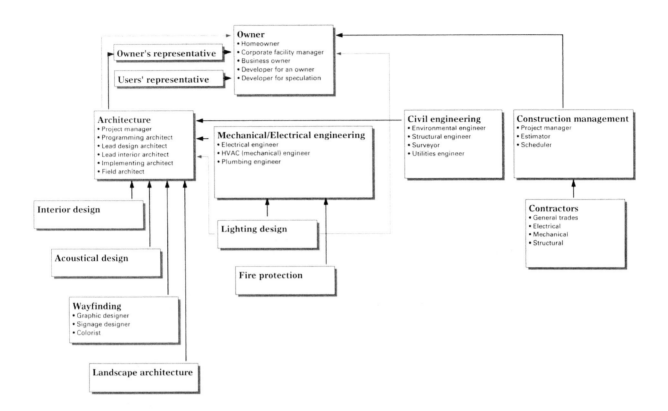

Figure 3.2

An organizational chart of what might be a team arrangement for a particular project. Direction of arrows indicates the reporting direction of respective team members. The dashed lines from lighting designer to architect and to owner, and from architect to owner represent other possible and common reporting directions. Bullet items suggest possible specific members of the team.

a lead restoration architect. Further, contractors are key members of the team on such projects—where exploration of existing physical conditions is necessary to appreciate what, how, and if lighting can be integrated into details or architecture, or mounted on the architecture in a way that is reminiscent of what might have been authentic to the original architecture or to discretely locate modern equipment. Figures 3.3, 3.4, and 3.5 illustrate a portion of the results of such an effort by a full complement of team members. It cannot be overemphasized that the work by all of the team members was crucial to the final result's success. This includes the owner's representative (for the project shown in Figures 3.2, 3.3, and 3.4, several owner's representatives were involved). The give and take, the breadth of ideas discussed and explored, and the robustness of the resolution greatly depend on this team approach. Unfortunately, many clients today believe such a team approach takes too much time and too much money. However, no shortcuts offer the same degree and success of results as a full team.

3.2 Programming

Programming a project is critical to understanding the kinds of living and working functions that are going to occur or at least are expected to occur on a given project. Programming may be nothing more than a survey of existing conditions (where do the users or owners now live or work and what kinds of living or working are done there) with a critical eye toward future desires or needs for their living and working. For example, if a client has workers using standard computer monitors with a few plasma screens interspersed as a test situation, then some detective work is in order. Are these plasma screen monitors (which for

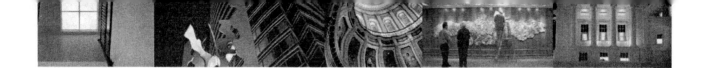

this example are flatter, are more matte, and exhibit better contrast than the standard computer monitor) being considered for mass implementation in the near future? Do users find these screens better or worse and why? Will the use of these screens coincide with more or less work on the computer by the users? Will users keep the old monitors in addition to the new and use both?

In addition to understanding the intended living and/or working functions and an understanding of the people doing the living/working, programming includes an inventory of existing conditions and project givens, establishing design goals, proposing lighting design criteria, and prioritizing that criteria. Project programming is discussed in Chapter 4 and project criteria are discussed in Chapters 5, 6, 7, and 8.

3.3 Design Strategies

Once programming aspects have been established, the designer(s) can strategize about how lighting can best address the programmed needs. For lighting, programming not only involves people and their intended functions, but any architectural givens which have been established. Strategizing typically involves cross-discipline influences. The architectural concept is probably fluid at this stage—indeed, the architecture may respond to lighting, mechanical, structural, or other systems.

Strategy(ies) will have much to do with programmed criteria. If a clear directive from the client is for a "LEED-certified building," then lighting strategy(ies) might address some or all of the LEED lighting-related credits. One strategy might be the exclusive use of fluorescent or LED lighting. Another strategy might be the use of only very low wattage downlighting on the exterior facade and site lighting. Although these are seemingly simple strategies in the abstract, they will be difficult to implement if all of the other lighting criteria are to be addressed. Therein lies the challenge of and rationale for schematic design and design development. Of course, many times clients "want it all"—a quality work or living environment, LEED-certified, on-schedule, under-budget, and so on. Code compliance is a requirement regardless. Yet a clearly focused strategy sets the bar for any project.

3.4 Schematic Design

As design strategy(ies) are considered and solidified, the designer can think about what lighting approaches might best embody the design strategy(ies) and address project lighting criteria. Schematic design records those thoughts for client and team consideration. A lighting schematic indicates that the design has progressed from nothing to at least general approaches and perhaps even preliminary plan or sketch diagrams illustrating the proposed scheme(s). Schematic lighting design typically results in an understanding and agreement among the client and team members of lighting criteria and general lighting approaches. Schematic design may result in the answering of a myriad of questions raised while attempting to advance the design strategy(ies) with viable lighting approaches.

fenestration
The opening(s) or aperture(s) in a building that permit the entry of daylight.

Lighting schematics may be driven by architecture. If daylighting emerged as the design strategy for a 30,000 ft^2 (about 2,800 m^2) office building, schematic lighting will drive the architecture of the building (see Chapter 9), then siting and form along with **fenestration** ideas should be explored in schematic design.

Architectural Lighting Design

In the best situation, work between the architectural schematic design and the lighting schematic design is iterative. That is, some preliminary thoughts on architecture are posed and lighting thoughts based on the program requirements *and* the newly conceived architectural thoughts are then posed. Here, there may be discussion regarding the lighting outcome *if* the architecture can be reconfigured in various ways. In a single-story 30,000 sf office building, the geometry of the building, its orientation, and active and/or passive daylighting schemes will combine to provide the best schematic design. This actively participative and iterative design process is not common. The effort takes the time and patience of the design team and client. Egos must be held in check. Ultimately, an arbiter, preferably a well-informed client, must guide the scheme if the team wrangles too much or too long without consensus. Otherwise, the architectural elements may be beautiful, but the lighting may render the architecture ugly or, at least, not to its fullest glory. Worse, however, the architecture may be stunning, but at the expense of ergonomically appropriate lighting. Can exciting, unique, and/or award-winning architectural forms and surfaces overcome glare? Most users are experts in seeing; few are experts in architectural design. In a sustainable-centric world, address functionality and comfort foremost, otherwise, why bother?

Electric lighting scheme(s) are also proposed. Depending on the extent of daylighting, electric lighting will be used to augment or supplant it. For example, if a light shelf scheme is proposed for daylighting, and if the facility is intended for long hours of operation outside of typical daylight hours, then electric light integrated with the light shelf scheme should be explored.

Once a schematic design(s) has been established, then feedback from the entire team is necessary—unless this feedback has occurred during the iterative process throughout schematic design. The other professionals and the client must have a chance to understand the lighting design scheme and respond to it, particularly if the lighting schematic poses a problem or problems with other systems' functions and/or their success. If feedback is significant, then additional lighting schematic iterations will be necessary to refine the scheme to a point where other disciplines are not negatively affected or have had a chance to modify their respective systems' schemes to work with the lighting scheme. Back and forth design ideas should be readily exchanged in an effort to home in on a viable, collaborative lighting scheme.

Schematic design is also the time to introduce intended lamping schemes. Defusing misconceptions or debunking myths is best addressed early. Such long-held public misconceptions may range from "use full-spectrum lamps for better health and vision" to "never use fluorescent lamps." During schematic design, clients can be educated on pros and cons of various lamping schemes. The electrical engineer will want to know if and where "slow-start" or "long-warm-up" lamps are proposed since this may help determine his/her emergency lighting strategy. At this stage, if a light shelf is part of a daylighting strategy, then an electric lighting strategy might be shelf-integrated indirect lighting. An idea toward lamping (fluorescent or LED or **CMH** for example) should be discussed if not proposed.

Once feedback has been received and addressed, the lighting scheme is finalized. This yields schematic or preliminary lighting plans illustrating the scope of various lighting strategies throughout the project and documenting preliminary light sources

CMH
Ceramic metal halide lamps are a part of the HID (high intensity discharge) family of lamps. CMH lamps are the most efficacious white light point sources today exhibiting excellent color rendering, long life, and available in a warm white 3000K color temperature.

Figure 3.3

Restoration of the 1879 Michigan Capitol was completed in 1992. The strategy was simple—restore the capitol. The lighting strategy involved identifying historic light locations and luminaire styles from historic documentation. However, introducing modern systems and infrastructure was a significant task—one that could not and would not have been so successful without the diligent teamwork of many professionals (see **Team** on next page). Here, the interior of the rotunda dome is viewed from the main floor. The lighting is the result of design **charrette**s during design development to review and develop options, at which stage it was determined that historic lights alone could not achieve an overall successful lighting approach without overly glary historic lights. From this view, the first view experienced by visitors, the decorative ceilings around the rotunda perimeter appear to be lit from early electric shades. See Figures 3.4 and 3.5. Image ©Balthazar Korab

2nd floor ceiling

charrette

A short, concentrated design or planning activity. Typically, a half- or full-day session when design team members engage in an intensive design meeting to sort through various design issues and assess the likely impact of various design options. The result is, typically, NOT a design, but a direction of one or several potential design options that are to be pursued further with pros/cons presented at a later session.

and some luminaire types. As the scheme is advanced for client review and hopeful approval, the stage is set for design development. Major changes in schematic approach after this point may wreak havoc on the team's efforts, perhaps resulting in a requirement for additional fees to develop a new schematic, and resulting in a longer project schedule.

3.5 Design Development

When a scheme is approved, the next step is to review and propose specific equipment alternatives and layouts to meet the intent of the scheme. For example, in the light-shelf-integrated uplighting the character of the uplight optics (optically active or passive), and physical parameters of luminaires (e.g., shallow

Figure 3.4

Floor-integrated uplights at the balconies were certainly not original to the 1879 building. Programming of the rotunda, however, called for a brighter appearance (more surface luminance). In addition to the near-original and relatively dim historic lighting, this meant introducing more period lighting (hanging from the balconies or walls) or discretely using modern lighting equipment (uplighting was one of several methods reviewed). After deliberation by the team, and after a mock-up in situ, it was agreed that the uplights were the least obtrusive means to introduce more overall luminance. The uplights accent specific architectural elements—the pilasters and the balcony armatures—thereby enhancing the effect of the electric shade lanterns on each armature. See Figure 3.5.
Image ©Balthazar Korab

Team/Michigan Capitol

Project: Rotunda and upper corridors, and façade and site
Owner: State of Michigan
Restoration architect: Richard Frank, FAIA
Implementing architects: Architects Four, Quinn Evans | Architects, and Wigen Tincknell Meyer & Associates
Lighting designer: Gary Steffy Lighting Design Inc.
Mechanical engineer: Shreve Weber Stellwagen
Electrical engineer: Shreve Weber Stellwagen
Structural engineer: Robert Darvas & Associates
Historian: William Seale
Art conservator: Detroit Institute of Arts
Stone conservator: Norman Weiss
Materials conservation and reconstruction: Washington University Technology Associates
Painting conservator: Darla Olson
Wayfinding: Corbin Design
Landscape architect: William Johnson & Associates
Construction manager: The Christman Company
Electrical contractors: F.D. Hayes Electric Co. and Quality Electrical, Inc.

and wide or deep and narrow) are explored. Not only is the electric uplight studied, but the effect of the luminaire on the effectiveness of the light shelf to reflect daylight is studied. There may come a time when a mock-up is necessary to determine if any distracting or disturbing light reflections will take place during the course of a day (recognizing that various sky conditions must be reviewed, including clear, partly cloudy, and overcast).

Now is also the time to review and, if needed, suggest modifications to architectural design aspects. For example, if the architectural design has advanced to include dark, polished granite walls in a small elevator lobby, but the lighting scheme is cove uplighting, then the walls will exhibit low luminance (and appear very dark). Will the money be well spent on the dark, polished granite, which can't be seen and which contributes to a dark, confining lobby space? If the wall

Figure 3.5

This view of the 2nd-floor rotunda illustrates the three lighting layers used to achieve the overall look of the 2nd floor ceiling seen in Figure 3.3.
Image right ©Balthazar Korab

Historic electric shade

Relatively dim to minimize glare, the historic electric shade gives the impression that it provides much of the light in the rotunda, when, in fact, its role is strictly for historic appearance.

Picture light

Highlights governors' portraits with warm tone 3000K fluorescent lamp for a relatively incandescent look. This lamp is shielded with a UV filter to protect the artwork from UV degradation. Although not seen in lighting catalogs much before 1900, this provides a more historic portrait lighting approach than any ceiling-recessed or **monopoint** would achieve.

monopoint

A single trackhead mounted to a ceiling canopy rather than on a linear track. *SOLUTION HINT: Monopoints are typically used where no ceiling plenum depth exists for recessed lights and/or where a more permanent, neat look is desired over tracklighting (monopoints cannot be readily moved/rearranged). See image below where four monopoints light an art wall.*
Image below ©Justin Maconochie

In-floor uplight

Accentuates detailed and decorated pilaster and decorative paint on ceiling panel, giving the impression that the light is provided by the historic electric shade.

material isn't changed, then the lighting scheme should be revised to include lighting of the granite walls (which, by the way, will provide a more pleasing, comfortable visual environment than just downlights alone spread throughout the lobby). Recognize the energy implications of the dark granite walls. It may be quite reasonable to argue that using more energy in such a highly public space that will be seen and enjoyed by all users of the building is a worthwhile endeavor, providing, of course, that this does not negatively impact the project's ability to meet energy code or, if a programmed requirement, LEED certification.

Light sources are the engines that propel any lighting solution. Before specific luminaires are selected, the lighting designer should consider the most suitable lamping for a given scheme. Once light sources are reviewed and a selection is narrowed, luminaires can be reviewed and a selection of these narrowed for

design team consideration. Light sources are covered in Chapter 9 (Daylighting) and in Chapter 10 (Lamps). Chapter 11 covers luminaires.

Where architectural details are part of the design scheme, these need to be further refined in the design development phase. This is not to be a final, construction-level detail, but should illustrate the size of the detail necessary to hold the lighting hardware and to permit its appropriate optical performance, its orientation, and required finishes for successful operation. Details are discussed throughout the text in appropriate related chapters, such as Daylight, Lamps, and Luminaires.

Controls (how lights are switched on/off or dimmed) should be developed by proposing which groups or individual luminaires are to be separately controlled from other groups or individual luminaires and which are to be on/off switched or dimmed and whether this process is to be manual, automatic, or some hybrid. Automation should play a significant role in controlling lighting to avoid energy waste during unoccupied conditions or when daylight is available. Special controls may be necessary in more functionally complicated spaces, such as presentation rooms, auditoriums, boardrooms, conference rooms, home theaters, and the like. Controls are discussed further in Chapter 12.

Design tools are necessary in the design development phase, or perhaps even in the schematic design that help illustrate the lighting ideas and offer some quantitative analyses of the proposed lighting. These tools range from labor-intensive model building, hand sketching, and airbrushing techniques to computer rendering and calculation techniques. The charge is to convince yourself and project team members that the proposed lighting will, indeed, offer an aesthetically pleasing appearance and also meet the programmed needs of users. Chapter 13 discusses design tools.

Development of at least **vignette** layouts and an outline specification is the result of the design development phase. This helps consolidate lighting ideas and clarify the proposed lighting for all team members. This also permits the registered professionals on the project to assess systems' integration issues and request clarifications or revisions by respective team members.

vignette
An abbreviated portion of a lighting layout that expresses the typical characteristics (such as dimensions, locations, orientations, and type of luminaires) of the lighting plan without developing a complete, entire plan(s).

3.6 Contract Documents

In order to formalize the lighting design, the lighting designer must pull together documents that finalize the lighting and provide a clear indication of where and what kind of lighting equipment is necessary to meet the needs of the users. Unless registered to practice architecture or electrical engineering, the lighting designer cannot offer sealed or stamped documents. However, the lighting designer should provide finished and complete reflected ceiling plans, clarification documents (such as lighting details and elevations illustrating wall-mounted lighting equipment), and lighting specifications. Part of the specification (an appendix) should include cutsheets for clarity of luminaire, lamp, and/or detail selection. The contractor can use cutsheets to procure more accurate **shop drawings** and installation instructions.

At the contract document phase, there is sufficient information to provide a complete cost magnitude. For lighting, this should include hardware cost magnitude and some sense of installation cost magnitude. Further, life cycle cost magnitude

shop drawings
Detailed luminaire drawings provided by the luminaire manufacturers and submitted through the contractor for the team's review and recommended disposition (e.g., rejected, accepted with changes, accepted). These shop drawings typically show detailed dimensional and material characteristics of the lighting equipment. Shop drawing review is considered a "check step" that helps the design team confirm that the contractor has indeed ordered the equipment as specified to meet the users' needs.

may be necessary in order to justify the use of more expensive (initially), longer-life, and/or more efficient lighting equipment.

All of the material the lighting designer generates in this phase must then be qualified and compiled by the registered professionals and issued as part of their respective contract documentation to contractors for pricing and/or bidding. Chapter 14 discusses the various aspects of contract documents.

3.7 Construction Admin

Once a project has been issued to a contractor (or to several contractors) for pricing and/or bidding, the CA (construction administration) phase begins for the lighting designer. Here, there may be a need for clarifications during the bidding process. As questions arise from bidding contractors, electrical distributors, or lighting equipment manufacturers' representatives, the lighting designer may be asked to provide answers or clarifications.

After bidding is complete and the project has been awarded to a contractor, additional questions may arise during the procurement of materials and/or as construction progresses. At some point (hopefully well in advance of lighting installation), the contractor submits shop drawings of the lighting equipment to the team for review and recommended disposition. These are typically more detailed drawings of the lighting equipment—showing precise dimensions, lamping configuration, intended operational orientation, and any mounting hardware, aiming, and/or rotational hardware and locking devices.

There may be times during construction when it becomes apparent that there are conflicts between lighting equipment and other systems. Depending on installation sequences, any field changes resulting from other systems' integration issues, and depending on the level with which the registered professionals compiled the documents, it may be necessary for site visits to assess the field situation(s) and address these as they develop.

As the project nears completion, the lighting designer visits the project to assess the lighting effects and to assess the visual aesthetic of the exposed lighting hardware. Incorrect lamping, luminaire finishes, aiming, lensing, and the like can lead to poor lighting effects—too little light, too much light, too narrow a light pattern, too broad a light pattern, and so on. Construction administration is discussed in more detail in Chapter 14.

Getting a handle on the problem involves assessment of the users' existing conditions and intended future living and/or work conditions. In other words, what is the program for the people in the to-be-designed space? Programming a project does not necessarily take much time, although large, rather unusual projects generally require a substantial amount of programming time. Lighting programming does require a concerned and committed designer interested in the kinds of criteria that make a space successful for the people who use it. The quality of the programming effort affects the quality and success of the lighting design. If the design is for speculative construction, then its prospective occupants may not be available, but it is reasonable to assume occupants' characteristics, their existing working conditions, potential tasks, and so on. The programming phase consists of inventorying conditions of existing space(s), inventorying givens for the planned space(s), establishing design goals, and defining and prioritizing criteria.

4.1 Inventory Conditions

Taking inventory of the existing conditions and/or design givens of any project is critical in assessing vision, perception, and subsequently lighting needs of users. It is preferable for the lighting designer to have knowledge of a variety of characteristics of the existing and proposed architecture. The process of getting to know the architecture, as well as the perceptions of the users, the owner, and the other designers, prepares the lighting designer for making rational, appropriate lighting decisions as the project progresses (see Figures 4.1 and 4.2). A checklist shown in Table 4.1 can be used as a guide for taking inventory of the conditions of existing and/or planned space(s) on a project. This can be gathered from a variety of sources. The architect and/or interior designer undoubtedly have made programming progress of his/her/their own. A memo, report, sketches, and/or drawings may exist that detail the existing conditions if these exist and/or of the proposed conditions being planned. Where such information is unavailable from other sources, the lighting designer will need to investigate the users' existing situation and/or the architectural plans and ideas first hand. Even where information is available from others, the lighting designer should investigate the existing conditions first hand. This entails visits to the facility or facilities in which the users are now living/working. A record can then be made of many of the items outlined in Table 4.1. To better understand the views of the owner and other designers on the conditions of the existing and planned space(s), meetings or at least voice conversations should occur.

Some of the inventory information is a matter of observation and measurement taking in users' existing environment(s) to better appreciate the conditions to which users have become accustomed and/or which users like or dislike or about which they have no opinion. Some information, however, requires interaction with users. Questions regarding users' opinions of existing lighting conditions will help in assessing the strengths and weaknesses of the existing environment and begin to direct the designer toward solutions to meet any shortcomings when planning the new construction or the renovation of the existing facility. A few points of etiquette, however. First, clear all site visits and any lines of questioning with the owner or owner's representative and/or with your client. Second, work up just a few simple,

Table 4.1 Inventory Existing and/or Planned Conditions

takeoffs
Related to quantities, as in the takeoff of each area, the number of each type of luminaire, or other elements necessary for establishing budgets. Usually taken off of plans—hence "takeoff."

indirect lighting
Architectural lighting achieved with luminaires exhibiting an indirect light distribution—90 to 100% of the light exits the luminaire upward; 0 to 10% of the light exits the luminaire downward. See Figure 11.15e.

semi-indirect lighting
Architectural lighting achieved with luminaires exhibiting a semi-indirect light distribution—60 to 90% of the light exits the luminaire upward;10 to 40% of the light exits the luminaire downward. See Figure 11.15d.

direct-indirect lighting
Architectural lighting achieved with luminaires exhibiting an indirect/direct light distribution—40 to 60% of the light exits the luminaire upward; 40 to 60% of the light exits the luminaire downward. See Figure 11.17.

LRV
Light Reflectance Value of the finish in question, typically reported by paint manufacturers. Sometimes referred to as simple reflectance or value (see Munsell discussion in Section 7.2). Represents percentage of light that will be reflected from a surface finished in the color/finish in question.[1] An LRV of 68 indicates 68% of the light striking the surface will be reflected. This value does not identify the specularity or gloss characteristics of the finish (e.g., matte or flat, semi-specular or semi-gloss, or specular or high-gloss). *SOLUTION HINT: Matte finishes are less glary (exhibiting less bling) and are very appropriate for work settings.*

Parameter	Inventory
☐ Space dimensions	• Lengths • Widths • Heights
☐ Spatial form	• Rectilinear • Curvilinear • Pie-shaped • Amorphous
☐ Space activities	• Primary (may be several) • Secondary (may be several) • Infrequent but critically important
☐ Visual tasks	• Prioritize by importance • Prioritize by time spent on each
☐ Occupants' ages by group	• 20 to 40 years old • 40 to 60 years old • 60 or more years old
☐ Furnishings	• Low and open • Low and closed • High and open • High and closed
☐ Surface finishes	• Degree of gloss • Colors • **LRV**
☐ Lighting	• Illuminances • Luminances • Luminaire types, layouts, and lamping • Daylighting
☐ Users' feedback	• Complaints about present environment • Compliments about present environment
☐ Owner's feedback	• Image • Users' satisfaction
☐ Designers' expectations	• Image • Monument to owner • Improve human condition

Significance

The size of the space has an impact on a variety of lighting issues. Quantitative lighting aspects are affected by space geometry. Subjective aspects are influenced by space geometry. Space dimensions also allow for some quick "**takeoffs**" of area (ft^2 or m^2) and assist in early cost guesses. Ceiling heights may influence general lighting approaches—limiting application for ceiling suspended **indirect**, **semi-indirect**, or **direct-indirect** lighting systems.

The geometry of the space affects the success of a variety of lighting techniques. Quantitative aspects, such as lighting efficiency, are greatly influenced with space shape and geometry. *SOLUTON HINT: Generally, larger, moderate ceiling spaces (10' to 12' in height) offer a more efficient use of daylight and electric light.* Subjective aspects, such as spatial comprehension, are also influenced by spatial form. Long, narrow spaces with low ceilings promote a sense of enclosure or confinement particularly when downlit with no wall lighting. See Figures 4.1 and 4.2.

Understanding activities can greatly help the lighting designer develop more appropriate lighting criteria. For example, in a retirement center, if the lobby is to be used for short-term socializing (greetings and good-byes) and for long-term socializing where users take up knitting, card playing, philately, or other hobbies, then simply addressing the space as a lobby and lighting it accordingly will result in serious underlighting.

One way to know the kinds of tasks that are likely to be involved in the planned spaces is to observe and query users regarding the tasks they typically perform and the importance and duration of these tasks. Users and/or the client should be asked to confirm that these kinds of tasks, in this priority of importance, and in these durations, are anticipated in the planned spaces. If not, then the lighting designer should ask for specifics about the kinds of tasks, their priorities, and duration of such tasks anticipated in the planned spaces.

Generally, 60-year-old eyes need two to three times as much light as 20-year-old eyes to perform a task to the same degree of accuracy and timeliness. Some assessment, then, of the ages of people likely to use the planned facility is appropriate. By observation, the lighting designer should attempt to categorize users' ages by percentage of population. Aging eyes are also more sensitive to glare than young eyes. General lighting and task lighting may elicit complaints of glare depending on the age of the population and on the degree (or lack) of optical control (e.g., lensing, louvering) or on the optical distribution of light. *SOLUTION HINT: Indirect or direct-indirect lighting is less glary than direct lighting.*

Lighting system efficiency is greatly influenced by furnishings. Further, some furniture configurations create shadows that can result in complaints of too little light. Tall workstation partitions (e.g., greater than 60 inches height) and low ceilings (e.g., a ceiling height at or less than 8' in height) along with the ubiquitous binder bins or shelves all combine to reduce lighting effectiveness and introduce strong shadowing. The furnishing configurations also influence subjective impressions. Greater density of workstations and/or taller partitions introduce a sense of confinement.

Surface finishes affect both the quantitative aspects of light and the subjective aspects of light. *SOLUTION HINT: High reflectances (LRVs approaching 90% for ceilings and 50% for walls and 20% for floors) greatly improve lighting efficiency and overall brightness impressions.* Additionally, surface reflectances greatly influence transient adaptation as users switch views between paper tasks, computer tasks, and background surfaces. Low-reflectance surfaces are likely to create transient adaptation problems—tired eyes and/or headaches may result during the course of a day. The gloss (degree of specularity or matteness) of surfaces will help in assessing glare (more gloss yields more glare).

See text for discussion.

Getting user feedback on existing conditions requires the designer to survey users. Table 4.2 suggests some questions for surveying users. This information can be used to develop more successful lighting solutions for the proposed spaces.

Although many times owners are not the users of planned spaces, the designer should take stock of the owner's expectations. Does the owner have an image to uphold or establish? Does the owner hold users' satisfaction in high regard? See text for additional discussion.

See text for discussion.

Figure 4.1

One outcome of inventorying conditions on this renovation project was understanding the conference room layout and wall details. This enables development of lighting solutions that are not only appropriate to meet the quantifiable lighting criteria, but that also enhance the architecture. Spending money and resources on visually stimulating architectural elements, forms, and details but not enhancing them with light seems shortsighted. Here the wall niche exhibits a colored-fabric insert for acoustics and is of sufficient depth to hold a lighting slot detail to ehance the niche and light the convenience surface.
Image ©Robert Eovaldi

Inventory

Select two projects from your Observation Journal. Assume one example is a renovation project and assume one project as the "old" environment from which a client will move to a new-construction environment. Inventory existing conditions for both projects. Using Table 4.1 as a checklist, provide each inventory in a short report format or a clearly labeled spreadsheet. Include digital photos of each space.

short, and unambiguous survey questions that relate to lighting (see Table 4.2).[2] Third, don't make a scene (don't get caught up in an employee rally of opinion; don't express disrespect of past designers' efforts or of owners). Although lighting is an important issue and although some information from the owner/user is better than none, the programming task is to garner information from the existing situation and/or the proposed situation and not to incite users with undue frustration or consternation.

Much of the inventory information should be relatively straightforward to collect. Lighting information and designers' expectations may require some extra level of detail and care in collection and/or interpretation. Humans are, indeed, creatures of habit. Regardless of their merit, there are certain postures, rituals, events, foods, and places of which people become accustomed, even desirous. A living or working environment may be quite inappropriate and ill-equipped to meet a user's needs, yet because it has been "home" or "the office" for a period of time, the user has adapted to it. To avoid negative reactions and complaints when users move into

In this renovation project, an inventory of space dimensions highlighted those areas where ceilings would be low and where daylighting access was simply impossible. Couple this with owner's image criteria of energy efficiency and sustainable design. These inventoried parameters quickly directed lighting to be recessed (there's simply not enough ceiling height to employ pendent-mounted indirect or direct/indirect lighting techniques that would help visually "lift" the ceiling). Recessed lighting tends to produce darker ceiling and wall conditions. Further, the space width is narrow. Hence, wall lighting—which helps brighten the appearance and make the space seem more spacious—was an early outcome of the low ceiling and narrow room dimensions. The very low wattage wallwashers using 20,000-hour life lamps minimize total power budget here to 1.2 W/ft^2 (exactly 12.9 W/m^2)—setting the bar in 1994 for what is today the norm for low-power-budget, more-sustainable lighting.[3] Improvements in ballast and lamp technology since then would yield an even lower power budget today.
Image ©Robert Eovaldi

new or refurbished environments, designers must either "account" or "educate." Illuminance measurements should be made both on horizontal work surfaces (or floors or laps) and on vertical work surfaces (computer screens, writing boards, and tack boards) in users' existing environments. Luminance measurements should be made of typical room surfaces and tasks. A record should be made of the types of luminaires and lamps in use and their layout. Notes should be made of typical control settings (are lights energized or dimmed or off when people are using the space[s]?). A record of the size and location of daylight-admitting openings should be made as well. In existing situations, are these openings treated in any way (e.g., inherent tint, applied tint, manual or automated shades or blinds, and are these actively used)? Are daylighting control methods employed, such as photocell activated on/off or dimming of lights? This allows for later comparison to proposed planned daylighting in the new or renovated space(s) and for assessment of the

Table 4.2   Existing Conditions' Survey

Parameter	Questions
☐ Space activities	• How is/will the spaced (be) used?
	• What does the user/owner consider to be the primary use?
	• Are there any secondary uses?
☐ Visual tasks	• What is the most important visual task?
	• Are there any other tasks of similar importance?
	• What are the visual aspects of the work?
	• How much time is spent in the space(s) each day?
	• How much time is spent on various tasks?
☐ Users' Input[1]	• The lighting is comfortable (agree/disagree)?
	• The lighting is uncomfortable (agree/disagree)?
	• The lighting is too bright (agree/disagree)?
	• The lighting is too dim (agree/disagree)?
	• The lighting causes serious shadows (agree/disagree)?
	• The lighting is functional (agree/disagree)?
	• The lighting is efficient (agree/disagree)?

importance of view and daylight controllability. All of this survey information should be used to develop new proposed lighting solutions and to avoid faux pas in the development of the new lighting. Indeed, the most problematic solution would be one that is nearly identical to the users' existing situation and that the users have identified as undesirable or problematic!

Where daylighting is intended to be a significant factor in the lighting of the new or renovated space(s), the architecture geometry must be inventoried. If proposed configurations are narrow with high ceilings, then fenestration on the long walls will be more effective than on the short walls. Alternatively, and particularly in retrofit or renovation projects where the architecture already exists, daylighting opportunities should be explored based on the available space geometry. Clarification from the users and/or owner should be sought regarding daylighting as a source of light to provide illuminance and luminance versus view. Daylighting as a means to providing illuminance and/or luminance throughout the day is one application known as "daylighting." Users may be more concerned about view aspects—hence another application of "daylighting" addresses views. Still a third application of "daylighting" is related to physiological well-being, including most notably seasonal affective disorder (SAD).

By accounting for the lighting aspects of the user's old environment, the designer may be able to greatly improve on what users' lived/worked with in the old environment, or may see the need to educate the client about benefits of proposed changes. In a classic example, users move from an office lighted with glary, lensed luminaires and untreated clear, high-transmissive windows to one lighted with low-brightness parabolic louver luminaires with little daylight. Although the parabolic

Significance

lighting system exhibits less direct glare than the lensed lighting system and the lack of daylight is the opposite of the old glary clear windows, the parabolic lights produce more directional (and, therefore, harsher) downlighting and no daylight results in much less perceived brightness. Further, because the parabolic luminaires concentrate the light downward, whereas the lensed luminaires distribute light more diffusely throughout a space, the parabolic lighting creates a "darker" look since the now windowless walls receive less light. Compounding this effect is the relatively great amount of light directed onto the horizontal surfaces (work surfaces and floors) from the parabolic luminaires. So the work surface may be perceived as overlit while the room is perceived as underlit. While all of this may save lots on energy, the resulting "dark" environment is undesirable if not unacceptable to the users. The lighting designer could account for the greater room brightnesses experienced in the daylit, lensed-luminaire environment by using higher-reflectance, matte-surface finishes, by introducing some uplighting onto the ceiling, or by introducing wall lighting to increase the perception of brightness. Of course, windows would help as well.

Educating users, though a noble goal, is a difficult process, as the designer usually cannot get an audience with all of the users of a new environment. If one-on-one discussion is possible, or if educational material (e.g., a project website) can be developed, then user education may be an effective means of presenting new concepts, thereby avoiding or minimizing complaints at project's end.

The designer should take stock of what the owner expects of the newly planned environment. Issues of environmental quality and budget should be addressed early in the programming phase to avoid later surprises and disasters in both the planning

Design Goals

and the financing of the project. Are there image requirements that need to be conveyed by the architecture, interior design, and lighting to users and/or visitors? Are there quality expectations that the owner has seen or experienced in other facilities and expects to see incorporated into the new or renovated space(s)? Finally, what ego issues, if any, need to be addressed? Is the owner after the largest structure, the tallest building, the highest-tech installation, etc., to achieve some notoriety?

Budget matters also need to be defined. The owner should be educated on the costs/benefits or lack of benefits of various approaches. For example, an owner may indicate initially that the setting is to have "no frills," which to him/her probably means no decorative lighting. Yet decorative lighting is responsible for the human-scale aspects of an environment, providing a more intimate, pleasing atmosphere. It also is responsible for establishing an image and alleviates the blandness of solely implementing general lighting techniques.

Designers' own expectations need to be accounted. Designers on the project will likely have opinions about the owner's existing space(s). These should be heard—helping the lighting designer understand potential biases of the other designers, and, in turn, this will assist in developing lighting ideas for the planned spaces. Opinions alone, however, are insufficient information. An understanding of the issue(s) surrounding the opinion will help unravel the real reason behind designers' likes and dislikes. For example, some design team members may dislike or even despise fluorescent lighting. Typically, this comes from past experiences with lousy color, cool-toned fluorescent lamps that flickered throughout the day. Further, much of the old fluorescent lighting equipment simply had poor glare control and was oversized to accommodate large lamps and ballasts. All has changed today.

Ego considerations are an inherent part of the design process and should be openly discussed with the owner. Some designers have "signatures" that are exhibited in nearly all of their projects, which may be responsible for the client's selection of the designer for a given project. Lighting can play an important role in expressing this signature. For example, it the architect or interior designer may insist on rich materials (e.g., marble, granite, or wood) in a building lobby. Such an upgrade in materials can play a profound role in developers' abilities to sign and retain lessees. Often, however, these expensive materials are left unaccented—visually expressing a lack of commitment and concern for quality, detail, and comfort—the very attributes for which designers hope to be recognized, and the very characteristics that landlords wish to promote! The lighting designer should express and address his/her own expectations early and follow through with lighting concepts and details that promote those expectations and those of others on the team.

4.2 Design Goals

With a clear understanding of the users' existing conditions and the givens of the planned space design, the designer is in a position to develop specific lighting design goals. Design goals are those attributes, both soft (art) and hard (science), that the lighting system will attempt to address. So, prior to designing, these goals need to be established. The programming discussed to this point is the basis for

defining the design goals. Design goals will then be used to establish specific criteria. It is important to note, however, that these design goals are not steadfast, finite requirements. These are goals toward which the design team should strive. For various reasons, these goals may not ultimately be attainable on a project. For example, at the last minute, the owner may experience financial problems that result in difficult but necessary cost cuts that will likely negatively affect previously established design goals. Other circumstances beyond the design team's control include owners' and users' opinions, change in staff, corporate takeovers, homeowners' change in finances, divorces, and the like.

Seldom are design goals conveniently straightforward and easily stated. Perhaps this is why many designers today elect simply to plop a uniform array of downlights or rectilinear recessed luminaires on an **RCP** or rely on factory representatives to provide layouts that, hopefully, generate "enough light." This approach may enable the designer to meet the legal requirements of a project without expending much time and money. In fact, it is ironic that as design has become more and more demanding, as the service sector of the economy has increased—deserving more attention to the human-scale aspects of design—designers may be joining the commodity-society by discounting fees. Unfortunately, this has the unintended effect of eliminating or drastically reducing the time and money the designer should have available to properly review the lighting and other systems needed for appropriate function and behavior. Ultimately, just providing "enough light" will not allay complaints and dissatisfaction and may lead to a reduction in performance, less time spent in the offending environment, and an overall morale problem and a lousy sustainability story (all of those resources expended to manufacture, transport, and operate a lighting system that isn't very supportive to users).

For a well-rounded and well-grounded approach, the designer should consider, even if only fleetingly, a host of issues. A comprehensive list of lighting design goals is outlined by categories: Spatial Factors in Table 4.3, Systems Factors in Table 4.4, Psychological and Physiological Factors in Table 4.5, and Task Factors in Table 4.6. Some goals are relatively straightforward (e.g., codes, although questions on exact interpretation may persist), but others may require considerable research and thought prior to their resolution (e.g., daylighting). There are many factors to consider on every project and these tabular checklists are not exhaustive. They may appear to be overwhelming, but after several reviews and repeated use, some or perhaps most of the checklist items will become second nature and may not involve much invested time. These tabular checklists are used to guide preliminary thinking and then intermittently throughout a project to confirm and reconfirm direction. They also serve throughout a project as confirmation that all relevant items are, indeed, still relevant and are addressed. As the project progresses, these intermittent reviews of the various factors and goals may actually spur new lighting strategies or tweaks on existing strategies or may even reset some of the architectural and/or interiors strategies. This is the nature of a good design process. These various factors are discussed in detail in Chapters 5, 6, 7, and 8 as they relate to developing specific criteria.

RCP
Reflected ceiling plan. A mirror-image (reflected) view of the ceiling—as if looking from above through the ceiling to a mirrored floor and seeing the reflection of the ceiling plan. Typically shows lighting and ceiling changes such as coves, slots, bulkheads, and the like. See Figures 12.7, 14.1, and 14.2.

Table 4.3 Spatial Factors

	Goal	Lighting Aspect
☐	Pleasantness	• Lighting hardware scale and shape
		• Lighting hardware styling
		• Lighting hardware spacing
		• Luminances
☐	Spatial Definition	• Wall lighting
		• Ceiling lighting
		• Architectural feature lighting
☐	Spatial Order	• Lighting layout
		• Luminance patterning
☐	Circulation	• Luminance intensity

4.3 Spatial Factors

Spatial Factors Assessment

Select two quite different project types from your Observation Journal. Make a spreadsheet similar to that shown in Table 4.3; however, in place of the "Significance" column, introduce a "Critique" column and fill this in with your assessment about how or even if Spatial Factors were addressed in the lighting design. Add a fourth column, "Strategy," and indicate what you suggest what should have been done with lighting to address Spatial Factors.

Design goals associated with spatial factors relate to the architecture of the building, the interior architecture of the spaces, and overall intended pleasantness of the visual setting. Table 4.3 outlines spatial factor goals and related lighting aspects and their significance. The designer must consider physical parameters of architectural form, surfaces, and modulation. For example, how can the lighting enhance the architectural strategy? How can lighting enhance the order and pleasant appeal of the architecture? Or for deconstructive architecture, how can lighting juxtapose with 3-dimensional aspects of the architectural form? In more traditional architecture, how can lighting be integrated with the architecture and building systems to best meet the programming needs without encumbering the space with out-of-scale hardware or hardware that is stylistically inappropriate for the architecture and interior furnishings? Figure 4.3 exemplifies the outcome of spatial-factor goal-making and systems-factor goal-making in establishing design strategies and ultimately in developing lighting, architectural, and interiors solutions that relate and work together to provide a successful environment.

A purposeful and methodical assessment of spatial factors will influence lighting design decisions and/or may influence architectural and interiors design decisions. If "good lighting" addresses systems factors, psychological and physiological factors, and task factors, but misses the mark on spatial factors, the environment may still fail its intended function. This could be something as seemingly innocent as lights laid out off center over a dining or conference table because the ceiling architecture or layout could not be reconciled with lighting equipment locations and the spatial goal of pleasantness and/or spatial order were not allowed to trump the expedience of the ceiling design and/or construction. If the table is centered on the room, the off-center lights will be obvious. If the table is centered on the lights, it will not be centered in the room—which will be obvious because of more space along one side and/or end of the table than the other side and/or end.

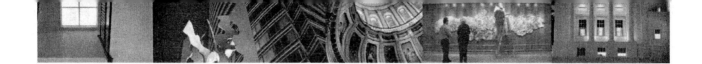

Significance

Scale and shape determine the visual impact of the lighting hardware in the context of the architecture.

Styling determines how well the lighting hardware fits with the architectural/interiors style.

Spacing, while based on quantitative needs, determines how lighting modulates with architectural/interiors elements and features.

Luminance patterns, intensities, and uniformities/nonuniformities determine how the room's features look.

Lighting walls can delineate or clarify room shape.

Lighting ceilings can delineate or clarify height and/or ceiling configuration.

Lighting such features as floor or ceiling apertures or bulkheads can clarify these features.

Lighting hardware layouts can enhance the architectural/interiors patterning.

Luminance patterns can delineate the architectural/interiors patterning.

Intense luminance creates visual attraction.

Systems factors relate to lighting's integration with a facility's operations, how or if lighting hardware integrates physically with other building systems. The impact of lighting on other building systems, and lighting's compliance with codes, ordinances, and certification programs. Table 4.4 outlines systems factors and Figure 4.3 exemplifies the outcome of systems-factor goal-making and spatial-factor goal-making. Although mundane compared to most other factors, systems factors must be addressed if the lighting is to integrate with architectural substrates and other systems and meet legal requirements necessary for building occupancy.

Facility operations can be enhanced dramatically if sufficient planning is given to flexibility and controls. Greater facility use and greater facility longevity are results of flexible and well-controlled lighting systems. Controls contribute immensely to efficient, sustainable practice. Even a small amount of lighting energy accidentally left "on" uses energy needlessly. Automated controls can prevent this.

Lighting equipment influences other systems and vice versa. Leaving these interactions to chance will usually result in shortcomings—some significant enough to lead to dissatisfied users. In music halls, for example, some lighting equipment—from lamps to ballasts to transformers and dimmers—can provide audible interference with audience listening and/or recordings.

Many sustainability goals are common-sense and enable the designer to limit the impact of the lighting design on Earth's environment. Undoubtedly, the best way to preserve Earth's resources is to not use them—building new buildings less frequently and renovating old buildings less frequently. However, when new buildings are built and old building restored, lighting design practice can at least conserve Earth's resources.

Codes cannot and should not be ignored. Ignoring codes simply delays the inevitable and may significantly affect the final look, feel, and function of a space or area.

Figure 4.3

Using the Spatial Definition Checklist, lighting goals were considered and discussed with the design team and owner for this indoor pool. Key aspects are outlined to the right, although others were also addressed. Once these lighting goals were resolved with other systems', interiors', and architectural goals, lighting design strategies emerged that then could be proposed together as a complete lighting design scheme for the space and later developed into specific product selections and design details during design development. Recognize the implications of avoiding the spatial definition discussion and proceeding directly to an easy, convenient, and cheap downlighting scheme. Take away the perimeter lighted valance and the large wall sconces, and what's left is a downlit hall (note how the perimeter valance adds an intimate proportion to the space—without it, the perimeter walls are relatively quite tall, contributing to a barn look rather than an elegantly proportioned and lighted indoor pool.
Image ©C.M. Korab

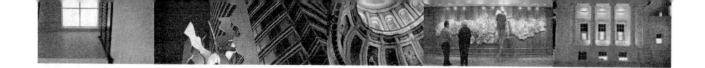

Key **Spatial Factors** ▼

Key **Systems Factors** ▼

HVAC: Layout and Details

Early mechanical schemes called for a significant air distribution system to address the large pool house satisfactorily in all seasons. Huge ducts would either traverse the center of the space, following the slope of the ceiling, or would encircle the space along the perimeter. After a design charrette to discuss the options and the impact with other systems, including lighting, it was decided to encircle the space with ductwork and develop a giant architectural valance to hide the ductwork and then develop a lighting detail—a giant lighting valance—in front of the ductwork to mask the real intent of the valance—to hide the ductwork. This and other factors outlined here set the stage for a lighting strategy.

Pleasantness: Hardware Scale and Shape

It is a big room. Early architectural concepts convey the scale of the space in new-construction projects or an actual site visit clearly establishes volume and scale in renovation projects. If lighting hardware is to have a presence—work as a visual part of the architectural design (something the team and owner must discuss and agree upon), then large luminaires and/or details will be needed. Would small, delicate lights work in such a large and rugged (albeit elegantly rugged) space?

Maintenance: Layout and Lamping

Any lighting hardware over the pool is difficult to maintain. Early architectural concepts called for large operable door walls to open onto exterior patios for summer use. The size of the door walls was checked against a motorized lift that could stand on the pool deck and extend to the peaked ceiling. Once confirmed, lighting at the upper extent of the ceiling could be considered. Nevertheless, to minimize downtime, it was agreed that lamping would be very long life sources—given the throw distance of light. This ultimately resulted in metal halide lamping.

Spatial Definition: Ceiling Lighting

The architectural scheme (lodge look) calls for a dark, wood ceiling. Lighting should be developed to enhance the wood tone (it is a relatively expensive and unique treatment for such a large-volume space) and add some "ceiling presence" to the space to avoid a dark cavern look.

Pleasantness: Hardware Styling

It has a lodge look. Early architectural schemes, which may be nothing more than words discussed or written, will influence lighting equipment styling and detailing. If modern, standard equipment is deemed necessary (such as the surface-mounted downlights here) in spaces not exhibiting simple lines of modern architectural schemes, then painting out the modern equipment to match the architectural background is one way to introduce the equipment without detracting from the architectural scheme. Which is what was done with the rectangular, surface-mounted downlight at the joists near the ceiling's peak (those lights exhibit a 1' [300 mm] square footprint and a height of 1' 6" [450 mm]).

Codes: NEC

Lighting hardware requirements and layout limitations for swimming pools (literally in the body of water and outside the body of water) are well-prescribed in the National Electrical Code.

Spatial Order: Layout and Luminances

The oblong, multifaceted room shape and truss ceiling scheme were an early response to the pool size and architectural design scheme (lodge look). During early design charrettes, it was agreed that lighting hardware and luminances would reinforce the multifaceted room shape—contributing to the lighting strategy. The perimeter luminances generated by the backlit "grand valance" reinforce the room proportions and make the perimeter wall appear somewhat shorter. This helps with adding more human-scale presence to the large space. This same perimeter valance is faced with a trellis motif enhancing the lodge look. Downlights overhead are arranged to correspond to the deep purlins.

Design Goals

Table 4.4

Systems Factors

in-service lamp life

All electric lamps have a rated life of operation based on industry standards. The more a lamp is used, the more frequent it will require replacement. Such frequent replacement means more frequent consumption of Earth's resources to make new lamps. This also leads to more frequent disposal or, preferably, recycling. Needless operation (e.g., a room is empty, but lights are energized) results in reaching end of life faster. Automated controls, such as motion or occupancy sensors or timers, can reduce hours of operation and extend the length of time that the lamp will remain in service—the in-service lamp life.

ADA

Americans with Disabilities Act, passed by the U.S. Congress and signed into law by the president in 1990, establishes guidelines for accessibility to public and commercial facilities by people with disabilities.

	Goal	Lighting Aspect
☐	Flexibility	• Movable lighting hardware
		• Consistent lighting throughout
		• Addressable lighting hardware
☐	Controls	• Automatic control
		• Manual control
		• Addressable lighting control
☐	Acoustics	• Lighting hardware size and construction
		• Lighting hardware ballasts and/or transformers
		• Lamps and controls
☐	HVAC	• Lighting layout and wattage
		• Lamping
		• Details
☐	Ceiling System	• Lighting layout
		• Luminaire trim
		• Luminaire distribution
☐	Codes	• NEC
		• ASHRAE/IESNA 90.1
		• IBC
		• ADA
☐	Ordinances	• Dark-sky
		• Illuminances
		• Disposal
☐	Sustainability	• Luminaires and lamps
		• Lamps
		• Operational energy
		• Recycling
		• Mains voltage
		• Room finishes
		• Synergies with other systems
☐	Certification	• UL
		• LEED
☐	Maintenance	• Lighting layout
		• Cleaning
		• Relamping
		• Finish

Significance

Affects reconfiguration of space(s) and tasks.

Affects reconfiguration of space(s), user comfort, and affects power budget.

Affects reconfiguration of lighting intensities to address reconfiguration of space(s) and tasks.

Affects functionality, energy use based on occupancy, daylighting, load shedding, time-of-day, and **in-service lamp life**.

Affects functionality and energy use based on user input.

Affects functionality and energy use based on preprogrammed space/use configurations and functions.

Affects sound reflections.

Affects noise impact.

Affects noise impact.

Affects cooling load requirements.

Affects air distribution (e.g., fluorescent lamps affected by cold air).

Affects lamp/ballast operational life (e.g., concentrated heat in details can affect lamp and ballast/transformer operation and life).

Affects ceiling and above-ceiling infrastructure integration.

Affects ceiling integration may impact flange type for trim.

Affects ceiling type and finish.

Affects specific hardware requirements and/or application limitations.

Affects layouts and lamping.

Affects minimum and/or average illuminance requirements.

Affects luminaire sizes and/or mounting heights.

Affects specific hardware requirements and/or application and/or operational limitations with respect to exterior lighting.

Affects minimum and/or average illuminance requirements typically with respect to exterior applications.

Affects disposal/recycling of luminaires.

Affects amount of embedded energy in lighting hardware production, shipping, and packaging.

Affects toxins and system efficiency.

Affects amount of power plant emmissions.

Affects process energy and landfill impact.

Affects resources required for hardware (wiring and switchgear) and operations efficiency (e.g., using 277V).

Affects system efficiency (e.g., higher reflectances more effectively distribute light throughout a space).

Affects systems integration.

Affects specific hardware requirements.

Affects specific hardware requirements and/or application and/or operational limitations.

Affects access for cleaning, relamping, and reballasting.

Affects efficiency and sustainability.

Affects efficiency and sustainability.

Affects durability and/or ability to hide fingerprinting, dirt.

Table 4.5 Psychological and Physiological Factors

Goal	Lighting Aspect
☐ Sensory Responses	• Aural
	• Thermal
	• Visual
☐ Hierarchies and Focals	• Surface lighting
	• Architectural feature lighting
	• Object feature lighting
☐ Subjective Impressions	• Clarity
	• Spaciousness
	• Preference
	• Relaxation
	• Intimacy
☐ Color	• Color of light
	• Color of surface
	• Color rendering
	• Color temperature
	• Spectral power distribution
☐ Daylighting	• View
	• Health
	• Luminance
	• Illuminance
	• Sustainability
☐ Night lighting	• Illuminance
	• Health
	• Spectral power distribution
☐ Health	• Illuminance
	• Spectral power distribution
	• Spectral power intensity

4.5 Psychological and Physiological Factors

Another set of lighting design goals revolves around the users' biological needs for light and reactions to light. Users' health can be affected by light. Most health aspects of architectural lighting are vision-related and appear to be short-term and beneficial, if not benign. Lighting can have therapeutic benefit; however, there is evidence that lighting also may have negative health implications.[4,5] The circadian rhythm is regulated by our light/dark cycles. Recent discoveries implicate the lack of total darkness during the dark cycles to melatonin suppression, which may increase the risk of breast cancer in women. More on this and other physiological and psychological factors in Chapter 7.

The way in which an environment is presented to its users is at least partly responsible for the way they perceive it and react to it. The distribution of luminances in a space can influence perceptions of the space's intended functions, level of comfort, and apparent spatial volume. Luminance levels and ratios are responsible

Significance

Affects actual or perceived noise level.

Affects perceived ambient temperature.

Affects glare.

Affects visual attraction/spatial hierarchy and/or perceived spatial delineation/configuration.

Affects visual attraction and visual interest.

Affects visual attraction and visual interest.

Affects perception of details, features, objects, people.

Affects perceived spatial volume.

Affects users' evaluation of space.

Affects users' perception of work atmosphere.

Affects users' perception of social atmosphere.

Affects subjective impressions and perceived color and distance.

Affects subjective impressions and perceived distance.

Affects color perception and vibrancy.

Affects color of light and preference.

Affects color perception and vibrancy.

Affects eyestrain and motivation.

Affects circadian rhythm.

Affects glare, task visibility, transient adaptation.

Affects task visibility.

Affects energy use and in-service lamp life.

Affects ability to detect hazards and/or perpetrators.

Affects circadian rhythm.

Affects visual acuity and ability to discriminate colors.

Affects circadian rhythm.

Affects circadian rhythm.

Affects exposure.

---

for visual attraction and visual comfort and appear to influence users' subjection impressions. Exterior views appear to be related to satisfaction and motivation.

Senses other than vision may be influenced by light. "Hushed" spaces and how "cool" or "warm" a space feels may be affected by lighting.

4.6 Task Factors

It is no secret: programming and designing toward many of the lighting design goals outlined as Spatial Factors (Section 4.3) and Psychological and Physiological Factors (Section 4.5) involve architectural and interior design and, thus, are fun to think about and resolve for most designers—and are more time-consuming compared to Task Factors. However, Task Factors, while perhaps not as much fun, are considered easy. This perception is based on a false assumption that lighting calculations are straightforward or, when done by computer, are infallible. This, no

Table 4.6 ## Task Factors

	Goal	Lighting Aspect
☐	Visual Tasks	• Contrast
		• Color
		• Size
☐	Luminances	• Work surface
		• Wall lighting
		• Ceiling lighting
		• Daylighting
☐	Surface Reflectances	• Degree of gloss or specularity
		• LRV (ρ — Greek letter for "r" for reflectance)
		• Color
☐	Surface Transmittances	• Diffusion
		• T_{vis} (τ — Greek letter for "t" for transmittance)
		• Color
☐	Illuminances	• Speed/Accuracy
		• Users' Ages
		• Visual tasks (see first goal above)

interreflection
Light reflecting back and forth among surfaces diminishing each time as a function of LRV. Higher LRVs result in better interreflection and more efficient lighting.

T_{vis}
T-vis represents the visible light transmittance in decimal form (e.g., 0.48 for 48%) of a light transmitting material (commonly available for glass and acrylics). May also be referred to as VLT for visual or visible light transmittance.

doubt, explains why most lighting design today revolves exclusively around task factors. Define a few tasks, establish (look up in a reference) some illuminance criteria, perhaps address some luminance criteria (and in the process look at surface reflectances), and voilà, this results in easily quantifiable criteria that can be solved with some straightforward arrangement of lights in or on a ceiling. Next project, please! This is an unfortunate view held by many in the building and construction industry. Keep in mind—these environments are being built or re-built for people to live in and/or work in for what is a good length of time. Yet, many folks focus on streamlining and cheapening the design and construction process. Designing just for task factors usually results in visually uninteresting, less people-oriented solutions (look at Figure 4.4 versus Figure 4.5). The challenge is to convince the owner, users, developers, or all that the project will be in place for 10, 20, 30, or more years. How is an easy, convenient, and lower-cost resolution that won't stand the test of time in equipment durability and in satisfying or at least enhancing the experience of the viewing eyeballs to which it will be exposed best in the long run for business or for living? How are we conserving Earth's resources if we're creating settings that most people won't like? Indeed, America's profligate construction activities are unsustainable. Because past attitudes of "build it cheap and quick" fostered a vicious cycle—if you don't like it or are now "tired of it," start anew since it was cheap in the first place. And yet another cheap and quick installation is commissioned! Designers can limit these vicious cycles by keeping the construction team focused on a long-term perspective rather than the how-soon-and-for-how-little-cost-can-we-complete-it

Significance

Affects illuminance, luminance, and visibility.

Affects spectral power distribution and visibility.

Affects illuminance.

Affects adaptation and visibility and brightness perception.

Affects transient adaptation, adaptation, and visibility and brightness perception.

Affects transient adaptation and brightness perception.

Affects transient adaptation, adaptation, visibility, and glare and brightness perception.

Affects glare and brightness perception.

Affects brightness perception and **interreflection** efficiency.

Affects spectral power distribution.

Affects source imaging, brightness perception, and glare.

Affects brightness perception and glare.

Affects spectral power distribution.

Affects illuminance.

Affects illuminance and luminances.

Affects illuminance and luminances.

attitude. Task factors as discussed here can be only one part of the programming of a project.

Programming appropriately for task factors involves a review of visual tasks, luminances (and, therefore, surface reflectances and transmittances), and illuminances. Making a full analysis of the kinds of visual tasks that are likely to occur is the best means of understanding tasks and to solve unique lighting challenges. First-hand review of these tasks (or even attempting to perform them) is beneficial. The designer will better understand task issues and will also see previous resolutions to their lighting. A complete review of tasks is likely to lead to a comprehensive lighting solution that will meet users' requirements for most all tasks most or all of the time.

Figure 4.4

Addressing task factors alone may result in functional space, but pleasantness, spatial definition, spatial order, and circulation— tenets of Spatial Factors—having been unattended yield uninteresting or less desirable places. Here, luminances are haphazard— varying scallops on the bulkhead— or missing—lack of luminances behind check-in desk and on front face of reception desk.

Figure 4.5

Here, Spatial Factors and Psychological and Physiological Factors played prominent roles in establishing design goals. The end result is a well-planned arrangement of luminances that make the space pleasant and create visual attraction to the key feature—check-in. Planned luminances or brightnesses are hallmarks of attractive, stimulating settings using energy to best advantage.
Image ©C.M. Korab

4.7 Programming

So, what to make of these checklists and where to go from here? The next few chapters will discuss specific criteria related to the lighting goals outlined in the checklists presented in Tables 4.3, 4.4, 4.5, and 4.6. A novice should review the checklists and become familiar with the related lighting aspects and the significance attached to the various goals. On a given project, some attempt should be made to determine if any of the goals are much more important than others or if any can be dismissed. An intermediate designer will use the checklists to assess the importance of the various goals, perhaps literally ranking most important to least important and eliminating those deemed of little or no importance for the project at hand. A seasoned designer will scan the checklists to confirm that relevant issues have been considered and, if applicable, dismiss the rest. Regardless, this planning task will determine ultimate success or failure. Review the lists thoroughly and with purposeful deliberation.

4.8 Programming Brief

A project is only as good as its programming. Without appropriate programming, the project is likely to fail, perhaps not entirely, but in some aspect. Indeed, many clients admit that their previous installation initially was deemed a success by all involved, including users, until time to downsize or upsize—in which case, perhaps, lighting flexibility was insufficient, or until a certain season (e.g., during the winter season the southern exposures exhibit greater glare potential, but when the project was commissioned in the mid summer, this glare wasn't evident). These are issues that could have been addressed with comprehensive programming. Programming can only be as good as the information the users/client allow designers to collect—this may be a function of fees, project schedule, and/or user accessibility.

The program should then be conveyed to the client. For most projects this may be nothing more than an oral presentation of "the facts" as defined by the team and based on a review of various design strategies, inventory items, and some or all of the lighting design goals considered. For other projects, this may necessitate a brief report that includes programmatic statements and very

Programming
Establish an inventory and design goals for a hotel reception lobby. With nothing more than the imagery and caption in Figure 4.6, a solid inventory and list of design goals can be established.

Phase I.1/Inventory
Based on Figure 4.6 and Table 4.1, write up a Program Inventory for the reception lobby. Review each parameter in Table 4.1 and glean whatever inventory information is available from image in Figure 4.6 and its caption. With the exception of knowing specific illuminances and lamping, all inventory items can be established, even if approximately. Take an educated guess at Users' and Owner's feedback. As the designer, identify the designer's expectations.
This should result in a PDF document titled "Phase I.1/Inventory," using 11 pt. Arial font. Use no more than 1000 words. Draft in hardcopy due next class period for discussion in class.

Phase I.2/Design Goals
Based on the Phase I.1 effort above, establish those design goals for this project that you believe are important related to Spatial Factors, Systems Factors, Psychological and Physiological Factors, and Task Factors. Write these up in a short report, being sure to indicate why you believe these to be important and how this will affect your design.
This should result in a PDF document titled "Phase I.2/Design Goals," using 11 pt. Arial font. Use no more than 1000 words. Draft in hardcopy due next class period for discussion in class.

Architectural Lighting Design

Figure 4.6

In this "lighting renovation exercise," the hotelier is seeking ideas to revise the lighting. The architectural layout and all finishes will remain unchanged. Other than a desire to explore relighting options, the hotelier offers no additional feedback. For color confirmation, the back wall consists of book-matched medium-tone, wood paneling exhibiting a copper color. The floor consists of marble tile. Columns are exposed concrete. Ceiling is painted plaster. The reception desk top and upper front fascia are also wood with the main front panel as stainless steel. A series of floor-to-ceiling windows separated by large stone piers comprise the wall behind the photographer, which extends the length of the lobby and opens to street level in an urban setting.

preliminary guidance on achieving the programmed needs. This should provide the client with a salient overview of the project's needs and likely ways to deal with those needs.

4.9 Endnotes

[1] Sherwin-Williams Pro Tips: The Ups and Downs of Dryfall Coatings—Light on the Subject (web page, 2007), http://www2.sherwin-williams.com/oem/pro-tips/dryfall/light.asp. [Accessed July 4, 2007.]

[2] Neil H. Eklund and Peter R. Boyce, The Development of a Reliable, Valid and Simple Office Lighting Survey, Conference Proceedings—1995 IESNA Annual Conference (New York: Illuminating Engineering Society of North America, 1995), 855–880.

[3] Kenneth J. Che, "Foundation Conservation," Lighting Design + Application, March 1995, 18–20.

[4] J.A. Veitch, Principles of Healthy Lighting: Highlights of CIE TC6-11's Forthcoming Report, National Research Council of Canada, http://irc.nrc-cnrc.gc.ca/pubs/fulltext/nrcc46749/nrcc46749.pdf. [Accessed July 14, 2007.]

[5] Catherine Guthrie, "The Light Cancer Connection," Prevention.com, http://www.prevention.com/article/0,5778,s1-1-55-179-6199-1-P,00.html. [Accessed July 15, 2007.]

4.10 References

Agoston, G.A. 1987. Color Theory and Its Application in Art and Design. Berlin: Springer-Verlag.

Rea, Mark S., ed., and Thompson, Brian J., general ed. 1992. Selected Papers on Architectural Lighting. Bellingham, WA: SPIE Optical Engineering Press.

Rea, Mark S., ed. 2000. The IESNA Lighting Handbook: Reference & Application, Ninth Edition. New York: Illuminating Engineering Society of North America.

Rea, Mark S., ed. 1993. The IESNA Lighting Handbook: Reference & Application, Eighth Edition. New York: Illuminating Engineering Society of North America.

Spatial Factors set criteria for lighting hardware selection and layout and luminances. When carefully considered, Spatial Factors will enhance the architecture and interiors. Pleasantness, spatial definition, spatial order, and circulation are the Spatial Factor goals addressed by criteria discussed in this chapter. These criteria are perhaps the most powerful and most interesting to the architect and interior designer. Yet, if these are the only lighting goals addressed, the respective project is only likely to be a celebrity success garnering architecture and/or interiors awards and press. Many figures in this chapter illustrate key Spatial Factor goals. Where available, vendor cutsheet thumbnails are shown for luminaires of interest. The specification for these luminaires on the respective projects is reported in the Project Data section at chapter's end.

5.1 Pleasantness

Visual environment pleasantness is the appropriate choreography of light and architecture toward a common goal of pleasantness—a very subjective, yet often attainable end. Pleasantness is achieved when the architecture, interiors, and/or landscaping and their support systems reinforce the visual setting. However, pleasantness is not blandness. In a poetic sense, pleasantness is the harmony of all things in the built condition. Typically, pleasantness is achieved when team interaction is genuine and high—on the contrary, if team members work in isolation and/or in haste, then there will likely be less harmony in architectural detailing, finishes, and systems' integration.

The lighting system is likely to remain in place for many years prior to any move or renovation. The environment is built to support people over that period of time. People are an expensive asset and Earth resources are limited—pleasantness would seem an important issue.

Lighting techniques that help with pleasantness include lighting hardware scale and shape; lighting hardware spacing and relationships to architectural elements and other building systems; and resulting luminance patterns, intensities, and uniformities.

Scale

A conscious decision should be made on luminaire scale. This affects the visual impact of the architecture, architectural elements, and interiors elements and furnishings. Luminaires that are large, particularly those that are purely functional r–ather than decorative/functional, may appear overbearing, institutional, and out of scale relative to human occupants, architectural elements, and interiors furnishings and elements. On the other hand, decorative/functional luminaires that are used to impart some of the architectural and interiors' character may be quite appropriate at large sizes in order to fit proportionally with the scale of the architecture and/or to create a sense of intimacy or place. Luminaires recessed into ceilings, walls, and/or floors can be visually discrete, visually obvious, or visually obnoxious. Where luminaires are intended to regress or disappear into the architecture, smaller sizes and simpler geometries are best. **Where ceilings are within 10′ (about 3 m) of the floor plane, where luminaires are recessed and purely functional but visible (not hidden in details), consider luminaires of less than 7″ (about 175 mm) square or diameter or for linear lights less than 12″ (about 300 mm) in width.** Figures 5.1 and

Pinhole (Type LMD1a)
www.lightolier.com

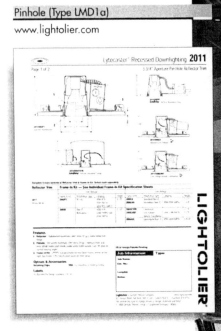

Mini-pendent (Type LTP1)
w.2thousanddegrees.com

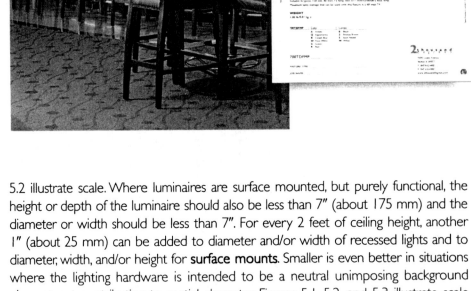

Figure 5.1

Pleasantness/Scale: The ceiling directly over the bar is drywall with an articulated bulkhead. The foreground ceiling is matte black to recede from view. To minimize visual attraction, small-scale downlights—pinholes—are painted out black (this technique works in any ceiling color, providing lights are factory or field painted with high-temperature paint to match the ceiling color).

Small red glass pendents are used at the bar. Small to maximize views to the monitors. Red to hold visual attraction. Such small elements express the curvilinear bar if used on frequent spacings and/or in bold color.
Image ©Justin Maconochie
Left Cutsheet ©Genlyte Thomas Group LLC
Right Cutsheet ©Encompass Lighting Group

surface mounts

Luminaires mounted to ceilings and walls. Sometimes purely functional and sometimes decorative/functional.

decorative luminaires

Luminaires typically providing functional light and having some decorative feature(s) and/or appearance. Where purely decorative and not functional, these are called "eye candy."

5.2 illustrate scale. Where luminaires are surface mounted, but purely functional, the height or depth of the luminaire should also be less than 7″ (about 175 mm) and the diameter or width should be less than 7″. For every 2 feet of ceiling height, another 1″ (about 25 mm) can be added to diameter and/or width of recessed lights and to diameter, width, and/or height for **surface mounts**. Smaller is even better in situations where the lighting hardware is intended to be a neutral unimposing background element not contributing to spatial character. Figures 5.1, 5.2, and 5.3 illustrate scale aspects with respect to recessed and surface-mounted functional luminaires.

Where architecture is grand and luminaires are recessed or surface mounted and purely functional, sizes should remain relatively small. However, where **decorative luminaires** are used, scale, proportions, and mass must be carefully assessed. Where luminaires are to contribute character to the architecture and/

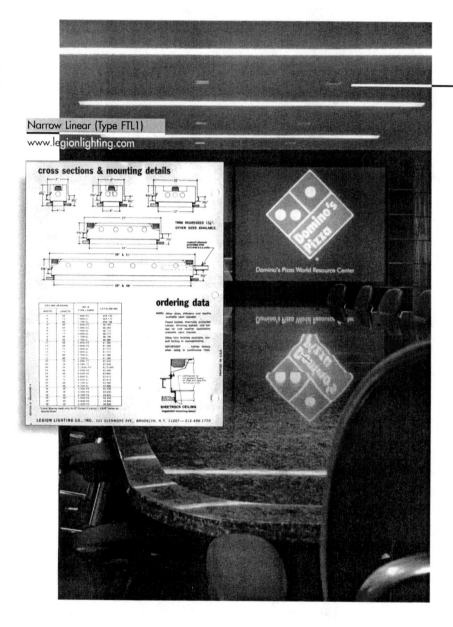

Narrow Linear (Type FTL1)
www.legionlighting.com

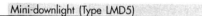

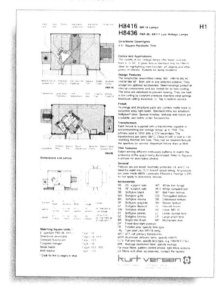

Figure 5.2

Pleasantness/Scale, Shape, and Spacing: Here the ceiling is relatively low and the room relatively narrow and long. To avoid emphasizing this aspect, lighting elements are of minimal dimensions. Fluorescent recessed narrow linear lights for general lighting are 6" (150 mm) wide. IR/MR16 mini-downlights for low-level notetaking are 4½" (about 115 mm) square. Image ©Justin Maconochie
Left Cutsheet ©Legion Lighting Co., Inc.
Right Cutsheet ©Kurt Versen Company

or interiors, the scale of luminaires needs to relate to the architectural scale of space and/or the interiors elements. This takes study in elevation and/or computer model form and should include review against the backdrop of planned architectural elements and human figures. Figure 5.4 illustrates application of relatively large decorative luminaires. A few generalizations: I) Decorative luminaires that are too small will look lost and/or out of character unless their lighted color is saturated and/or their spacing is sufficiently tight to create an expression of lights and lighting, 2) Decorative luminaires that are too large will overtake and detract from the architectural and interior elements. However, there are times when a sense of intimacy can be enhanced with oversized luminaires. There are times when a sense of glitter and vibrancy can be enhanced with a massing of miniature luminaires.

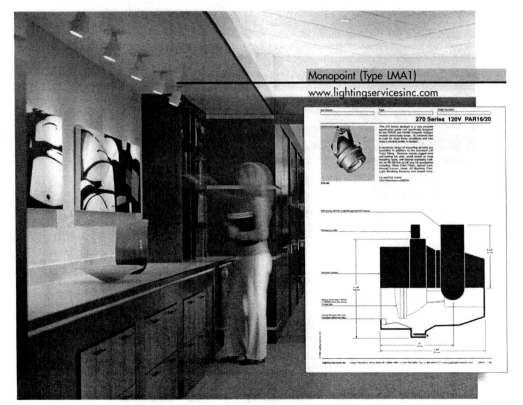

Monopoint (Type LMA1)
www.lightingservicesinc.com

270 Series 120V PAR16/20

Shape

Recessed luminaires are available with face geometries of round, oval, square, and rectilinear. With some thought, these shapes can fit in most any ceiling configuration and have a purposeful, pleasant look. Where ceiling plans are round or curvilinear, any luminaire face geometry works providing the relationship between the ceiling edge condition and between other luminaires is consistent (see Figures 5.4 and 5.6) or even consistently inconsistent (much like a series of lights that spiral inward with increasing distance from ceiling edge to luminaire). This works best in drywall or plaster ceilings where there is no visible grid to limit luminaire spacings and orientations.

Spacing

The spacing of luminaires should relate in some way to architectural or landscape components, such as structural bays, pilasters, beams, joists, trees, planters, pavement patterns, flooring patterns, and the like while providing the functional light required. Where lighting hardware is "sharing" space or surfaces with other systems, such as mechanical (HVAC) diffusers, sprinklers, speakers, and construction joints, or street furniture, such as drains, benches, planters, and the like, the proximity to these elements and consistent spacing and position with respect to these repeating elements are important for minimizing visual clutter or visual noise.

Figure 5.4

Pleasantness/Scale, Shape, and Spacing: Here the ceiling is relatively low and the art wall consists of segmented wood panels on a radius. 1- and 2-lamp accents are spaced consistently along the arc. Each accent luminaire is positioned perpendicular to the tangent of the curved wall. This consistently lights the artwork and enhances the visual aesthetic of the curvilinear wall/ceiling. Accents are 6½" (about 160 mm) in width to minimize their visual impact in such a low ceiling. The low ceiling also precluded use of surface-mounted monopoints since these would have hung too low into the space. The "before art lighting" image at the bottom shows the relatively drab appearance with just room ambient lighting.
Art: Terrain ©Glen Michaels
"After" image below ©Jack Butler
Cutsheet ©Cooper Industries, Inc.

Square and Slot Accent (Types MPA1, 2)

www.rsalighting.com

After art lighting

Before art lighting

Figure 5.5

Pleasantness/Scale, Shape, and Spacing: With a ceiling height of nearly 12' (about 3.7 m), curvilinear space flow, and a desire to accommodate many table layouts, a large-scale shallow chandelier was explored. Few chandeliers of the desired style (transitional/contemporary) and size (about 6' in length by 5' in width by 2'-plus in height [about 1.8 m by 0.6 m]) are available (see image below left for preliminary sketch showing three nestled shades). The chandelier size was determined after reviewing room elevations and plans. Luminaires are oriented. The amorphous shape was selected to work with the curvilinear space flow and ceiling details. The nestled shades, which exhibit varying degrees of warm white, amber, and orange coloration, were kept within a limited height range for maximum flexibility. Image at lower right illustrates proposed dimensional and seam aspects.
Image ©Justin Maconochie
Sketches ©GarySteffyLightingDesign

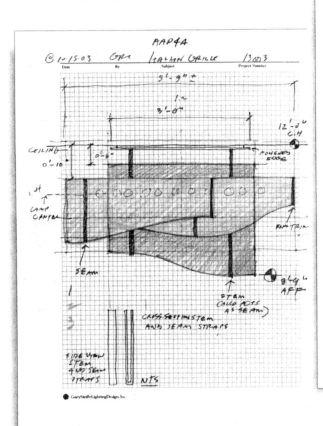

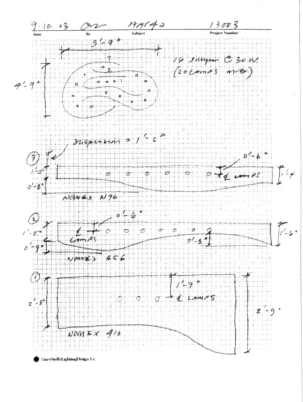

The previous few paragraphs deal with the visual impact of the lighting hardware on, in, and with the architecture and/or landscape. Just as important toward maintaining a pleasant visual setting is how the lighting effects—the luminances—influence the view of the setting. The luminances—patterns, intensities, and uniformities of light and dark—should support the architectural setting. **In many situations, patterns that are consistent and noticeable, yet not too bright and not too dim, contribute to a pleasant scene. Uniformity establishes the softness or harshness of the luminances, with softer considered more pleasant in situations where occupants are expected to spend long periods of time.** For example, in Figures 3.3 and 3.4, note how the in-floor uplights introduce consistent luminance patterns enhancing the pilasters and decorative ceiling brackets and panels. In Figure 4.3, downlights are spaced to prevent harsh scallop patterns (sharp luminance patterns) on the upper member of the deep wood trusses (at the ceiling plane) and on the bottom cord of the trusses spanning below the ceiling. Hence, in the total view of Figure 4.3, the luminance patterns enhance the architectural elements presented by the cathedral wood ceiling rather than introduce harsh, distracting streaks or patterns. Luminance patterns can be visualized only with extensive experience, or alternatively with mock-ups and/or extensive calculations and renderings to assess light patterns and distributions within given settings.

Harsh and/or oddly patterned luminances are best used where visual excitement is most important and occupants spend relatively short periods. Some retail, lobby, hospitality, lounge, club, gaming, and game-room environments may be candidates for harsher and/or oddly patterned luminances.

The importance of luminances, their intensities, patterns, and uniformities (or not) cannot be overstated. With an eye toward luminances (light reflected from walls and ceilings or transmitted through windows and skylights), carefully review all of the photographic figures in this book and in other references and trade magazines and journals. Do these luminances contribute to a more pleasant setting? Are these luminances the result of daylight or electric light or both? Observation journal efforts should include review of luminances and accompanying descriptive text to indicate success or failure—are wall, ceiling, and/or other surface luminances (reflected and transmitted light) patterned in pleasant arrays, intensities, and uniformities? How could luminances be improved—different surface reflectances and transmittances, different lighting techniques, or both? In daylighted spaces, review the space during the day and at night and compare the luminances. While they are expected to be quite different, do both conditions (day and night) result in pleasant experiences?

Luminances

Observation Journal
Include review of luminances with specific attention paid to wall, ceiling, and/or other surface luminances. Indicate how reflected and/or transmitted light could be improved. Distinguish between daylight and electric light luminances.

5.2 Spatial Definition

Walls and ceilings are used to define space physically. Lighting key surfaces or portions of surfaces can enhance the spatial definition intended by the architecture of walls and ceilings. This is not to say all walls and/or ceilings should be lighted. Indeed, very selective lighting can offer distinct, interesting, and visually compelling spatial definition. The key, then, is to develop patterns of light that support the architecture, rather than work against the architecture or leave it sufficiently

Figure 5.6

Pleasantness/Scale, Shape, and Spacing, **Spatial Definition**, and **Spatial Order**: An indoor pool is bounded by relatively simply finished walls, two of which are curvilinear. Very narrow linear lights (2½" in width by 4' in length [about 64 mm by 1220 mm]) are arrayed in the ceiling and wall. The wall lights are lamped with blue lamps while the ceiling lights are lamped with white. These narrow linear lights on relatively tight, consistent spacings enhance spatial definition and a sense of spatial order.
Cutsheet ©SELUX Corp.

Narrow Linears (Types FTG1, FTQ1)
www.selux.com.au/

unlighted and thereby limiting occupants from experiencing the forms of space boundaries in a way that is visually stimulating and pleasing. Figure 5.7 is but one example of lighting supporting spatial definition.

Walls

solution

Although wall lighting (the act of lighting the wall) can also serve as a decorative treatment, it is an important means of setting appropriate brightness levels as well as visually defining space (see Figure 5.7). Lighting walls may simply introduce luminance to what could be a drab backdrop. This helps occupants more quickly identify and appreciate room boundaries. Lighting walls helps with adaptation and transient adaptation by introducing brightness as backdrop to tasks. More articulated wall surfaces such as brick or stone or those specially treated with wood or wallcovering are well-enhanced with light—making the most of the material cost and labor involved in constructing/installing these decorative wall treatments. These are the very elements that help to define place. Although the effect of lighting walls is the primary technique which comes to mind when discussing wall lighting, it is also possible to introduce glowing lights as wall lighting as shown in Figure 5.6. *SOLUTION HINT: Some form of wall lighting on at least one or some of the walls is recommended for most situations.* Luminances from wall lighting are most effective and most efficient where wall finishes exhibit a LRV of at least 50. Unless highly dramatic contrast is desired and can be tolerated by occupants, dark wall materi-

Figure 5.7

Spatial Definition/Wall Lighting: The stair is bound on the inside by a brick wall and on the perimeter by a painted drywall wall following respective floor landing passages. Both walls create cylinders as they define the stair. Creating a light slot at the juncture of the outside wall and landing/passage ceiling washes the wall and pleasantly defines the cylindrical enclosure. Image: ©Robert Eovaldi

als should be avoided or, at most, relegated to very small areas of walls or to a single, small wall in any given space. This is key for lighting efficiency and sustainability and/or for occupant comfort. This is also important to the visual aesthetic and occupant acceptance of the space. Most dark finishes are scrutinized and selected under daylight or high ambient electric light conditions where these small samples of dark materials look visually interesting if not stunning. **In typical efficient daylight and electric light situations in most living and working environments, these same dark materials appear lifeless and contribute to a perception of foreboding darkness that most occupants find unpleasant and unacceptable.** Worse, to "brighten" these dark surfaces requires a significantly greater amount of electric

Figure 5.8

Spatial Definition/Feature Lighting: An opening in the floor between an entrance lobby/ reception area and the 2nd floor circulation serves as the aperture for a series of pendent lights. The aperture is detailed with a slot containing lighting that then washes down the face of the bulkhead that is defined by the floor plane of the 2nd floor and the ceiling plane of the 1st floor.
Image ©Robert Eovaldi

lighting energy or daylighting, which frustrates energy efficiency goals—or requires a replacement wall surface treatment that exhibits a LRV of at least 50 in work settings, conference rooms, and toilet rooms. Toilet rooms are singled out as they tend to be small and subdivided by partitions and therefore inefficient for effective light distribution.

There may be situations where dark walls are desirable for the sense of mystery they may bring to a space or for strong contrast to highlighted elements or objects in the foreground or to provide an illusion of no wall boundaries. For transitory experiences, this may be appropriate, but beware dark finishes regardless of their perceived esteem.

Spatial definition can be enhanced with lighted ceilings in addition to or instead of lighted walls. Sometimes this is achieved with coffer conditions, beam details, perimeter coves, or simply wall- or ceiling-mounted uplights. Uniformity of ceiling lighting is most important in work settings but can be employed to good effect in more casual areas. Colored lighting and/or dim effects should be limited to casual areas. **For functional efficiency, ceilings should exhibit LRVs of at least 85 in work settings, conference rooms, and toilet rooms. Ceilings exhibiting LRV of 90 are available and highly efficient.** As with walls, there may be situations where dark or blacked-out ceilings are desired for dramatic effect or to direct focus to other areas (see blacked-out upper lay-in ceiling in Figure 5.1).

Ceilings

Architectural features can be used to define space and place. Figure 5.8 illustrates a floor opening feature and its lighting. Columns, bulkheads, niches, water features, and the like can be lighted. Figure 5.5 shows bulkhead slots and column slots used to help define space. Regular arrays of these elements can be used to further refine/define space within space just as the columns in Figure 5.5 define the loose-table dining area and, in the same figure, as the bulkhead slots define the booth-table dining area. Every project exhibits walls, ceilings, and perhaps architectural, landscape, or interior features. The challenge is to consider how or if lighting some or all of these aids in defining and enhancing space without overdoing it. *SOLUTION HINT: In work settings, typically only a few key architectural features are lighted. In more casual areas, including lobbies, some regular array of architectural features should be considered for lighting. Creating and lighting many architectural features is typically limited to hospitality (hotel and gaming), retail, and entertainment facilities where such visual variety and stimulation is desirable.*

Features

solution

5.3 Spatial Order

Architecture generally promotes some sense of order and/or hierarchy through structure, pattern, and wall and/or ceiling aperture arrangement. Lighting can augment and intensify or even introduce this order. Using lighting hardware in layouts and spacings that are sympathetic to the architecture will help strengthen the architectural order. In its 2-dimensional plan view, a particular lighting layout may look appropriate, but in 3-dimensional space, the lighting hardware and/or the luminance patterns may not support the order and hierarchy of the architecture.

Here's the problem. It is convenient to plan lighting on paper plans or on computer paper-space plans, both of which are 2-dimensional. This encourages layouts of downlights to light the floor or worksurfaces. Unless elevations, perspectives, isometrics, or real or virtual models are employed, the designer may not readily see all of the surfaces that luminaires will light (by accident) or which surfaces are prominent or where features exist that deserve lighting. 2-dimensional planning may explain the annoying luminance patterns (odd scallops) on the angular bulkhead in Figure 4.4. Look at how lighting is used in Figure 4.5 to

 establish the visual hierarchies of the interior plan and architecture. *SOLUTION HINT: Develop lighting layouts only with a good understanding of 3-dimensional space. Use elevations, models, and other drawing or CAD documents along with discussion with the architect(s) to best understand the 3-dimensional attributes.*

Lighting also can enhance architecture of a deconstructive style. Lighting hardware and/or luminance patterns can be used to accentuate the varied planar and/or compound curvilinear elements that form the architectural space envelope. Indeed, lighting these elements in a nonuniform fashion can itself promote the style of deconstructive architecture.

Layout

Luminaire layouts are inevitably based on cost and power budget. While these might well be appropriate priorities for establishing general layout parameters on many projects, they should not be the end-all to layouts! For purposes of pleasantness, attractive layouts are de rigueur. Many times, this simply means respacing lights in one direction, the other, or both in order to better align with architectural elements such as centering lights on doors, windows, walls, niches, and so on. *SOLUTION HINT: In order of priority, 1) layout luminaires according to task locations—ranging from where work is to occur to where art is to be positioned to which architectural surfaces are to be lighted, 2) then adjust the layout to relate and respond to architectural room/ceiling geometries, and 3) confirm light level and power budget are not compromised.*

Nearby architectural elements should be evident on plans and elevations. These include windows, doors, columns, pilasters, beams, coves, coffers, niches, bulkheads, panelized/modular walls, ceiling grids, etc. Of course, some of these elements may not exist until lighting design is undertaken, at which point some interactive design work between the lighting designer and architect/interior designer may lead to adding architectural elements to help "contain" or array lighting layouts.

Working up layouts is a challenge. This is an iterative process. Seldom is the first, second, or even third layout the "definitive" layout. Usually look at a minimum of three layout options before settling on a layout for the team's review.

Luminance Patterns

photometrically accurate
Many computer rendering programs provide some "light" modeling. However, most of these use basic "sources" to simply introduce shade and shadow or use simple algorithms that do not account for the effects of multiple light reflections from many surfaces. These are not accurate representations of luminance patterns. Online searches and demos and/or review of published listings are recommended.[3]

Luminances, when planned well, will contribute to spatial order. Since most lighting design layouts are solely based on illuminances, no effort is made to assess luminance patterns—yet we see luminances, not illuminances. Luminances are affected by surface reflectances/transmittances and by the distribution and intensity of light falling on the surface.

Assessing the resulting luminances of luminaire layouts will help avoid odd luminance patterns or misidentified focals. Although this is readily evident and accurately predicted in **photometrically accurate** computer models, it can be eye-balled with plans and elevations and some practice. In Figure 5.9, high-wattage flood downlights at the elevator doors on the far left image produce harsh luminances on the bulkhead above the doors. A downlight near the front corner of a nearby column also produces a harsh luminance pattern. A lower-wattage

Architectural Lighting Design

Figure 5.9

Spatial Definition/Luminance Patterns: The elevator lobby at far left is lighted with relatively large diameter flood downlights positioned very close to the walls and column. Arguably appropriate at the elevators, although a change in material finish above the elevator doors could result in a more subtle effect as shown on the right. In the far left lobby, only one column corner is brightly grazed resulting in an odd spatial character.

spot light accent at each elevator door in the right image is aimed onto a wood panel above the door, creating a pleasant glow from the wood panel and simultaneously creating a threshold accent on the floor. The selection of materials plays a crucial role here. Light-colored wall covering in the far left image exacerbates the bright patterns above the doors. Further, the polished elevator doors, reflecting very little light to most observer positions (as evidenced by the camera view—and a common misconception by designers that "polished" means "bright"), appear that much darker relative to the brightness above the doors. *SOLUTION HINT: Confirm that no odd luminance patterns will result in 3-dimensional space (e.g., if lighting layout is arranged such that a bulkhead or wall edge/corner is oddly lighted, then revise the layout to eliminate or greatly soften the odd effect or reposition/add lights to create a symmetric luminance pattern).*

5.4 Circulation

Lighting can be used to help direct people from one zone to another. Greater luminances (typically at walls and/or the ceiling as opposed to the floor) will attract attention. A single area of high luminance or a series of high-luminance areas can then lead people through a space or from one space or area to another. This technique can be used in open areas even where architecture does not define "the path." These luminances are at walls and/or ceiling surfaces for maximum "distant" effect where the intent is to attract occupants from some distance away. Greater luminances at floor surfaces are used for "local" effect where the intent is to maintain occupant attention once he/she is in the vicinity of these luminances. The image on the right in Figure 5.9 illustrates wall luminances on wood panels above the elevator doors used for distant focal attention with floor luminances at the elevator threshold used for local attention. See Section 7.2 for more discussion on visual attraction and focal centers. Figure 5.10 illustrates an extension of the concepts shown in Figure 5.9 where an elevator lobby in close proximity to hotel check-in is simply lighted with the planned luminances accentuating the wood panels. The richness of the wood grain and coloration, not evident in these black-and-white photos, also contributes to the overall visual attraction. These are not intended to be "solutions in isolation" of other systems. Interior finishes and materials should be enhanced with light, creating luminances that make visual sense.

Figure 5.10

Spatial Definition/Circulation: The elevator lobby near hotel check-in to the far left is lighted with relatively large diameter flood downlights positioned very close to the walls and column. Arguably appropriate at the elevators, although a change in material finish above the elevator doors could result in a more subtle effect as shown on the right. In the far left lobby, only one column corner is brightly grazed resulting in an odd spatial character. Cutsheet ©Genlyte Thomas Group LLC

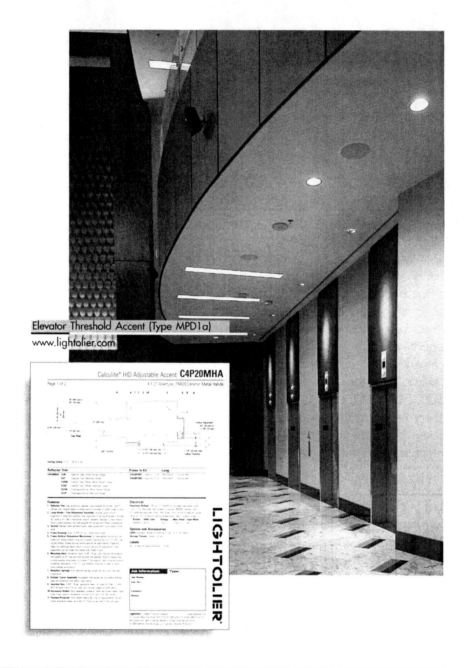

Elevator Threshold Accent (Type MPD1a)
www.lightolier.com

5.5 Endnote

[1] IESNA Computer Committee, 2006 Lighting Software Directory, LD+A, November, 2006, 59–69.

5.6 Project Data

Here are lighting specification excerpts for select projects. The catalogic for lamps and luminaires are specific to projects cited here and may be incorrect for other projects or may have changed or may be retired since the date of their specification. Final specifications for any project must be developed by the responsible professional for the specific project at hand.

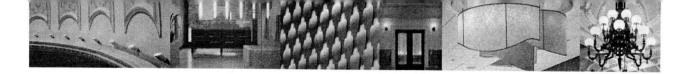

Figure 5.1 Specified 2004
Type LMD1a Pinhole
Recessed (lay-in ceiling) mounted low voltage incandescent adjustable accent luminaire shall be about 0 feet/3¾ inches in diameter by 0 feet/5½ inches in recessed depth (see respective vendor's current datasheets for actual dimensions). Luminaire shall consist of a recessed frame-in kit and an adjustable accent trim with a round pinhole aperture nominally 0-feet/1¾-inches in diameter with a faceplate with a factory-standard white painted finish. Luminaire shall be furnished with an integral magnetic transformer. Luminaire shall be lamped with one [1] Philips 35MRC16/IRC/FL36 (#36351-5) 35-watt, halogen infrared MR16 flood lamp. Luminaire shall be UL listed and labeled for application. Luminaire shall be aimed straight downward.
- Halo H1499T/1419P
- Lightolier 2011/2000LV

Type LTP1 Mini-pendent
Surface (cable from ceiling) mounted line voltage incandescent pendant shall be nominally 0 feet/5 inches in diameter by 1 foot/1 inches height with an overall suspension length of 6 feet/6 inches (subject to ceiling height confirmation by Contractor) so that the bottom of the luminaire is 7 feet/0 inches above finished floor or as directed by the Architect and Interior Designer. Luminaire shall consist of a red glass sphere with a clear spiral finial suspended on a black power cord from a satin nickel canopy. Luminaire shall be UL listed and labeled for application. Luminaire shall be lamped with one [1] vendor supplied 120-volt, 40-watt T3 mini-candelabra base E11 krypton augmented incandescent lamp. Components and entire assembly shall be of sufficient structural integrity to allow for maintenance and to maintain plumb appearance, consistency in alignment and elevational aspects, and to support themselves/itself freely without any auxiliary visible bracing or continual readjustment. Coordinate structural support requirements with all respective trades. Provide three [3] spare lamps in addition to each initial-installation lamp.
- 2Thousand Degrees "Fume" 700TDFMP-R- S-78"OAS[fieldConfirm]-3SpareLamps

Figure 5.2 Specified 2004
Type FTL1 Narrow Slot
Recessed (drywall ceiling) mounted fluorescent luminaire shall be nominally 0 feet/6 inches in width by 12 feet/0 inches by 0 feet/7 inches in overall recessed depth (see vendors' current datasheet for accurate dimensions—Contractor shall confirm fit prior to order placement). Exposed metal components shall be painted to match RAL color selected by Architect. Luminaire shall consist of a deep, straight-vertical white regress and a matte opal structural acrylic lens of single contiguous sheet or alternatively three [3] equal sheets of 0.156 (or greater as vendor determines) thickness with an overlap joint. Coordinate luminaire integration with ceiling system and installation sequencing. Luminaire shall be furnished with Lutron ECO10 dimming ballasts suitable for operation at 277V. Luminaire shall exhibit two lamps in cross section. Luminaire shall be lamped with six [6] GE F28W/T5/830(#39982) or Philips F28T5/830 (#23084-7) 28-watt, 3000K color temperature, 20,000-hour rated life T5 high-efficiency linear fluorescent lamps. Luminaire shall be UL listed and labeled for application. Luminaires shall be fused subject to confirmation by Electrical Engineer.
- Legion 86-628T5-F28T5-277-LutronECO-Fuse-Drywall/Plaster/RAL

Type LMD5 Mini-downlight
Recessed (drywall) mounted low voltage adjustable accent luminaire shall be similar to Type LMD2, except all exposed trim plate and reflector cone metal shall be factory painted to match RAL color selected by Architect. Luminaire shall be installed flat/flush/plumb and shall be installed orthogonally square with nearby walls. Where a series of units is spaced regularly in one area, all trims shall be square with respect to all other trims. Luminaire shall be furnished with integral transformer exhibiting 12V secondary suitable for operation at 277V primary as specified by the Electrical Engineer. Luminaire shall be lamped with one [1] Philips 20MRC16/IRC/SP8 (#36345-7) 20-watt, 5,000-hour rated life, halogen spot lamp. Luminaire shall be UL listed and labeled for application. Lamps shall be aimed under observation of Architect or Lighting Designer.
- Kurt Versen H8416-RALcone-RALtrim-FLT4MP-V277
- RSA QCT-1875RAL/QCT-901-277-LN21SP

Figure 5.3 Specified 2004
Type LMA1 Monopoint
Surface (ceiling) mounted line voltage PAR20 adjustable accent monopoint shall exhibit a diameter of nominally 0 feet/4¼ inches with a depth of 0 feet/4½ inches and a ceiling canopy of 0 feet/5 inches in diameter. Lamp aiming shall include at least a 45° tilt and a 358° rotation and shall be self-lockable. Luminaire shall consist of a formed steel housing painted factory-standard white. Luminaire shall be lamped with one [1] GE 50PAR20/H/SP10 (#17866) 130V narrow spot lamp. Lamps shall be aimed under observation of Interior Designer or Lighting Designer after artwork is installed.
- Lighting Services 270-5A-W

©Justin Maconochie

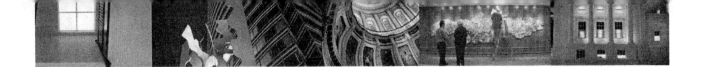

Type FTC11 Cove Light

Surface (architectural cove as detailed by Architect) mounted asymmetric cove luminaire shall be similar to Type FTC1a except detail and orientation may be different as developed by Architect and shall use nominal 3-foot, 4-foot, 6-foot, and 8-foot luminaire sections to make up a total lighted length of about 21 feet (subject to field confirmation by Electrical Contractor). Luminaire sections shall be butted tightly end-to-end and centered in the detail with any dead space equally divided between the ends of the run and not exceeding 0 feet/6 inches. Luminaire detail shall be lamped with three [3] GE F25T8/SPX30/ECO (#25611) or Philips F25T8/TL830 (#31984-8) 25-watt and three [3] GE F32T8/SPX30 (#22648) or Philips F32T8/TL830/ALTO (#24667-8) 32-watt, 3000K color temperature, 20,000-hour rated life, T8 linear fluorescent lamps. Luminaire shall be UL listed and labeled for application.

* Birchwood ASH-T8-21-ISEB0.88BF
* Corelite CI-S-N-1T8-1C-120-21-ISEB0.88BF

Figure 5.4 Specified 2004

Type MPA1 Square Accent

Recessed (existing drywall ceiling) ceramic metal halide accent luminaire shall exhibit an aperture of nominally 0 feet/6½ inches in width by 0 feet/6¾ inches in length with a housing footprint above the ceiling of about 0 feet/8¾ inches in width by 1 foot/7¼ inches in length and an overall height of 0 feet/10 inches (see respective vendor's current cutsheet for actual dimensions). SPECIAL NOTE: The short dimension of the luminaire aperture (0 feet/6½ inch width) shall be installed running parallel with the tangent of the art wall—this is imperative for a consistent appearance—and in alignment with the front edge of nearby linear fluorescent lights. Refer to lighting plan for orientation of luminaire housings subject to field confirmation by Contractor in coordination with above-ceiling elements prior to placing order for luminaires. Contractor shall provide and coordinate structural support requirements with respective trades and ceiling finish work as necessary to provide a complete, aesthetically satisfactory, fully functional installation. Luminaire shall be installed flat/flush/plumb and shall exhibit no light leaks at ceiling juncture. As with all recessed luminaires, luminaire housing shall be appropriately and securely attached to structure to meet code and to prevent settlement shifting over time and to prevent inadvertent heaving or rotation of housing during servicing and/or aiming. Stapling, nailing, screwing, or otherwise attaching ceiling substrates or supports to luminaire housing which precludes complete access to lamp and ballast mechanisms or which is not code compliant shall not be permitted. All interior and trim flange metal components shall be finished in factory standard white. Luminaire shall exhibit one [1] lamp and shall be furnished with an electrically fused, integral electronic ballast suitable for operation at 120V or 277V subject to confirmation by Contractor and coordination with hospital engineering. Lamp shall exhibit rotation of 380 degrees and tilt of up to 45 degrees and shall be mounted on a retractable yoke. Luminaire shall be lamped with one [1] GE CMH39/PAR30L/SP10 (#45066) or Philips CDM35/PAR30L/M/SP (#22329-7) 39-watt, 3000K color temperature, 9,000-hour rated life, ceramic metal halide PAR30 long neck spot lamp. For each lamp include one complete set of the following accessories which shall be installed by Contractor as requested by Artist: [1] snoot, [1] linear spreadlens, [1] universal spreadlens, [1] beam softener, and [1] 40-percent light-blocking screen. Lamp retainer accommodates any two of these accessories at one time. Any accessories not used during aiming shall be boxed and marked "MPA1" and turned over to the Owner. Lamp shall be aimed and locked as observed by Artist or Lighting Designer. Aiming shall be a "white thermal glove" operation to avoid fingerprinting painted housing, trim, and mechanism elements. Luminaire shall be UL listed and labeled for lamping and application. Provide one complete set of spare lamps for first group relamping. Subject to confirmation by Contractor with hospital engineering, Contractor shall provide and install an astronomical timeclock which compensates automatically for daylight savings time to provide at least two automated scenes as follows: Scene 1) ON at 8 AM and OFF at 8 PM weekdays and Scene 2) ON at 10 AM and OFF at 6 PM weekends.

* RSA CO310MH-WH-WH-39-SNP30WH-LN31-LN32-LN33-RS4030-RT-[120/277]-Fuse

Type MPA2 Slot Accent

Recessed (existing drywall ceiling) ceramic metal halide accent luminaire shall be similar to Type MPA1, except shall exhibit an aperture of nominally 0 feet/6½ inches in width by 1 foot/2¼ inches in length with a housing footprint above the ceiling of about 0 feet/8¾ inches in width by 2 feet/2¾ inches in length and an overall height of 0 feet/ 10 inches (see respective vendor's current cutsheet for actual dimensions). SPECIAL NOTE: The short dimension of the luminaire aperture (0 feet/6½ inch width) shall be installed running parallel with the tangent of the art wall—this is imperative for a consistent appearance—and in alignment with the front edge of nearby linear fluorescent lights. Luminaire shall exhibit two [2] lamps and shall be furnished with electrically fused, integral electronic ballasts suitable for operation at 120V or 277V subject to confirmation by Contractor and coordination with hospital engineering. Luminaire shall be lamped with two [2] GE CMH39/PAR30L/SP10 (#45066) or Philips CDM35/PAR30L/M/SP (#22329-7) 39-watt, 3000K color temperature, 9,000-hour rated life, ceramic metal halide PAR30 long neck spot lamps. For each lamp include one complete set of the following accessories which shall be installed by Contractor as requested by Artist: [1] snoot, [1] linear spreadlens, [1] universal spreadlens, [1] beam softener, and [1] 40-percent light-blocking screen. Lamp retainer accommodates any two of these accessories at one time. Any accessories not used during aiming shall be boxed and marked "MPA2" and turned over to the Owner. Lamps shall be aimed and

locked as observed by Artist or Lighting Designer. Aiming shall be a "white thermal glove" operation to avoid fingerprinting painted housing, trim, and mechanism elements. Luminaire shall be UL listed and labeled for lamping and application. Provide one complete set of spare lamps for first group relamping.
• RSA CO320MH-WH-WH-39-SNP30WH-LN31-LN32-LN33-RS4030-RT-[120/277]-Fuse

Figure 5.5 Specified 2003

Type AAP3 Booth Pendent

Surface (cable from ceiling) mounted line voltage incandescent pendant shall be nominally 0 feet/4½ inches in diameter by 0 feet/10¼ inches height with an overall suspension length of 4 feet/0 inches (subject to ceiling height confirmation by Contractor) so that the bottom of the luminaire is 5 feet/6 inches above finished floor or as directed by the Architect and Interior Designer. Luminaire shall consist of an ivory glass cone with suspended on a black power cord from a clear anodized aluminum canopy. Luminaire shall be lamped with one [1] Philips BC60BT15/HAL/W (#24926-8) 60-watt, 3000 hour rated life, BT15 envelope, medium base, halogen incandescent lamp. Luminaire shall be UL listed and labeled for lamping and application. Components and entire assembly shall be of sufficient structural integrity to allow for maintenance and to maintain plumb appearance, consistency in alignment and elevational aspects, and to support themselves/itself freely without any auxiliary visible bracing or continual readjustment. Coordinate structural support requirements with all respective trades.

©Justin Maconochie

• Resolute "Jane" 364-IV-48"OAS[fieldConfirm]

Type AAP4a Chandelier

Surface (stems from ceiling) mounted line voltage chandelier shall consist of three vertical planes of FlexLume material painted in a faux Dupont Nomex wrapped in a loosely formed concentric arrangement and shall exhibit an overall dimension of about 5 feet/10 inches by 4 feet/2 inches. Overall suspension shall be 2 feet/6 inches (subject to ceiling height confirmation by Contractor) so that the bottom of the luminaire is 8 feet/6 inches above finished floor or as directed by the Architect and Interior Designer. Inner most vertical sheet (call this Sheet 1) of FlexLume shall be material of sufficient density to preclude direct lamp imaging and yet supple enough to allow for the concentric arrangement and shall be finished in white/amber on clear and REVERSED so that the typical "outside" surface faces to inside of fixture. The middle vertical sheet (call this Sheet 2) of FlexLume shall be white/amber on opal with normal "outside" surface facing outside. The outermost sheet (call this Sheet 3) of FlexLume shall be finished in white/cream on clear with normal "outside" surface facing outside all subject to vendor's confirmation on durability and UL compliance. Sheets shall be arranged in such a manner that lamps are never more than 0 feet/8 inches on center from face of sheet, and preferably less providing same meets all UL requirements. All sheet edges shall be trimmed and framed as necessary to hold shape. Stems shall be clustered to fit into a ceiling plate of brushed nickel exhibiting dimensions of 3 feet square and itself exhibiting an edge reveal with edges polished. Stems shall be of square tubular forms finished in factory-standard matte aluminum paint and shall be formed into elongate tight U-shapes to engage and support the Nomex and to support the medium base sockets (to accommodate lamps in a base up configuration). Socket supports shall be finished in brushed chrome. Components and entire assembly shall be of sufficient structural integrity to allow for maintenance and to maintain plumb appearance, consistency in alignment and elevational aspects, and to support themselves/itself freely without any auxiliary visible bracing or continual readjustment. Coordinate structural support requirements with all respective trades. Manufacturer to submit finished paint samples, shade material samples, and complete shop drawing as part of luminaire equipment product data submittal process. Luminaire shall be lamped with twenty four [24] Philips 30A15/CL (#30452-7) 30-watt, 22,000-hour rated life, clear incandescent lamp. Luminaire shall be UL listed and labeled for lamping and application. Components and entire assembly shall be of sufficient structural integrity to allow for maintenance and to maintain plumb appearance, consistency in alignment and elevational aspects, and to support themselves/itself freely without any auxiliary visible bracing or continual readjustment. Coordinate structural support requirements with all respective trades.

• Baldinger
• Winona

Type APS3 Grazing Column Wash

Surface (architectural slot) mounted linear incandescent channel shall consist of medium base, incandescent sockets spaced 0 feet/6 inches on center with flat blade baffles centered in between each socket. Channel shall be about 34 feet/11 inch in overall length made up of four segments—one leg about 4 feet/6 inches, a 90-degree corner, one leg about 10 feet/10 inches, a 135-degree corner, one leg about 12 feet/1 inch in length, a 90-degree corner, and one leg about 7 feet/6 inches in length, subject to field confirmation by Contractor. Channel housing and baffles shall exhibit a factory-standard baked satin aluminum painted finish. Channel shall be lamped with sixty-nine [69] Osram/Sylvania 35PAR20CAP/SPL/NFL30 (#14459) 35-watt, 130-volt PAR20 narrow flood lamps rated for 5000 hours life operating at 120-volts subject to field confirmation of final length (which may affect number of sockets). Luminaire shall be UL listed and labeled for lamping and application.

• Litelab LTX-1-6M-D-419(Pattern)-120-Cover-Baffles-AL-35PAR20WFL-GSLD

Type LMD1a Pinhole Downlight

Recessed (lay-in ceiling) mounted low voltage incandescent adjustable accent luminaire shall be about 0 feet/3¾ inches in diameter by 0 feet/5½ inches in recessed depth (see respective vendor's current datasheets for actual dimensions). Luminaire shall consist of a recessed frame-in kit and an adjustable accent trim with a round pinhole aperture nominally 0-feet/1¾-inches in diameter with a faceplate with a factory-standard white painted finish. Luminaire shall be furnished with an integral magnetic transformer. Luminaire shall be lamped with one [1] Philips 35MRC16/IRC/FL36 (#36351-5) 35-watt, halogen infrared MR16 flood lamp. Luminaire shall be UL listed and labeled for application. Luminaire shall be aimed straight downward.
• Halo H1499T/1419P
• Lightolier 2011/2000LV

Type NTS1 Curvilinear Bulkhead Slot

Surface (architectural slot as detailed by Architect) mounted luminous neon slot lighting shall consist of a two curvilinear parallel tubes of 15mm diameter, 60ma operating current tubing with one row of 3000K triphosphor white and one row of "Copper" cold cathode in a curvilinear pattern with a nominal length of about 98 feet/0 inches subject to field confirmation by Contractor and Vendor. Each tube shall be independently dimmed for cross fade effects from intense copper to pale amber to very warm white to warm white. Tubes shall exhibit no flicker nor create audible hum through dimming range or when maintained in static color state. Contractor shall coordinate architectural detailing and sizing with Neon Vendor's hardware size requirements and with Architect to assure fit and optical performance. Entire run shall be symmetric and shall exhibit no socket shadows or variations in output along the length. All interior details of slot shall be painted out to match the accent bulkhead. Transformer(s) shall be remote located in a well ventilated, easily accessible, code compliant space as agreed by Architect, Electrical Engineer, Neon Vendor, and Contractor. Transformer(s) shall have the highest sound rating available. Contractor shall coordinate Neon Vendor's installation process with the overall installation of the electric lighting for the project. Cove detail shall be coordinated by Contractor and Neon Vendor with Architect for a clean, neat appearance. Entire installation shall meet all code requirements and shall meet a standard of care expected of architectural installations of this caliber.
• Heller Signs

Type QTT1 Demo Kitchen Studio Light

New, surface (ceiling/cove) mounted theatrical studio light shall be about 1 foot/1 inch in width by 0 feet/10¾ inches in length by 0 feet/11¾ inches in overall height and shall weigh about 13 pounds (see respective vendor's datasheet for actual dimensions and weights). Luminaire shall consist of a die-cast aluminum housing with a specular die-cast aluminum reflector with a snap-in tempered prismatic glass lens. Luminaire shall be yoke mounted to a ceiling canopy. Contractor shall coordinate structural support requirements with all respective trades. Luminaire housing and yoke shall be painted factory-standard black. Luminaire shall be furnished with a wide flood lens in place and a top hat. Three spare lenses (one each of very narrow spot, narrow spot, and medium flood distributions) shall be turned over to Owner for potential future use. Luminaire shall be furnished with an electronic ballast suitable for operation of specified lamping at 120V. Luminaire shall be lamped with one [1] vendor-supplied Philips CDM70/T6/830 70-watt, 120-volt, 12,000 hour life, 3000K color temperature ceramic metal halide lamp. Luminaire shall be UL listed for lamping and application. Luminaires shall be controlled via Lutron system as an on/off metal halide electronic ballast load type. Two [2] steel mesh, properly sized, and framed neutral density filters shall be available for possible use for each luminaire. One [1] framed neutral density filter of 30 percent blocking and one [1] framed neutral density filter of 40 percent blocking shall be provided (available from City Theatrical at 800.230.9497).
• Altman CDM StarPar SPCA-HardwireCanopy-Black-8SN-120V-9070CDMT6/830
• ETC Source Four HID PAR-EA-Black-400PTH3-400CK-120V-70-watt Option-GSLD

Figure 5.6 Specified 2006
Type FTG1 Recessed Narrow Linear

Recessed (drywall ceiling as detailed by Architect) mounted fluorescent slot luminaire shall be nominally 0 feet/3 inches in width by 4 feet/0 inches in length by 0 feet/3¾ inches in overall recessed depth (see respective vendor's current datasheets for actual dimensions). Contractor shall coordinate final ceiling type/thickness and mounting with Vendor. Luminaire housing and gear tray shall be constructed of aluminum. Exposed metal components shall be painted in natatorium-rated paint to match RAL color selected by Architect. Luminaire shall consist of a flush diffuse lens. Luminaire shall exhibit a flangeless trim and Contractor shall coordinate with plaster worker to obtain flangeless appearance. Luminaires shall be installed flat/flush/plumb and shall be installed radially as indicated on plan. Luminaire shall be furnished with a fused, integral, metal-cased, high power factor (0.95 or greater), 1.0 ballast factor, program-start electronic fluorescent ballast with end-of-lamp-life protection mode suitable for operation at 120V subject to confirmation by Electrical Engineer. Luminaire shall be lamped with one [1] GE F28WT5/830 (#39982) or Philips F28T5/830 (#23084-7) 28-watt, 3000K color temperature, 20,000-hour rated life linear fluorescent lamp. Luminaire shall be UL listed and labeled for lamping and "damp" application. Luminaire shall be operated on GFCI subject to confirmation by Electrical Engineer.
• Selux M60-1T5F28W-OD-SF1/2-004-SPnatatoriumRAL-120-FS-DL

Type FTQ1 Recessed Sconce

Recessed (drywall wall as detailed by Architect) mounted fluorescent sconce luminaire shall be similar to Type FTG1, except for application as wall sconce and shall be oriented vertically. Luminaire shall be centered at 11 feet/0 inches AFF. Luminaires shall be installed flat/flush/plumb and shall be installed orthogonally square with floor/ceiling planes. Where a series of units is spaced regularly in one area, all trims shall be square with respect to all other trims. Luminaire shall be furnished with a fused, integral, metal-cased, high power factor (0.95 or greater), 1.0 ballast factor, program-start electronic fluorescent ballast with end-of-lamp-life protection mode suitable for operation at 120V subject to confirmation by Electrical Engineer. Luminaire shall be lamped with one [1] Osram F28W/67/HE/UNV1 (#4050300646657) 28-watt, 24,000-hour rated life, blue T5 linear fluorescent lamp. These lamps and an attic stock quantity equal to the original installation count shall be supplied by luminaire vendor. Luminaire shall be UL listed and labeled for lamping and "damp" application. Luminaire shall be operated on GFCI subject to confirmation by Electrical Engineer.

• Selux M60-1T5F28W-OD-SF1/2-004-SPnatatoriumRAL-120-FS-DL-SeluxProvideLampsAndOneSetSpares

Type MTD2 Downlight

Recessed (drywall ceiling as detailed by Architect) mounted ceramic metal halide lensed downlight luminaire shall be similar to Type MTD1, except reflector shall exhibit a parabolic shape to provide a medium beam distribution suitable for downlighting in high ceilings. As with all recessed luminaires, luminaire housing shall be appropriately and securely attached to structure to meet code and to prevent settlement shifting over time and to prevent inadvertent heaving or rotation of housing during servicing and/or aiming. Stapling, nailing, screwing, or otherwise attaching ceiling substrates or supports to luminaire housing which precludes complete access to lamp and ballast mechanisms or which is not code compliant shall not be permitted. Reflector cone shall be finished in factory standard matte aluminum with an overlap polished flange. Luminaire shall be furnished with fused, integral, metal-cased, high power factor (0.95 or greater), low harmonic distortion (10% or less) electronic ceramic metal halide ballast suitable for operation at 120V subject to confirmation by Electrical Engineer. Luminaire shall be lamped with one [1] GE CMH70/T/U/830/G12 (#92582) or Philips CDM70/T6/830 (#22337-0) 70-watt, 3000K, 12,000-hour rated life, T6 ceramic metal halide lamp. Per Electrical Engineer's direction, luminaire shall exhibit an electronic standby system and DCB socket and 100-watt T4DCB lamp supplied by luminaire Vendor all subject to confirmation by Electrical Engineer. Contractor shall align T4DCB socket position in a consistent orientation on all units. Luminaire shall be powered by GFCI circuit subject to confirmation by the Electrical Engineer. Luminaire shall be U.L. listed and labeled for damp application and specified lamping.

• Kirlin HRR-06225-28-45-70-120V-96-FS-65-LS/100T4DCB

Figure 5.10 Specified 2006
Type FCD3 Lensed Downlight

Recessed (ceiling substrate as detailed by Architect) mounted compact fluorescent lensed downlight luminaire shall be similar to Type FCD1, except shall exhibit a wattage rating label of 32 watts and shall be lamped with one [1] F32TBX/830/A/4P/EOL (#39378) or Philips PLT32W/830/4P/ALTO (#26832-6) 32-watt, 3,000K color temperature, 10,000-hour rated life triple tube compact fluorescent lamp. Luminaire shall be UL listed and labeled for application and lamping.

• Cooper Portfolio C6132-E-6181H-1-120-Fuse
• Kirlin FRR06014-17-70-120-FS-99(WRL32)
• Kurt Versen P921-SC-LP-120-Fuse
• Lightolier 8091-PCCDP-6132BU-120-Fuse

©GarySteffyLightingDesign

Type FTL2b Artistic Visual Effect

Surface (ceiling slot wall as detailed by Architect) mounted linear fluorescent uplight luminaire shall be similar to Type FTL2a, except shall be 6 feet/0 inches in length, shall be furnished with fused, integral, metal-cased, high power factor (0.95 or greater), 1.0 ballast factor, program-start electronic fluorescent nondim ballasts and shall be lamped with two [2] Osram FQ39W/67/HO (#4050300938899) 39-watt, 10,000-hour rated life blue T5/HO linear fluorescent lamps. These lamps and an attic stock quantity equal to the original installation count shall be supplied by luminaire Vendor. Luminaire shall be UL listed and labeled for application.

• Neoray 790S-1-2F39T5HOSylvania BlueByNeoray-6ft-120V-EB-SI-Fuse-modGSLDcustompaint(including reflector systemMatchBenMooreLinenWhiteMatteFinish)

Type MPD1a Elevator Threshold Accent

Recessed (ceiling as detailed by Architect) mounted ceramic metal halide adjustable accent luminaire shall exhibit an aperture of about 0 feet/4¼ inches in diameter and shall exhibit a recessed footprint of about 1foot/2 inches in width by 1 foot/4 inches in length by 0 feet/9 inches in overall recessed depth (see vendor's current datasheet for actual dimensions). Luminaire shall be installed flat/flush/plumb and shall exhibit no light leaks at ceiling juncture. As with all recessed luminaires, luminaire housing shall be appropriately and securely attached to structure to meet code and to prevent settlement shifting over time and to prevent inadvertent heaving or rotation of housing during

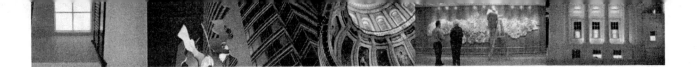

servicing and/or aiming. Stapling, nailing, screwing, or otherwise attaching ceiling substrates or supports to luminaire housing which precludes complete access to lamp and ballast mechanisms or which is not code compliant shall not be permitted. Reflector cone shall exhibit a straight cut (0°) and shall be finished in matte clear aluminum with a polished overlap flange. Luminaire shall be furnished with a soft diffusion lens. Luminaire shall be furnished with a fused, integral, metal-cased, high power factor (0.95 or greater), low harmonic distortion (10% or less) electronic ceramic metal halide ballast suitable for operation at 120V subject to confirmation by Electrical Engineer. Luminaire shall be lamped with one [1] GE CMH39/UPAR20/SP10 (#42069) or Philips CDM35/PAR20/M/SP (#23365-0) 39-watt, 3000K color temperature, 9,000-hour rated life, ceramic metal halide PAR20 spot lamp. Lamp shall be aimed and locked by Contractor as observed by Architect. Aiming shall be a "white thermal glove" operation to avoid fingerprinting painted housing, trim, and mechanism elements. Luminaire shall be UL listed and labeled for application.

• Kurt Versen R7408-39120-SC-Fuse-FF20-8-LightFrostClearLens-STC
• Lightolier C4P20MHACCDW-C4A39P20E1-0DegreeCone-CAH4-AF3LF-Fuse

Type MPS1 Slot Uplight

Recessed (in fireplace mantle pocket as detailed by architect) mounted linear ceramic metal halide extruded socket channel indirect luminaire shall be about 6 feet/9 inches in length (subject to field confirmation by Contractor) by 0 feet/10¾ inches in height by 0 feet/6¾ inches in width and fitted with linear spreadlenses. Channel shall consist of fabricated heavy gage and extruded metal for rigidity, consistency of run alignment, durability, and to provide heat sink capability. Exposed metal components shall be finished in factory standard white paint. Channel shall exhibit 9 sockets on 9-inch centers in a straight linear run of 6 feet/9 inches (subject to field confirmation by Contractor with Architect). Detail shall be vented as detailed by Architect. Sockets shall be screw base type for ceramic metal halide PAR20 lamping. All dead space shall be split equally at each end. Each socket shall be furnished with a fused, integral, metal-cased, high power factor (0.95 or greater), low harmonic distortion (10% or less) electronic ceramic metal halide ballast suitable for operation at 120V subject to confirmation by Electrical Engineer. Each socket shall be lamped with one [1] GE CMH39/UPAR20/SP10 (#42069) or Philips CDM35/PAR20/M/SP (#23365-0) 39-watt, 3000K color temperature, 9,000-hour rated life, ceramic metal halide PAR20 spot lamp. Luminaire shall be UL listed and labeled for application and specified lamping. Every other lamp shall be looped on one control channel, for a total of 5 lamps. Remaining lamps shall be looped on a second control channel for a total of 4 lamps.

• Specialty Lighting 803UP-PAR20-CMH39W-9inchCenters-120-FS-2Circuit/6ft/9in-734TLG-WHT

G od is in the details, as Mies van der Rohe so famously quipped in the New York Herald.[1] That's the more positive reflection of "the devil is in the details." In the context of this chapter, details aren't the physical architectural elements that support or express lighting hardware and/or light. Details means those characteristics or attributes of lighting that combined together make a project a complete and finished work, but that individually may go unnoticed or unacknowledged. In the view of some, these are relatively minor issues. However, it is the details that collectively will make or break a project. Systems Factors epitomize the details. Many times unheralded and typically uninteresting to the occupants and even some design team members, Systems Factors help address systems integration, codes, maintenance, and sustainability.

6.1 Flexibility

Owners and/or occupants of many project types are likely to want if not need lighting that is flexible. Addressing flexibility where it is needed will yield a significantly more sustainable approach than the alternative—trashing and replacing the lighting system. Flexibility has many meanings. So, the design team must agree on what kind of flexibility, if any, the lighting system is to have for a specific project. For example, flexibility may mean that:

- lighting quantities and quality remain constant (people/furniture can be moved around without changing lighting)
- all or most luminaires are readily physically moveable and/or reconfigurable
- lighting quantities and qualities are changed by addressing (controlling) luminaires

It is important then to define the degree of flexibility required, if any. Initially, many owners/occupants will indicate flexibility to be an important *want*, but is it a *need*. On closer scrutiny, it may be determined that the owners/occupants have not reconfigured their existing environment in many years—not because they couldn't, but because there was never a need. Or, it may be determined that some limited reconfiguration occurs once every 10 to 15 years—perhaps not enough to warrant the costs in design effort and lighting system hardware necessary for complete, repetitive reconfiguration.

Consistent lighting quantities and qualities throughout an area or large portions of a building allows for easy furniture and people reorganization. However, the design of such a lighting system must be carefully monitored to confirm it can address a myriad of furniture reconfiguration options without introducing an energy-intensive and/or vapid lighting solution. Nevertheless, this can be a convenient, cost-effective (in both initial and life-cycle costs) approach.

Physically moving luminaires to respond to furniture, wall, and people moves can be costly and time-intensive unless quick-connect/disconnect modular wiring systems are used and fully and easily accessible ceiling systems are used. Further, where linear pendent lights are used, their modularity is crucial to reconfiguration. Lay-in ceilings are most appropriate and preferably the lift-and-shift tile type to avoid laborious puzzle-like deconstruction/reconstruction exercises. Although more disruptive than the consistent lighting approach, this reconfigurable approach typically allows for a more tailored lighting solution that may be more energy efficient (better using the available watts).

The addressable lighting approach, when designed to its fullest potential, literally allows the owner/occupants to address every luminaire separately—from switching on/off individual lights as needed to dimming individual lights to different intensities as needed. Although most costly and requiring sophisticated computer control to manage the number of control points (a minimum of one control point per luminaire), this approach offers the most energy and sustainability benefits while making reconfiguration of lighting seamless and least disruptive. More on this in 6.2.

6.2 Controls

temporal control
Dynamic control over time. Involves a time machine or programmed computer program to control light intensity, color, motion (e.g., chasing effects), flashing, and the like. Static control or the traditional definition of "control" is the simple act of turning a light or series of lights on and off, or dimming them from one steady state to another.

Energy use, sustainability, flexibility, and Spatial Factors, Physiological and Psychological Factors, and Task Factors are all influenced by lighting controls. Switching lighting effects on/off and/or dimming lighting over the course of a day can change the impact of the architecture and of energy use. When integrated with daylighting techniques, this can even further impact energy use. **Temporal control** or dynamic control can itself help establish and/or modulate some of the Spatial Factors previously discussed (e.g., visual hierarchy, circulation, and focal centers). Task factors, discussed later in this chapter, can significantly influence the need for controls as well. There will always be some sort of lighting control (to control both electric lighting and daylighting quantities and qualities) in built environments. Manual controls—simple wall switches—with timeclock sweeps are the bare minimum required by many codes. Smart switches and/or motion sensors are de rigueur. Add in automated timeclock control and/or preset scenes, and potential exists for significant energy savings and sustainability. Controls make sense in terms of economics, global environment protection, and occupant protection and satisfaction. For electric lighting, controls may include: smart switches and/or dimmers, time-of-day control, occupancy sensors, photocell sensors, and centralized building energy management. For daylighting, controls may include photocell sensors and/or local manual switches for control of window treatment. Controls are discussed at length in Chapter 12.

6.3 Acoustics

Lighting can have a negative impact on spatial acoustics. The lighting designer should be in a position to address goals established by the acoustician. Nevertheless, it is incumbent on the acoustician or on the architect (as the design leader and coordinator) to relay any lighting-related acoustics goals to the lighting designer as early as possible—during the programming of the project—so that informed lighting design can proceed in the schematic design phase.

Luminaire ballasts and transformers can introduce noise into spaces and/or into audio amplification systems. Chokes are available to minimize this noise. Using remote ballasts or transformers can reduce noise, but this is providing the remote equipment is sound isolated from noise-sensitive spaces. Further, remote equipment needs to be easily accessible and well ventilated as determined by the registered professionals on the project. Electromagnetic ballasts and transformers are notorious noise generators. Some electromagnetic transformers are quiet, but still require review by the acoustician. Certain versions of electronic ballasts and transformers may also cause problems. Electronic components

operating above 20,000 **Hz** are not audible to humans, although frequencies should be reviewed by the acoustician for feedback through audio amplification and/or recording systems.

The makeup of the lighting hardware can also have a negative influence on architectural acoustics. For example, in open plan offices, ceiling-recessed lensed luminaires, ceiling-recessed small cell (paracube) louver luminaires, and large, flat-bottomed pendent indirect luminaires all of which are exhibiting a width of at least 1′ (about 300 mm) can easily reflect sound from one workstation or area to another. *SOLUTION HINT: In these office situations, consider narrow profile luminaires (less than 8″ in width or very small square cross-section [3″ or about 75 mm]), or in the case of pendent lights, consider round cross-sectional profiles (to avoid a flat bottom).*

Hz
Hertz. The SI metric for frequency of wavelengths of energy. 1 Hz represents one wavelength cycle per second. Audible sound ranges from 20 to 20,000 Hz.[2]

6.4 HVAC

Heating, ventilating, and air-conditioning can be influenced by lighting—both by lighting loads or power budgets (total wattage of lights) and lighting equipment air-handling capabilities. As with acoustics, the responsibility for HVAC lies with another design professional—in this case the mechanical engineer. The lighting designer, however, needs to be in a position to meet the goals the mechanical engineer establishes. It is incumbent on the mechanical engineer to convey these goals as early in a project as possible—during the programming of the project—so that informed lighting design can proceed in the schematic design phase. Similarly, the lighting designer should alert the mechanical engineer of any HVAC requirements that the lighting system may demand. This may be an alert of heat-intensive details such as the cavity of backlighted surfaces or of heat- and/or cool-sensitive areas such as applications of compact fluorescent lamps (CFL) and linear T5 fluorescent lamps. **CFL and T5 lamps exhibit relatively long warm-up times to full-on and this is exacerbated in environments exhibiting cooler ambient temperatures.**

Lighting power budgets are particularly important to the mechanical engineer in establishing cooling loads and in sizing air-conditioning and heating equipment.

Some recessed luminaires have the capability to extract air (return air through the luminaire housing into ductwork or plenum spaces and ultimately back to the central conditioning units) and/or to supply conditioned air into the environment. Although such a feature may be convenient for the mechanical engineer, it should never be the sole or primary reason for selecting a particular lighting solution.

6.5 Ceiling Systems

The architect establishes the ceiling system or systems to be used in a particular project. These ceiling systems establish other design goals for the lighting designer. Here, however, the lighting designer should work to influence the architect on establishing ceiling surface reflectance characteristics—as these significantly affect the efficiency of the lighting system (higher-reflectance finishes are more efficient and sustainable as less lighting equipment is required) and the glare potential of the lighting system (more specular surfaces are prone to glaring reflections). **Matte, white ceiling surfaces exhibiting LRVs of at least 85 and preferably 90 are best.** If recessed lighting is used, then the type of recessed luminaire trim and mounting version will be influenced by the ceiling system.

Figure 6.1

Ceiling systems: This office installation is fitted with a suspended, exposed T grid system arranged in a 2' by 2' pattern (about 600 by 600 mm). The acoustic ceiling tiles exhibit tegular edges to slip over the corner of the T. This creates a shadow line for a more textured appearance to the ceiling. Laying out the grid at 45° to the main direction of the corridor and cove provides additional texture and interest. [This is a close-up of Figure 5.3.]
Image ©Justin Maconochie

tegular edge
A reference to ceiling tile edge conditions. A tegular edge is a notched corner rather than a full square corner. Tegular edges are also known as shadowline.

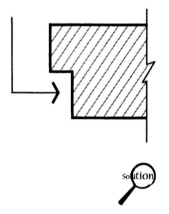

Ceiling systems can be categorized as suspended, drywall, and structural. Each of these ceiling systems typically requires that the lighting equipment has specific trim/mounting configurations to fit into or onto the respective ceiling type. In more typical construction, drywall or gypsum panels are attached to structure to provide a ceiling plane. Where cost, future flexibility, acoustics, and/or accessibility are key criteria, ceilings are likely to be suspended. In these situations, a grid system of metal runners or inverted Tees (Ts) is suspended from the building structure. These Ts, depending on their exact cross-section, are either exposed or concealed. Exposed Ts include the common T grid and the slot grid. In any event, the grid work can then accept panels to create a finished look and to provide some acoustic capability. Ceiling panels or tiles may have a right-angle edge to simply fit or lay into the inverted T grid. Alternatively, ceiling tiles may have a **tegular edge** to allow the bottom face of the panel to float about ¼" to ½" below the grid line in the case of standard inverted Ts (see Figure 6.1), or to allow the bottom face of the panel to flush out to the same elevation as the bottom of a slot-T (see Figure 6.2).

The layout of T grid systems influences the lighting layout. Typically, for best appearance—enhancing pleasantness—recessed and surface mounted lights are centered in the tiles of T grid ceilings. This can influence optical distribution if lights are too close to walls and my require readjustment of the grid layout. *SOLUTION HINT: Layout lighting first and then layout ceiling grid.*

Drywall ceilings are also known as gypsumboard, Sheetrock®, wallboard, plasterboard, or plaster ceilings. In construction prior to the mid-20th century or even in some new construction where more ceiling character and mass are desired, plaster is common. Drywall has a more traditional appearance than lay-in ceilings. Its monolithic planar appearance also makes it suitable for a clean, crisp, modern look (see Figures 5.6 and 5.7). As such, it is considered a higher-end treatment.

Sheetrock® is a registered trademark of USG Corporation.

Figure 6.2

Ceiling systems: A slot-T grid system (Fineline®) with a tegular edge fiberglass tile.

Because drywall reflects sound well, it is not considered appropriate in large, open office areas or in areas where a "loud" setting need not be exacerbated (e.g., pediatricians' waiting rooms).

Structural ceilings are typically exposed wood, metal, or concrete decks of the floor or roof above. Many times, the depth between the bottom of the structural ceiling plane and the next floor surface or the roof surface is sufficiently shallow so lights cannot be recessed into these ceilings. Hence, lights are surface mounted or suspended from these ceilings.

In lay-in ceilings, recessed luminaires are typically sized to fit the T grid module (typically 1′ by 4′, 2′ by 2′ or 2′ by 4′ luminaires [about 300 by 1200 mm, 600 by 600 mm, or 600 by 1200 mm]). Figure 6.3 illustrates a recessed luminaire capable of accommodating various types of T grids.

Recessed luminaires that are smaller than the T grid module or used in drywall require a flange or trim to conceal the rough edge of the hole cut into the ceiling to accommodate the recessed luminaire, resulting in an "island" look (see Figures 6.4 and 6.5). This flange may project below the ceiling by as much as an eighth of an inch (about 3 to 4 mm), which may be objectionable when a large ceiling plane has many luminaires. For an even cleaner, less-cluttered look in drywall or plaster ceilings, some small recessed luminaires are available in trimless or flangeless versions (see Figures 6.5 and 6.6). The drywall skimcoat or plaster is applied right up to the luminaire trim edge for a flush look.

```
more online @
www.armstrong.com/
www.bpb-na.com/us/english/acoustical_ceilings/index.php
www.ceilingsplus.com/
gordongrid.com/
www.nortonceilings.com/
www.usg.com/
```

Fineline® is a registered trademark of USG Corporation.

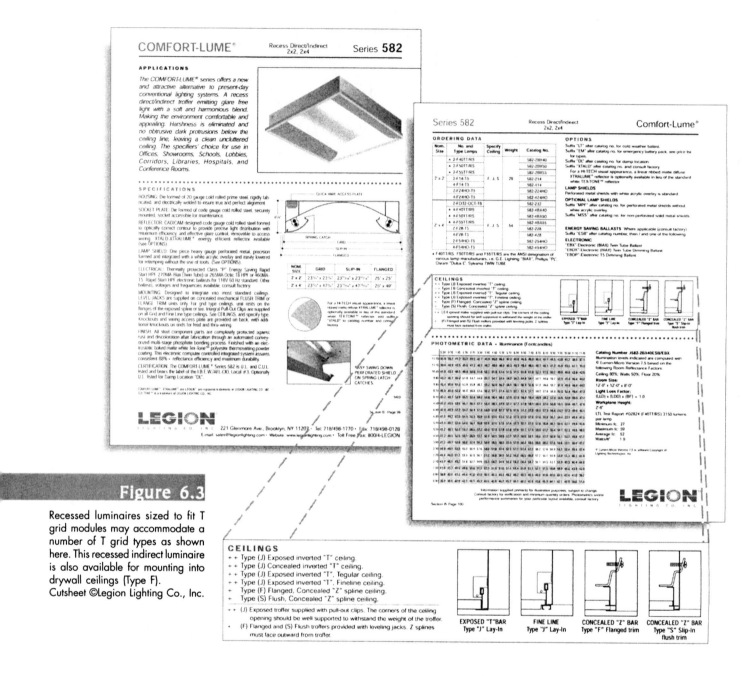

6.6 Codes

ordinance
A law enacted by the legislators or council of a local governing body (e.g., county, city, town, township, or village).

Codes, of course, are law. A building code is a collection of laws, regulations, **ordinance**s, or other statutory requirements adopted by a government's legislative authority.[2] Building codes establish predictable and consiste—nt minimum standards for the quality and durability of construction materials. "Minimum requirements" means that construction meets the criteria of being both "practical and adequate for protecting life, safety and welfare of the public."[2] The registered professional (the architect or engineer) on every project must assure that all code requirements are met prior to a project's completion. If the lighting designer is not also acting in the capacity of one of these registered professionals, then the architect or engineer must define lighting-related code issues and direct

Architectural Lighting Design

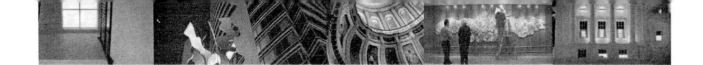

Figure 6.4

Ceiling systems: A small rectilinear recessed compact fluorescent wallwash luminaire is island mounted in an acoustical tile pad. An even more refined look is achieved with mitered-joint frames (frame shown here exhibits butt-joint configuration).

the lighting designer as or if necessary. Ultimately, the registered professionals must check the work of the lighting designer and that of any nonregistered consulting specialty. Some of the more typical and universal code requirements include egress lighting, luminaire insulation-contact and air-tight requirements, ADA-compliance, power limits, and recycling requirements. What follows are some typical requirements, but these may change from jurisdiction to jurisdiction and may be interpreted differently by different code officials and professionals. Always seek out local code requirements.

more online @
www.constructionweblinks.com/Industry_Topics/Building_Codes_
    and_Regulations/building_codes_and_regulations.html
www.bpcnet.com/codes.htm
www.municode.com/Resources/OnlineLibrary.asp

Egress Lighting

Egress lighting relates to providing a lighted path of egress during emergency-power conditions and during nonemergency (or **normal power**) conditions. Egress lighting requirements are typically 0.1 and 1 fc (about 1.1 and 11 lx) minimum, maintained on the path of egress for emergency and normal power conditions respectively, as well as exit signs of appropriate size, luminance, and color located at paths and egress ways indicating the direction of exit and the actual exit point. In the past decade, many codes have evolved to require signage to be mounted low to the floor to account for smoke buildup and the ultimate obscuration of those exit signs mounted high on walls and/or above exits. Registered professionals should select egress lighting hardware and establish quantities and locations on plans in accordance with current code requirements for the jurisdiction in which the project is located or, for state and federal projects, the current state and/or federally mandated code requirements.

normal power
A reference to the electrical power service provided by the electric utility. When normal power is interrupted, some sort of emergency power system is energized, which is then used to power select or all lighting and equipment.

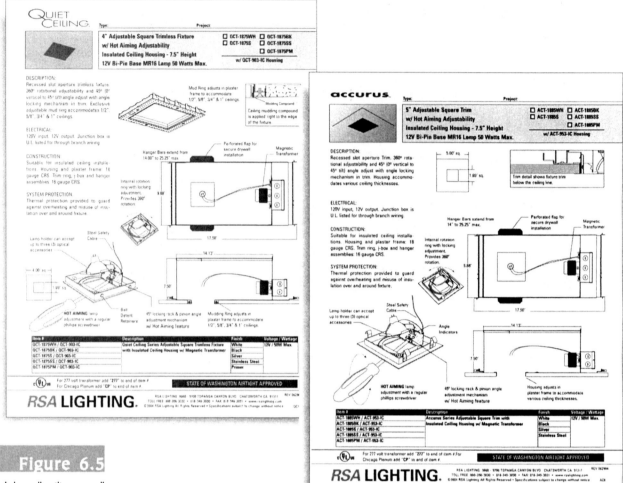

Figure 6.5

For lay-in and drywall ceilings, small recessed luminaires are available with flanged trims to hide the rough cut of the hole opening (as shown on far right). In drywall ceilings, another option is a flangeless or trimless version shown on the near right. The trimless version results in a cleaner ceiling appearance.

Egress lighting can be achieved by several means. Some more costly and typically more aesthetically pleasing than others. To some degree, the selection of egress lights will depend on the project style, budget, and/or source of the emergency power—centralized, decentralized, or localized. All systems are required to provide power for a minimum amount of time defined by the code (e.g., 90 minutes). Centralized systems consist of generator(s) or very large arrays of batteries known as UPS systems (uninterruptible power supply aka inverter). Decentralized systems consist of smaller UPS systems located in various designated UPS rooms throughout a floor or floors of a building. Localized systems consist of batteries located within each egress luminaire.

With emergency-power generators, entire lighting systems can be operated depending on the efficiency of the lighting system, size of building, and size of generator(s) (see Figure 6.7). In these situations the normal-power lights also act as egress lights. From the occupant's perspective, there are no extraneous lights on ceilings or walls to clutter the view or the places where art, signage, etc., might be hung. Money is not spent on additional luminaires. Additional earth resources

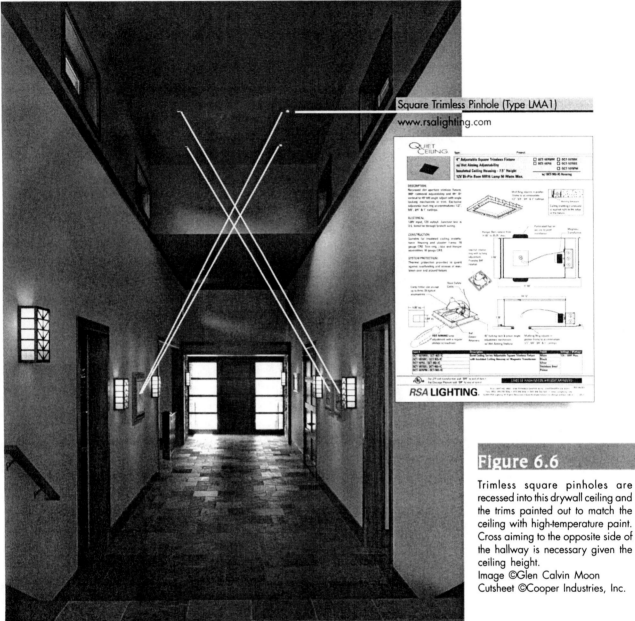

Square Trimless Pinhole (Type LMA1)
www.rsalighting.com

Figure 6.6

Trimless square pinholes are recessed into this drywall ceiling and the trims painted out to match the ceiling with high-temperature paint. Cross aiming to the opposite side of the hallway is necessary given the ceiling height.
Image ©Glen Calvin Moon
Cutsheet ©Cooper Industries, Inc.

are not expended on the production and transportation of egress luminaires. Conventional emergency-power generators are very large and expensive, and during operation pollute the air, which limits their application and siting.

Where smaller generators or UPS systems are employed, egress lighting can be accommodated by selecting specific normal-power lights that are identified by the registered professionals as sufficient to meet the egress lighting requirements Where normal-power lights are deemed undesirable or inefficient for egress

Figure 6.7

At the Virginia State Capitol, egress lighting is accomplished by placing normal-power electric lights on an emergency-power generator. Here, the wall brackets and column bands in the foreground and pendents in the background are using very efficient 13-watt (F13Triple/4P) compact fluorescent lamps in 2700K color for a more historical incandescent appearance. Custom historic luminaires by Crenshaw Lighting (www.crenshawlighting.com/). Image ©Tom Crane Photography

lighting, it may be necessary to specify lights solely for purposes of egress lighting. These might be architectural luminaires that are simply not used during normal-power conditions, but are connected to a generator or UPS.

Where no generator(s) or UPS is practical, egress lighting consists of normal-power luminaires fitted with batteries, emergency luminaires fitted with batteries, or some combination of both. Emergency luminaires might be simple, low-cost wall- or ceiling-mounted exposed lights and battery box (see Figure 6.8) or where aesthetics are more critical these might be concealed versions that are activated under emergency-power situations (see Figure 6.9).

more online @
www.concealite.com/
www.emergi-lite.com/usa/catalogue.html
www.lithonia.com/products/groups/Emergency/Velare/default.asp
www.surelites-lighting.com/

IC/AT

IC-rated

A reference to a luminaire rated for insulation contact. IC-rated luminaires are typically required in residential construction where lots of insulation is used in most all walls and ceilings. Non-IC-rated indicates that the ceiling or wall recessed luminaire is not rated for insulation contact—more common in commercial installations.

Thermal protection is a necessity for most luminaires when they are recessed into typical ceiling and wall construction. In general, use luminaires with thermal protectors. The thermal protector is an internal heat-sensitive switch. The thermal protector "trips" or disengages if the luminaire overheats due to improper lamping or because the luminaire is surrounded by inappropriately positioned insulation that does not allow for proper heat dissipation.

In today's efficient buildings where thermal insulation is present and/or where sound insulation is present, luminaires are likely to come in contact with or to be surrounded by insulation. So, codes require that luminaires be made to withstand the effects of the insulation surrounding and in direct contact with the luminaire housing. However, the physical sizes of these luminaires may preclude their use in certain construction types (e.g., the stud spacings and heights may prohibit use of all but the lowest-wattage—and, therefore, smallest—**IC-rated** luminaires).

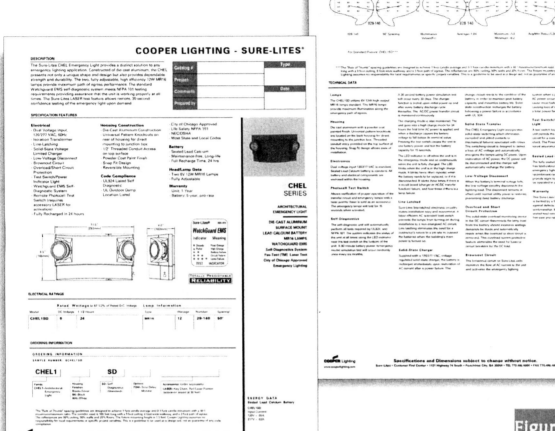

The higher quality versions are typically smaller and have a wide variety of finish, lamping, and aperture options. Further, the higher-quality luminaires tend to exhibit better glare control and better aiming and locking mechanisms (important for adjustable accents aimed onto artwork or features).

In some instances, commercial-grade luminaires are deemed appropriate for their lighting effects in residential settings, yet are to be installed in insulation-filled walls or ceilings. Here, the local inspector and electrician must be consulted to determine if the construction of "thermal breaks" around the luminaires designed to keep insulation at least 3" (about 75 mm) from any component of the luminaire will meet with approval.

Most residential codes and some commercial codes also stipulate use of **AT-rated** luminaires. These lights do not allow the conditioned air in the rooms to escape through the housings. Figure 6.5 illustrates IC- and AT-rated luminaires. These lights are also used in commercial construction even if not required by code. Where sound transmission from one office to another is a design issue (sound travels through luminaire openings into the plenum and

AT-rated

A reference to a luminaire rated as air tight. AT-rated luminaires are typically required in residential construction to limit air flow between the conditioned rooms and the unconditioned attic or plenum—which would essentially require increased heating or cooling depending on the season and thereby waste energy.

Figure 6.9

Egress lighting: Emergency lights with concealed lamps and integral batteries are useful where normal-power luminaires are inappropriate for egress situations or cannot be connected to generators or UPS systems and where an uncluttered aesthetic is desirable.
Cutsheet ©Concealite

to adjacent space back out through luminaire openings), IC/AT-rated luminaires can minimize sound transfer. Their sealed housings and sealed ceiling apertures act to limit sound transfer.

ADA

AFF
Above finished floor. The distance from the finished floor plane to the imaginary or real plane of interest. For example, work surfaces are typically 2' 6" (about 750 mm) AFF. Typically used to reference interior dimensions. Not to be confused with **AFG** (see sidebar on next page).

The Americans with Disabilities Act (ADA) of 1990 requires, among other things, that lighting equipment not impede the movement of people. Obvious, perhaps, but not well observed by designers prior to this act's signing. Wall sconces may not protrude more than 4" (about 100 mm) beyond the face of the wall or, alternatively, they need to be mounted so that the bottom of the wall sconce is at least 6' 8" (about 2 m) **AFF**. Where torchieres are used, elements may not protrude more than 1' 0" (about 300 mm) from the torchiere post. As noted in the discussion on controls, the ADA also has requirements for the mounting of wall switches. An illuminance of 5 fc (about 50 lx) is required at elevator thresholds.

ADA compliance may not be a requirement for certain single-family residential projects. A local code check is necessary. Even if not required, compliance may provide better resale value and result in a more user-friendly experience.

Typical Power Budget Requirements

Table 6.1

Space Type	Power Budget Limit[a]	Typical Qualified Adder(s)[b, c]
Classroom	1.4 w/ft²	plus 0.35 w/ft²
Conference room	1.3 w/ft²	plus 1.0 w/ft²
Corridor	0.5 w/ft²	plus 1.0 w/ft²
Lobby (office)	1.3 w/ft²	plus 1.0 w/ft²
Open office	1.0 w/ft²	plus 0.35 w/ft² plus 1.0 w/ft²
Retail	1.7 w/ft²	plus 1.0 w/ft²

[a] Refer to specific code documents for exact requirements and metric conversions — which many times are rounded. Values typical of ASHRAE/IESNA 90.1/2004, which may be superceded.

[b] For those spaces where visual display terminals (computers) are the primary viewing task and ambient lighting equipment meets low-glare requirements, additional connected load of 0.35 w/ft² is permitted solely for the ambient lighting so that more comfortable, less glary lighting equipment can be used.

[c] For those spaces where decorative lighting such as chandeliers, sconces, and/or art accents is deemed necessary, additional connected load of 1.0 w/ft² is permitted solely for the decorative lighting.

Energy

Power-limit codes (or power budget codes or just energy codes—even though many of the requirements address power [kilowatts] rather than energy [kilowatt hours]) were initially established as a direct result of the oil embargoes of 1973 and 1979. These power limits were intended to simply reduce connected load (watts) and, thereby, reduce energy consumption. These codes have evolved to be more holistic in their approach and result. Although connected loads are still limited, controls requirements and daylighting requirements also need to be addressed. As such, these codes are now better targeting energy use and sustainability. For example, automatic controls are mandatory for many lighting applications. Table 6.1 cites a few space types and typical respective power limits as defined by ASHRAE/IESNA 90.1/2004. Other prominent energy codes include California's Title 24/Section 6 and the International Energy Conservation Code (IECC). Most of these are revised every three or four years. However, in an effort to be "new" and "revised," there is a trend with energy codes to simply cut the power allowances regardless the effect on the living/working conditions.

Seek out the most efficient *certified* lighting solutions. For example, **specifying incandescent luminaires with screwbase CFL lamps and taking credit for the reduced wattage of the CFL lamp is not a code certified approach**. Dedicated-socket luminaires or **wattage reduction labels** must be specified for proper wattage credit in accordance with the energy code. To help maximize the lighting efficiency, specify room surface finishes of very light colors and/or white. Exceptions and exemptions in most energy codes should also be pursued to avoid dim and vapid settings that themselves waste energy because few folks are willing to live or work in them—or at least not to the full potential of living and working. A recurring issue that can trip up designers is the lack of coordination between various codes. While energy codes continue to cut connected load allowances,

AFG
Above finished grade. The distance from the finished grade plane to the imaginary or real plane of interest. For example, an exterior wall sconce might be mounted so that its bottom is 6′ 8″ (about 2 m) AFG. Typically used to reference exterior dimensions.

dedicated-socket luminaires
Luminaires fitted with sockets that only accept one type and a limited wattage-range of lamps, such as pin-based CFL luminaires.

other codes ratchet up illuminance requirements for occupied spaces and stairs to excess. In any event, safety and security should not be sacrificed to save energy.

more online @
/ www.energy.ca.gov/title24/
www.energycodes.gov/implement/state_codes/state_status_full.php

Recycling

wattage reduction labels
Luminaires that are fitted with the ubiquitous medium screwbase sockets can have wattage reduction labels factory-applied to limit the lamp wattage to significantly less than the original luminaire's rating. For example, a luminaire UL-listed and labeled for a 100-watt A19 incandescent lamp may be suitably functional using a 20-watt screwbase CFL. A wattage reduction label can be specified as a means to comply with the energy code requirements of accounting luminaire wattage based on the maximum rated wattage of the luminaire.

WEEE
Waste of Electrical and Electronic Equipment (European Union). Outlines directives on reuse, recycling, and recovery of waste associated electrical and electronics equipment, including lighting.

Many jurisdictions have regulations on lamp disposal—typically targeted toward lamps containing mercury and other heavy metals. However, the whole issue can be avoided by recycling spent lamps. Further, using the most efficient and longest life lamps will at least reduce the number of times and amount of recycling necessary for any particular project. Lamps containing mercury and/ or other hazardous materials include fluorescent, high pressure sodium, and metal halide lamps, as well as cold cathode and neon lamps and mercury vapor lamps. Lamp manufacturers have low-mercury lamps that are TCLP-compliant. That is, these lamps meet the EPA's toxicity characteristic leaching procedure and, therefore, are exempt from the regulations. Nevertheless, even these TCLP-compliant lamps should be recycled. Handling any of these lamps in bulk should be done with great care and only by professional maintenance personnel or licensed electricians.

Of course, lamps are just one part of the lighting system. Recycling luminaires, ballasts, and related packaging should be pursued, as should using recycled equipment or equipment made from recycled materials/components. These aspects are all new to the lighting industry and may take some time to enter manufacturing and marketing procedures. Regulations (e.g., **WEEE** in Europe) and certification programs (e.g., LEED, the EU Greenlight Programme, the EU Green Building Programme) will accelerate this, as will designers' inquiries.[3]

more online @
/ ec.europa.eu/environment/waste/weee/index_en.htm
www.eere.energy.gov/
www.energystar.gov/ia/partners/promotions/change_light/downloads/
    Fact_Sheet_Mercury.pdf
www.eu-greenbuilding.org/fileadmin/Greenbuilding/gb_redaktion/modules/
    Lighting_Module_GB.pdf
www.eu-greenlight.org/
www.healthlinkeurope.com/landing-weee-registration.php?gclid=
    CK3G6brRk44CFQYjWAod3zJ2Dw
www.lamprecycle.org/
www.lif.co.uk/dbimages/doc/techstatements/LOTECH.doc
www.lumicom.co.uk/
www.rohs.gov.uk/
www.rohs-news.com

Other Ordinances

Ordinances are statutes or regulations typically enacted by local governments. As with codes, the registered professional (the architect or engineer) on every project must assure that all ordinances are met or appropriately exempted prior to a project's completion. If the lighting designer is also not acting in the capacity of one of these registered professionals, then it is imperative that the architect or

engineer address lighting-related ordinance issues and direct the lighting designer as necessary. Ultimately, the registered professionals must check the work of the lighting designer and that of any nonregistered consulting specialty. Some of the more typical ordinance requirements are exterior lighting related and include light pollution and light trespass. Because these ordinances are locally generated and because building commissions will likely review the proposed work, the designer can anticipate some degree of flexibility by the building authority. However, this is a double-edged sword, and seemingly more stringent and/or more inclusive requirements may be established during the review(s).

Light pollution (not to be confused with light trespass—see below) relates to light being dispersed in the air. Water vapor and air pollution offer sufficient light refraction and light reflection characteristics to, in the eyes of some, adversely interact with exterior electric lighting at night. Common sense, if practiced, would be sufficient to limit light pollution. Overlighting exterior areas does not effectively reduce crime or improve nighttime seeing. Hence, illuminances should be limited to criteria espoused by the IESNA, CIE, or other recognized lighting authority. Further, the application of light should be carefully established and limited. For example, lighting a façade should depend on the materials with which the façade is made. Vision-glass walls (clear glass) will simply redirect any accenting or floodlighting up to the sky. The façade is left to appear unlighted. These surfaces act like mirrors and should simply not be lighted. Even opaque-surface façades (e.g., brick, stone, and wood, etc.), need not be wholly flooded with light. Many times, this is ineffectual in highlighting any architectural character or features. Light-colored surfaces need not be lighted to the same illuminances as darker-colored surfaces. High-wattage floodlights (anything over 150 watts) and/or with uncontrolled wide beam spreads are most likely to cause light pollution and should be avoided. Using high-color-rendering white light (e.g., ceramic metal halide) with coated lamps for softer light and less glare at IESNA-proposed illuminances is much more effective than using the yellow light of high pressure or low pressure sodium at higher illuminances (more on this below). Check jurisdictional ordinances for design requirements associated with light pollution. If none exist, use common sense.

Light trespass occurs where light is perceived to trespass, if it not actually does trespass onto adjoining property and/or into nearby buildings, and is found to be annoying. To some extent, common sense application of light and of window treatment can help mitigate light trespass. However, there will generally be problems with exterior nightlighting since some folks will simply be offended that any lighting that they can detect on their property and/or exterior building surface(s) is used after their bedtime. As such, this can be a highly charged issue and is one that follows the travails of development, urban sprawl, and greenways. Light trespass can be divided into two categories—light source glare and light spill. Light source glare occurs when lights are either designed or aimed in such a way that the light source is then directly visible from nearby property(ies), and/or are of sufficiently high intensity, causing nearby surfaces and objects to reflect too brightly to neighboring properties. Light spill occurs when some measurable

Table 6.2   Environmentally Sensitive Exterior Lighting Design Guidance

	Aspect	Goal	Tactic
☐	Neighborhood	• Tailor lighting to neighborhood	• Limit illuminances to degree of activity and security required.
☐	Need-basis	• Establish need (or no need)	• Identify through programming the degree of desire/need
☐	Limit Duration of Lighting	• Limit duration in areas with windows/skylights	• Automated controls
		• Limit duration in exterior areas	• Automated controls
☐	Limit Illuminances	• Design to reasonable, practical light levels	• Follow good practice guidelines
☐	Interior Lighting (through windows)	• Minimal brightness • Limit blue and ultraviolet radiation	• Automated window/skylight treatment • 3000K or lower color temperature lamps for general use
☐	Exterior Façade Lighting	• Limit blue and ultraviolet radiation • Trade luminance contrast for chromatic contrast • Judicious coverage	• 2700K to 3000K color temperature lamps for general use • High CRI lamps (≥80 CRI) • Accent key features rather than flood/flatly light façade
☐	Roadways w/o Pedestrians	• Limit blue and ultraviolet radiation • Direct all light downward • Limit glare and spill	• 2200K to 3000K color temperature lamps for general use • Full cutoff (no light above the horizon line) luminaires • Full cutoff, low wattage (≤150W) with house-side-shield luminaires on short poles (≤30 ft)
☐	Roadways w/Pedestrians	• Limit blue and ultraviolet radiation • Limit glare and spill • Trade luminance contrast for chromatic contrast	• 2700K to 3000K color temperature lamps for general use • Full cutoff, low wattage (≤150W) with house-side-shield luminaires on short poles (≤30 ft) • Low wattage (≤70W) with mostly-downlight luminaires on very short poles (≤18 ft) • High CRI lamps (≥80 CRI)
☐	Pedestrian Paths	• Limit blue and ultraviolet radiation • Limit glare and spill • Trade luminance contrast for chromatic contrast	• 2700K to 3000K color temperature lamps for general use • Low wattage (≤70W) with mostly-downlight luminaires on very short poles (≤18 ft) • High CRI lamps (≥80 CRI)
☐	Parking Lots w/Pedestrians (high-activity lots)	• Limit glare and spill • Limit blue and ultraviolet radiation • Trade luminance contrast for chromatic contrast	• Full cutoff, low wattage (≤150W) with house-side-shield luminaires on short poles (≤30 ft) • 2700K to 3000K color temperature lamps for general use • High CRI lamps (≥80 CRI)
☐	Parking Lots w/Pedestrians (low-activity lots)	• Limit glare and spill • Limit blue and ultraviolet radiation	• Full cutoff, low wattage (≤150W) with house-side-shield luminaires on short poles (≤30 ft) • 2200K to 3000K color temperature lamps for general use
☐	Landscape	• Limit glare and spill of uplighting	• Precise optics with louver/snoot, low wattage (≤70W), quality aiming/locking mechanisms.
☐	Security	• Limit glare and spill • Limit duration	• Full cutoff, low-wattage (≤70W) downlights on short mounting heights (≤18 ft) • Motion sensors

Significance

Projects in urban, suburban, country locales, and dark-sky-preserves require different degrees of lighting. Follow ordinances and good practices accordingly.

No light avoids the issue. Usually, the less critical the need, the more likely cost cutting during design/construction will result in use of fewer, cheaper, higher-wattage, unshielded or poorly shielded, low-quality floodlights, at which point the lighting in question should be reconsidered.

No light spill by dimming back/switching off lights in vicinity of windows/skylights when not in use (motion sensors, timeclocks) and especially during reasonable curfew (e.g., 11 pm to 6 am).

No light spill by switching off lights after reasonable curfew (e.g., 11 pm to 6 am).

Minimize spill and reflected light, which exacerbate light pollution and light trespass.

Limit amount of light spill by controlling window transmittance.

Warm white light less disruptive, provides more familiar look/feel.

Warm white light less disruptive to environment, provide more familiar look/feel for people.

Higher color rendering improves visual contrast and allows reduction in light levels up to 50% for noncritical viewing situations such as façades.

Accenting features typically generates less light pollution and more visual interest.

Yellow (monochromatic) to warm white light less disruptive to environment.

Minimize environmental impact beyond roadway.

Minimize environmental impact beyond roadway.

Warm white light less disruptive to environment, provide more familiar look/feel for people.

Minimize environmental impact beyond roadway.

Higher color rendering improves visual contrast and reduces need for greater light levels.

Warm white light less disruptive to environment, provide more familiar look/feel for people.

Minimize environmental impact beyond path.

Higher color rendering improves visual contrast and reduces need for greater light levels.

Minimize environmental impact beyond parking lot.

Warm white light less disruptive to environment, provide more familiar look/feel for people.

Minimize environmental impact beyond parking lot.

Minimize environmental impact beyond parking lot.

Yellow (monochromatic) to warm white light less disruptive to environment.

Minimize environmental impact beyond landscape area.

Minimize environmental impact beyond immediate security zone.

Lights only energized when motion is sensed (recognize potential issue of false positives with animals).

amount of light (illuminance) falls onto adjoining or nearby property(ies). Check jurisdictional ordinances for design requirements related to light trespass. If none exist, use common sense. Table 6.2 outlines guidance for useful, efficient exterior lighting that is environmentally sensitive.

In many situations, making serious sacrifices of the nighttime users' vision and function in order to alleviate light pollution is not a reasonable method of addressing this problem, but it remains such a politically charged issue that many municipalities have implemented highly restrictive light pollution/light trespass ordinances. Monochromatic light sources, such as high pressure sodium and low pressure sodium, may be preferred by some astronomers and environmentalists (plants and animals are affected by night lighting), for example.[4,5] However, these light sources create impressions of dim, dingy lighting and promote a sense of unsafe, insecure nighttime settings. Indeed, to counteract such dim appearances, shopping centers, big-box retailers, service stations, toll road ticket plazas, and the like have resorted to increasing illuminances well above recommended levels in an attempt to offer users a brighter, cheerier, and safer-feeling environment even when using the requisite monochromatic sources. In an ironic twist, this overlighting exacerbates light pollution and light trespass and uses more energy (thereby creating more industrial air pollution onto which more light is thrown, albeit reflected from pavement) than carefully designed lighting solutions with white light sources meeting reasonable illuminances for nighttime viewing situations. **One smart practice**, regardless of ordinances, political rhetoric, light levels, and lamp color, **is the introduction of automated nighttime lighting setbacks**. Commercial curfews at most establishments could be 10 p.m. or perhaps as late as midnight where façade lighting is greatly reduced (if some is required for security) or switched off and parking lot lighting also reduced (to the lowest IESNA guidance or, say, 0.2 fc minimum maintained (about 2 lux) or switched off. This darkens the environment considerably and saves energy and extends in-service lamp life.

Aggressive retailers and developers and overly cautious inspectors, engineers, and designers have, unfortunately, seriously and negatively affected light pollution and light trespass, helping to ignite a grass-roots political charge. As retailers and developers look for methods of differentiating their locale, many have resorted to increasing exterior parking lot and building lighting to ridiculous levels. Parking lots are lighted to between 5 and 10 fc (about 50 and 100 lx), literally two to five times the highest levels recommended by the IESNA as recently as 1993 for even the busiest of parking lots. Building façades are now bathed with 1000-watt floodlights, causing reflected glare and direct glare problems—not to mention all of the wasted light flooding into the night sky. Many service station fueling islands, in a misguided attempt to address security issues, are lighted to more than 50 fc (about 500 lx). Car lots' sales' areas are lighted to more than 20 fc (about 200 lx), with first rows lighted to 40 fc (about 400 lx), 50 fc (about 500 lx), or even greater levels in an attempt to attract attention (and so they have). These practices are foolish, environmentally unfriendly, and plain garish and they serve to inflame those calling for sharp restrictions in all night lighting of all applications. See Section 8.6 for more discussion about establishing appropriate illuminance targets for various applications.

Architectural Lighting Design

Overly cautious designers are sufficiently concerned about the liability and legal ramifications of "just meeting criteria" with what juries might be swayed to think is too little light or light concentrated in small areas of large sites or light exhibiting poor color rendering. What happens (in a legal sense) if a rape takes place between the pools of low-wattage dim downlighting or after curfew? What happens if someone trips on a curb along a private development darkened street/sidewalk or on a temporary obstacle (e.g., tree limb or tricycle) or down a step or two along a darkened path? What happens if someone is mugged under 0.5 fc (5 lx) of low pressure sodium lighting and is unable to identify the clothing color or skin tone of the mugger? The scenarios go on and on. In all cases, there is a chance some compensation could be and would be sought for the victim. Those who might be expected to pay are the (insurers of) landlords, developers, retailers, engineers, designers, luminaire and/or lamp vendors (if they had involvement in the lighting design), and no doubt other potential players with sufficient insurance coverage or deep pockets. The point—there are too many issues with exterior night lighting to simply apply broad draconian measures for the unqualified pleasure of viewing some more stars. Designers should address each situation quite independently and certainly with knowledge of all regulatory requirements, but in a way that also addresses the whole premise for exterior nightlighting.

6.7 Sustainability

Sustainability is a relatively new term in the construction industry used to express the concept of meeting the needs of the present without compromising the ability of future generations to meet their needs. In other words, cut the cycle of "dispose of the old and build new or refurbish with virgin materials/products." Some designers have practiced sustainability's ethos for some time. More recently, however, some elements of sustainable practice have been codified or certified. To some extent, energy codes have a similar end, yet their area of influence is limited to the reduction of energy—targeting fossil fuel use—and do not address the content or reuse of equipment.

Sustainability should simply be intrinsic in the entire design process—not an extra step as this text outline might suggest. Codes and certifications are intended to encourage this mindset. In its ultimate form, sustainability is a practice whereby the design, construction, maintenance, and rebirth of any installation are to use as few, nontoxic, and preferably all-natural resources as practical, and/or to use recycled materials, with all materials themselves made for recycling/reuse at end of life. The intent is to minimize the amount of energy and pollution expended in extracting resources from the Earth, making products and buildings, and operating buildings. Further, the intent is to minimize the environmental harm of throwing away spent materials. While early practice promoted **cradle-to-grave** concepts, an even more holistic approach to sustainability is **cradle-to-cradle**. These concepts involve a comprehensive review of the life cycle of the material or product or system of interest in environmental terms, such as CO_2 emissions, mercury emissions, fossil fuel use, and/or in cost terms.

For some components of lighting such as luminaire housings, sustainabiilty is an emerging issue, while for others, like lamps, significant progress has been made

cradle-to-grave
Reference to life cycle analysis of a product from the extraction of needed resources from earth to its disposal.[6]

cradle-to-cradle
Reference to life cycle analysis of a product from the extraction of needed resources from earth to its rebirth (refreshing for reuse again or reformation to another use), taken from the concepts espoused in William McDonough's and Michael Braungart's seminal *Cradle to Cradle*.[6,7]

toward more sustainable practices and products since 1990. Nevertheless, electric lighting by its nature is not environmentally friendly either in its production (making the luminaires and lamps) or its use (operating the luminaires/lamps)—at this time it appears we can make strides in *minimizing* electric lighting's impact on the environment. For example, great reductions in lead content and mercury content have been made.[8]

Although many lamp types had long been made with a variety of toxic materials, many of these toxins have been removed or greatly reduced. The glass in some lamps, including linear fluorescent, is now lead-free. Some vendors' medium screwbase lamps of any type (incandescent, fluorescent, metal halide, cold cathode) no longer use lead solder.[8] However, the most efficacious white-light lamp available for general lighting at this printing, fluorescent, can only exhibit such efficiency by using some minute amount of mercury. Although mercury is a highly toxic material, its use in many of the most modern and efficient lamps is limited to less than 8 mg and in some of the newest lamps is as low as 2 mg (by comparison, typical mercury thermometers contain 500 mg of mercury and the button cell batteries in digital thermometers typically contain 3.5 to 11 mg of mercury).[9]

How is it that a lamp (fluorescent) with traces of toxic materials is better than a lamp (incandescent) without? Here, the concept of reviewing the cradle-to-grave or crade-to-cradle aspects of each product is used to better assess a lamp's production, its operation, and its disposal. Unfortunately, at printing, sufficient data is unavailable on the **embodied energy** for the various incandescent, fluorescent, HID, and LED lamps (and luminaires) made today.[11] However, as an example, even if incandescent lamps require much less energy in their production than fluorescent, the very frequent replacement cycle (short life) relative to fluorescent means they are produced and transported much more frequently than fluorescent lamps (assuming the same use periods). In any event, the operation and disposal aspects of using fluorescent over incandescent are significantly compelling at this time. Most energy today in the US is produced by burning fossil fuel. Figure 6.10 illustrates the breakdown of net electricity generation by source. Today's coal-fired power plants release mercury into the atmosphere. So, as lamps are switched on or energized, they use electricity—nearly 50 percent of which is generated using fossil fuels and, therefore, releasing mercury into the atmosphere. **Compact fluorescent lamps are so much more efficient than incandescent lamps, that over their lifetime of operation, they will be responsible for the release of about 75 percent less mercury than their incandescent counterparts.**[14] This assumes that the fluorescent lamps are recycled at the end of life and that most of their mercury content will be reused rather than released into the environment.

For architectural lighting applications, **every attempt should be made to use highest-efficacy, longest-life, white-light-producing lamps for nearly all applications** (except where colored light is necessary). If any toxic materials need be used, they should be limited in application and should yield maximum benefits. Today's energy-efficient lighting not only contains smaller amounts of toxic materials, but long life limits the frequency of reintroducing toxins into the lighting chain and limits the energy required to remake products more frequently. Further, efficient lighting reduces electricity demand and therefore reduces

embodied energy
Reference to the energy necessary to extract raw materials from earth, to transport those to a manufacturing plant, to manufacture the product in question, and to ship that product to its place of sale or use.[10]

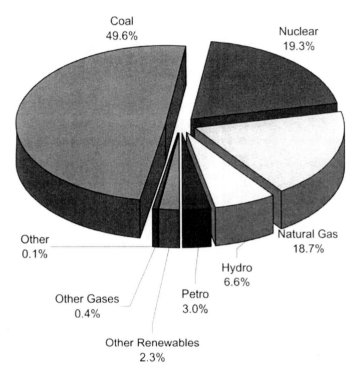

Coal
49.6%

Nuclear
19.3%

Natural Gas
18.7%

Hydro
6.6%

Petro
3.0%

Other Gases
0.4%

Other
0.1%

Other Renewables
2.3%

Figure 6.10

According to 2005 data, just over 70% of the electricity generation in the US comes from burning fossil fuels which produces many pollutants including nitrogen oxides and CO_2 and, in the case of coal, sulfur dioxide and mercury—although the amounts of these pollutants should decline with more restrictive pollution controls on power plants.[12, 13]

environmental toxins resulting from the production of electricity. Lamps discussed in Chapter 10 meet these tenets of highest efficacy, longest life, white-light sources.

As sustainable practice broadens, look for the industry to become more savvy in its use of energy and resources and its respect for the environment. Table 6.3 outlines some aspiring sustainable aspects. Some vendors have begun to address sustainable practices. GE, Osram, and Rebelle Lighting are now reporting their progress. Most notably, Litecontrol has earned the Cradle to Cradle Silver Certification^{CM} from McDonough Braungart Design Chemistry. Soon, these more sustainable practices will become de rigueur.

```
more online @
www.weeenetwork.com/
www.gelighting.com/na/business_lighting/education_resources/
    environmental/msd_sheets.htm
h2e-online.org/docs/h2e10stepfluorescent121802.pdf
www.informinc.org/fact_P3fluorescentlamps.php
www.litecontrol.com/contentmgr/showdetails.php/id/4218
www.ncat.org/greentree/welcome.html
www.rebellelighting.com/environmental-statement.php
www.sylvania.com/AboutUs/EnergyAndEnvironment/OSIEnvironment/
www.sylvania.com/AboutUs/EnergyAndEnvironment/OSIEnvironment/
    EnvironmentalAchievements/OSRAMSYLVANIA/ProductImprovement/
    MercuryReduction/
```

6.8 Certification

Related to Systems Factors, there are two certifications with some significance to the US lighting industry—that of lighting products and of sustainable practice. Products that are UL listed and labeled or NRTL listed and labeled in accordance with UL standards identify lighting equipment that is considered "physically and environmentally safe" in an effort to "prevent or reduce loss of life and property." Although equipment with no UL listing may be safe, its use may not satisfy insurance requirements for a given property. Further, should any calamity occur

Cradle to Cradle Certified^{CM} is a certification mark of McDonough Braungart Design Chemistry

Table 6.3 | Sustainable Practices

Aspect	Goal
☐ Packaging (for anything)	• Minimal but robust packaging • Environmentally friendly packing if packing necessary • Recycled and/or renewable content
☐ Finishing (for luminaires)	• Powder coatings • Low/nonhazardous metal finishing
☐ Processes (for lamps and luminaires)	• Low/renewable energy use • Minimal waste • Quality production • High-efficiency machinery and facilities
☐ Materials (for luminaires)	• Lead-free • Recycled content • Quality • Recyclable content and/or return program
☐ Transportation (for all lighting components)	• Maximum local content • Efficient palletizing/loading • High-efficiency transport
☐ Electric Lighting	• Local production • Efficient luminaires • Efficient, long-life lamps • Efficient room finishes • Automated controls
☐ Daylighting	• Account daylighting • Efficient room finishes • Controls
☐ Maintenance	• Specified or-better replacements • Regular spot relamping/extended group relamping • Regular cleaning (luminaires, room surfaces, fenestration) • Recycle
☐ End-of-life	• Recycle base materials • Refurbish/reuse (recycle product) • Reformation to another use

and be attributable to the nonlisted product, liability ramifications may be skewed toward the specifier and/or installer and/or purchaser rather than the original equipment manufacturer. If UL/NRTL-listed/labeled lighting equipment is modified in any way in the field (after production), it is likely the listing is voided. While this modification may be safe, any calamity attributed to the modified lighting equipment may skew liability to the entity responsible for the modification. In short, specify UL/NRTL-listed/labeled lighting equipment. If any modifications are desired, inquire if these modifications can be made at the factory and if the equipment will remain UL/NRTL-listed and labeled after the modification is made. **Note that UL/NRTL-listing and labeling should be a requirement for all off-**

Significance

Limit amount of resources used in packaging and amount to be recycled, but sufficient to prevent damage in transit.

No plastics, oil-based materials, or expanded polystyrene, no hazardous materials.

Limit amount of resources used in packaging.

Require no solvents, release no hazardous air pollutants (HAP), low/no volatile organic compounds (VOC), durable long-life.

Minimize environmental impact of production.

Minimize environmental impact of production.

Minimize environmental impact of production.

Long life, fewer returns.

Minimize environmental impact of production.

Minimize in situ hazard and disposal issues.

Minimize use of raw earth resources and minimize environmental impact of production.

Long life, fewer returns.

Minimize disposal issues.

Minimize resource use and pollution in obtaining materials and components for production.

Minimize resource use and pollution in product transit to site.

Minimize resource use and pollution in product transit to site.

Minimize resource use and polluiton in product transit to site.

Maximum benefit from minimum resources.

Maximum benefit from minimum resources.

Maximum benefit from minimum resources.

Provide "lighting on demand" based on occupancy and daylighting availability.

Reduce use of electric lighting.

Maximum benefit from daylighting.

Reduce use of electric lighting.

Maintain maximum benefit from minimum resources.

Minimize use of raw earth resources, maintain maximum benefit from minimum resources.

Maintain maximum benefit from electric lighting and daylighting.

Limit landfill hazardous waste.

Minimize use of raw earth resources.

Minimize environmental impact of production.

Minimize use of raw earth resources and minimize environmental impact of production.

the-shelf (standard) lighting equipment, factory-modified lighting equipment, and factory-custom lighting equipment regardless country of origin.

It is popular to specify lighting equipment of foreign origin, usually for reasons of style (foreign products always seem to have a unique look relative to the home-country's standard fare), but sometimes for cost reasons (some foreign imports are very low cost). If not evident on product datasheets, **the designer must confirm these products are UL/NRTL-listed and labeled for the intended applications.**

UL/NRTL markings relate to the luminaire types and their application(s). While there are extensive listing markings, for purposes of this text two are key—re-

UL/NRTL Listing
Find the UL listing note and any references to the location application on the luminaire cutsheets in Figures 5.3, 5.4, 5.6, 5.10, 6.3, and 6.5.

cessed luminaires and environmental location.[15] Recessed luminaires may need to be listed/labeled for IC/AT applications (see Section 6.6). Where luminaires are used in a location not normally subject to dampness (typically interior dry situations), the listing/labeling mark is "DRY LOCATIONS ONLY." Where luminaires are used in damp locations, an interior or exterior location that is periodically or typically subject to condensation of moisture, the listing/labeling mark is "SUITABLE FOR DAMP LOCATIONS." A damp location might be an exterior protected soffit location. If there is any doubt, select luminaires suitable for wet locations. Where luminaires are used in wet locations, a location where water may drip, splash, or flow on the face of the luminaire, the listing/labeling mark is "SUITABLE FOR WET LOCATIONS." A wet location might be a tub or shower or an exterior exposed soffit location. In any event, these luminaires are not intended to be submersed in water. A luminaire rated for damp locations can also be used in dry locations. A luminaire rated for wet locations can also be used in dry or damp locations. Similar certifications are used in the EU, Canada, and other jurisdictions.

A process is in place to guide designers interested in seeking certification for sustainable practice on a given project. The U.S. Green Building Council's (USGBC) Leadership in Energy and Environmental Design (LEED) is a benchmark for the design, construction, and operation of high-performance green buildings. LEED promotes whole-building sustainability by recognizing performance in five areas of human and environmental health: sustainable site development, water savings, energy efficiency, materials selection, and indoor environmental quality. Lighting is recognized in the areas of sustainable site development (for addressing light pollution), energy efficiency (for addressing lighting efficiency), and indoor environmental quality (for addressing daylighting and view). The degree to which the design addresses these various areas determines the level of certification with "Certified" being the basic level, "Silver" being the next, "Gold" the next, and "Platinum" the premium level of certification.

more online @
www.ul.com/about/
www.ul.com/regulators/luminaries.pdf
www.usgbc.org/DisplayPage.aspx?CategoryID=19

6.9 Maintenance

Although maintenance procedures and convenient access to lights should not drive lighting solutions to the exclusion of other lighting aspects—the lighting is intended to best meet the visual needs of the occupants, which should not be sacrificed for the convenience of the maintenance staff—an effort should be made to limit the degree of difficulty and/or frequency of maintenance. Luminaire selection, architectural detailing, and layout can influence the ease with which luminaires are accessed for cleaning and replacement of lamps and ballasts. The significance of cleaning, relamping, and reballasting cannot be overstated. Dirt buildup on luminaires and room surfaces can degrade illuminances and luminances 2 to 5 percentage points over a period of a few years in most typical office and hospitality settings. This is equivalent to wasting 2 to 5 percentage points of energy and taking the ever-elusive, but real hit on user comfort and productivity.

Lamps deteriorate over time. Most of the best fluorescent lamps may lose 10 percent or more of their light output over life. This is equivalent to wasting 10 per-

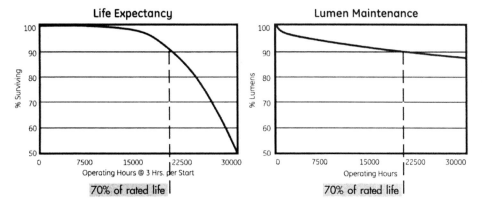

Life Expectancy

70% of rated life

Lumen Maintenance

70% of rated life

Figure 6.11

The graph on the far left is the mortality curve (life-expectancy) for a GE Starcoat® T5 lamp with a rated life of 30,000 hours (the point in time at which half the lamps are expected to have failed). Somewhere between 70% and 80% of rated life (21,000 hours and 24,000 hours respectively), lamp burnouts occur at ever-increasing frequency. To spot replace the burnouts becomes an ever-bigger burden for maintenance as ladders, lamps, and disruptions throughout the facility increase in frequency. At the same time, the light output of the lamps diminishes (see the lumen maintenance graph on the near left). At about 70% of rated life, the lamps will have lost about 10% of their light output. Therefore, at between 70% and 80% of rated life, the economics favor group relamping—change out all lamps at one time.
Image courtesy of General Electric Company (from Starcoat® T5 Ecolux® sell sheet, 01/2006)

centage points of energy—and still spewing associated power plant pollutants. Lamp failures increase precipitously at the end of rated life. Although economic analyses are necessary for each situation, group relamping might make economic and environmental sense between 70 percent and 80 percent of rated life (see Figure 6.11). Of course, lamps must be recycled regardless of their operating condition, although some quantity of the still-surviving lamps might be retained as "spares" for spot relamping. Alternatively, another maintenance strategy is to purchase "attic stock" of 10 to 15 percent more lamps than needed for group relamping, then use these for spot relamping after the group relamping is completed. Once the attic stock is depleted, it should be time for another group relamping.[16] Ignoring spot relamping (replacing lamps as they burn out) is the equivalent of wasting the energy associated with the lamp wattage rating. This spot relamping is especially critical as designs are "fine-tuned" to "just" meet lighting criteria in an effort to avoid the waste of extra equipment and wattage associated with overlighting.

For convenience of maintenance and storage, if possible specify same lamps in similar luminaire types. For example, if linear pendent lights are specified with 28-watt T5 fluorescent lamps, then where cove details or luminous ceiling details are used, attempt to specify the same 28-watt T5 fluorescent lamp. However, this should not be done at the expense of other lighting criteria—illuminances, luminances, color, etc.

An ever-increasing issue is with lamps and their sockets. Many lamps now use the same socket design as the standard household lamp of nearly 100 years. Halogen accent lamps use medium screwbase sockets. Compact fluorescent retrofit lamps use medium screwbase sockets. Ceramic metal halide accent lamps use medium screwbase sockets. And yet none of these lamps are technically interchangable and may pose a safety hazard if interchanged with their medium screwbase counterparts. If practical, attempt to not mix these lamp types on a project. Regardless, maintenance must carefully review luminaire, lamp, and wattage labels, and lamp instructions and also cross-reference all replacements for compatibility with original specifications.

Lamp replacements should always be as-specified. If sufficient time has passed for product improvements to have been made that do not affect lamp color and lamp optics or negatively affect light output and do not result in increased wattage, or a change in socketry or ballasting or wiring, then improved lamp replacements should be considered. Beware cheap and abundantly available "alternates." Secure published data on lamp performance. If vendors are unknown, seek out feedback from other purchasers/specifiers and determine country of origin and number of years the vendor(s) has been in business under the same name.

If luminaires are adjustable, specify units with locking tilt and rotating mechanisms. Regardless, relamping should be done in such a way so as not to affect the aiming or, alternatively, all aiming adjustments should be recorded prior to relamping in order to re-aim properly after relamping. This might best be resolved by photographing the objects/surfaces onto which the lights are aimed so that where re-aiming is unavoidable, the same effect can be recreated.

Luminaire finishes, room finishes, and fenestration affect electric lighting and daylighting efficiency and appearance. Selection of these surface finishes with an eye toward maintenance is worth consideration. For example, specular reflectors in downlights are difficult to keep clean and readily show fingerprinting. Samples of the various vendors' versions of specular, semi-specular, and matte aluminum trim finishes should be reviewed on typical downlights and lay-in recessed luminaires.

Maintenance calendars and procedures should be developed and adopted to keep lighting maintenance aspects in the forefront of building operations to sustain lighting system efficiencies and quality and quantity of light for the occupants.

more online @
h2e-online.org/docs/h2e10stepfluorescent121802.pdf

6.10 Endnotes

[1] James P. Simpson, Simpson's Contemporary Quotations, http://www.bartleby.com/63/19/5519.html. [Accessed August 11, 2007.]

[2] Building Codes: What are Building Codes (web page, 2007), http://growth-management.alachua.fl.us/building/buildcode.php. [Accessed August 18, 2007.]

[3] Dieter Schornick, Survey of the European Commission activities on Lighting and Environment (web page, 2007), http://www.celma.org/pdf_files/Survey%20of%20EU%20activities%20on%20Lighting%20and%20Environment.pdf. [Accessed August 26, 2007.]

[4] Bob Mizon, Light Pollution Responses and Remedies (London: Springer-Verlag, 2002), p. 70.

[5] Catherine Rich and Travis Longcore, editors, Ecological Consequences of Artificial Night Lighting (Washington: Island Press, 2006), p. 55, p. 163, p. 299, p. 333, and p. 424.

[6] Wikipedia, Life cycle assessment (web page, 2007), http://en.wikipedia.org/wiki/Life_cycle_assessment. [Accessed September 1, 2007.]

[7] William McDonough and Michael Braungart. Cradle to Cradle/Remaking the Way We Make Things (New York: North Point Press, 2002).

[8] Mercury Reduction (web page, 2007), http://www.sylvania.com/AboutUs/EnergyAndEnvironment/OSIEnvironment/EnvironmentalAchievements/OSRAMSYLVANIA/ProductImprovement/MercuryReduction/. [Accessed September 1, 2007.]

[9] Frequenty Asked Questons About Mercury Fever Thermometers (web page, 2001), http://www.p2pays.org/ref/06/05732.htm. [Accessed September 3, 2007.]

[10] Wikipedia, Embodied Energy (web page, 2007). http://en.wikipedia.org/wiki/Embodied_energy. [Accessed September 3, 2007.]

[11] Jeff Miller, What Will be the Fate of the Incandescent Lamp (web page, 2007), http://www.archlighting.com/industry-news.asp?sectionID=1311&articleID=498755. [Accessed September 3, 2007.]

[12] Energy Information Administration, Net Generation by Energy Source by Type of Producer (web page, 2006). http://www.eia.doe.gov/cneaf/electricity/epa/epat1p1.html. [Accessed September 3, 2007.] and Energy Information Administration, U.S. Electric Power Industry Net Generation (web page, 2007). http://www.eia.doe.gov/cneaf/electricity/epa/figes1.html. [Accessed January 8, 2008.]

[13] U.S. Environmental Protection Agency, How does electricity affect the environment: Air Emissions, (web page, 2007), http://www.epa.gov/solar/energy-and-you/affect/air-emissions.html. [Accessed March 15, 2008.]

[14] Ohio EPA Public Interest Center, Compact Fluorescent Light Bulbs What Consumers Need to Know, (web page, 2007), http://www.epa.state.oh.us/pic/cfl_info.html. [Accessed September 3, 2007.]

[15] Underwriters Laboratories Inc., Marking Guide Luminaires, July 2004, http://www.ul.com/regulators/luminaries.pdf. [Accessed September 3, 2007.]

[16] John L. Fetters, Maximizing Lighting Maintenance (web page, 2006), http://www.maintenancesolutionsmag.com/article.asp?id=1699&keywords=. [Accessed September 8, 2007.]

6.11 Reference

Sharon Koomen Harmon and Katherine E. Kennon. 2001. The Codes Guidebook for Interiors, Second Edition. New York: John Wiley & Sons.

T he previous chapter outlined lighting criteria related to the architectural systems. Another set of lighting criteria revolves around the users' biological need for light and reaction to light. The way in which an environment is presented to its users is at least partly responsible for the way they perceive and react to it. Lighting can play a significant role in people's psychological and physiological responses to an environment. Light seemingly influences other sensory responses. The distribution of luminances in a space or area influences perceptions of spatial form and volume, the space's intended functions, security, and safety, and degree of comfort and well-being. Luminance levels and ratios are responsible for visual comfort and visual attraction. Exterior views appear to be related to satisfaction and motivation. However, it is luminances, their distribution, location or position in the setting, and intensities that are key to any lighting design regardless whether electric light or daylight. Lighting is all about planning and maintaining luminances.

7.1 Sensory Responses

While no definitive links are known to exist between light and other sensory responses, a few studies and/or some experience indicate light can influence other sensory responses. For example, very low and nonuniform brightnesses, particularly when coupled with some intermittent accent lighting on perimeter objects (e.g., wall art), seem to promote quieter settings. Alternatively, high uniform brightnesses seem to promote louder settings. The auditory senses are, it seems, affected by light intensities.

The thermal sense may be affected by the color of visual experience. A study in the mid-1970s indicated that people in warm-tone settings lighted with warm-tone light tended to feel 2 to 3°F (about 16 to 17°C) warmer than the actual room ambient temperature.[1] Likewise, people in cool-tone settings lighted with cool-tone light tended to feel 2 to 3°F cooler than the actual room ambient temperature. Regardless of a designer's intent, then, light and color may have an impact on other senses. These affects should be considered during the design process to avoid disappointment upon project completion. For example, when a designer plans a retirement community, if interior finishes are cool-toned, it may not be advisable to enhance this palette with cool-toned light sources. This may exacerbate the elderly populations' sensitivity to cold.

7.2 Hierarchies and Focals

Visual hierarchies are quite appropriate to signify varying degrees of importance among various areas, surfaces, and objects. Using light to help identify these visual hierarchies is crucial to their effectiveness. Figures 7.1, 7.2, and 7.3 illustrate one such application of visual hierarchies and focal accenting with light to help set the architectural scene and direct users' attention into and around a space.

Focal centers are specific objects or elements (e.g., artwork, floor medallions, and ceiling domes, etc.) that are a special feature of the environmental setting. Enhancing these focal centers with light is almost always a must, and this can contribute to several design goals already discussed: spatial order, visual hierarchy,

Figure 7.1

Focal Center: Here the sculptural wall panels are a focal center defining the registration desk. This focal center is a key feature in the lobby and is lighted as brightly as the ceiling medallion above the chandelier. Track lights in a ceiling slot detail (which hides the lights from view) provide good positioning and aiming flexibility to make the sculptural wall panels bright. A somewhat grazing angle adds some distinct shadow for texture and contrast.
Image ©C.M. Korab

and circulation. There are times, however, when a focal center is developed specifically for visual interest, visual identity, and/or eye muscle relaxation (which is particularly important in work-related settings). As a design goal, those focal centers that are important and necessary to add interest or bring attention to an area should be identified. Figure 7.4 illustrates a focal center being used to help direct people through a large public space. It is worth noting, however, that the 3-dimensional aspects of space and light interaction must be carefully reviewed as well. Otherwise, light patterns may not properly enhance the focal centers and may inadvertently create distracting luminance patterns. This is a common issue. If artwork is planned for a wall, for example, and the exact location is not established during the lighting planning process, then it is likely that the lighting equipment won't be in the right place to best highlight the artwork upon project completion. This results in odd-angled luminance patterns as lights are aimed toward the artwork.

- Strong luminance (ceiling and chandelier)
- Moderate luminance (decorative lights)
- Subtle luminance (back wall)
- Intense luminance (sculptural wall)
- Subtle luminance (desk front)

Figure 7.2

Hierarchies: Layering luminances establishes hierarchies and helps define the architectural setting and draw attention to registration. This approach is known as layered lighting.

Discrete wall lighting behind the sculptural wall panels provides depth and relief. The wall lighting, ceiling lighting, and the feature lighting all help define the space. The lighting equipment layout and luminance patterning reinforce spatial order.
Image ©C.M. Korab

Over the past thirty years, there have been a number of studies and assessments on people's reactions to various lighting situations. Much of this work shows that luminance patterns, intensities, contrasts, and locations (horizontal versus vertical planes) can influence how people perceive a given space and respond to it. Table 7.1 outlines the attraction power associated with luminance contrasts regardless of their location and size. These contrasts can be used to help attract attention and develop visual hierarchies in the built environment. Luminance contrasts can be used to guide people to objects or spaces and can lead people through spaces. This requires careful planning of both illuminance and surface/material finish. Luminance is a result—actually the product—of illuminance and surface reflectance or of illuminance and surface transmittance. So, for example, the surface/material reflectance of the background versus the surface/material reflectance of the focal element is as critical to establishing luminance contrast as the illuminance on the background versus the illuminance on the focal element. Think of it this way: To make an object barely stand out against a wall when the illuminance on both the object and wall is the same, the wall will need to be painted half the reflectance value of the object (then the luminance contrast from the object to the wall would be 2-to-1). If the object and wall have the same reflectance value, then the object will need to be lighted to twice the illuminance of the wall in order to achieve a 2-to-1 luminance contrast from the object to the wall. Alternatively, if a piece of art is half the reflectance of the background wall, then illuminance on the artwork needs to be four times the illuminance on the background wall in order to achieve a 2-to-1 luminance contrast. It should be obvious that medium to low reflectance surfaces, objects, and materials are difficult to sufficiently accent without using lots of power. So, **the designer must decide where visual attraction requirements need to occur on a project and to what degree or attraction power. Then surface finishes and illuminances must be planned accordingly.**

Figure 7.3

Hierarchies: This is the view from the hotel entry into the reception lounge. From the front door, the highlighting of the fireplace sculpture and the brightness surrounding the custom chandelier establish the focal destination to the visitor. Once in this transition zone, the front desk is off to the right (see Figure 7.1).
Image ©C.M. Korab

additive color

This is a phenomenon of light—the mixing or adding of various colors (wavelengths) of light. Wavelengths work in an additive fashion, combining or adding together to form a different color of light. For this discussion, the primary colors of light are red, green, and blue. When at least two of these specific wavelengths are combined, in varying degrees (or intensities), they create other colors. If all three primary colors of light are added together, the result is white light.

subtractive color

This is a phenomenon of pigments (inks, paints, and dyes)—the mixing of various colors of pigments. Pigments react to light by absorbing (subtracting) some wavelengths and reflecting others. When pigments combine, they subtract more and more wavelengths from the white light striking them. For this discussion, the primary colors of subtractive color are cyan, magenta, and yellow. When at least two of these specific pigments are mixed, in varying degrees, they create other colors. If all three primary subtractive colors are mixed together, the result is technically a black pigment.

Chromatic contrast can also be used to advantage in establishing visual attraction and visual hierarchy. Surface color and/or colored light offer great, largely untapped resources for visual attraction. Table 7.2 outlines approximations of the effect of color on visual attraction.[3] However, the mixture of colored light onto colored surfaces can result in disaster if not carefully understood and planned. Alternatively, when carefully studied, some visually powerful effects result with colored light on colored surfaces. This is achieved through tests and mock-ups.

To understand these effects, the designer needs to appreciate the difference between **additive color** and **subtractive color**. Additive color occurs with visible energy or light. Colors of light add together to create more colors of light or, when all colors are combined, white light. Subtractive color occurs with pigments, dyes, inks—surface material coloration. Pigments, when lighted, actually subtract out (absorb) some colors of light and selectively reflect others. So, a pure red surface material will appear red (or at least reddest) only when lighted with a source (lamp) that has some red energy present in it. Hence, a blue light on a red surface will result in a gray or near-black surface appearance.

Herein lies a common problem. In many installations, the selector of the architectural/interior finishes does not fully appreciate the impact of the lighting on these surfaces. Finishes are selected under one light source (typically high-level incandescent or daylight), while the lighting design is ultimately based on fluorescent lamps with SPD properties different from the incandescent or daylight references used for surface finish selection. Colors end up drab and dingy or overly intense in appearance. For lighting design, the **hue, value,** and **chroma** (as defined by the Munsell Color System) of surfaces and objects are either important lighting design parameters or should be selected based on the lighting design. Hue should depend

hue
Based on the Munsell Color System, hue refers to the color family (e.g., red) and is reported by color abbreviation of which there are ten (R=red; YR=yellow-red; Y=yellow; GY=green-yellow; G=green; BG=blue-green; B=blue; PB=purple-blue; P=purple; and RP=red-purple).

value
Based on the Munsell Color System, value refers to color lightness and is reported on a scale of 0 (black) to 10 (white). The Munsell value is roughly the square root of the color's reflectance.

chroma
Based on the Munsell Color System, chroma refers to color saturation (e.g., intense red or dull red).

on, or affect the selection of the lamp SPD (i.e., the wavelength makeup of light will influence how the surface color looks). Value should depend on, or will affect, lighting system efficiency (i.e., higher values more efficiently reflect light than lower values). Chroma should depend on, or will affect, the light intensities on various surfaces (i.e., duller color may require more light than saturated color to be appropriately visible as something other than a grayed tone). On the aspect of value, it cannot be overstated that color value significantly (and usually negatively) affects lighting system efficiency. Depending on the general lighting approach(es) in a space (e.g., all indirect, all direct, some indirect and some direct), ceiling values and/or some portion of the four-wall color values of 5 or 6 (exhibiting a reflectance of about 25% to 35%) will reduce light levels by up to 50 percent compared to ceiling values and/or some portion of the four-wall color values of 8 or 9 (exhibiting a reflectance of about 65% to 80%). **The energy consequences are enormous. The brightness consequences are enormous. This cannot be overstated. Use higher-value (higher-reflectance) walls and ceilings as a normal practice.**

more online @
web.archive.org/web/20030813092028/www.adobe.com/support/techguides/
color/colormodels/munsell.html

Table 7.1 Luminance Contrasts for Attraction[2]

Attraction Power	Effect	Potential Application	Luminance Contrast[a]
Negligible (low luminance)	barely recognizable focal	• museum displays (fugitive materials) • office artwork • retail sales racks	2 to 1
Marginal (subtle to moderate luminance)	minimum meaningful focal	• fine dining artwork • office lobby artwork • residential artwork • retail special displays	10 to 1
Dominant (strong to intensive luminance)	strong significant centerpiece	• retail high-end display • premiere architectural or artwork feature	approaching 100 to 1

[a] Focal-to-background luminance ratio.

7.3 Subjective Impressions

Over the past thirty years, research has resulted in some understanding of the relationships between luminances and luminance patterns and people's preferences, sense of visual clarity, and sense of spatial volume.[4, 5, 6, 7] Figure 7.5 exemplifies the kinds of light settings that people evaluated in one study. Evaluations were based on scalar (opposing pair) descriptor survey forms (see Table 7.3) completed by subjects and interviews with subjects. This work was done in the early 1970s, so the environmental furnishings and finishings appear dated to us now. However, based on continued practical experience, the reactions to luminances and their patterns remain valid today. This work ultimately led to the definition of five specific impressions influenced by various luminance aspects. These five impressions are visual clarity, spaciousness, preference, relaxation, and privacy. The influencing luminance aspects derived from these studies can be categorized by uniformity, location, and intensity. Luminance uniformity is an indication of how smoothly or uniformly luminance is distributed over surfaces or objects throughout the room. Location is an indication of the primary plane(s) or surfaces of luminance application—horizontal (ceiling surfaces, work surfaces, and/or floor surface) or vertical (wall surfaces). Intensity is an indication of the degree of luminance of the **horizontal activity plane** (work plane or floor plane)—relatively low or dim versus relatively strong or bright.

Ignoring these subjective impressions does not mean occupants won't have subjective reactions to the finished project. Indeed, many projects where little emphasis is placed on anything other than illuminance criteria result in spaces that are likely to elicit negative reactions because subjection impressions weren't considered or were ignored. Because these are *subjective* impressions, there may not be any overt or recognized reaction or complaint by users. Negative impressions of the visual environment may simply result in users wishing to spend less time in the setting, but not knowing why or even realizing a causal relationship exists. Or perhaps negative impressions result in poorer attitudes. In any event, such negative impressions are a further waste of energy and resources—

horizontal activity plane
The work plane or floor plane. In work settings, the work plane, desktop, or tabletop qualifies as the horizontal activity plane. In transition and circulation spaces, the floor qualifies as the work plane. In classroom settings, desktops qualify as the work plane. In churches or auditoriums, laps qualify as the horizontal activity plane. Referring to any one of these as simply a work plane would imply that the situation is indeed one of concentrated, long-term work, which is not always the case. Hence, the more generic reference to horizontal activity plane.

Chromatic Contrasts (of transmitted light) for Attraction[3]   Table 7.2

Color[a]	Relative Luminance[b]	Relative Brightness[c]
Warm White	1.0	1.0
Gold	0.6	0.7
Red	0.1	0.2
Green	1.4	2.0
Blue	0.4	0.6

[a] Color of transmitted light. Modeled with fluorescent lamps exhibiting named color of light commonly available in the 1970s (the time of the cited study).[3]

[b] Photometric luminance (as measured in laboratory setting).

[c] Brightness as judged by most observers. Blue, for example, has the brightness appearance of about 60% of that of warm white, while measured luminance of blue is about 40% of that of measured luminance of warm white.

minimizing the value of the installed hardware and the energy used to operate it. The point is this: **subjective impressions affect human use. Lighting should be developed to promote or evoke the positive attributes**.

The following subjective impressions are key criteria in developing lighting solutions for many types of spaces. In fact, the impressions deemed appropriate to a given project could and should help guide the lighting solution on that project. The specific luminance uniformity, location, and intensity offer explicit guidance on how light should be applied in the space and, therefore, what kind of lighting solutions should be considered.

ambient lighting
Referring to the general background lighting in a space. Typically considered as one of three layers of light—task lighting, ambient lighting, and architectural feature or accent lighting. Because ambient lighting is the background lighting, it will likely affect all people in a space.

Visual Clarity

Visual clarity refers to the users' perceptions of how well architectural and interior detail, features, objects, and other people's features are distinguished. Scalar or opposing-pair descriptors are *clear* versus *hazy*. The more crisp and distinct architectural and people's features seem to appear, the greater the clarity perception rating. Flat, shadow-free lighting yielding low-to-moderate and uniform luminances (particularly of the horizontal activity plane) tends to elicit a perception of haziness. Figure 7.6 uses two of the comparative images from the lighting study previously discussed to illustrate the difference between the hazy and clear scalars. Visual clarity is believed to be an important subjective impression for work settings. It is best enhanced with higher luminance of the horizontal activity plane in the central area of a workspace. Some wall luminance is helpful in eliciting visual clarity. Luminance uniformity does not seem to be a particularly strong determinant.

Several lessons here. First, relatively low levels of general lighting and/or relatively dark surfaces will, if used alone, result in impressions of haziness. Second, regardless of the use of direct, indirect, or indirect/direct lighting systems for general lighting then, emphasis is necessary at the work surface and, to a lesser extent, on the walls. Third, three lighting layers need attention—the **ambient** layer, **task** layer, and **accent** or architectural layer. Finally, attention must be given to the impact of

task lighting
Referring to the lighting in a space specifically designed to light the task. Typically localized lighting—using lights positioned close to the task surface or area or using architecturally mounted lights arranged to light the task area.

accent lighting
Referring to the lighting in a space specifically designed to light special features or details such as artwork and architectural elements (columns, pilasters, coves, and niches).

Figure 7.5

Subjective Impressions: This series of six images illustrates six lighting conditions in one of the conference rooms used in a seminal study in the 1970s on how light influences subjection impressions. Based on many study subjects' responses to many room types and lighting conditions, researchers were able to categorize subjective reactions and identify the luminance trends responsible for those reactions. Look beyond the decorative styling of the room furnishings and architectural elements in these studies—what matters for lighting purposes is how the luminances are applied (or not). This helps to determine people's reactions to lighting in a space. Image ©GarySteffyLightingDesign Inc.—a gift of the John E. Flynn Estate

Condition 1: Overhead/direct low illuminance (10 fc [100 lx] on table) setting (incandescent downlights). **Evokes impressions of haziness, quiet, and confinement.**

Condition 2: Peripheral/indirect low illuminance (10 fc [100 lx] on table). Fluorescent lighting on long walls and incandescent lighting on short walls. **Evokes impression of spaciousness. Considered somewhat pleasant.**

Condition 3: Overhead/indirect low illuminance (10 fc [100 lx] on table). Indirect fluorescent lighting. **Evokes impressions of haziness and quiet. Elicits strong negative reaction (impression of tenseness).**

surface finishes—with a need to consider **higher-reflectance work surfaces and wall surfaces** to **enhance the subjective impression of visual clarity while minimizing energy use**.

Spaciousness

Spaciousness refers to the users' perception of spatial volume. Scalar descriptors are spacious versus cramped. A lack of peripheral luminances make for a dark appearance and apparently elicits negative reactions and a sense of confinement from many people except where the conditions are expected (e.g., home theaters, conference rooms set for AV). Higher (greater) luminance applied rather uniformly to all or many of the walls enhances the sense of spaciousness. Figure 7.7 uses two of the comparative images from the lighting study previously discussed to illustrate the difference between the cramped and spacious scalars. Spaciousness is believed to be an important subjective impression for high occupancy areas, such as circulation spaces, transition spaces, assembly halls, and the like. It is best enhanced with higher or greater luminance of the walls. Luminance uniformity does seem to be a particularly strong determinant; however, the more uniform the wall luminances, the stronger the impression of spaciousness.

Several lessons here. First, downlighting alone typically evokes a sense of cramped space or confinement. Second, dark wall finishes exacerbate this impression of confinement. Third, the application of peripheral lighting can also serve to assist with architectural definition. Finally, as with visual clarity, attention must be given to the impact of surface finishes—with a need to consider **higher-reflectance wall surfaces** to **deliver the sense of spaciousness while minimizing energy use**.

Condition 4: Overhead/direct and selected peripheral/indirect low illuminance (10 fc [100 lx] on table). Incandescent downlighting (like Condition 1) and incandescent lighting on short walls.
Elicits strong positive reaction (impression of relaxation).

Condition 5: Overhead/indirect high illuminance (100 fc [1000 lx] on table). Indirect fluorescent lighting (like Condition 3) but greatly increased illuminance.
Evokes impression of visual clarity. Considered somewhat spacious. Elicits strong negative reaction.

Condition 6: Overhead/direct, overhead/indirect, and peripheral/indirect moderate illuminance (30 fc [300 lx] on table). Combination of Conditions 1, 2, and 3.
Evokes impressions of visual clarity and spaciousness. Elicits strong positive reaction.

Subjective Impressions Scalar Descriptors[7]   Table 7.3

General Evaluative Scalars	Clarity Scalars	Spaciousness Scalars
friendly vs. hostile	clear vs. hazy	large vs. small
pleasant vs. unpleasant	bright vs. dim	long vs. short
like vs. dislike	faces clear vs. faces obscure	spacious vs. cramped
harmony vs. discord	distinct vs. vague	
satisfying vs. frustrating	focused vs. unfocused	
beautiful vs. ugly	radiant vs. dull	
sociable vs. unsociable	noisy vs. quiet	
relaxed vs. tense		
interesting vs. monotonous		

Preference

Preference refers to the users' general evaluation of lighted space—their preference (or lack thereof) for a space. Scalar descriptors are dislike versus like. Typically, the more uniform the luminances in the central portion of a space, and simultaneously the lower the luminances of the periphery, the less preference for the space. Relatively nonuniform luminances throughout a space, along with peripheral luminances, enhance preference. Figure 7.8 uses two of the comparative images from the lighting study previously discussed to illustrate the difference between the like and dislike scalars. Preference is an important subjective impression for any space where users are expected to live and/or work for ex-

Figure 7.6

Subjective Impressions/ Visual Clarity: The 1970s space on the left (and other spaces like it) prompted negative sentiment and impressions of haziness and quiet. The same space, but with different luminance patterns and intensities on the right prompted positive sentiment and impressions of visual clarity. This information was used to develop the lighting design for the 1993 boardroom (below this page) and the 2004 meeting room restoration/refurbishment (shown on the opposing page).

Top two images this page ©GarySteffyLightingDesign Inc.—a gift of the John E. Flynn Estate
Bottom image this page ©Robert Eovaldi
Image opposing page ©Tom Crane Photography

■ Moderate to strong luminance (from luminous ceiling and cove on neutral ceiling/baffles)

■ Moderate to strong luminance (from daylight through low-transmittance windows and image-preserving MechoShade®)

■ Low to moderate luminance (from wallwashers on dark wall)

■ Low to moderate luminance (from luminous ceiling, cove, and downlights on medium-dark table)

MechoShade® is a registered trademark of MechoShade Systems, Inc.

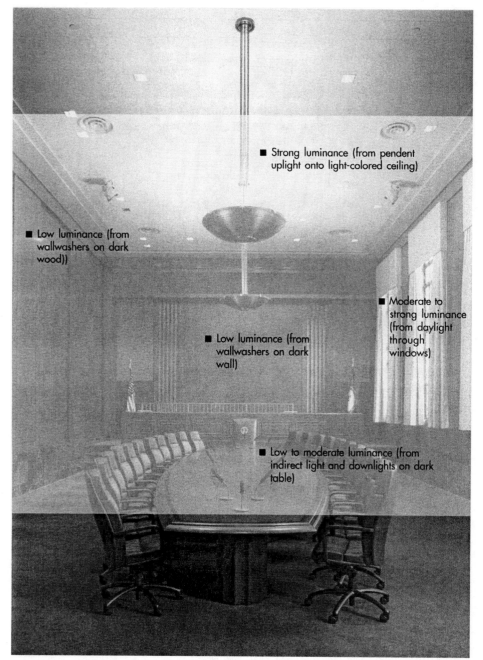

- Strong luminance (from pendent uplight onto light-colored ceiling)

- Low luminance (from wallwashers on dark wood))

- Moderate to strong luminance (from daylight through windows)

- Low luminance (from wallwashers on dark wall)

- Low to moderate luminance (from indirect light and downlights on dark table)

visual clarity applications
- Meeting settings
- Work settings

visual clarity luminances
- Luminance uniformity: not a key factor, but uniformity helps
- Luminance intensity: higher rather than lower
- Luminance location: at central, horizontal activity plane and some peripheral (wall) surfaces

visual clarity solution hints *solution*
- Higher (greater) luminance of horizontal activity plane, and higher (greater) luminance in central area
  - select light finishes for activity planes (e.g., light-colored desktop—30 to 40% reflectance—and very-light-colored ceilings—60 to 90%)
  - illuminate work surface(s) to greater intensity than adjacent areas (e.g., use task-oriented direct lighting that could include task lights or some ceiling-integrated direct lighting)
  - illuminate ceiling above work area
- Some peripheral luminance
  - select lighter finishes for wall surfaces (e.g., 30 to 50% reflectance)
  - illuminate walls with accenting on artwork, wallwashing, or sconces
- Use daylight and/or electric light to achieve luminances

tended time periods. Preference is best enhanced with higher or greater luminance of the periphery (walls). Luminance nonuniformity does seem to be a particularly strong determinant—the less uniform the luminances throughout the space, the stronger the preference.

Several lessons here. First, **downlighting alone typically evokes a sense of dislike**. Second, **dark wall finishes mixed with lighter wall finishes can assist in eliciting preference**. Third, the application of **peripheral lighting, particularly in conjunction with varied wall finishes, can also serve to address preference**.

Figure 7.7

Subjective Impressions/ Spaciousness: The 1970s space on the left (and other spaces like it) prompted negative sentiment and impressions of confinement. The same space, but with different luminance patterns and intensities on the right prompted positive sentiment and impressions of spaciousness. This information was used to develop the lighting design for the 2007 corridor (below this page) and the 2004 waiting lobby restoration/refurbishment (shown on the opposing page).
Top two images this page ©GarySteffyLightingDesign Inc.—a gift of the John E. Flynn Estate
Bottom image this page ©Gary Steffy Lighting Design Inc.
Image opposing page ©Feinknopf Studio

- Low-luminance ceiling and floor emphasize wall lighting effect
- Moderate to strong luminance (from wallwashers and sconces on light-colored walls)
- Moderate luminance (from wallwashers on light-colored artwork)

Relaxation

Relaxation is the original reference to users' perceived degree of expected work intensity. Scalar descriptors are relaxed versus tense. However, tranquility more clearly expresses the lighting effect, whereas relaxation may be misunderstood as "laid back," restful, and leisure-related. Nonuniform peripheral luminances elicit a sense of relaxation. Uniform, central luminances elicit a sense of tenseness. Figure 7.9 uses two of the comparative images from the lighting study previously discussed to illustrate the difference between the tense and relaxed scalars. Relax-

Architectural Lighting Design

■ Low-luminance ceiling and floor help emphasize wall lighting effect

■ Moderate luminance (from wallwashers and torchieres on medium-light walls)

■ Moderate luminance (from wallwashers on medium-light walls)

spaciousness applications
- Circulation spaces
- Assembly spaces
- Any space that may feel cramped

spaciousness luminances
- Luminance uniformity: uniform
- Luminance intensity: higher or greater wall luminances than horizontal activity plane
- Luminance location: peripheral (wall) surfaces

spaciousness solution hints
- Higher (greater) luminance of walls
  - select light finishes for walls (e.g., light-colored desktop—30 to 50% reflectance)
  - illuminate walls to greater intensity than horizontal activity plane
- Peripheral (wall) luminance
  - select lighter finishes for wall surfaces (e.g., 30 to 50% reflectance)
  - illuminate walls
- Use daylight and/or electric light to achieve luminances

ation is believed to be an important subjective impression for more casual spaces, such as waiting rooms, lounges, many dining establishments, and conference spaces. This attribute is considered important for hospitality-type spaces and, therefore, is an acceptable technique in commercial facilities where these kinds of spaces exist. Relaxation is best enhanced with nonuniform luminance of the periphery (walls). Luminance intensity does not seem to be a particularly strong determinant.

Several lessons here. First, downlighting alone typically elicits a sense of tenseness, not of tranquility. This should signal that **uniform, direct lighting for any setting, including workspaces, is typically undesirable if it is the only lighting technique employed**. Second, the intermittent need for peripheral luminance means that **art accenting and/or wall sconces are reinforcing lighting techniques where a sense of relaxation or tranquility is desired**.

Figure 7.8

Subjective Impressions/ Preference: The 1970s space on the left (and other spaces like it) prompted strong negative sentiment overall. The same space, but with different luminance patterns and intensities on the right, prompted strong positive sentiment. This information was used to develop the lighting design for the 2005 chapel (below this page) and the 2003 residential dining room (shown on the opposing page).

Top two images this page ©GarySteffyLightingDesign Inc.—a gift of the John E. Flynn Estate
Bottom image this page ©Gene Meadows
Image opposing page ©Glen Calvin Moon

■ Low to moderate ceiling luminance (from uplights on medum-dark ceiling)

■ Moderate luminance (from wallslot on medium-light wall)

■ Strong luminance (from accent on light-stone panel)

- Low to moderate ceiling luminance (from uplights on medium-light ceiling [bright appearance here due to daylight from foreground window])

- Moderate to strong luminance (from wallslot in niche on medium walls)

- Moderate to strong luminance (from accents on medium walls)

preference applications
- Most any occupied space

preference luminances
- Luminance uniformity: nonuniform
- Luminance intensity: not a key factor
- Luminance location: some emphasis of peripheral (wall) surfaces

preference solution hints Solution
- Nonuniform luminances
  - light walls selectively and/or somewhat dramatically (e.g., wallslots and accent lighting)
  - illuminate ceiling areas selectively and/or somewhat dramatically
- Peripheral (wall) luminance
  - mix some dark finishes (e.g., 10 to 20%) with some lighter finishes (30 to 50% reflectance)
  - illuminate walls somewhat dramatically
- Use daylight and/or electric light to achieve luminances

Privacy

Privacy or intimacy is the original reference to the users' perception of private space. Scalar descriptors are private versus public. However, privacy or seclusion more clearly expresses the lighting effect, whereas intimacy may be misunderstood as related to more seductive space. Relatively uniform and high (great) luminances in the zone of the user elicit a sense of public space. Higher (greater) peripheral luminance applied nonuniformly (intermittently around the periphery) enhances the sense of intimacy or privacy. Privacy is believed to be an important subjective impression for more intimate casual spaces, such as some lounges, clubs, restaurants, and residential living spaces. However, it can be used quite well in any space where privacy or seclusion is an important attribute, as Figure 7.10 illustrates. It is best enhanced with relatively higher or greater luminance of the periphery (walls), but in a nonuniform manner, and is further enhanced with relatively low luminance in the zone of the users. Luminance nonuniformity does seem to be a particularly strong determinant—the more nonuniform the peripheral luminances, the greater the sense of seclusion.

Several lessons here. First, **downlighting alone typically elicits a sense of more public space**—the users are highlighted as if on stage. Second, wall finishes are ultimately not as significant here as with the other four subjective impressions. Indeed, **darker wall finishes that are intermittently lighted will enhance the sense of intimacy**. Third, **low luminance in the zone of the user is critical** to the sense of intimacy. Overly bright casual settings will be perceived as public and less inviting to those seeking a private or secluded setting.

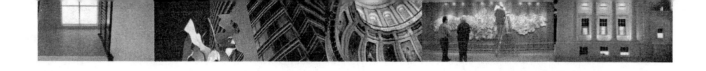

Figure 7.9

Subjective Impressions/ Relaxation: The 1970s space on the left (and other spaces like it) prompted strong negative sentiment as promoting sense of tenseness. The same space, but with different luminance patterns and intensities on the right prompted strong positive sentiment as promoting sense of relaxation.

Images ©GarySteffyLightingDesign Inc.—a gift of the John E. Flynn Estate

relaxation applications
- Waiting rooms
- Lounges
- Sit-down restaurants
- Conference rooms
- Casual areas

relaxation luminances
- Luminance uniformity: nonuniform
- Luminance intensity: not a key factor, but lower helps
- Luminance location: peripheral (wall) surfaces

relaxation solution hints
- Nonuniform luminances
  - accent selective walls (e.g., wallwashers, wallslots and consistent accent lighting)
- Peripheral (wall) luminance
  - use light finishes for selective wall surfaces (e.g., 30 to 50% reflectance)
  - illuminate selective walls
  - accent artwork
  - use sconces
- Use daylight and/or electric light to achieve luminances

7.4 Color

Color of light, surface color, color rendering, and color temperature also appear to be factors influencing subjective impressions. Color of light here refers to more saturated color—red, green, amber, and blue light. Long wavelengths, red light, focus behind the retina and red appears to advance or be closer to the observer. Short wavelengths, blue light, focus in front of the retina and blue appears to recede or be farther from the observer.[8, 9] This effect is known as chromostereopsis and is most pronounced with single wavelength sources and helps explain why it is impossible to focus on the blue-security-phone lights or on some red signals. This effect can be used to advantage in varying degree. For a dramatically spacious or expansive room, in addition to the techniques outlined under Spaciousness, or where one wall or architectural feature is to appear to dramatically recede, strong blue light on blue surface(s) (matched to the wavelength of light) is used. For more subtle effect, use blue-white or blue light on white or pale blue surfaces. Alternatively, for a dramatically confined or enclosing room or where one wall or architectural feature is to appear to advance dramatically, strong red light on red surface(s) (matched to the wavelength of light) is used. For more subtle effect, use red-white or red light on white or pale red surfaces. There are many less-powerful ways to use this chromostereopsis effect. However, even wood walls washed with warm-toned white light still evoke the sense of spaciousness. Of course, chromostereopsis can be confounded by the designer. Strong blue color on strong red background in print or paint or video presents the observer with a focusing nightmare.

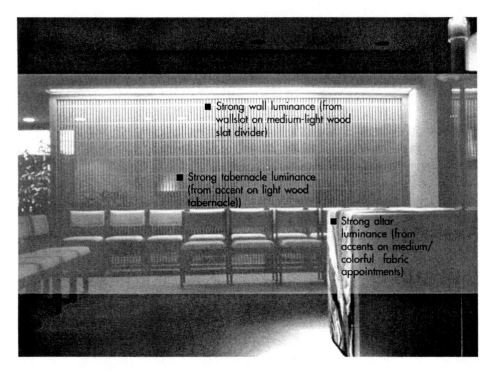

- Strong wall luminance (from wallslot on medium-light wood slat divider)
- Strong tabernacle luminance (from accent on light wood tabernacle)
- Strong altar luminance (from accents on medium/ colorful fabric appointments)

Figure 7.10

Subjective Impressions/Relaxation/Privacy: This chapel (foreground) and meditation area (background behind lighted wood screen) were modeled around relaxation (for the foreground chapel) and privacy (for the background meditation area) information taken from the 1970s' study. With strong luminance on the tabernacle, visitors readily recognize the available private meditation area in the background of his hospital chapel where personal reflection is possible in very low light.
Image ©INAI Studio

privacy applications
- Upscale clubs and restaurants
- Some residential spaces
- Meditation spaces

privacy luminances
- Luminance uniformity: nonuniform
- Luminance intensity: low, particularly in the zone of the occupant(s)
- Luminance location: some emphasis of peripheral (wall) surfaces

privacy solution hints
- Nonuniform luminances
  - light a few walls very selectively and/or somewhat dramatically (e.g., accent lighting)
- Peripheral (wall) luminance
  - primarily dark finishes (e.g., 10 to 20%) with few lighter finishes (30 to 50% reflectance)
  - illuminate select walls, features, or art dramatically
- Use daylight and/or electric light to achieve luminances

Color rendering is an indication of how well colors are rendered under a given light source and depends on the lamps' spectral power distributions. A system of measuring and calculating color rendering exists. Lamps are rated on a color rendering index (CRI) scale up to 100. There is no bottom end to the scale. Indeed, some lamps have negative color rendering indices—an indication that these lamps actually skew color perception quite significantly and quite negatively. For most applications, high color rendering lamps are suggested. A high CRI (greater than 80) generally results in crisper color appearance to materials and objects and better skintone appearance than a low CRI. This is especially important in low light environments. Here the color contrast boost offered by high color rendering lamps can help, to some extent, make up for the loss in luminance contrast of the lower illuminances. Poor color rendering lamps (e.g., CRI less than 80) should be limited to zones where few people are anticipated to occupy the area and/or occupancy is limited to very short time periods, and tasks are not color sensitive. Many limited access and suburban roadway applications where the task is essentially identifying lane markers and large objects (other vehicles) are good candidates for lamps with color rendering less than 80. However, **where pedestrians are involved and encouraged (shopping, dining, and entertainment districts), color rendering should be greater than 80. This helps with quicker recognition and reaction and, in the event of crime, improves color and skintone recognition**.

Although CRI is a convenient means to select lamps, it is flawed. The CRI system was established in the late 1950s and is based on an array of 8 basic, somewhat muted colors relative to today's color tastes. Further, as lamp technology has advanced and manufacturers have found the "sweet spot" for efficiency—resulting in a greenish cast since our eyes' peak sensitivity is at green (see Figure 2.3)—many lamps with CRIs of 80 or greater are simply deficient in red or blue or both. So, the designer should make preliminary lamp selections based on published CRI. However, final lamp selections should only be made after reviewing operational lamps and their effects on the designed color palette. Be especially suspicious of lamps exhibiting CRIs greater than 80 and color temperatures higher than 4000K or of CRI ratings for colored lamps of any kind or of white or colored LEDs. Also be suspicious of lamps with CRIs greater than 90 regardless of color temperature. Some of these lamps may actually provide good-to-excellent color rendering and be "rated" at 2800K to 3200K "warm" color temperatures, but when energized may exhibit an odd purplish character. Although colors and skin tones may be appealing under these lamps, the lamps themselves have a distinctly weird appearance.

Color temperature identifies the whiteness of the light produced by a light source. Figure 7.11 outlines the color temperatures of various daylight and man-made light sources. There is some indication that warmer-toned lamps (also known as lower color temperature lamps—exhibiting a color temperature less than 3500K) have several influences. First, for equal illuminance, the lighted space may appear somewhat dimmer under the warmer-tone lamps to many users. Second, and probably because this color temperature range approximates that of incandescent light, many users consider this color of whiteness more homelike and comfortable and less institutional. Lower color temperature reinforces the impressions of privacy and haziness. Experience shows great success with lamps in the 2700K to 3000K for many residential, hospitality, new, and restoration projects. 3500K seems the upper limit accepted in most commercial applications. Any introduction of 3500K or cooler (higher) color temperature in residential and hospitality applications generally results in some complaint(s) except where a cooler color temperature lamp is hidden in a detail with expectations of providing a more "daylight" rendition (e.g., false clerestory or skylight or an ultramodern miniature cove or slot detail).

```
more online @
www.sizes.com/units/color_temperature.htm
```

7.5 Daylighting

Daylighting is a physiological and psychological driver. As discussed briefly in Sections 2.8 and 2.9, Seasonal Affective Disorder and the circadian rhythm are affected by light levels associated with daylight and more efficiently delivered by daylight. Spectral distribution including nonvisible radiation of daylight is also beneficial. Highlights from a 2003 literature review.[10]

- no electric light source mimics the variation in light spectrum that occurs with daylight at different times of the day, in different seasons, and under different sky conditions
- physiologically, daylight is an effective stimulant to the human visual system and the human circadian system
- psychologically, daylight and view are highly desirable
- daylight exposure has both positive and negative effects on health—the strongest effects occur outdoors

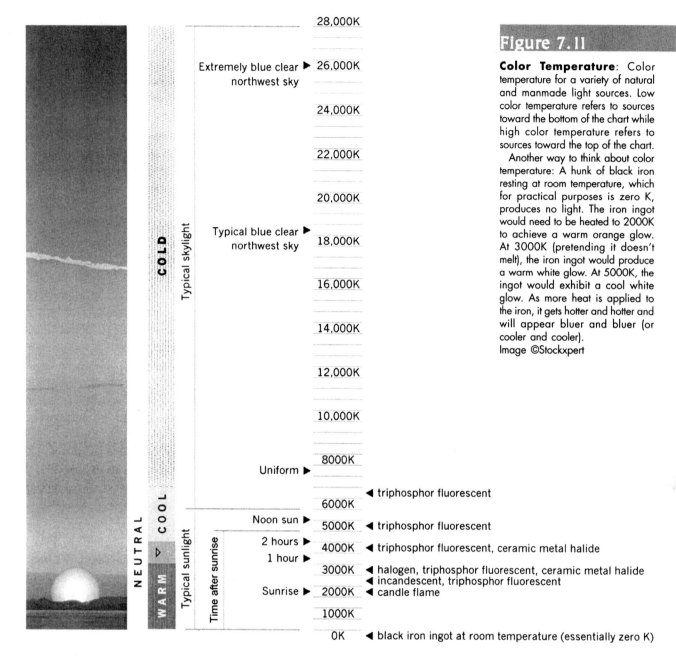

Figure 7.11

Color Temperature: Color temperature for a variety of natural and manmade light sources. Low color temperature refers to sources toward the bottom of the chart while high color temperature refers to sources toward the top of the chart.

Another way to think about color temperature: A hunk of black iron resting at room temperature, which for practical purposes is zero K, produces no light. The iron ingot would need to be heated to 2000K to achieve a warm orange glow. At 3000K (pretending it doesn't melt), the iron ingot would produce a warm white glow. At 5000K, the ingot would exhibit a cool white glow. As more heat is applied to the iron, it gets hotter and hotter and will appear bluer and bluer (or cooler and cooler).
Image ©Stockxpert

Although mimicking daylight variability with electric light—in intensity and color—is certainly a challenge that is not insurmountable, the cost and controls hardware and programming requirements would be staggering. Not to mention the unsustainability of such rigmarole. The point—this variability is highly desirable and the best way to address it is with the introduction of daylight into buildings in such a way that the variability in intensity and color can be experienced.

The performance aspects associated with daylighting are evermore compelling. Research over the past decade intimates that some significant performance enhancement is made with **sidelighting** and/or **toplighting** techniques.[11] In educational facilities, it was generally found that students in classrooms with the most daylighting progressed at the fastest pace. It was also found that skylight design plays a significant role in the success of daylight. Perhaps not surprisingly,

sidelighting
Referring to daylighting that enters a space from the side, typically through windows.

toplighting
Referring to daylighting that enters a space from above, typically through skylights.

clear skylights with no provision for daylight control were unsuccessful in delivering beneficial daylight. However, diffuse skylights with provision for daylight control were quite successful in delivering beneficial daylighting. Daylighting design is discussed in Chapter 9.

Daylight and its day/night cycle is critical to our own cycle—the human circadian rhythm. The control of electric light at night and its spectral distribution can enhance the nighttime portion of the cycle (see Section 7.6) when darkness is crucial. However, establishing "waking light" conditions in homes and offices with architectural electric lighting to simulate circadian-quality daylight levels and/or to address SAD is, for the most part, folly. For four reasons. First, these aspects of light and health should be carefully established and monitored by medical professionals. While there is therapeutic benefit, side effects such as glare, visual fatigue, and headache are possible.[12] Second, implementation of such "waking light" electric lighting systems on any meaningful scale will seriously jeopardize energy efficiency and sustainability measures since a significant quantity of light is required to effect a result—typically in the range of 250 to 1200 fc (about 2500 to 12,000 lx).[12] Third, daylight is available in many highly populated geographies at no cost monetarily or environmentally to anyone with access to outdoors or, at a minimum, access to windowed or skylighted rooms. Lastly, research now suggests that wavelength of light source may be a stronger trigger than light intensity—all the more reason such lighting should be developed only with the consultation of medical personnel.

The glare issues associated with daylighting are significant. For all of the talk about energy efficiency, sustainability, and desirability associated with daylight, users' perception of too much glare can mitigate any daylight benefit. The ultraviolet issues associated with daylight are significant and may have serious health side affects. UV accelerates the development of cataracts—yellowing the lens to the point that vision is obscured. UV is linked with melanoma and less deadly forms of skin cancer. UV also accelerates fading of many fabrics, materials, and paints. The point is this: too much of a good thing is bad. Although most interior daylight exhibits less UV than outdoor daylight, good daylight control must be a part of the daylighting system—controlling intensity and/or duration of daylight.

more online @
www.epa.gov/sunwise/uvandhealth.html
www.lrc.rpi.edu/programs/daylighting/pdf/DaylightBenefits.pdf

7.6 Night Lighting

As reported in Section 2.3 (Color Vision), our ability to detect detail and color depends both on our eyes and on the lighting situation. In the recent past, lamps were tested and evaluated based on laboratory reference standards that presumed the users' eyes would be photopically adapted—operating under relatively high light intensity situations (greater than 2 fc [20 lx]). Experience and recent research shows that the spectral power distribution of the light source significantly influences most people's visual acuity under scotopic and mesopic vision—low light intensities (less than 2 fc [20 lx]). Where scotopic vision is anticipated (e.g., intensities less than 0.2 fc [2 lx]), bluer, whiter light sources may offer more than a twofold improvement in visual acuity. As light intensities increase to the threshold for pho-

topic vision, this improvement diminishes. So, **for night situations, particularly exterior environments where light intensities are quite low and where people are interacting socially or where security is of concern, the use of monochromatic yellow light sources, such as high pressure sodium or low pressure sodium, are discouraged, as are many of the LED sources with CRIs less than 80.**

On the other hand, however, light that is rich in blue inhibits melatonin production in humans, which occurs at night. As noted in Section 7.5, electric light, actually the lack thereof, enhances the nighttime aspect of the circadian rhythm—when melatonin production is intended to be high. Complete and total darkness is best, but if some light is necessary or desired for nightlighting, this should be done with very few and very low-energy sources exhibiting 600 nm or greater wavelengths typified by shielded ½- or 1-watt amber (~590 nm), red-orange (~617 nm), or red (~625 nm) LED steplights.[12,13] Where outdoor light might filter into interior sleeping quarters the outdoor lighting should be appropriately designed to limit spill light and/or sleeping quarters should be fitted with black-out window treatment that exhibits no light leaks. Where sleeping quarters are used solely for sleeping functions, consideration to low-reflectance room surfaces exhibiting very little blue pigmentation will further serve to filter blue light from the nighttime setting. Also recognize the implication of TV-watching in bed. TVs exhibit a rather strong blue-white component and typically exhibit relatively high luminances—both aspects that work against melatonin production and the night cycle. Many of these are design aspects that the design team directly affects if not designs and specifies.

7.7 Health

Over the past 40 years, there has been much ado about light and health. Indeed, light affects health profoundly, as discussed in Chapter 2 and here in Sections 7.5 and 7.6. However, many products and "studies" espouse the spectral power distribution (the wavelength makeup) of light as significantly altering physiological behavior and performance. Some of this is the "extension" of previously cited daylighting studies to electric light, which is an inappropriate extension unless intensities and spectral distribution of the electric lights can match those of daylight—which they simply cannot. Perhaps the most common myth is the "fact" that so-called full-spectrum electric light significantly improves academic achievement, mood, and health in general, and work productivity. It is reasonable to conclude that there is no panacea—indeed, so-called full-spectrum electric light has no substantive impact (positive or negative) on people.[14] While there is certainly evidence of health effects of specific intensities of light (e.g., relatively high illuminance intensities to set circadian rhythm), little evidence of health effects related to spectral quality of light exists, except that ultraviolet (UV) radiation helps the skin produce vitamin D. However, it is also clear that too much UV exposure will result in sunburn and, ultimately, in melanoma. So, introducing electric light (or even daylight) in living and working environments with significant amounts of UV radiation is inappropriate. Attempting to introduce illuminance levels like those experienced outdoors is also inappropriate. In the absence of any new research or of corroboration of previous research by independent researchers and reviewers, there is no need to heed the hype surrounding "full-spectrum" electric lighting.

As noted, light affects the circadian rhythm. As such, light can be used to benefit when/if the circadian rhythm is upset. For example, shift workers may experience upset circadian rhythms. Here, high doses of light at the beginning of the shift can help with resetting circadian rhythms.[15] This might be done at the shift workers' homes with light treatment from localized light boxes or at work in light rooms. Similarly, folks experiencing SAD can be treated with localized light boxes or light rooms. The programming phase should establish if such treatment is necessary, and, if so, if it should be addressed with localized light boxes (a specified, purchased item) or by light rooms (an architectural lighting design and specification item). Consultation with a specialized physician or opthalmologist should be made to establish appropriate intensities, spectral distributions, and durations of exposure.

7.8 Endnotes

[1] Rohles, F. H., Bennett, C. A. and Milliken, G. A. The effects of lighting, color and room decor on thermal comfort. ASHRAE Transactions, 1981.

[2] John Flynn, "The Psychology of Light, Article 2, Orientation as a Visual Task," Electrical Consultant, January, 1973, 10–21.

[3] D. H. Alman, "Errors of the standard photometric system when measuring the brightness of general illumination light sources," Journal of the Illuminating Engineering Society, 1977, no. 1: 61.

[4] John Flynn, "The Psychology of Light, Article 5, Attitude Reinforcement through Lighting Design," Electrical Consultant, May, 1973, 42–45.

[5] Dale Tiller, Lighting Quality, National Research Council of Canada, http://www.nrc.ca/irc/bsi/92-5_E.html. [Accessed October 7, 2000.]

[6] Belinda Collins, Evaluation of Subjective Response to Lighting Distributions: A Literature Review/NISTIR 5119 (Gaithersburg, MD: National Institute of Standards and Technology, 1993).

[7] John E. Flynn, et. al., "Interim Study of Procedures for Investigating the Effect of Light on Impression and Behavior," Journal of the Illuminating Engineering Society, 1973, no. 3: 94.

[8] Ming Ye, Arthur Bradley, Larry N. Thibos, and Xiaoxiao Zhang, Interocular Differences in Transverse Chromatic Aberration Determine Chromostereopsis for Small Pupils, Indiana University, http://research.opt.indiana.edu/Library/chromostereo/chromostereo.pdf. [Accessed September 16, 2007.]

[9] Alan Hedge, Vision and Light, DEA 350 Human Factors: Ambient Environment, Cornell University (web page, January 2007), http://ergo.human.cornell.edu/studentdownloads/DEA350pdfs/vision.pdf. [Accessed September 16, 2007.]

[10] Peter Boyce, Claudia Hunter, and Owen Howlett, The Benefits of Daylight Through Windows, Lighting Research Center Rensselaer Polytechnic Institute, September 13, 2003, http://www.lrc.rpi.edu/programs/daylighting/pdf/DaylightBenefits.pdf. [Accessed September 22, 2007.]

[11] Heschong Mahone Group, Daylighting in Schools, The Pacific Gas and Electric Company, August 20, 1999, http://www.pge.com/003_save_energy/003c_edu_train/pec/daylight/di_pubs/SchoolsCondensed820.PDF. [Accessed September 22, 2007.]

[12] George C. Brainaird, et. al., "Action Spectrum for Melatonin Regulation in Humans: Evidence for a Novel Circadian Photoreceptor," The Journal of Neuroscience, August 15, 2001, 21(16): 6405–6412.

[13] Luxeon I product data, September 22, 2007, http://www.lumileds.com/products/line.cfm?lineId=1. [Accessed September 22, 2007.]

[14] Jennifer A. Vietch, ed. Full-Spectrum Lighting Effects on Performance, Mood, and Health, Institute for Research in Construction Internal Report No. 659, June, 1994, http://www.nrc.ca/irc/fulltext/ir659/contents.html. [Accessed November 26, 2000.]

[15] Lynne Lamberg, Medical News and Perspectives: Dawn's Early Light to Twilight's Last Gleaming…, The Journal of the American Medical Association, November 11, 1998, http://www.websciences.org/sltbr/jama.htm. [Accessed November 26, 2000.]

7.9 References

Agoston, G.A. 1987. Color Theory and Its Application in Art and Design. Berlin: Springer-Verlag.

Flynn, John E., Kremers, Jack A., Segil, Arthur W., and Steffy, Gary R. 1992. Architectural Interior Systems, 3rd ed. New York: Van Nostrand Reinhold.

Hedge, Alan. 2007. Vision and Light, DEA 350 Human Factors: Ambient Environment (web page, January 2007), http://ergo.human.cornell.edu/studentdownloads/DEA350pdfs/vision.pdf. [Accessed September 16, 2007.]

Rea, Mark S., ed., and Thompson, Brian J., general ed. 1992. Selected Papers on Architectural Lighting. Bellingham, WA: SPIE Optical Engineering Press.

Rea, Mark S., ed. 2000. The IESNA Lighting Handbook: Reference & Application, Ninth Edition. New York: Illuminating Engineering Society of North America.

I t is no secret: programming and designing toward many of the lighting design factors outlined in Chapters 5 and 7 involve architectural and interior design and, thus, are of greater interest to most designers but typically less interesting to engineers. Systems Factors in Chapter 6 and Task Factors here, while perhaps not as enjoyable for designers, are more appealing to many engineers. For any lighting design to be successful, all of these factors need to be reviewed and addressed to some degree. Many times, to limit fees and schedule issues, Task Factors may be the only set of factors addressed. Define a few tasks, establish (look up in a reference) some illuminance criteria, perhaps address luminance criteria related to glare, and voilà, this results in easily quantifiable criteria that can be solved with a regular array of lights in or on a ceiling. Next project, please! This is unfortunate. Designing just for task factors usually results in vapid, insensitive solutions. The challenge at this stage is to convince the owner, users, or both that the project being designed will be in place for 10, 20, 30, or more years—in a sustainable society, even longer. So, is an easy, convenient, and low-initial-cost resolution best in the long run for business or for living or for the Earth? Task factors as discussed here are intended to be only one part of the programming of a project.

Programming appropriately for task factors involves a review of visual tasks, luminances (and, therefore, surface reflectances and transmittances), and illuminances. Making a full analysis of the kinds of visual tasks that are likely to occur is the best means of preparing the designer to solve unique lighting challenges. A complete review of tasks is most likely to lead to a comprehensive lighting solution that will meet users' requirements for most all tasks most or all of the time. This may also result in a more unique or thoughtful way of looking at the lighting problem and developing better solutions.

vertical illuminance
Light falling onto a vertical plane (e.g., walls or partitions) or, where facial recognition, or teleconferencing, or viewing computer or television monitors are an issue, then light falling onto an imaginary vertical plane representing the plane of the face and/or monitors.

8.1 Visual Tasks

Solutions for lighting the visual tasks can only be as good as the programming and this programming needs to be all-inclusive. Tasks such as facial recognition tend to be overlooked or ignored, but require **vertical illuminance**. This is particularly important for circulation areas and gathering spaces where facial recognition is a key component of the task of conversing. Sidewalks are another application where vertical illuminance is important, particularly if security is of concern—vertical light helps people identify and assess the demeanor of other people.

Establishing the amount of time that users spend on given visual tasks may help the designer determine the ambient lighting requirements for a space. For example, if **VDT** tasks are performed for less than an hour a day, and if handwritten paper tasks or reading of small-print hardcopies are performed most of the day, then it may not be reasonable to design an ambient lighting system for the VDT task operation. Generally, the tasks people perform most of the time are the tasks that the lighting should accommodate. An exception is when a critically important task is performed for only a short period of time. Then it is reasonable to design the lighting to accommodate the very important task(s).

VDT
Visual display terminal, computer screen, or computer monitor or just monitor.

As noted previously, users' ages have an impact on lighting requirements. Typically, **older eyes require two to three times more light than younger eyes to see a task equally as well. For practical purposes, however, light levels are usually increased by 50 percent over those for younger-than-40-year-olds when designing for occupants between 40 and 55 years of age, and increased by 100 percent for occupants over 55.** Further, older eyes tend to require some sort of lens correction—resulting in eyewear. The frames and lenses can exacerbate glary lighting situations and shadows that are predominant with direct (downlighting) solutions. These increases should be carefully considered before implementation and are most appropriate where people are performing sight-dependent tasks for extended periods.

8.2 Luminances

disability glare
Glare sensation experienced as a result of viewing a light source or reflection of such great luminance as to be visually disabling—the observer cannot see or can see in only such a limited capacity that his/her vision is essentially disabled.

discomfort glare
Glare sensation experienced as a result of viewing a light source or reflection of sufficient luminance to cause discomfort, but the observer is still capable of seeing.

reflected glare
Considered a misnomer, but used by many people to identify light reflections that interfere with vision. See veiling reflection below.

veiling reflection
Reflection(s) of light(s) from task surfaces (e.g., computer monitors, TV screens, glossy paper, glass-enclosed artwork, and wet roadways, etc.) that veil some or all of the task from view.

Luminances and the resulting contrasts (the differences between luminances), as well as chromatic contrasts (the differences between chromas or colors), are the external or environmental effects responsible for our sight. As discussed in Section 7.2, luminances play a significant role in how we see, react to, and accomplish tasks. For purposes of general comfort, absolute luminances of any surface, window or daylight element, or luminaire should be limited to avoid glare. To what degree, however, remains a tough question. Our response to luminance depends on several key factors, including the background luminance (the overall luminance to which the eyes are adapted), the luminance of the area or source in question, the size of the area or source in question, the color of the area or source in question, and the condition of the eyes doing the observing. A classic example of the dilemma that luminances pose is to ponder if car headlights are glary. During the night, on an unlit, asphalt, country road where the background luminance is very low, and if the headlights are near the line of sight, then most folks will judge them to be glary. However, if the headlights are out of the line of sight, they pose less of a **disability glare** problem and, perhaps, pose only a **discomfort glare** problem. If those same headlights are viewed against the background of a relatively new concrete lighted freeway, even discomfort glare may not be an issue. Further, during daytime conditions, the headlights are not judged as glary (the background is quite bright) even when directly in the line of sight. Less extreme situations are downlights in an office setting. When are they glary? A more important issue is when surface luminances (particularly wall luminances, window luminances, and luminaire luminances) become significant enough to create **reflected glare** or **veiling reflection** problems for users of VDT screens.

Computer monitors exhibit very high resolution and luminance capabilities today. However, for the most detailed computer-aided design work, such as that for architectural and engineering planning and for scientific molecular study and drug design, dark screen backgrounds offer the viewer the best visual acuity. These are called positive contrast displays—the background is dark and the information content (text, lines, graphics) is light (see Figure 8.1). Depending on the character of the monitor glass (see Figure 8.2), the dark background creates a near-mirror like situation where light-colored walls that are lighted, windows, and most any luminaire (except dim, totally indirect luminaires) will cause the detailed text, lines, and graphics to wash out (similar to looking out a window at

Figure 8.1

VDT Screen Contrast/Positive and Negative: The image on the far left is called positive contrast—background is black or nearly black and the text, graphics, and/or lines are white or colored. Screen luminance for such positive contrast displays is typically 1.5 cd/ft² (15 cd/m²) and depends on the density of text and graphics. On the near left, the image is called negative contrast—background is white or very light gray and the text, graphics, and/or lines are black or colored. Screen luminance for such negative contrast displays is typically 9 cd/ft² (90 cd/m²) and depends on the density of text and graphics.
Images ©Stockxpert

night where most of the view is veiled by the interior light reflections on the window). In these situations, luminaire selection and room surface reflectances and overall light levels must be carefully assessed.

If and how people judge glare depends on the luminance of the light source or lighted area of concern, the size of the source or area of concern, the luminance of the surrounding visual field, the position of the source or area of concern in the visual field, the number of sources or areas of concern in the visual field, and the configuration (layout) of the sources or areas of concern.[1] The luminance of the source is a function of the source itself—is this a bare lamp or a lamp completely enclosed by luminaire reflector, lens, and/or louver, or is it an area of wall or ceiling, or is it the view out a window during daylight hours (in which case does the view consist of dark foliage, deep blue sky, and/or bright clouds, the solar disc, and/or all of this). Table 8.1 identifies luminances for some typical exterior scenes. Note the influence of glazing and window-treatment transmission. In many situations, a 30% to 40% T_{vis} media arrangement is considered a reasonable compromise between excessive glare, dinginess, and daylight efficiency. Yet even this arrangement will likely be problematic on at least southern exposures in the northern hemisphere (and on northern exposures in the southern hemisphere) where a 5% T_{vis} glazing/window treatment arrangement may be necessary on those partly cloudy days where the sun is reflected from or barely hidden by the clouds. Hence, a 40% T_{vis} glazing system and a 10% or 12% T_{vis} window shade may be best for an overall 4 to 5% T_{vis}. In any event, complaints about glare typically far outpace complaints about dinginess or gloominess—do not be tripped up by promotions for "sustainable" practices or "clear" (aka high-transmission view) glazing. Compare the data for 30% T_{vis} in Table 8.1 to the luminance limits outlined in Table 8.2. See Chapter 9 for more on daylighting.

Although most people will tolerate a source of high luminance if the source is quite small, they are much more likely to accept a window (a large source of high luminance) more readily than a direct luminaire (also a large source of high luminance) of high luminance. Since the window offers significant perceived benefits (e.g., view and connection to the outdoors) over "an ordinary light fixture," it is easier to cope with the high, sometimes blinding luminance associated with it. Sources in the periphery can typically exhibit greater luminances without being considered offensively glary than sources near the central line of sight.

Figure 8.2

Computer Screen Character: Screen surface affects the intensity and angle of reflections from the screen. Matte or diffuse screens are most forgiving (ISO Type I), semi-specular screens are moderately forgiving (ISO Type II), and specular (mirror-like) screens are least forgiving (ISO Type III). However, a Type III screen used in negative contrast mode is usually sufficiently bright to negate reflections. θ_i represents the angle of incidence. θ_r represents the angle of reflection, which, in the case of specular screen surfaces and semi-specular screen surfaces, is equal to the angle of incidence.

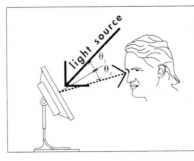

Specular Reflection

Whatever percentage of light that is reflected from the monitor screen surface will reflect in one specific direction. If viewing geometry/lighting geometry is wrong, the specific direction is back to the observer's eyes. ISO Type III—specular or polished, glossy surface could be light, medium, or dark tone.

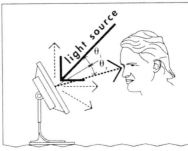

Semi-specular Reflection

Most of the light reflected from the monitor screen surface will reflect in one specific direction with some diffuse reflection in many other directions. ISO Type II—semi-specular or lightly etched or brushed surface could be light, medium, or dark tone.

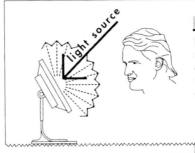

Diffuse Reflection

Light reflected from the monitor screen surface will reflect equally and softly in all directions. ISO Type I—matte or textured surface could be light, medium, or dark tone.

Given all of the variables influencing glare, luminance guidelines for luminaires and room surfaces are elusive. Further, glare is dependent on the condition of the viewer's eyes and on the viewer's experiences and cultural background. In other words, seldom will the condition arise where all people find a given situation glare-free. However, based on consensus opinion over the past half century, based on some research, and based on experience, some guidance can be offered for luminance limits for some situations. Table 8.2 outlines luminance limits for a variety of applications and a variety of luminance sources. Figure 8.3 illustrates how luminances, luminance limits, and luminance ratio guidelines were followed for better environments.

Luminance limits are helpful in avoiding discomfort glare situations and limiting the extent of veiling reflections for many tasks. However, for people viewing computer and TV monitors, and digital readout displays, luminance ratios are critically important. These are the ratios of the luminance of one source or area as compared to a nearby source or area. For direct lighting systems, this means that the luminaires themselves need to be relatively dim or low-brightness in order not to create harsh contrasts or ratios with the surrounding darker ceiling. For indirect lighting systems, this means that the ceiling luminance directly above

Architectural Lighting Design

Exterior Surfaces/Objects[a, b]	Seen Outdoors	Thru 70% T_{vis} Media[c]	Thru 30% T_{vis} Media[c]	Thru 5% T_{vis} Media[c]
Sky, north near horizon	605 cd/ft^2 (6500 cd/m^2)	425 cd/ft^2 (4550 cd/m^2)	180 cd/ft^2 (1950 cd/m^2)	30 cd/ft^2 (325 cd/m^2)
Sky, north nearly overhead (deep blue)	90 cd/ft^2 (980 cd/m^2)	65 cd/ft^2 (685 cd/m^2)	25 cd/ft^2 (295 cd/m^2)	5 cd/ft^2 (50 cd/m^2)
Sky, south near horizon	1670 cd/ft^2 (18,000 cd/m^2)	1170 cd/ft^2 (12,600 cd/m^2)	500 cd/ft^2 (5400 cd/m^2)	85 cd/ft^2 (900 cd/m^2)
Ground, snow covered	560 to 1020 cd/ft^2 (6000 to 11,000 cd/m^2)	390 to 715 cd/ft^2 (4200 to 7700 cd/m^2)	170 to 305 cd/ft^2 (1800 to 3300 cd/m^2)	30 to 50 cd/ft^2 (300 to 550 cd/m^2)
Ground cover, winter vegetation	150 cd/ft^2 (1600 cd/m^2)	105 cd/ft^2 (1120 cd/m^2)	45 cd/ft^2 (480 cd/m^2)	10 cd/ft^2 (80 cd/m^2)
Brick pavers, medium value	230 cd/ft^2 (2500 cd/m^2)	160 cd/ft^2 (1750 cd/m^2)	70 cd/ft^2 (750 cd/m^2)	10 cd/ft^2 (125 cd/m^2)
Trees, deciduous, facing south[d]	60 cd/ft^2 (650 cd/m^2)	40 cd/ft^2 (455 cd/m^2)	20 cd/ft^2 (195 cd/m^2)	5 cd/ft^2 (35 cd/m^2)

[a] Winter conditions at 42°N latitude.

[b] Exact conversions rounded to nearest five between US Customary and SI.

[c] Any combination of vision glass and image-preserving window treatment to achieve cited visible light transmittance (e.g., 70% clear glass with 7% solar mesh shade ~ 5% T_{vis}).

[d] View is north to stand of trees that face south and are washed in sunlight.

the luminaires must be of similar intensity as the area between luminaires. Further, with indirect luminaires, the bottom of the luminaire either needs to be relatively small (less than several inches), needs to be rounded (to capture and reflect a bit of the light from the ceiling), or needs to have some soft transmitted light through it so that the luminaire is not harshly contrasted against the lighted ceiling.

Table 8.3 outlines luminance ratios to consider in various applications. The ratios help adaptation luminance—the luminance to which eyes become adapted. As eyes scan from the background to tasks, transient adaptation occurs. The greater the luminance change, the greater the adaptation effect and the more annoying. Research suggests that most people have a preference for background luminances that are nearly identical to the task luminance.[3, 4] So, a negative contrast computer screen exhibiting a typical luminance of 9 cd/ft^2 (exactly 97 cd/m^2) suggests nearby surfaces exhibit a similar luminance. A paper task should not be more than three times the luminance of the computer screen—the paper's luminance should not be greater than 27 cd/ft^2 (exactly 290 cd/m^2). Since white paper has a reflectance of about 80 percent, the illuminance on the paper should be no more than 105 fc (exactly 1130 lx) and preferably closer to 35 fc (exactly 375 lx).

8.3 Reflectances

Luminances are the result of reflected light or transmitted light. Reflected light is a result of illuminances (light levels) and surface reflectances interacting. Therefore, surface reflectances need to be a conscious design goal. They have a significant and direct bearing on energy use. Lighter surfaces reflect more light and can yield energy savings by as much as 20 percent.[11]

The degree of surface gloss affects the direction or directions in which light is reflected and not how much light is reflected. Matte or diffuse surface finishes are better for many situations, but especially work environments, than are specular surface finishes. Diffuse surfaces spread light reflections in

Table 8.2 Luminance Limits for Task Visibility and Visual Comfort

Source[a]	Task[b]	Application[c]	Maximum Luminance[d]				Maximum CP[e]
			ISO Types I and II Monitors[f]		**ISO Type III Monitors[f]**		
			Negative Contrast	Positive Contrast	Negative Contrast	Positive Contrast	
Luminaire	secondary	• Industrial[g]	240 cd/ft² (2570 cd/m²) at 65°				
		• Conference space[g]	160 cd/ft² (1715 cd/m²) at 65°				300 cd @65°, 185 cd @75°, 60 cd @85°
		• Transitional space[g]					
	normal	• Classroom	140 cd/ft² (1500 cd/m²) at 65°	95 cd/ft² (1000 cd/m²) at 65°	45 cd/ft² (500 cd/m²) at 65°	20 cd/ft² (200 cd/m²) at 65°	300 cd @65°, 185 cd @75°, 60 cd @85°
		• High-tech industrial					
		• Office					
	sensitive	• Call centers	140 cd/ft² (1500 cd/m²) at 55°	95 cd/ft² (1000 cd/m²) at 55°	45 cd/ft² (500 cd/m²) at 55°	20 cd/ft² (200 cd/m²) at 55°	300 cd @55°, 220 cd @65°, 135 cd @75°, 45 cd @85°
		• Computer programming[h]					
	highly sensitive	• Air traffic control	20 cd/ft² (200 cd/m²) at 55°				less than 300 cd @55°, 220 cd @65°, 135 cd @75°, 45 cd @85°
		• Auto/Arch CAD					
		• Computer programming[i]					
		• Emergency command centers					
		• Medical lab					
		• Security monitoring					
Surfaces[j]		secondary computer task apps	160 cd/ft² (1715 cd/m²)				
		normal computer task apps	80 cd/ft² (855 cd/m²)				
		sensitive computer task apps	80 cd/ft² (855 cd/m²)				
		highly sensitive computer task apps	55 cd/ft² (615 cd/m²)				
Daylight Media[k]		secondary computer task apps	• Conference space • Transitional space	320 cd/ft² (3425 cd/m²)			
		secondary computer task apps	• Industrial	240 cd/ft² (2570 cd/m²)			
		normal computer task apps	80 cd/ft² (855 cd/m²)				
		sensitive computer task apps	80 cd/ft² (855 cd/m²)				
		highly sensitive computer task apps	55 cd/ft² (615 cd/m²)				

[a] The source of luminance.

[b] The degree of sensivitty of the primary computer task. "Secondary" indicates computer task is not a key task in the respective application(s).

[c] Although luminance is somewhat application specific, many applications include similar visual tasks—viewing LCD screens, monitors, and readouts along with fine 2- and 3-dimensional detail. Hence, many luminance limits are the same for various applications.

[d] The values are based on a variety of reference sources and experience.[4, 5, 6, 7] Exact conversions rounded to nearest five between US Customary and SI.

[e] Candlepower maximums are based on guidelines introduced by the IESNA Office Lighting Committee in 2004.[8]

[f] Type I monitors exhibit good anti-reflection/anti-glare properties typified by matte finish). Type II monitors exhibit moderate anti-reflection properties (typified by semi-matte finish). Type III monitors exhibit little or no anti-reflection properties (typified by glossy finish).

[g] Spaces where computer task performance is limited to intermittent use and where room surfaces are light in color and/or washed with light to balance contrast.

[h] Programming of typical commercial software.

[i] Programming of critical commercial and military software.

[j] Wall and ceiling surfaces presumed to have matte finishes to diffuse reflections.

[k] Light transmitting wall (e.g., windows, clerestories) and ceiling surfaces (e.g., skylights, monitors).

[l] Some applications, such as air traffic control, may require image preserving shading.

ISO
International Standards Organization.
www.iso.org/iso/home.htm

Consider

See diagram below for clarification on candlepower angles of interest

Normal-to-high output indirect or indirect/direct luminaire or lensed/louvered direct luminaire	see Figure 8.3a
Normal output indirect or indirect/direct luminaire or louvered direct luminaire	
	see Figure 8.3b
	see Figure 8.3c
Normal-to-low output indirect or indirect/direct luminaire with very little downlight or specially lensed/louvered/low wattage direct luminaire	
Normal-to-low output indirect or indirect/direct luminaire with well-shielded downlight or specially louvered well-controlled low wattage direct luminaire	
Low output wide-distribution indirect luminaire	
	see Figure 8.3d

Specify mostly wall materials with semi-gloss or matte finishes

Specify mostly wall materials with matte finish, avoid great illuminances and strong scallops on walls

Specify mostly wall materials with matte finish, avoid great illuminances and strong scallops on walls

Specify wall materials with matte finish and moderate reflectance value, use gentle and low illuminances on walls and ceilings

Specify manual or automated shading on windows and skylights

Specify manual or automated shading on windows and skylights

Specify automated shading on windows and skylights or low transmission glass

Specify dense or opaque automated shading on windows and skylights and low transmission glass

Specify dense or opaque automated shading on windows and skylights and low transmission glass[1]

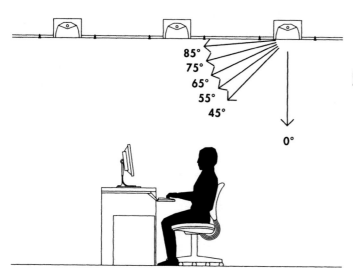

Luminaire Luminance-Limit Angles

Luminance limits are based on the angle of light distribution. See table for luminance limits at various angles for various computer monitors. Nadir (0°) is directly downward from the luminaire toward the floor.

Figure 8.3

a

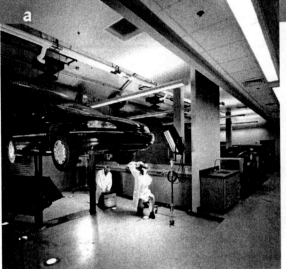

b

Visibility and Visual Comfort/
Indirect and direct/indirect lighting offer several significant luminance benefits over direct-only lighting approaches. First, uplighting diffuses comfortably across the ceiling plane. This background of luminance allows for the introduction of direct downlighting without glare where more light is necessary for low contrast and detailed visual work like the forensics inspection garage in 8.3a. Second, this background of luminance works to minimize the contrast of windows (8.3b and 8.3c). Third, indirect lighting allows for good visibility of projected images (8.3c), computer screens and equipment readouts (8.3d).
Image 8.3a ©Christopher Lark Photography
Image 8.3b ©Justin Maconochie
Image 8.3c ©Bill Lindhout Photography and courtesy BETA Design Group, Inc.
Image 8.3d ©Christopher Lark Photography

all directions. These eliminate the harsh, glary reflections that are problematic when electric light or daylight reflects from specular or polished surfaces at a specific angle (the angle at which people happen to view the task or areas), which can change based on occupant viewing position and light source position (which is everchanging with daylight). Figure 8.4 graphically represents the three basic categories of directional characteristics of light reflections—specular surface reflections; semi-specular or spread surface reflections; and matte or diffuse surface reflections.

Total light reflectance value (LRV) affects how *much* light is reflected, but not in which direction(s). For most office furniture, LRV of 20 percent should be a minimum for worksurfaces and 40 percent a minimum for partitions and walls. For worksurfaces, this can be achieved with some light woods and most medium-to-light laminates. For partitions and walls, this can be achieved with light woods, light laminates, and light paint and wallcoverings. Combined with surface gloss, LRV provides the designer with an effective means of specifying surfaces for comfortable, efficient visual work and energy efficiency. Table 8.4 outlines guidelines for typical surface reflectances in work environments for good lighting efficiency. However, as is many times the case with well-intentioned efforts, other factors may also influence final finish selections—there may be a code or legal requirement for some minimum amount of "contrast difference" between key building surfaces for visually impaired people, for example. This may require adjacent surfaces to exhibit at least a 30-point difference in LRV.[12]

There is a common misbelief that changing a given surface finish from matte to specular will increase total reflectance. In some cases, for example, kitchen countertops have been specified as honed (matte) black granite. When the designers are reminded that this countertop will appear dark and that the "counter should have a higher reflectance," the countertop

136 Architectural Lighting Design

specifications are changed from honed granite to polished (specular) granite in the belief that this will reflect more light. This is incorrect—the total visible light reflectance is unchanged from honed to polished. Instead, what little light is reflected from the black granite, will, in the case of polished granite, all reflect in one very specific direction—usually toward the user standing at the countertop attempting to prepare food. This harsh reflection causes veiling reflections and, perhaps, even reflected glare. If the user's eyes happen to be located in the same position as the reflected light is directed, he/she will see a relatively high amount of light in a small area (veiling reflection and/or reflected glare). If the user's eyes are not located in the position of reflected light, he/she will see no reflected light (hence, a black countertop will look dark). The point is this: **unless the user is made aware of the issue in advance and still wishes for dark countertops or work surfaces, the designer should not specify dark countertops or work surfaces, regardless of the finish gloss.**

Reflectances of typical surfaces are reported in Table 8.5. This list is intended to illustrate reflectance values of surfaces that are commonly considered for many applications. However, final selections for the majority of the surfaces in most environments should follow the guidelines in Table 8.4 to achieve best lighting system efficiency.

8.4 Transmittances

Although luminance can be a result of light being reflected from surfaces, they also can result from light being transmitted through various surface types. Surface transmittances as a design goal will depend on the luminance and luminance ratio goals established. Surfaces with high transmission are likely to result in luminance ratios greater than the 1:10 limit between task and distant lighter surfaces (such as windows and bright door sidelights). Even relatively low transmission surfaces, if backlighted by intense sources (e.g., daylight) can result in exceeding

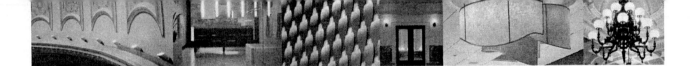

Table 8.3 Luminance Ratios[1, 9, 10]

Intent	Ratio of Interest	Maximum Luminance Ratio
Maintain task attention	• Paper task to computer screen	3:1 or 1:3
	• Task to immediate background surfaces	3:1
	• Task to darker distant background	10:1
	• Task to lighter distant background	1:10
Minimize discomfort glare	• Task to daylight media	1:40
	• Task to luminaires	1:40
	• Daylight media to adjacent surfaces	20:1
	• Luminaires to adjacent surfaces	20:1
Minimize veiling reflections	• Adjacent ceiling zones (positive contrast and/or intensive computer tasks)	4:1
	• Adjacent wall zones (positive contrast and/or intensive computer tasks)	4:1
	• Adjacent ceiling zones (negative contrast and/or intermittent computer tasks)	8:1
	• Adjacent wall zones (negative contrast and/or intermittent computer tasks)	8:1

image-preserving
A transmissive material that allows view through and permits light to pass through.

non-image-preserving
A transmissive material that does not allow view through, but permits light to pass through. Not to be confused with **opaque**.

the luminance ratio of 4:1 from one zone to another (e.g., wall area to window area). Hence, some sort of transmission reduction or light source intensity reduction (the light source behind the transmitting surface) is necessary. If an **image-preserving** transmitting surface has a high transmission, then changing the surface to a **non-image-preserving** surface will not necessarily decrease luminance. Since non-image-preserving materials exhibit either spread or diffuse transmission characteristics, the transmitted light is directed in many directions and, therefore, creates an overall glow or luminance. In fact, luminance may increase, on average, across the entire transmitting surface. This action also negates view benefit through the transmitting surface (which may or may not have been the design intention—for example, a privacy screen

Significance

With negative contrast computer screen, the paper task can be as much as 3 times the luminance of the screen or can be as little as $^1/_3$ the luminance of the screen. Consider 9- to 15-watt LED or CFL task lights. With positive contrast computer screen, the paper task can be as much as 3 times the luminance of the screen. Consider 3- to 9-watt LED or CFL task lights (preferably dimmable).

Task can be as much as 3 times the luminance of the worksurface and surrounding partition/tack surfaces. Can only be achieved with partitions exhibiting 40 percent or greater reflectances.

Task can be as much as 10 times the luminance of distant walls. Requires dark wall surfaces to be accented or washed with light.

Task should not be any less than $^1/_{10}$ the luminance of distant walls. Requires daylighted walls and ceilings to be moderated with medium surface reflectances or shading.

Tasks should not be any less than $^1/_{40}$ the luminance of windows/skylights. Requires window/skylight treatment. Paper tasks require task lighting. Negative contrast computer screens work better than positive contrast screens.

Tasks shouldn't be any less than $^1/_{40}$ the luminance of luminaires. Requires indirect or direct-indirect lights or very-well-controlled, moderate-to-low wattage direct lights. Beware "bare lamp" task lights.

Windows/skylights should not be more than 20 times the luminance of nearby ceiling and wall surfaces. Requires window/skylight treatment and walls exhibiting reflectances of 50% or greater and ceilings exhibiting reflectances of 80% or greater. Dark wall and ceiling finishes create significant problems.

Luminaires should not be more than 20 times the luminance of nearby ceiling and wall surfaces. Requires indirect or direct/indirect lights or very-well-controlled, moderate-to-low wattage direct lights.

One ceiling zone should not be more than 4 times the luminance of an adjacent ceiling zone. To keep "splotchiness" to a minimum, use wide-distribution low-wattage uplights to softly wash the full ceiling. A requirement for work with positive contrast computer screens and/or detailed computer viewing is critical (e.g., CAD work, scientific modeling, medical, and forensics labs).

One wall zone should not be more than 4 times the luminance of an adjacent wall zone. Avoid strong light scallops on walls. If using direct lighting, keep direct lights sufficient distance from wall. A requirement for work with positive contrast computer screens and/or detailed computer viewing is critical (e.g., CAD work, scientific modeling, medical, and forensics labs).

One ceiling zone should not be more than 8 times the luminance of an adjacent ceiling zone. Use wide-distribution indirect or direct-indirect lights to light the ceiling or use well-controlled, moderate-to-low wattage direct lights. A requirement for comfortable working conditions.

One wall zone should not be more than 8 times the luminance of an adjacent wall zone. Use wallwashing or low-wattage art accents. A requirement for comfortable working conditions.

may be a non-image-preserving surface to permit some room light to pass through, but preventing identification of the people in the adjoining space and/or preventing identification of their facial expressions. Figure 8.5 illustrates the concepts of direct transmission, spread transmission, and diffuse transmission respectively. The resulting luminance issue is dependent on both the light source hitting the transmitting surface and the transmission character of the surface.

opaque
A material that does not permit view through and does not permit light to pass through. In other words, opaque materials are not light transmissive.

Illuminances are partly responsible for luminances. As illuminance interacts with surface reflectance or surface transmission, the result is reflected or transmitted light—luminance. As a design goal, then, illuminances are important. Illuminance

8.5 Interior Illuminances

Figure 8.4

Light Reflection/From top to bottom, specular, semi-specular, and diffuse. Specular or mirror-like surfaces have a microscopically smooth surface finish that reflects light in one direction—at an angle opposite but equal to the angle of the incoming light. Specular surfaces are distracting and glary and can be a nuisance in work settings. Specular materials are also known as high-gloss, polished, or shiny and can be light, medium, or dark in value.

Semi-specular surfaces exhibit a microscopically etched surface finish that reflects a majority of the light in one direction and the remainder of the light more diffusely in many other directions. Semi-specular surfaces can be distracting and depending on ambient light conditions may actually veil the true character and quality of the underlying surface material. Semi-specular materials are also known as etched, honed, or brushed and can be light, medium, or dark in value.

Diffuse surfaces exhibit a microscopically textured surface finish that reflects the light rather equally in many different directions. Diffuse surfaces are best for work settings or where user comfort is paramount. Diffuse materials are known as matte or textured or heavily etched and can be light, medium, or dark in value.

This is the angle of incidence (the angle Theta).

This is the angle of reflectance (which is equal to the angle of incidence for specular materials).

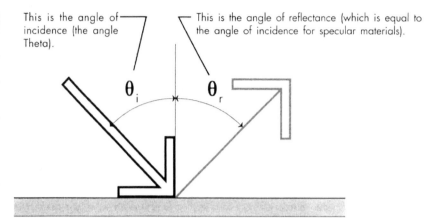

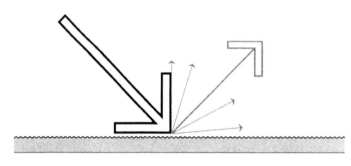

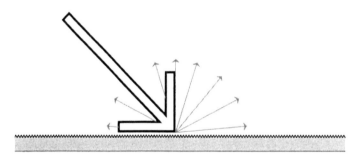

requirements depend on the task or tasks to be performed, on the criticality of the task, and on the users' ages.

Tasks themselves are reflective and/or transmissive in nature. The degree of reflectivity and/or transmissivity involved help to determine the illuminance necessary for accurate, timely task assessment by users. For example, if office workers are decoding special forms that have black dots on dark gray paper (considered a low-contrast task), a fair amount of illuminance will be required just so the workers can detect the black dots against the gray background and identify their location on the form. Alternatively, if the black dots are on white paper (considered a high-contrast task), less illuminance will be necessary to detect the black dots and identify their location on the form.

Indeed, quite a few visual tasks have been reviewed over the years by the Illuminating Engineering Society of North America (IESNA) and for which illuminance criteria are suggested.[13, 14] These listings of visual tasks need to be scrutinized carefully. Footnotes detail special circumstances or conditions surrounding various tasks. Some tasks may sound identical to other visual tasks, but occur in different situations (e.g., health care situation versus office situation) or have a different relationship to the user (e.g., intensive task work or intermittent task work). Illuminance requirements are known to vary depending on task criticality (task importance) and users' ages (see Section 2.6). Previous editions of the *IESNA Handbook* addressed these issues by providing illuminance ranges—lower ends of the ranges were considered appropriate for tasks where criticality was not an issue and/or where users were typically under 40 years of age; middle values of the ranges were considered appropriate for most typical commercial environment situations where task criticality deems some attention and users' ages might typically range from 40 to 55 years of age; higher ends of the ranges were considered appropriate for tasks where criticality was a serious consideration (e.g., pharmacist reading a doctor's prescription and/or reading drug vial labels) and/or where users were over 55 years of age.[15] Unfortunately IESNA documentation as of this publication date no longer provides definitive direction on modifying illuminance values to address issues of task criticality and users' ages. Based on previous editions of the *IESNA Handbook*, on issues cited previously in Section 2.6, and on design experience, Table 8.6 is offered as The Essential Illuminance Guide. Of course, code requirements always take precedent. And other criteria should figure as prominently on any project as illuminance (that's the purpose of the preceding pages of this text). Figure 8.6 illustrates zones of various illuminance needs within a hospitality application.

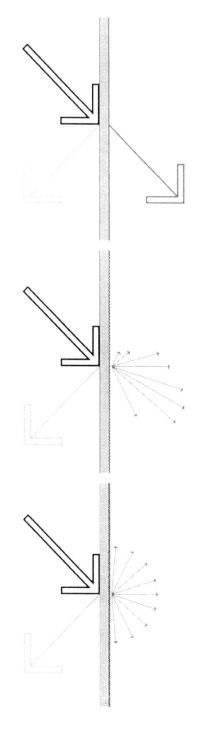

Figure 8.5

Light Transmission/From top to bottom, direct, spread, and diffuse. Direct transmission materials are clear and have a microscopically smooth surface finish that transmits light in a single direction consistent with the direction of incoming light. This may be so concentrated as to cause discomfort or disability glare. In work environments, direct transmission surfaces can be a distraction because light transmits harshly in specific directions. Direct transmission materials are known as image-preserving and can be high, medium, or low in transmission capability.

Spread transmission materials exhibit ribbed or patterned surface finishes and/or lightly translucent fill material that transmit a majority of the light in one direction and the remainder of the light more diffusely in many other directions. Spread transmission materials can be high, medium, or low in transmission capability. Spread transmission surfaces can be distracting and depending on ambient light conditions may actually cause glare or veiling reflections when seen from the wrong viewing angle(s).

Diffuse transmission materials exhibit microscopically textured surface finishes and/or translucent fill material that transmit light in many directions resulting in a soft glow unless the incoming light is too intense, in which case the result is discomfort glare and/or veiling reflections (once the transmitted light hits other surfaces or tasks and reflects back to the user). In work environments, diffuse transmission can be extraordinarily uncomfortable if it is associated with daylight. Not only does the user have no exterior view because of the diffuse glazing, but experiences high degrees of discomfort glare and/or veiling reflections. Diffuse transmission materials are known as matte, textured, heavily etched, or opal, and can be high, medium, or low in transmission capability.

Table 8.4 Reflectance Guidelines

Surface	Suggested Reflectance (matte)[a]	Complying Material (matte)[b]
Ceilings	85 percent or greater	• Premium white tile • Ultra-white tile • White paint
Floors	20 percent or greater	• Medium-to-light carpet • Medium-to-light wood • Medium tile
Partitions and Walls	40 percent or greater	• Light fabrics[c] • Medium-to-light laminates • Medium-to-light paint • Medium-to-light vinyl wall covering • Very light stone • Very light woods

Window Treatments
   image preserving
    (preserve view)
	Match wall reflectances	• Medium value mesh shade[d]
		• Medium value frit pattern
		• Light-to-medium opaque frit pattern

Worksurfaces	20 to 40 percent	• Light woods • Medium-to-light laminates • Medium-to-light ink blotters or desk pads

[a] Some specular trim materials can provide visual interest, but too much is distracting. Contiguous and larger surfaces should be matte finish. Values intended for commercial, institutional work spaces.

[b] See Table 8.5 for a selected list of building materials, some of which comply with these suggested reflectances.

[c] Best acoustically for open plan partitions.

[d] For residential applications, sheer fabrics of high reflectance may be considered traditionally appropriate, however, in sunlight these create significant glare. Sheer fabrics should not be used in commercial, institutional, or hospitality applications. Mesh shades are not sheer and are typified by MechoShade®.

® MechoShade is a registered trademark of MechoShade Systems, Inc.

frit

A ceramic coating that is an integral and permanent part of the glass lite or pane. Usually consists of patterns of white, gray, or black round or square dots or lines. White frit, unless backed by a coating of black frit, exhibits significant luminance when lighted by the sun and becomes a glare source.

Horizontal illuminances are important where visual assessment is of things relatively horizontal in orientation, such as small objects on a floor, irregularities in a floor, or a paper on a table or desk. A fair number of visual tasks, however, are oriented vertically or near-vertical. A significant example is the task of conversation that includes the visual task of facial assessment. Another significant example is in a work environment—the VDT screen. Here, too much light on the screen can wash out text and graphics, so vertical illuminance should be relatively low. Where people use VDTs exclusively, vertical illuminance should be near zero on VDT screens. Where VDTs are used intensively (e.g., typical office situation), vertical illuminances should be moderate.

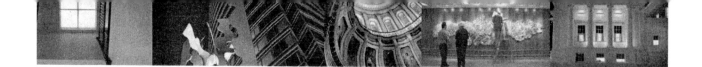

Significance

With available reflectances approaching 90 percent, this is a simple way to greatly improve electric and daylighting efficiency.

Most ceiling manufacturers have a "standard, best" white tile exhibiting reflectance of 85 percent with little or no first-cost impact.

Most paint manufacturers have a "bright white" paint exhibiting reflectance of 85 percent with little or no first-cost impact.

Enhances overall room perception. Greatly improves overall workstation perception. Lighter flooring will require more frequent maintenance cycles.

Efficient means of meeting luminance limits outlined in Table 8.2 and balancing luminance ratios outlined in Table 8.3. Enhances overall room perception. Greatly improves overall workstation perception.

Although dark mesh shade best preserves view to exterior, the interior may feel oppressive and/or the mesh shade may contrast too greatly with other interior walls. Avoid white or very light value mesh shade.

Light-value frit coatings may be too transparent and may create a greater glare problem than if no frit is used.

Opaque frits best limit daylight glare and best preserve view. May require a double-frit coating to achieve opacity.

Avoid dark woods and dark stains. Consider lighter-finished maple, poplar, pine, oak, birch, ash, and bamboo. For worksurfaces where paperwork and/or negative-contrast computer screens are prevalent, select matte surfaces with 30 to 40 percent reflectance.

Avoid saturated colors as backdrops for worksurfaces. Where paperwork and/or negative contrast computer screens are prevalent, select matte surfaces with 30 to 40 percent reflectance.

Black or dark ink blotters or desk pads are too much contrast against white paper and/or negative contrast computer screens. Avoid glass "protectors" as polished surface results in harsh, glary reflections.

To minimize energy use and to maximize visual interest in any environment, it is recommended that several layers of lighting be used to achieve all of the appropriate horizontal and vertical illuminances for a given situation. The three layers of light are 1) ambient, 2) task, and 3) accent (or architectural). Ambient or general lighting is intended to be a base level of general light throughout an area or space. Task light is intended to augment the ambient light so that appropriate illuminances are achieved on task areas. Accent light is used to provide illuminance on elements of visual interest, such as special architectural details or artwork. This accent light also serves to help balance luminances in a space (see Tables 7.1 and 8.3).

Table 8.5   Typical Reflectance Values[16]

Category	Material	Typical Reflectance (%)[a]
Diffuse	• Brick	
	Dark buff	35 to 40
	Light buff	40 to 45
	Red	10 to 20
	• Granite	20 to 25
	• Gray cement	20 to 30
	• Limestone	35 to 60
	• Marble	30 to 70
	• Sandstone	20 to 40
	• White paint	75 to 90
	• White Plaster	90 to 92
	• White terra cotta	66 to 80
	• Wood	
	Beech[b]	26
	Birch[b]	35
	Cherry[b]	20
	Mahogany	6 to 12
	Maple[b]	54
	Oak, dark	10 to 15
	Oak, light	25 to 35
	Pine, Oregon[b]	38
	Pine, Red[b]	49
	Pine, White[b]	51
	Poplar[b]	52
	Walnut	5 to 10
Specular	• Aluminum	
	Alzak® polished	85
	Coilzak® polished	90
	Polished	60 to 70
	• Chromium	63 to 66
	• Clear vision glass (high transmission)[c]	5 to 20
	• Silver	90 to 99
	• Stainless steel	55 to 65
	• White porcelain enamel	65 to 90

[a] Some specular trim materials can provide visual interest, but too much is distracting. Contiguous and larger surfaces should be matte finish. Values intended for commercial, institutional work spaces.

[b] From *Energy Design Guidelines for High Performance Schools*, 2002, U.S. Department of Energy.

[c] Reflectance value is percent of reflected light from the *inside* surface of the glass. From a survey of glass manufacturers' literature.

® Alzak and ® Coilzak are registered tradenames of Alcoa.

8.6 Exterior Illuminances

The illuminance targets outlined in Table 8.6 are for interior and exterior spaces/ areas and tasks and are based on high-CRI, white-light sources. Studies and experience show that white light is more effective in low-light situations than monochromatic yellow sources.[17, 18, 19] Most exterior applications have much different requirements—for two reasons. First, outdoor applications of electric light are important for nighttime situations. Here, the eyes are essentially dark-adapted, and

not much illuminance is necessary to elicit a response. Second, most nighttime outdoor tasks involve relatively large objects (e.g., are there obstacles on the sidewalk, are there pedestrians in the street, etc.). The single largest issue with exterior lighting is the preponderance of overlighted applications. Unfortunately, particularly in the United States, an attitude of "more is better" is pervasive. Competition among retailers, particularly fueling stations and auto dealerships, has resulted in ratcheting of illuminances to absurd levels. The illuminance criteria outlined here are intended as maintained targets—see the discussion below on targets. Gross overdesigning is not an option—this results in energy waste and exacerbates light pollution and light trespass. The uniformity criteria help maintain senses of safety and security and serve to minimize unsettling shadows. Exterior focals should be based on luminance ratios cited in Table 7.1. So, for example, a car sales lot in an urban setting should be lighted to 2.4 fc (exactly 25 cd/m^2). If there is a desire to accent special vehicles, and using Table 7.1 guidance of 10 to 1 for "retail select displays," then the special vehicles should be lighted to 24 fc (exactly 260 cd/m^2) or less. With high color rendering lamps (lamps with a CRI greater than 80), these accented vehicles will command attention without gross glare or energy consumption. Of course, the accent lighting should be timed off at a reasonable curfew to further limit energy use and to reduce light annoyance to neighbors.

8.7 Targets

With the exception of egress lighting requirements, illuminance targets are intended to be just that—the target to which the designer should design the lighting system. Calculational inaccuracies, as well as in situ voltage and construction fluctuations (e.g., actual paint reflectance), and field measurement accuracies affect final illuminance outcomes. Designs are considered to be in compliance with target criteria when calculational predictions show illuminances to be within 10 percent. End results in the built setting that are within 20 percent are considered in compliance. However, where surface finishes vary significantly from commonly accepted norms for efficient lighting (see Table 8.4), end results may be as much as 25 to 50 percent of criterion target. This can be a point of contention between decorators/interior designers/architects and lighting designers/engineers. To develop efficient, more sustainable lighting solutions and since lighting is designed early in the project sequence, most lighting designs are based on very high surface reflectances. Except as minor accents, using dark finishes for drama or visual impact or as a designer's signature is simply bad practice in today's environment.

Illuminance Targets
Propose illuminance targets for the various spaces observed in Figures 7.6 (bottom), 7.7 (bottom and opposite), 7.8 (bottom and opposite), 8.3a, b, c, and d. Include all assumptions.

8.8 Endnotes

[1] Matthew Luckiesh and S. K. Guth, "Brightnesses in Visual Field at Borderline Between Comfort and Discomfort (BCD)," *Illuminating Engineering*, November 1949, vol. 44: 650–670.

[2] Gary R. Steffy, *Lighting the Electronic Office* (New York: Van Nostrand Reinhold, 1995), p. 55.

[3] James E. Sheedy, Rob Smith, and John Hayes, John, 'Visual effects of the luminance surrounding a computer display," Ergonomics, 2005, 48:9, 1114–1128.

[4] G.R. Newsham, R.G. Marchand, J.A. Vietch, Preferred surface luminances in offices, by evolution, 2004, http://irc.nrccnrc.gc.ca/pubs/fulltext/nrcc46976/nrcc46976.pdf. [Accessed October 6, 2007.]

[5] Gary R. Steffy, *Lighting the Electronic Office* (New York: Van Nostrand Reinhold, 1995), pp. 79–84.

[6] CIBSE, *Addendum to CIBSE Lighting Guide 3* (London, Chartered Institution of Building Services Engineers, 2001), p. 4.

[7] Mark S. Rea, ed. *The IESNA Lighting Handbook: Reference and Application, Ninth Edition* (New York: Illuminating Engineering Society of North America, 2000), chapter 11.

Table 8.6 The Essential Illuminance Guide[13, 14, 15]

Tasks	Discussion	Typical Application Examples
Exterior/Low Activity —low activity urban or suburban —country	• Casual passage, low-activity pedestrian zones, low-activity parking	• Ceremonial publicways • Park walkways, typical sidewalks • Small commercial parking zones, local roadways • Small-town college campus
Exterior/High Activity —high activity urban or suburban	• Pedestrian zones, parking	• Community plazas • Town squares/city centers, busy sidewalks • Large commercial parking zones, major roadways • Large or city university campus
Exterior/Interior —important nodes	• Destination/arrival zones where vehicles and pedestrians interact • Interior areas of casual passage	• Dropoffs (small-town commuter stations, apartments), building entries, car lots, service stations • Clubs • Historic and/or elegant interiors' circulation
Exterior/Interior —congested and significant nodes —residential interiors —historic interiors —hospitality interiors	• Key destination/arrival zones with much vehicular and pedestrian traffic interface • Interior areas of passage, leisure, respite and/or where tasks are internally lighted	• Porte cocheres (hotels, malls) • Dropoffs (metro commuter stations, malls) and building entries • Atria (add task lighting as necessary) • Ceremonial public spaces, lobbies, vestibules • Concourses, interior passages (stairs/ramps/horizontal circulation) • Historic and/or elegant interiors, restaurants and bars • Rotundas • Exclusively computers (CAD, call centers, drug design)
Interior —simple orientation for short visits —restful interludes —commercial interiors	Areas of deliberate and necessary passage and/or of conversational activity and/or of limited casual reading	• Atria • Dining rooms • Elevators • Lobbies, vestibules • Restrooms • Concourses, interior passages (vertical/horizontal circulation) • Rotundas
Working spaces where simple visual tasks are performed	Areas of casual and/or recreational reading or where periodic paper task performance is required and/or extensive VDT use occurs	• Restrooms, residential master bathrooms • Copyrooms, casual reading, religious naves • Dining rooms/multipurpose meeting rooms • Library stacks (K-12/youth, vertical at 30" AFF) • Lounges, reception areas, waiting areas, fitness centers • Ceremonial offices, computer-intensive offices
Performance of visual tasks of high contrast or large size	Areas of prolonged discourse and/or where visual work is typically easy to read, or where hard-to-read paperwork is intermittent	• Committee rooms, hearing rooms, intermittent reading • Conference rooms, meeting rooms, classrooms, videoconferencing • Hair-styling studios (on faces) • Library stacks • Offices—computer/paper tasks mixed
Performance of visual tasks of medium contrast or small size	Areas of prolonged assessment of consistently difficult to read documents or detailed 3-dimensional tasks	• Accounting ledgers (hardcopy) • Bank tellers' stations • Commercial research laboratories • Hair-styling studios (on tops of heads) • Blueprints or hardcopy drawings • Intermediate and high school science labs • Detailed/laborious/critical visual tasks

(solution) *SOLUTION HINT: In many situations with targets of 10 fc or more, efficiency improves when ambient lighting provides $1/3$ to $1/2$ of the illuminance with task lighting providing the remainder.*

[a] All values cited are guidelines for consideration and intended to be average, maintained targets achieved on the task area.

[b] Where circulation spaces are listed, targets are intended to apply to floor plane. Where workspaces are listed, targets are intended to apply to horizontal work surface. Where tasks are listed, targets are intended to apply to the plane of interest on which task is located.

[c] For dark pavement or dark surface finishes and/or where users' ages are 40 to 55 years, consider increasing base illuminance targets by 50% as represented here.

Baseline ~ *exterior*: country/*interior*: casual/transient task situations or work settings for people under-40

First Degree ~ *exterior*: suburban/*interior*: typical life/work task situations

Second Degree ~ *exterior*: urban/*interior*: pressured task situations or work settings for people over-55

Baseline[a,b]	First Degree[a,b,c]	Second Degree[a,b,d]	Uniformity		IESNA[f]
Illuminance Target Value (average, maintained)[e]			Average-to-minimum	Maximum-to-minimum	Target
0.3 fc	0.4 fc	0.6 fc	2:1	4:1	Varies

horizontal on grade and either half-this-level vertical at face height for normal situations or
full-level vertical at face height where pedestrian activity is high and/or senses of security/safety are considered crucial

0.6 fc	0.8 fc	1.2 fc	2:1	4:1	Varies

horizontal on grade and either half-this-level vertical at face height for normal situations or
full-level vertical at face height where pedestrian activity is high and/or senses of security/safety are considered crucial

1.2 fc	1.6 fc	2.4 fc	2:1	6:1	3 fc

horizontal on grade or floor and either quarter-this-level vertical at face height for normal situations or
half-this-level vertical at face height where people activity is very high and/or senses of security/safety are considered crucial

2.4 fc	3.2 fc	5.0 fc	2:1	6:1	3 fc

exterior: horizontal on grade and either quarter-this-level vertical at face height for normal situations or
half-this-level vertical at face height where people activity is very high and/or senses of security/safety are considered crucial

interior: horizontal on "task" surfaces (counters, desks, laps) and
half-this-level vertical at face height for social situations and even less for exclusively-computer-work

5.0 fc	7.5 fc	10 fc	3:1	6:1	5 fc

horizontal on "task" surfaces (counters, desks, laps)
full-level vertical at face height for grooming
quarter-this-level vertical at face height for social situations

10 fc	15 fc	20 fc	3:1	6:1	10 fc

horizontal on "task" surfaces (counters, desks, laps)
full-level vertical at face height for grooming
half-this-level vertical at 30" AFF for library stacks
quarter-this-level vertical at face height for social situations and even less for computer-intensive offices

20 fc	30 fc	50 fc	3:1	6:1	30 fc

horizontal on "task" surfaces
half-this-level to full-level vertical at face height for videoconferencing (camera dependent)
full-level vertical at face height for hair-styling
half-this-level vertical at 30" AFF for library stacks

50 fc	75 fc	100 fc	3:1	6:1	50 fc

horizontal on "task" surfaces

[d] For dark pavement or dark surface finishes or where visual component of tasks are life- or fiscally-critical and/or where most users' ages are 55 years or greater or where motorized personal mobility devices/pedestrian interfaces occur (e.g., electric wheelchairs, scooters, Segways, etc. interfacing with pedestrians) or where monochromatic sources (e.g., high pressure sodium) will be used, consider increasing base illuminance targets by 100% as represented here.

[e] Calculations within 10 percent of target values are considered acceptable. Field results within 20 percent of target values are considered acceptable.

[f] IESNA targets are based on interpretation of reference 13. Alternative interpretations may result in lower or higher values.

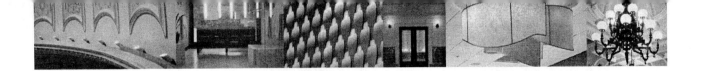

Figure 8.6

Illuminances/Target illuminances (taken from Table 8.6 and its references) for a variety of space/task types are outlined for a hospitality project. Although illuminances help with code compliance, liability issues associated with traversing areas, and performing such other visual tasks as reading, it is the luminances that set the mood, establish sense of place, and elicit users' positive (or negative) reactions.

Images ©2007 Kevin Beswick.

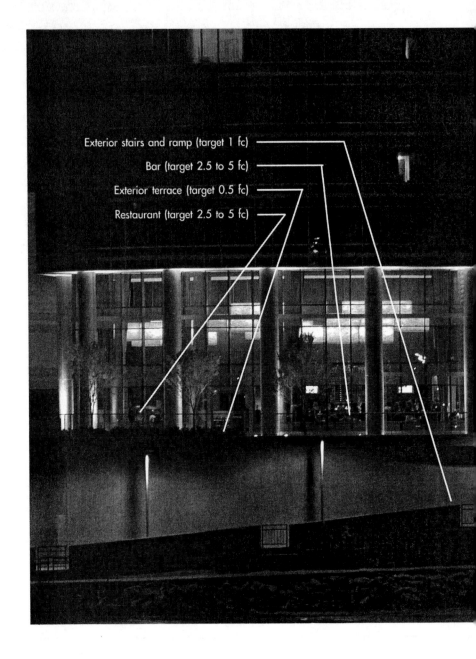

Exterior stairs and ramp (target 1 fc)

Bar (target 2.5 to 5 fc)

Exterior terrace (target 0.5 fc)

Restaurant (target 2.5 to 5 fc)

porte cochere

A feature of large French homes is an entrance, typically of two large wooden carved doors, through which a wheeled carriage or vehicle can pass to an interior, open court. The term is commonly used in America to identify a canopy under which vehicles may pass to disembark passengers. For example, many large hotels have porte cocheres. See Figure 11.6.

[8] IESNA Office Lighting Committee, *American National Standard Practice for Office Lighting* (New York: Illuminating Engineering Society of North America, 2004), p. 45.

[9] Mark S. Rea, ed. *The IESNA Lighting Handbook: Reference and Application, Ninth Edition* (New York: Illuminating Engineering Society of North America, 2000), pp. 11-3 and 19-4.

[10] Illuminating Engineering Society, *IES Lighting Handbook, Second Edition* (New York: Illuminating Engineering Society, 1952), pp. 10-58 and 10-69.

[11] Gary Steffy, *Time-Saver Standards for Architectural Lighting* (New York: McGraw-Hill, 2000), p. 9-9.

[12] Office of the Deputy Prime Minister, The Building Regulations 2000 Access to and use of Buildings Approved Document M, 2004 edition (London: NBS, 2006), p. 16.

[13] Mark S. Rea, ed. *The IESNA Lighting Handbook: Reference and Application, Ninth Edition* (New York: Illuminating Engineering Society of North America, 2000), chapter 10.

[14] Gary Steffy, Rational Illuminance, *Leukos*, 2006, no. 4, pp. 235–261.

[15] Mark S. Rea, ed. *The IESNA Lighting Handbook: Reference and Application, Eighth Edition* (New York: Illuminating Engineering Society of North America, 1993), chapter 11.

[16] Mark S. Rea, ed. *The IESNA Lighting Handbook: Reference and Application, Ninth Edition* (New York: Illuminating Engineering Society of North America, 2000), p. 1-22.

Elevator lobby (target 5 fc)

Elevator lobby (target 5 fc)

Atrium or lobby (target 5 fc)

Reception (target 20 fc with task to 100 fc for focal on granite counter)

Lobby (target 10 fc with task to 15 fc for casual reading)

Exterior stairs and ramp (target 1 fc)

Exterior terrace (target 0.5 fc)

[17] Y. He, M. Rea, A. Bierman, and J. Bullough, Evaluating Light Source Efficacy Under Mesopic Conditions Using Reaction Times, *Journal of the Illuminating Engineering Society*, Winter 1997, (IESNA JIES, 1997), pp. 125–138.

[18] A. L. Lewis, Equating Light Sources for Visual Performance at Low Luminances, *Journal of the Illuminating Engineering Society*, Winter 1998, (IESNA JIES, 1998), pp. 80–84.

[19] Alan Lewis, Visual Performance as a Function of Spectral Power Distribution of Light Sources at Luminances Used for General Outdoor Lighting, *Journal of the Illuminating Engineering Society*, Winter 1999 (IESNA JIES, 1999), pp. 37–42.

8.9 References

Agoston, G.A. 1987. *Color Theory and Its Application in Art and Design*. Berlin: Springer-Verlag.

Rea, Mark S., ed., and Thompson, Brian J., general ed. 1992. *Selected Papers on Architectural Lighting*. Bellingham, WA: SPIE Optical Engineering Press.

Rea, Mark S., ed. 2000. *The IESNA Lighting Handbook: Reference & Application, Ninth Edition*. New York: Illuminating Engineering Society of North America.

Rea, Mark S., ed. 1993. *The IESNA Lighting Handbook: Reference & Application, Eighth Edition*. New York: Illuminating Engineering Society of North America.

Energy crises, renewable energy sources, sustainability, and health and well-being have renewed the interest in daylighting. Although these are, indeed, serious issues, it is much too easy to get caught in the whirlwind of political correctness and jump headlong into "daylighting" without appreciating the issues. Treating daylighting solely as an architectural design feature or strictly as a means to generating more illuminance will likely wreak havoc on the occupants. Indeed, all light and dark need to be treated with great care, regardless of their source(s). Daylight's dynamic qualities are both a bane and a boon and must be addressed accordingly for success. Figure 9.1 illustrates this variability in monumental and dramatic fashion.

Daylighting, like all lighting, should be considered from the occupants' perspectives. While many, if not all, occupants want a view to the exterior, few, if any, can discern a daylight footcandle (or lux) from an electric light footcandle (or lux). So, while no one wants to waste energy or earth resources, neither does anyone want to be debilitated by glare, reflected glare, or uncomfortable extreme contrasts or solar heat to get a few footcandles "free." Indeed, a steep price to pay for this free light is an uncomfortable occupant. Unfettered daylight, or worse, daylight restrained improperly, can result in glare, task washout, veiling reflections, and adaptation effects that can seriously limit the occupants' levels of comfort, desire to remain in the space, and ability to perform tasks whether for work or pleasure.

Any light that the sun produces and that strikes the earth directly, indirectly, or both is daylight. This includes sunlight (direct from the solar disc), sky light (whether clear or cloudy or somewhere in between), and sunlight and/or sky light reflected from other surfaces (e.g., the ground, other buildings, bodies of water, and the like, except the moon—which is considered moonlight).

Many books have been written on daylight—as a design and engineering medium, as a health medium, and as a sustainable medium. So, the following text covers the primary issues and offers some direction toward avoiding serious blunders. This is presented on the basis that improperly using an ostensibly sustainable source like daylight will lead to discomfort and human inefficiency—a real waste of energy and resources and the ultimate slap to sustainability.

Daylighting involves several distinct criteria—view, health, illuminance, and sustainability. It is common to develop a daylighting approach on any project based on any one of these criteria, several of these criteria, or all of these criteria. However, daylighting's best implementation is as a holistic approach—one where the site, architecture, interiors, and lighting *all* are designed to best take advantage of and successfully deliver daylighting. This requires a new-construction or significant-reconstruction project, a dedicated client, dedicated teamwork, and sufficient fees, schedule, and budget. This might be called an integrated or **holistic daylighting** approach. Another way to approach daylighting is simply more traditionally as another light source—perhaps rather reactive given daylighting's potential. In this situation, whatever siting is given and whatever **fenestration** is provided, the best scenarios with window treatment, interior finishes and layouts, luminance balancing, and control of electric lights are explored.

holistic daylighting

Making a conscious decision at project commencement to develop the building architecture, interiors, and lighting to maximize the impact of daylighting—daylighting is *the* priority driving lighting techniques and fenestration, which drive building siting, massing, proportions and skin, interior layouts and finishes, etc. A paradigm shift in design.

fenestra

Latin for window. In the context of this discussion, used to mean any daylight aperture. Fenestration, then, is the arrangement of daylight apertures—which might be windows, skylights, clerestories, roof monitors, etc.

Figure 9.1

Daylight is desirable for its dynamic qualities. Here, the roughly south-facing Mount Rushmore illustrates these varying qualities of daylight. (Top) On clear days, early morning sun exhibits relatively horizontal light. Details are subtle, but evident. For interior situations, any occupants on east exposures with untreated vision glass experience harsh direct glare for perhaps an hour or so. Same situation occurs late afternoon on west exposures.

(Second) On clear days, mid-morning to mid-afternoon sun exhibits strong angled light. Details are crisp and sharp. For interior situations, any occupants on south exposures (in the northern hemisphere) with untreated vision glass and/or no architectural shade control experience harsh direct glare for perhaps much of the day.

(Third) On cloudy days, daylight exhibits relatively flat light. Details are softened, but distinctly evident. For interior situations, occupants on any exposure with untreated vision glass may experience fatique from overlighting and high background luminance of the sky.

(Bottom) When daylight is insufficient, electric light is used. Of course, electric light cannot match daylight intensities or quality. By comparison, then, details are washed out and orientationally altered. Nevertheless, the monument can be seen and enjoyed after sunset. NOTE: Gary Steffy Lighting Design did not provide lighting consultation on this project.

First (Top) Image ©Corbis Singles 027 Collection/Corbis
Second Image ©Photodisc Green Collection/Getty Images
Third Image ©Purestock Singles Collection 8/Superstock
Fourth (Bottom) Image ©2007 JupiterImages Corporation

Architectural Lighting Design

Since most projects are renovation or rehabilitation efforts, architectural siting and envelopes are not design opportunities. Here, **conditional daylighting** is the only practical approach if daylighting is identified and agreed as an important role-player in the project. New glazing and shade-control may be opportunities for maximizing the daylight potential as may new interior layouts and finishes.

Many projects are designed with priority on appearance and/or cost and/or schedule. Any one or all of these priorities significantly affects the success of daylighting. Indeed, in these situations **fractional daylighting** is often the only approach to be implemented by any one or several or all of the team members. Whatever daylighting strategy or strategies can be implemented with little or no influence on the overall appearance, cost, and/or schedule are implemented. Although this catch-as-catch-can approach is likely not to be the success of holistic or even conditional daylighting approaches, anything is better than nothing providing user satisfaction and performance are not sacrificed. Unfortunately, these fractional strategies are easy targets for so-called value engineering and many times are deleted with unintended consequences on lighting qualities and quantities.

Regardless of the holistic, conditional, or fractional approach, the more successful daylighting strategies demand that the design team work together closely. Ultimately, addressing daylighting luminances is crucial for success from the occupants' perspectives. Since daylight exhibits luminances readily capable of creating glare or veiling reflections, these aspects must be addressed meticulously and collectively. For example, if the architect and lighting designer collaborate on a daylighting scheme, but the interior designer is not part of the design process or makes decisions based on style over functionality, then errors in interiors aspects might include use of low (dark) reflectance surfaces, specular (shiny or polished) surfaces, misorientation and/or positions-relative-to-windows of workstations and computer screens, and/or selection of improper shading treatments, to name a few.

conditional daylighting
Making the most of the given siting and architectural situation — daylighting is conditional on siting and architecture, but is the priority driving interior layouts and finishes, glazing selections and shade treatments, and electric lighting design and integration.

fractional daylighting
Daylighting is overshadowed by such priorities as appearance, cost, and/or project schedule. Convenient and low-or-no-cost daylighting strategies might be implemented on a piecemeal basis.

9.1 Benefits

Daylighting has many benefits, some not so obvious. Daylighting can improve operating costs, reduce emissions, and enliven the setting. Although succinct, this is a list rich with opportunities.

Operating costs for electric lighting and HVAC can be influenced by daylighting—in a good way with appropriate design. Where daylighting is used as a primary or supplementary source of illuminance and/or luminance, electric lights can be continuously dimmed, step-dimmed, step-switched to partial off, or switched off completely. These actions reduce **electricity costs** for the lighting, may extend the life of some or all of the lighting system components, and in the cooling season may reduce energy costs associated with air conditioning. With daylighting, baseline direct energy costs for electric lighting are simply reduced in proportion to the percentage of electric lighting watts not used. Additionally, demand charges are less when electric lighting watts are reduced during "prime use" hours (usually 9 a.m. to 9 p.m.). Finally, as the amount of total electricity used is reduced, the premium electricity charges are reduced.

electricity costs
Electricity costs for most commercial buildings in the US are comprised of baseline energy cost (which depends on source of electricity— coal-generated power usually exhibits a lower retail cost to the consumer than nuclear), demand charges based on time-of-day (costs are higher when demand is higher, typically midday), and cost for any amount required over and above the utility's baseline rate (essentially a premium charge for ever greater amounts of energy).

Where lights are step-switched to partial off or switched off completely in response to daylight, the lamps and ballasts will experience extended in-service life. This reduces replacement cycles, reduces landfill waste, recycling energy, fabrication energy associated with new replacement components, and transportation energy associated with disposal and new replacement components. This is similar to results which can be achieved with motion sensors and timeclocks.

Daylighting may also reduce HVAC operating and initial system costs. During the cooling season or whenever the air conditioning system is engaged to cool interiors, the use of electric lights contributes to a higher heat load that must be cooled. Daylighting allows for some electric lights to be dimmed or switched off, thereby eliminating some heat and allowing the air conditioning to operate less frequently or to a reduced capacity. This further reduces electricity use. Recognize, however, that there must be a balance between visible light transmittance and **shading coefficient** or **solar heat gain coefficient** when selecting the various fenestration media. Many media which exhibit high T_{vis} also exhibit relatively high infrared transmission. Even if daylighting is comfortable for the occupants, solar gain through the glazing may be undesirable if not unbearable. Coordinate glazing selections with the mechanical engineer.

Reduction in electricity use will yield a reduction in noxious emissions if local utility power plants are coal or gas driven. There is a bonus effect whereby the daylighting reduces electricity use during the same hours when ozone formation is most likely. If power is generated by hydro or nuclear, then electricity reductions from daylighting will effectively reduce the need for additional power plants for other new construction or new manufacturing processes.

The dynamic quality of daylight enlivens the built environment. Color temperature varies with time of day and sky conditions. Color rendering also varies with time of day and sky conditions and is usually considered superior to any manmade light source. Luminances and illuminances vary with time of day and sky conditions. These variations arguably serve to motivate and exhilarate occupants.[1] Many occupants have a preference for daylight, but this seems related most strongly to view out.[2]

Daylight resets the circadian rhythm. As discussed in Sections 2.9 and 7.5, daylight of sufficient intensity and duration during waking hours is necessary. While best achieved with daily exposures to the outdoor environment, daylighting situations in the built setting can meet this need. However, and this cannot be overstated, the intensities of daylight needed are greater than most people are willing to tolerate throughout most daily tasks (e.g., 250 fc [about 2500 lx] for a few hours or 1000 fc [about 10,000 lx] for about twenty minutes). A "bright daylight" break room or "sun porch" would be one means of introducing high levels of daylight without negatively affecting typical work and living environments.

more online @
www.lrc.rpi.edu/programs/daylighting/pdf/DaylightBenefits.pdf

shading coefficient (SC)
The ratio of solar heat gain through a specific glazing system to that through a reference glazing system comprised only of $^1/_8''$ glass (about 3 mm). Lower values represent better shading (less heat entering the building through the glazing system). Look at/through glazing samples before making selections based solely on technical performance data.

solar heat gain coefficient (SHGC)
Replaces shading coefficient. The ratio of solar heat impinging on the exterior of a glazing system to that exiting the interior of a glazing system. Lower values represent better shading (less heat entering the building through the glazing system). Look at/through glazing samples before making selections based solely on technical performance data.

9.2 Design Aspects

There is one overarching philosophy with any daylighting design. Daylighting cannot be considered as an architectural option or "add-on" if the building is to be successful. Daylighting and architecture must be one. Even if fractional daylighting is as good as can be had on a project, the architecture and/or interiors must work in

concert with the daylighting technique(s) for best benefit. This is a crucial aspect of sustainability—making the most of Earth resources. Does it make Earth-sense to cut a hole in the roof if the floor below will be dark in finish, and/or the ceiling will be unfinished, and/or the room will be relatively tiny and/or the space seldom used—like a toilet room, for example? Does it make sense to cut in floor-to-ceiling windows where the perimeter space will be left to circulation or where furnishings will be shoved up against the outside wall? Do windows on the sunny exposure of a tall-ceiling office building in a predominantly sunny clime (see Table 9.1 and related Figure 9.2) with no surrounding structures and little natural shading make sense if **light shelf** or shading techniques can't be employed?

Although powerful design tools exist for evaluation of daylighting strategies and development of daylighting techniques, many of the design decisions are based on common sense. The lighting design parameters associated with electric lighting *and* daylighting are discussed in Chapters 4, 5, and 6. Key aspects particularly associated with daylighting success or failure are visual comfort, surface reflectances, surface configurations, and uniformity.

more online @
www.energydesignresources.com/category/daylighting/
www.energydesignresources.com/docs/dl-02.pdf
windows.lbl.gov/daylighting/designguide/dlg.pdf
www.lrc.rpi.edu/programs/daylighting/dr_designguides.asp
www.newbuildings.org/lighting.htm
www.wbdg.org/design/daylighting.php

light shelf
A horizontal or near-horizontal shelf located inboard of wall and positioned above standing eye height (to allow exterior views) and above which a window or clerestory extends several feet. Top of shelf is finished in high-reflectance matte white in order to capture and diffusely reflect sunbeams onto the interior ceiling. See Figure 9.3.

Visual Comfort

Glare is always a potential deal-breaker with lighting, regardless of how the light is generated. With daylighting, the magnitude of the issue is many times greater than possible with electric lighting. Two important points about daylight visual comfort—1) elimination or limitation of direct view of the glare source and 2) magnitude of surrounding luminances—will determine the success of the solution. To reduce the severity of daylight glare, avoid direct view of the solar disc, minimize sunbeaming onto readily viewed or seen interior surfaces, and establish an overall uniformly bright background.

First, what is the potential for glare? If the climate is predominantly clear and/or partly cloudy, the solar disc will be visible in the sky quite frequently (Table 9.1 outlines average sky conditions for some US cities). Siting the building can limit direct visual access to the solar disc—in the northern hemisphere, this results in primarily north-exposure views. Integrated fenestration elements can limit direct visual access to the solar disc—fixed-view-orientations away from primary sun angles require more significant architectural form work, while overhangs, **brise soleils**, horizontal or vertical louvers, landscaping, and awnings require less architectural forming, but still affect aesthetics and overall appearance to varying degrees (see Figure 9.3). However, **any one of these techniques alone will not alleviate the problem**. Again, daylighting is much like electric lighting. Just like insisting that a 4-foot-long, 32-watt, T8 fluorescent lamp must be used exclusively as the lamp for a given project, insisting that landscaping, for example, will solve the glare problems is foolish. **Multiple techniques need to be reviewed and some combination implemented to achieve good results most of the time for most occupants.**

brise soleil
French for sun break. A device mounted on the exterior of the building that consists of appropriately spaced/proportioned louvers, mesh, and/or tubular elements that effectively limit direct view of the sun without the mass of overhangs or impermanence of awnings. See Figure 9.4.

Table 9.1 — Annual Average Sky Conditions/Select US Cities[3]

Predominant conditions can be used to establish the design parameters and priorities. For example, areas where clear and/or partly cloudy sky conditions prevail year-round are good candidates for light shelves—to act both as shade control and reflectors—or for fixed shading devices. Where clear conditions are seasonal (the source data for this table are available by month), shade treatments need only respond to limited sun angles and/or need not be permanent to allow greater access to the diffuse cloudy-sky conditions. Figure 9.2 outlines latitude, longitude, and daylight-relevant astronomic parameters.

CL (clear)
Denotes 0 to 30 percent average sky cover during daylight hours.

PC (partly cloudy)
Denotes 40 to 70 percent average sky cover during daylight hours.

CD (cloudy)
Denotes 80 to 100 percent average sky cover during daylight hours.

Location[a]	Latitude/Longitude	CL[b]	PC[b]	CD[b]
Alabama, Montgomery	N 32:22:54/W 86:18:30	107	107	151
Alaska, Anchorage	N 61:13:5/W 149:54:1	61	65	239
Arizona, Phoenix	N 33:26:54/W 112:4:24	211	85	70
California, Los Angeles County	N 34:3:8/W 118:14:33	186	106	73
California, San Francisco	N 37:46:30/W 122:25:6	160	100	105
District of Columbia, Washington	N 38:53:42/W 77:2:12	96	106	164
Florida, Miami	N 25:46:26/W 80:7:49	74	175	115
Georgia, Atlanta	N 33:44:56/W 84:23:16	110	107	149
Illinois, Chicago	N 41:50:59/W 87:39:0	84	105	176
Indiana, Indianapolis	N 39:46:6/W 86:9:29	88	99	179
Kansas, Topeka	N 39:2:53/W 95:40:40	114	97	154
Louisiana, New Orleans	N 29:57:16/W 90:4:29	101	118	146
Massachusetts, Boston	N 42:21:30/W 71:3:37	98	103	164
Michigan, Detroit	N 42:20:32/W 83:3:39	75	105	185
Minnesota, Minneapolis	N 44:58:47/W 93:15:48	95	101	169
Mississippi, Tupelo	N 34:15:26/W 88:42:11	119	97	150
Nevada, Las Vegas	N 36:10:29/W 115:8:11	210	82	73
New York, New York	N 40:42:51/W 74:0:22	96	117	153
Ohio, Columbus	N 39:57:40/W 82:59:55	72	103	190
Oklahoma, Oklahoma City	N 35:28:2/W 97:30:58	139	96	130
Oregon, Portland	N 45:31:23/W 122:40:33	68	74	222
Pennsylvania, Philadelphia	N 39:57:7/W 75:9:51	93	112	160
Tennessee, Nashville	N 36:9:56/W 86:47:4	102	106	156
Texas, Dallas	N 32:46:52/W 96:47:34	135	97	133
Utah, Salt Lake City	N 40:45:39/W 111:53:24	125	101	139
Virginia, Roanoke	N 37:16:14/W 79:56:29	102	112	151
Washington, Seattle County	N 47:36:22/W 122:19:51	71	93	201
Wisconsin, Madison	N 43:4:22/W 89:24:3	89	96	180

[a] 20-year-plus data for this city from United States National Oceanic and Atmospheric Association (NOAA).

[b] Average number of days for respective sky condition.

Figure 9.2

In the northern hemisphere, summer solstice occurs when sun is over Tropic of Cancer, winter solstice occurs when sun is over Tropic of Capricorn, and equinoxes occur when sun is over equator. Equinox exhibits 12 hours of darkness and 12 hours of daylight (Latin for equal night and day). Spring equinox is vernal equinox and fall equinox is autumnal equinox.
Image ©Photodisc/Global Perspectives/ Getty Images

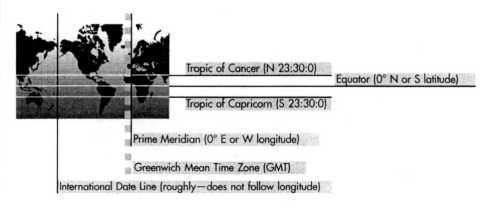

Tropic of Cancer (N 23:30:0)

Equator (0° N or S latitude)

Tropic of Capricorn (S 23:30:0)

Prime Meridian (0° E or W longitude)

Greenwich Mean Time Zone (GMT)

International Date Line (roughly—does not follow longitude)

Reflectances

Surface reflectances are the single most important contribution that can be made to lighting system efficiency (daylight and/or electric light) beyond the selection and layout of the daylighting and/or electric lighting devices. Both exterior and interior surfaces must be addressed. Exterior ground planes and neighboring vertical surfaces (e.g., other building façades, retaining walls, fences) can be used to better distribute daylight into the building under design or redesign. These surfaces are best if matte in finish rather than specular, although obviously existing neighboring glass façades will be specular (in which case siting for the building under design should be reviewed for glary reflections from sun or sky). If the building under design or redesign is in a snowy climate, a review of frequency and duration of snow cover on the ground plane and anticipated glare should factor in to window glazing selections and window treatment methods.

Interior reflectances should be matte but high in value. Ceiling reflectance has a significant influence on the depth of daylight penetration, the uniformity of daylight, the luminance and illuminance levels, and the balance of exterior sky luminance to interior luminance (the harshness of contrast). Baseline ceiling reflectance should be 85 percent, but with 90 percent and even greater ceiling reflectance, the opportunity exists to reduce electric lighting consumption even further. The greater ceiling reflectance has an added benefit of reducing the energy necessary to power the electric lighting for equivalent illuminance levels. **Ceiling reflectance of 90 percent or greater is recommend.** Walls also have an influence on daylight efficiency (and electric light efficiency), but to a lesser extent. **Wall reflectances of 50 percent or greater are recommended.** Although floor reflectance has little influence on efficiency of electric lighting, it can affect daylighting efficiency, particularly if the zone immediately adjacent to the window wall or under a skylight is used for circulation where no furnishings and task work are likely to vary day-to-day and alter reflectance properties. Floor reflectance of 30 percent or greater is recommended where daylight has access to an uninterrupted floor plane.

Configurations

Surface configurations influence the effectiveness of daylighting. Surfaces are most effective at "catching" and reflecting light if they are oriented directly at the light source. Surfaces that are simply angled or tilted toward the daylight aperture will better reflect the daylight. This can lead to angled and vaulted ceilings, and angled and curved walls to better capture and reflect the daylight. This also effectively reduces the distance the light travels before striking a reflecting surface—and reducing the distance results in greater light intensity. Figure 9.5 illustrates the concept of ceiling configurations to more effectively use daylight. No different than electric lighting, the more layers of techniques employed, the more likely the overall system will be successful for the occupants—and the more likely initial costs will be greater than with the simple and cheap lighting techniques that have come to be "standard" in the states. As pressure mounts to reduce energy, cut emissions, and simultaneously provide healthier, more pleasant environments that endure for the long term, incrementally higher initial costs will be seen for what they have always been—a small price for the benefits.

Figure 9.3

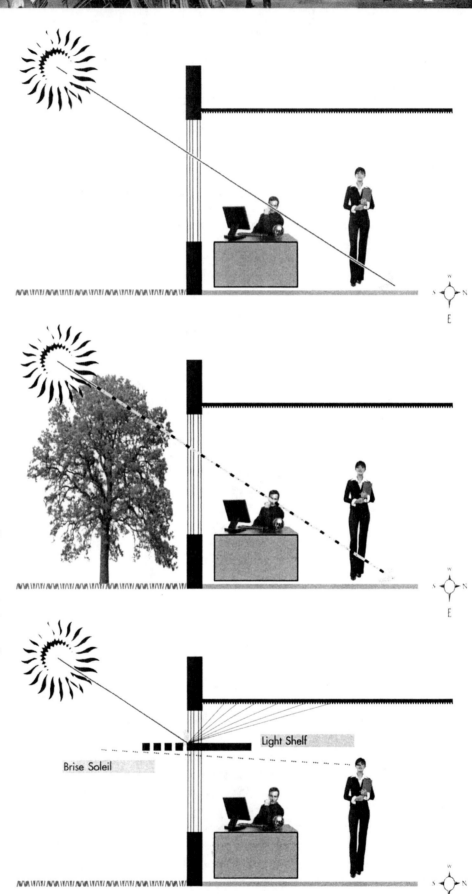

Direct view of the solar disc is undesirable. Window treatments, themselves a typical fractional strategy, are the usual fix, but studies show manually controlled treatments are usually set once and left alone for days or even weeks, thereby limiting benefits of daylight availability.[4] Window treatments that are automated to track sun angle during clear and partly cloudy sky conditions will limit glare situations and simultaneously take advantage of the daylight. It is worth noting that since some amount of solar heat enters through the glazing system, the usual interior window treatments may not yield the cooling load benefits of landscaping and/or brise soleils or overhangs or awnings.

Landscaping, typically a fractional strategy, can be used to minimize, although usually not complete block view of the solar disc. Must be well-executed for varying sun angles and seasonal conditions. Landscaping can work in conjunction with automated window treatments.

Brise soleils and/or light shelves (a combination of both is shown in the bottom graphic) can effectively limit view of the solar disc over a significant time of the year and significant portion of the day. These devices have the added benefit of reflecting sunlight onto the ceiling and further into the space. The top surfaces of these devices should be matte in finish and white (high reflectance neutral so as not to skew color rendering). Mounting heights of these devices should be arranged to permit unobstructed views.

Images used in development of graphics ©Stockxpert

Figure 9.4

Brise soleils are employed to shade the glass façade and interior occupants. Here, the device exhibits a luminous appearance (perhaps of stainless steel or anodized aluminum). There is a fine balance between too luminous and too dark. The intent is to provide a soft transition from the sky beyond to the interior ceiling so that occupants are not bothered by overly bright (glary) brise soleils nor by the harsh contrast of a black or very dark material viewed against the background sky. NOTE: Gary Steffy Lighting Design did not provide lighting consultation on this project.
Image ©Stockxpert

Figure 9.5

Two ceiling configurations are illustrated that are different from the "normal" flat horizontal ceiling configuration (shown in light gray). The top graphic illustrates a flat ceiling angled up toward the window. The bottom graphic shows a curvilinear ceiling profile arched up toward the window. Notice in both graphics that the diffuse light rays reflected from the light shelf strike (and therefore reflect from) the different ceiling configurations sooner than they would if left to strike the normal horizontal flat ceiling. This results in greater ceiling luminance, better ceiling luminance uniformity and therefore greater illuminance and illuminance uniformity on the workplane or floor. In any event, ceiling finishes should be matte and ceiling reflectances should be 90 percent or so.

Images used in development of graphics ©Stockxpert

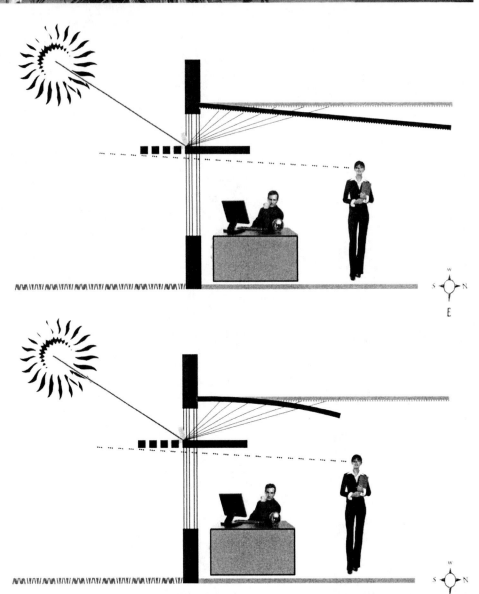

Although these configurations work well for improving daylight effectiveness, their utility is best realized on sunny façades in sunny climes where the direct beam of the sun produces significantly greater light intensities throughout the course of the day than that from the indirect light of the sky dome. In predominantly cloudy situations, surface configurations are less successful.

Uniformity

bilateral daylighting
Daylighting from two directions.

For most work settings, lighting uniformity is important for comfort and task performance throughout the space(s). Lighting uniformity (both electric light and daylight) will be enhanced with implementation of the shading devices, high surface reflectances, and surface configuration techniques previously discussed. However, particularly for larger and deeper buildings, **bilateral daylighting** or multilateral daylighting is suggested to more uniformly light the space. This minimizes strong

contrasts that can arise from fenestration at one side or area of a larger building or room. As a basic rule, daylighting from windows can be expected to distribute into a room a distance that is roughly 1½ to 2 times the height of the window above the workplane or floor plane (assuming a reasonably sized window and assuming the ceiling is within 6″ to 12″ [about 150 to 300 mm respectively] of the window head).[5] So, for example, if the depth of the room is greater than twice the height of the window above the workplane, a second daylight source is recommended—sidelighting from the wall opposite the original window wall or toplighting (e.g., skylight or **laylight**, roof monitor) more distant from the original window wall.

laylight
An architectural feature or element that is a decorative light diffuser. Consists of a pattern of decorative or plain glass or acrylic panels (typically obscuring) that usually sits below or near-below a skylight to allow daylight to enter a room below. See Figure 9.6.

9.3 Design Practice

Briefly noted previously, there are three approaches to programming daylighting—called here holistic, conditional, and fractional. Much like electric lighting, the type and number of daylighting strategies implemented on any given project will depend on the programming. Holistic daylighting begins with the building site selection and works through siting (orientation on site), proportions (length, width, and height), daylight availability (lattitude, seasonal aspects, and sky conditions). maximizing daylight (exploring sidelighting and toplighting strategies and surface configurations and reflectances), maintaining visual comfort (exploring shading strategies), and minimizing electric light use (developing controls strategies). Figure 9.7 shows a plan-view snapshot of what a daylighting study on a particular development and site might look like. In these situations, daylight availability is more closely tied to neighboring structures' heights, massings, and finishes. In suburban or country settings, geology and landscape affect daylight availability (a structure sited in a north/south-running valley might be sited in such a way to avoid early morning [east] and late afternoon [west] solar disc glare problems). Before making such site studies, understand the kinds and magnitude of available daylight by studying average sky conditions (such as those outlined in Table 9.1) and studying illuminance magnitudes (see Figures 9.8 and 9.9). Preliminary work assessing daylight availability and magnitudes can be done to narrow strategies prior to computer modelling—usually reserved for assessing specific daylighting strategies and refining techniques and details.

Conditional daylighting might begin with proportions, but more likely commences as an effort to maximize daylight given pre-established proportions. Here, while the architectural form and/or fenestration *might* be influenced by daylighting, the building site and the siting (orientation/position) of the building will not. As such, daylighting design now must react to these conditions. If the building is sited in a southeast or southwest orientation and the footprint is very large, glare control and daylight penetration will be nearly mutually exclusive (i.e., to limit glare for most of the day will likely require dense shade treatments and/or low visible-transmittance glazing that prevent much daylight penetration—and this is even a problem on the northeast and northwest façades given early morning and late afternoon glare control). While some daylight is better than no daylight, just recognize that in these situations significant electric light energy savings and sustainability benefits will not be realized.

Figure 9.6

A laylight below a skylight introduces toplight to this hearing room. With the west-facing window, the room has bilateral daylighting. The diffuse laylight helps distribute daylight high onto the perimeter walls and uniformly onto the floor and seating area. With such diffuse light, faces are rendered fully with no harsh shadows to confound interpretation of facial expressions. The plenum or interstital space between the top of the laylight panel and the skylight above can be designed to accommodate electric lights as was done here. With controls and skylight shades, the laylight can then also provide lighting during darkness.
Image ©Feinknopf Studio

Fractional daylighting might commence with maximizing daylight, but more often than not is likely limited to maintaining visual comfort or just minimizing electric light use. Not that these are insignificant or unimportant program items, but the magnitude of their success, if success is even a likelihood, is greatly diminished without having influence on the other program items.

Table 9.2 summarizes important program items, key related design aspects, and some suggested design guidelines for daylighting. The guidelines are intended as starting points. Refinements, whole-building energy analyses, and other-than-lighting criteria may very well lead to less glazing, greater shading of glazing, and/or lower-T_{vis} glazing. There is a tendency to overlight with daylight (just as there is with electric light). No doubt an American thing—more must be better! Don't fall victim to this mantra. Overlighting with daylight is as problematic as overlighting with electric light, if not more so. Glare issues are compounded and energy savings are diminished if not entirely negated, not to mention increased pressure on the HVAC system to accommodate the heating or cooling issues associated with ever-more glazing. Simply using more "thermally best" glazing will skew costs even higher where less glazing will meet lighting criteria. See Chapter 8 for discussions on illuminance and luminance criteria—which, by the way, are to be met by daylighting and electric lighting combined or individually. Daylighting should never be considered "icing on the cake."

Additionally, these lighting design efforts must be integrated with other building systems' designs and engineering. With light shelves and tilted or vaulted ceiling configurations, integration with other systems will require detailed analysis. Sprinkler systems, HVAC systems, acoustics, and even electric lighting are just several of the building systems and aspects that may be impacted or that may impact the details of the daylighting technique(s).

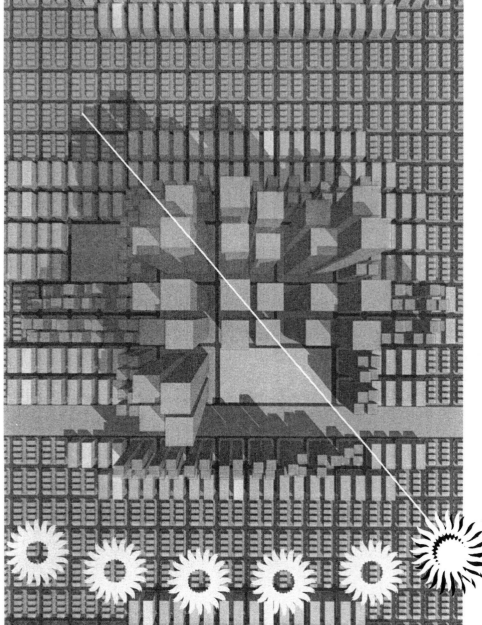

Figure 9.7

Site studies assess influence of neighboring structures and landscaping and daylight availability for at least the equinoxes and solstices and for several key times of the day. For occupancies of "normal working hours," this might include 9 a.m., noon, and 3 p.m. These studies influence the architectural scale, proportions, layouts, and block diagrams and ultimately individual building form, proportions, and fenestration elements. Here, sun path for summer solstice (see Figure 9.2 and diagram below) in northern hemisphere is shown with a 9 a.m. **solar time** assessment. Latitude and longitude help establish **solar azimuth** and **solar altitude** for various times of the day throughout the year. Background Image ©Stockxpert

solar time
Time that is defined based on the sun's actual position (e.g., highest position in sky is noon). So-called standard time is solar time.

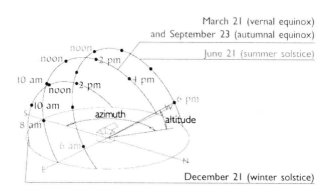

March 21 (vernal equinox) and September 23 (autumnal equinox)

June 21 (summer solstice)

December 21 (winter solstice)

solar azimuth
Viewing a site plan view of the building in question in the northern hemisphere, solar azimuth is the angle between due south and the horizontal position of the sun (if the sun is aligned with due south, the solar azimuth is 0°). Sun path shown for northern hemisphere (interchange June 21 and December 21 for southern hemisphere).

solar altitude
Viewing a section of the building in question, solar altitude is the angle between the ground plane and the vertical position of the sun.

Figure 9.8

Average Mostly-clear-sky Incident Illuminance/Phoenix, AZ: The charts graph illuminance on the horizontal ground plane, and on imaginary north, east, south, and west façades for March (top), June (middle), and December (bottom). Since Phoenix has a preponderance of clear to partly cloudy days (see Table 9.1), this data is for mostly clear days.

In March, illuminance on the ground plane and the south façade is consistently quite high. Not surprisingly, horizontal illuminance in June remains high—approaching 11,000 fc (about 110,000 lux) in the early afternoon. However, because of the steep angle with which the sun strikes the south façade, illuminance in June on the south façade is about half what it is in March. Nevertheless, these values indicate glare control will be critical to successful implementation of daylighting. Further, such great and consistent illuminances suggest that light shelves at least along the south façade should be pursued.

In all three months, note how the east and west façades are essentially identical opposites—the east façade having strong illuminance in the morning and low illuminance in the afternoon, but vice versa for the west façade. Although relatively fleeting, the magnitude of the high illuminances is sufficiently great to demand attention to glare control.
Data from *Solar Radiation Data Manual for Buildings.*[6]

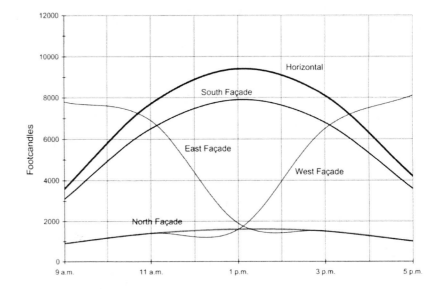

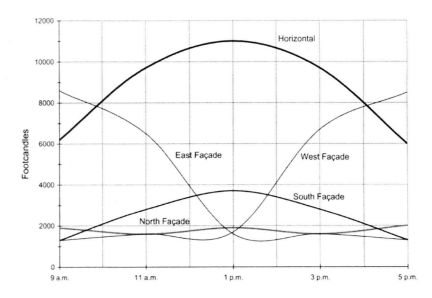

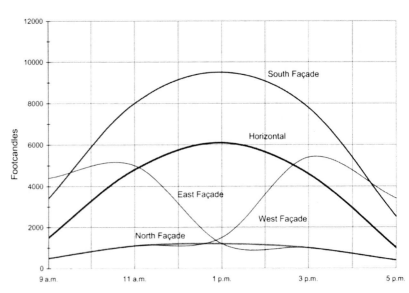

Architectural Lighting Design

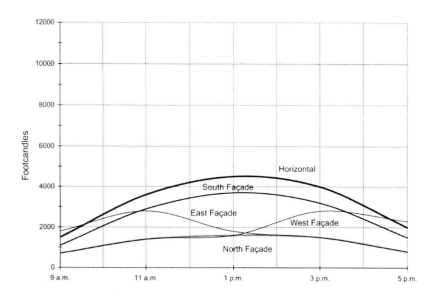

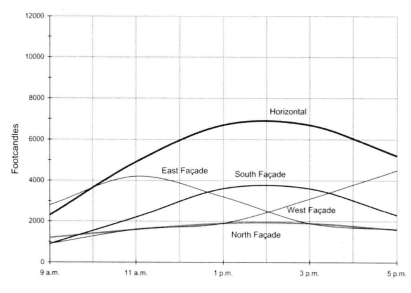

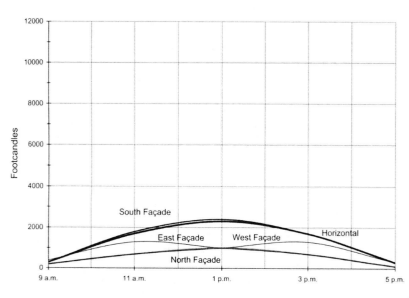

Figure 9.9

Average Mostly-cloudy-sky Incident Illuminance/Detroit, MI: The charts graph illuminance on the horizontal ground plane, and on imaginary north, east, south, and west façades for March (top), June (middle), and December (bottom). Since Detroit has a preponderance of partly cloudy to cloudy days (see Table 9.1), this data is for mostly cloudy days.

In March, illuminance on the ground plane and the south façade is consistently high. Horizontal illuminance in June increases significantly—approaching 7,000 fc (about 70,000 lux) in the early afternoon. This is likely about the time peak demand occurs, so skylights could significantly reduce the need for electric light providing these do not contribute to the cooling load. South façade illuminance in June is nearly identical to that in March, indicating one daylighting strategy on the south façade would yield consistent results for March to September and should be pursued. With the lower probability of direct sun, fixed elements like brise soleils or overhangs are probably not cost effective.

The June south façade illuminance in cloudy Detroit is nearly identical to that of clear Phoenix in June. The north façade illuminance in March and June is nearly identical to that of the north façade conditions in March and June in Phoenix, AZ (See Figure 9.8).

Data from *Solar Radiation Data Manual for Buildings.*[7]

Table 9.2 Daylighting Design Practice

Program Item	Design Aspects		Design Practice
Site Selection	• Visual comfort		Limit east and west exposures
			Maximize native landscaping
	• Site daylight availability		Latitude
			Sky conditions
	• Daylight penetration		Maximize north and south exposures
	• Impact on neighboring structures		Consider setback potential and topology
Siting	• Visual comfort		Limit east and west exposures
			Maximize native landscaping
	• Daylight penetration		Maximize north and south exposures
			Assess neighboring building's projected shade/sun-blocking
	• Impact on neighboring structures		Consider setbacks
			Assess proposed building's projected shade/sun-blocking
			Consider affects of building skin reflecting qualities
Proportions	• Daylight penetration		Long, narrow footprints (long façades facing south and north)
			High ceilings
	• Daylight uniformity		Long, narrow footprints and/or bilateral or multilateral daylight strategies
Daylight Availability (Building interior)	• Sky conditions		Establish primary condition for design (clear, partly cloudy, cloudy)
	• Maximize daylight penetration		Consider light shelf on sunny elevation(s) in predominantly sunny climes
			Consider tall ceilings regardless climate
Maximizing Daylight	• Sidelighting		Consider continuous (along length of façade) windows
			Consider tall window head height
		Predominantly Cloudy	North view glass: consider T_{vis} of 50% ±
			South, east, and west view glass: consider T_{vis} of 30 to 50% ±
			Daylight glass: consider T_{vis} of 50 to 70% ± above light shelf
		Predominantly Clear	North view glass: consider T_{vis} of 50% ±
			South, east, and west view glass: consider T_{vis} of 30% ±
			Daylight glass: consider T_{vis} of 30 to 50% ± above light shelf
	• Light shelf		Consider on sunny elevation(s) in predominantly sunny climes
	• Ceiling height		Consider 10' to 12' ceiling heights
	• Toplighting		Consider skylights or roof monitors in areas more distant from sidelighting
	• Surface configurations		Considered angling/tilting ceiling and wall surfaces toward daylight apertures
	• Surface reflectances		Consider matte finishes
			See Table 8.4 (generally, greater reflectance values are better)
	• Workstation configurations		Open plan with low/no paritition or transparent upper partitions along perimeter
Maintain Visual Comfort	• Shading	Sidelighting	Consider fixed architectural shading on sunny elevation(s) in predominantly sunny climes
			Consider automated image-preserving shading on inside of glazing
			Consider horizontal blinds on inside of sunny-elevation glazing
			Consider vertical blinds on inside of east and west elevation glazing
		Toplighting	Consider roof monitors (facing north in northern hemisphere)
			Consider deep-well skylights (well height ~ narrow dimension of skylight)
			Consider light-well louvers
			Consider perforated, translucent, or opaque interior reflectors
	• Efficient room finishes		See Table 8.4
	• Automated controls		Automate shading and electric lighting for best luminance balancing
Minimize Electric Light	• Zoning		Zone electric lights in conjunction with daylight zones
	• Controls		Automate with astronomical timeclocks and photocells
			Manual control should be limited to task light on desk

Like most other technologies, daylight's ebb and flow with the interest in the topic. The next decade promises to be a time of significant development in daylight technologies. Political and economic forces are converging in a way that will make fenestration media, shades, controls, light shelves, and the like more readily available, more cost effective, and more feature-rich. New terms will apply to old techniques and will be needed to define new techniques or metrics. No doubt, some old techniques will be redeveloped and some old metrics redefined. Daylighting, for example, is now also called **daylight harvesting**. Daylighting designs are now accredited in some circles based on their **daylight factor**s (which themselves vary in definition from country to country). In any event, it is the appropriate application of techniques and technologies that result in successful daylighting project. Sometimes simplest is best.

Even seemingly simple daylighting problems, however, demand attention on every project. For example, diffuse north skylight luminances can exceed 950 cd/ft^2 (exactly 10,220 cd/m^2), which is more than ten times the luminance limit criteria for daylight media in a typical computer-intensive work environment (see Table 8.2). So, if 80 cd/ft^2 (exactly 860 cd/m^2) is a design target (taken from Table 8.2/Daylight Media/ normal computer task apps), then shade control techniques are advisable even for north-oriented glazing unless glazing transmittance is limited to just 8 percent (8 percent of the 950 cd/ft^2 sky luminance yield about 80 cd/ft^2—but this is for the worst-case sky luminance, which may not occur frequently so, arguably, glazing transmittance could be somewhat greater). If, however, 50 percent transmissive glazing is desired on the north face, then interior shades will need to exhibit a transmission of about 17 percent to achieve a transmission of 8½ percent for the window/shade assembly.

more online @
www.learn.londonmet.ac.uk/packages/clear/visual/daylight/analysis/hand/
daylight_factor.html

9.4 Technologies

daylight harvesting
Synonymous with daylighting, although originally meant to distinguish those daylit projects that actually saved energy by switching off or dimming lights from those that did not. Now considered an integral part of daylighting.

daylight factor
Daylight factor (DF) is essentially the ratio of all non-sunbeam daylight reaching a point in the building versus that reaching the same point if no building enclosure were present. Although considered a decent "gross assessment" of daylighting for a particular design, this does not account for specific geographic locations and sky conditions and may lead to overdesigned or underdesigned conditions if daylight is not carefully modelled and designs modified accordingly.[8] Projects in the states with a DF of 0.02 (2%) have been considered daylight-worthy. Do not use DF as a final assessment.

Shading

Shading can be done with building architecture (e.g., deep window recesses), with permanent devices integrated with the building architecture (e.g., exterior horizontal and/or vertical baffles, external and/or internal light shelves), or with transient devices (e.g., exterior awnings and exterior or interior shades). Window recesses on the sunny façade have the benefit of also limiting rising and setting sun glare. However, the depth of these recesses will limit occupants' fields of view. Permanent devices integrated with the architecture are typically affixed to the exterior and must be detailed to align with architectural features and/or glazing frames if they are to have an appearance of purposeful integration. Figure 9.4 shows brise soleils while horizontal and vertical overhangs that are window-specific are shown in Figure 9.10. Projection of these devices are based on a variety of factors from structural stability, cost, shading aspects (selecting a "worst case" condition such as the equinox and knowing that the device will then work from equinox to equinox), and aesthetics. Depending on the building type, consistent overhangs can serve the purpose of an exterior porch such as that shown in Figure 9.11. Exterior transient devices may be most appropriate in climates where seasonal shading is sufficient or where initial cost may be a higher priority. Figure 9.12

Figure 9.10

Fixed shade treatment is developed to respond to either typical sun angles, a range of sun angles, or "worst-case" sun angles. Here, vertical treatments help limit either early morning or late afternoon sun—that is, when the sun is low in the east or west sky, some windows on the south façade are shaded either early morning or late afternoon without sacrificing both view angles. The finish treatment on the south face is presumably for thermal reasons—to reflect radiant heat. Recognize the implications of this "reflected light" on adjacent buildings (the surface luminance of this south façade is quite high, serving to reflect some light into windows of adjacent buildings, which can be considered in daylighting strategies for adjacent building[s] or might be considered a glare source).
NOTE: Gary Steffy Lighting Design did not provide lighting consultation on this project.
Image ©Stockxpert

Architectural Lighting Design

Figure 9.11

On some building types, an extended porch can serve as a fixed shade device. Manually-adjustable louver panels allow for additional shading and privacy.
NOTE: Gary Steffy Lighting Design did not provide lighting consultation on this project.
Image ©Stockxpert

shows some awnings, while Figure 9.13 shows interior shading. Many of these techniques can and should be layered—used collectively to address daylighting. For example, for sunny climes in the northern hemisphere, exterior overhangs on the south elevation might be designed to address conditions anticipated with high sun angles for roughly the six-month period from vernal equinox to autumnal equinox, while interior shades are used to address conditions anticipated with low sun angles from autumnal equinox to vernal equinox.

Light shelves and horizontal blinds not only shade occupants, but when designed properly can also improve interior luminances with daylight. These are additional benefits not available with exterior overhangs, interior vertical blinds, or interior solar shades. Of course, the scale and finish and angular tilt of light shelves and horizontal blinds influence their success. For interior blinds, automated sun tracking

Daylighting

Figure 9.12

Transient shade treatments can have a distinctly modern appearance (top) or traditional (below). Typically less costly than fixed permanent devices, maintenance and deployment can be labor intensive. In both situations note the apparent desire, if not need, for interior shades.

NOTE: Gary Steffy Lighting Design did not provide lighting consultation on this project.

Image ©Stockxpert

Figure 9.13

An overhang provides some shading on this west façade. Since low sun angles occur during some times of the year when services are performed at this chapel, interior shades were specified (also see Figures 12.8 and 13.5). Criteria for the shades included **image-preserving** and low transmission to mitigate the solar disc. The window glazing is Viracon Solarscreen VE 3-40 exhibiting a gray tint and an overall T_{vis} of 18% (SHGC of 0.19). Window shade is Mechoshade® 1302 dense Basket Weave in beige with a transmittance of 5%. Total visible light transmittance for the entire window/shade assembly when shade is employed is just under 1%—necessary to address the solar disc late in the afternoon in the west sky.

A black finish on the shade would alleviate the "luminous washout" created by the sunbeam striking the shade and would improve the view of the scene beyond. However, it was decided that the black finish would create an unacceptably dark wall.

Although the shades are motorized, they are not automated with photocell or **astronomical time-clock** as automated function might unintentionally interrupt services. Images ©Gene Meadows

image-preserving

A reference to window shades, glass, and acrylic, etc., that permit a view through. Image-obscuring indicates no view is available through the media, but light is allowed to pass through it.

astronomical timeclock

A timeclock that has built-in software to keep track of the solar calendar and, if so programmed, track daylight savings time and standard time changes. Such a timeclock, then, knows, for example, sunrise and sunset times and can program lights on or off accordingly. Astronomical timeclocks can perform complete operation of lights without the need for photocells, providing there is no concern about darkness due to impending storms (which only a photocell could detect).

on the sunny façade(s) provides consistent glare control and more consistent interior luminance distribution from daylight. Manual blinds tend to be set very infrequently, and only then to control glare, but with little regard for daylight distribution and intensity.[9] Such manual control would obviously defeat plans to interconnect and control electric light with daylight availability in order to "harvest daylight" and save energy on electric lights. No doubt many cultures will need tutoring and even attitude change with such automation. Some form of manual intervention seems appropriate in private offices; however, both to avoid extreme conditions and place some degree of control in the hands of the occupants. In open office situations, however, this approach deserves scrutiny—who's to be in charge of manual intervention?

Some clients and designers may shun the "burden" that shading devices place on the architecture. However, regardless how spartan the "daylighting treatment," somehow, somewhere the issue of daylighting and occupant comfort will need to be addressed. A demand for no window shades (ostensibly to minimize maintenance or to maintain an "uncluttered façade") will force selection of very low transmittance glazing. Even this won't solve glare from low-angle early-morning or late-afternoon sun. Occupants will tape up butcher paper or cardboard (anything sufficiently dense to mitigate the solar disc) and/or complain until the issue is resolved.

Unless blackout conditions are necessary for sleeping or work functions, interior transient shade devices should permit some degree of view. Where daylight will not interfere with the occupants' functions, the shade should transmit enough light to supplant electric light. For maximum energy savings, the shade should be automated to track the sun or daylight intensity and interlocked with electric lights to dim or switch off lights.

```
more online @
www.alcoa.com/global/en/products/product.asp?prod_id=1852
www.bendinglight.co.uk/serraglaze_canopy.asp
www.brisesoleil.com/
gaia.lbl.gov/hpbf/techno_a.htm
www1.hunterdouglascontract.com/HDWeb/Cultures/en-US/Products/
  SolarControl/
www.insolroll.com/index.php?id=1
www.levolux.com/L_products/walkway.htm
www.mechoshade.com/site/home.cfm
www.naco.co.uk/ellip.html
www.parlouvres.co.uk/
```

Glazing

Glazing used in sidelighting and toplighting fenestration must not only allow daylight to enter, but must meet thermal, acoustic, and weather requirements. And in order to serve its arguably primary purpose, glazing must allow view. The designer must weigh transmittance for useful light versus transmittance for glare control versus transmittance for acceptable view.

Transmittance values for useful daylight depend to some degree on the available daylight, the fenestration technique, the likelihood of viewing the solar disc, and the position of the solar disc in the field of view. Typical daylight-useful transmittances for sidelight view glazing range from about 30 percent to 50 percent for sidelight view glazing (see Table 9.2 for additional guidance).

There are two basic types of glazing—static and dynamic. Static glazing exhibits a fixed transmittance and color and is available in a range of transmittances from about 1 percent to about 70 percent. The lowest transmittances are achieved with fritted and/or heavily tinted and/or mirror-coated glass lites or panes arranged in a window assembly. Dynamic glazing exhibits a continuously variable transmittance and/or color. This introduces a means to limit some of the layering of daylighting techniques needed for success. Whereas a 35 percent fixed-transmission window layered with an automated interior image-preserving shade addresses multiple sky conditions throughout the seasons, dynamically transmissive glazing enables transmissions to range from a low of perhaps 2 percent to a high of 80 percent depending on manufacturer. Figure 9.14 illustrates one manufacturer's offering. So, during the most intense sunny conditions the 2 percent setting can be employed while during the most cloudy conditions the 60 percent setting can be employed. Although these systems cannot enhance daylight penetration like light shelves or interior adjustable blinds, an initial study found occupants to be comfortable with their function and the daylight results.[10] This glazing is known generically as electrochromic and is part of the chromogenic technologies.[11] Electrochromic glass is also known as smart or switchable glass. A small amount of energy is necessary to change the state of electrons in the glass—depending on their alignment with each other, they block more or less light. Systems using liquid crystals can be designed to yield visual privacy.[12] Other chromogenic techniques are photochromic and thermochromic—automatically responding to ambient light or ambient heat respectively.

Much has been reported about window sizes and color, but with little definitive consensus, undoubtedly because of the extreme difficulty in separating occupants' aesthetic preferences, which are highly variable and unstable from long-term impacts on visual comfort and productivity. Window transmittance should be based on balance between useful light and energy savings and visual comfort. A mockup is always desirable, but budgeting the cost and time for this may be out of reach given the current construction paradigm (at least in the states). When mockups are possible, care must be taken to limit the "grass is greener" aspect of one condition compared to another. Inevitably, neutral-colored glass of high transmission will always be the preference unless observers must actually relax and/or work in the setting under several sky conditions during several seasons. Side-by-side comparisons are a bad idea, even for the design professional. Indeed, here's where color constancy helps. Immersed in a room of daylight that's passed through blue-tinted windows, people will observe colors of objects and faces as normal—our memory of color helps us perceive the blue-tinged objects and faces as we would see them under "true" outdoor daylight. However, viewing two windows, one with a blue tint and one clear, most observers will object to the blue window—it is obviously "blue" by comparison to the clear glass. Similarly, immersed in a room of blue-tinted windows, people's views outdoors will still perceive tree trunks as brown, deciduous leaves as green, male cardinals as red, and the like.

Window sizes should be based on common sense, code requirements, and thermal energy issues in addition to their daylighting intent. Very small punched openings singularly or clustered may look attractive from the designer's perspective,

Figure 9.14

Sage Glass (test installation illustrated below with detailed information available at www.sage-ec.com) offers electrochromic glazing with continuously variable transmittances from about 3½ percent to 63 percent. Manipulation of the transmittance can be automated with photocell or time of day control or manual. The top image illustrates a condition where too much sun/luminance is available immediately adjacent to the work area. Changing the transmittance of the glass, either manually or automatically, results in better work conditions without loss of view (shown in the bottom image). The test installation exhibits sensors on each pane not found in commercial installations. Recognize the potential for varying transmittances based on orientation (north windows operating at different trransmittances than the south windows, for example) and time of day (east windows versus west windows). This degree of control also assists in the reduction of solar heat gain.
Images ©Sage Electrochromics, Inc.

but offer little in the way of view or helpful daylight. Continuous floor to ceiling glazing may also look attractive from the designer's perspective, but the first 24″ to 30″ (about 600 mm to 750 mm) above the floor are likely to be filled with unsightly (at least from the exterior) clutter of desks, chairs, tables, and power and data cords unless the perimeter is used for circulation. Further, the thermal issues associated with such a monolith of glazing are unsustainable. The designer must work with the mechanical engineer and review various iterations of daylighting strategies and studies to optimize window size for a given location and sky condition(s).

In addition to the chromogenic glazing media discussed earlier, advances in optical control embedded within glazing allow for direct solar control while also redirecting daylight to interior ceilings. These systems are, thus far, fixed in nature—with daylight control set typically for noon sun on façades facing the equator. One system is known as Serraglaze® while the other is known as Okasolar®. The Serraglaze technology is available in both window form and an exterior overhang or canopy form whereby the canopy (which is tilted toward the sky) sees more sky than a traditional window, collects that skylight, and redirects it onto the interior ceiling. The Serraglaze system is based on very minute and precisely shaped air pockets embedded within an acrylic glazing sheet. These air pockets cause some amount of daylight to refract toward the ceiling—maintaining an exterior view while assisting with daylight penetration. The Okasolar system consists of an insulated glass assembly with precisely shaped louvers embedded in the insulating air space. The louvers are polished and contoured based on building latitude and respective sun angles in order to reflect direct sun to the exterior while redirecting sky light to the interior ceiling. Both the Okasolar and Serraglaze techniques are categorized as angular selective solar control.[13]

```
more online @
www.bendinglight.co.uk/serraglaze.asp
gaia.lbl.gov/hpbf/techno_a.htm
gaia.lbl.gov/hpbf/techno_b.htm
gaia.lbl.gov/hpbf/techno_c.htm
gaia.lbl.gov/hpbf/techno_d.htm
windows.lbl.gov/materials/chromogenics/default.htm
www.sage-ec.com/
www.us.schott.com/architecture/english/products/insulated_solar_glass/
    okasolar/index.html
www.viracon.com/index.php
```

Pipes and Tubes

Although skylights (with or without laylights) and roof monitors are the prevalent toplighting methods, recent advances in light piping technologies have enabled the packaging of very cost effective light tubes. These are relatively small tubes that collect and direct sky light through a configured tube to a diffuser, which itself looks more like an electric light diffuser. Some of these devices can be fitted with electric light for dark conditions and can be fitted with "dimmers" to modulate the incoming daylight. Many of these are made to work around plenum and structure obstructions. These devices do not provide an exterior view.

Serraglaze® is a registered trademark of Serra Technologies/Bending Light
Okasolar® is a registered trademark of SCHOTT North America, Inc.

Architectural Lighting Design

more online @
www.solatube.com/commercial/brightenup.php
squareflex.com/index.html
www.veluxusa.com/products/sunTunnels/

9.5 Color

Color of daylight and electric light need not "match." Indeed, there are two problems with attempting a match. First, most daylight conditions from a few hours after sunrise to a few hours before sunset for cloudy, partly cloudy, and clear, color temperature exceeds 6000K (see Figure 7.11). Even direct sunlight during these times is about 5500K. Electric light sources exhibiting such color temperatures are considered very cold and "blue white" in appearance. Second, color of daylight *is* so variable throughout the day and different day-to-day, that even if a comfortable and pleasing "match" could be made with electric light, the match would occur infrequently. The beauty of daylight is that it is daylight. Attempts to somehow seamlessly merge it with electric light (or vice versa depending on one's perspective) would simply lessen its attraction. The author's design practice suggests that many people actually prefer warmtone electric-light lamps—those in the 2700K to 3000K range.

Suggestions circulate from time to time that 4100K electric light sources are better suited for the sunnier equatorial climes, while warmer electric light sources are better suited for the more cloudy and colder climates more distant from the equator. A study in the 1970s suggested this to be an effect if the room surface finishes were also part of the overall design (see Section 7.1). If this effect were so pronounced solely because of lamp color temperature, then energy savings on cooling and heating loads could be dramatically affected by simply changing lamp color temperature seasonally. The fact that equatorial regions seem filled with 4100K lamps may be simple economics—the lousy-color halophosphate cool white lamps of the mid-twentieth-century have been some of the cheapest lamps available (without downgrading to the lowly standard tungsten filament lamp). While not nearly as efficacious as today's T5 and T8 deluxe triphosphor lamps, these lamps appear to be an artifact of outdated technology and machinery that continue production elsewhere.

9.6 Controls

Controls for daylighting technologies and for daylighting/electric lighting interface are a critical aspect of sustainable design. At the very least, some means must be provided to allow the reduction or elimination of electric lights when daylight suffices. Daylighting is not an energy efficient nor a sustainable practice if electric lighting is not interactively linked with daylighting. So the development of an electric lighting solution that works with the daylighting is paramount to an efficient and sustainable project. In most applications, automated controls are crucial to the success of daylight and electric light integration on a large project. Here, as daylight becomes available, electric light should be dimmed or switched to lower levels, while luminance

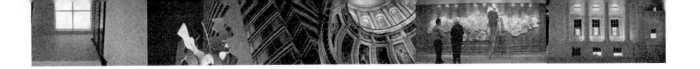

balances are maintained. This typically results in the use of a photocell or photocells, depending on the fenestration orientations, the configuration(s) of interior space(s), and the zoning of the electric lighting (see Figure 9.15). Astronomical timeclocks may be desirable to offer time-of-day control beyond that offered by photocells, such as lunch hour or morning or afternoon breaks, or peak demand time, or simply to offer a change in light quality and/or quantity over time. Dimming of lights seems least annoying to occupants, particularly if electric lights are only fully extinguished when daylight is at its maximum. Stepped switching of lights is more noticeable than dimming, but is much less costly and may be less problematic. For example, the effects of dimming on fluorescent lamps and ceramic metal halide lamps is not well understood. Periodically, some lamp manufacturers do not endorse dimming of their respective fluorescent and/or ceramic metal halide lamps. Lamp manufacturers and dimming ballast and controls manufacturers offer differing opinions on lamp life, quality of light, and ease of dimming. With legislated measures and public pressure to reduce energy use, however, dimming is likely to significantly increase in the near term.

DALI®
Digital Addressable Lighting Interface. A commercially open-source protocol to address lighting devices.

The advent of commercially available addressable ballasts and luminaires may offer improved and more finite localized control as well as rearrangement advantages (always desirable for sustainability). **DALI®** has been available for several years and some control systems now take advantage of this digital standard for electronic operating devices. However, at least some of these control systems use proprietary devices and/or control front-ends that preclude convenient change-out from one device to another or interfacing with other manufacturers' devices or interfacing one system with another for aggregated control and/or energy savings or even preclude common programming and diagnostics. Nevertheless, DALI® brings to reality a long-held desire—individual control of each and every light on a project. The benefits for daylighting integration and for reconfiguration of lighting as furniture and task layouts change are significant.

In any event, all of this automation offers another layer of complexity to the system installation, commissioning, and maintenance. Tracking lighting circuits and aligning these with control zones is an increasingly difficult task for the contractor and controls manufacturer. Regardless of the types of control devices and daylighting and electric lighting techniques used, system commissioning is de rigueur. However, specification of this aspect is at times difficult if the control system is not a complete package supplied by a single manufacturer. Even then, self-interests during the commissioning process may impede success. The designer should investigate these aspects during the design and specification process. Maintenance must be undertaken with much greater care on both the electronic devices and the programming. See Chapter 13 for more discussion on controls.

```
more online @
www.aboutlightingcontrols.org/about.shtml
www.dali-ag.org/
```

DALI® is a registered trademark of Elektrotechnik- und Elektronikindustrie e.V. (The German Electrical and Electronic Manufacturers' Association)

Architectural Lighting Design

Figure 9.15

Here, indirect/direct linear pendent lights exhibit two lamps in cross section. At the window wall, lamps are controlled by a photocell, with the outboard lamps separately controlled from the inboard lamps. Here, daylight is sufficient to allow one-half of the lamps to be switched off in the linear pendent nearest the window.
Daylighting Consultant: Moji Navvab, The University of Michigan Building Technology—Lighting and Daylighting Simulation Laboratory Image ©Bill Lindhout and courtesy BETA Design Group, Inc.

9.7 Maintenance

Maintenance of daylighting and electric lighting controls is one component of the maintenance program. Glazing systems need to be cleaned regularly to maintain the design lighting targets and energy savings. Cleaning schedules will depend on environmental air quality and any available self-cleaning from weather. Light shelves require periodic cleaning to maintain appropriate reflectance qualities. Interior dirt buildup should be monitored to establish cleaning schedules. Horizontal blinds and image-preserving shades need to be cleaned. Manufacturers of these devices should be consulted on cleaning techniques. Even room surfaces should be cleaned and refinished periodically to maintain appropriate light reflecting properties. Awnings and brise soleils may not require cleaning to remain effective; however, their appearance may suffer if not maintained on a regular basis.

Maintenance is probably the most significant way to achieve greater gains in sustainability. Equipment in place represents some amount of Earth resources in both material and embodied energy. Although material quality establishes a sound base for building systems, it is maintenance that will enable these systems to lead long and productive service lives. The designer has little, if any, influence on the quality and degree of maintenance brought to any project. This should not deter design and specification of systems that are most appropriate for the occupants and the environment. In other words, do not design to a "lowest-common-denominator" mentality of simple, cheap, easily maintained unless that design happens to meet all or most of the lighting criteria on the project.

more online @
msucares.com/pubs/publications/p2269.html
windows.lbl.gov/daylighting/designguide/section10.pdf

9.8 Modelling

Figure 9.16

heliodon

A sun machine of sorts. *Helios* is Greek for sun. A heliodon is a large adjustable table (which is used to represent the Earth ground plane) onto which scale models of buildings are placed (usually a single model, but could be multiple models to study effect of one on the other). An electric light source positioned some distance away is used to mimic the photometric properties of the sun. The table adjusts to various tilt and rotation angles to represent latitude of the actual building site and sun angle and position for specific times/days of the year. Building mass, shading techniques, and fenestration schemes can then be assessed before designs are finalized. A ring heliodon is shown in top image below. For more detailed study, a platform heliodon (shown bottom below) is often used.

Images ©GarySteffyLightingDesign

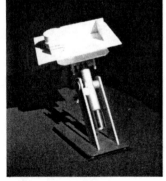

In analyzing daylight at a given location, there are three basic components to consider: direct sunlight, which impinges intermittently on the east, south, or west exposures of a building in the northern hemisphere; sky light, which impinges simultaneously and somewhat more consistently on all exposures of a building; and reflected light from the ground and nearby man-made structures. Each of these components will vary wildly with time of day, season, and prevalent atmospheric conditions.

Like any design task, daylighting design is an iterative process. Establish preliminary schemes, test these schemes by hand or computer renderings and/or physical scale models (for aesthetics) and computer calculational models or physical scale models (for technical attributes), review and revise, and test again. Scale models can be tested in "artificial sky" devices and on **heliodon**s (see Figure 9.16). A number of calculational techniques exist, but computer software allows for greatest depth and speed of study. Figure 9.17 reports in simple graphic fashion some output from an AGi32® study on the daylighting potential from a skylight/laylight design option. Crude to very refined imagery is also available from such software to study sun patterns and aesthetics. Figure 9.18 illustrates a sunlight study of a physical model on a ring heliodon. All of these methods are a means to predicting performance and/or appearance. Interior lighting aspects that are studied with any or all of these modelling techniques include visual comfort assessment (by tracking direct sunbeam), uniformity, façade configurations and shading techniques, and spatial and building geometry (to assist in uniformity and to establish daylight effectiveness). Exterior lighting aspects that are studied include building orientation on site, shadowing of neighboring structures, and shadowing on neighboring structures. Where physical models are studied, photographs are used to record the findings and provide a storyboard series for team review and possibly for client and/or planning commission presentations. Where computer models are studied, screen captures or images are typically generated in addition to the numeric data. These, too, are used for team review and perhaps for presentations to others.

Each building project is, by its nature, unique from every other building project. Before committing designs to paper, there is a desire, if not a need, to establish a degree of certainty on the proposed outcome. As such, all of these methods are very helpful when used simultaneously or sequentially in project design phases. Full-scale mockups are pursued where there is an interest to confirm approach(es) with a very high degree of certainty. This is especially helpful when attempting new technologies and/or techniques. Of course, this does require time and fee, but assists in the quest for more sustainable buildings—confirming with greater certainty that what is proposed will perform satisfactorily and, therefore, remain in successful employ for some time.

more online @
www.bsu.edu/web/ceres/heliodon/htmlside/CERES_home.htm
www.hpd-online.com/products/model_126_heliodon.asp
www.learn.londonmet.ac.uk/packages/clear/visual/daylight/analysis/physical/sim_sky.html
www.learn.londonmet.ac.uk/packages/clear/visual/daylight/analysis/physical/sim_sun.html
www.pge.com/003_save_energy/003c_edu_train/pec/info_resource/pdf/Heliodon_Studies.pdf

AGi32® is a registered trademark of Lighting Analysts, Inc.

Architectural Lighting Design

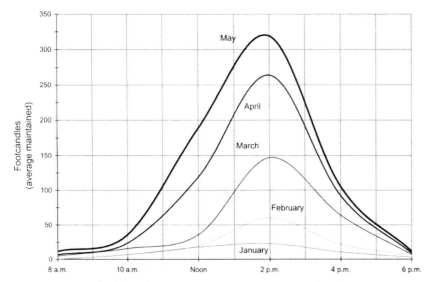

Figure 9.17

The AGi32 lighting software was used to predict the average maintained illuminance from a skylight/laylight configuration for the restoration of the Virginia Capitol House of Representatives Legislative Chamber. Legislative sessions typically convene in January and adjourn in March each year. The finished laylight is shown below. Image ©Tom Crane Photography

[1] Heschong Mahone Group, *Daylighting in Schools: An Investigation into the Relationship Between Daylight and Human Performance* (San Francisco, CA: Pacific Gas and Electric Company, 1999).

[2] Peter R. Boyce, *Human Factors in Lighting, 2nd Edition* (London: Taylor & Francis, 2003). pp. 250–256.

[3] NOAA, Cloudiness—Mean Number of Days (Clear, Partly Cloudy, Cloudy). http://ols.nndc.noaa.gov/plolstore/plsql/olstore.prodspecific?prodnum=C00095-PUB-A0001. [Accessed December 24, 2007.]

[4] D. Maniccia, B. Rutledge, M.S. Rea, and W. Morrow, Occupant Use of Manual Lighting Controls in Private Offices, *Journal of the Illuminating Engineering Society*, Winter 1999, (IESNA JIES, 1999), pp. 42–56.

[5] U.S. Department of Energy Building Tool Box/Daylighting (web page June 13, 2006), http://www.eere.energy.gov/buildings/info/design/integratedbuilding/passivedaylighting.html#daylight. [Accessed December 28, 2007.]

[6] National Renewable Energy Laboratory, *Solar Radiation Data Manual for Buildings* (Golden, Colorado: NREL, 1995), p. 38.

9.9 Endnotes

Figure 9.18

A sunlight (or alternatively a shading) study is made on a ring heliodon at the Center for Energy Research/ Education/Service at Ball State University (www.bsu.edu/ceres/) to review form and massing influences on daylight availability.
Images ©GarySteffyLightingDesign

40° N latitude equinox 8 a.m.

40° N latitude equinox 10 a.m.

40° N latitude equinox noon

40° N latitude equinox 2 p.m.

40° N latitude equinox 4 p.m.

40° N latitude equinox 6 p.m.

[7] National Renewable Energy Laboratory, *Solar Radiation Data Manual for Buildings* (Golden, Colorado: NREL, 1995), p. 109.

[8] John Mardalijevic, Examples of Climate-Based Daylight Modelling, *CIBSE National Conference* (London: Chartered Institution of Building Services Engineers, 2006), Paper No. 67.

[9] Anca D. Galasiu and Jennifer A. Veitch, Occupant preferences and satisfaction with the luminous environment and control systems in daylit offices: a literature review, *Energy and Buildings*, July 2006 (Elsevier B.V., 2006), pp. 731–733.

[10] R.D. Clear, V. Inkarojrit, and E.S. Lee, Subject responses to electrochromic windows, *Energy and Buildings*, July 2006 (Elsevier B.V., 2006), pp. 758–779.

[11] Carl M. Lampert, Chromogenic smart materials, *Materials Today*, March 2004 (Elsevier B.V., 2004), pp. 28–35.

[12] Switchable Glazing Windows, http://www.toolbase.org/Technology-Inventory/Windows/switchable-glazing-windows [Accessed April 18, 2008.]

[13] High Performance Commercial Building Façades—Solar Control Façades, http://gaia.lbl.gov/hpbf/techno_a.htm. [Accessed December 30, 2007.]

9.10 References

ASHRAE Special Project 102 Committee. 2004. *Advanced Energy Design Guide for Small Office Buildings.* Atlanta: American Society of Heating, Refrigerating and Air-Conditioning Engineers, Inc.

Brown, G.Z., et. al. 1992. *Inside Out, Second Edition.* New York: John Wiley & Sons, Inc.

Daylighting Committee. 1999. *Recommended Practice of Daylighting.* New York: Illuminating Engineering Society of North America.

Evans, Benjamin. 1997. *Daylighting Design, Time-Saver Standards for Architectural Design Data, Seventh Edition.* New York: McGraw Hill.

Lam, William M. C. 1986. *Sunlighting as Formgiver for Architecture.* New York: Van Nostrand Reinhold Company.

Rea, Mark S., ed. 2000. *The IESNA Lighting Handbook: Reference & Application, Ninth Edition.* New York: Illuminating Engineering Society of North America.

Rea, Mark S., ed. 1993. *The IESNA Lighting Handbook: Reference & Application, Eighth Edition.* New York: Illuminating Engineering Society of North America.

Robbins, Claude L. 1986. *Daylighting Design & Analysis.* New York: Van Nostrand Reinhold Company.

Wulfinghoff, Donald R. 2003. *Energy Efficiency Manual.* Wheaton, Maryland: Energy Institute Press.

Establishing daylighting and electric lighting solutions is the crux of the design development stage. Lamps, luminaires, and controls must be selected and orchestrated into a lighting system that meets the project's needs. This chapter reviews electric light sources or lamps that are worthy of consideration during design development. Lamps (colloquially called bulbs) are the source of electric light. We might shade them, reflect them, refract them, louver them, dim them, or bare them, but these devices that produce visible electromagnetic radiation are called lamps. Many people have grown accustomed to and prefer filament lamps. As our sensibilities about the Earth have quickly shifted recently, these preferences, while probably universally held, have come under scrutiny. Now, many people want to prefer fluorescent lamps for their efficiency. Also, as technologies advance, our common impressions of lamps become outdated. Recently, **LED**s have, at least, garnered favor of those enthralled with that technology's promise. The knowledgable designer will conclude that, as yet, there is no lamp panacea. This chapter will discuss lamps as the technologies exist today. However, energy, sustainability, maintenance, and life-cycle issues, and lighting manufacturers' desires to "hit a home run" with any product, including lamps, will continue to influence lamp preferences and pressure product development, as will legislation. While many of the design principles and procedures outlined in this text are relatively unchanging, lamp and luminaire technologies evolve rather rapidly. Hence, what follows is a review based on today's marketplace—in terms of what's available, most efficient and worthy of consideration. Continuing education on lamps on at least a 2-year cycle is a must (see Section 1.8).

Figure 10.1

LED
Light emitting diode. A solid state or fully electronic light source with no filament and/or gaseous compounds to deteriorate or fail. Typically a point source (small button) of light which offers excellent optical efficiency potential. See Figure 10.1 above illustrating a tiny, low-wattage LED indicator (e.g., $1/8$" in diameter [about 3 mm] at 0.05 watts).
Image ©Stockxpert

For purposes of architectural lighting design, there are six general families of electric lamps (listed here according to chronological age as architectural lighting sources): filament, cold cathode, fluorescent, high intensity discharge (HID), electrodeless, and solid state (encompassing LED, and emerging **OLED** technologies). These lamp families provide the palette from which most lighting designers choose lamps. Halogen and halogen-infrared filament, cold cathode, and LED lamps are used sparingly as decorative and accent sources for commercial (meant here to included offices, institutional, healthcare, educational) and hospitality facilities. Halogen and halogen-infrared filament lamps are used in residential applications. Fluorescent lamps are making significant inroads in residential applications and remain a staple in commercial, hospitality, and retail facilities for both general lighting and decorative lighting. Until recently, HID lamps were used nearly exclusively in industrial and exterior applications. However, advances in the metal halide sector of HID lamps puts ceramic metal halide lamps in commercial, hospitality, and healthcare facilities. Electrodeless lamps offer very long **rated life** as the absence of electrodes (present in most other lamp technologies and which wear out and cause failure) promise extraordinary longevity. The lamps have been available for nearly a decade to architectural lighting, but remain appropriate only for a very small segment of parking lot, roadway, and industrial applications. For nearly a decade, LEDs have been touted as the next great light source and have finally made their way into decorative and even a few functional

10.1 Lamp Families

OLED
Organic light emitting diode. A solid state or fully electronic light source with no mechanical component using film of organic compounds to produce light. Typically an area source (small to moderate sheets) of light.

rated life
Industry standard to mean that point in time at which half of the lamps in a very large group under laboratory conditions will have failed. However, read manufacturers' literature footnotes for specifics for each family of lamps. Two important notes. First, this means a good number of lamps will fail before rated life. Second, LED lamps purportedly never fail, but just fade away (get dimmer). LED vendors are attempting to develop a "rated-life" standard.

luminaires; however, these lamps are hyped to far greater performance than they can achieve in real-world projects. One common and over-hyped issue with electrodeless and solid state lamps is extraordinary (some would say unbelievable) claims of long-life operation (on light sources that haven't existed in commercial applications for any real great lengths of time) and efficacies.

Certainly, as manufacturers continue lamp development and as designers become increasingly innovative in meeting a host of lighting criteria, we should see adoption of all higher-efficiency lamp types. Fluorescent lamps will continue to make inroads in residential and hospitality applications. HID lamps will gain in popularity in commercial and retail applications, both interior and exterior. If energy supplies become too scarce and if global warming takes priority, then designers will see rapid shifts to the most efficacious lamps. Table 10.1 outlines the general lamp families and their relative respective operating characteristics. Discussions follow on each family. Nearly all lamps made today have some serious limitations or "side effects." Most exhibit some hazardous materials. Read all caveats in vendors' literature.

These lamp discussions introduce some specific qualities about lamps. For example, there is a distinction that must be emphasized between efficacy (lumens per watt [LPW]) and **candlepower** (cp). Candlepower is a much better indication of a lamp's (and also a luminaire's) effectiveness in directing light to the area where light is desired. So, while LPW is a favored metric of efficacy, it does not tell a complete story about a light's effectiveness. The following example about a water hose might help. Suppose you have a spigot that can supply 3 gallons of water per minute (11.3 liters [L] per minute). If you connect a typical hose to the spigot, water flows out the end of the hose at 3 gallons per minute. Now, put a nozzle on the end of the hose. The nozzle concentrates or directs the water—making the water more effective for cleaning or "hosing down" objects. Think of "gallons per minute" as the equivalent of "lumens per watt," and think of the nozzle as the equivalent of a reflector and/or lens assembly on a lamp or luminaire. Lighting technologies that are point sources of light, such as filament, miniature metal halide, and LED lamps are much better suited as directional or concentrated sources of light because reflectors and/or lenses work very well with the point-source of light to concentrate or spread it. **Point sources are typically more efficient at generating illuminance on a specific target than relatively large linear or area light sources. Most times, lower wattage point sources are more effective than higher-wattage linear or area sources.** So, for accent lighting or areas where little or no spill light beyond the object or area of interest is desired, filament, miniature metal halide, and LED lamps are primary candidates for consideration. **Even though some linear or area sources exhibit higher lumens per watt, the lumens cannot be sufficiently concentrated and directed. Don't fall victim to selecting lamps based solely on LPW ratings.**

candlepower
The light intensity in a specific direction from a lamp or luminaire. Measured in candelas (cd).

more online @
www.gelighting.com/eu/index.html
www.gelighting.com/na/
www.lrc.rpi.edu/programs/Futures/index.asp
www.osram.com/osram_com/Professionals/index.html
www.lighting.philips.com
www.sylvania.com/BusinessProducts/LightingForBusiness/
www.sylvania.com/AboutUs/EnergyAndEnvironment/RegulationsLegislation/
  Energy/StateProductRegulations/

Architectural Lighting Design

Incandescence is light emission from a heated filament. In a traditional incandescent lamp, an electric current passes through a filament, heating the filament to the point of producing visible radiation (see Figure 10.2). Filament lamps with tungsten filaments as we know them today are better heaters than illuminators. For architectural lighting, halogen and halogen infrared filament sources are the most efficient filament lamps at time of this printing. Even these lamps, however, pose a cooling load issue for HVAC systems, and use more energy to produce light than cold cathode, fluorescent, metal halide, or even some LED counterparts. Because most people prefer the color quality of filament lamps, they are the reference against which all other lamp types are judged. Hence, for cold cathode, fluorescent, metal halide, and LED lamps to have popular success, they must compare quite favorably in both color temperature and color rendering with filament lamps.

Filament lamps remain the most popular lamps in America and in the rest of the world. There are simply too many incandescent screwbase sockets in place in existing construction (most of it residential) to effect a significant and fast switch to other lamp types. However, in response to energy consumption and security concerns and energy pollution issues associated with the electricity needed to operate standard incandescent filament lamps, manufacturers are improving filament lamp technology and exploring alternatives. The latest source development, commercialized by GE, is the halogen infrared plus technology.

Standard tungsten filaments boil away as the standard incandescent lamp ages. A typical household table light's incandescent lamp is likely to have a blackened zone or area on the bulb envelope when it fails. This is where the evaporated tungsten has settled on the inside of the glass envelope or bulb. During the several hundred hours of its life, a standard tungsten filament incandescent lamp loses light output—the filament boils away, leaving less filament to produce light and blackening the inside bulb wall, thereby reducing the overall transmittance of the bulb glass. In the 1950s, it was discovered that halides or salts enclosed in a quartz capsule (as in quartz rock—then the only material able to withstand the temperature and pressure involved) and heated to high temperatures would help capture the evaporating tungsten and redeposit it back onto the filam-ent—sort of a self-perpetuating filament. The halogen cycle (aka halogen regenerative cycle) enables lamp manufacturers to offer lamps that are more efficient, are longer-lived, and have better **lumen maintenance** than standard tungsten counterparts. The early versions of these lamps were called quartz halogen—quartz being the only light-transmitting substance at the time that could withstand the very high temperatures and serve to envelop the filament and contain the halide. Many capsules today use ceramics.

In the 1980s, GE introduced a coating that could be applied to the halogen capsule that would take some of the heat (infrared radiation) generated by the tungsten filament and redirect this heat back onto the filament. More heat on the filament produces more light and permits a reduction in power (watts) required. This, in turn, allows the use of fewer watts of power to achieve the same amount of light. At the moment, **halogen infrared (HIR™) incandescent lamps are about twice as efficient as standard tungsten filament incandescent lamps.** As this HIR™ technology finds its way into the various bulb shapes, residential lighting and accent lighting in hospitality and religious applications will become more efficient.

HIR™ is a registered trademark of GE.

lumen maintenance
Referring to a lamp's ability to maintain light output over life. As all lamps age, they produce incrementally less light. Some lamps have better **lamp lumen depreciation (LLD)** than others.

lamp lumen depreciation (LLD)
A percentage value indicating the total light output available from a given lamp at a certain time in its life versus its original light output value at initial installation. For example, a halogen lamp that has a rated life of 2000 hours will have 100% of its rated light output at the start of its operation (or life). At 1400 hours of operation, enough filament will have burned away that the lamp produces 95% (0.95) of its initial rated output. At the end of rated life (2000 hours), the halogen lamp will produce 92% (0.92) of its initial rated output. In this text, LLD is reported at 70% of life.

Table 10.1 Lamps and Respective Characteristics

Lamp Category	The Good	The Bad
Filament/Standard Tungsten (cited for historical reference)	• Very well accepted • Extremely low initial cost • Very easy to dim, electrically simple[c]	• Most inefficient • Shortest life • Extremely high operating cost
Filament/Halogen	• Very well accepted • Very low initial cost • Very easy to dim, electrically simple[c]	• Very inefficient • Very short life • Very high operating cost
Filament/Halogen Infrared	• Very well accepted • Low initial cost • Very easy to dim, electrically simple[c]	• Inefficient • Short life • High operating cost
Filament/HIR Advanced	• Very well accepted • Moderate initial cost • Very easy to dim, electrically simple[c]	• Baseline-efficient • Short life • Moderately high operating cost
Cold Cathode/Retrofit Versions (using screwbase sockets)	• Well accepted at 2700K to 3000K • Moderate initial cost • Easy to dim, relatively simple[c]	• Limited wattages • Poor power factor and/or harmonics bad for electrical system • Mercury content requires handling care and recycling
Cold Cathode/Architectural Versions	• Well accepted at 2700K to 3000K • Easy to dim • Lamps formed to shape of details	• High initial cost • Relatively complex[c] and complicated maintenance • Mercury content requires handling care and recycling
Fluorescent/Retrofit Versions (using screwbase sockets)	• Well accepted at 2700K to 3000K • Low initial cost • Relatively simple[c]	• A, B, R, and PAR versions least efficient • Very poor power factor and/or harmonics bad for electrical system • Not dimmable • Mercury content requires handling care and recycling
Fluorescent/Dedicated Compact Versions (using plug-in or pin-base sockets)	• Well accepted at 2700K to 3000K • Low-to-moderate initial cost • Dimmable	• No very-low-wattage quality electronic versions • Limited lamp form factors[d] • Costly to dim • Mercury content requires handling care and recycling
Fluorescent/Linear Versions	• Well accepted at 3000K and new 2700K • Low-to-moderate initial cost • Dimmable • Most efficient general white-light	• No very-low-wattage quality electronic versions • Costly to dim • Mercury content requires handling care and recycling
Ceramic Metal Halide	• Well accepted at 3000K • Most efficient accent white-light • Low operating cost	• No 2700K option • High initial cost • No very-low-wattage versions • Not instant-on: requires 5 to 10 minutes warmup to full output • Very costly to dim/dims only to 60% • Mercury content requires handling care and recycling
Electrodeless	• Acceptable at 3000K • Very long life • Low to very low operating cost	• No 2700K option • Very high initial cost • No very-low-wattage versions • Not dimmable • Mercury content requires handling care and recycling
Light Emitting Diode	• Fair at 3000K • Very long life (using "unique" rating) • Low to very low operating cost	• Highly inconsistent color temperatures • Extremely high initial cost • Requires (sometimes many) extra auxiliary devices for dimming • Supposedly never expires, but fades over time (questionable long term efficacy) • CRI barely tolerable

[a] Efficacies are based on "system" data that includes high-efficiency ballast or transformer losses. For "warm white" lamps typical of architectural lighting applications. Higher efficacies from higher-wattage lamps. Even higher efficacies are possible with very high-wattage lamps and/or the higher color temperature lamps.

[b] If these lamps were available today, this represents the likely candelas per watt for lamps exhibiting a 9° to 12° beam spread.

Efficacy[a]		Targeted Candlepower		Color Aspects		Status of Use	Applications
LPW	Focused Lamps Available		9° to 12° CBCP Cd/Watt	CRI	CCT		
8–13	NO		85[b]	100	2700	Very Rare	Historic Landmarks
use very, very rarely in special historic or public monuments for historic dimmable lighting effect							
10–15	YES		200	100	2800	Rare	Hospitality Residential
use rarely in residences or historic or public monuments for traditional dimmable lighting effect							
15–20	YES		300	100	2800	Limited	Hospitality Residential Retail
use in residences and sparingly in select hospitality applications for dimmable accenting and general downlighting (e.g., restaurants, ballrooms)							
20–25	YES		330	100	2850	Some	Hospitality Retail
use in select hospitality and retail applications for dimmable, instant-on accenting and general downlighting							
35–45	YES BUT WEAK[d]		Questionable Utility	82	2700 to 4100	Some	Hospitality Residential
use in residential and sparingly in hospitality applications for dimmable, instant-on general lighting							
70–80[e]	NO		NA	85+[f]	2700 to 6500+	Limited	Commercial Hospitality
use in select commercial and hospitality applications for dimmable, instant-on detail accenting							
35–65	YES BUT WEAK[d]		Questionable Utility	82	2700 to 4100	Some	Hospitality Residential
use in residential and sparingly in hospitality applications for interior general lighting (the more efficacious lamps are the exposed-tube "spiral" and "biaxial" versions)							
50–60	NO		NA	82	2700 to 4100	Significant	Commercial Hospitality Residential Retail
use in many applications for general interior lighting and exterior lighting and surface washes							
70–90	NO		NA	85	2700 to 4100	Significant	Commercial Hospitality Residential Retail
use in many applications for general interior lighting and surface washes							
40–80	YES		400–900	80+	3000 and 4200	Some	Commercial Hospitality Retail
use in many applications for interior and exterior general and accent lighting							
60–80	NO		NA	80	3000 to 4000	Rare	Industrial Exterior
use in some roadway and parking lot applications							
15–50	YES BUT WEAK[d]		Questionable Utility	75 common	2700 to 6500+	Limited	Commercial Hospitality Retail
use in "eye candy" accent situations, custom situations, steplights							

SPECIAL NOTE: These data "improve" monthly. However, bonafide, independently verifiable efficacy, color temperature, and color rendering data obtained in accordance with architectural lighting-industry standards are scarce. Higher efficacies are tied to higher (typically less desirable) color temperatures.

[c] Degree of simplicity is used here to indicate the need (or lack thereof) for additional control/power devices independent of the lamp for operation.

[d] Lamps may be available in so-called "MR" and "R" and "PAR" type bulbs, but typically these lamps are useless for accenting and "punchy" downlighting.

[e] For triphosphor white lamps.

Lamps

Figure 10.2

The typical traditional tungsten filament incandescent lamp (in the "A" or Arbitrary shaped bulb). Shown here as reference to understanding lamp components and operation. Close-up on opposite page shows filament, support wires, and electrical contact wires viewed from above. Lower image on opposite page illustrates the coiled coil tungsten filament. Filament is coiled multiple times to introduce as much surface area in as small a space as practical to produce as much light as practical.
Images ©Stockxpert

screwbase
Referring to the type of base a lamp exhibits for fit into a traditional table light or ceiling light socket.

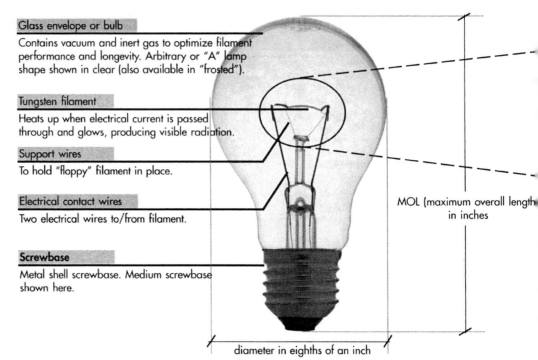

Glass envelope or bulb

Contains vacuum and inert gas to optimize filament performance and longevity. Arbitrary or "A" lamp shape shown in clear (also available in "frosted").

Tungsten filament

Heats up when electrical current is passed through and glows, producing visible radiation.

Support wires

To hold "floppy" filament in place.

Electrical contact wires

Two electrical wires to/from filament.

Screwbase

Metal shell screwbase. Medium screwbase shown here.

MOL (maximum overall length in inches

diameter in eighths of an inch

mains voltage
Referring to the primary or main operating voltage of a typical electrical system. Typically, 120V or 277V in America, 230V in much of Europe, and 347V in Canada.

low voltage
Referring to the secondary operating voltage of some lamp types. Typically, 12V or 24V operation as opposed to the mains voltage of 120V or 277V in America, 230V in much of Europe, and 347V in Canada.

Other technologies are allowing lamp manufacturers to squeeze more efficiency from HIR™ lamps. Osram Sylvania and Philips have pioneered special reflectors for accent lights that capture the light from the HIR™ capsules and redirect it more efficiently than has been possible or practical in the recent past. GE's latest generation of HIR™ lamps, HIR™ Plus, combine a special silver reflector coating on the bulb wall with a new thin-film infrared coating on the filament capsule. These HIR+ lamps are 20 percent more efficient than their HIR™ counterparts and 60 percent more efficient than their halogen counterparts with lamp life 30 percent greater than HIR™ and 50 percent greater than halogen. Halogen infrared **mains voltage** lamps are the lamps of choice for architectural applications where an incandescent color, color rendering, and dimming quality is a necessity and/or where instant-on lamps with significant candlepower punch are appropriate.

Finally, for the most efficient and discrete accent lighting, smallest filaments are best. **Low voltage** (typically 12V) lamps permit filaments to be quite small—as close to a theoretical point source as is practical—and, therefore, allow for optically precise reflectors to be developed around them. Recent advances in low voltage halogen infrared lamps result in relatively long life (4000 and 5000 hours), very precisely controlled accent lights.

The HIR™ technologies are possible only because of extremely high operating temperatures near the filament. These lamps need to be used with great care. They should be used only in luminaires that are UL listed for operation of such a lamp; should be kept sufficient distances from flammable materials; should never be touched when in operation or soon after extinguishing; should never be in close proximity to human skin; should be enclosed in a protected outer bulb envelope or shielded with a tempered glass lens; and should not be used in portable lights that are easily tipped or are used without adult supervision.

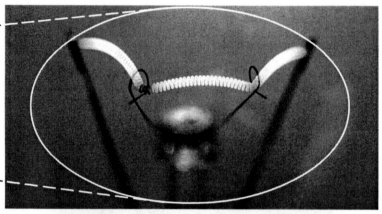

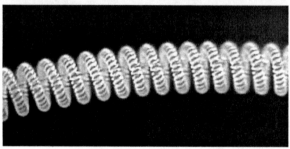

Dimming of HIR™ lamps is very easy and costs little. Dimming has the advantage of increasing lamp life by as much as 400 percent. However, since the halogen cycle works only under high temperature conditions and since dimming reduces filament temperature, extensive dimming (to less than 90 percent of full output) for extended periods (more than 100 hours) may reduce lamp life. Therefore, periodically (perhaps once a month), HIR™ lamps that are consistently dimmed should be operated at full output for an hour or so. Dimming also affects light output (lumens) and wattage (power) consumption. Filament lamps become progressively less efficient as they are dimmed. Figure 10.3 offers several graphs showing the changing relationship of these various parameters as filament lamps are dimmed.

Filament lamps may contain a number of hazardous materials, including lead solder. Review the manufacturers latest material safety datasheets (MSD or MSDS). **All lamps should be recycled,** although finding a recycler for all lamp types may prove difficult in the near term. Relative to other lamp types, filament lamps are suspected of exhibiting low embodied energy from manufacture although this information is yet unavailable.

As of this writing, legislation now seems poised to ban incandescent lamps. Given the state of energy codes and sustainability initiatives, filament lamps are already relegated to an extremely minor role in commercial construction. Even then, HIR™ filament lamps should be used for long life and best efficiency of the filament family. GE recently announced plans to introduce a new, presumably filament-based, technology by 2010 that promises an efficacy of 30 LPW with up to 60 LPW by 2012. If this comes to pass, energy requirements for lighting could plummet. However, adoption in the residential marketplace will likely be very sensitive to initial cost.

more online @
www.ul.com/consumers/halogen.html

Figure 10.3

Dimming an incandescent lamp significantly influences its life, output (lumens), wattage (power), and efficacy (lumens per watt [LPW]).

Lamp Life Function
Dimming an incandescent lamp significantly increases lamp life. Halogen and HIR™ lamps, however, do require full run-up periodically in order to maintain the halogen cycle.

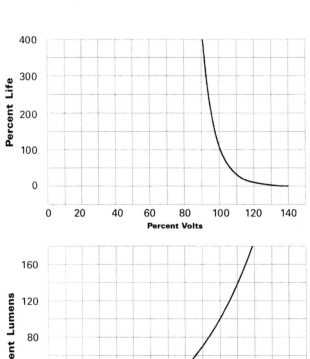

Lumen Output Function
Lumen output drops with dimming, but not in a linear fashion as shown here. When dimmed below 20%, little useful light is produced— although the effect can be much like candlelight.

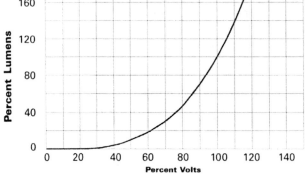

Power Function
Lamp watts decline nearly linearly as volts are reduced.

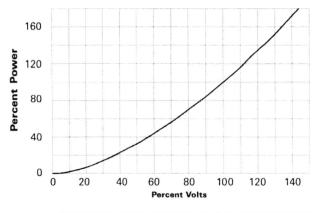

Lumens per Watt Function
Lamp efficacy is seriously reduced as incandescent lamps are dimmed since light output falls faster than power used.

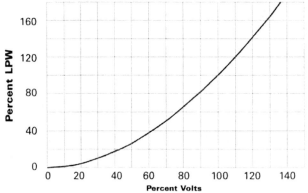

Architectural Lighting Design

BT/TB/Mains Voltage

BT- (near right thumbnail) and TB- (far right thumbnail) shaped lamps are the modern-day equivalent to the A bulb shape (A stood for Arbitrary shape—the soft curvilinear bulb profile shown in Figure 10.2). Some halogen capsules require protective shielding or circuitry on the off-chance that the capsule experiences a nonpassive failure—in other words, explodes. While not a common occurrence, if/when one of these halogen capsules explodes (perhaps by coming in contact with moisture), the hot shards of glass and filament can cause a fire unless contained—hence, the protective shield, which is typically tempered glass. To develop the first halogen A bulb, manufacturers had to come up with a thick glass bulb envelope. The first of these, by GE, was also covered in Teflon® hence, a Teflon® bulb, or TB lamp. Since the glass is cast (for tempering) and not blown, the bulb has a more angular shape than the traditional A bulb. These lamps are frosted or diffuse-coated to provide a general-purpose lamp. Lamps are available in the "19" size (TB/H/19) only. As with any lamp designation, the numeric value immediately succeeding the bulb shape/type indicates the lamp's diameter in eighths of an inch (see Figure 10.2). This size aspect is very important when selecting luminaires, or conversely when selecting lamps. If a wall sconce cutsheet indicates that the sconce can accommodate an A15 lamp, then an equivalent-size lamp is needed at or below the rated wattage of the sconce. The TB/H/19 won't fit.

A more recent development in halogen capsule design now allows for use of soft-glass bulbs since these new capsules are not prone to nonpassive failure. For these capsules, the BT-lamp shape is popular. Although smaller in diameter than the TB-shape, the overall length is slightly longer to accommodate the more-linear halogen capsule. BT and TB lamps are best suited for low-level applications where a filament lamp is required for color or dimming such as a special table light or a few key wall sconces in residential spaces and some ceremonial commercial and hospitality spaces. These lamps should be used rarely and preferably in situations where they are not operated continuously for long hours. For example, good applications might be a toilet room fitted with motion sensors in low-occupancy situations or an infrequently used formal living room. For most applications requiring screwbase, low-wattage lamps, consider cold cathode or fluorescent retrofit lamps (see discussions below).

PAR/Mains Voltage

PAR is an acronym for parabolic aluminized reflector, which describes the shape and type of the bulb. Made of cast glass and a precisely formed parabolic internal reflector, some varieties of PAR lamps can withstand direct contact with rain and snow, so they have been popular, albeit unsightly, as household security floodlights. Since this application contributes to light trespass and light pollution, such security floodlights should be used in conjunction with motion detectors to limit use. The large lens on a PAR lamp has a partially stippled, mostly stippled, to fully stippled pattern that, in conjunction with the PAR reflector, establishes the intensity and spread of light. PAR lamps are the most versatile of the filament lamps. Given their various beam spreads, wattages, and resulting candlepower, these lamps can be used as accents in low, moderate, or high ceiling applications, or can be used for general lighting where low-end dimming for note-taking is important and/or where group dining occurs (place settings look their best under these lamps).

Teflon® is a registered trademark of E. I. duPont de Nemours and Company.

Figure 10.4

Anatomy of a PAR lamp designation. Check each lamp manufacturer's catalog for respective actual catalog designations and beam spreads. Unfortunately, the industry seems unable to settle on common **beam spread** definitions. The following beam spread designations are suggested:[1]
- VNSP = very narrow spot (≤7°)
- NSP = narrow spot (8 to 10°)
- SP = spot (11 to 14°)
- WSP = wide spot (15 to 18°)
- VWSP = very wide spot (19 to 23°)
- NFL = narrow flood (24 to 32°)
- FL = flood (33 to 44°)
- WFL = wide flood (45 to 55°)
- VWFL = very wide flood (≥56°)

Image courtesy of General Electric Company

beam spread

The total angle within which a directional lamp exhibits at least 50 percent of the lamp's maximum light intensity. If a 10° beam spread lamp exhibits 15,500 candelas CBCP, then at 5° either side of the center beam the lamp generates 7750 candelas. This is used to determine the diameter and magnitude of the beam at various aiming angles and distances.

instant-on

Not long ago, this meant "full light instantly" when switching on a lamp. Typically filament and fluorescent lamps were instant-on and HID lamps were not. However, some latest technology high-efficiency fluorescent lamps only provide about 40 percent of their light output instantly, taking 3 to 8 minutes to provide 100 percent light output. This can be an issue with code requirements and/or with users.

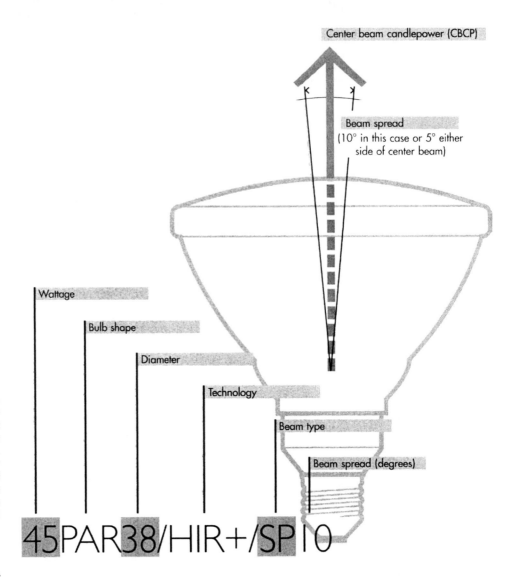

Center beam candlepower (CBCP)

Beam spread (10° in this case or 5° either side of center beam)

Wattage

Bulb shape

Diameter

Technology

Beam type

Beam spread (degrees)

45PAR38/HIR+/SP10

Similar to the TB lamp designation, PAR lamps have a numerical designation indicating the lamp diameter. However, other alphanumerics are used to distinguish the various versions of PAR lamps from one another. Figure 10.4 illustrates the extent of the typical PAR lamp designation.[1]

PAR lamps can be used in bare sockets, in luminaires with little or no special reflectors, or in luminaires with reflectors specially designed to accommodate them. The higher-wattage halogen infrared and HIR+ versions have efficacies of 20 and 24 LPW respectively as of this printing. In the relatively large PAR38 reflector (diameter of $3\frac{8}{8}$" or $4\frac{3}{4}$"), excellent candlepower intensity is possible. For this reason, however, these lamps can be quite glary. Their best use is in deep downlights, deep adjustable accents, accents fitted with louvers, or spreadlens wallwashers in limited areas requiring **instant-on**, dimmable lighting such as ballrooms (see Figure 10.5). **These lamps should be used sparingly and preferably in situations where they are not the sole source of light operated continuously at full output for long hours. For most commercial and institutional applications requiring directional lights operating at full power for long periods of time and where dimming is unnecessary and on/off switching is infrequent, consider ceramic metal halide lamps** (see discussion below).

PAR38/HIR+/NFL25 Downlight
www.epl.com

Image courtesy of General Electric Company

Figure 10.5

PAR/HIR+ Application: High ceiling spaces where focused downlight is needed to highlight features (e.g., table top finishes, place settings, etc.) and/or provide full-range dimming (e.g., for various lecture-style programs and various dining settings) are candidates for HIR+ lamps. Consider luminaires with relatively large diameter reflectors to allow for pole relamping (a pole with suction cup is used to replace the lamp from the floor).
Image ©Kevin Beswick

The quartz halogen tubular bulb, or T bulb, (see Figure 10.6) is so named because the bulb is a linear, cylinder shape. These are commonly known as "halogen bulbs" to the consumer and have been responsible for a number of fires in the past because of users' carelessness. Table lights and floor lights which use T lamps are not recommended.

T3/HIR™ lamps exhibit efficacies of 30 LPW. These lamps are particularly well-suited for wallwash and uplighting applications. The tiny, linear source allows for very efficient linear reflector designs to "shovel" the light toward walls or ceilings. Figure 10.7 shows uplights using HIR™ T3 double-ended lamps. Relatively few hours of use each week, the need for continuous dimming, sparkle on silver and gold gilt only achievable with small sources, and low initial cost made these lamps an appropriate choice for this cathedral. **These lamps should be used sparingly and preferably in situations where they are not the sole source of light operated continuously at full output for long hours. For most commercial and institutional applications requiring wallwash and uplighting with sparkle operating at full power for long periods of time and where dimming is unnecessary and on/off switching is infrequent, consider ceramic metal halide lamps** (see discussion below). For wallwash and uplighting applications where flatter and softer lighting is desired and operating at full- or dimmed-power for long periods of time and/or with frequent on/off switching, consider triphosphor fluorescent lamps (see discussion below).

T3/Mains Voltage

Figure 10.6

The halogen cycle and the thin-film infrared IR coating greatly improve the efficacy and life of a tubular filament lamp. The halides in the lamp react with vaporized tungsten to recycle it back to the filament. This regenerative cycle allows a doubling or tripling of useful filament life. The IR coating allows visible radiation to pass through, but reflects infrared wavelengths back to the filament. This infrared radiation provides additional heat to the filament and therefore requires fewer watts to produce more light. A double-ended T3/HIR has this appearance and operational aspects. Actual lamp depends on manufacturer and wattage.

Image ©Fuzzphoto—Fotolia.com

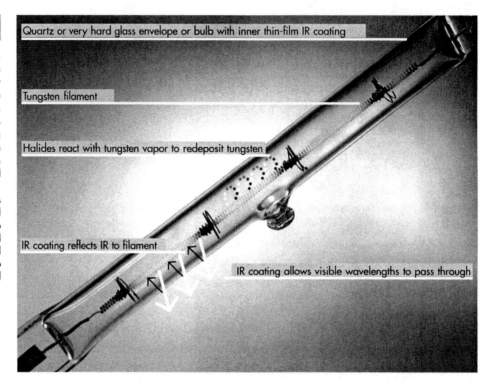

Quartz or very hard glass envelope or bulb with inner thin-film IR coating

Tungsten filament

Halides react with tungsten vapor to redeposit tungsten

IR coating reflects IR to filament

IR coating allows visible wavelengths to pass through

MR16/12V

Image courtesy of General Electric Company

MR is an abbreviation for multifaceted reflector—a highly polished, many-faceted mirror reflector surrounds a small halogen capsule to direct light quite precisely and efficiently (see Figure 10.8). Traditionally, these lamps were used exclusively in slide projectors. As technologies and manufacturing quality control have advanced, these lamps now have sufficiently long lamp life and efficiencies to make them suitable for many architectural lighting applications.

Because of their tiny size yet high light output, these lamps are inherently glary. The best luminaires are relatively deep or offer an optional louver to control glare. Their tiny size, however, makes them very popular for architectural applications. MR16 lamps fit into downlights and adjustable accents that are about 4" in diameter and some with apertures less than 2". Appropriate applications include lighting objets d'art and artwork, as well as merchandise feature accenting (see Figures 10.9 and 10.11), wallwashing, and downlighting.

Because of the possibility, albeit unlikely, of non-passive failure, an auxiliary, protective, tempered glass lens is required in front of the MR lamp. Most versions of the MR/IR are available from lamp manufacturers with an integral cover glass. However, some integral glass cover lenses are convex and limit the use of auxiliary filters (e.g., ultraviolet and spreadlenses). Review samples before writing specifications.

Some 50-watt MR/IR lamps exhibit such high operating temperatures that they prematurely fail in some luminaires. Check with lamp and luminaire manufacturers before writing specifications.

The IR coating on the halogen capsule in MR/IR lamps is responsible for 25 percent improvement in efficiency—the same amount of light as standard MR16 counterparts at 25 percent fewer watts. The MR/IR lamps exhibit a rated life of

T3/HIR Uplight
www.elliptipar.com

Figure 10.7

T3/HIR Application: Very high ceiling spaces where strong uplight is needed to highlight colorful ceilings (e.g., sky blue, gilt decoration, decorative painting) and where use is limited to select hours and/or where full-range dimming is needed (e.g., for various ceremonial programs) are candidates for T3/HIR lamps. Consider luminaires with enhanced reflector optics for best efficiency.
Image ©GarySteffyLightingDesign

4000 to 5000 hours. **These lamps should be used in moderation as accents and feature lighting in retail applications demanding the sparkle of filament lamps with high degree of focused light (e.g., jewelry displays, crystal, glassware, etc.) and dining and residential applications where discrete accenting and dimmability are required. For most commercial and institutional applications requiring feature accenting with sparkle operating at full power for long periods of time and where dimming is unnecessary and on/off switching is infrequent, consider ceramic metal halide lamps** (see discussion below).

Two other low voltage lamps are worth discussion which are halogen, not HIR. 12V halogen AR (aluminum reflector—top thumbnail to right) lamps and PAR (parabolic aluminized reflector) lamps operate much like the MR lamps—taking a small halogen capsule and putting a reflector around it. Here, however, the reflectors are relatively large, so that they can achieve extremely tight (very narrow spot) pinspots. For high-impact focal lighting in retail, and hospitality spaces or where ceilings are relatively high and/or the objects to be highlighted are relatively small, these lamps are useful. One benefit of these lamps over MR lamps is the use of a filament cap. A cap placed over the filament, preventing its direct view, results in much less glare. 12V halogen AR and PAR lamps are so well controlled optically that there is no spill light, yielding very dramatic presentation with very little glare.

Other Bulb Types

Image courtesy of General Electric Company

Figure 10.8

The MR16 lamp is only 20 in diameter. With the multifaced mirror reflector system, the halogen cycle and the thin-film infrared IR coating, these lamps offer exceptional light intensity in concentrated beams for accenting. MR/IR lamps have this appearance and use the bipin base. Actual lamp depends on manufacturer and beamspread.
Top image ©Thorsten Jahns—Fotolia.com
Bottom image ©Gufh—Fotolia.com

The 12V halogen AR version may require a tempered glass protective lens—check with the lamp manufacturer. The 12V halogen PAR36 lamp does not require a protective lens. The AR lamp is a quieter lamp upon dimming. Dimming causes lamp filament hum or singing on many filament lamps. For many of the halogen and HIR™ lamps, however, the bulb envelope is sufficiently thick and the internal halogen capsule offers another acoustic isolation mechanism. For PAR36 lamps, however, likely because of their design originally as automotive lamps, filament hum is significant when dimmed. **These lamps should be used very rarely for significant focal features where glare control and dimmability are critical.** No other light source is comparable.

There are many other bulb types of mains and low voltage filament lamps. However, these are standard tungsten or halogen filament lamps, not halogen infrared lamps. Because of their inefficiencies and short life, these lamps are not recommended.

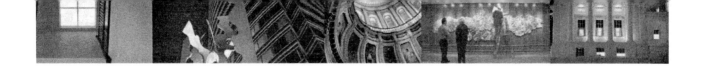

MR/IR Pinhole Accent
www.iris-lighting.com

Figure 10.9

MR16/IR Application: In a restaurant with relatively high ceilings and the desire to light fabric and metal mesh curtains used to separate two dining areas the MR16/IR lamp offers full-range dimming and can be used in pinhole trims. Pinholes painted out to match the ceiling (using high-temperature paint or custom painted at the factory) reduce ceiling clutter. All lamps are hot, but IR and HIR lamps especially. Check with lamp and luminaire manufacturers on specific use limitations. Sufficient distance must be maintained from lights to flammable materials. This depends on wattage, beam spread (concentrated beams may concentrate heat in the center of the beam), luminaire, and adjacent and lighted materials. When in doubt, consult with lamp and luminaire manufacturers. Mockups can help, but these must be carefully monitored and scrutinized.
Image ©Kevin Beswick

Several of these include BR, ER, and R types. Existing installations with these kinds of **tungsten filament lamps should be considered as retrofit candidates with the newer more efficient halogen and HIR™ lamps. Check with lamp and luminaire manufacturers for lamp compatability before retrofitting existing lights.**

12V Transformers

The low voltage lamps previously discussed require 12 volts of power for operation. To achieve this, transformers (which transform the mains or high voltage down to 12 volts) must be used at the lamp (integral to the luminaire) or remotely. Using a remote transformer eliminates hardware from each luminaire and typically allows the operation of more than one lamp from a single transformer. However, sizing the remote transformer and the wiring from the transformer become critical engineering assignments in order to maintain proper operating voltage at the lamp (remember, under voltage, or dimming, results in significantly longer life but less light, while over voltage results in significantly shorter life). Also, the location of the remote transformer(s) becomes a critical architectural and engineering issue. Transformers, which could be at least 8 by 8 by 12" (200 by 200 by 300 mm), must be easily accessible, well ventilated, and sound-isolated, and located in a code-compliant space.

Transformers that are used adjacent to lamps and are intended to operate just a single lamp usually are available in either an electromagnetic version (the original-style iron core with a continuous coil of wire wound around it—simply called magnetic) or an electronic version (solid state components). Each type has its benefits. The magnetic transformer is bulky and relatively heavy, but is also relatively quiet, today, and easily dimmed. These are available with various "taps" whereby the transformer output can be set to slightly less than 12V to permanently dim lamps ever so slightly for improved life with little light loss, or can be set to slightly more than 12V to allow for voltage drop created by long distances between lamps and the transformer location. The electronic transformer is smaller and lightweight, but can be noisy when dimmed, and requires a special dimmer. However, electronic transformers are better at limiting the secondary voltage (the 12 volts) to any fluctuations. This better preserves lamp life if the mains power is subject to over-voltage fluctuations.

Low voltage transformers consume some energy just in the transforming process. Typically, this extra load is between 5 and 10 percent of the lamp wattage. This is a particularly important consideration when determining electrical loads for energy code compliance and for cooling loads.

more online @
www.q-tran.com/

10.3 Cold Cathode

Cold cathode lamps are so named because of the use of a filament-like device known as a cathode at each end of the lamp. These cathodes, installed in a tubular glass structure, strike an arc from one end of the tube to the other. Unlike many fluorescent lamps that retain a bit of heat at the cathodes (hence, "hot" cathodes) to help strike an instant light with ease, the cathodes in cold cathode lamps are not preheated (which would help start the arc through the tube), but rather are simply energized with very high voltages that drive an arc through the tube. This is an important distinction because cold cathode lamps, thus, require high voltage transformers that have the potential to be noisy and hot, and require careful wiring/connecting by the installer. The reference "cold cathode" is at times used interchangeably with "neon." Technically, however, neon is a type of cold cathode lamp—one filled with neon gas and of small diameter (typically 15 mm). Red light results when the tube is filled with neon. Blue light results when the tube is filled with argon and a minute amount of mercury. If the glass tube is coated with various phosphors, then other colors of visible light can be generated, including shades of white (from very pink or warm white, to very blue or daylight white).

Cold cathode lighting, initially developed as signage lighting in the early 20th century, was a precursor to today's fluorescent lighting. Each cold cathode installation is essentially custom. Tubing is purchased by a sign or local lamp manufacturer or a national manufacturer and is then shaped into the various configurations and lengths required for the given project. Tubes are cleaned, vacuum-pumped, and filled with the appropriate mixture of gas and elements needed to achieve the specified color. Cold cathode lamps using the most efficacious triphosphor coatings in 2800K, 3000K, 3500K, and 4100K typically are up to times as efficient as the most efficacious filament

lamps. Cold cathode lamp life ratings can be as high as 25,000 hours. However, because these are custom lamps, when one lamp in a long run burns out, it may be necessary to replace all of the lamps or alternatively, if the lighting system can be "down" for a brief period, all lamps can be recharged. In any event, any components or elements, especially the minute amount of mercury in each lamp, should be recycled. The new lamp will likely have a brighter appearance than and may even exhibit some color shift from the original lamps if just one lamp is replaced or recharged. If the lamps are exposed or backlighting signage, this brightness and color difference can be readily apparent and distracting. Even in cove lighting applications, this difference may be sufficiently bothersome. Group relamping is typically best. Finally, the custom nature of these lamps makes them somewhat expensive.

Cold cathode tubing diameters range from 12 to 25 mm. The smaller-diameter lamps can be neatly tucked into relatively small architectural coves, niches, and ledges as illustrated in Figures 10.10, 10.11, and 10.12. Cold cathode lamps have the added benefit of being continuous "lines" of light that can be bent to almost any shape. The serpentine slot detail in Figure 5.5 and Figure 11.29, the curvilinear slot detail in Figure 5.7, and the cove detail in Figure 11.29 consist of cold cathode tubing following the configurations of the details. Because these lamps are handmade to order from stock tubes that are usually 4' (1200 mm) in length, the tubes can be molded end to end to 8 to 12' (2.4 to 3.6 m) runs. Alternatively, special socket configurations called "bend backs" allow for a continuous lighted appearance with short lamp segments.

Cold cathode lamps should be used in moderation to accentuate details or for soft general lighting in coves and wall slots in applications where curvilinear architectural forms and detailing are prominent and/or affordable dimmability and/or color are required. Cold cathode lamp life is typically extended with fewer on/off switching cycles. This makes cold cathode appropriate where lighting is intended to be energized 24/7 or for relatively long operational periods. All lamps are to be recycled after use.

The National Electrical Code cites requirements regarding neon tubing. In residential applications, for example, the transformers must be specially sized and relatively low voltage. Check with the registered electrical engineer on the project and with the local building authorities for specific interpretation and guidance.

```
more online @
www.americancathode.com/
www.cathodelighting.com/index.html
www.cathodelightingsystems.com/
www.egl-neon.com/
www.nationalcathode.com
www.neonshop.com/krypton/neonfaq.html
www.tecnolux.com/
www.voltarc.com/NeonTubing.htm
```

The light output of cold cathode tubing depends on: the glass tube color, if any (many times the tube is clear); the glass tube phosphor, if any; the tube diameter; the electric current in milliamperes (ma); the gas fill in the tube; and the quality with which the tube is blown, vacuum pumped, filled, and sealed (in other words, the manufacturing quality control). Generally, 25 mm tubes with a phosphor coating

Light Output

Figure 10.10

These three ceiling murals are painted on shallow coves that are uplighted by 15 mm cold cathode tubing. Since the diameter of each cove is relatively small, and to maintain a continuous lighted ring, the cold cathode lamp was selected. A high-efficacy triphosphor, high color rendering (85 CRI), 3000K color temperature lamp was used. The 15 mm tubing allowed for a relatively small cove detail to be developed that is proportionally appropriate for the diameter of each cove. This provides most of the ambient light to the main floor elevator lobby in a hotel resort. Image ©C.M. Korab

and some argon and minute amount of mercury operating at the relatively high current of 120 ma will produce the greatest light output—as much as 700 lumens per linear foot for the various high-color-rendering whites.

Small-diameter tubes (12 to 15 mm) can be very bright—the smaller the tube, the brighter the appearance—to the point of being glary. However, it is the larger diameter tubes (20 and 25 mm) that produce the most light.

Light output is also dependent on the ambient temperature of the environment in which the cold cathode is to operate. Especially sensitive are tubes based on the mercury fill. At cold temperatures, below 50°F (11°C), the output of mercury-based cold cathode lamps is reduced. At freezing temperatures and lower, some mercury-based lamps may not start or may flicker dully. Neon-based lamps are best where temperatures are expected to be low for extended time periods.

Architectural Lighting Design

Figure 10.11

A cold cathode cove detail was developed using 15 mm copper neon tubing. Since this detail occurs at the intersection of two long corridors, and to help guests in the hotel readily identify such intersections from some distance, the copper color was selected. An added "surprise" as one approaches the intersection is the impact of the MR16 downlight accenting the carpet detail.
Image ©C.M. Korab

Color

With the variables of glass tubing color, glass tubing phosphor coatings, and fill gases, cold cathode lamps can produce a rainbow selection of colored light. Saturated (ruby) red, orange, gold, emerald green, and cobalt blue are relatively standard. There are also variations of these saturated colors (intense neon red to bright cherry red, for example). Softer colors include peach, lavender, creamsicle, turquoise, orchid, and the like, are also available (visit www.eurocom-inc.com/color_chart.htm for a sample color chart). RGB (red, green, blue) cold cathode

Figure 10.12

This installation features an oculus between the first and second floors. Above the oculus on the ceiling of the second floor is a cove detail. All of the details are lighted with triphosphor 3000K cold cathode. To provide additional visual interest to the coved ceiling, the architect developed a plan of progressively smaller slabs or sheets of drywall. The edge of each sheet then catches the light from the cove. The inset shows a view through the oculus (the photographer was on the first floor) to the second floor coved ceiling detail.
Top image ©C.M. Korab
Bottom image
©GarySteffyLightingDesign

installations with each color separately dimmed yield many color options. Even mixing two colors relevant to a specific project can result in visually interesting architectural lighting. The cove in Figure 10.11 is lighted with a single row of copper-colored tubing. The serpentine bulkhead in Figure 5.5 is lighted with a row of copper and a row of 3000K triphosphor and the bulkhead is painted a complementary orange. By fading or dimming the cold cathode from just 3000K to copper/3000K to all copper, the orange bulkhead reads creamsicle to orange to deep rich orange/copper. This dimming can be done automatically over several hours of time so as not to overtly affect diners but to provide subtle shifts.

more online @
www.egl-neon.com/chart1.html
www.egl-neon.com/chart3.html
www.egl-neon.com/chart5.html

Transformers

Cold cathode lamps require transformers for starting and operation. Because these transformers are relatively high voltage, particularly on the secondary side (the electrical connection between the transformer box and the cold cathode lamps), they must be out of reach of the casual occupant. At the same time, these transformers need to be easily accessible for electrical connections, replacement, or repair.

Many of these high voltage transformers are electromagnetic and have a tendency to hum or buzz. For this reason, they should be located in a sound-isolated, code-compliant area. Operation at these high voltages also requires well-ventilated locations. Finally, to minimize magnetic interference, lamp/socket hum, and potential code compliance issues, transformers need to be located as close as practical to the cold cathode lamps and the wiring between the transformers and lamping needs to properly shielded and sized.

Retrofit Versions

Cold cathode tubes can be very small diameter—$\frac{1}{8}$" or about 3 mm—and can be formed into relatively small loops or concentric circles that are then mounted to a small electronic transformer or ballast, enclosed (sometimes) in a plastic "bulb" envelope and fitted with a medium screwbase or candelabra screwbase (base on second lamp from left is candelabra while all others are medium screwbase). These lamps are used as retrofits in existing luminaires intended for incandescent lamping but where better lamp life and better energy efficiency are desired or required. These lamps are usually available in a variety of bulb shapes such as G (globe), B (blunt tip or torpedo), A (arbitrary), and PAR (parabolic aluminized reflector) as shown in the icon to the right. Wattages typically range from 3 to 15 watts and are considered replacements for 15 to 50 watts.

Cold cathode retrofit lamps exhibit such small envelopes that they are excellent retrofits for picture lights, small task lights, and small decorative shaded candelabra-based sconces and table lights. They are less successful in larger table and floor lights as the lumen packages are not sufficient for most of those applications.

Cold cathode retrofit lamp life may be up to 25,000 hours. Confirm with lamp vendors if this is regardless of number of on/off switching cycles and/or dimming cycles. Also, many of these lamps are not produced or vended by the major lamp manufacturers—GE, Osram, and Philips—and may not be subjected to the same testing procedures or quality scrutiny.

The designer needs to take great care in specifying these retrofit lamps. Just like any other lamp, color rendering and color temperature are critical to the success of the application. Since these lamps are directly replacing incandescent lamps (within minutes an incandescent lamp can be swapped out for a cold cathode retrofit lamp allowing for near side-by-side comparison), color temperature and color rendering should very closely match incandescent—2700K and 80-plus respectively. Deviations from this are likely to fail. Indeed, the more commonly available, higher (cooler in appearance) color temperature retrofits exhibit an institutional, flat, cold appearance. Even if higher color rendering options exist from higher color temperature lamps, consider a mockup first. The tradeoff may not be acceptable.

harmonic distortion

Referring to how smoothly electrical current flows through an electrical device. Reported as a percentage. For lighting devices, THD or third harmonic distortion is considered most relevant and should be 10 percent (0.1) or less (0 indicating no distortion). High distortion devices, particularly those of high wattage and/or if there are many of these devices hooked up to the building electrical system, adversely affect the **power factor** of the electrical system and can cause system overloading.

power factor

Referring to how well an electrical device maintains the integrity of the electrical power flowing to it. Reported as a percentage. For lighting devices, PF should be close to 100 percent (1.0) and certainly greater than 95 percent (0.95).

For these retrofits to be successful on very large-scale projects, the integral transformer or ballast should be electronic to avoid flicker and hum and maximize efficacy. Additionally, ballasts should exhibit low **harmonic distortion**s (THD of 0.1 or less) and high power factors (PF of 0.95 or greater). Most retrofits do not exhibit these properties due to small ballast sizes and manufacturers' desires to keep component costs low. Hopefully, as the market size and sophistication increases, THDs and PFs will improve.

Since many of these retrofit lamps are intended for incandescent sockets (shorthand for intended for replacement of incandescent lamps), dimming may be an important criterion. User requirements should be confirmed and, if necessary, retrofit lamps that can operate on "standard" dimmers should be specified. A mockup is suggested to confirm satisfactory lamp operation under dimmed conditions.

Where retrofit lamps are specified as part of renovation, restoration, or new construction work (in other words, more than just replacing a few light bulbs in existing lights in a residential application or more than a maintenance group-relamp upgrade), the designer is obligated to meet requirements of the energy code in the project's jurisdiction. Inevitably, this will require that wattage reduction labels be specified by the designer on at least most, if not all, luminaires with medium screwbase or candelabra base lamps (of which there should be few, if any).

Some might consider retrofit lamps an interim or short-term solution to energy reduction, with dedicated-socket lamps considered a long-term solution. However, this perspective is shortsighted. First, there are billions of medium screwbase sockets installed now throughout the world. A mass exchange of all of these sockets to some other socket type would require an immense amount of resources—in both Earth resources to make and transport the new sockets and in labor resources to make the change-out. Not to mention the surge in recycling the old sockets. Second, dedicated sockets, if they are to be in use for at least 20 years and preferably 50 or more years, will require a stream of "upgrade" dedicated-socket lamps that will work in the respective dedicated sockets and yet enable the implementation of enhanced future technologies. Otherwise, society will be stuck in the near future with obsolete lights that themselves perpetuate the throw-away mentality that is not sustainable.

 Cold cathode retrofit lamps should be considered for decorative, general lighting in medium and candelabra screwbase socket luminaires originally intended for filament lamps. Although cold cathode lamps are available in R and PAR formats, they do not offer the candlepower punch associated with filament R and PAR lamps and should be avoided or, at the least, mocked up. Lamps with bulb enclosures (no exposed cold cathode tubes) may be preferred in residential applications to limit breakage and the hazards and cleanup aspects associated with minute amounts of mercury. All lamps are to be recycled after use.

more online @
www.tcpi.com/commercial/commercialHome.aspx

Fluorescence is light emission from an ultraviolet (UV)-radiated material (the phosphor coating—a white, powdery substance—in lamps). When phosphors are radiated or bombarded by UV radiation, they react by emitting visible light. Typically, 20 to 35 percent of the radiation produced is visible, with the remainder being thermal. In a fluorescent lamp, the UV radiation is produced when gas in the tube is electrically charged and a minute amount of mercury is vaporized. Like cold cathode lamps, fluorescent lamps have cathodes that strike an electric arc from one end of the lamp to the other. With fluorescent lamps, these cathodes require preliminary heating to ease the electric arc through the lamp and, therefore, require less voltage "kick" from a transformer or ballast (an energy savings and a safer, more cost-effective method for mass production than the requirements for cold cathode lamps). Thus, fluorescent lamps are also known as hot cathode lamps. The most efficient and common fluorescent lamps today are rapid start varieties using deluxe triphosphor coatings. Lamp families commonly available and deemed most efficient for present-day and immediate-future use are linear and compact. In linear lamps, the most appropriate versions are: T5 (standard and high output [HO]), T8, and T2. In compact lamps, the most appropriate are the dedicated socket versions of single-tube, double-tube, and triple-tube. See Table 10.2 for application characteristics of these fluorescent lamps. Figure 10.13 graphically illustrates the respective lamp types. Figure 10.14 outlines basic fluorescent lamp aspects of today's most efficient white light sources.

Fluorescent lamps are longer-lived than filament lamps. Typical rated life ranges from 10,000 to 30,000 hours. Most life ratings are based on 3-hours-per-start. That is, if the lamp is allowed to remain energized for three hours or more every time the switch is turned "on," then the lamps rated life should equal the ratings the manufacturers provide. This is an important aspect of lamps with cathodes. Recall that filament lamps produce light by heating a filament to the point of filament glow. In cathode lamps, like cold cathode and fluorescent lamps, the cathodes have to be heated sufficiently to actually cause an arc of electricity to travel the length of the lamp. This significant and sudden voltage surge obviously wreaks havoc on the cathodes, and eventually they fail. Since this voltage surge is only required when the lamp is energized, it is reasonable to presume then that the fewer times the lamp is energized (turned on), the less likely the cathodes are to fail. Indeed, most fluorescent lamp manufacturers admit (and in some instances advertise) that where lamps are used in situations where the on-cycle is 12-hours-per-start, rated life increases significantly. Conversely, where lamps are switched off/on quite frequently (and, therefore, the "on" cycle might be limited to half an hour or an hour at a time), lamp life will be reduced significantly—apparently by 50 percent or even more). Another factor affecting lamp life is the ballast type used to start and operate a fluorescent lamp (more on this in Ballasts).

Fluorescent lamps operate considerably cooler than filament lamps. However, the newer, smaller-diameter and high-wattage fluorescent lamps will exhibit quite a bit of heat at or near the sockets (where cathodes are located). The lamps themselves

Table 10.2 Fluorescent Lamp Selection Matrix

Techniques	▼ Applications[a]	T5[b]	T5HO[b]	T8[b]	T2[b]	FS/4P[b]	FL/4P[b]	FD/4P[b]	FT/4P[b]
	Dimmable[c] ▶	Yes	Yes	Yes	No	No	Yes	Yes	Yes
EXTERIOR									
Bollards	• Baseline							■	■
	• First degree							■	■
	• Second degree								■
Decorative Postlights	• Baseline							■	■
	• First degree	■		■				■	■
	• Second degree		■				■		■
Sconces	• Baseline							■	■
	• First degree	■		■				■	■
	• Second degree		■						■
Steplights	• Baseline					■		■	■
	• First degree					■	■	■	
	• Second degree						■	■	■
Uplights	• Baseline							■	■
	• First degree							■	■
	• Second degree								■
INTERIOR DECORATIVE									
Architectural Details e.g., decorative coves, slots, display cases	• Baseline				■	■			
	• First degree					■	■		
	• Second degree						■	■	■
Chandeliers	• Baseline						■	■	■
	• First degree	■		■		■		■	■
	• Second degree	■	■	■		■		■	■
Pendents	• Baseline					■	■	■	
	• First degree							■	■
	• Second degree							■	■
Picture Lights	• Baseline				■	■			
	• First degree					■	■		
	• Second degree	■					■		
Sconces	• Baseline					■		■	
	• First degree							■	■
	• Second degree							■	■
INTERIOR FUNCTIONAL									
Architectural Details e.g., functional coves, slots, retail displays	• Baseline				■	■			
	• First degree	■		■				■	■
	• Second degree		■	■				■	■
Recessed Ambient e.g., direct/indirect basket lights, direct lights	• Baseline								
	• First degree	■		■				■	■
	• Second degree	■	■	■				■	■
Downlights	• Baseline							■	■
	• First degree							■	■
	• Second degree							■	■
Indirect Ambient	• Baseline	■		■					
	• First degree	■		■					
	• Second degree		■						
Task Lights	• Baseline				■	■		■	■
	• First degree						■	■	■
	• Second degree	■		■					

[a] Reference illuminance criteria outlined in Table 8.6, The Essential Illuminance Guide. Baseline = low illuminance; First degree = moderate; Second degree = high.

[b] See discussions/definitions of lamps in respective sections of this chapter.

[c] Dimming ballasts only available for interior applications and are not yet commercially available for all lower wattage

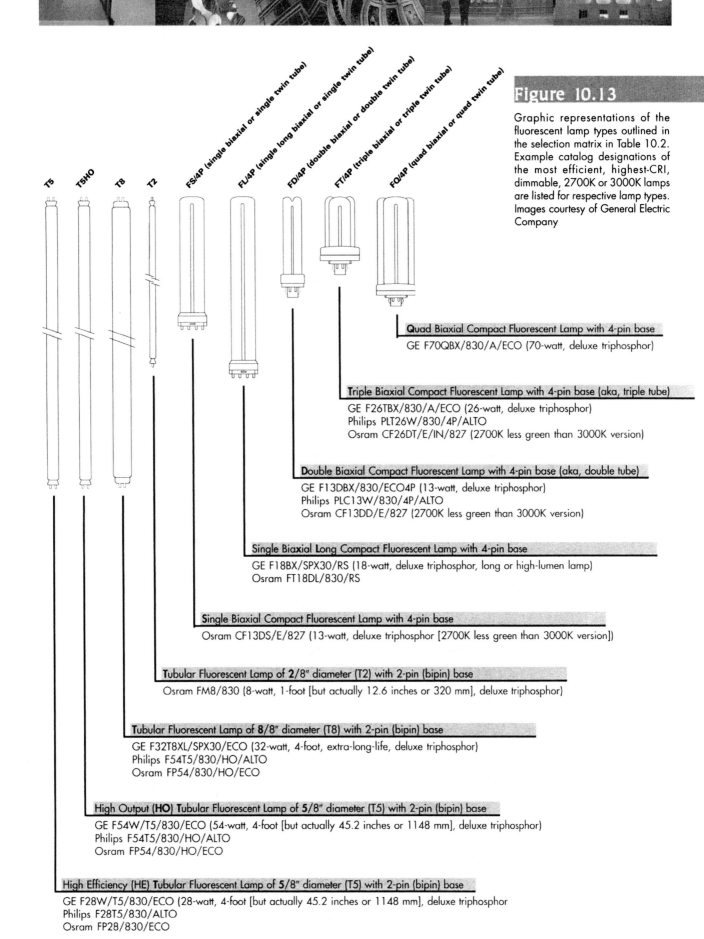

T5 T5HO T8 T2 FS/4P (single biaxial or single twin tube) FL/4P (single long biaxial or single twin tube) FD/4P (double biaxial or double twin tube) FT/4P (triple biaxial or triple twin tube) FQ/4P (quad biaxial or quad twin tube)

Figure 10.13

Graphic representations of the fluorescent lamp types outlined in the selection matrix in Table 10.2. Example catalog designations of the most efficient, highest-CRI, dimmable, 2700K or 3000K lamps are listed for respective lamp types. Images courtesy of General Electric Company

Quad Biaxial Compact Fluorescent Lamp with 4-pin base

GE F70QBX/830/A/ECO (70-watt, deluxe triphosphor)

Triple Biaxial Compact Fluorescent Lamp with 4-pin base (aka, triple tube)

GE F26TBX/830/A/ECO (26-watt, deluxe triphosphor)
Philips PLT26W/830/4P/ALTO
Osram CF26DT/E/IN/827 (2700K less green than 3000K version)

Double Biaxial Compact Fluorescent Lamp with 4-pin base (aka, double tube)

GE F13DBX/830/ECO4P (13-watt, deluxe triphosphor)
Philips PLC13W/830/4P/ALTO
Osram CF13DD/E/827 (2700K less green than 3000K version)

Single Biaxial Long Compact Fluorescent Lamp with 4-pin base

GE F18BX/SPX30/RS (18-watt, deluxe triphosphor, long or high-lumen lamp)
Osram FT18DL/830/RS

Single Biaxial Compact Fluorescent Lamp with 4-pin base

Osram CF13DS/E/827 (13-watt, deluxe triphosphor [2700K less green than 3000K version])

Tubular Fluorescent Lamp of 2/8″ diameter (T2) with 2-pin (bipin) base

Osram FM8/830 (8-watt, 1-foot [but actually 12.6 inches or 320 mm], deluxe triphosphor)

Tubular Fluorescent Lamp of 8/8″ diameter (T8) with 2-pin (bipin) base

GE F32T8XL/SPX30/ECO (32-watt, 4-foot, extra-long-life, deluxe triphosphor)
Philips F54T5/830/HO/ALTO
Osram FP54/830/HO/ECO

High Output (HO) Tubular Fluorescent Lamp of 5/8″ diameter (T5) with 2-pin (bipin) base

GE F54W/T5/830/ECO (54-watt, 4-foot [but actually 45.2 inches or 1148 mm], deluxe triphosphor)
Philips F54T5/830/HO/ALTO
Osram FP54/830/HO/ECO

High Efficiency (HE) Tubular Fluorescent Lamp of 5/8″ diameter (T5) with 2-pin (bipin) base

GE F28W/T5/830/ECO (28-watt, 4-foot [but actually 45.2 inches or 1148 mm], deluxe triphosphor
Philips F28T5/830/ALTO
Osram FP28/830/ECO

are temperature sensitive. This means that luminaire design and ballast selection are important to the lamps' starting and operating abilities in cold settings. Manufacturers' data list the minimum starting temperature for each variety of fluorescent lamps. In cold-climate exterior applications, fluorescent ballasts with starting temperatures of 0°F (-18°C) or even lower should be used.

Operating orientation for fluorescent lamps is universal—lamps can be oriented vertically, horizontally, or any position in between without significant adverse effect on color of light or lumen output. However, in the case of the smaller fluorescent lamps, the orientation of the lamp and/or the construction of the luminaire greatly influences how heat is retained or carried away from the lamp—and this factor can influence light output. Further, most fluorescent lamps have an optimum operating temperature (at which point the lamp produces its rated light output) that is different from typical room ambient temperature. So, when lamps are first energized, they are "cool" (at whatever ambient temperature is available in the room or the exterior environment). As the lamps warm, light output increases. If too much heat is retained in the luminaire over a period of time, then light output will, after having risen, actually fall to a point where equilibrium is reached with final operating temperature and final light output. What's this mean for the designer? First, recognize that such light output/temperature relationships exist and ask luminaire and lamp manufacturers about specific situations. A reduction factor may have to be applied to calculations or, alternatively, expect potential complaints if too little or too much light is provided in a given application. Second, recognize that most any fluorescent application will have a time lapse or run-up at the first "switch on" after perhaps a 30-minute off period until full light output is achieved. Hence, occupants may enter a space, switch on the lights, and over the first 10 to 20 minutes experience a "warm-up" period where lights transition from perhaps 30 percent output to 100 percent output. Although this is gradual, it may be annoying to users that lights are "dim" or "too dark" on initial startup.

T5/HE

These fluorescent lamps, known as high efficiency (HE—not to be confused with high output, or HO, versions), are the latest development in tubular, linear fluorescent lamps. T signifies a tubular lamp and 5 indicates the lamp's diameter in eighths of an inch (just like incandescent lamp designations). At just over ½" (15 mm) in diameter, **T5 lamps are significantly smaller than their T8 counterparts. The circumference of the tube is 40 percent less than that of a T8 tube, thereby significantly reducing the amount of glass, mercury, and rare earth phosphors necessary to make each lamp—more sustainably appropriate than the T8. The T5 size also reduces packaging and transportation volume significantly.** Further, the T5 lamp more closely approximates a line source than the T8 lamp, thereby greatly improving luminaire efficiencies—again, more sustainably appropriate.

Lamp efficacy is a direct result of the deluxe triphosphor (rare earth) coatings used inside the tube. The standard T5 lamp is the most efficacious white light source currently available on a large scale—104 LPW (without ballast losses). This is significant, and is not to be confused with the T5HO lamp that, while certainly producing lots of lumens, has an efficacy of 90 LPW (a result of its much higher

Figure 10.14

In a fluorescent lamp, cathodes at each end of the lamp are like filaments—and these help to strike an arc of electricity (much like controlled lightning) from one end of the lamp to the other. This arc vaporizes the minute amount of mercury in the lamp, which then produces an ultraviolet glow. A triphosphor coating on the inside of the glass tube reacts with the ultraviolet radiation to produce light. By tweaking the triphosphor coating, the visible radiation can be very warm white to very cool white in appearance. This also changes color rendering with deluxe triphosphor lamps offering the best color rendering.
Image ©Bosko Martinovic—Fotolia.com

Glass envelope or bulb

Contains slightly pressurized inert gas and very small amount of mercury. Tubular or "T" lamp shape shown.

Deluxe triphosphor coating

Ultraviolet radiation electrically excites the phosphor coating on the inside of the bulb to create visible radiation. Typical tones are warm white (3000K), neutral white (3500K) and cool white (4100K). Standard triphosphor coatings result in lower efficiency and poorer color rendering.

Cathodes

Cathodes or electrical filaments (which look much like the filament in Figure 10.2) at each end of lamp strike an electrical arc from one cathode to the other. This vaporizes the minute amount of mercury which creates ultraviolet radiation. Note how the lamp on the right exhibits a large patch of gray at the foreground end. Here, the cathode filament has boiled away and sufficiently collected on the inside of the bulb wall to cause the gray patch. Eventually the cathode filament fails and the lamp needs to be recycled and replaced.

wattage relative to the light output). T5 lamps are also the first metric lamp introduced in the United States. The so-called 4′ equivalent lamp, which requires 28 watts of power, is 45.2″ (1148 mm) in overall length. Other lengths are 21.6″, 33.4″, and 57.1″ (549 mm, 848 mm, and 1450 mm with wattages of 14, 21, and 35 watts respectively).

The deluxe triphosphor coatings result in a high CRI of about 85 for all T5 lamps and four basic color temperatures—2700K, 3000K, 3500K, and 4100K. The 4100K lamps result in the most vapid and institutional appearance although users will likely consider this "brighter" than the warmer-tone lamps. Where a filament-lamp color quality is desirable, consider 2700K and 3000K varieties. Where some "crispness" to the environment is deemed necessary, consider 3500K.

Operating such small diameter tubing at such high levels of efficiency requires use of the higher-quality triphosphors—so T5 lamps are available only in the 800-color series. Therefore, the quality of light from T5 lamps is excellent. LLD is 0.95 at 70 percent life.

The small size of the T5 lamp has empowered luminaire manufacturers to introduce very small luminaires with excellent efficiencies. Figure 5.6/Type FTG1 illustrates one example. Small luminaires can result in less material volume and weight, further advancing sustainability. This has been particularly dramatic in indirect luminaires. Since the T5 lamp is nearly half the diameter of a T8 lamp, but produces nearly as much light as an equivalent length T8, the brightness of the T5 bulb is extremely high. Hence, these lamps work well in indirect or well-shielded or lensed direct luminaires. T5 lamps are dimmable on interior applications, although dimming gear is costly.

T5 lamps will likely continue the evolution that began with T8 lamps. Indeed, the T5 lamps are nearly a paradigm shift in lighting. The optical characteristics of such a small, 30,000-hour lamp enable task lights under shelves or binder bins to use a single 21.6″ (549 mm) lamp in a 2′, 3′, or 4′ long housing to comfortably light a task area at just 14 watts when combined with low-to-moderate ambient lighting. Lamp and luminaire costs are rapidly decreasing as use and replacement volume increases.

Consider T5/HE lamps for general (ambient) lighting, for task lighting, and for display details and architectural details such as coves and slots in all applications, including residential applications where relatively high light levels are required, including, but not limited to, living rooms, family rooms, fitness rooms, bathrooms, kitchens, walk-in master closets, workrooms, and garages. All lamps are to be recycled after use.

T5/HO

T5HO lamps are the high output (HO) version of the T5 standard output lamps. Many times confused as the most efficacious lamps, these lamps offer the most lumens for a given lamp length. These lamps have many of the same characteristics as standard output counterparts, except lumen output and efficacy. HO lamps have efficacies of about 93 LPW (without ballast losses) and, therefore, are nearly 12 percent less efficacious than the standard output T5HE counterparts. Additionally, **these high-wattage lamps have lumen outputs that make them significant glare sources and potential over-lighters.** Unfortunately these lamps are erroneously specified on projects because many times the prevailing attitude is since T5 lamps are efficient, then "more or higher output must be better." On the other hand, HO lamps are appropriate and successful where ceiling heights are sufficiently generous to yield acceptable luminance ratios, where lamps are well-hidden, and/or where low surface reflectances need enhancement. Otherwise, these lamps are not as helpful in meeting project energy goals as are the T5/HE fluorescent lamps. These lamps are more costly than their T5/HE counterparts, but depending on luminaire design, lighting and glare criteria, and ceiling heights, fewer HO lamps may be needed than T5/HE lamps. Figure 10.15 shows a T5/HO application. Like T5/HEs, HO lamps are dimmable on interior applications, although dimming gear is costly.

Architectural Lighting Design

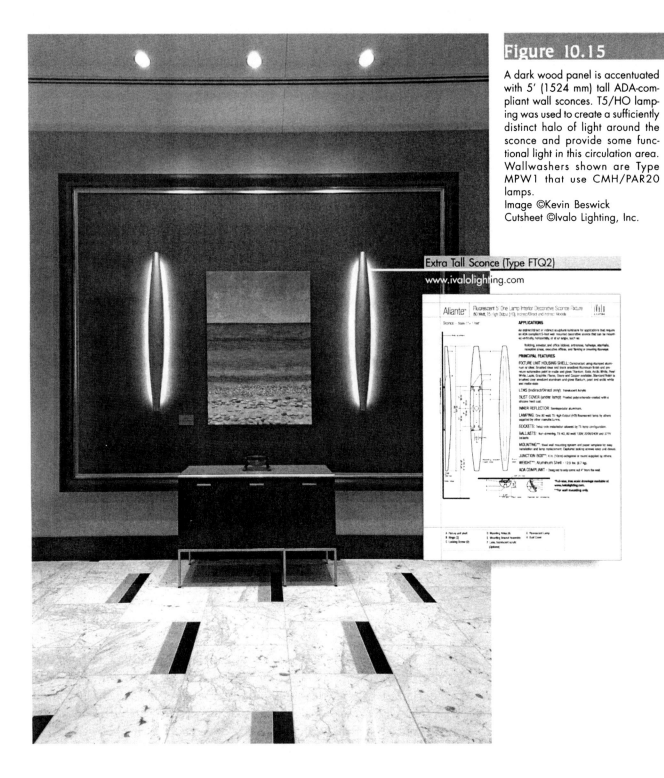

Figure 10.15

A dark wood panel is accentuated with 5' (1524 mm) tall ADA-compliant wall sconces. T5/HO lamping was used to create a sufficiently distinct halo of light around the sconce and provide some functional light in this circulation area. Wallwashers shown are Type MPW1 that use CMH/PAR20 lamps.

Image ©Kevin Beswick
Cutsheet ©Ivalo Lighting, Inc.

Extra Tall Sconce (Type FTQ2)
www.ivalolighting.com

T8

instant start

A method of starting fluorescent lamps by applying a relatively high voltage to the lamp cathodes to strike an arc from one cathode to the other. This "shock" of high voltage more rapidly deteriorates the cathodes and results in shorter lamp life if lamps are switched on/off frequently. However, this starting process uses slightly less wattage than the program start or rapid start methods and results in less costly ballasts. Most appropriate where lamps are energized just once or twice a day and then needed for large blocks of time, say 4, 8, or 12 hours. Not recommended for use with occupancy sensors or photocells.[2, 3]

program start

[aka program rapid start or programmed rapid start] A method of starting fluorescent lamps by applying an optimal amount of heat to the lamp cathodes programmed to the specific lamp type and wattage before striking an arc of relatively low voltage from one cathode to the other. This heating of the cathodes limits the "shock" of high voltage to the cathodes and better preserves them leading to longer life regardless the frequency and number of on/off switching cycles. However, this starting procedure uses a very small amount of wattage and results in slightly higher cost ballasts. Most appropriate where lamps are frequently switched on/off. Recommended for use with occupancy sensors and photocells.[2, 3]

The introduction of T8 lamps in the early 1980s initiated a significant trend toward more compact, better color, and more efficient fluorescent lamps. Since these lamps are somewhat small in diameter, they lend themselves to good luminaire efficiency.

Lamp efficacy is a direct result of the triphosphor (rare earth) coatings used inside the tubes. With these phosphors, T8 lamp efficacy is about 90 LPW (without ballast losses). T8 lamps are available in 2', 3', 4', and 5' (610 mm, 914 mm, 1219 mm, and 1524 mm with wattages of 17, 25, 32, and 40 watts respectively).

There are two color rendering categories of T8 lamps—the 700 series and the 800 series. These designations indicate the color characteristics of triphosphor coatings. The 700-series lamps has a CRI of 75. The 800 series has a CRI of 85—considered deluxe triphosphor lamps. Lamp manufacturers have established a standard designation within each series that relates to the color temperature of the lamps. A "30" indicates a lamp with 3000K color temperature. A "35" indicates 3500K, and a "41" indicates 4100K. The most efficient, longest-lived, and best color rendering T8 fluorescent lamps are the 800 series. Figure 10.16 shows use of an F25T8/830 lamp (exterior sconce). T8 lamps are available in the same color temperatures as T5 lamps.

Another important difference between the 700- and 800-series lamps is lamp lumen depreciation (LLD). The 700-series' LLD is 0.87, while the 800 series have an LLD of 0.92. So, to maintain a certain light level over time, fewer 800-series lamps are needed—a more sustainable approach.

T8 lamps have revolutionized architectural lighting design over the past 25 years. Combined with the compact fluorescent lamps used in wall sconces, downlights, and wallwashers, T8 lamps have allowed designers and, hence, owners, clients, and users, to experience energy-efficient, cost-effective, comfortable, attractive, human-scale lighting approaches. T8 lamps are dimmable on interior applications; however, dimming gear is costly.

Continuing technological developments have enabled T8 lamps to dominate the fluorescent lamp market. Long-life versions offer 30,000-hour life. High-performance versions offer 97 LPW efficacies (without ballast losses). Low-mercury versions offer improved sustainability. As lamps become more efficient with longer rated life, confirm with manufacturers operating characteristics such as optimal ambient temperature, dimming, run-up to full output upon cold-start, and ballast type (e.g., **instant start**, **program start**, and **rapid start**).

Consider T8/800-series lamps for general (ambient) lighting, for task lighting, and for display details and architectural details such as coves and slots in all applications, including residential applications where relatively high light levels are required, including, but not limited to, living rooms, family rooms, fitness rooms, bathrooms, kitchens, walk-in master closets, workrooms, and garages. All lamps are to be recycled after use.

T2

The smallest and newest fluorescent lamp commercially available today is this ¼" (6 mm) diameter lamp. Indeed, the ballast gear that powers the lamp is itself larger than the lamp. Available in wattages of 6, 8, 11, and 13 watts, and corresponding lengths of 8½" (216 mm), 12½" (318 mm), 16½" (419 mm), and 20½" (521 mm),

Figure 10.16

Wall sconces are used at the ground-floor level to introduce a more human scale element and provide better street-level presence. However, to maintain an appropriate proportion to the scale of the building, each sconce is 2' (600 mm) in width by 4' (1200 mm) in height. Sconces are lamped with F25T8/830 fluorescent lamp and ballasted with low-temperature ballasts. The F25T8 lamp is 3' in length an centers nicely in the 4' sconce. The 830 color yields a warm, welcoming appearance and enhances the stone facade. CMH/PAR38 lamps at ends of flagpoles highlight the American Indian ornament.
Image ©Glen Calvin Moon

rapid start
A method of starting fluorescent lamps by constantly applying heat to the lamp cathodes and, when switched "on," striking an arc of moderate voltage from one cathode to the other. This method yields better lamp life than instant start, but worse lamp life than program start. Rapid start uses more wattage than program start and an even greater amount than instant start. Costs less than program start and more than instant start.[2, 3]

these lamps appear well suited for task lighting and architectural detail lighting situations. Lamp life is rated at 10,000 hours, and lamps are available in the 830 color series. Efficacies range from 55 to 71 LPW (without ballast losses) depending on wattage. This lamp so closely approximates a virtual line source that excellent optical systems could be developed in relatively small luminaires to provide excellent light distributions and efficiencies. Cove luminaires and task luminaires come to mind as those where size and performance are significant positive attributes. Pitfalls include the potential heat of the lamp and the brightness of the lamp. Given the

very small-diameter tube, cathodes at each end of the lamp are in very close proximity to the glass bulb wall, and, therefore, surface temperatures of the glass bulb can get quite high. So the lamp is hot to the touch and requires sufficient space volume. Another fallout of the tiny bulb diameter is the brightness of the bulb wall. So much light exits from such a small source that a glare problem exists if direct view of the lamp is permitted. Finally, given their relatively new stature and low-volume use, these lamps and their respective luminaires are expensive. As experience is gained with the lamp and applications increase, look for cost and availability to improve.

 Consider T2 lamps for task lighting, and for display details and architectural details such as coves and slots in all applications. With UV filters, these lamps can be used in picture lights made to accommodate T2 lamping. All lamps are to be recycled after use.

CFL: FSingle/4P

Compact fluorescent lamps (CFLs) were first introduced by Philips under the PL brand designation and many folks erroneously refer to the entire family of compact fluorescent lamps as PLs. These were essentially miniature-diameter fluorescent lamp tubes of relatively short length that were then bent in half for an even shorter lamp. These bent-tube lamps were called twin tubes. Soon manufacturers were able to combine several twin tubes into a single lamp. So, a lamp with just one twin tube is called a single tube. A lamp with two single tubes combined is called a double tube. A lamp with three single tubes combined is called a triple tube. A generic reference to any of these small lamps is CFL (compact fluorescent lamp). The first single twin tube lamps were available in 5, 7, 9, and 13 watt versions in either electromagnetically ballasted or electronically ballasted versions. Today, only 4-pin or 4P electronic versions should be used for best life, efficacy, and reliability. Each manufacturer has, unfortunately, elected to introduce its own "designation" for identifying the various versions of CFL lamps. Hence, this text uses a generic designation system (see Figure 10.13)— review lamp manufacturers' literature for specific catalogic for the various lamp types.

To maintain high efficacy and offer a stable, relatively long life lamp, manufacturers use the deluxe triphosphor or 800 series of phosphors. This has the added benefit of offering the best color rendering available. Depending on manufacturer and the wattage, the FS/4P lamps are available in 2700K, 3000K, and 4100K. Unfortunately, not all colors are available in all wattages This leads to a potential hodgepodge when specifying various luminaires or severely restricts the designer's luminaire options. In short, the 2700K versions were originally thought to be most appropriate for residential applications and might be considered too pink for many applications The 4100K versions are extremely cool white in appearance—the availability of this lamp is apparently driven by the old school of design where only cool white lamps were readily available and/or where the thinking was that in warm climates the cooler-toned lamps are somehow more appropriate. Of course, these lamps are perceived by most folks as too institutional in appearance, and wash out skin tones and warm tones. Since manufacturers continue to review and consider tweaking color temperatures and color renderings, these lamps should be periodically reviewed in operation by the designer. This also suggests maintenance relamping may result in a hodge-podge of lamp colors and apparent brightnesses.

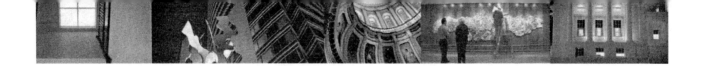

Efficacy for these single twin-tube, 4-pin compact fluorescent lamps ranges from 45 to 60 LPW (without ballast losses). However, the rated lamp life of 10,000 hours and the low-brightness, all-around glow available from these lamps make them **excellent candidates for steplights, wall sconces, and task lights. These lamps are not useful in downlighting or wallwash lighting applications. Any exterior applications require the use of lamps with minimum starting temperatures of 0°F (−18°C).** Further, with these low-wattage lamps, consider limiting exterior use to well-protected luminaires very close to or integrated into building architecture. All lamps are to be recycled after use.

CFL: FLong/4P

These long versions, also known as high-lumen versons, of the single twin-tube lamps offer excellent life and performance when the rapid-start, electronically ballasted versions are used. Efficacies range from 70 to 79 LPW (without ballast losses). Wattages are 18 and 40 watts. The F18L-version is 10½" (267 mm) in overall length and the F40L is 22½" (572 mm) in length, and each has a rated life of 20,000 hours. These lamps are available in the 830, 835, and 841 color series. **The F18L is typically used in sconces, small linear wallwashers, small rectangular downlights (lamps oriented horizontally), small cove striplights or asymmetric cove luminaires, and freestanding tasklights. The F40L is typically used in indirect pendent luminaires (linear or large bowl type), and cove striplights or asymmetric cove luminaires.** The F40L is typically too bright for direct lighting applications unless placed on dimmer or behind materials with good diffusion and/or relatively low transmission. Figure 10.17 shows an application with dimmable F40L lamping. An inherent problem with early compact fluorescent lamps was their tendency to have base meltdowns and/or cracked tubes near the base at the end of life. There are now two ways to avoid this messy and hazardous situation—by specifying lamps with end-of-life (EOL) protection and ballasts with EOL detection. All lamps are to be recycled after use.

CFL: FDouble/4P

Manufacturers soon realized that the single twin-tubes could be combined together on a single lamp in wattage and light output packages similar to their longer counterparts. While 2P and 4P versions are available, only the 4P versions offer high-quality, flicker-free, no-hum, instant-on (no start-up flutter) light. Typical applications include wall sconces, downlights, wallwashers, and tasklights. However, **lower wattages such as the F13Double are best in more decorative tasklight situations, otherwise the task area is overlighted and becomes too harsh and/or the task light glare risk increases.** On the other hand, the F13Double do not produce sufficient output for commercial downlight and wallwash applications.

Double-tube, 4-pin compact fluorescent lamps have efficacies of 66 to 69 LPW (without ballast losses) and exhibit the 800 series color characteristics. Rated lamp life is up to 12,000 hours, manufacturer-dependent. Some of these lamps are not suitable for exterior, cold-climate applications. Check each manufacturer's data for starting temperature requirements. As noted above, specify lamps with EOL protection and ballasts with EOL detection. All lamps are to be recycled after use.

Figure 10.17

A light box behind a mirror is deep enough to house striplights. A strip of mirror roughly 4″ in width by 24″ (102 mm by 610 mm) in height is etched away, leaving a swath of diffuse glass. A single F40L lamp of 3000K on a striplight is positioned behind each etched swath. All opaque surfaces of the inside of the light box are painted out white for best efficiency and diffusion. Lamps are operated by a dimmer control. Image ©Glen Calvin Moon

CFL: FTriple/4P

Soon after the double-tube lamps were introduced, manufacturers developed a triple-tube version in response to demands for even smaller, high-lumen light sources for downlight and wallwash applications. These lamps are only available in 4P versions for high-quality, flicker-free, no-hum, instant-on (no start-up flutter) light. Figure 10.18 illustrates an application with FTriple/4P lamps (the pendent luminaires) as does Figure 6.7. In a short amount of time, **the triple-tube lamps have become the standard. These lamps are found in decorative sconces, pendents, chandeliers, table lights, steplights, torchieres, bollards, and postlights. They are also found in downlights, wallwashers, and in-grade uplights. Custom lights are frequently based on triple-tube lamps because of their efficiency, small size, good color, and dimming capability**. All lamps are to be recycled after use.

Triple-tube lamps have efficacies of 66 to 76 LPW (without ballast losses) and exhibit the 800 series color characteristics. Rated lamp life is 10,000 to 12,000 hours, manufacturer-dependent. Some of these lamps are not suitable for exterior, cold-climate applications. Check manufacturers' data for starting temperature requirements. Recognize that these lamps have a warm-up time to full on.

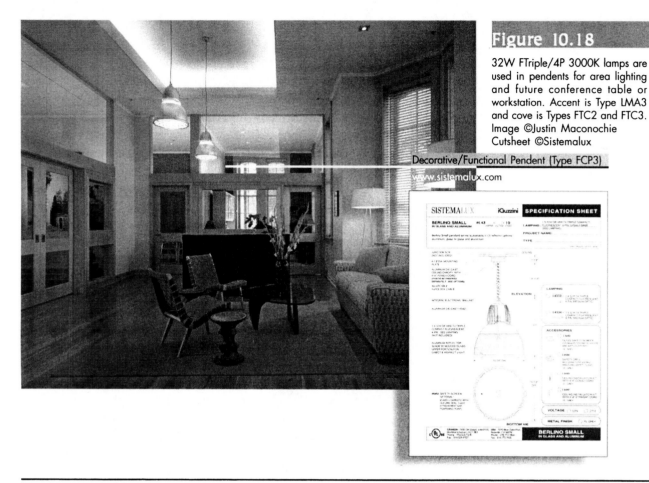

Figure 10.18

32W FTriple/4P 3000K lamps are used in pendents for area lighting and future conference table or workstation. Accent is Type LMA3 and cove is Types FTC2 and FTC3. Image ©Justin Maconochie Cutsheet ©Sistemalux

Decorative/Functional Pendent (Type FCP3)
www.sistemalux.com

CFL: FQ/HO/4P

The latest evolution of the compact fluorescent lamp is development of a quad-tube high-output (HO) version that isn't exactly compact. These lamps are about 8″ (about 200 mm) in length. These lamps have efficacies of about 75 LPW (without ballast losses), exhibit the 800 series color characteristics and a rated life of 12,000 hours. These lamps exhibit such high-lumen output that they are more typically used in industrial or utility applications. All lamps are to be recycled after use.

Ballasts

Fluorescent lamps require a voltage surge to energize the lamp and then, once started, need a constant current flow to assure continuous, stable operation. The devices that serve these two functions are known as ballasts. As recently as the 1990s, most ballasts were relatively large, heavy black boxes—heavy because they were filled with lots of windings of copper wire around an iron block or core. Those kinds of ballasts were called electromagnetic and, besides being bulky and heavy, operated fluorescent lamps in such a way that the lamps flickered and the ballasts themselves hummed. This is noticeable by some folks and can be quite annoying. More than twenty-five years ago, electronic ballasts were in initial development and production. The promise of electronics was to operate fluorescent lamps at high frequency (25,000 Hz or greater). Such operation increases lamp/ballast system efficiency by as much as 15 percent, and has the benefits of no audible hum (25,000 Hz is above human hearing) and no flicker. Up until 1995,

however, these electronic ballasts were unreliable. Every three or four years from 1980 to 1995, a new electronic ballast model or manufacturer or both was introduced to the marketplace. By 1995, manufacturing processes and electronic technologies were sufficiently refined to permit mass production of good (not great or excellent) reliability. Since the mid-1990s, electronic ballasts have made significant progress in quality control and in the production chain for luminaire manufacturers. Today, electronic ballasts are commonplace and fairly reliable. When issues arise, the manufacturers typically respond quickly and decisively to correct the problem.

Electronic ballasts, like most fluorescent ballasts, are available for single- or multiple-lamp operation. Generally, multiple-lamp operation results in greater system efficiency and uses fewer Earth resources since one ballast operates at least two lamps. Multiple-lamp-operation ballasts are available for series or parallel wiring of the lamps. Lamps operating in series will each receive the same amount of electrical current. When one lamp fails, all lamps in the series will cease operation until the failed lamp is replaced. This can increase maintenance troubleshooting since a 2-lamp system results in a 50/50 chance of selecting the wrong lamp for replacement (fluorescent lamps typically do not exhibit telltale signs of failure, such as blackened bulb walls that were common with old-style filament lamps). Lamps operating in parallel will each receive the same amount of voltage. When one lamp fails, only the failed lamp extinguishes and the other lamp or lamps on the parallel ballast remain in operation. Figure 10.19 graphically represents the concepts of parallel and series circuits.

Electronic ballasts are quite small today—this has been evolutionary as the electronic components have shrunk. Today, these small ballasts permit the design of smaller luminaire housings. The electronic components also allow ballast manufacturers to change ballast operating characteristics with relative ease or to assign functionality to chips. This is likely the next frontier for ballasts—inserting additional code on chips to track operating hours and conditions and to report optimal relamping cycles and lamp failures and allow control assignments for specific scenes or light settings without rewiring.

Seven specific characteristics must be correctly specified to assure satisfactory operation of the lighting system: lamp starting sequence, end-of-life protection, electromagnetic interference protection, current crest factor, ballast factor, power factor, and total harmonic distortion. The lamp starting sequence is, perhaps, the single most important aspect with regard to maximizing lamp life. The three basic starting sequences are instant start, rapid start, and program start (see sidebars under T8 lamping). Instant-start operation uses the least amount of energy, but is not well-suited where lamps are switched on/off more than four or five times each day. Rapid start uses a bit more energy than instant start, but is more suitable where lamps are switched on/off frequently throughout the day. Program start also uses a bit more energy than instant start, but is quite well suited for frequent on/off switching and is intended to offer the best lamp life.

EOL protection is desirable to avoid any physical meltdown and/or cracking of the fluorescent glass tube when the lamp fails. A ballast with EOL protection senses the lamp failure and disconnects electricity from the lamp until a new lamp is installed.

Parallel Circuit/All Lamps Operational

a

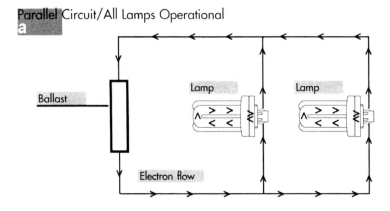

Ballast

Lamp   Lamp

Electron flow

Parallel Circuit/One Lamp Fails

b

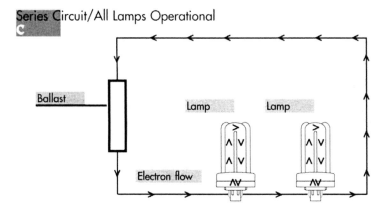

Ballast

Lamp fails   Lamp

Electron flow

Series Circuit/All Lamps Operational

c

Ballast

Lamp   Lamp

Electron flow

Series Circuit/One Lamp Fails

d

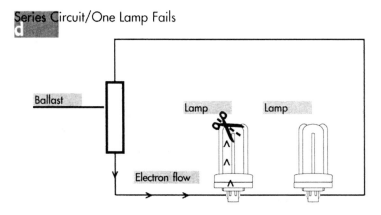

Ballast

Lamp   Lamp

Electron flow

Figure 10.19

Multi-lamp ballasts (ballasts operating more than a single lamp) are available for parallel circuit wiring and for series circuit wiring. In parallel circuits, electrons flow from the ballast independently to each lamp (a). When one lamp fails, the electron flow through that lamp is cut, but the electron flow through the other lamp remains intact and electrons flow uninterrupted back to the ballast (b). The circuit is not broken.

In series circuits, electrons flow from the ballast to and through the first lamp in the series and then from that lamp to the next lamp (c). When one lamp fails, the electron flow is cut and unable to complete the circuit back to the ballast. Regardless which lamp in the series fails (d), all lamps will cease operation since the entire circuit is broken.

NOTE: This is not a wiring diagram, but simply represents the concept of parallel and series circuits. Each ballast and lamp exhibit specific wiring requirements to be addressed by luminaire manufacturers. Wiring and rewiring should be performed by qualified factory representatives and licensed electricians. Image courtesy of General Electric Company
Diagram ©GarySteffyLightingDesign

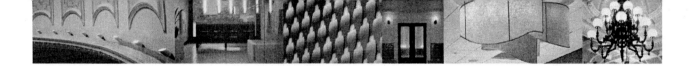

Electromagnetic interference (EMI) protection helps minimize ballast interference with other electrical devices, such as radios or televisions.

Current crest factor relates to the ratio of the peak electrical current and the operating current requirements of the lamp. The ballast should meet lamp manufacturers' current crest factor specifications. Typically this factor is 1.6 or so, and the ballast should not exceed 1.7.

Ballast factor (BF) expresses the percentage of rated light output to be expected from a lamp when operated on the given ballast. Based on an unfortunate and outdated industry standard, many standard ballasts operate lamps to only 88 percent output (a BF of 0.88)! Admittedly, lamp wattage is also reduced to about 88 percent of full rating, but this certainly misleads the public and can foul up designs if not properly accounted in calculations or specifications. Lamps are rated to produce a certain and expected amount of light. Many production ballasts, however, are purposely designed to operate lamps at 88 percent output. This means, of course, that to meet a specific light intensity, 14 percent more lamps, luminaires, and ballasts need to be used than would be required if the BF were 1.0 (100 percent). This is not sustainable practice. Hopefully all ballast manufacturers will expand the range of BFs available to include 1.0 across all ballast lines, voltages, and number of lamps operated.

There are situations where BFs other than 1.0 are helpful. For example, sometimes very low light levels are desired, but to maintain reasonably uniform intensity, luminaires must be spaced on a given pattern. While ballasts are available for many but not all lamp wattages that have BFs of 0.78, 0.88, 0.98, and 1.18, these vary from manufacturer to manufacturer and do not all offer the same starting sequences, EOL protection, and EMI characteristics. Most of the compact fluorescent lamp electronic ballasts are available with BFs of only 1.0.

Power factor relates to a building's wiring system and the electrical load that the ballast appears to place on that wiring. A power factor of 1.0 is best and is referred to as "high" power factor. As the power factor is reduced, a building's wiring systems are increasingly burdened. A sufficient number of low power factor ballasts can actually create an electrical wiring distribution problem in a building. As such, power factors should be 0.95 to 1.0.

Total harmonic distortion (THD) and third harmonic distortion also relate to a building's electrical power distribution system. The lower a ballast THD, the better. The THD should not exceed 0.20, and third harmonic distortion should not exceed 0.10.

Electronic ballasts are available to dim fluorescent lamps. Dimming, however, remains a somewhat elusive feat. Cost, lamp life, lamp **seasoning**, and system reliability are seemingly unresolved issues amongst lamp, ballast, and controls manufacturers. Further, dimming ballasts are not available for all of the more popular lamps and wattages. Finally, integration with dimming systems is not universal—some dimming ballasts require proprietary dimming controls, resulting in serious hardware aesthetic challenges with respect to the non-dim switches throughout a facility. When reviewing dimming ballasts, check low-end dimming ability (preferably down to 10 percent or less with no flicker), and check lamp/ballast warranty with the respective manufacturers. Dimming of fluorescent lamps will result in some shift in both color temperature and color rendering. The dimmer the setting, the greater the color shifts. When a group of fluorescent lamps must be dimmed, it is advisable that all of the lamps be

seasoning
A reference to "burning-in" fluorescent lamps at full output at the time they are first installed. This seasoning apparently burns off any remaining impurities within the lamps and results in smoother dimming and more uniformly lighted fluorescent tubes. NEMA suggests fluorescent lamps be seasoned for 12 hours at 100 percent full-bright prior to dimming.[4] Not to be confused with seasoning necessary for photometric testing (which is a required 100 hours) or for stabilized and matched color character from lamp-to-lamp (which is recommended to be 100 hours and is particularly useful in ceramic metal halide installations).

identical in size, wattage, and color. Otherwise, noticeable and annoying color shifts will occur from lamp to lamp. For example, if a dimmable fluorescent cove is being designed for a conference room, and the cove is 15' (about 4.6 m) long, then use five 3' lamps rather than three 4' lamps and one 3' lamp. The single 3' lamp may not dim at the same rate or to the same color as the 4' lamps.

Use only ballasts that are UL listed and labeled. Ballasts should be warranted for a minimum of two years and preferably for three or even five years. While the newer electronic ballasts have not been in operation long enough to tell, it is anticipated that ballasts will last twenty years.

Finally, electronic ballasts do offer excellent potential for precise, energy efficient operation of lamps. Computer chip circuitry allows for addressable ballasts, which can actually be addressed via handheld wireless control devices. Look for continued development of electronic ballasts in the near future that will offer greater functionality (e.g., 2- and 3-level switching, and more reliable and lower cost dimming).

more online @
www.advancetransformer.com/products/fluorescent-electronic.jsp
www.berkeleypoint.com/learning/parallel_circuit.html
www.fulham.com/
genet.gelighting.com/LightProducts/Dispatcher?REQUEST=
    BALLASTLANDINGPAGE&PRODUCTLINE=Ballasts&CHANNEL=Commercial
www.hatchtransformers.com/default.asp
lansing.apogee.net/foe/
lansing.apogee.net/foe/fcspp.asp
lansing.apogee.net/foe/fcsps.asp
www.sylvania.com/BusinessProducts/LightingForBusiness/Products/Ballasts/
www.tridonicatco.com/kms/static_nav/index.php
www.unvlt.com/

Retrofit Versions

Compact fluorescent lamps, when fitted with medium or candelabra screwbases, make reasonable retrofits for existing luminaires intended for incandescent lamping but where better lamp life and better energy efficiency are desired or required. These lamps are usually available in a variety of bulb shapes such as G (globe), B (blunt tip or torpedo). A (arbitrary), and PAR (parabolic aluminized reflector) as shown in the icon to the right. Wattages typically range from 5 to 42 watts and are considered replacements for 15 to 150 watts. Some are available in 3-way switching versions and in dimmable versions. Figure 10.20 shows several variations.

CFL retrofit lamp life may be up to 15,000 hours. Confirm with lamp vendors if this is regardless of number of on/off switching cycles and/or dimming cycles.

The designer needs to take great care in specifying these retrofit lamps. Just like any other lamp, color rendering and color temperature are critical to the success of the application. Since these lamps are directly replacing incandescent lamps (within minutes an incandescent lamp can be swapped out for a CFL retrofit lamp allowing for near side-by-side comparison), color temperature and color rendering should very closely match incandescent—2700K and 80-plus respectively. Deviations from this are likely to fail. Similar to the Cold Cathode Retrofit Versions, the more commonly available, higher (cooler in appearance) color temperature retrofits exhibit an institutional, flat, cold appearance. Even if higher color rendering options exist from higher color temperature lamps, consider a mockup first. The tradeoff may not be acceptable.

Figure 10.20

A variety of medium screwbase CFL retrofits are shown. Lamps with enclosed globes or bulbs are most appropriate where lamps will be directly visible and in residential applications where there may be a greater likelihood of accidental breakage without qualified maintenance cleanup.
Image ©Stockxpert

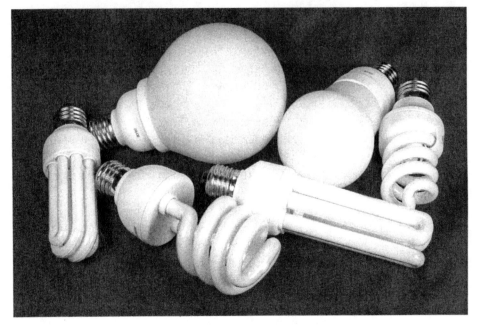

For these retrofits to be successful on very large-scale projects, the integral transformer or ballast should be electronic to avoid flicker and hum and maximize efficacy. Additionally, ballasts should exhibit low harmonic distortions (THD of 0.1 or less) and high power factors (PF of 0.95 or greater). Most retrofits do not exhibit these properties due to small ballast sizes and manufacturers' desires to keep component costs low. Hopefully, as the market size and sophistication increases, THDs and PFs will improve.

Since many of these retrofit lamps are intended for incandescent sockets, dimming may be an important criterion. User requirements should be confirmed and, if necessary, retrofit lamps that can operate on "standard" dimmers should be specified. A mockup is suggested to confirm satisfactory lamp operation under dimmed conditions.

Where retrofit lamps are specified as part of renovation, restoration, or new construction work (in other words, more than just replacing a few light bulbs in existing lights in a residential application or more than a maintenance group-relamp upgrade), the designer is obligated to meet requirements of the energy code in the project's jurisdiction. Inevitably, this will require that wattage rating labels be specified by the designer on at least most, if not all, luminaires with medium screwbase or candelabra base lamps (of which there should be few, if any).

Some might consider retrofit lamps an interim or short-term solution to energy reduction, with dedicated-socket lamps considered a long-term solution. However, this perspective is shortsighted. First, there are billions of medium screwbase sockets installed now throughout the world. A mass exchange of all of these sockets to some other socket type would require an immense amount of resources—in both Earth resources to make and transport the new sockets and in labor resources to make the change-out. Not to mention the surge in recycling the old sockets. Second, dedicated sockets, if they are to be in use for at least 20 years and preferably 50 or more years, will require a stream of "upgrade" dedicated-socket lamps that will work in the respective dedicated sockets and yet enable the implementation of

enhanced future technologies. Otherwise, society will be stuck in the near future with obsolete lights that themselves perpetuate the throw-away mentality that is not sustainable.

CFL retrofit lamps should be considered for decorative, general lighting in medium and candelabra screwbase socket luminaires originally intended for filament lamps. **CFLs in R and PAR formats do not offer the candlepower punch associated with filament R and PAR lamps and should be avoided or, at the least, mocked up.** It is truly a waste of resources to use lamps that do not perform as users expect and therefore require users to add even more lamps and luminaires or simply to not use the area in question. Lamps with bulb enclosures (no exposed fluorescent tubes) may be preferred in residential applications to limit breakage and the hazards and cleanup aspects associated with minute amounts of mercury. All lamps are to be recycled after use.

A very recent CFL socket and lamp development is the GU-24 lamp/ballast system, which essentially permits luminaire manufacturers to readily adapt filament-lamp luminaires to use these small CFL lamps. Although industry standards in the states are still under development by ANSI, these lamps appear to an interim, if not long-term, means of using decorative lights on projects without the high energy load and/or short life of filament lamps and without the cumbersome and odd "humps" and "cylinders" on the luminaire bodies or ceiling canopies to house standard CFL ballasts. The GU-24 lamps are available with or without integral ballasts. The self-ballasted lamps are small and fit into the special "twist and lock" socket. Of course, on every relamping cycle, the lamp *and* the ballast are replaced, leading to a more costly recycling effort and less sustainable than the socket-ballast version where the ballast remains in the socket. As industry standards are finalized, look for formalized introduction of these lamps from the lamp manufacturers. **As with all lighting equipment, and particularly equipment relatively new to the market, check with manufacturers' local representatives on product warranties, durability, and return and replacement policies as well as country or countries of origin to assess quality aspects. On lamps, also check luminaire vendors' recommendations and experiences with various lamp and/or ballast options.**

Fluorescent lamps, in order to operate efficiently, require the use of a minute amount of the heavy element mercury. Mercury is hazardous. Although the doses in fluorescent lamps are quite low, combining lots of these lamps (as might be expected to happen in landfills) is cause for concern. Recycling is always a preferred method of dealing with spent lamps. See Section 6.8 for additional information.

Sustainability

Because sustainability is concerned with minimizing the number of Earth resources used to make anything, including lamps and ballasts, then it is arguably prudent to use the longest-life systems and the systems with the smallest (in physical size) components. T5 lamps, for instance, use nearly 40 percent less glass and less phosphor than T8 lamps, and last longer. Program-start ballasts are the same size as other electronic ballasts, yet these ballasts promise longer lamp life. So, pulling together lighting systems that use as little in the way of hazardous components as practical but that also promise long life and energy efficient operations is a model design target for lighting designers.

Figure 10.21

The typical ED-bulb metal halide lamp. Shown here as reference to understanding lamp components and operation. The "T" or tubular ceramic metal halide lamps do not have the advantage of a protective shroud around the ceramic arc tube, which requires "T" lamps to be used only in fully enclosed luminaires exhibiting tempered glass lenses. Image ©Stockxpert

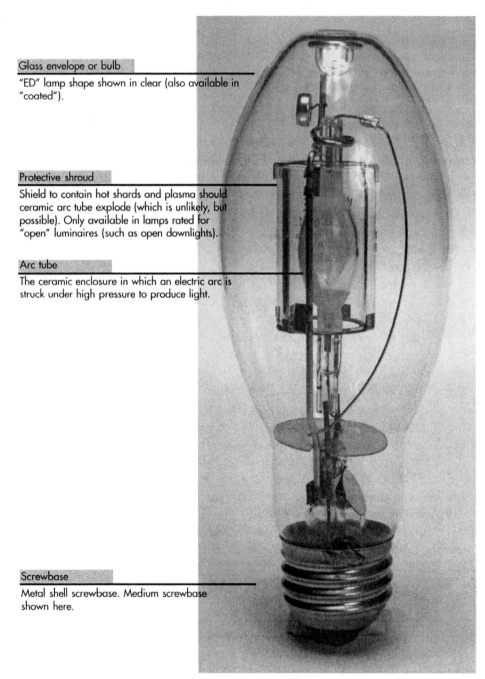

Glass envelope or bulb

"ED" lamp shape shown in clear (also available in "coated").

Protective shroud

Shield to contain hot shards and plasma should ceramic arc tube explode (which is unlikely, but possible). Only available in lamps rated for "open" luminaires (such as open downlights).

Arc tube

The ceramic enclosure in which an electric arc is struck under high pressure to produce light.

Screwbase

Metal shell screwbase. Medium screwbase shown here.

10.5 CMH

CMH or ceramic metal halide lamps are a member of the high intensity discharge (HID) lamp family. HIDs are so named for their ability to produce significant amounts of light by discharging electricity through a high-pressure vapor. There are three types of HID lamps: mercury vapor, metal halide, and high pressure sodium. These lamps are characterized by their warm-up time, restrike time, and color rendering (or lack thereof). For architectural lighting, ceramic metal halide lamps are most appropriate and discussed here. Mercury vapor lamps are inefficient. High pressure sodium lamps, although seemingly efficient according to technical standards of pho-

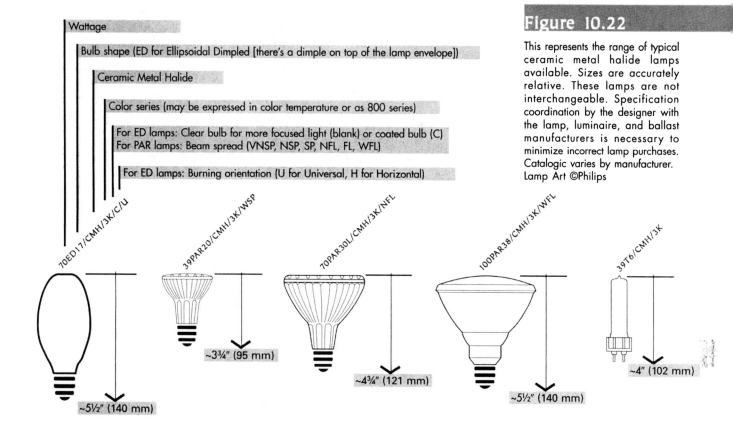

Wattage

Bulb shape (ED for Ellipsoidal Dimpled [there's a dimple on top of the lamp envelope])

Ceramic Metal Halide

Color series (may be expressed in color temperature or as 800 series)

For ED lamps: Clear bulb for more focused light (blank) or coated bulb (C)
For PAR lamps: Beam spread (VNSP, NSP, SP, NFL, FL, WFL)

For ED lamps: Burning orientation (U for Universal, H for Horizontal)

70ED17/CMH/3K/C/U

39PAR20/CMH/3K/WSP

70PAR30L/CMH/3K/NFL

100PAR38/CMH/3K/WFL

39T6/CMH/3K

~5½" (140 mm)   ~3¾" (95 mm)   ~4¾" (121 mm)   ~5½" (140 mm)   ~4" (102 mm)

tometry, have proved woefully inadequate for most lighting applications as they exhibit very poor color rendering—these lamps cannot produce environments with decent chromatic contrast.

CMH lamps are not instant-on, requiring up to five minutes for full light output. If there is a power interruption while these lamps are on, they typically must cool down before they will restrike and warm back up to full light output. Therefore, where emergency lighting is required, auxiliary lighting systems are used to provide instant light during and immediately after power outages. This can be achieved with a quartz halogen restrike option—CMH luminaires fitted with a quartz halogen lamp that switches on instantly in the event of a power outage, and remains on until the CMH lamp is back to reasonable light output.

Like other lamp families, several bulb shapes are available for CMH lamps. For most architectural lighting applications, bulb shapes include BD (bulbous dimpled), ED (ellipsoidal dimpled), PAR (identical to filament PAR shapes), and T (identical to filament T shapes). Figure 10.21 illustrates some of the key components in a typical metal halide lamp. Figure 10.22 graphically represents the range of CMH lamp shapes available.

In general lighting applications—that is, where uniform, relatively low-to-moderate illuminances are desired—CMH lamps are not especially efficient compared to the newest deluxe triphosphor fluorescent lamps. However, CMH lamps are extremely effective at accenting and/or providing high illuminances. Further, the small "T" lamps (e.g., T4.5 and T6 envelopes) are especially effective where relatively large luminaire reflectors of precision glass and polished aluminum can be used for focused beams

Figure 10.23

The 19′ (about 5.8 m) tall sculpture, Ad Astra, at the top of the dome on the Kansas Capitol, is lighted with eight very narrow beam spot lights using precision glass reflectors and 150-watt T6/G12 ceramic metal halide lamps. The beam is so narrow, very little light escapes beyond the sculpture.
Image ©Wayne Pierce

(see Figure 10.23) or where emphatic indirect or wallwashing is desired relative to the softness of fluorescent (see Figure 10.24).

CMH lamps are more appropriate for most exterior lighting because they are less affected by temperature than fluorescent lamps. Further, CMH lamps better approximate point sources and are, therefore, more easily controlled optically—

Figure 10.24

A detail at the base of a decorative wood wall houses a linear uplight luminaire fitted with CMH 39W PAR20/SP10 3000K lamps on 9' centers (about 229 mm) and fitted with linear spreadlenses to graze the wall. Lamps are on two control circuits (every other lamp on one circuit and the remaining on a second circuit) for night setbacks and alternating between lamp sets every other day.
Image ©GarySteffyLightingDesign

resulting in more efficient luminaires and more carefully controlled nighttime lighting (see Figure 10.23). Ceramic metal halide lamps are excellent candidates where efficient, long-life, near-incandescent color accent or general lighting is desired (e.g., retail, commercial accenting, façade accenting, etc.). Rated life for CMH lamps ranges from 7500 to 15,000 hours. These life ratings are expected to rise after more field application experience is achieved.

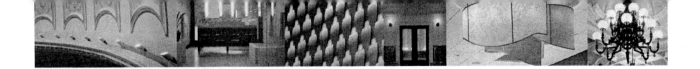

Like fluorescent lamps, CMH lamps are enjoying the benefits of miniaturization and electronics. Luminaire sizes are smaller than ever, and electronic operation yields efficiency gains previously unanticipated. Further, electronic operation is quiet and flicker-free. Ballasts for CMH lamps are typically best if electronic. These versions now offer smaller, lighter-weight options.

CMH dimming can be done technically, but with limited dimming range and relatively high cost. Dimmed CMH lamps typically change drastically in color temperature and color rendering (both going "bad"). The range of dimming might be 60 to 100 percent without objectionable color shifting. Cost might be as high as several hundred US dollars per lamp. Further, similar to fluorescent dimming, no comprehensive study has been undertaken to establish the effect of dimming on lamp life.

Color rendering of ceramic metal halide rivals that of deluxe triphosphor fluorescent—ranging from 82 CRI to 93 CRI. Available color temperatures are 3000K and 4200K. The 3000K lamps have a halogen color quality.

Color consistency has traditionally been a problem with metal halide lamps. Apparently, the doses of halide could not be sufficiently controlled to such minute degrees to minimize color shifting from lamp to lamp. Further, construction of the arc tubes could not be sufficiently controlled to prevent some eventual loss of halides during operational life, resulting in some color shift over time. Both problems have been addressed with ceramic metal halide.

Although ceramic metal halides are the promise of the present and future in HID lighting, some operational issues remain. These lamps, to date, are not available in instant-on versions. As with all metal halide lamps, there is potential for nonpassive failure (a kind reference to the lamp failing violently—exploding). Hence, some versions (notably all T4.5 and T6 single-ended lamps and the T6 and T7 double-ended lamps) of these lamps need to be used in enclosed luminaires (check with lamp and luminaire manufacturers before finalizing specifications on the lamp and luminaire combination). Another issue is that of LLD. Historically, metal halide lamps have exhibited LLD as much as 50 percent over life. The ceramic metal halide lamps are better, exhibiting LLDs of about 35 percent over life. Nevertheless, this reduction needs to be accounted in the designer's calculations and might also suggest that group relamping is appropriate prior to end of rated life.

CMH lamps should be considered for general lighting, focal lighting, indirect lighting, and wallwash lighting in interior and exterior commercial, hospitality, and retail applications where dimming is unnecessary and on/off switching is infrequent. All lamps are to be recycled after use.

10.6 Electrodeless

These lamps are the newest family in architectural lighting. Without electrodes or cathodes, there is, apparently, no "weak link" to fail. These lamps typically have rated life in the range of 40,000 to 100,000 hours, which was heretofore unheard. For purposes of this text, there are two categories of electrodeless lamps—light emitting diode lamps (LEDs) and induction lamps. LEDs are of such popular acclaim, that these are discussed separately in 10.7.

Induction lamps operate on the principle of generating visible radiation by inducing high magnetic currents in order to generate atomic-level activity within the bulb. Philips and Osram have production lamps available in relatively high wattages. Specific operating conditions are required for various wattage and lamp types. While the lighting equipment is relatively expensive, it does have rated life of 100,000 hours (about four times greater than the best T8 fluorescent lamp and three times greater than the best T5 fluorescent lamp). Lamps are available in 3000K, 3500K, and 4100K versions and offer a CRI of 80. This is an emerging technology. At the moment, Osram classifies its induction lamp as fluorescent, while Philips classifies the lamp as HID. **This technology has not advanced rapidly, perhaps due to the limited wattages and apparent vapid color characteristics, which bely the 80 CRI.** Experience with the induction process in various application settings will likely lead to improved guidance on system application recommendations. Frequently check with lamp manufacturers for updates.

more online @
www.nam.lighting.philips.com/us/ecatalog/catalogs/ql_oem_guide.pdf

10.7 LED

Light emitting diodes, or LEDs, are also known as solid state lighting (SSL) devices. LEDs as visible-light sources were developed in 1962, although their discovery dates to the turn of the 20th century (1907) with later practical developments for radio in the 1920s that apparently were not commercialized.[5, 6, 7] LED lamps are fully electronic or solid state devices with no traditional filaments or cathodes that are subjected to high voltages or currents, which ulimately wear out in traditional lamps and which can be a significant power drain. LEDs can be tuned to produce discrete wavelengths of radiation, thereby deleting the heat-causing infrared wavelengths from the source. LEDs are quite tiny, as Figures 10.1 and 10.25 illustrate, and with optical lensing, as shown in 10.25, can be very effective directional or focused sources. In fact, regardless of their LPW ratings, their optical efficiency can be very high.

LEDs are touted for consisting of no harzardous materials (like mercury or lead solder), exhibiting excellent efficacies, and very long life. They are considered a significant part of the solution to global warming. However, the present-state of commercially available LEDs has yet to prove these parameters in a light source fit for typical commercial applications at a cost competitive with traditional lamps. In other words, LEDs have been over-hyped. Unfortunately, this may ultimately delay their adoption by consumers. LEDs at this writing are best used as **eye candy** where costs are of little consequence.

Apparently LEDs contain no hazardous materials. Like other lamps, it is unclear what kinds of hazardous materials are used or generated in the production of LEDs. Since LEDs may be adopted with such speed and force that billions will be in sockets in a decade, and since the technology advances significantly in "lab-efficacy" every few years, there may soon be a need for mapping recycling and replacement strategies for LEDs to avoid pitfalls of massive quantities being landfill.

Efficacy on LEDs is elusive. Although lab experiments have shown 150 LPW to be achievable, commercially available LEDs exhibit, at best, 40 to 50 LPW. However, even for these real-world efficacies, caveats abound—primarily centered on driver compatability, **p-n junction** temperature, and luminaire heat-sinking (or lack thereof).

eye candy
Lighting hardware and/or lighting effect that is visually attractive but serves little other purpose (e.g., provides little or no functional light).

p-n junction
An LED has no filament or arc tube. Instead, a layer of positively charged material (p) is placed over a layer of negatively charged material (n), essentially forming the LED chip. The area where they touch is referred to as the junction. When electricity flows to the LED, the negative electrons move from the n material to the p material across the junction. As these positive and negative charges combine, they produce visible radiation emitted out the top of the "p" layer.[8] The junction has an optimal design temperature for operation. If this temperature is exceeded, light output is reduced. Many LED manufacturers report light output data based on junction temperatures of 77°F (about 25°C).

system integrator
The party responsible for bringing to-gether the components necessary to have an operable LED. With tradi-tional lamps, operational parameters of lamps (e.g., CFLs) are defined by/ agreed-upon as industry-standard. Lamp manufacturers and ballast manu-facturers make their products mutually compatible by meeting these stan-dards. With LEDs, no such industry standards exist. So, in order to have an operational LED, someone must marry the LED to a power supply and, if needed, a dimming module. The system integrator might be the lumi-naire manufacturer, the LED manufac-turer, or a third party. If the LED isn't correctly tuned to the power supply and dimming module, or vice versa, the LED might produce too little light, too much light, or face premature fail-ure.

driver
A black-box-device much like a ballast or transformer that transforms incoming voltage and current to meet the requirements of operating an LED lamp.

LEDs are extremely sensitive to heat. While they generate little heat, what is generated is concentrated at the LED light source and must be conducted or convected away, otherwise performance drops or even failure of the LED's electronics occurs. Heat sinks are de rigueur and can add significant bulk and weight to luminaires, not to mention the embodied energy added to the system. LEDs work best in cold settings such as cold exteriors or refrigerated displays and walk-ins. Interestingly, most commercially available decent color LEDs achieve between 7 and 35 LPW (without driver losses) in interior settings once actual driver currents are accounted. In other words, at this writing, LEDs are about as good as halogen infrared filament lamps in terms of actual efficacy. LEDs are superior, however, in longevity, probably.

Life rating for LEDs is not defined as that for traditional lamps (filament, cold cathode, fluorescent, and ceramic metal halide). Indeed, LED life isn't defined by any codified, certified industry standard. A trade-group has proposed two definitions—one for functional LEDs and one for decorative LEDs.[9] Functional LED life is proposed to be that point in time at which the LED will exhibit 70 percent of its initial light output. Decorative LED life is proposed to be that point in time at which the LED will exhibit 50 percent of its initial light output. In other words, LEDs are more likely to fade away rather than extinguish. This fading or dimming aspect is based in part on the current flow to the LED. The current also establishes light output and is determined by the **system integrator**'s selection of a **driver**. Fantastic claims on life range as high as 100,000 hours, but few of these commercially-available LEDs have even been in existence for such a period. A more realisitic perspective is probably 50,000 hours, although some colored LEDs may be rated as low as 40,000 hours. To avoid the appearance of conflicts of interest and to maintain public trust, parameters such as lamp life, color temperature, color rendering, and the like, should be defined by technical societies rather than trade groups. Further, new definitions, if deemed necessary, should be universally adopted for all lamp types to avoid market confusion and maintain integrity.

In an effort to avoid the fading or dimming of LEDs over time, some luminaire manufacturers have developed LED/driver/control systems that hold the light output constant over time. In order to do this, however, the system wattage must increase over time. In any event, the designer must recognize the energy implications. If LED lights are used to generate a specified light level, then to achieve that light level over the anticipated life of the LEDs, the designer either must add a certain percentage of extra lights to cover at least some, if not all, of the dimming-effect over time (so, this could be as much as adding 30 percent more lights to the project) or taking a hit for the "final" wattage load that is anticipated with the manufacturers "constant light/ increasing wattage" solution. To further confound matters, LDD is typically addressed during relamping. With their long life, LEDs will exhibit a significant amount of dirt buildup unless periodic intermittent cleaning is initiated. If the cleaning cycle is tied to relamping, an additional loss factor for dirt depreciation needs to be accounted.

array
A collection of LEDs into a single "lamp" to provide more light, larger area of source, and/or variable color selections of light.

The auxiliary components, such as the drivers and dimming modules are themselves significantly larger than the LEDs or LED **array**s which they operate and control. This equipment must be housed either in the LED luminaire housings (in which case the LED luminaire manufacturer has addressed this), which are quite large and thefore no longer capable of fitting into small lighting details, or remotely. Remote mounting

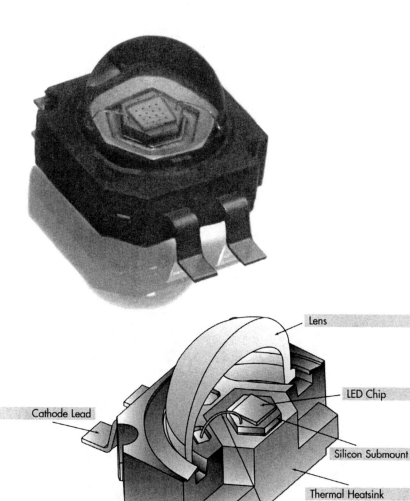

Lens

LED Chip

Cathode Lead

Silicon Submount

Thermal Heatsink

Outer Package

Bond Wire

Figure 10.25

A detail view and cutaway of a high-quality, high-output LED—Philips' Lumileds LUXEON K2 power LED. Both views are greatly overscaled here for clarity. The lens dome is nearly ¼" in diameter (about 5.5 mm). A 3W version of this LED is shown in linear arrays in Figure 10.26. The highly collimated light provides functional illuminance even at great distances.
Image ©Philips Lumileds Lighting Company

requires careful attention to the run distances involved and driver- and wire-sizing and to code-compliant access for maintenance.

LEDs are available in very discrete spectral distributions—red at 627 nm, green at 530 nm, and blue at 470 nm—such that RGB (red/green/blue) arrays allow for tantalizingly brilliant colored light in an ever-changing intensity and color, including white. And 2700K white will be available soon. The RGB versions require control devices and respective wiring and data cabling. Remote location of these control devices and their programming need to be addressed as part of the specification and installation. However, this usually involves some degree of theatrical equipment and programming/control knowledge.

Although LEDs are available in a range of discrete colors and white, manufacturing tolerances have not yet perfected the preciseness of color and whiteness. It is now common for LED manufacturers to **bin** the LEDs.

bin
A method of sorting LEDs based on their respective tolerance from color and/or brightness specifications (color binning and intensity binning respectively). Close or tight binning suggests LEDs from such a "batch" or bin would look very much the same when energized—producing the identical wavelength of light or degree of whiteness and the same brightness or output. This affects cost. Where LEDs are not seen directly or where they are part of a very large group or array of LEDs, the color or brightness tolerance or binning may not be important.

Lamps

Figure 10.26

Traditional chandelier beads are lighted from linear arrays of Philips' Lumileds LUXEON K2 power LED—3W high output LEDs. The foreground row consists of 6500K LEDs, the second row consists of blue (470 nm) LEDs, and the third row consists of amber (590 nm) LEDs. By fading or dimming respective rows, the chandelier beads glow white, warm white, blue white, blue, amber, and a near-magenta. The highly collimated light from the 3W LEDs provides functional light on the stairs below. Although a custom array, these LED luminaires are warranted for five years parts and labor. Here, LEDs offer improved maintenance situation over the alternative CMH lamping and require much lower wattage and more vivid color than filtered CMH. Also see Figure 11.25. Custom chandelier by Winona Lighting (www.winonalighting.com). Image ©Kevin Beswick

White LEDs are achieved with a phosphor coating on the lens. The most efficacious white LEDs are those at high color temperatures (6500K to 8000K), which are typically considered unacceptable for many architectural lighting applications where users are anticipated to be in the settings for any amount of time. These are typically the LEDs with the worst color rendering indices. These are some of the same parameters that ultimately turned most consumers away from standard cool white fluorescent, mercury vapor, and high pressure sodium lighting—all touted as highly efficacious, but saddled with such lousy color temperature and/or color rendering

characteristics that consumers came to hate them. LEDs will need to be engineered to provide consistently high color rendering light (at least 80 CRI) in color temperatures of 2700K to 3000K if they are to be well received by consumers. Further, if these lamps are to have a real impact on global warming, their efficacies must improve dramatically and costs must decline significantly *and* they will be made available in candelabra and medium screwbase retrofits—to fill the billions of existing incandescent sockets—and will be made to look and function like common household lamps.

LEDs should be considered for decorative interior and exterior applications and especially where bold, vivid color is desired. Functional lighting might include steplights, path lights, subtle downlighting and wallwashing, backlighting, and cove details (see Figure 10.27).

What's this all mean for the designer? Two plans of action—one for consideration of LED lamps and one for consideration of LED luminaires. **For LED lamps, including screwbase retrofit lamps, obtain and mock up at least two samples.** Check color and output consistency. Review these under intended environmental conditions (if these are to be used in a retirees' apartment and the ambient temperature is maintained quite high, test the lamps in the appropriate temperature setting for several days or even a week or two). For accent lamps, check intensity on intended objects such as sculpture, 2D artwork, cocktail table, dining table, etc. If these lights are to be used on dimmers, check lamp manufacturer's data on dimming, confirming that lamps can be dimmed and what kind(s) of dimmer is necessary. Check with the dimming vendor to confirm compatability between dimmer and LED lamp. For dedicated lamps (nonretrofits), understand the extent of auxiliary hardware required to properly operate the LED. Confirm lamp manufacturer's intentions—check references, Better Business Bureau, length of term producing LED lamps and/or auxiliary hardware for LEDs, warranties, local representative support in locale of project and locale of specifier's office. Inquire of recycling programs.

For LED luminaires, specify entire luminaires that have been designed by the luminaire manufacturer around specific LEDs and auxiliary components supplied as part of the luminaire. **These should be manufactured or sold by name-brand or recognized manufacturers and should carry a warranty of at least two years and preferably five years for parts and labor. Any LED luminaires under consideration should be sampled—obtain an operable sample. If dimming is desirable, have the manufacturer demonstrate dimming. Obtain photometric data for the luminaire to confirm its characteristics and efficiency. Understand the extent, if any, of auxiliary hardware required to properly operate the luminaire. This includes dimming aspects. Check with the dimming vendor to confirm compatability between dimmer and LED luminaire.** Confirm LED luminaire manufacturer's intentions—check references, Better Business Bureau, length of term producing LED luminaires, warranties, local representative support in locale of project, and locale of specifier's office. Inquire of recycling programs and ease of replacing LED lamp components and auxiliary components such as drivers and dimming modules.

more online @
www.epl.com/bulletin.cfm?FixtureIDs=640,641,642,643&bulletinID=41
www.lightingservicesinc.com/product.asp?productID=175
www.lightolier.com/MKABrochures/LOL%20SOLID-STATE%20BROCHURE.PDF
www.luxeon.com/pdfs/DS60.pdf
www.luxeon.com/products/line.cfm?lineId=18

Lamps

Figure 10.27

A pocket detail behind the banquettes in the distant background is fitted with a linear LED luminaire comprised of amber LEDs on roughly 3" centers (about 76 mm). The LEDs produce a starburst effect on the tightly-woven fabric, which has a sheen. In addition to lighting the wall, the collimated beam of LED-generated light creates a ceiling halo.
LED luminaire by Winona Lighting (at www.winonalighting.com).
Image ©Kevin Beswick

10.8 Mixing Lamps

On any given project, it is highly unlikely that a single lamp from one lamp family will meet all of the lighting criteria for all of the situations encountered. This has always meant that lamps must be mixed and matched on projects. Traditionally, this has been difficult. However, with the latest advances in deluxe triphosphor fluorescent lamps and in ceramic metal halide, these lamps can usually be mixed on projects with a good degree of success, providing color temperatures are matched. Today it is more an issue with luminaire reflectors and/or lenses causing unexpected color shifts than the lamps themselves. Further, these lamps can usually be mixed with halogen and HIR™ lamps. When mixing lamps on a project, it is preferable to maintain consistency with luminaire types at least in each space, if not across the entire project. In other words, when downlights in a space, don't change lamping unless the function of the down-light changes (e.g., all "general lighting" downlights might be 3000K CFL, but all "spot" downlights to enhance a floor medallion or seating centerpiece might be 3000K CMH). Additionally, within the same space, mix lamps only if there are distinct functional differences between the various lights (such as the aforementioned "general" lights versus "spot" lights). Consider, for example, a building lobby. One wall is programmed to have many pieces of art on it, and it has been determined that wallwashing will permit most any size art to be positioned most anywhere (this also allows for future flexibility as the art changes). An opposite wall is to be fitted with the corporate logo that, based on its design, should be accented with pinspots. The wallwashing can be achieved with spreadlens wallwashers. Two varieties of wallwashers come to mind for such a commercial application—compact fluorescent and ceramic metal halide. One variety of adjustable spot accents come to mind—ceramic metal halide. To avoid the subtle but visible differences among these various sources, consider using the same lamp family for both the wallwashing and the logo accenting. Downlights, if used, could then be a different lamp type (e.g., compact fluorescent downlights). In any event, for a consistent appearance across the space in terms of color temperature

and color rendering, it is suggested that all lamp color temperatures match (within 200K) and that all lamp CRIs match (within 5 CRI points or so). Where distinct visual attention is required, a distinct change in color temperature may suffice.

Of course, to minimize maintenance lamp stocking requirements and to minimize confusion on relamping, it is desirable to minimize the variety of lamp types and wattages. Nevertheless, programming criteria established previously for the users of the space(s) should not be compromised just to make maintenance simpler. Maintenance staff should be NCQLP-certified (LC) in order to maintain an efficient yet program-compliant installation.

10.9 Other Lamps

There are many other lamps available, at least for now, for commercial and residential applications. This chapter covers the more efficient, white-light lamps. The allure of most other lamps will be cost, or rather low initial cost. Steer clear of the 700-series fluorescent lamps as these are less efficient and less colorful than their 800-series counterparts. Although 900-series fluorescent lamps exhibit better color rendering than even the 800-series, the 900-series lamps are less efficient and, arguably, the CRI is little changed from the 800-series. Beware "new" T6 fluorescent lamps. These apparent T8-retrofits, are typically not as efficacious as high efficiency T8 lamps or the metric T5 lamps.

Standard metal halide lamps (non-CMH) exhibit relatively low CRI and sometimes are only available in odd color temperatures (e.g., 3600K). These lamps render the environment dull.

A host of filament lamps not covered here will likely be retired in the near future as these do not meet the requirements of the Energy Independence and Security Act of 2007. These range from popular low voltage T3 single-ended bipin lamps to standard tungsten filament household lamps to a wide range of candelabra-based decorative lamps. Avoid these. Their relatively short life combined with their inefficiencies make these unattractive for most all applications.

High pressure sodium lamps are the monochromatic yellow lights seen on freeways and rest stops. Their monochromatic nature make these useless. The luminaires in which many of these are found are glary because of lousy optics and/ or high-wattage lamping. Any use of these should be a rare exception.

Mercury vapor lamps are the monochromatic blue lights seen fading away along urban or rural streets or in very old factories. These lamps have been legislated out of existence and will no longer be available.

10.10 Future

The near-term future in lighting technologies will likely be very active. In the United States, the Energy Independence and Security Act of 2007 legislates that minimum lamp efficacy standards be implemented no later than 2020 with the minimum efficacy of **general service lamps** at 45 LPW. This same legislation also establishes prize categories and funding to award the individuals or entities capable of producing SSL lamps meeting specific efficacy, wattage, CRI, and CCT thresholds. Although the prize awards clearly recognize only SSL lamp developments, the performance

general service lamps
Lamps exhibiting such a common shape and/or all-around general-diffuse light distribution that they are appropriate for many lighting applications. For example, filament amd LED "A" lamps and CFL triple biaxial lamps are general service lamps.

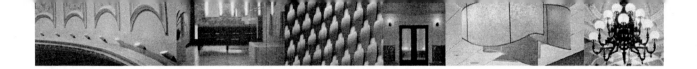

mandates of 45 LPW are applicable to all general service lamps. In other words, although standard tungsten incandescent lamps are targeted for obsolescence, new filament lamp technologies that exhibit efficacies of at least 45 LPW meet the mandate.

General Electric's High Efficiency Incandescent (HEI) lamp promises to exhibit 30 LPW by about 2010 and 60 LPW by about 2014—about the same time that the 2007 Energy Act lamp efficacy performance mandates are hoped to take effect. Although difficult to know what future characteristics these future lamps may exhibit, it is likely these lamps will have relatively short life compared to CFL and LED options.

OLEDs are essentially very thin films that glow—operating on principals similar to LEDs. OLEDs are very flexible, but at the moment are expensive to produce and available in relatively small panel or sheet sizes.[10] At press, OLEDs are used extensively in consumer products, with new ultrathin televsions just entering the marketplace. OLEDs use significantly less energy than their LCD and LED counterparts. OLEDs exhibit less of a heat issue than LEDs since OLEDs have the entire area of the thin film sheet over which to dissipate the heat. Life on OLEDs is expected to be much shorter than that of LEDs, but the hope is that OLEDs will be entirely recyclable. Watch for more development of OLEDs as commercial light sources over the next five to ten years.

Recent word of a very tiny metal halide electrodeless capsule exhibiting an astounding 140 LPW indicates that LEDs may not be the only future technology with promise of great efficacies.[11]

In any new lamps henceforth, nanotechnology may play a significant role or roles. Nanotechnology is technology that deals with the atomic level or scale of materials and/or devices. At such minute scales of engineering and manufacturing, new understandings and new performances of materials are realized. Subminiature lighting components such as filaments, coatings, and reflector and refractor surfaces might see significant performance benefits.

10.11 Caveats

There are plenty of caveats on lamps, their limitations, intended uses, and operating characteristics. A specification cannot be written based solely on the material in this textbook. Determining the actual performance of any given manufacturer's product and establishing final specifications require review of manufacturers' literature on all products, including lamps. For lamps, some of the more common caveats include: base orientation or burning position (some lamps are only meant for certain operation positions); protection from moisture (many lamps fail—some violently—if they come in contact with moisture); temperature sensitivity (some lamps do not operate well under conditions that are too cold or too hot); immediately replacing lamps with broken filaments, bulb walls, or bases (all of today's efficient lamps should be replaced immediately if any defects are detected in the bulb envelope or the base or visible within the bulb envelope, such as broken filament or arc tube supports); avoiding lamp shock while the lamp is operating (the HIR filament lamps are particularly susceptible to shock—sudden jolts—when energized); never changing lamps when the circuit is energized (all switches and circuit breakers controlling the lamp[s] being changed must be in the "off" position); high lamp operating temperatures and risk of burn or fire; using lamps only in luminaires with UL listings and labels indicating luminaire capacity to accommodate said lamps; and UV and/or IR radiation warnings. Carefully read luminaire cutsheet data and lamp data, including any footnotes.

Beware of claims that sound too good or on which there is no bona fide scientific research or independent testing data. Beware documentation from trade groups. Long-life and super-long-life lamps, while no doubt lasting many thousands of hours, sometimes do so at the sacrifice of efficiency—and in a big way (primarily relates to filament lamps). These lamps are typically half as efficient as their "standard-life" counterparts. So, a maintenance person can be frugal on the labor budget (the money needed to change lamps frequently), but will be contributing to increased energy consumption and the resulting pollution. Full-spectrum lamps typically are not. Yes, these may be "fuller" spectrum lamps than their common counterparts of ten or twenty years ago. However, given the latest lamp technologies, most high-quality lamps offer a relatively full spectrum of radiation. Further, many so-called full-spectrum lamps have bluer cast to the light quality—actually making warm tones and skin tones look poor. Many times their efficacies are lower than their "standard" deluxe triphosphor counterparts. As noted in Section 7.7, there is no known and scientifically recognized benefit from full-spectrum lamps. As Sections 2.8 and 7.7 indicate, light therapy is based on intensity rather than spectrum, and the intensity needs to be much greater than that experienced in most architectural lighting situations.

Finally, specify the lamps you believe are best for a given project. Do not fall victim to a lamp agenda espoused by a maintenance crew, an electrical distributor, or a lighting rep. Furniture system manufacturers may wish to force a specific (usually cheap) lamp on a project if they are supplying the task lights (which, of themselves, are typically overpriced and ergonomically inappropriate from lighting intensity, distribution, and control perspectives). Don't succumb to their tactics. The lighting design is intended to help people be comfortable and to be as productive as possible while maintaining reasonable energy use and maintenance strategies for many years. The easy decision today usually isn't right for the long haul.

10.12 Endnotes

[1] Gary Steffy Lighting Design Inc., *Time-Saver Standards for Architectural Lighting* (New York, New York: McGraw-Hill, 2000), p. 3-16.

[2] Yunfen Ji and Robert Davis, *High Frequency Lighting Supplies* (J. Webster, ed. *Wiley Encyclopedia of Electrical and Electronics Engineering*, New York, New York: John Wiley & Sons, Inc., 1999).

[3] Glossary of terms, Light Corporation (web page, 2007), http://www.lightcorp.com/glossary.cfm. [Accessed December 9, 2007.]

[4] NEMA Lighting Systems Division, *LSD-23-2002 Recommended Practice—Lamp Seasoning for Fluorescent Dimming Systems* (Rosslyn, Virginia: National Electrical Manufacturers Association, 2002).

[5] Smithsonian, Quartz Watch Inventors (web page, 2007), http://invention.smithsonian.org/centerpieces/quartz/inventors/biard.html. [Accessed December 16, 2007.]

[6] H.J. Round, "A Note on Carborundum," *Electrical World*, February 9, 1907.

[7] Nikolay Zheludev, "The life and times of the LED—a 100-year history," *Nature Photonics*, April 2007, 189-192.

[8] Susan Wyckoff, Fundamentals of Physical Science PHS 110, Experiment: What is a Light Emitting Diode? Arizona State University (web page, 2003), http://acept.asu.edu/courses/phs110/expmts/exp13a.html. [Accessed December 16, 2007.]

[9] Jennifer Taylor, "Industry alliance proposes standard definition for LED life," *LEDSMagazine*, April 2005, 9-11.

[10] Craig Freudenrich, Ph.D., How OLEDs Work (web page, 2007), http://electronics.howstuffworks.com/oled.htm. [Accessed December 22, 2007.]

[11] Michael Graham Richard, Luxim Plasma Light Bulb Kicks Some Serious LED Butt (web page, 2008), http://www.treehugger.com/files/2008/04/luxim-plasma-lifi-light-bulb-led-cfl.php#ch02. [Accessed April 20, 2008.]

10.13 References

Energy Savings, Inc., 2000: *The Guide for Lighting Designers and Specifiers.* Schaumburg, IL, Energy Savings, Inc.

Gary Steffy Lighting Design Inc., 2000: *Time-Saver Standards for Architectural Lighting.* New York: McGraw-Hill.

IESNA Light Sources Committee, 2005, *IESNA TM-16-05 IESNA Technical Memorandum on Light Emitting Diode (LED) Sources and Systems.* New York: Illuminating Engineering Society of North America.

Roush, Mark L. 2007. "Lighting People Are from Mars, LED Folks Are from Venus," *Lighting Design + Application,* December 2007, 57-60.

10.14 Project Data

Here are lighting specification excerpts for select projects. Specific catalogic for lamps and luminaires are specific to projects cited here and may be incorrect for other projects or may have changed or may be retired since the date of their specification. Final specifications for any project must be developed by the responsible professional for the specific project at hand.

©Kevin Beswick

Figure 10.15 Specified 2006

FTQ2 Sconce

Surface (exterior wall substrate as detailed by Architect) mounted linear fluorescent wall sconce shall consist of a sculpted stamped steel housing shell of stamped steel, gasketed polycarbonate lampcover, and semispecular aluminum reflector. Luminaire shall be nominally 5 feet/2 inches in height by 0 feet/6¾ inches in width with an overall projection out from the wall of 0 feet/4 inches. Luminaire shall exhibit a factory standard silver paintfinish. Luminaire power feed shall be centered on bracket wallplate and shall be 6 feet/3 inches AFF subject to field confirmation by Contractor with Architect for each respective location of FTQ2. Luminaire shall be furnished with an electrically fused, integral, high power factor, program-start electronic fluorescent ballast suitable for operation at 120V subject to confirmation by the Electrical Engineer. Luminaire shall be lamped with one [1] GE F80W/T5/830 (#90266) 80-watt, 3000K color temperature, 20,000-hour rated life T5 high output linear fluorescent lamp. Luminaire shall be UL listed and labeled for application and lamping.
• Ivalo AL-INSC-INNL-060-1-T5HO-120-INWMT-NOD-NAM-PCP-PCSI-Fuse

MPW1 Wallwasher

Recessed (drywall ceiling as detailed by Architect) mounted ceramic metal halide spreadlens wallwash luminaire shall exhibit an aperture of about 0 feet/4¼ inches in diameter and shall exhibit a recessed footprint of about 1 foot/2 inches in width by 1 foot/4 inches in length by 0 feet/9 inches in overall recessed depth (see vendor's current datasheet for actual dimensions). Luminaire shall be installed flat/flush/plumb and shall exhibit no light leaks at ceiling juncture. As with all recessed luminaires, luminaire housing shall be appropriately and securely attached to structure to meet code and to prevent settlement shifting over time and to prevent inadvert heaving or rotation of housing during servicing and/or aiming. Stapling, nailing, screwing, or otherwise attaching ceiling substrates or supports to luminaire housing which precludes complete access to lamp and ballast mechanisms or which is not code compliant shall not be permitted. Reflector cone shall be finished in matte clear aluminum with an overlap polished flange. Luminaire shall exhibit a spreadlens to uniformly spread light over adjacent wall surface. Luminaire shall be furnished with fused, integral, metal-cased, high power factor (0.95 or greater), low harmonic distortion (10% or less) electronic ceramic metal halide ballast suitable for operation at 120V subject to confirmation by Electrical Engineer. Luminaire shall be lamped with one [1] GE CMH39/UPAR20/FL25 (#42068) or Philips CDM35/PAR20/M/FL (#23364-3) 39-watt, 3,000K color temperature, 10,000-hour rated life PAR20 ceramic metal halide lamp. Luminaire shall be oriented to wash the adjacent wall with light. Luminaire shall be U.L. listed and labeled for application.
• Cooper Portfolio MSP5394-E3LWW-39PAR20-120-H-Fuse
• Kurt Versen R7526-39120-SC-Fuse
• Lightolier LW4PCCDP-AA4P35HD-120-Fuse

DEDUCT ALTERNATE for MPW1 AT OWNER'S DISCRETION
Provide line-item deduct for this item which may be accepted or rejected at the owner's discretion. Same as described above but exhibiting an aperture of about 0 feet/6 inches in diameter and an overall recessed depth of about 0 feet/10¼ inches.
• Kirlin HRR-06010-43-39PAR20-120V-96-70-FS

Figure 10.18 Specified 2003
FCP3 Pendent
New, surface (ceiling) mounted pendent shall be similar to Type FCP2 except bottom of luminaire shall be mounted at 7 feet/6 inches AFF.
• Sistemalux 4333-10-4444Frosted-4447-EPRSEOL-cordtosetbottom90inchesAFF

FTC2 Cove (detail—long sides)
Fluorescent architectural cove detail shall consist of two [2] units of 8 feet/0 inches in length butted end-to-end, subject to field confirmation and with any dead space split equally at each end of detail. All units shall be nominally 0 feet/8¾ inches in width by 0 feet/2¾ inches in height and shall accommodate one [1] lamp in cross section. Interior clear dimensions of cove detail shall be nominally 0 feet/9 inches or greater in depth by 0 feet/3 inches in height (a critical dimension). Luminaire shall be furnished with an electronic program start, high power factor, THD <10%, high ballast factor ballast suitable for operation at voltage as specified by the Electrical Engineer. Cove detail shall be lamped with a total of four [4] GEF32T8/SPX30/ECO (#25611) or Philips F32T8/ADV830/ALTO (#27064-5) 32-watt, 3,000K color temperature, high color rendering, linear T8 fluorescent lamps. Luminaire shall be mounted as detailed by architect (with at least 1 foot/0 inches clear from top of luminaire detail to upper ceiling).
• Peerless 16542a

FTC3 Cove (detail—short sides)
Fluorescent architectural cove detail shall be similar to Type FTC2, except shall consist of one [1] unit of 8 feet/0 inches in length subject to field confirmation. Cove detail shall be lamped with a total of two [2] GEF32T8/SPX30/ECO (#25611) or Philips F32T8/ADV830/ALTO (#27064-5) 32-watt, 3,000K color temperature, high color rendering, linear T8 fluorescent lamps.
• Peerless 16542b

LMA3 Accent
Recessed (ceiling) mounted low voltage MR16 pulldown adjustable accent shall be similar to Type LMA1, except shall exhibit two independently adjustable lamp modules and an aperture nominally 0 feet/5¼ inches in width by 0 feet/9¼ inches in length. Luminaire shall consist of a formed steel housing with a rectangular trim factory painted silver/gray. Luminaire shall be powered by a remote transformer suitable for dimming and sized by Electrical Engineer and located in a sound-isolated, easily-accessible, well-ventilated, code-compliant area as agreed by Architect, Electrical Engineer, and Contractor. Luminaire shall be lamped with one [1] Philips35MRC16/IRC/SP8 (#36348-1) spot lamp and fitted with a "Spread Lens" diffusion lens. Lamp shall be aimed and locked in position under observation of Architect after artwork is installed. NOTE: Unit is not IC rated.
• Sistemalux 4602-10-00SPL

Lamps

Luminaires are the devices that deliver light. They house lamps, ballasts, drivers, dimming modules, data interfaces, and/or transformers, sockets and wiring components. Luminaires also typically house reflectors and/or lenses that are, in theory, designed to best distribute the light from the lamp to the functional area or zone intended. Luminaires should be built around lamps or, conversely, lamps should be built around luminaires. Some luminaires are more decorative than others. But ultimately these devices need to meet vision needs efficiently. This chapter will discuss and give examples of some of the more important physical and photometric attributes of luminaires, as well as the various families of luminaires available.

Luminaires are responsible for how light is distributed on room surfaces, work surfaces, tasks, plants, architectural elements and details, and people. Luminaires can be very noticeable—a significant part of the overall look of a setting may come from the actual hardware appearance of the luminaires (see Figures 5.5, 6.7, 7.3, and 10.15). Ironically, the lighting hardware may have as much or more to do with the appearance of a setting when the luminaires themselves are unlit (see Figures 11.1 and 11.2). On the other hand, luminaires, or at least their application, can be discrete, yet this too contributes to the overall look of a setting (see Figures 3.5 [in-floor uplights], 5.7, and 11.2 [lighted handrails at entry steps]). There are many off-the-shelf or standard luminaires available to meet many of today's lighting needs. The key is to begin by defining all of the appropriate lighting needs for a project (see Chapters 4, 5, 6, 7, and 8) and then, based on these needs, to formulate daylight/electric light schemes. Once the schemes are established, the designer is in a position to define daylight devices and lamps and luminaires to bring those schemes to reality.

Luminaires can be either off-the-shelf, modifications of standard equipment, or totally custom. Many times, using off-the-shelf equipment in architectural details will lead to a successful project. The buffet niche in Figure 4.1 is lighted with standard striplights in an architectural slot detail—a drywall detail finalized by the architect that washes the niche wall with light. Arriving at such a solution did not mean starting with the assumption that somehow, some way a striplight would be used on the project. The lighting program identified the need for spaciousness and daylight balancing in the conference room, while the architectural schematic presented a clean, modern aesthetic. Lighting of the niche would introduce a bright vertical surface corresponding to the acoustic and color enhancement of the niche.

Understanding lighting hardware is critical to knowing if and how light can be introduced into a given space or architectural setting. Light reflection (see Figure 8.4) and light transmission (see Figure 8.5) are both important concepts in developing lighting solutions. Understanding luminaire photometric qualities is also crucial to resolving lighting design challenges.

more online @
www.lightsearch.com/

11.1 Hardware

Clearly, lighting design is much more than just applying available equipment, more than tacking luminaires onto or into the architecture—hence, the importance of programming and schematic design. There comes a time, however, when hardware must be selected if the designer is to maintain control over the quality of the

Figure 11.1

The postlights were selected to provide a hardware look and a lighting quality similar to that of the era of the building's construction—1913. 3000K 39-watt T6 ceramic metal halide lamps are enclosed in a refractor inside an opal globe. Simple globes mark each entry portal. Miniature linear uplights provide a subtle wash to the stone window frames. Lights integrated with the handrail illuminate the entry steps. A single in-pavement uplight at each column accentuates the columnar shape and further defines the more active entry area.
Image ©Per Kjeldsen

photometry
The intensity and distribution characteristics of a luminaire or lamp, typified by intensity measurements and data in various directions. Typical photometric data include candlepower (reported in candelas), lumens (from the luminaire after reflector losses), and coefficients of utilization (CUs).

project, in terms of both aesthetics and performance. Lighting hardware is generally judged on quality of construction, quality of appearance, and quality of **photometry**. The degree to which each of these factors contributes to luminaire selection depends on the use and/or location of the equipment. For example, the luminaires used to uplight the columns in Figure 11.3 need not be particularly attractive or decorative. Given the scale of the application and the relative diminutive size of the luminaires, they simply need to be painted out to match the stonework—the quality of appearance is not so important if the units are relatively small and painted out to match the background. However, the quality of the luminaires' construction and photometry are critical to its success in this exterior application. Rugged and durable are keywords when exterior lighting is involved. The luminaires shown

Figure 11.2

In daylight, the decorative cast postlights exhibit a mass and proportion appropriate to the time of the building's construction. Globes are relatively diminutive, also a hallmark of the 1913 time period. The simple globes are visible at each entry portal, but the handrail lights and the upper facade linear uplights are not evident.
Image ©Balthazar Korab

have cast and spun components of heavy gauge aluminum, along with tempered glass lensing, and are UL wet-labeled. In this example, the choice of lamp—100PAR38/CMH/3K/WSP—offers the photometric distribution required to fully light the column sides bottom to top. The luminaire, a Sterner PD41270, need not provide any optical benefit except the clear domed glass front lens (to allow for ready water runoff and to minimize debris buildup) in a light straw color (to ever-so-slightly warm the color of the light for best enhancement of the limestone).

Another example is the steplights shown in Figure 5.7. Given close proximity to people (readily seen and easily touched), such luminaires should maintain a susbstantive quality over time—requiring a cast housing with no blemishes and a high-quality paint job (so the quality of appearance is high). Additionally, the cast

The scale of the architecture is so large and the style so grand that the column uplights need not exhibit any detailing. At just over 10″ in height and 8″ in diameter (about 250 mm and 200 mm respectively), the uplight hardware is insignificant. However, it is sometimes difficult to convince other team members and/or the client that simple relatively standard-size hardware will not itself detract from the architecture. Uplights use CMH/PAR38 lamps. Image ©Glen Calvin Moon

housing provides the durability needed to withstand an accidental foot kick or vacuum-cleaner hose hit (so quality of construction is high). Photometry needs to be sufficient to light the treads relatively uniformly without introducing glare. Clearly, then, whenever selecting a luminaire, the questions of construction quality, aesthetic quality, and photometric quality need to be asked—and the degree to which each, if any, of these is important needs to be established. Some luminaires offer quality construction, others offer quality aesthetics, still others offer quality photometry, and some offer some combination of these qualities. Some of this information can be teased from published literature, but, in the end, the designer should review working samples or visit installations of the lighting hardware under consideration.

Custom luminaires are sometimes unique assemblies of various off-the-shelf components. How these components are brought together makes a unique aesthetic and/or photometric character (see Figure 11.4). Here, it is critical to develop hardware that will be UL listed and labeled once completed. Further, for durability and quality of fabrication to maintain integrity of luminaire construction and warranty, it is strongly suggested that the entire luminaire assembly and some significant portion of constructed components (e.g., 50 percent or so) be made by the specified vendor. Sometimes custom luminaires are remakes, reworks, reconstructions, or restorations of existing (or previously existing) luminaires.

Figure 11.4

The lighting program for this hospitality space called for warm, more intimate, and human-scale lighting, both in terms of the lighting effects and in terms of the lighting hardware. The aesthetic was decidedly modern. No off-the-shelf luminaires could simultaeously meet the challenge of the scale, styling, and lamping/wattage requirements for the floor lights (right background) or the table lights (center foreground). Winona Lighting made the custom floor lights and table lights. All use GE F13DBX/SPX30/4P (#10580) lamps and Hatch electronic ballasts.
Image ©Kevin Beswick

For remakes, photographs or drawings of the missing luminaire are necessary for redevelopment. For reworks, reconstructions, and restorations, the existing luminaire is specified with new wiring, a new or refinished finish, new sockets, new lamps, new shades, and the like, all, which when completed, are UL listed and labeled as a complete lighting assembly. Any work on custom luminaires requires a bit of back and forth with luminaire manufacturers. The designer develops drawings as "cutsheets" to be used with the specification as part of the contract documents to convey an intent. The successful luminaire manufacturer then develops a shop drawing for review by the design team. The team marks up the shop drawing to clarify any issues not entirely understood in the process. For larger and more complicated custom luminaires, or for projects where time and team interest permit, the design team might review samples of various components for quality and aesthetics. For luminaires that are intended to have a significant photometric function, portions of reflectors/lenses and lamp assemblies should be reviewed as sample mockups to assure photometric performance. This entire back-and-forth process may take from 12 to 24 weeks or more from the date that the manufacturer is awarded the project, to final shipment of finished luminaire(s). This timeframe depends on the complexity and scale of the project and the status of the economy.

Table 11.1 outlines the various components that may be involved in a luminaire's construction and their specification characteristics. This checklist can be used to assess luminaires for a given project and can be used to assist in the writing of the lighting specification for a given project.

11.2 Construction

Luminaires are likely to remain in a given installation for many years—longer is certainly preferable from a sustainability perspective. Retail applications may be the least stable because these lighting systems change with fashion, purchasing trends, economic conditions, and the like. Commercial and hospitality installations will likely remain intact for twenty or thirty years. Luminaires' abilities to withstand the environment, both indoor and out; their ability to withstand building system interaction (e.g., vibration due to mechanical equipment); and their ability to withstand, indeed encourage, proper maintenance are key construction qualities necessary for long life. Heavy-gauge steel, extruded aluminum, and/or cast metal are good base construction methods for long-life luminaires. Connections are the most likely points of failure in any luminaire, and mechanical fasteners (e.g., screws or rivets) are more permanent than tab/slot construction or some of the "cost-creative" methods of double-sided tape and Velcro®.

Baffles and **louvers** should be of sufficient gauge, if formed metal, and/or of such cell size to minimize torquing. Extruded aluminum baffles or double-sided (U-shaped) steel baffles lead to more sturdy, monolithic construction. Acrylic lenses and baffles should be UV-stabilized to resist discoloration over time. Where luminaires are in vandal-prone areas, consider UV-stabilized polycarbonate lenses for greater durability.

In order to judge luminaire construction, several techniques are available: review of manufacturers' literature; view and handle samples, preferably an operational sample; and/or view a mockup. These techniques should be used in a linear progression toward decision making. For example, if six different manufacturers' luminaires are under consideration, then carefully review the manufacturers' literature—including online resources that may include various installation examples. Of the six, perhaps three manufacturers indicate the use of heavier-gauge steel than the others. Order and review samples of these three remaining luminaires. After this review of the physical samples, perhaps two luminaires will surpass the third. Finally, consider a mockup to review the construction quality of the luminaires after installation by electrical contractors. The mockup also provides an excellent opportunity to review the quality of the installed aesthetic appearance and of photometry.

baffles

A series of metal or plastic "blades" arranged in a consistently spaced pattern usually perpendicular to the lamp, and which shield (or cut off) the lamp(s) from view in at least two directions (view perpendicular to the width of the baffle blade). See Figure 11.5.

louvers

Two series of metal or plastic "blades" arranged in a consistently spaced pattern, and each series of baffles oriented perpendicular to the other series so as to create an eggcrate effect (hence, also termed "eggcrate louver"). Louvers shield the lamp(s) from view in at least the four cardinal viewing directions. Louvers are typically less efficient (they block more light) than baffles. Louvers are necessary, however, whenever the likelihood is high that folks will view the luminaire from at least three if not four major viewing directions.

Velcro® is a registered trademark of Velcro Industries B.V.

Architectural Lighting Design

LITECONTROL

Type:
Project:

Wall/Slot®-II
85N
Recessed Perimeter

Specifications

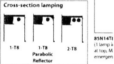

baffle shown in flush F/position

FIXTURE SUPPORT RAIL. Extruded white aluminum, wall-mounted rail provides continuous support and true alignment of fixtures and components. Rail is designed to provide a reveal at the wall to compensate for irregularities in wall construction. Galvanized splines are included for continuous alignment. A hook-and-lock system provides quick installation and horizontal adjustment.
FIXTURE HOUSING. Components are manufactured using computer controlled dies to assure precise tolerance. Housing is with an 18-gauge steel integrated rear support channel having captive leveling screws to provide field adjustment.
FIXTURE REFLECTOR SHIELDS. Die-formed 24-gauge steel having a continuous channel at ceiling juncture with locking and splining clips for attaching to ceiling trims. Shields are designed to provide 1 1/2" vertical adjustment.
LAMPING. Available in one- and two-lamp T8.
BALLAST. Electronic Ballast (**ELB**), high power factor, thermally protected Class P, Sound Rated A, less than 10% THD, manufactured by a UL Listed manufacturer, as available, determined by Litecontrol. Ballasts with a voltage range of 120 to 277 will be used when fixture configuration and ballast availability allow. The minimum number of ballasts will be used.
CEILING TYPE. Compatible with most types of ceiling systems, including grid and plaster. Fixture system must be installed prior to installation of ceiling. Finish of wall should extend 11" above finished ceiling height. See Wall/Slot-II Pre-Installation Manual for specific ceiling type details.
CERTIFICATION. Fixture and electrical components shall be UL and/or CUL Listed and shall bear the I.B.E.W., A.F. of L. label.

Note: Litecontrol reserves the right to change specifications without notice for product development and improvement.

Ordering guide

Product, lamping, & length				Options	
85N -		**T8 -**		**CWM -**	

Series	Lamp Count	Nominal Length(ft)	Lamp Type
85N	1,2 → 2		T8
	1,2 → 3		
	1,2 → 4		
	2,4 → 6		
	2,4 → 8		
	see notes		

Shielding Position
S/
R/
F/
see Shielding position

Cross-section lamping

1-T8   1-T8   2-T8
Parabolic Reflector

Questions to Ask
1. 120 or 277 volt? 2. Row information
3. Diffuser type? 4. Tandem wiring?

SHIELDING TYPES

BW Blade Baffle   **PBSS** Parabolic Baffle   Lens or Diffuser (various types available)

BW Blade Baffles. S/ position: White, 3/4" high x 3/4" OC. 20-gauge steel. Linear shielding is 45°. R/ or F/ positions: White, 1 1/2" high x 1 1/2" OC. 20-gauge steel. Linear shielding is 45°.
PBSS Parabolic Baffles. R/ or F/ position: semi-specular anodized aluminum. 1.4" high x 2" OC. Linear shielding is 40°.
PAT. 12 (XA) Lens. Diagonal 3/16" conical prisms, .100" thick extruded acrylic.
FP Lens. White acrylic diffuser, .100" thick.

BALLAST OPTIONS

Specify in place of ELB, contact factory for availability.
ELB10 Electronic ballast, same specification as "Ordering Guide", except less than 10% THD.
MKV/ELB Advance Mark V electronic ballast.
DA-ELB Advance Mark VII dimming ballast.
HEL/ELB Motorola Helios dimming ballast.
ECO/ELB Lutron ECO-10 dimming ballast.

CEILING TYPE

G Lay-in   CT Concealed Tee   CZ Concealed Zee   DP Drywall/Plaster

Specify the applicable ceiling trim. Detailed fixture shield information is available from your sales representative.

OTHER OPTIONS

DS Double Shields
Specify when a corridor intersects a row of Wall/Slot. Specify DS in OTHER OPTIONS column. Not intended for use as row fixtures in ceilings.

SDS Special Depth Shield
Standard fixture height is 10 1/2". A lower height shield is available for installations where obstructions occur. Specify SDS in OTHER OPTIONS column and contact factory.

OTHER ELECTRICAL OPTIONS
EF Emergency fluorescent ballast. Battery-powered ballast from a UL Listed manufacturer will operate one T8 lamp in a 3', 4' or 8' fixture for 1 1/2 hours.
F Fuse. Slow or fast blow, determined by Litecontrol.
TW Tandem Wiring. For two-lamp cross-section fixtures wired to switch in-line lamps separately; providing two levels of light.

LITECONTROL   an employee owned company
100 HAWKS AVENUE   HANSON   MA   02341   781 294 0100   FAX 781 293 2849   info@litecontrol.com   www.litecontrol.com

Table 11.1 Luminaire Specification Checklist

Aspect	Parameter	Significance
Dimensions	• Length/width/depth/diameter	US Customary vs. metric
		Integration with modular systems
		Interferences in room space or in walls/ceilings
		Scale appropriate to architecture and/or occupants
	• Projection	US Customary vs. metric
		ADA-compliance
		Comfort
	• Maintenance access	Accessibility vs. comfort vs. frequency
Mounting	• Recessed	Necessary clear depth in ceilings/walls/floor/ground
		Mounting surface (smooth, rough, very rough, articulated, flat, angled)
	• Surface mounted	Necessary clear space around luminaire
		Mounting surface (smooth, rough, very rough, articulated, flat, angled)
	• Suspended	Mounting surface (smooth, rough, very rough, articulated, flat, angled)
		Desired overall suspension vs. overall available height
		Stem, aircraft cable, chain
		Safety cable
	• Furniture or millwork mounted	Wire management/routing
		Exposed (visible) or hidden (detail)
		Control (at luminaire or remotely)
	• Freestanding (floor or furniture)	Hardwired or cord+plug
		Control (at luminaire or remotely)
Ceiling Type	• Lay-in Grid-type	Standard T, narrow T, screw-slot T, concealed T
	• Hard Flange-type	Drywall, plaster, plaster-on-lathe, wood
	• Metal	Standard T or concealed T, linear
	• Other	Concrete, special modular, special fabric (e.g., Barrisol), special acoustic (e.g., BASWAphon)
Thermal	• Insulation contact	IC rated or maintain at least 3" clear all around housing (or as otherwise required by code)
	• Insulation nearby	IC rated or maintain at least 3" clear all around housing (or as otherwise required by code)
	• No insulation	IC rated or non-IC rated (both are acceptable)
Flange	• Overlap trim	Self-flanged/same metal finish as reflector (best for most all ceiling colors/types)
		Self-flanged/white paint (best for white ceilings)
		Self-flanged/custom paint (best for other-than-white ceilings where custom look is desired)
		White acrylic/polymer flange (two-piece, less attractive, but quick and cheap)
	• Flangless	Cleanest, most minimal look, but requires precision drywall/plaster work
Reflector	• Optics	Precision formed and finished
		Diffuse
	• Finish	Anodized/low-irridescent (matte vs. specular vs. semi-specular)
		Painted
	• Material	Metal (for best durability)
		UV-stabilized acrylic
		Glass
Lensing	• Glass	Tempered vs. laminated vs. untreated (application and/or lamping dependent)
		Optically-active (prisms) or diffuse (opal) or decorative (colored, faux stone)
	• Acrylic	UV-stabilized
		Optically-active (prisms) or diffuse (opal) or decorative (colored, faux stone)

Barrisol® is a registered trademark of Barrisol-Normalu SAS
BASWAphon® is a registered trademark of BASWA AG of Switzerland

	Aspect	Parameter	Significance
☐	Function	• Fixed	Narrow, medium, wide spread
		• Adjustable	Narrow, medium, wide spread
			Max rotation, max tilt angle, friction or locking mechanisms, hot aim
		• Wallwash	Narrow, medium, wide spread
☐	Photometric	• Luminances	Maximum, average
		• Candlepower	Center beam
			Maximum
			Beam spread
		• Luminaire lumens	Luminaire efficiency
		• Power	Number of lamps and lamp wattage
			Total wattage with ballast/driver/transformer losses
☐	Lamping	• Configuration	Layout and number of lamps
			Base type (screwbase, pin base)
		• Type	HIR, CFL, fluorescent, CMH, LED
		• Internal Circuiting	Number of internal luminaire control circuits for mutliple-lamp units
		• Color	CCT
			CRI
		• Lamp lumens	Lumens
		• Lamp life	Hours
☐	Ballasts (electronic)	• Voltage	Specific voltage or universal voltage
		• Lamps	Quantity of lamps controlled
		• Operating characteristics	Ballast factor
			Total harmonic distortion (<0.1)
			Power factor (>0.95)
		• Control method	Non-dimming
			Dimming
			DALI
		• Start method	Instant start, program start, rapid start (fluorescent options)
		• End method	End-of-life shutdown protection
		• Protection	Thermal fuse (required)
			Electrical fuse (may protect more costly lamps/ballasts)
		• Location	Internal to luminaire
			Remote from luminaire
☐	Lamp Containment		Required for some halogen, HIR, CMH lamps
☐	Environment	• Dry	UL listed/labeled for Dry
		• Damp	UL listed/labeled for Damp
		• Wet	UL listed/labeled for Wet
		• Hazardous	Vapor/dust-proof, explosion proof, marine, etc. UL listed/labeled
☐	Shielding	• Baffles	Visual cutoff in one viewing direction
			Material and finish
		• Louvers	Visual cutoff in two viewing direction
			Material and finish
☐	HVAC	• Static	Door frame appearance (reveal or no reveal)
		• Air handling	Supply

11.3 Appearance

Selecting a luminaire for its appearance simply on the basis of reviewing some brochures, ads, magazine articles, or online photographs may produce surprising and disappointing results. For any luminaire, it is necessary to ascertain several factors firsthand: the consistency, sheen, and durability of the finish; methods of attachment to the architecture; methods of connecting various components to one another; baffle, louver, reflector, and/or refractor (lens) fit and finish; and for linear luminaires, long-run connector components and straightness of edges. The lighting designer is not reviewing these sorts of details in an engineering nor installation role, but rather needs to determine if any of these details will result in a bad appearance of either the luminaire or the architecture. For example, a beautiful sconce, particularly if imported and retrofitted for the local market, may have a wall escutcheon or canopy that is bolted into the wall with exposed bolts! To review such details, an actual working sample or a visit to an installation using the luminaire in question is required. Reviewing an installation (a project or application) sometimes is preferable to obtaining a sample because the sample can be commandeered and perfected at the factory prior to presentation to the designer.

Quality of fit and finish cannot be overstated. Not only do these affect the installed appearance, but will affect the maintenance and long-term appearance. In general, lower cost products are that way because some aspect of appearance, photometry, fit, finish, and/or construction is/are compromised. Metal finishes should be checked for integrity, color consistency, and finish consistency. Polished finishes will show fingerprints and typically require constant cleaning for good appearance. Further, cleaning will inevitably leave a light etch to the polished finish. Polished finishes more readily exhibit glare—a concern in work settings. Brushed finishes should be reviewed for finesse. Some of these are finely or lightly brushed while others exhibit a grossly deep and/or wide grain.

Where paint finishes are desired, the durability of the paint should be verified—is the finish easily marked? Is the paint matte/satin or eggshell or glossy? A more refined look is achieved with matte finishes while a more industrial look is achieved with a glossy finish.

Door latches and hinges should be checked for durability, ease of operation, and consistency in closure. Is the frame torqued and does this lead to an uneven door closure? Where downlights are involved, do the trims suck up tight into the housing and seal neatly at the ceiling line? Is gasketing provided to limit light leaks? Are lamps easily changed? Are there sharp edges and exposed (unfinished) metal (which may cause cuts during installation or maintenance or aiming and/or which may result in oxidation and deterioration)? Are auxiliary devices like ballasts and transformers and drivers reasonably accessible?

When luminaires are illuminated, are the optics consistently lighted or are there odd patterns or splotches of light/dark visible on lenses and/or reflectors and/or louvers or baffles? Not all light/dark patterns are problematic. Some glass shades may, in fact, exhibit inherent shadows because glass depth and coloration cannot be perfect.

The photometry or optical performance of a luminaire is quite critical to the success of the lighting design. Even decorative luminaires need to have some sort of particular optical performance if they are to serve their decorative function. Such photometry may rely solely on the lamp. For example, the crystal chandelier in Figure 10.26 is illuminated only because of the very narrow beam distribution exhibited by the 3-watt LEDs in the overhead channels. Only such small and yet "punchy" point sources show off the long crystal strands in a glittery fashion. Figure 11.6 illustrates two luminaires where the inherent lamp photometry provides the photometric character of the luminaires.

11.4 Photometry

With the exception of the most decorative custom luminaires, photometric information from manufacturers should be readily available. In Figure 11.7, initial illuminance data is shown in the "Performance at a Glance" section for 32- and 42-watt lamps. Candlepower data (for computer calculations and simulations) and coefficient of utilization data (for hand calculations) are shown in the "Detailed Photometry" section. Whenever assessing any photometric information, clearly understand the luminaire optics that were used by the manufacturer to generate the data. In Figure 11.7, the "Features" outline an upper reflector of specular (polished) Alzak® aluminum and a lower reflector of low-iridescent specular Alzak aluminum, one piece, self-flanged. Therefore, with no other notations to the contrary, the data reported in the "Performance at a Glance" section and in the "Detailed Photometry" section are for the upper and lower reflector finishes. Reduction multipliers are reported in the "Options" section for respective finish options (hidden from view in Figure 11.7).

Dimensional information is also reported as are specification options. Key features are outlined—this luminaire's ballast has a starting temperature of −22°F (so this is an option for exterior canopies at entries/exits, for example) and the housing is aluminum (presumably greater embodied energy, but likely more durable than steel and therefore greater installed life).

Data

Reviewing actual working samples is recommended. Some aspects of light distribution are not reported in published photometric data (unintentionally—the photometers simply are not required to measure data at every possible angle [an infinite amount of data would be generated, requiring a never-ending process]). A classic example is with indirect fluorescent luminaires. Many, but not all, indirect luminaires that are fitted with specular reflectors will likely produce striations or streaks on the ceiling or upper wall. These striations are very annoying disturbances, particularly if they exhibit movement caused by even subtle air circulating across/around the indirect lights or from mechanical vibration. These striations, as obnoxious as they might be to some observers, do not show up in photometric reports and can be experienced only first hand. This is a good example of needing

Samples

Alzak® is a registered trademark of Alcoa

Figure 11.6

Recessed downlights (the very small, flush circles of light) consist of a cluster of three 3-watt white LEDs and a clear lens for wet rating. These downlights exhibit a narrow beam distribution and light the pavement (creating the circular light pattern). The marquee lights (the small glowing cylinders) are clear acrylic cylinders with a pattern etched into the bottom side lighted with a 3-watt blue LED. In both of these luminaires, the LED lamps provide the photometric character of the luminaire unaided by reflectors or refractors.

Custom LED luminaires by Winona Lighting (at www.winonalighting.com). Image ©Kevin Beswick

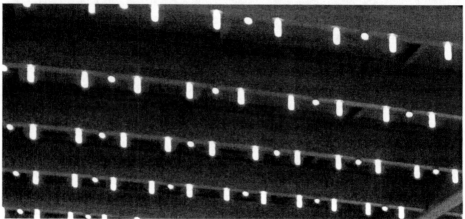

nothing more than a working sample, plugging it in and holding it near a light-colored, matte wall with the light oriented upward or toward the wall; and looking for striations on the ceiling or wall. Another example is with parabolic (direct) luminaires. No matter how the parabolic baffle or louver is formed and if specular or semi-specular aluminum material is used, if lamps are aiming light directly onto the baffle or louver assembly, then there will be some viewing angle when a flash or hot streak of light is observed. This is the angle-of-incidence/angle-of-reflectance phenomena (see Figure 8.4) doing its magic (or horror, if this angle is near a typical viewing position). Photometric tests will, in all likelihood, show that the parabolic luminaires exhibit low, consistent luminance. Viewing a sample is important to discovering if such a photometric glitch exists and evaluating its glare or annoyance, if any.

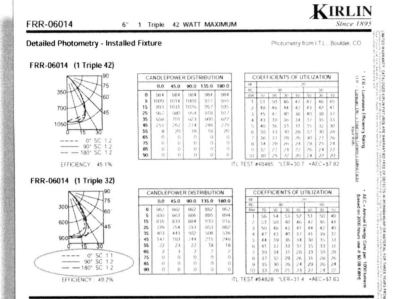

FRR-06014   6" 1 Triple 42 WATT MAXIMUM

KIRLIN
Since 1895

Detailed Photometry - Installed Fixture

Photometry from I.T.L., Boulder, CO

FRR-06014 (1 Triple 42)

EFFICIENCY 45.1%

FRR-06014 (1 Triple 32)

EFFICIENCY : 49.2%

Figure 11.7

This compact fluorescent downlight is suitable for wet, damp, or dry applications, works in lay-in or dry-wall ceilings, is IC-rated, available in a variety of reflector finishes, in lensed or open reflector, and accommodates either a 26-, 32-, or 42-watt CFL. A wattage reduction label is necessary to meet energy code if either the 26- or 32-watt lamp is used to meet the power budget limit on a project. Available at www.kirlinlighting.com. Cutsheet ©Kirlin

Options

SUBMITTAL DATA

KIRLIN
Lighting Since 1895

6" 1 Triple 42 WATT MAXIMUM   FRR-06014

Type IC Dual Reflector with Multiple Trims

Recessed Round
Open
Dual Reflector
Shallow Plenum
Type IC

Performance at a Glance

FRR-06014 (1 Triple 42W)

FRR-06014 (1 Triple 32W)

THE KIRLIN COMPANY

RENAISSANCE SERIES
COMPACT FLUORESCENT LIGHTING

Reflectors

It is worth noting that aluminum is a predominant reflector material. The finish on this material varies significantly from manufacturer to manufacturer. Also, the specular reflectors are typically most efficient, but also the most harsh with respect to glare. While specular reflectors may generate higher illuminances on workplanes or floors, ironically they create the "darkest" looking rooms—a phenomenon caused when the reflector sends more light downward and less light outward to walls. The walls go dark in appearance, which is compounded by the brighter workplane. Semi-specular or even matte reflectors are usually a better choice. This needs to be seen first hand for full appreciation.

Lamp Exposure

cutoff angle
The angle from nadir (nadir being directly straight downward—or 0°—from a luminaire) to the line of sight at which a lamp just becomes visible. Not to be confused with **shielding angle**. See Figures 11.8 and 11.9.

shielding angle
The angle from horizontal ceiling plane to the line of sight at which a lamp just becomes visible. See Figures 11.8 and 11.9.

Some people have an aversion to viewing bare fluorescent lamps. In some cases, people may have had issues with flicker with previous-generation lamps and ballasts. In other cases, people simply object to fluorescent lighting. Downlights, like the kind illustrated in Figure 11.7, are available with lenses to hide direct view of the lamping. These virtually eliminate any perceptible flicker. If the lamp is 2700K or 3000K in color with CRI greater than 80, the downlight will have an incandescent appearance. Some manufacturers offer pale champagne, pale bronze, pale wheat, or other warm-toned reflector finishes to mimic an incandescent appearance. Downlights are also available with lamps oriented vertically much like the old-style A-lamp incandescent downlight. Because the long side of the CFL is not visible and because lamp and reflector brightness are sufficiently great, it is difficult to know if these vertical-lamp downlights are fluorescent or incandescent when they're energized. A further detail to consider is **cutoff angle**. A smaller cutoff angle (which corresponds with a larger shielding angle) means less direct lamp glare from more viewing positions within the room—people must get ever closer to the luminaire to see the lamp. This inevitably requires the designer to make tradeoffs with glare and efficiency. Where occupants are not performing intensive "heads-up" tasks like reading computer screens or conversing in meeting settings, cutoff might be sacrificed for efficiency.

The lensed downlights are likely less efficient than open counterparts. Efficiencies for the vertical-lamp downlights vary from manufacturer and reflector style and shape—some are more efficient than the horizontal-lamp versions and some are less efficient. While efficiency is certainly an attribute to track, it should not be the sole determinant. If people object to the lighting quality of a space, for whatever reason including the fact they can "see bare lamps" or "experience glare," then real or perceived comfort should trump efficiency.

Efficiency

On the topic of efficiency, greater overall inefficiencies are experienced by poor lighting choices and layouts than by percentage-point-differences between specular and matte reflectors, lensed and open lights, or indirect and direct lights. A glary lighting system that's "efficient" (usually this means "efficient at delivering illuminance for the wattage input") will result in greater societal inefficiencies as occupants attempt to deal with the glare, associated headaches, and eyestrain. No attention is paid to luminaire and environmental luminances. Regardless, there is

Architectural Lighting Design

a dearth of photometry on luminaires with up-to-date lamping and ballast combinations. The accuracy of final luminaire layouts is simply a function of the accuracy of the calculations used in assessing those layouts. Calculations are only as good as the dataset. The designer must seek out the most current photometry for luminaires under consideration—meaning photometry using the desired optics, including reflector finishes/configurations, using the desired ballast, using the desired lamping configuration with the latest-available lamp. As energy codes become ever-tighter and sustainability becomes ever-more-important, up-to-date photometry from manufacturers is a necessity. As noted elsewhere many times, room surface reflectances are crucial to the assessment of lighting. Higher reflectances result in much greater lighting system efficiencies. Of course, all of this efficiency makes no sense if the lighting system doesn't set a pleasant, funtional, and comfortable scene.

11.5 Literature

Luminaire manufacturers offer a wealth of catalog information in hard copy and online. Online viewing offers the most up-to-date information, easier search options for those unfamiliar with specific brands, and less waste. Information typically available includes a photo or line drawing (or both) of the luminaire, along with product features, construction materials and techniques or features, finish, energy and photometric data, ordering information, and sometimes application photos. As discussed above, detailed photometric data are available. This data might be presented in graphic and tabular form on cutsheets or might be available in online photometric files for convenient use in lighting calculation and lighting simulation programs. For the contractor, installation instructions are available online for many manufacturers' products.

Finding lighting hardware is easy with the Internet. Finding efficient, durable, safe, and long-life lighting hardware is more challenging. Use precaution on anything that is incandescent, most simply because this is not efficient, probably looks pretty, and no doubt has little photometric benefit. Use precaution on foreign manufacturers with foreign-language or foreign-address websites—this might be an indication that the manufacturer has yet to build strong sales and distribution service networks and, therefore, may not be familiar with your market. Inquire about the manufacturer's longevity—how long has the firm been in business making lighting equipment (generally, longer is better). How much of the material that they sell is made by their employees in their factory? Where is their factory? What are the typical leadtimes for their equipment? Use extreme caution on anything that does not exhibit a UL or NRTL (nationally recognized testing lab) listing and label mark indicating the product has been tested against and passed UL standards (for the states) or the respective EU labels/standards or Canadian Standards labels/standards, etc. for respective markets. Some manufacturers assume that you know their products are so listed and labeled. If you see no mention of these listings and labels, ask the manufacturer before considering this equipment for a project. If you intend to specify options that are not listed as common options, confirm with the manufacturer that such special options are available and that this/these will not void any safety listings and labels.

Figure 11.8

This compact fluorescent downlight is suitable for damp or dry applications, works in lay-in or drywall ceilings, is not IC-rated, is available in a variety of reflector finishes, and accommodates a 26-watt CFL (other luminaires in the same family exhibit other wattages). A companion wallwash luminaire is available and some data is provided for the wallwasher as well as for the downlight. Shielding angle is 38° (so cutoff angle is 90° minus 38° or 52°). Available at www.epl.com.

Cutsheet ©Edison Price Lighting
Image ©Stockxpert

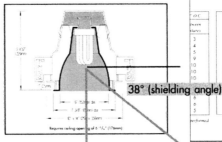

TRIPLES-V 26/6

PHOTOMETRIC REPORT

Report No. 44958. Original Independent Testing Laboratories Inc. (ITL) test report furnished upon request.

Luminaire .... recessed compact fluorescent downlight with spun aluminum reflector, specular finish
Lamp .... Philips 26-watt triple-tube compact fluorescent, 4-pin GX24q-3 base, 1800 lumens
Efficiency 62.9%
Spacing Criteria .... 0°-1.1, 90°-1.1

BALLAST INFORMATION

Voltage	120	277
Input Watts	28	28
Line Current (A)	.25	.11
Power Factor (%)	>98	>98
THD (%)	<10	<10
Min. Starting Temp* (°F)	0	0

*Consult lamp manufacturers for specific temperatures

CANDLEPOWER DISTRIBUTION (Candela)

Vertical Angle	Horizontal Angle		
	0.0	45.0	90.0
0	843	843	843
5	945	897	853
15	858	872	842
25	702	656	714
35	518	482	505
45	208	218	230
55	0	0	0
65	0	0	0
75	0	0	0
85	0	0	0
90	0	0	0

LUMINANCE DATA (Candela/m²)

Vertical Angle	Average 0° Longitude	Average 90° Longitude
45	14858	16429
55	0	0
65	0	0
75	0	0
85	0	0

To convert cd/m² to footlamberts, multiply by 0.2919

ZONAL LUMEN SUMMARY

Zone	Lumens	% Lamp	% Fixture
0 - 30°	650	36.1	57.4
0 - 40°	963	53.5	85.1
0 - 60°	1132	62.9	100.0
0 - 90°	1132	62.9	100.0
90 -180°	0	0.0	0.0
0 -180°	1132	62.9	100.0

COEFFICIENTS OF UTILIZATION – ZONAL CAVITY METHOD
Effective Floor Cavity Reflectance 20%

Ceiling Reflectance (%)	80			70			50			30			10			0
Wall Reflectance (%)	70	50	10	70	50	10	50	30	10	50	30	10	50	30	10	0
Room Cavity Ratio																
0	75	75	75	73	73	73	70	70	70	67	67	67	64	64	64	63
1	71	69	68	70	68	66	65	64	63	63	62	61	61	60	59	58
2	67	64	61	66	63	60	61	59	57	59	57	56	57	56	55	54
3	63	59	56	63	62	58	55	53	57	54	52	55	53	51	54	52
										51	49	47	50	48	46	45
										48	45	43	47	44	42	41
										45	42	39	44	41	39	38
										42	39	36	41	38	36	35
										39	36	34	38	36	33	33
										37	33	31	36	33	31	30
										34	31	29	34	31	29	28

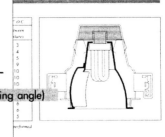

TRIPLES-V 26/6

recessed compact fluorescent downlight/wallwasher

COMPACT
FLUORESCENT
1-130

FEATURES

Triples-V 26/6 is an efficient 6" aperture low brightness downlight designed for use with one 26-watt triple-tube compact fluorescent lamp of the 4-pin types made by GE, Sylvania or Philips. Triples-V 26/6 provides a shielding angle of 38°.

One housing allows interchangeable use of downlight and wallwash reflectors, permitting housings to be installed first and reflectors to be installed or changed at any time.

Triples-V 26/6 uses one 26-watt lamp providing 1800 lumens (more than a 100-watt incandescent), a 10,000-hour life, a color rendering index (CRI) of 82, and color temperatures as warm as 2700°K (nearly duplicating the color qualities of incandescent).

Reflectors are available in clear, natural aluminum in three finishes: **EvenTone**, our standard clear finish, partially diffuse, anti-iridescent and gently luminous in appearance; **OptiTone**, specular and anti-iridescent, with minimum brightness and maximum efficiency; and **EasyTone**, diffuse and luminous. Additionally, reflectors are available in champagne gold, wheat, pewter and bronze. Wallwash (120°), corner wallwash (210°) and double wallwash (2x120°) reflectors are also available.

Triples-V 26/6 includes a pair of mounting bars (¾" x 27" C channel). Specialty bars for wood joist and T-bar installations are also available.

APPLICATIONS

Fixture is suitable for downlighting or wallwashing in nearly all architectural environments, especially those spaces where non-directional luminaires are preferred over rectangular troffers. These include offices, stores, lobbies, corridors, restrooms and public areas.

Fixture is UL listed for Damp Location (may not be suitable for some outdoor environments). Fixture is in compliance with the component based efficiency standards of the 1995 New York State Energy Conservation Code. Fixture is prewired with high power factor Class P electronic ballast, suitable for use in a fire rated ceiling, and approved for ten #12 wire 75°C branch circuit pull-through wiring. Removal of the reflector allows access to the ballast and junction box.

Requires ceiling opening of 6 15/16" (176mm)

38° (shielding angle)

0° (nadir)

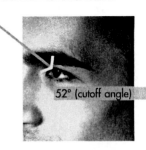

52° (cutoff angle)

PRODUCT CODE
For a complete product code, list basic unit and selections from each following box.

Basic Unit		TRPV 26/6
Reflector Type		
Downlight .... no suffix	Corner Wallwash	CWW
Wallwash .... WW	Double Wallwash	DWW
Voltage		
120 volt service 120	277 volt service	277

Reflector and Flange Color		Overlap	Flush
EvenTone Clear		VOL	VFL
OptiTone Clear		COL	CFL
EasyTone Clear		ECOL	ECFL
Champagne Gold		GOL	GFL
Wheat		WHOL	WHFL
Pewter		POL	PFL
Bronze		ZOL	ZFL

Other reflector finishes are available on special order.

OPTIONS
Specify by adding to the basic unit.

Dimmable 3-wire ballast; not for outdoor application .... DM

Emergency battery pack operates lamp in event of power outage. Fixture footprint increases to 10 x 17½" (254 x 444mm). Not available with a CWW reflector. Not for outdoor application .... EM

⅛" (3mm) thick **clear acrylic shield**, spring-mounted within reflector .... PS

► For combinations of the Options above, contact factory or Edison Price Lighting representative.
► A modified fixture suitable for 2" maximum ceiling thickness is available on special order. Contact factory.
► A modified fixture suitable for 34-watt service is available on special order. Contact factory.
► An install-from-below version of this fixture, suitable for installation outside North America, is available on special order. Contact factory.
► Decorative reflector rings are available on special order. Contact factory.

EDISON PRICE LIGHTING
41-50 22nd STREET, LIC NY 11101 tel 718.685.0700 fax 718.786.8530 www.epl.com
©Copyright Edison Price Lighting 2007

TRIPLES-V 26/6 DS

recessed compact fluorescent downlight/wallwasher

COMPACT FLUORESCENT
1-132

FEATURES

Triples-V 26/6DS is an efficient 6" aperture low brightness downlight designed for use with one 26-watt triple-tube compact fluorescent lamp of the 4-pin types made by GE, Sylvania or Philips. Triples-V 26/6DS provides a shielding angle of 45°.

One housing allows interchangeable use of downlight and wallwash reflectors, permitting housings to be installed first and reflectors to be installed or changed at any time.

Triples-V 26/6DS uses one 26-watt lamp providing 1800 lumens (more than a 100-watt incandescent), a 10,000-hour life, a color rendering index (CRI) of 82, and color temperatures as warm as 2700°K (nearly duplicating the color qualities of incandescent).

Reflectors are available, natural aluminum in three finishes. **EvenTone**, our standard clear finish, partially diffuse, anti-iridescent and gently luminous in appearance; **OptiTone**, specular and anti-iridescent, with minimum brightness and maximum efficiency; and **EasyTone**, diffuse and luminous. Additionally, reflectors are available in champagne gold, wheat, pewter and bronze. Wallwash (120°), corner wallwash (210°) and double wallwash (2x120°) reflectors are also available.

Triples-V 26/6DS includes a pair of mounting bars (¾" x 27" C channel). Specialty bars for wood joist and T-bar installations are also available.

APPLICATIONS

Fixture is suitable for downlighting or wallwashing in nearly all architectural environments, especially those spaces where non-directional preferred over rectangular troffers. These include offices, corridors, restrooms and public areas.

Fixture is listed tion (may not be sui outdoor environment complianc ponent b standards Ne En tion Co prewired with hi

Class P electronic ballast, suitable for use in a fire rated proved for ten #12 wire 75°C branch circuit pull-through v of the reflector allows access to the ballast and junction b

PRODUCT CODE

For complete product code, list basic unit and select one item from each following

Basic Unit				TRPV 26/6DS
Reflector Type				
Downlight	no suffix	Corner Wallwash	CWW	
Wallwash	WW	Double Wallwash	DWW	
Voltage				
120 volt service	120	277 volt service	277	
Reflector and Flange Color		Overlap		Flush
EvenTone Clear		VOL		VFL
OptiTone Clear		COL		CFL

45° (shielding angle)

0° (nadir)

45° (cutoff angle)

TRIPLES-V 26/6 DS

PHOTOMETRIC REPORT

Report No. 51043. Original Independent Testing Laboratories, Inc. (ITL) test report furnished upon request

Luminaire .... recessed compact fluorescent downlight with spun aluminum reflector, specular finish
Lamp .... Philips 26-watt triple-tube compact fluorescent, 4-pin GX24q-3 base, 1800 lumens
Efficiency 51.3%
Spacing Criteria .... 0°-1.2, 90°-1.1

BALLAST INFORMATION

Voltage	120	277
Input Watts	28	28
Line Current (A)	.25	.11
Power Factor (%)	>98	>98
THD (%)	<10	<10
Min. Starting Temp* (°F)	0	0

*Consult lamp manufacturers for specific temperatures.

ZONAL LUMEN SUMMARY

Zone	Lumens	% Lamp	% Fixture
0 - 30°	529	29.4	57.2
0 - 40°	796	44.2	86.1
0 - 60°	924	51.3	100.0
0 - 90°	924	51.3	100.0
90 -180°	0	0	0.0
0 -180°	924	51.3	100.0

CANDLEPOWER DISTRIBUTION *(Candela)*

Vertical Angle	Horizontal Angle		
	0.0	45.0	90.0
0	668	668	668
5	761	710	674
15	705	683	671
25	584	551	587
35	454	434	410
45	152	154	172
55	0	0	0
65	0	0	0
75	0	0	0
85	0	0	0
90	0	0	0

LUMINANCE DATA

(Candela/m²)

Vertical Angle	Average (0° Longitude)	Average (90° Longitude)
45	11305	12792
55	0	0
65	0	0
75	0	0
85	0	0

To convert cd/m² to footlamberts, multiply by 0.2919.

COEFFICIENTS OF UTILIZATION – ZONAL CAVITY METHOD
Effective Floor Cavity Reflectance 20%

Ceiling Reflectance (%):	80			70			50			30			10			0
Wall Reflectance (%):	70	50	30	10	70	50	30	10	50	30	10	50	30	10	50	30	10	0
Room Cavity Ratio:																
0	61	61	61	61	60	60	60	60	57	57	57	55	55	55	52	52	52	51
1	58	56	55	54	57	55	54	53	53	52	51	51	51	50	50	49	48	48
2	55	52	50	48	54	51	49	48	50	48	47	48	47	46	47	46	45	44
3	52	48	45	43	51	47	45	43	46	44	42	45	43	42	44	42	41	40
4	49	45	42	39	48	44	41	39	43	40	38	42	40	38	41	39	38	37
5	46	41	38	36	45	41	38	36	40	37	35	39	37	35	38	36	35	34
6	43	38	35	33	43	38	35	33	37	34	32	36	34	32	36	34	32	31
7	41	36	32	30	40	35	32	30	35	32	30	34	31	30	33	31	29	29
8	39	33	30	27	38	33	30	28	32	30	27	32	29	27	31	29	27	26
9	36	31	28	26	36	31	28	26	30	27	25	30	27	25	29	27	25	25
10	35	29	26	24	34	29	26	24	28	26	24	28	25	24	28	25	23	23

TRIPLES-V 26/6 DS WW

WALLWASH INFORMATION

Distance From Ceiling (Feet)	2'6" From Wall; 2'6" O.C.		3' From Wall; 3' O.C.	
	Below Fixture	Between Fixtures	Below Fixture	Between Fixtures
1	4	4	2	2
2	8	7	5	5
3	12	12	7	6
4	14	14	9	9
5	13	13	10	10
6	11	11	9	9
7	9	9	8	8
8	7	7	7	7
9	6	6	6	6
10	5	5	5	5
11	4	4	4	4
12	3	3	3	3

All vertical footcandles are initial values with no contribution from ceiling or floor reflectances. Computation performed with at least five wallwashers.

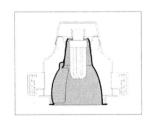

Figure 11.9

A "deep socket" version of the downlight shown in Figure 11.8 is available with a 45° shielding angle (equivalent to a 45° cutoff angle). Available at www.epl.com. Cutsheet ©Edison Price Lighting Image ©Stockxpert

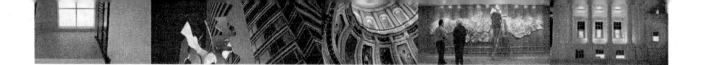

Listings of manufacturers and their respective luminaire capabilities appear annually in such magazines as *LD+A*, *Architectural Lighting*, and *Interiors & Sources*. Many of these resources have websites where additional listings are available, along with links to specific manufacturers' sites. Also see Section 1.9.

```
 more online @
/ www.archlighting.com/
 www.iesna.org/
 www.isdesignet.com/
 www.lightsearch.com/resources/magazines/
```

11.6 Specific Types

Getting to know specific luminaires takes hands-on review. Visiting local lighting representatives showrooms or offices can help, although the selection of hardware is likely to be limited since optional trims, finishes, and optical packages abound. Visiting luminaire manufacturers' studios, research and development facilities, or manufacturing facilities will likely lead to a greater breadth of equipment to see. Recognize the propriety or impropriety of such visits, however. If the luminaire manufacturers fund these junkets, then perhaps the designer will be more likely to specify those manufacturers' products over others that may better meet a given project's needs. Sessions that the designer funds may qualify toward CEU credits for, say, NCQLP recertification. Another method for viewing products is attending annual trade shows. In the United States, the premiere show is LightFair (also see Section 1.8). Finally, requesting samples for review is also a good way to ascertain a luminaire's various operational and aesthetic qualities in addition to lighting qualities. However, these samples can be reviewed for only limited time before being returned to manufacturers, otherwise the local lighting representative or the designer may be charged the cost of the sample.

Besides the downlights already discussed, a few other luminaire categories include wallwashing, ambient lighting, accent lighting, and decorative lighting. The discussions here are only intended as broad-brush introductions. There are many more luminaire types and specific luminaires at the designer's disposal. Indeed, two issues come to mind: overwhelmed and the easy way out. Luminaire types and selections and finishes and options and lamping and styling are so abundant that it is easy to be overwhelmed to the point of not making any but the simplest of decisions or those that come early, which leads to the easy way out. Because it is presented here and discussed, albeit briefly, does not mean the author endorses it or that it should be used nearly exclusively on any and all projects.

Downlights were discussed earlier. Downlights are ubiquitous. Obviously some are nicer than others, but these devices should not be considered the first and only lighting hardware for spaces. Chapters 5 and 7 outline the need for wall and/or ceiling luminances in varying intensities and uniformities or nonuniformities. Downlights do not address these issues. Wallwashers and uplights contribute significantly to the success of lighting as do many functionally—decorative or "all-around-glow" lights (which, for lack of better terminology, will be called decorative lights in the following discussion).

Wallwashing is a more important means of introducing brightness into a space than is downlighting. If lighting design had to be compressed to three steps, it would go something like this: Step 1—wash walls, Step 2—wash ceilings, Step 3—downlight for tasks. Washing walls with light so affects people's adaptation levels and impressions of brightness, that more can be done with energy used for wallwashing to influence people's satisfaction with lighting than can be done with energy used for downlighting. Indeed, increasing energy in downlighting only exacerbates the contrast problem (too much light on the horizontal workplane or floor and not enough on walls and ceilings—the walls and ceilings look dark, adaptation levels are low, and people respond that the environment is "dim." Yet over and over, many designers fall victim to cheapness by specifying as few, high-wattage downlights as calculations prove will "meet criteria" (illuminance criteria, and nothing more). Survey the photos in this text and see how many times wallwashing is used to make the environment comfortable, pleasant, spacious, and ultimately more productive and efficient as overdriven downlights.

Which walls to pick? **Walls opposite daylight sidelighting are good candidates for either daylight toplighting or, if unavailable, electric light wallwashing. Feature walls that identify a key area or function are good candidates as are walls that are treated with special materials and/or graphics and/or messages. Areas where ceilings are quite low or where spaciousness is a desired impression are good candidates for wallwashing.** Some walls are better candidates for grazing techniques and others are best suited for frontal/flat lighting techniques. Sometimes the wallwashing technique itself helps emphasize the special nature of the wall or helps make a "vanilla wall" a feature of interest. Figure 11.4 (also see Figure 10.24) has a feature wall of decorative wood that is accented with a grazing wallwash—but from the bottom of the feature rather than the top. This adds even greater visual interest.

Wallwash luminaires are available in two versions—those that graze a wall with light and those that provide a flat frontal flood. The grazing light is typically used to accentuate architecture—the wall as a slab of architecture itself—without introducing multiple perforations into the architecture. This is primarily of interest where ceilings are drywall, stone, or wood and the architecture is decidely modern. The flat frontal flood is typically used to offer more uniform overall glow—highlighting relatively unadorned wall surfaces and/or artwork (see Figure 13.3 for several studies of frontal/flat wallwashing). However, depending on the art and other criteria, such as cost and/or energy use, there are instances where grazing light works for art highlighting and where a flooding wash works for architectural highlighting. Grazing options are also typically used where a more frontal flood would create harsh glary reflections from the wall surface or where the wall has some translucency, in which case frontal floods would direct some glare through the wall to people on the opposite side.

Grazing wallwashing is achieved with wallslots—continuous linear luminaires available in many trim, lamping, and baffling/louvering options. The construction of the slot luminaire is very important. Since these run for full lengths of walls, thin-gauge housings are undesirable since they result in snaking of the luminaire

along the length of the wall, which is itself hopefully quite true/straight. Louver construction, as discussed in 11.2, is also important to the finished appearance. There are times, however, where wallslots occur on "dead end" walls—walls that are at the end of a corridor or perhaps at the end of a vestibule where users must make a path choice between left and right, but never can walk beneath or sight down the length of the slot. Here, inexpensive slots or slot details with striplights can be used to good advantage. Standard wall slots typically require some shielding. If wall lengths are not on a module with lamps, some fiddling with end conditions is necessary. Corner conditions can be problematic. Many manufacturers do, however, have techniques to minimize these issues—from telescoping ends, to overlapping lamps, to indirect slot lighting techniques. In any event, some dark end conditions may result if care is not taken in selecting and specifying the wallslot. Overlapping of lamps will help avoid socket shadows that are common in many, though not all, wallslots. However, the extent of the overlap may actually create a "brightened" or reverse socket shadow condition. Here, visual inspection of an installation or mockup is necessary to appreciate the degree of socket shadowing or end darkening, if any.

While the grazing wash is achieved with continuous wallslots, the flat flood wash has quite a few variants. The flood wash is typically achieved with open bottom downlight/wallwash combinations (see the lower right corners of the "second sheets" shown in Figures 11.8 and 11.9); spreadlens wallwashers; small, rectilinear CMH asymmetric lensed luminaires; or discrete linear fluorescent and CFL asymmetric rectangular luminaires. Each of these is intended to work best when placed several feet from the wall with center-to-center spacings of one to two times the distance from the wall (e.g., a wallwasher located 2' from the wall should be spaced on 2 to 4' centers if the wall is to be uniformly lighted). From experience, and by reviewing the photometric data—even just the illuminance data included for wallwashers—downlight/wallwash combinations and spreadlens wallwashers provide a relatively soft light. These seem to have best impact when used relatively close to the wall (e.g., 1' 6" [450 mm] to 2' 0" [600 mm] where ceilings are 10' [3 m] in height or less) and spaced on a one-to-one ratio (spaced the same distance on center as they are spaced from the wall).

Figure 11.10 shows a stone feature wall in a hotel lobby. Highlighting this feature serves to attract visual attention to this area even from the exterior as seen in Figure 11.6—helping arriving guests clearly identify the lobby zone from some distance. Indeed, the lighting and the wall help define the sense of arrival. A sense of spaciousness is introduced with this consistent wallwashing. Highlighting this feature makes the most of the material cost and labor involved in its construction.

In Figure 11.11, a potentially dark shadow at an entry niche is avoided with wallwashing. A grazing wallslot detail was used to maintain the architectural integrity of the overhead soffit. The warmth of the wood paneling is greatly enhanced with the 3000K, 82 CRI fluorescent lighting, making the most of that natural material and its contribution to the interior environment. Figure 11.12 also illustrates a fluorescent slot, this one grazing a brick wall and using a simple drywall pocket detail.

Figure 11.13 shows a wall housing integrated file cabinets. These file cabinets need some degree of light for the filing tasks. A series of nearby downlights might be considered an answer, but downlights would need to be placed very close to the wall to be functional for open file drawers. This would create a series of harsh and distracting scallops. Further, in order for the downlights to exhibit less direct glare, the lamping would need to be recessed sufficiently or lensed. Resulting in selection of a nice downlight of perhaps 26 watts when, in fact, an asymmetric wallwasher throwing all of its light to the wall and thereby creating no direct glare, could be more effective with an 18-watt lamp—and the 18-watt lamp exhibits a 20,000-hour life compared to 12,000 hours for the 26-watt lamp. On several levels, then, the wallwash solution makes sustainable sense. It is more efficient, uses longer-life lamping, and provides a better ergonomic solution (people-energy is better tapped!). The wallwash light reflects from the white wall back to the tops of the opened file drawers avoiding shadow problems common with downlights. Figure 11.14 also illustrates flat/frontal lighting, but with CMH lights using lensing and lamping to achieve a more scalloped effect.

Ambient Recessed

Ambient lighting or general lighting is that which provides "stumble light" to traverse a space or provides "background light" to limit harsh contrasts between task-lighted worksurfaces and surrounding surfaces or provides "task light" sufficient to allow for performance of visual tasks without additional task lighting. Ambient lighting is typically achieved with recessed luminaires or surface mounted luminaires or pendent luminaires. A CIE classification system is used to identify ambient luminaires based on photometric character—direct, semi-direct, general diffuse, semi-indirect, and indirect. Figure 11.15 illustrates these classifications.

Recessed luminaires are so named because the housing actually recesses into the **plenum** above the ceiling plane. Several varieties are common for general lighting in many applications. These include lensed luminaires, parabolic luminaires, and shielded-lamp (or basket or recessed-indirect) luminaires. All of these luminaires depend on a rigid housing. The thinner the gauge of metal used in the housing, the greater the likelihood that luminaires will not sit firmly into or be aligned with the ceiling grid or drywall flange. Further, most of these luminaires require some sort of mechanical door to access lamps for relamping. Again, thinner gauge metals and/or poor fitting lift-and-shift access doors will lead to a poor look soon after the first relamping cycle.

Lensed luminaires are typically used in laboratories, healthcare facilities, and foodservice facilities where easy cleaning and/or the need to contain broken lamp fragments (by code in the case of foodservice facilities) are required. With proper gasketing, these luminaires are available in wet-rated versions. A wide range of lensing is available. However, the higher-efficiency lenses typically are also the most glary and/or most unattractive. Usually, lenses with smaller prisms (e.g., the generic A20) have a better appearance and offer a softer distribution of light and less glare. Lens thickness will depend on the size of the luminaire, but is particularly important on luminaires with a footprint larger than 4 square feet (0.35 square

plenum
The void above the ceiling used to route ductwork, piping, electrical services.

Figure 11.10

Grazing Stone: The laid stone wall is a focal to the hotel entry shown in Figure 11.6. For this reason and to maintain a spacious lobby presentation, wallwashing was identified as a necessary lighting layer. Laid stone is best rendered by grazing light. The wall height of over 13' (about 4 m) demanded a strong light source. Further, the stone wall was detailed with an "infinity" look at the top with the stone continuing up into a pocket (seen more clearly on far right). A grazing wallslot using GE CMH39/UPAR20/SP10 (#42069) 39-watt CMH lamps was determined to be the best technique. Luminaire is Edison Price SPR-20-MH-DL-12 modified for a curved wall and circuited with every-other-lamp on one control zone and the remaining lamps on a second control zone for automated alternating-lamp-use-half-level-lighting setbacks to extend in-service lamp and ballast life. Available at www.epl.com.
Main Image ©Kevin Beswick
Image ©GarySteffyLightingDesign
Cutsheets ©Edison Price Lighting

meters). Thicker lenses exhibit less sag. Some luminaire manufacturers, including Legion, Lightolier, LSI/Lightron, Neoray, Prudential, and Selux offer deep regress lensed luminaires with opal lenses. The regress is achieved in most of these luminaires with an extruded edge, offering a clean, neat look. Regressing indicates that the lens itself sits at least an inch (about 25 mm) above the ceiling plane. If the lens is etched on the bottom surface, there are no glossy reflections—offering a more distinctive look than run-of-the-mill shiny plastic. Although these luminaires are quite nice in appearance, they are sometimes relatively inefficient and therefore better left to areas where appearance is a critical criterion. The recessed linear luminaires in the ceiling and in the wall in Figure 11.14 are very narrow (3" or about 75 mm) lensed units.

SPREDLITE 20 MH DL/12

cove mounted baffled metal halide wall grazing system

FEATURES

Spredlite 20 MH DL/12 is a baffled system designed to provide uniform grazing illumination on vertical surfaces between 10' and 20' high utilizing metal halide 20-watt or 39-watt PAR-20 spot lamps. Lamp sockets and integral spread lenses, as well as interposed baffles, are mounted at 12" (305mm) centers.

System is designed for surface mounting in an architectural light cove (see page 2 for dimension detail). Modular segments are installed end-to-end as needed to form a continuous run.

Parabolic baffles located between the sockets provide a 26° shielding angle down the length of the Spredlite and minimize lamp brightness.

Spredlite 20 MH DL/12 provides 0° to 10° angular adjustment of the set of lamps in a segment, allowing precise illumination of the wall surface below. The lamp angle of the segment can be locked in place, and the system may be cleaned or relamped without disturbing its adjustment.

Standard finishes are a matte black housing and a matte white back panel. Housing may be ordered with a custom color paint finish as an option. Reflective back panel must remain white.

Baffles are available in clear, champagne gold or black Alzak®.

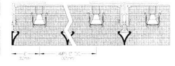

In the boxes below, record the number of segments you will need for your Spredlite order. The worksheet on page 3 will help you decide.

PRODUCT CODE

The product code for a Spredlite segment includes the Basic Unit and a Segment Length. The product code for a Spredlite run includes a list of the segments required; see example below.

Basic Unit	SPR-20-MH-DL-12
Segment Length	
two-lamp segment, 24" long	-24
three-lamp segment, 36" long	-36

APPLICATIONS

System is suitable for use in offices, hotels, malls, stores – especially in lobbies, atriums and public spaces. System provides illumination of specular wall surfaces with no distracting r[...]

System is (UL) listed for Damp Location. System is prewired [...] ballasts and approved for 90°C supply wiring. Electrical sup[...] from adjacent accessible outlet boxes (supplied by others) [...]

INSTALLATION

Dimensions: the segment lengths listed under "Product Co[...] segments can be bolted end-to-end to ensure uniform lamp [...]

Mounting: secure segments to wood or metal framing me[...]

Ends and Corners: leave at least 1" between the end of [...] nearest segment, and at least 2" between segments at cor[...]

SPREDLITE 20 MH DL/12 WORKSHEET

This sheet will help you pick which segments in which quantities will add up to a Spredlite run for the architectural cove or trough on your project.

Spredlite 20 MH DL/12 is made in four segment lengths:

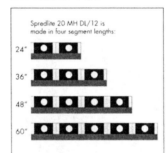

24"

36"

48"

60"

INSTALLATION GUIDELINES

Remember:

- the segment lengths listed are precise "out-to-out" dimensions
- segments can be bolted together to ensure uniform lamp spacing
- leave at least 1" between the end of the cove and the end of the nearest segment
- leave at least 2" between segments at corners

SUGGESTED RUN LAYOUTS

Length of Run	Spredlite Segments			
	24"	36"	48"	60"
2' 0"	1			
3' 0"		1		
4' 0"			1	
5' 0"				1
6' 0"		2		
7' 0"		1	1	
8' 0"			2	
9' 0"			1	1
10' 0"				2
11' 0"		1	2	
12' 0"			3	
13' 0"			2	1
14' 0"			1	2
15' 0"				3
16' 0"			4	
17' 0"			3	1
18' 0"			2	2
19' 0"			1	3
20' 0"				4
21' 0"			4	1
22' 0"			3	2
23' 0"			2	3
24' 0"			6	
25' 0"				5
26' 0"			4	2
27' 0"			3	3
28' 0"			2	4
29' 0"			1	5
30' 0"				6
31' 0"			4	3
32' 0"			3	4

Figure 11.11

Grazing Wood: A tall niche lined in light-toned wood paneling houses the entrance to a large meeting room. To provide a welcoming entry, to warm the wood, and to maintain a sense of spaciousness, highlighting the niche was identified as a necessary lighting layer. Downlights in the overhead soffit would, by their very nature, perforate the soffit monolith, which was deemed architecturally undesirable. The niche can be fully opened such that the circulation/breakout becomes an extension of the meeting room. For this, instantly controllable lighting was necessary. A grazing wallslot using 3000K T5/HO lamps of various lengths/wattages was determined to be the best technique. Luminaire is Focal Point FW4-NS-1T5HO. Available at www.focalpointlights.com. Image ©Tom Crane Photography Cutsheets ©Focal Point

overhead glare

A new form of glare common with parabolic luminaires. Although parabolics exhibit little glare when viewed from some distance, the multiple-lamp versions exhibit a powerful downlight component that creates an overhead glare when seated underneath—something not directly seen, but perceived. Can be eliminated by wearing a head-visor.

Parabolic luminaires, introduced in the 1960s, had, until recently, replaced lensed luminaires as the commodity light for most commercial applications. Four-lamp lensed 2' by 4' (about 600 by 1200 mm) were the popular, cheap way to achieve illuminances exceeding 100 fc (1000 lux). For the few employers who cared and the few architects who fought the battle, 4-lamp parabolic luminaires were a welcome reprieve from the institutional-glare of the lensed luminaires. By the mid-1980s, however, the energy crises had made their collective mark and 3-lamp parabolic luminaires became the standard. Engineers, in an attempt to maximize illuminance, minimize connected load, and minimize first costs, were laying out parabolic lighting systems that resulted in dark, cavelike spaces, and/or inflexible open plan offices, with **overhead glare** and severe VDT screen washout problems. A VDT screen positioned under a large, 2- or 3-lamp parabolic luminaire may

focus™ 4

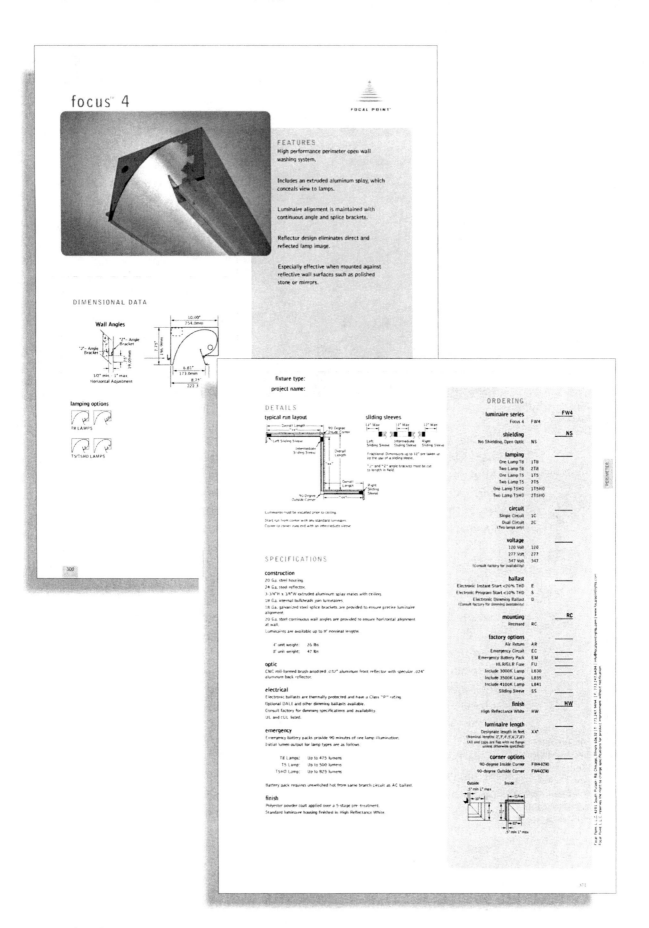

△
FOCAL POINT®

FEATURES

High performance perimeter open wall washing system.

Includes an extruded aluminum splay, which conceals view to lamps.

Luminaire alignment is maintained with continuous angle and splice brackets.

Reflector design eliminates direct and reflected lamp image.

Especially effective when mounted against reflective wall surfaces such as polished stone or mirrors.

DIMENSIONAL DATA

Wall Angles

"Z" - Angle Bracket
"J" - Angle Bracket
1/2" min. 1" max Horizontal Adjustment

10.00" / 254.0mm
7.75" / 196.9mm
6.81" / 173.0mm
8.74" / 222.3

lamping options

T8 LAMPS

T5/T5HO LAMPS

fixture type:

project name:

DETAILS

typical run layout

Overall Length
90 Degree Inside Corner
Left Sliding Sleeve
Intermediate Sliding Sleeve
Overall Length
Right Sliding Sleeve
90 Degree Outside Corner
Overall Length

Luminaires must be installed prior to ceiling.
Start run from corner with any standard luminaire.
Corner to corner runs end with an intermediate sleeve.

sliding sleeves

12" Max   12" Max   12" Max

Left Sliding Sleeve   Intermediate Sliding Sleeve   Right Sliding Sleeve

Fractional Dimensions up to 12" are taken up by the use of a sliding sleeve.

"J" and "Z" angle brackets must be cut to length in field.

SPECIFICATIONS

construction

20 Ga. steel housing.
24 Ga. steel reflector.
3-3/4"H x 3/8"W extruded aluminum splay mates with ceiling.
18 Ga. internal bulkheads join luminaires.
18 Ga. galvanized steel splice brackets are provided to ensure precise luminaire alignment.
20 Ga. steel continuous wall angles are provided to ensure horizontal alignment at wall.
Luminaires are available up to 8' nominal lengths.

4' unit weight:	26 lbs
8' unit weight:	47 lbs

optic

CNC roll-formed brush anodized .032" aluminum front reflector with specular .024" aluminum back reflector.

electrical

Electronic ballasts are thermally protected and have a Class "P" rating.
Optional DALI and other dimming ballasts available.
Consult factory for dimming specifications and availability.
UL and cUL listed.

emergency

Emergency battery packs provide 90 minutes of one lamp illumination.
Initial lumen output for lamp types are as follows:

T8 Lamps:	Up to 475 lumens
T5 Lamp:	Up to 500 lumens
T5HO Lamp:	Up to 825 lumens

Battery pack requires unswitched hot from same branch circuit as AC ballast.

finish

Polyester powder coat applied over a 5-stage pre-treatment.
Standard luminaire housing finished in High Reflectance White.

ORDERING

luminaire series			FW4
Focus 4	FW4		

shielding			NS
No Shielding, Open Optic	NS		

lamping			
One Lamp T8	1T8		
Two Lamp T8	2T8		
One Lamp T5	1T5		
Two Lamp T5	2T5		
One Lamp T5HO	1T5HO		
Two Lamp T5HO	2T5HO		

circuit			
Single Circuit	1C		
Dual Circuit (Two lamps only)	2C		

voltage			
120 Volt	120		
277 Volt	277		
347 Volt (Consult factory for availability)	347		

ballast			
Electronic Instant Start <20% THD	E		
Electronic Program Start <10% THD	S		
Electronic Dimming Ballast (Consult factory for dimming availability)	D		

mounting			RC
Recessed	RC		

factory options			
Air Return	AR		
Emergency Circuit	EC		
Emergency Battery Pack	EM		
HLR/GLR Fuse	FU		
Include 3000K Lamp	L830		
Include 3500K Lamp	L835		
Include 4100K Lamp	L841		
Sliding Sleeve	SS		

finish			HW
High Reflectance White	HW		

luminaire length			
Designate length in feet (Nominal lengths: 2',3',4',6',&7',8') (All end caps are flat with no flange unless otherwise specified)	XX'		

corner options			
90-degree Inside Corner	FW4IC90		
90-degree Outside Corner	FW4OC90		

Outside   Inside
.5" min 1" max
.5" min 1" max

PERIMETER

Focal Point, L.L.C. 4201 South Pulaski Rd. Chicago, Illinois 60632 | T: 773.247.9494 | F: 773.247.6494 | info@focalpointlights.com | www.focalpointlights.com
Focal Point, L.L.C. reserves the right to change specifications for product improvement without notification.

Figure 11.12

Grazing Brick: In this rehabilitation project, an original-construction brick wall was uncovered and left exposed. This created a "natural" focal element for lighting. Bookshelves were built into the old door frames. Ductwork created an opportunity for a slot detail that best accentuates the character of the brick. Given the room function, there is little opportunity for people to look into this slot. Middle right is a close-to-the-wall view of the slot. Far right is a head-against-the-wall view into the slot. A simple striplight detail was identified as the best technique. Striplights are lamped with GE F17/F25/F32T8/SPX30 lamps (single-lamp cross-section in length combinations necessary to fill the length of the run). Luminaire is LSI Industries Channel (S1) series. Available at www.lsi-industries.com/media/SpecSheets/pdf/s1.pdf. Images and detail graphic ©GarySteffyLightingDesign Cutsheet ©LSI Industries Inc.

low iridescent
Exhibiting a slight or no oil-canning appearance that is obvious and distracting with standard untreated aluminum when lighted with the triphosphor fluorescent lamps—the three phosphor wavelength peaks are actually reflected at slightly different angles, thereby causing a rainbow effect on the aluminum.

exhibit washout. A user seated under such a luminaire may experience a form of glare, even if the luminaire is not in the overhead peripheral field of view. On the other hand, a user seated between luminaires may have a "dark hole" experience—the contrast between the relatively brighter surround and the immediate low brightness results in an impression of a very dark zone. The key is using low-lumen luminaires (e.g., a 2' by 2' (about 600 by 600 mm) parabolic using three (3) F17T8/830 lamps, or a 1' by 4' (about 300 by 1200 mm) parabolic using one (1) F32T8/830 lamp) on relatively close spacings (e.g., on staggered patterns of 4' by 4' [about 1.2 by 1.2 m] or on regular patterns of 6' by 6' [about 1.8 by 1.8 mm] for 8' or 9' [about 2.5 or 2.75 m respectively] ceiling heights). As computer tasks became predominant, upgraded parabolic luminaires were developed to maintain low luminances and illuminances. Figure 11.13 illustrates one such parabolic luminaire (above the workstation). One way to quickly assess a parabolic luminaire's glare control is to check the depth and cell size of the louver or baffle. The deeper the louver, in general, the better the glare control. Some louvers and baffles actually surround and almost engage the lamp for a very low glare situation (as is the case in the parabolic luminaire shown in Figure 11.13). Louvers or baffles that are less than 3" (about 75 mm) in depth should have blade spacings equal to their depth in order to maintain a 45-degree cutoff angle. Finally, the finish of the aluminum reflector and louver or baffle has a significant impact on the glare, the aesthetic quality of the luminaire, and on the overall brightness impression. Three basic finishes are available, and all should be **low iridescent** These three finishes are specular, semi-specular, and diffuse. Diffuse is the current favorite where some sense of brightness is desirable (which is most applications). Diffuse finishes also hide fingerprinting—a very practical benefit with luminaire relamping.

Architectural Lighting Design

S1

PRODUCT HIGHLIGHTS

- Premium housing crimped along sides for extra rigidity and straight alignment
- Accepts optional plug-in wiring feature for continuous row installation
- Alignment couplers furnished for continuous row installation
- Channel cover equipped with quarter-turn, captive fasteners for easy access to ballast compartment

CONSTRUCTION - Fixture housing, lampholder brackets, end sections and channel cover constructed of code-gauge, die-formed steel.

ELECTRICAL - All devices UL/CUL listed. Suitable for damp locations. Damp location emergency pack must be specified separately. Ballasts are energy-saving solid-state electronic or electromagnetic. Ballasts and lampholders replaceable without removing from ceiling. Discrete voltage must be specified for emergency pack options when wired with flex.

FINISH - All metal parts painted after fabrication following treatment with phosphate rust inhibitor. Finish coating of housing reflecting surfaces is with white, high reflectance (minimum 92%) polyester powder.

PHOTOMETRICS - Please visit our web site at **www.lsi-industries.com** for detailed photometric data.

ONE LAMP STRIP (T8/T12)

CHANNEL SERIES

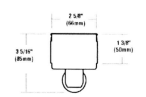

LUMINAIRE ORDERING INFORMATION

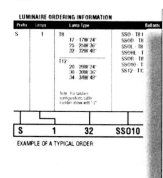

Prefix	Lamps	Lamp Type	Ballasts
S	1	T8	SSO - T8
		17 - 17W 24"	SSOO - T8
		25 - 25W 36"	SSOL - T8
		32 - 32W 48"	SSOHL - T
		T12	SSOR - T8
		20 - 20W 24"	SSO10 - T
		30 - 30W 36"	SS12 - T1
		34 - 34W 48"	

Note: For tandem configurations, suffix number above with "/2".

| S | 1 | 32 | SSO10 |

EXAMPLE OF A TYPICAL ORDER

Project Name _____

Catalog # _____

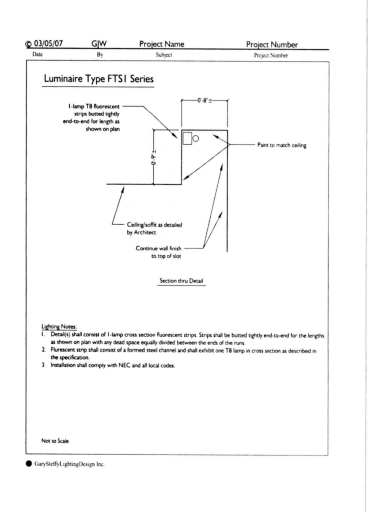

© 03/05/07   G|W   Project Name   Project Number

Date   By   Subject   Project Number

Luminaire Type FTS1 Series

1-lamp T8 fluorescent strips butted tightly end-to-end for length as shown on plan

0'-8" ±

Paint to match ceiling

0'-6" ±

Ceiling/soffit as detailed by Architect

Continue wall finish to top of slot

Section thru Detail

Lighting Notes:

1. Detail(s) shall consist of 1-lamp cross section fluorescent strips. Strips shall be butted tightly end-to-end for the lengths as shown on plan with any dead space equally divided between the ends of the runs.
2. Flurescent strip shall consist of a formed steel channel and shall exhibit one T8 lamp in cross section as described in the specification.
3. Installation shall comply with NEC and all local codes.

Not to Scale

● GarySteffyLightingDesign Inc.

Figure 11.13

Flat/Frontal Drywall: A wall plane of painted drywall contains file drawers to limit furnishings and paperwork clutter. Some sort of task lighting was necessary for the filing tasks. The wall was further identified as an opportunity to create an impression of spaciousness and brightness, particularly if left white, in this relatively small space with little access to daylight. This helps to avoid the cave effect so common with low ceilings and direct ambient lighting. Luminaire scale was deemed important in the relatively confined space—smaller lighting hardware to minimize a crowded look. Design priorities were low-energy use and long life as part of a sustainabiity effort. Frontal lighting consisting of an 8″ by 12″ (about 200 mm by 300 mm) recessed open-aperture wallwasher with kicker reflector and using GE F18BX/SPX35/RS (#17175) was identified as the best technique. Luminaire is Columbia Parawash PW81-1-18TTRS-G-LD-K-EPRS-U-PWFK1. Available at www.columbialighting.com/products/pw.html.
Image ©Robert Eovaldi
Cutsheets ©Hubbell Lighting, Inc.

A relative newcomer to recessed lighting, and fast overtaking parabolic as the commodity light for commercial applications, is an approach whereby the lamps are actually hidden from direct view. The recessed luminaire acts as a miniature cove—a recessed indirect light. Although the effect is somewhat like indirect lighting, the proximity of the lamps to the luminaire reflecting surface result in sufficient luminances that this luminaire may not be appropriate for large open areas where intensive or even normal VDT use is anticipated. Further, the optics tyically do not drop below the ceiling line (most of these luminaires are fully recessed), so that the surrounding ceiling looks quite dark compared to the indirectly-lighted luminaire housing. This depends on the size of the luminaire and

Parawash

Linear Wall Wash

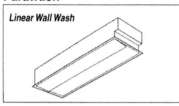

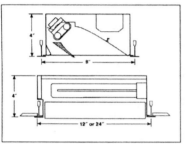

4"

8"

4"

12" or 24"

Ceiling Compatibility

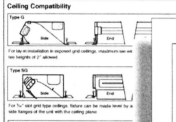

Type G

Side   End

For lay-in installation in exposed grid ceilings, maximum tee width, tee heights of 2" allowed.

Type SG

Side   End

For 9/16" slot grid type ceilings, fixture can be made level by adjusting side flanges of the unit with the ceiling plane.

Flange Kit Trim

Side   End

For hard ceiling applications fixtures are provided with a flange kit that into the concealed ceiling opening for a clean finished appearance. In row configurations contact your local Columbia representative.

Flange kit cut out dimensions for single
PWFK1: (1') - 8¾" x 12¾", PWFK2: (2') -

Complete ordering information on back. Dimensions and specifications subject to

HUBBELL Hubbell Lighting, Inc.

www.columbi

PW81, PW82 Kicker
8" x 12", 8" x 24"
Twin Tube Compact Fluorescent
or T8 Lamps

Type: _____

Job Description: _____

Description

The Parawash is an exciting advancement in the art of wall washing and display lighting. The unique kicker (linear baffle) reflector in the Parawash optimizes the lamp output effectiveness by directing the majority of the light on the vertical surface where it is needed. Precise optics provide excellent spread laterally, enabling fixture spacings unattainable with conventional wall wash downlights. Additionally, the kicker reflector directs light to the ceiling line with no visible horizontal cut-off lines. The Parawash is an ideal luminaire for wall washing and display lighting and also can be used to eliminate the so-called "cave effect" associated with parabolic troffers. When mounted at the ends and sides of the parabolic rows, the Parawash will eliminate the dark wall scalloping that the parabolics produce.

Construction

The luminaire housing is constructed of die formed code gauge cold rolled steel. The reflector assembly is constructed of anodized aluminum and is designed to present a clean uninterrupted reflecting surface. The kicker reflector is highly polished extruded aluminum and is not adjustable. The kicker reflector shields the lamp completely from room side and 9° from nadir on the wall side. Ballast is housed above front reflector and is totally accessible from below. Neither the optical system nor kicker has to be removed for lamp maintenance. Standard fixture has no reveal. A spread lens is also available as an option. The spread lens is only available with the twin tube compact fluorescent lamp and shields 75% of the lamp.

Finish

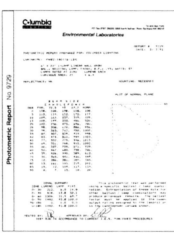

Columbia LIGHTING

Environmental Laboratories

Photometric Report No. 9729

2' Linear Baffle, LWW - One F40BX Lamp

Vertical Footcandles

Fixture Mtg. 2'6" from wall to Ctr.	Single Unit Distance from Corner				Multiple Units on 6' Center			Multiple Units on 8' Center		Multiple Units on Continuous Row	
	0'	2'	4'	6'	0'	3'	0'	4'	0'		
3'	5	3	1	1	7	4	7	7	15		
6"	40	18	4	1	42	15	42	42	86		
1'	72	35	7	2	71	32	78	74	160		
2'	71	39	11	4	79	46	79	75	179		
3'	38	28	10	4	46	34	46	44	118		
4'	23	17	6	4	27	31	27	16	84		
5'	14	11	6	5	26	18	20	18	56		
6'	8	7	4	3	14	12	14	10	38		
7'	5	4	3	2	9	8	9	7	25		
8'	3	3	2	2	7	6	7	5	19		

Vertical Footcandle Distribution on Wall Surface

Energy Data

LER: FP-29 **Energy Cost: $8.28***
Input Watts: 47 **BF: .95**

The above energy calculations were conducted using a specific lamp/ballast combination. Actual results may vary depending upon the lamp and ballast used. Lamp and ballast specifications are subject to change without notice.

*Comparative annual lighting energy cost per 1000 lumens based on 3000 hours and $0.08 per KWH.

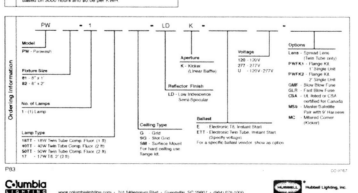

Ordering Information

PW — 1 — LD K — — —

Model
PW - Parawash

Fixture Size
81 - 8" x 1'
82 - 8" x 2'

No. of Lamps
1 - (1) Lamp

Lamp Type
18TT - 18W Twin Tube Comp. Fluor. (1 ft)
40TT - 40W Twin Tube Comp. Fluor. (2 ft)
50TT - 50W Twin Tube Comp. Fluor. (2 ft)
17 - 17W T8, 2' (2 ft)

Reflector Finish
LD - Low Iridescence
Semi-Specular

Ceiling Type
G - Grid
SG - Slot Grid
SM - Surface Mount
For hard ceiling use flange kit.

Aperture
K - Kicker
(Linear Baffle)

Ballast
E - Electronic T8, Instant Start
ETT - Electronic Twin Tube, Instant Start
(Specify voltage)
For a specific ballast vendor, show as option.

Voltage
120 - 120V
277 - 277V
U - 120V-277V

Options
Lens - Spread Lens
(Twin Tube only)
PWFK1 - Flange Kit
1' Single Unit
PWFK2 - Flange Kit
2' Single Unit
GMF - Slow Blow Fuse
GLR - Fast Blow Fuse
CSA - UL listed or CSA
certified for Canada
MS9 - Master-Satellite
Pair with 9' Harness
MC - Mitered Corner
(Kicker)

P83

CO 4107

Columbia LIGHTING   www.columbialighting.com • 701 Millennium Blvd. • Greenville, SC 29607 • (864) 678-1000   **HUBBELL** Hubbell Lighting, Inc.

Figure 11.14

Flat/Frontal Drywall and Tile: Two angled wall planes define the ends of this indoor pool and angle toward the east-facing window wall. The distant wall is Zolatone®-painted drywall. Foreground-left wall is combination glass tile and Zolatone. For overcast day and night situations, wallwashing was deemed important to maintain impressions of spaciousness and pleasantness. The Zolatone and glass tile are features worth lighting. Design priorities were low-energy use and long life as part of a sustainabiity effort. Frontal lighting consisting of a 6" (about 150 mm) diameter clear lens wallwasher and a GE CMH39/UPAR20/FL25 (#42068) 39-watt CMH lamps was determined to be the best technique. (Note: The clear lens and FL25 beam spread results in a more scalloped, less uniform wash.) Luminaire is Kirlin HRR-06010-43-39PAR20-120V-96-45-70-FS. Available at www.kirlinlighting.com. Image ©Kevin Beswick Cutsheets ©Kirlin

the output of the lamps, the finish of the upper reflector, and the number of lamps per luminaire. The more light that comes from a smaller package, the more glare and veiling reflections to be expected. These luminaires are best suited for small areas, such as private offices, conference rooms, copier centers, and the like, or circulation and transition spaces, or larger areas where VDT viewing is intermittent or VDT tasks consist of matte-finish flat-screens. Figure 11.16 shows an example of a recessed-indirect luminaire and Figure 6.3 illustrates a cutsheet of such a luminaire.

Ambient Pendent

Where ceiling heights are greater than about 8' 9" (about 2.65 m) and preferably 9' 3" (about 2.8 m) or more, pendent mounted lighting generally has promise. Indirect lighting can provide virtually glare-free conditions while giving the impression of brightness. Just as with parabolic luminaires, the success of this approach is driven by the lamping and spacing of the luminaires. Luminaire optics can vary significantly from manufacturer to manufacturer and from luminaire type to luminaire type. Luminaires using T5 fluorescent lamps tend to be very efficient with widespread distribution. In large areas, single-lamp cross-section indirect luminaires are best in order to meet energy code requirements and offer best sustainable practice—using fewer lamps, ballasts, and luminaires, while maintaining comfortable, attractive, and functional settings.

Two key criteria for indirect lighting of electronic office applications are the ceiling luminance and the uniformity of this luminance. As reported in Table 8.2, office ceilings should not be any brighter than 80 cd/ft^2 (855 cd/m^2), and as reported in Table 8.3, the luminance ratio on the ceiling surface should be 4:1 where computer use is intensive. The indirect lighting shown in Figure 8.3d (and in 11.15e) meets these criteria—compliance depends on luminaire optics and lamping.

Zolatone® is a registered trademark of Surface Protection Industries

KIRLIN *lighting since 1895*

Features and Options

Recessed Round PAR Lamp Lensed Wall Washers: 39 to 150 Watt

6"	150W	**HRR-06010**
7"	150W	**HRR-07011**

Features

Lamp
- Designed for metal halide PAR lamps. See chart below for standard and optional lamps and wattages.
- See Option -43 and chart below for lower wattage.

Socket Assembly - Wall Washers
- Fixed tilt optimizes wall wash pattern.

Socket
- Medium base. Pulse rated. Glazed porcelain.
- Nickel-plated brass screw shell. Silicone leads.

Reflector
- Self-flanged clear specular Alzak® aluminum.
- Thirteen optional reflector finishes available.

Lens
- UV absorbing, tempered and frosted linear glass mounted above trim assembly.

Ballast Assembly: Specify Voltage
- WhisperPack™ fully encapsulated 180°C rated HPF pulse start ballast.
- Premium Class H, High reactance for 120 volt, linear reactor for 277 volt.
- Capacitor and ignitor supplied.
- Dimming (-39) and electronic (-96) ballast available. See Options.
- Cool, quiet, long life. Silicone leads.
- Visible and easily serviced in all ceilings, including dry wall.

Fuse
- Fused primary. Renewable. Aids servicing.

Housing
- Acrylic enameled aluminum.
- Cool. Dissipates heat across entire surface area. Ventilated.
- Rustproof. Exceeds 1000 hour ASTM 5% salt spray test.

- Entire luminaire serviced through removable reflector. For top access, see Option -TA.
- Built-in plaster frame.

Outlet Box
- Prewired 14 GA (NEC) galvanized steel. UL listed, with removable insulated cover.
- 1/2" and 3/4" knockouts.

Installation
- 27" galvanized hanger bars supplied (2).
- Fully adjustable universal mounting brackets supplied (2).
- Recesses indoor or outdoor in covered locations.

UL, C-UL (Canada) Listings
- Wet, damp or dry locations, covered ceilings.
- Through-branch circuit conductors (6 #12).

Three Year Limited Warranty
- Complete standard fixture, including ballast.

Thermal Protection
- Per current NEC.

Wattage / Lamp Availability and Cut-Out Dimensions

Catalog No.	Designed For: Standard Lamp	Optional Lamp(s)	Option -43: Lower Wattage	Ceiling Cut-Out Diameter	Fixture Style
HRR-06010	150 PAR 38 · 20° SP	35° MFL · 65° FL	70-100	6.5"	Lensed Wall Wash
HRR-07011	150 PAR 38 · 20° SP	35° MFL · 65° FL	70-100	8.0"	Lensed Wall Wash

Options

Sources and Ballasts
- -39 Electronic dimming ballast instead, for pulse start metal halide. Consult factory for wattage and voltage availability.
- -96 Regulating electronic MH ballast instead.

Wattage and Voltage
- -43 Lower wattage. See Option -43 chart above for available lower wattages. Specify voltage.
- -120 120 volt, 60 Hz ballast.
- -277 277 volt, 60 Hz ballast.
- -347 347 volt, 60 Hz ballast. Consult factory for dimming or electronic.
- -97 Other voltage ballast instead. Consult factory.

Lamps (See Chart)
- -LP With lamp. Choose standard lamp shown above or specify wattage, beam spread, style (PAR 20, PAR 30, PAR 38), brand and color temperature.

KIRLIN *lighting since 1895*

Performance at a Glance

HRR-06010
HRR-07011

Plan View

C.U. (Coefficients of Utilization) Tables are available on request. Please contact your Kirlin representative.

HRR-06010 150W

LAMP and TRIM ASSEMBLY SHOWN 90° OUT OF POSITION

10-1/8" 257 mm

6"=152 mm
7-1/8"=180 mm

HRR-07011 150W

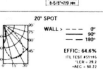

LAMP and TRIM ASSEMBLY SHOWN 90° OUT OF POSITION

10-1/8" 257 mm

7-1/2"=190 mm
8-5/8"=279 mm

20° SPOT

WALL > — — — 0°
———— 90°
——— 180°

EFFIC: 57.5%
ITL TEST #51351
*LER = 26.0
•AEC = 58.24

20° SPOT

WALL > — — — 0°
———— 90°
——— 180°

EFFIC: 64.6%
ITL TEST #51195
*LER = 29.2
•AEC = 50.22

35° MEDIUM FLOOD

WALL > — — — 0°
———— 90°
——— 180°

EFFIC: 54.7%
ITL TEST #51354
*LER = 24.2
•AEC = 58.71

35° MEDIUM FLOOD

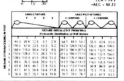

WALL > — — — 0°
———— 90°
——— 180°

EFFIC: 60.6%
ITL TEST #51196
*LER = 27.4
•AEC = 58.76

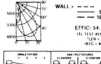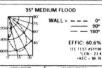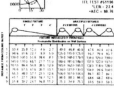

* LER (Luminaire Efficacy Rating) = Luminaire Effic. x Total Lamp Lumens x Ballast Factor / Input Watts

• AEC = Annual Energy Cost per 1000 lumens (based on 3000 hours use @ $0.08 KWH).

SUBMITTAL DATA

JOB NAME *Click here to edit*

TYPE *Click here to edit*

WATTAGE *Click here to edit*   VOLTAGE *Click here to edit*

CATALOG NUMBER *Click here to edit (include voltage and option #s after catalog number)*

APPROVAL STAMP

Figure 11.15a

CIE Direct Lighting—90% to 100% of the light is directed downward. Luminaire housing types take many forms and exhibit many distributions (from narrow to widespread). Graphic and image illustrate different housing types and distributions. Image is thumbnail of Figure 11.14. Image ©Kevin Beswick

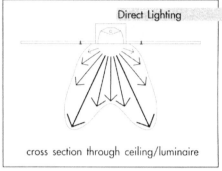

Direct Lighting

cross section through ceiling/luminaire

Figure 11.15b

CIE Semi-direct Lighting—60% to 90% of the light is directed downward. Here, 10% to 30% of the light is uplight. Photo shows uplighting excaping from the top of the reflector on the two CFL pendent luminaires. Image is thumbnail of Figure 8.3b. Image ©Justin Maconochie

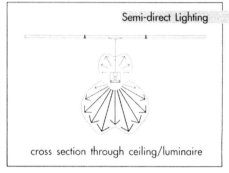

Semi-direct Lighting

cross section through ceiling/luminaire

Figure 11.15c

CIE General Diffuse Lighting—light is distributed more-or-less uniformly in all directions from the luminaire. Direct-indirect is a special category within General Diffuse (see Figure 11.17). Photo shows general diffuse lighting from CFL column collar luminaires. Image is thumbnail of Figure 6.7. Image ©Tom Crane Photography

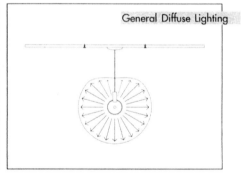

General Diffuse Lighting

cross section through ceiling/luminaire

Figure 11.15d

CIE Semi-indirect Lighting—60% to 90% of the light is directed upward. Photo shows semi-indirect lighting from linear fluorescent pendent luminaires. Image is thumbnail of Figure 8.3c and 9.15. Image ©Bill Lindhout Photography and courtesy BETA Design Group, Inc.

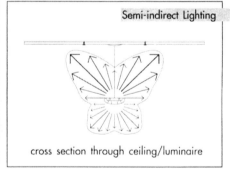

Semi-indirect Lighting

cross section through ceiling/luminaire

Figure 11.15e

CIE Indirect Lighting—90% to 100% of the light is directed upward. Photo shows indirect lighting from linear fluorescent pendent luminaires. Image is thumbnail of Figure 8.3d. Image ©Christopher Lark Photography

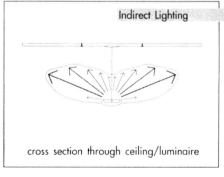

Indirect Lighting

cross section through ceiling/luminaire

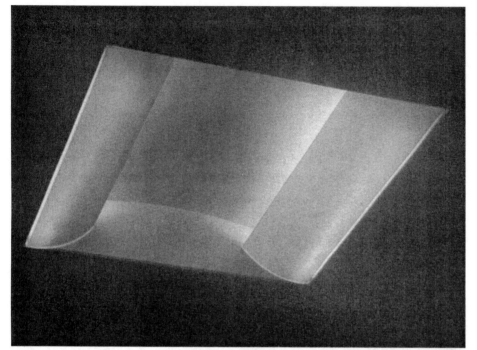

Figure 11.16

Recessed indirect luminaire typically exhibits perforated side baskets that house lamps. Light is directed on the upper reflector of the luminaire and then reflected back into the room. This qualifies as a CIE Direct Lighting luminaire since 100% of the light from the luminaire is directed downward. Figure 6.3 illustrates a catalog cutsheet for such a luminaire.
Image ©GarySteffyLightingDesign

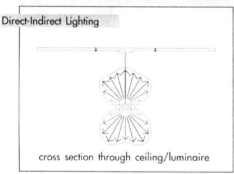

Direct-Indirect Lighting

cross section through ceiling/luminaire

Figure 11.17

Direct-indirect Lighting—a special category within the CIE General Diffuse Classification, where little light is emitted from the sides of the luminaire, but uplight is nearly equal to downlight. Image is thumbnail of Figure 8.3a.
Image ©Christopher Lark Photography

Other pendent luminaire types include the semi-indirect (see Figure 11.15d) and direct-indirect (see Figure 11.17) versions. These tend to offer the most efficient lighting systems available today that also have the capability of providing the most comfortable environments. For any pendent lighting solution, including the indirect version, luminaires can be extruded aluminum or formed steel. They can be modular or essentially built to suit (usually in 1' [about 300 mm] increments), although as the commodity manufacturers consolidate this portion of the business, this feature that helps distinguish one project from another may disappear. Pendent luminaires can be suspended by aircraft cable (see Figures 11.15e and 11.18), which is essentially invisible, or via tubular stems. These suspension components need to be on some consistent spacing that the manufacturer recommends for the given luminaire to assure structural stability and safety and a plumb and true run. Power feeds need to occur every so often and are available in straight or coiled white or black cords. The coiled cords, while initially looking cute and neat, eventually sag so that the coils are all bunched toward the bottom of the cord. With aircraft cable, luminaires can be attached to some grid systems,

Figure 11.18

Aircraft cable is used to suspend this CIE General Diffuse (Direct-Indirect) luminaire. Here, a straight, white power cord is used to feed power to the luminaire. In areas where multiple similar luminaires are used, a specification requirement that "all power feeds shall be consistently positioned at the same end and consistently aligned" may be appropriate. Otherwise, one luminaire may have power feed at one end, while the next luminaire in a series may have the power feed at the other end.
Image ©GarySteffyLightingDesign

depending on the local code requirements. Otherwise, cable attachment points are typically located in the center of ceiling tiles, at least laterally (with the luminaire width).

Accent

Accent lights help with visual attention, visual relief (from task work), and helping to balance luminances. Artwork (2D and 3D) and special architectural features or finishes are candidates for accenting. Sometimes, accenting is nothing more than a scallop pattern of light or even a projected pattern of light. Key aspects to consider on accent lights include lamp access, ballast/transformer access, maximum tilt, maximum rotation, aiming lock, filter and accessory capacity, available accessories, robustness of housing, mechanisms, finish, number of fitting types, and, of course, aesthetics. CMH accents are well received in most commercial, hospitality, and institutional applications. HIR/MR16 accents are well received in residential applications. Figures 5.10, 11.19, and 11.20 illustrate a few accent applications.

Lamp access is important for optic changeout in exhibit and museum or rotating display situations where spot lamps may be appropriate for one situation, but narrow flood or flood lamps are appropriate for others. Ballast/transformer access is important for maintenance. However, ballasts and transformers typically exhibit 15- to 20-year service life, so access is infrequent.

Maximum tilt is important in determining the mounting position for the luminaire. If the desired mounting position isn't available (e.g., there's a sprinkler, duct, pipe, or other immovable device in the way), does the luminaire have sufficient tilt to accommodate its forced placement on the ceiling? In exhibit situations, aiming tilt

Figure 11.19

Low-wattage ceramic metal halide PAR lamps are excellent for accenting—offering relatively long life at very low wattage for significant candlepower punch. At far left, a continuous slot detail houses 5" (about 125 mm) diameter by 8" (about 200 mm) deep monopoint wallwashers with CMH 20W/T4.5 lamps spaced on 12" (about 300 mm) centers to uniformly graze the pebble wall. Monopoint luminaire by Amerlux (www.amerlux.com).

At near left, a recessed 8½" wide by 17¼" long (about 215 mm by 440 mm) slot luminaire houses two adjustable fittings each lamped with a CMH 39W PAR30L/FL25 lamp. Recessed slot light by RSA (www.rsalighting.com/). This is a prayer inscription in the same project space as shown in Figure 9.13.

Far left image ©GarySteffyLightingDesign
Near left image ©Gene Meadows

should be at least 40° and preferably 45° to accommodate the unknown and untold number of exhibit piece locations and sizes. In high ceiling spaces, a tilt of up to 45° may be necessary to highlight art or features low on walls without having long (tall) scallops on the wall, which would occur with 30° or 35° tilts positioned closer to the wall. The means to tilt adjustment is important. This should be readily accessible particularly if lights are reaimed frequently.

Maximum rotation affects how well the accent can rotate around the room. Rotation should be at least 359° to allow the luminaire free aiming access to most any location in the immediate vicinity of the luminaire. This is particularly important for accent luminaires in exhibit situations or in space where 3-dimensional artwork is likely to be placed and perhaps periodically moved (e.g., a corporate lobby, hotel lobby, or airport concourse). The means to rotation adjustment is also important. Again, if lights are reoriented frequently, then rotation means should be easily accessible.

Aiming lock is a feature that might be most desirable if maintenance (relamping) is likely to be frequent and/or if maintenance is not performed by a professional trained in the importance of maintaining tilt and rotation. Some luminaires work on friction tilt and rotation. This can be acceptable providing the friction mechanism is tight. Some luminaires have locking wingnuts or other mechanisms that can be tightened once the luminaire is aimed.

Figure 11.20

Theatrical ellipsoidal luminaires lamped with CMH 150W T6 lamps and fitted with leaf-pattern **gobos** and aimed to project a tree/leaf pattern onto the wall. Ellipsoidal luminaires by ETC (www.etcconnect.com/). Image ©Bill Lindhout Photography and courtesy BETA Design Group, Inc.

gobos

A device consisting of a thin stainless steel sheet with cutout patterns that, when placed in front of a pattern-projector spotlight, will project corresponding light patterns. Might also be made of glass with aluminized coating. Can be customized and can exhibit very detailed patterning. Also see Figure 2.5 where the pattern on the floor is generated by a gobo in a CMH ellipsoidal luminare. See www.rosco.com/us/gobocatalog/index.html for more on gobos.

Most accent luminaires can accommodate accessories such as UV and IR filters to protect artwork. Other accessories include snoots, glare louvers, neutral-density filters, and barndoors (see Figure 11.21 for a sampling). Snoots and barndoors are only available for track or monopoint accents that accept them or some recessed accent slots—these do not work with traditional recessed accent luminaires. Neutral-density filters are essentially mechanical dimmers. Most art curators prefer to use "white" light to render artwork. If lights are too bright, dimming turns halogen infrared lamps to a warm candleflame color, which skews artwork. A neutral-density filter is intended to be placed in front of an undimmed lamp to preserve the whiteness of light, but cut the intensity. Think of a window screen mesh in front of a lamp—output is cut by 30% or 50% or 60% depending on the density of the screen mesh. Neutral-density filters work well with ceramic metal halide lamps since these are not easily dimmable. Filters include "warming" filters to make ceramic metal halide lamps have the color quality of standard tungsten incandescent (2700K). Some accents accept no accessories while others accept a single accessory. A few take two and three accessories.

Since accent luminaires are handled frequently, housing robustness is more important here than for downlights, ambient recessed luminaires, or ambient pendent luminaires. Thin gauge housings and trims will more readily warp and torque when pressue is applied to change lamps and accessories or adjust aiming.

Architectural Lighting Design

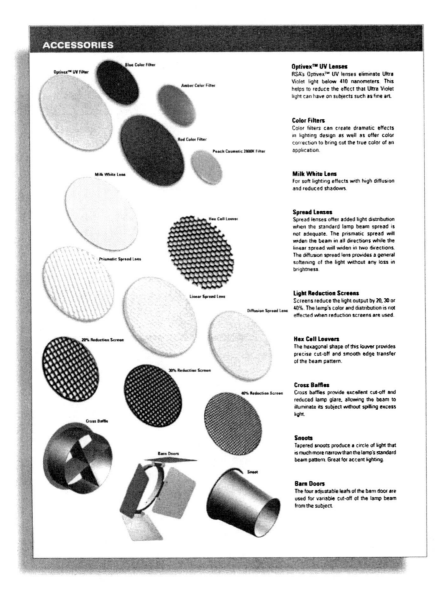

Optivex™ UV Lenses
RSA's Optivex™ UV lenses eliminate Ultra Violet light below 410 nanometers. This helps to reduce the effect that Ultra Violet light can have on subjects such as fine art.

Color Filters
Color filters can create dramatic effects in lighting design as well as offer color correction to bring out the true color of an application.

Milk White Lens
For soft lighting effects with high diffusion and reduced shadows.

Spread Lenses
Spread lenses offer added light distribution when the standard lamp beam spread is not adequate. The prismatic spread will widen the beam in all directions while the linear spread will widen in two directions. The diffusion spread lens provides a general softening of the light without any loss in brightness.

Light Reduction Screens
Screens reduce the light output by 20, 30 or 40%. The lamp's color and distribution is not effected when reduction screens are used.

Hex Cell Louvers
The hexagonal shape of this louver provides precise cut-off and smooth edge transfer of the beam pattern.

Cross Baffles
Cross baffles provide excellent cut-off and reduced lamp glare, allowing the beam to illuminate its subject without spilling excess light.

Snoots
Tapered snoots produce a circle of light that is much more narrow than the lamp's standard beam pattern. Great for accent lighting.

Barn Doors
The four adjustable leafs of the barn door are used for variable cut-off of the lamp beam from the subject.

Figure 11.21

This accessories cutsheet from RSA illustrates the various kinds of filters, glare control, and light control devices available for some RSA accents.
Available at www.rsalighting.com.
Cutsheet ©Cooper Industries, Inc.

Accessory holders or cartridges should exhibit sturdy construction and should easily and consistently accept and firmly hold accessories. Durability of finish is also important since these lights are handled frequently. For track or monopoint units, consider extruded or machined aluminum housings, lamp holders, and accessory holders. Natural aluminum finish is most durable.

For track and monopoint luminaires, there may be a number of fitting options, including track, busway, and monopoints (see Figure 11.22). Luminaires with all three options offer the widest application of the same luminaire throughout a project. This helps reduce the number of different luminaires, maintain a consistent appearance throughout a project, and maintain accessories that can be universally swapped between the luminaires.

Aesthetics will depend on the designer's taste, the owner's taste, the users' taste, and/or the style of the project. Recessed accent luminaires can be quite discrete. CMH luminaires are available with pinhole apertures as small as 2″ (about 50 mm) in diameter.

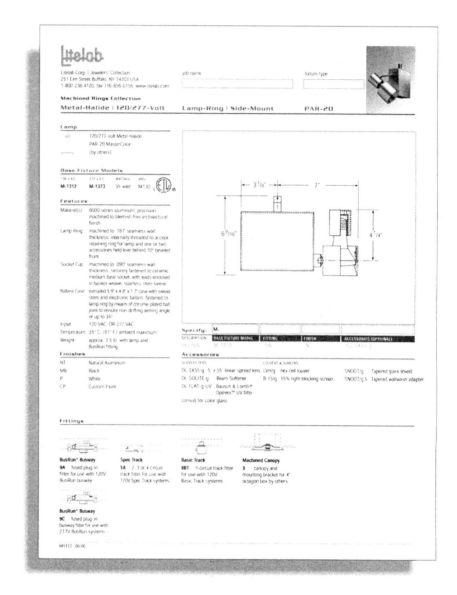

Figure 11.22

An example of a CMH adjustable accent available with a variety of fitting options for a variety of applications—track, busway, or monopoint with ceiling canopy for mounting to junction box. Available at www.litelab.com.
Cutsheet ©Litelab Corp.

Decorative Decorative lighting, of course, is best if it is also functional. Therein lies the challenge for the designer—seek out and specify functional decorative lighting. This should not be an exercise in decorating with lights. Decorative lights can set the scene for a project. To endear them to a project, they need to be efficient and long-life. If these are custom, then the opportunity exists to lamp these with CFL, CMH, or LED lamps. If these are to be off-the-shelf, then limit the search to CFL, CMH, or LED lamped versions. Beyond lamping, consideration should be given to some aspects discussed in previous luminaire categories—UL listing/labelling, fit and finish, durability, and ease of lamping and ballast maintenance. Other aspects important to decorative luminaires are scale, proportion, and mounting height, diffuser finish and color, metal finish, and lighting effect.

As noted in Section 11.5, luminaires should be UL or NRTL (nationally recognized testing lab) listed and labeled or exhibit respective labels/listings that the EU standards or Canadian Standards are met for respective markets. This is the most elusive aspect for decorative lights. In the states, many decorative lights are imported. Seemingly many of these are not UL/NRTL listed and labeled. Most use standard tungsten incandescent lamps. Avoid these, although it doesn't hurt to alert the respective manufacturers or importers that their equipment, while aesthetically pleasing, isn't functionally appropriate without UL listing/labeling and efficient, long-life lamping options.

Fit and finish on decorative luminaires is more important than on other luminaire types. Since the fit and finish impart quality and since these luminaires are more likely to be scrutinized by users of the space and, in fact, may be viewed up close (such as in the case of wall sconces), fit and finish are a critical consideration. If more than a few of these luminaires are considered and/or if these are costly, a sample should be reviewed for fit and finish. Look for square and true edges, lines, and corners. Look for light leaks around the diffuser and/or access door (if one exists). No light leaks are desirable.

Durability is perhaps more important here than with other luminaire types, especially with wall sconces. If these are in an area where people may brush up against the luminaires and/or they might be handled periodically, consider heavy-gauged or extruded framing and body components. Diffusers may need to be glass for form, color, and/or heat resistance, so insisting on acrylic may not be practical or appropriate. Where the look of fabric is desired, consider fabric on acrylic backers. Nomex® is another shade material that is quite durable, but only appropriate where a parchment look is desired.

Relamping needs to be easy enough to limit the time and amount of contact with decorative elements. Etched glass sconces can collect oil and dirt from fingers depending on the method of etching. If the glass diffuser must be handled directly (rather than handling a metal frame that holds the diffuser), and/or held open with one hand while changing the lamp with the other hand, then significant fingerprint or even handprint patterns may develop. These are difficult to clean from some types of etched glass.

Scale and proportion requirements of a decorative luminaire depend on the intended application setting. The plaza shown in Figures 11.1 and 11.2 is a historic setting with a monumental building—a university auditorium. The heft or solidity or mass of the postlights needs to work with the background building and the wide extent of the plaza. At the same time, these particular postlights need to complement the historic setting—they themselves had to exude history. Spring City Electrical Manufacturing Company (www.springcity.com/) provided a customized cast post and globe luminaire using CMH 39W T6 lamping. To determine scale usually requires studying elevations and/or perspectives of the area(s) in question with varying luminaire options of varying dimensions. Sometimes this further requires FomeCor® mockups or 3D rendering studies on computer. Where a specific luminaire is

Nomex® is a registered trademark of E.I. du Pont de Nemours and Company
FomeCor® is a registered trademark of Alcan Composites USA, Inc.

considered a must-have, but its scale too small, consider developing a massing of several of these luminaires (as was done in Figures 4.1, 5.1, and 5.8). Recognize, however, cost and installation aspects as well as a possibility of overlighting unless lamp/ballast configurations and wattages are tempered to account for the use of additional luminaires. Finally, the massing technique should be reserved for areas of special interest or focal attention such as lobby or foyer arrival points or dining rooms.

Mounting heights are related to scale and proportion. Where wall sconces are involved in all but residential projects, ADA requirements in the states stipulate that luminaires can project no more than 4″ (about 100 mm) unless the bottom of the sconce is elevated at least 6′ 8″ (about 2 m) AFF. So, in grand spaces with relatively tall ceilings, scale of sconces, if used, must be managed with respect to mounting height. Since there are few appropriately scaled and proportioned wall sconces or **wall brackets**, most of these will need to be mounted so their bottoms are at least 6′ 8″ AFF. Where sconces are planned for stairs, assessment of the sconce elevation with respect to the tread elevations is necessary to understand the implications of mounting large sconces at 6′ 8″ AFF—above the tread over which the sconce is centered or above the highest-elevation-tread over which the sconce straddles. As people walk down the stairs, this height arrangement will still be too low for sconces that project more than 4″. Why the obsession with 6′ 8″ AFF? Most of the typical off-the-shelf sconces are relatively small. For these to feel appropriately human-scale, they should be mounted so that some part of their body or luminous lens is at about standing eye height (somewhere between 5′ 3″ and 5′ 9″ AFF for most people [about the same centerline mounting height for most 2D artwork]). The sconces in Figure 6.6 are centered at 5′ 9″ AFF in a residential application (these are 10¾″ in width by 1′ 3½″ in height with a projection of 5¼″) and are by Brass Light Gallery (model Prairie Sunrise PA-1213-A16-PC-AC-GW and available at www.brasslight.com/). The sconces in the bottom image of Figure 7.7 are centered at 5′ 4″ AFF in a hospitality application (there are 5¾″ in width by 1′ 4″ in height with a projection of 4″) and are by Boyd Lighting (model Niagara 9785-Fluorescent-Champagne-Fuse and available at www.boydlighting.com/). Sometimes, the mounting height of the sconce will dictate its projection requirements and its overall height requirements. Obviously, this greatly reduces the number of sconces that are appropriate and results in longer searches for "the right light." The wall sconce shown in Figure 10.15 is one such example. Here the ceiling is about 14′ in height and the framed wood panel is about 10′ in height. Any sconces need to relate to both the scale of the entire wall and the scale of the wood panel. The sconce needs quite a bit of overall height. Since the centerline of the sconce wants to be at about 7′ AFF, this means the bottom of any reasonably scaled sconce will certainly be below the ADA requirement of 6′ 8″ and therefore any sconce here will need to comply with the ADA projection requirement of 4″ or less. The Ivalo Aliante sconce (available at www.ivalolighting.com) was selected as most appropriate to the style requirements of the project while meeting the ADA requirement. Since the details of the framed

wall brackets
Term reserved for large, more ornate and typically historic wall sconces—which were traditionally bracketed off the wall by a fair distance to avoid candle or gas flame source from igniting the architecture.

Architectural Lighting Design

wood panel, its elevation, and the elevation of the art were finalized by the interior designer and architect, they determined the actual final centerline location for the sconce.

Diffuser finish and color depend on the application, the functional lighting requirements, and the aesthetic. Most diffusers for commercial applications are glass or acrylic. However, a host of additional materials might be deemed appropriate for certain special areas or projects, including residential. Manmade synthetic materials meant to mimic fabrics and papers are available as shades for luminaires. Other more common materials are glass and acrylic. Mica, alabaster, and onyx are a few natural materials that, when properly cut and finished, transmit light. These all need to be experienced visually by the designer under the lamping desired or required for a given project. This review might result in some tinting or coloring of the diffuser material to more closely approximate an authentic incandescent look or, alternatively, to provide a crisper, whiter light. It is worth noting that deep saturated colors on diffusers will have a dramatic and likely undesirable color shift from one lamp type to another. Also, saturated color diffusers are generally extremely dim compared to their white-shade counterparts, with, typically, yellow being the brightest, green and red moderately bright, and blue least bright. Finishes on these materials can run from highly polished to dull matte. Generally, with the exception of some glass diffusers, the matte finishes actually exhibit a richer look than the polished finishes. However, much of this is in the eyes of the beholder—and especially on residential projects, the polished look may be the client's pick.

Metal finishes for frames, housings, canopies, backplates, luminaire bodies, and the like can run the gamut. White metals, yellow metals, painted, stressed, etched, brushed, polished, rusticated, and more are all possible. Off-the-shelf selections will typically offer a limited choice, but even these, if quantities are sufficient, can be customized. Polished surfaces typically are more maintenance intensive as they hold fingerprints, or they will simply look unkempt if not periodically polished.

Until now, many decorative lights were eye candy using a relatively high amount of energy. Their lighting effect was an afterthought—usually provided by a 25- or 40-watt candelabra-based standard tungsten-filament incandescent lamp. While eye candy is an appropriate "layer" of light to help set the mood or define architectural features or portals, it should be done now with CFL, CMH, or LED sources that use fewer watts and last many times longer than their incandescent counterparts. Even the smallest lighting effect from these lights can and should be included in all calculational assessments. Many times, appropriately lamped sconces can contribute at least some amount if not all of the illuminance required in an area and can also provide some or all of the wall and/or ceiling luminance needed in an area. Of course, this requires photometric data for the decorative lights, something many manufacturers have yet to provide—and something that should be a mandated requirement in such an energy-conscious, sustainable atmosphere. If careful planning with a half dozen pretty sconces eliminates just one or two downlights, that's one or two fewer lights that need to be made, installed, and operated over the life of the building.

Historic pendent re-creations are sized with 18" deep by 36" diameter arcylic bowls with bottom elevation at 10' AFF. Bowls were specially etched to create an intricate engraved pattern, shown below, of the 1913-era of the building. Each bowl is lamped with eight (8) F26TBX/3000K lamps. Luminaires custom made by St. Louis Antique Lighting (www.slalco.com).
Image ©Balthazar Korab

11.7 Custom

There may be a time when the project cannot be well served by off-the-shelf decorative lights. Usually for reasons of scale, style, and/or lamping, standard lights are unworkable. Applications where custom lights are more likely to be used include grand public spaces such as atria, lobbies, and concourses, gigantic spaces where lighting is a critical functional and aesthetic component such as ballrooms, convention center breakouts, and auditoria, special projects or landmark civic projects such as performing arts centers and judicial centers, and corporate headquarters' lobby spaces, dining rooms, and board rooms, and projects where historic recreations are needed.

For these applications, the designer can specify styling, shape, scale, proportions, shade and metal finishes, lamping, ballasting, and control needs (e.g., half the lamps are dimmed separately from the remaining half of the lamps in the custom luminaire). This is also an opportunity to specify spare parts, should a bowl or diffuser break several years after project completion, and to outline warranty requirements (e.g., "luminaire assembly and all parts shall be warranted for a period of two (2) years from date of shipping, including necessary labor costs"). Figure 11.23 illustrates a restoration project where historic pendents were scaled

to better "fill" the architecture. Figure 4.3 shows a new-construction project where a custom light valance, itself huge, helps provide scale and character to a large indoor-pool room. In Figure 5.5, note the scale, form, and proportions of the custom chandeliers and how these fit the architectural proportions of the available dining room space. Custom historic column bands were created for the Visitor Concierge space shown in Figure 6.7. Scale and styling cues were taken from an original lighting catalog dating to the period of historical significance of 1904 and from a historic postcard (see Figure 11.24).

Sometimes custom luminaires may be more about the massing and layout of traditional components combined with state-of-the-art lamping. Figure 11.25 illustrates the end result for lighting a grand stair in a hospitality project (see also Figure 10.26). Here, the lighting had many design objectives. First and foremost, safety on the stairs. A very close second, the visual impact of the lighting—the grand stair is a significant focal element both inside and outside the building. Seemingly bunched in a close third were such issues as maintenance, efficiency, lamp life, cost, and leadtime—a microcosm of most all lighting on most all projects. Certainly, the lighting had to provide sufficient light for easy, convenient, and safe travel up and down the stairs by all patrons. The image was significant. Develop lighting that isn't sufficiently bright and/or colorful or lighting that is overwhelmed by the scale and crispness of the architecture or lighting that doesn't promote the "edge" this hotelier has over many others, and the solution will be unsuccessful. Of course, if a fantastic design is had but it can't be maintained or it is high maintenance, then within a short period the project will look disheveled and unkempt—losing the edge. Efficiency is important as part of the hotelier's desire to minimize its carbon footprint. Lamp life gets to the issues of maintenance and appearance over time. Cost and leadtime are issues on many projects. Establish budgets and timeframes early in the project.

To address aesthetics, maintenance, and lamp life, a design concept was developed that considered using traditional chandelier beads that were to be lighted with optically efficient, narrow-beam LEDs (in hopes of addressing the functional aspect of lighting the stairs). To limit the amount of bead material needed (which reduced cost and weight), a skewed layout (at least in the orthogonal plan view) was developed that produced a significant amount of "chandelier projected area" for drivers' and pedestrians' views as they passed the exterior and patrons' views as they circulated the interior. This layout scheme is shown in the far right of Figure 11.25 along with an elevation view. These were the culmination of mini-mockups and elevational studies of various massings, skew-angles, bead arrangements, etc. Mockups were critical to understanding the failure or success of various LED wattages and optics.

11.8 Details

Some luminaires are intended for use in architectural details, and others intended for use in or on ceilings and/or walls can sometimes be used in details. Here, the designer must develop concept sketches indicating the relevant detail dimensions around which the architect and/or engineer will then develop structural and archi-

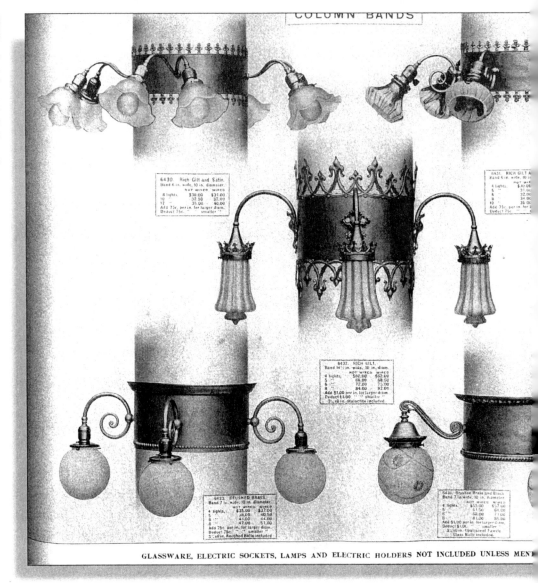

Figure 11.24

Styling cues and precedent were established for the column bands shown in Figure 6.7 with plate 1349 from the R. Williamson & Company, Chicago, Catlog No. 12, ca 1904 and with a postcard of the Michigan State Capitol from the turn of the 20th century.
Images ©GarySteffyLightingDesign

tectural finish details to support and hide the luminaire. Perhaps the most significant issue for any detail is its intended function—decorative, functional, or both. The more functional details will have to be developed around the photometric qualities of the luminaire. Fluorescent asymmetric distribution cove lights, for example, are intended to spread light across a ceiling above the cove detail. Calculations prove that the height of the cove opening is critical to optimal performance of the asymmetric cove luminaire. For lights intended for details, if the manufacturer offers no catalogued guidance, forward intended application sketches for review of heat and/or photometric deficiencies. For lights not originally intended for details, review the potential application with the manufacturer(s) and the design team prior to any detail development as there may be serious issues of photometric malfunction and/or heat buildup that preclude the luminaire from use in

Architectural Lighting Design

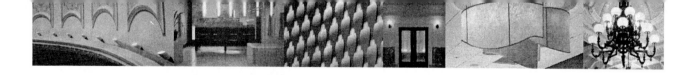

CORRIDOR IN STATE CAPITOL, LANSING, MICH

details. Ask the question: Is the luminaire UL listed/labeled for such an application? Figure 11.10 shows a wallslot detail used with a CMH lamp channel intended for the detail application. Figure 11.12 shows a wallslot detail used with a striplight intended for the detail application. Other details that are common in many commercial and even some residential applications include reverse coves, indirect wallslots, and indirect coves. Figure 11.26 illustrates reverse coves and the equipment and detail used to create the effect. With dimming ballasts, these details can be appropriate for residential applications and restaurants. Additionally, experimenting with paint color of the cove detail and the upper ceiling can significantly affect the drama and effect for these applications. An indirect wallslot is illustrated in Figure 11.27. These, too, can be used in residential applications with or without dimming ballasts. Other applications include spas, restaurants, and restrooms.

An indirect cove, shown in Figure 11.28, is an effective way to introduce ambient light with no glare in a clean, architecturally crisp style. These are effective in lobbies, conference rooms, living areas, kitchens, courtrooms, classrooms, libraries, and offices. They are available in single or double-lamp cross-sections depending on illuminance requirements. With dimming ballasts, they are appropriate in residential applications. Figure 11.29 illustrates two details, both using cold cathode. Here, cold cathode can actually provide a sophisticated look with clean, minimal architectural detailing. Issues of ventilation, transformer noise and remote mounting locations and distances, connection and wiring details for purposes of aesthetics (if cold cathode tubes are visible), and color and intensity should be reviewed with cold cathode (neon) installers.

Figure 11.25

During design, the lighting of this grand stair, which has a high-profile interior and exterior presence, was the subject of much review and many ideas. Ultimately, a skewed array of six sets of three bead arrays and corresponding six sets of three LED arrays was determined to be the most appropriate approach addressing aesthetics, uniqueness, efficiency, longevity, and cost. The 129 wide by 459 long chandelier has a total connected load of 7,074W (7.1KW), but will rarely see more than 3KW in use at any one time since there are three channels—6500K white, saturated blue, and saturated amber. The total load is about ¼ what had been predicted for a similarly colored CMH 39WPAR20 system and dichroic color filters.

Lower near right image shows interior view of "background fill" bead arrays. Figure 10.26 shows stair view (and street view) of "water sheet" and "bubbles" bead arrays. Custom LED chandelier by Winona Lighting (www.winonalighting.com). Top near right image ©Kevin Beswick Iconic person ©Stockxpert All other images/graphics ©GarySteffyLightingDesign

11.9 Exterior

Much of the preceding discussion centered on interior luminaires. Many of the same aspects for interior luminaires apply here—construction, fit, finish, appearance, and the need to review samples. Most significantly, exterior lighting equipment needs to be rated for wet applications or damp applications. In some instances, typically under overhangs and porch roofs, lighting eqiupment can be damp-rated. However, since heavy rains, snows, and winds can force

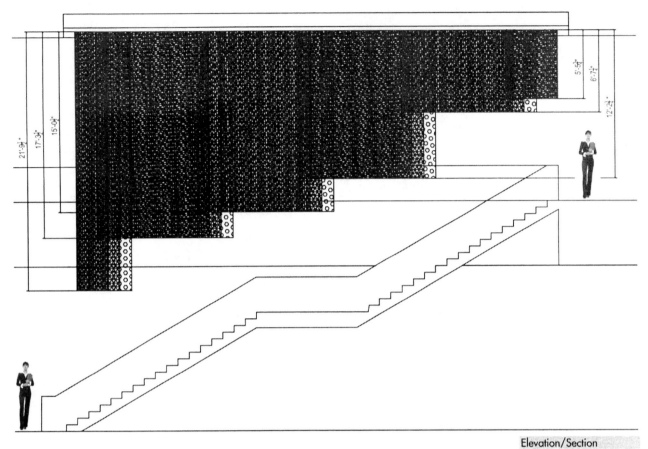

Elevation/Section

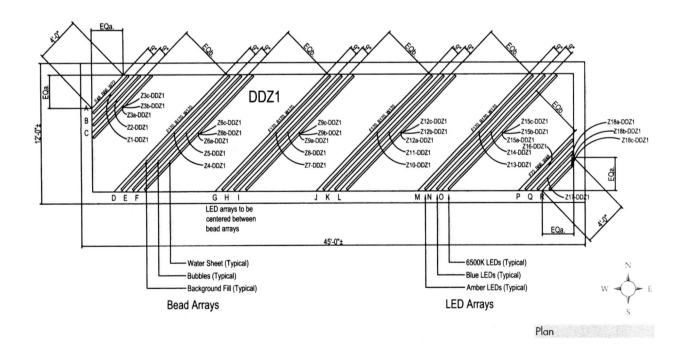

DDZ1

LED arrays to be
centered between
bead arrays

45'-0"±

Water Sheet (Typical)
Bubbles (Typical)
Background Fill (Typical)

6500K LEDs (Typical)
Blue LEDs (Typical)
Amber LEDs (Typical)

Bead Arrays

LED Arrays

Plan

Figure 11.26

Details/Reverse Ceiling Cove: In this hospitality project, entry lobbies and circulaton concourses use reverse ceiling cove details to define main entry/exit points (also seen in the bottom image of Figure 11.25). A reverse cove (not to be confused with the wallslot nearby in the top image) introduces a floating ceiling plane in what normally would be a coved or coffered ceiling. On top of the floating ceiling, a light cove is developed to uplight the ceiling above creating a glowing void between the floating ceiling and the main ceiling. Here, flexible miniature fluorescent striplights are used with GE F18BX/SPX30/RS (#17174) lamps that exhibit 20,000-hour rated life. Luminaire is CV CV6-series. Available at www.cvlightingusa.com/.
Images ©Kevin Beswick
Cutsheets ©CV Lighting
Detail graphic ©GarySteffyLightingDesign

Architectural Lighting Design

CV6FE SERIES COVE LIGHTING
FLEXIBLE END-TO-END FLUORESCENT
LAMPS IN 3 3/16"X 2 3/16" CHANNEL

CV LIGHTING

TYPE FE FLEX END TO END

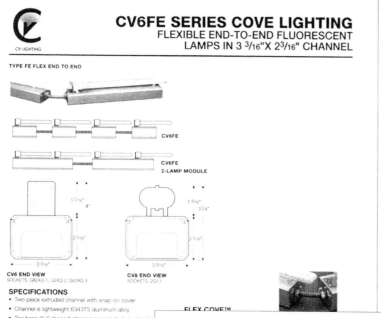

CV6FE

CV6FE
2-LAMP MODULE

1 5/16" 4"

2 3/16"

3 3/16"

CV6 END VIEW
SOCKETS: GX24Q-1, G24Q-2, GX24Q-3

1 9/16"
3 3/4"

2 3/16"

3 3/4"

CV6 END VIEW
SOCKETS: 2G11

SPECIFICATIONS
- Two piece extruded channel with snap-on cover
- Channel is lightweight 6343T5 aluminum alloy
- The base ("U" shaped) channel is easily fastened to the mounting surface
- Factory cut to specifications; sections up to 8' for of handling. Continuous runs with unlimited length possible with connectors
- Standard finish: Natural Aluminum

LAMP
- 13-40W compact fluorescent lamps
- Lamps supplied by others

AVAILABLE BALLASTS
- Electronic, 1 or 2 lamp ballast
- Dimming, 1, 2, or 3 lamp ballast (on specific watt
- 120V or 277V; 347V (Canada) consult factory

LABELS
- UL listed
- UL listed raceway
- Listed for damp location

c(UL)us

FLEX COVE™

CV LIGHTING, LLC

© 06/25/06 | G|W/GRS | Project Name | Project Number
Date | By | Subject | Project Number

Luminaire Type FCC1 Series

Independently supported 1-lamp-
cross-section F18 compact fluorescent
strip with flex connector to conform
to curvilinear layout along top of
suspended ceiling and independently
supported

Paint out to match ceiling

1'-0"

0'-9"

0'-4"

2'-0"

Section thru Detail

Lighting Notes:
1. Fluorescent luminaires shall be independently supported above upper surface of the ceiling as detailed by Architect.
2. Fluorescent strips shall exhibit a 1-lamp cross section as described in the luminaire specification.
3. Installation shall comply with the NEC and all local codes.

Not to Scale

● GarySteffyLightingDesign Inc.

Figure 11.27

Details/Indirect Wallslot:
Where wallslots occur at thresholds where people can readily look into the slot (see the niched entry to the restrooms), a detail can be constructed where the striplight is placed in a cove of sorts to indirectly light the slot. No lamp is visible when passing under the slot. Of course, this arrangement is not as efficient as the direct slot shown in Figure 11.12. The inside height and the width of the open slot determine the efficiency of the detail (to a limited degree, the greatrer the height, the better; and the greater the width of the opening, the better). Striplights are lamped with GE F17/F25/F32T8/SPX30 lamps (single-lamp cross-section in length combinations necessary to fill the length of the run). Luminaire is LSI Industries Channel (S1) series. Available at www.lsi-industries.com/media/SpecSheets/pdf/s1.pdf.
Image ©Kevin Beswick
Cutsheets ©LSI Industries Inc.
Detail graphic ©GarySteffyLightingDesign

water horizontally and sometimes vertically upward, it may be prudent to specify luminaires that are wet-rated. These are luminaires that have been constructed to keep water out of the lamp chamber. Most lamps, when operating, are sufficiently hot and made of soft glass that will violently shatter if they come in contact with water. Of course, water and electricity pose a very hazardous situation.

The finish on exterior luminaires should be resistant to weathering. Stainless steel generally weathers well, as does bronze. Aluminum and steel weather well when properly treated and factory finished. Aluminum can be anodized or painted. Steel can be painted. Cast iron, used on certain historic luminaires, can withstand weather providing the iron is primed and painted and constantly maintained. Aluminum, steel, and cast iron do not hold up well in settings where salt is used to clear ice and snow. Similarly, in salt-water enviroments, aluminum, steel, and cast iron will require periodic maintenance to maintain finish integrity. Refinishing/repainting may be necessary from time to time.

Finally, the construction of exterior luminaires needs to be sufficiently robust to take the potential abuse, albeit accidental, that may occur. Lights in landscaping may be subject to walkover or lawn-mower-drive-over situations and/or to weed wackers. Bollards and postlights are likely to be heavily trafficked by pedestrians, bikes, and perhaps a periodic car kiss. Setbacks from curbs can help with vehicular interactions. Permanent installations intended for long-term survival require foundation bases.

11.10 Reference

Gary Steffy Lighting Design Inc. 2000. *Time-Saver Standards for Architectural Lighting Design.* New York: McGraw-Hill.

S1

ONE LAMP STRIP (T8/T12)

PRODUCT HIGHLIGHTS

- Premium housing crimped along sides for extra rigidity and straight alignment
- Accepts optional plug-in wiring feature for continuous row installation
- Alignment couplers furnished for continuous row installation
- Channel cover equipped with quarter-turn, captive fasteners for easy access to ballast compartment

CONSTRUCTION - Fixture housing, lampholder brackets, end sections and channel cover constructed of code-gauge, die-formed steel.

ELECTRICAL - All devices UL/CUL listed. Suitable for damp locations. Damp location emergency pack must be specified separately. Ballasts are energy-saving solid-state electronic or electromagnetic. Ballasts and lampholders replaceable without removing from ceiling. Discrete voltage must be specified for emergency pack options when wired with flex.

FINISH - All metal parts painted after fabrication following treatment with phosphate rust inhibitor. Finish coating of housing reflecting surfaces is with white, high reflectance (minimum 92%) polyester powder.

PHOTOMETRICS - Please visit our web site at **www.lsi-industries.com** for detailed photometric data.

CHANNEL SERIES

2 5/8" (66mm)
1 3/8" (50mm)
3 5/16" (85mm)

cULus LISTED

LUMINAIRE ORDERING INFORMATION

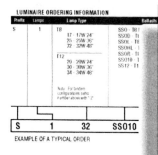

Prefix	Lamps	Lamp Type	Ballasts
S	1	T8	SSO - T8
		17 - 17W 24"	SSOD - T
		25 - 25W 36"	SSOL - T8
		32 - 32W 48"	SSOHL - T
		T12	SSOR - T
		20 - 20W 24"	SSO10 - T
		30 - 30W 36"	SS12 - T1
		34 - 34W 48"	

Note: For tandem configurations (who number above with "2")

S	1	32	SSO10

EXAMPLE OF A TYPICAL ORDER

Project Name
Catalog #

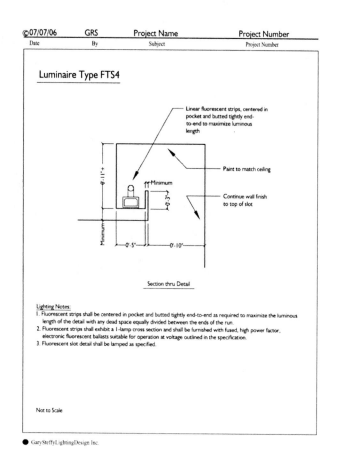

©07/07/06   GRS   Project Name   Project Number

Date   By   Subject   Project Number

Luminaire Type FTS4

Linear fluorescent strips, centered in pocket and butted tightly end-to-end to maximize luminous length

Paint to match ceiling

Continue wall finish to top of slot

Section thru Detail

Lighting Notes:
1. Fluorescent strips shall be centered in pocket and butted tightly end-to-end as required to maximize the luminous length of the detail with any dead space equally divided between the ends of the run.
2. Fluorescent strips shall exhibit a 1-lamp cross section and shall be furnished with fused, high power factor, electronic fluorescent ballasts suitable for operation at voltage outlined in the specification.
3. Fluorescent slot detail shall be lamped as specified.

Not to Scale

● GarySteffyLightingDesign Inc.

Figure 11.28

Details/Indirect Cove: Where depth permits, ceiling cove details introduce ceiling luminances in an architectural clean and simple fashion. Even where ceilings are relatively low, an indirect cove light helps to lift the ceiling visually. Luminaires are made with an asymmetric light distribution to throw light up and out into the center of the cove area. The cove lights used here are lamped with GE F17/F25/F32T8/SPX30 lamps (single-lamp cross-section in length combinations necessary to fill the length of the run). The brand of asymmetric cove light and clear distance from the top of the cove lip to the ceiling determines the uniformity of the ceiling luminance and the efficiency of the uplighting detail (greater clear distance is better). Luminaire is Peerless 9ECXM5-1-series. Available at www.acuitybrandslighting.com/Library1/PL/Documents/E51-58.pdf.
Image ©Justin Maconochie
Cutsheet ©Acuity Brands Lighting, Inc.
Detail graphic ©GarySteffyLightingDesign

Architectural Lighting Design

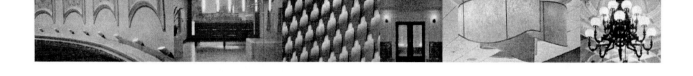

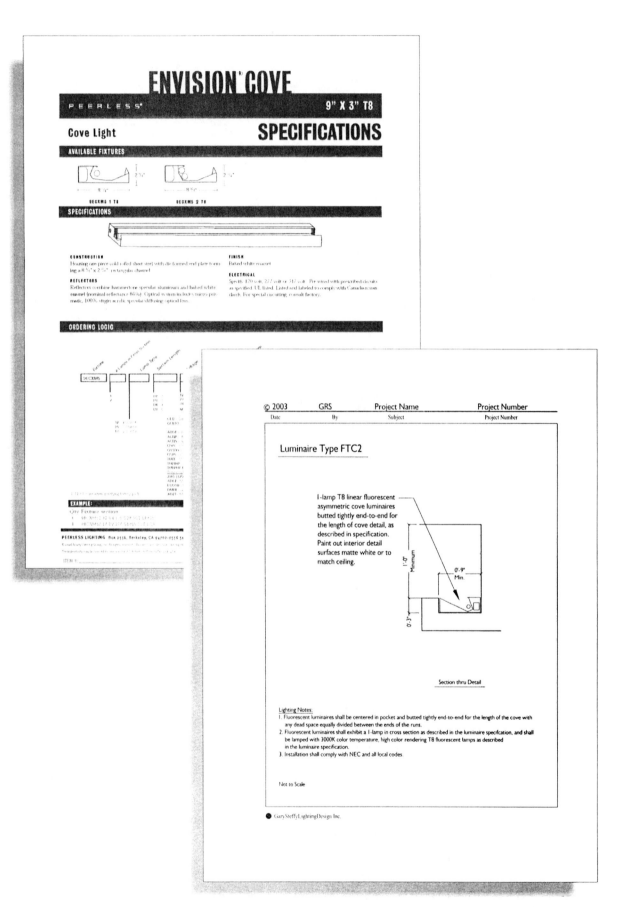

Figure 11.29

Details/Cold Cathode Cove:
Where domed coves (at the demonstration kitchen to the right) of relatively tight radius are considered, uplighting of the cove will provide comfortable, diffuse light and visually lift the ceiling. CFL, LED, or cold cathode lamping may be appropriate. In this situation, a cool, sky-blue effect was desired with a relatively significant amount of brightness. CFL could not provide the sky-blue and LED was too weak to provide the brightness. Here, two curvilinear parallel tubes each of 15mm diameter, with 60ma operating current are placed side by side. One tube is 3000K triphosphor white and one tube is "Neo Blue." These tubes are laid out in a closed circular pattern with a nominal radius of 8' 4" (about 2.5 m). By dimming between the two colors, the cove can exhibit a deep blue color (where little light is needed, but a nice effect is desirable from the diners' perspectives) or a bright white with both tubes energized (for cooking demonstration). The top graphic on the opposite page illustrates the schematic detail for the domed cove. Consult with cold cathode/ neon installers on such issues as ventilation, transformer noise, finished tube appearance, and the like.

Details/Cold Cathode Slot:
Where curvilinear bulkheads are considered, lighting of these bulkhead surfaces can significantly influence the mood. The cleanest architectural approach is to develop a slot detail. LED or cold cathode lamping may be appropriate. Here, the intensity and color of cold cathode was superior to that achieved with LED. Further, cold cathode is acceptable to view directly, providing the luminance of the tube is relatively low and providing the installer takes care in laying out the tubing and making electrical connections. Here, two curvilinear parallel tubes of 15mm diameter, with 60ma operating current are placed side by side. One tube is 3000K triphosphor white and one tube is "Copper" cold cathode in a curvilinear pattern with a nominal total length of about 98' 0".
Images ©Justin Maconochie
Detail graphic ©GarySteffyLightingDesign

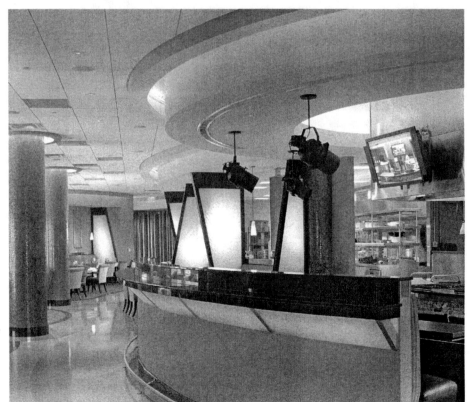

Architectural Lighting Design

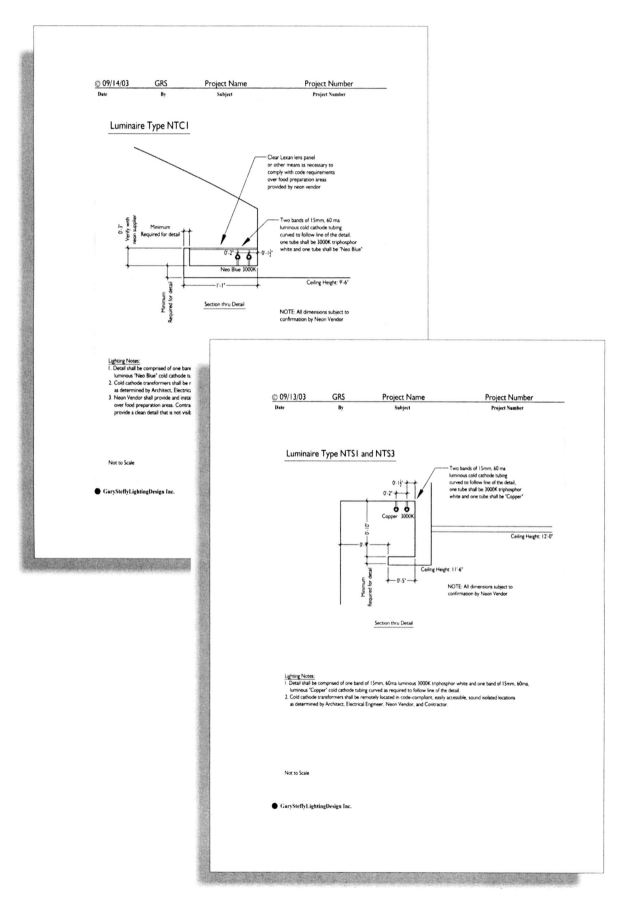

Luminaire Type NTC1

Clear Lexan lens panel
or other means as necessary to
comply with code requirements
over food preparation areas
provided by neon vendor

Two bands of 15mm, 60 ma
luminous cold cathode tubing
curved to follow line of the detail,
one tube shall be 3000K triphosphor
white and one tube shall be "Neo Blue"

0'-3"
Verify with
neon supplier

Minimum
Required for detail

0'-2"   0'-1½"

Neo Blue 3000K

Minimum
Required for detail

Ceiling Height: 9'-6"

1'-1"

Section thru Detail

NOTE: All dimensions subject to
confirmation by Neon Vendor

Lighting Notes:
1. Detail shall be comprised of one band
   luminous "Neo Blue" cold cathode tu.
2. Cold cathode transformers shall be r
   as determined by Architect, Electrica
3. Neon Vendor shall provide and insta
   over food preparation areas. Contra
   provide a clean detail that is not visik

Not to Scale

● GarySteffyLightingDesign Inc.

© 09/14/03   GRS   Project Name   Project Number
Date   By   Subject   Project Number

© 09/13/03   GRS   Project Name   Project Number
Date   By   Subject   Project Number

Luminaire Type NTS1 and NTS3

Two bands of 15mm, 60 ma
luminous cold cathode tubing
curved to follow line of the detail,
one tube shall be 3000K triphosphor
white and one tube shall be "Copper"

0'-1½"
0'-2"

Copper 3000K

0'-10"

0'-9"

Ceiling Height: 12'-0"

Ceiling Height: 11'-6"

Minimum
Required for detail

0'-5"

NOTE: All dimensions subject to
confirmation by Neon Vendor

Section thru Detail

Lighting Notes:
1. Detail shall be comprised of one band of 15mm, 60ma luminous 3000K triphosphor white and one band of 15mm, 60ma,
   luminous "Copper" cold cathode tubing curved as required to follow line of the detail.
2. Cold cathode transformers shall be remotely located in code-compliant, easily accessible, sound isolated locations
   as determined by Architect, Electrical Engineer, Neon Vendor, and Contractor.

Not to Scale

● GarySteffyLightingDesign Inc.

Controls

Controls for lighting can be simple electromechanical devices that literally connect a light to electricity or disconnect a light from electricity—depending on the position of the switch that a given user has manually configured (a typical single-pole toggle switch has an up position for "on" and a down position for "off"—see Figure 12.1). However, with the great developments and size and cost reductions in electronics, controls for lighting are increasingly capable of many functions. Because of their direct interface with the electrical distribution system, controls are devices that ultimately are the responsibility of the registered engineer on the project. The designer needs to indicate how lights are grouped and where switches are to be located. The designer might provide suggestions on or specify the style of control involved and its degree of functionality. Controls are just behind lamps in terms of their impact on system efficiency. Controls can greatly influence power consumption and thereby limit carbon emissions and can significantly affect in-service lamp life, thereby reducing manufacturing and transportation resources and reducing waste. Controls, particularly automated, empower users to take sustainable action.

12.1 On/Off Switches

Traditional on/off switches need to be addressed in terms of type (e.g., toggle, slide, electronic push-button, or rocker), location, and quantity. Typical locations for switches include somewhere on the wall, in door jambs or frames, or, with programmable systems, a phone or handheld infrared or radio frequency device can act as a switch. For wall-mounted switches, the height above finished floor (AFF) and the lateral location from nearby walls or door jambs or frames must be established by the architect or interior designer for aesthetic and code compliance. It should be noted that consistent lateral dimension from door jambs and consistent mounting height from floor are desired for the most reliable "find" by users and for the best look. To be ADA-compliant, switches need to be no lower than 15″ and no higher than 48″ (about 380 mm and 1220 mm respectively) AFF.

For any user, the number of switches increases the complexity of use. Typically, more than three switches introduces significant confusion. Further, more than three switches will consume a significant amount of wall space. This introduces at least two problems. First, the wall area may be sufficiently full that artwork or other wall-mounted niceties are prohibited. Second, this looks awful (examples shown in Figures 12.2 and 12.3). If more than three wall switches are a necessity, then consideration should be given to networked or preset switching systems. If three wall switches are used, these should be ganged if practical and safe (see Figure 12.1).

Switches are identified on plan as "S" with or without some identifying subscripts. Table 12.1 outlines some typical controls designations that might be considered when indicating controls on drawings. Reference to these designations is then required in the Controls' Specification or on a tabular schedule on the drawings so that the contractor purchases appropriate devices. For spaces where preset **scene** controls are specified or where switches are the networked or preset type, it is suggested that the control designation be $S_{\#\text{-Room No.}}$ in order to attract specific attention to its special nature.

scene
A specific setup whereby groups of lights are on, off, and/or dimmed to accommodate a specific aesthetic, functional, and/or task requirement.

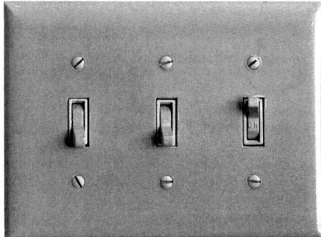

Figure 12.1

A single-gang toggle wall switch is shown near right. Far right illustrates a 3-gang wall plate with three toggle switches. These are basic switches. Decorator versions are available with matte finish in a variety of colors, with and without visible mounting screws.
Image ©Stockxpert

Switches should be selected based on intended function, users' needs, and always with an eye toward minimizing the energy used. Toggle switches are extremely easy to comprehend (up is "on" and down is "off" at least on the single-pole switch) and easy to use. Other switch types are available, including push-button and rocker (Figure 12.2 illustrates rocker-type). These are typically considered more decorative than the toggle switch; however, a review of switch type with the building owner and/or users may be advised to confirm that these styles are acceptable. Also, screwless plates are considered more aesthetically pleasing in most situations, and screwless-plate switches are now available in many styles, colors, and finishes. Typically, the screws are hidden beneath a snap-over switch plate. Where security is an issue, switches can be the keyed type, where insertion of a key into the switch is necessary for its function. However, the registered professional(s) on the project needs to ascertain the code requirements for switching types and locations.

```
more online @
www.cooperwiringdevices.com/index.cfm
www.geindustrial.com/cwc/Dispatcher?REQUEST=PRODUCTS&famid=
   18&lang=en_US
www.homeselect.net/Catalog2.htm
www.leviton.com/OA_HTML/ibeCZzpHome.jsp?minisite=10026&respid=22372
www.lithonia.com/controls/SynergyOnlineBrochure/Default.htm
www.lolcontrols.com/
www.lutron.com/
www.passandseymour.com/
```

12.2 Dimmers

Where filament lamps are used and/or where fluorescent lighting intensity is intended to change based on space use, time of day, or daylight availability, dimming switches are appropriate. Dimming for incandescent lamps has the added benefit of extending lamp life. As Figure 10.3 illustrates, dimming incandescent lamps just 5 percent can yield a 200 percent increase in lamp life.

Dimming of low voltage filament, LED, and fluorescent lamps requires special dimmers. When selecting and specifying dimmers, then it is necessary to determine

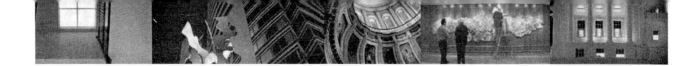

Figure 12.2

Where more than three control devices are used, users are likely to be confused about which switches operate which lights. Additionally, the issue of wall clutter becomes more serious. In some cases, depending on the type of switch or dimmer and the kind and wattage of lighting load it controls, it may require a certain amount of free area around it. It becomes difficult to align these exactly and the real estate consumed is rather large. Networked and preset controls alleviate these issues (or at least move them to an electrical closet that's out of sight). Of course, if other devices are on the wall (see Figure 12.3), then the management and design issue is far more significant, where only integrated networked controls and displays can reduce the clutter.

Image ©ImageSource/inmagine

if the desired dimmer can safely and satisfactorily dim the lighting that is intended to be dimmed. Manufacturers' literature is clear in this regard. However, where questions arise, contact respective switch and luminaire manufacturers. It may be necessary to specify interface devices that assist the dimmer and luminaire in communicating and proper operation. This is more "black box" stuff that needs to be accommodated, typically in the luminaire or nearby.

As with on/off switches, dimmers should be selected based on anticipated use. If users are elderly, then the ease of the on/off function and the ease of the dimming function (and the clarity of how these are done) will be crucial. Sliders might work best. If users are likely to set the dimmer setting once in a while (rather than changing the setting periodically or every time the dimmer is switched on), then dimmers that have a small, nearly hidden slider immediately adjacent to the toggle, push-button, or rocker might be appropriate (the slider is so small that it is not convenient for intermittent dimming control throughout the day—see Figure 12.4). Rotary dimmers are considered old-fashioned by many people and may be difficult to operate for the elderly. Slider dimmers may be easier to use, but, depending on the version, may have an inherent flaw with the "off" mode. "Off" is when the slider is pushed down and "clicked" off. Since the lights dim to what appears to be "off" at the downward push just prior to clicking off, most folks fail to realize that the final "click to off" is necessary. Hence, the lights continue to draw (and waste) a bit of power, but not enough for the lights to glow.

more online @
www.cooperwiringdevices.com/index.cfm
www.geindustrial.com/cwc/Dispatcher?REQUEST=PRODUCTS&famid=
 18&lang=en_US
www.homeselect.net/Catalog2.htm
www.leviton.com/OA_HTML/ibeCZzpHome.jsp?minisite=10026&respid=22372
www.litetouch.com/
www.lithonia.com/controls/SynergyOnlineBrochure/Default.htm
www.lolcontrols.com/
www.lutron.com/
www.passandseymour.com/
www.vantagecontrols.com/

Figure 12.3

Although it starts with wall switches or lighting control stations, wall clutter can expand significantly. Devices such as local lighting control, whole-building lighting control, phone, security keypad, audio control, thermostat, Ethernet port, intercom, and camera monitor must all be addressed by the interior designer or architect (or left to the installers' discretion).
Image ©fstop/inmagine

12.3 Networks

Depending on the size of the project and the number of switch and/or dimmer devices ultimately used on the project, it may be desirable or necessary to network the devices for centralized control. ASHRAE 90.1 requires automatic shut-off of building lighting for building's over 5000 ft^2 (about 465 m^2). There are two basic systems—one for residential and some smaller hospitality and commercial applications, and one for large-scale commercial applications. In residential applications, the desire for centralized control from specific locations is a convenience and an energy-saver. For example, in a large residence, it is tedious at bedtime for the owner to check all rooms to make certain lights are off. Further, it is desirable, perhaps, to have centralized function of exterior security lights. There may be a desire to have quick access to all or many house lights in the event of an emergency or an intrusion. It may be desirable to interconnect some or all lights with the security alarm system. It also may be desirable to set easily accessible scenes. When guests are expected for dinner, a preset scene can turn on the appropriate lights in the dining room, living room, foyer, and exterior entry to a comfortable, dimmed intensity. All of these desires can be achieved if lighting controls are networked together and then are made centrally programmable. These systems typically have such available features as photocell control (to automatically switch some or all landscape lights on at dusk or when a storm passes, for example) and astronomical timeclock control. Some systems also have special features, such as vacation mode and "lighted path home." Here, the system tracks and memorizes weekly lighting rituals (which lights are turned on/off and at what times by users of these spaces) and then can play back the previous week's lighting when occupants go on vacation—giving the residence the "someone's home" appearance due to oddly timed on/off and varied room lighting schedules. The "lighted path home" feature allows users to call ahead on a cell phone to activate certain lighting scenes (such as site lighting or security lighting). A similar feature interfaces the garage door opener with lighting scenes—when the garage door opener is activated, certain lights can also be switched on. These networked systems are quite popular in large residences or where the

Control Device Designations Table 12.1

Designation	Lighting Intent	Design Aspects
S	Single on/off switch (may be ganged with other devices)	• Switches on/off one or more lights from a single location • Should be convenient/obvious upon entering the room • Should permit switching off lights immediately prior to exiting (avoid walking through dark room) • Should be simple to operate and provide immediate feedback (lights "on" or "off" immediately upon activating/deactivating switch) • Typically controls all lights in room or combines with other switches for full room control
S_d	Single dimmer switch (may be ganged with other devices)	• Dims one or more lights from a single location • Should be convenient/obvious upon entering the room • Should permit switching off lights immediately prior to exiting (avoid walking through dark room) • Should be simple to operate and provide immediate feedback (lights "on" or "dimmed" or "off" immediately upon adjusting switch) • Typically controls all lights in room or combines with other devices for full room control • Derate load according to manufacturer's directions
S_3	3-way switch (may be ganged with other devices)	• Switches on/off one or more lights from two locations • At least one of the two switches should be convenient/obvious upon entering room • Many times used at each of two doors into/out of room • See other aspects outlined for Single on/off switch
S_4	4-way switch (may be ganged with other devices)	• Switches on/off one or more lights from three locations • At least one of the three switches should be convenient/obvious upon entering room • See other aspects outlined for Single on/off switch
S_L	Single on/off switch with indicator light	• Switches on/off one or more lights in another area that is unseen from the switch location • Might be used outside walk-in refrigerator or closet • Indicator or pilot light used as a visual cue to others that room is (probably) in use • Typically controls all lights except nightlight if one exists
$S_{\langle M \rangle}$	Single on/off switch with occupancy sensor (integral occupancy sensor)	• Switches on/off one or more lights manually from a single location or based on occupancy • Occupany sensing typically ultrasonic and infrared based • Digital technologies allow for greater sensitivity to sedentary task activities • Mounting height and furniture layouts/configurations may influence success/failure • Typically not ganged with other devices • Typically controls all lights in room
$\langle M \rangle$	Occupancy sensor ("M" for motion sensing)	• Switches on/off one or more lights based on occupancy • Typically wall or ceiling mounted • Area to be covered may require more than one sensor
S_T	Single on/off switch with integral timer	• Switches on/off one or more lights manually from a single location but with a timer • Timed-off function programmed for typical-length stays • Typically used in walk-in coat closets, electrical, mechanical and storage rooms • More reliable than motion sensors in rooms cluttered with objects that block sensing
PC	Photocell	• Switches on/off and/or dims one or more lights based on daylight availability • Typically controls a specific set of lights most influenced by daylight • Improves energy efficiency
CS_{1-201}	Control Station (Occurrence #—room designation)	• Switches on/off and/or dims one or more lights in preset scenes or settings • Greatly reduces wall clutter • Improves energy efficiency and in-service lamp life by controlling all lights to predetermined levels for specific functions • Can be programmed to function according to time of day, occ sensor(s), and/or photocell(s) • See other aspects outlined for Single on/off switch

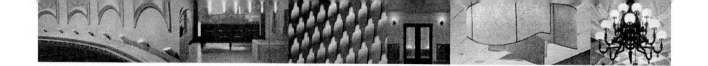

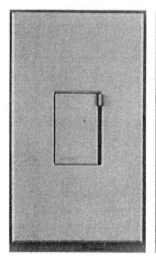 

Figure 12.4

A single-gang dimmer switch is shown near right. The center square acts like a push-button for on/off control. The small slider dims lights (to bright in the up position). This device is Lutron's Vareo control. Far right illustrates a matching duplex outlet from the Vareo collection. See cutsheets on opposite page. Several manufacturers offer control device collections with matching devices.
Images ©GarySteffyLightingDesign
Cutsheets ©Lutron Electronics Co.

occupant is looking for convenience. However, they are also appropriate in smaller hospitality and commercial applications. Country clubs, conference centers, conference suites, executive office suites, multiroomed dining facilities, and the like are potential applications.

In commercial buildings, networked systems offer significant energy benefits and in-service-life-extension for lamps. Of course, automatic timeclock control can be used to control the hours of operation. More significantly, however, networked controls can allow for group overrides through programming. Each networked switch and dimmer is addressable. If the third-floor accounting group is working late, an override function can be programmed to allow for the networked devices on that floor to remain active. This also works for cleaning operations—based on a timetable, each floor's networked devices are active for an hour to allow the cleaning crew to work the floor. Alternatively, programmed sweeps can occur "sweep" lights off every hour after 7 p.m.

Networked systems can range in cost from just US$1500 or so for a series of rooms to several tens of thousands of dollars for an entire commercial building.

```
more online @
www.cooperwiringdevices.com/index.cfm
www.geindustrial.com/cwc/Dispatcher?REQUEST=PRODUCTS&famid=
    18&lang=en_US
www.homeselect.net/Catalog2.htm
www.leviton.com/OA_HTML/ibeCZzpHome.jsp?minisite=10026&respid=22372
www.litetouch.com/
www.lithonia.com/controls/SynergyOnlineBrochure/Default.htm
www.lolcontrols.com/
www.lutron.com/
www.passandseymour.com/
www.pcilightingcontrols.com/
www.vantagecontrols.com/
```

12.4 Presets

For some facilities or spaces, the time comes when a bunch of dimmer switches on the walls to each room or area offers occupants and/or passersby too many choices. Examples include entire or partial buildings or whole floors, or individual spaces such as auditoria, restaurants, conference facilities, building lobbies and

Architectural Lighting Design

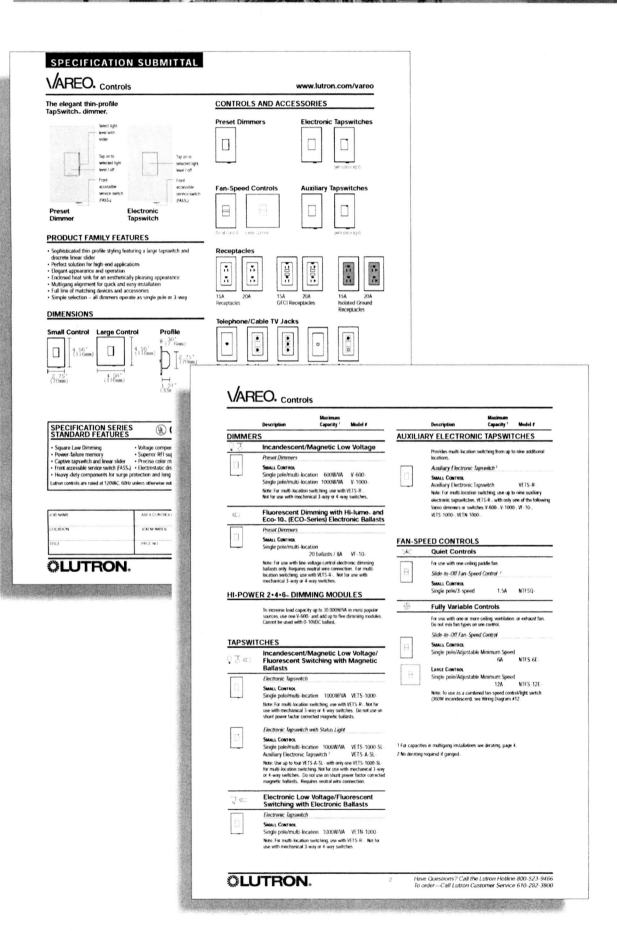

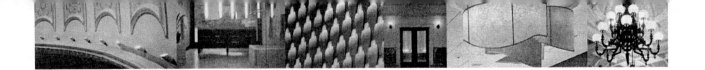

Figure 12.5

A preset control station or keypad greatly reduces wall clutter and allows access to a variety of lighting scenes. Here, scenes are labeled according to room type. This particular control station uses an LCD screen to allow scrolling to various layers or levels of control and to additional scenes—all in an intuitive manner without clutter.
Image ©Stockxpert

control zone
A specific light or group of lights identified to be separately controlled from all other light and/or groups of lights in a space or area. See Figure 12.7 for a control zone loop diagram.

atria, ceremonial reception and/or office areas, and home dining rooms, family rooms, living rooms, and even kitchens. Because of the various functions that might occur, or because of varying daylight conditions, or because of specific time-of-day functionality, it is desirable to "set the scene" for each specific function, sky condition, and/or time of day. With a wall full of switches and dimmers, this means some sort of marking code for the dimmers along with a legend on when each marked code is to be employed and when switches are to be "on" or "off" to create the various scenes. Obviously, this is tedious for the users and soon is dismissed as an annoyance if not downright impractical—and folks resort to simply switching on all lights to full intensity for the duration. Preset controls are based on a control system that actually keeps track of all the lights, their respective and "switch legs" or **control zone**s and which are dimmable and which are just switchable in a room, a suite of rooms, a floor, a building, and/or an exterior façade and/or site. This allows the specification of usually one, two, four, six, eight, twelve, sixteen, etc., preset scenes. These scenes can be established within rooms, areas, floors, or the entire building. Figure 12.5 shows a preset keypad or control station.

A preset scene is established when the lights in a room or area have been grouped and controlled to provide a specific light intensity and/or aesthetic look. For example, in a hotel circulation concourse (see Figures 12.6 and 12.7) the lighting consists of CFL downlights, a CFL reverse-cove, CMH spot downlights, CMH wallwashers, and linear fluorescent sconces. Late at night, only minimal circulation lighting with some accenting is necessary and later still, even the accenting is unnecessary. So, to save energy, a preset system was established to allow for various grouping of these lights to switch on/off throughout the late-night hours. This also accommodate the "one-hour-off-a-week" requirement for CMH lamps (lamp manufacturers require CMH lamps be switched off at least an hour a week as part of the lamp-failure cycle and to prevent nonpassive [violent]

lamp failures). Further, if the full extent of the programming capabilities are employed, the system can track which lights are on and off each night, thereby extending in-service lamp life of those lights alternating on/off each night.

Another example, one where dimming is involved, would be a restaurant with wall sconces, pendents over banquettes, recessed art accents, a special highlight accent for the maitre d' station, and special display lighting onto and in the wine cooler. There is a desire to set each of these groups of lights to specific intensities for breakfast, lunch, cocktails, dinner, late night, for clean up, and for closed—a total of seven scenes. An eight-button preset control station (or wall switch plate) is used—seven scene-select buttons and an off button. There are seven zones of lights. One zone for dimmable CFL sconces, one zone for two of the five non-dim CFL lamps in the pendents, one zone for the remaining lamps in the pendents, a zone for the dimmable MR16 art accents, a zone for the maitre d' station dimmable AR111 accent, a zone for the dimmable AR111 frontal spots on the wine cooler, and a zone for the internal non-dim LED lighting of the wine cooler. Table 12.3 outlines the various scenes and the proposed settings for each zone of lights. Most preset systems are easily reprogrammed, so that after several days or weeks of operation, changes can be made. However, any staff member can readily set lights properly for each scene with the push of a button. Of course, scene buttons need to be properly labeled. If staff is unable to manage the presets, these can be automated to specific time-of-day functions (e.g., breakfast runs from 6 a.m. until 11 a.m., then lunch until 5 p.m., then cocktails, etc.).

A final example of presets is unique because most of the lights are non-dim CMH. This project, a chapel, is illustrated in Figure 12.7 and 12.8 as well as Figures 7.8 and 9.13. Working with non-dim CMH lamps in a project with preset scenes can only be done with great discipline on the part of the users in operating the scenes in a strict sequence to avoid switching on/off/on CMH lamps that exhibit a 3- to 5-minute warm-up to full output and excellent color. However, the rewards are big—energy efficiency, better sustainability, and long life when compared to HIR lamps. Using fewer lights compared to HIR-lamped luminaires results in less material on the initial installation and less equipment to service over life. Figure 12.7 shows five of the eight scenes listed in Table 12.4. Figure 12.8 shows the linear accent luminaires housing the 39PAR30L/CMH/3K lamps.

more online @
www.cooperwiringdevices.com/index.cfm
www.geindustrial.com/cwc/Dispatcher?REQUEST=PRODUCTS&famid=
    18&lang=en_US
www.homeselect.net/Catalog2.htm
www.leviton.com/OA_HTML/ibeCZzpHome.jsp?minisite=10026&respid=22372
www.litetouch.com/
www.lithonia.com/controls/SynergyOnlineBrochure/Default.htm
www.lolcontrols.com/
www.lutron.com/
www.passandseymour.com/
www.pcilightingcontrols.com/
www.vantagecontrols.com/

Figure 12.6

A preset scene system is used for lighting control of this hospitality project. Here, the concourse just off the ballroom dropoff is illustrated. Luminaire types are identified along with respective control zones in the RCP showin in Figure 12.7. These are then used to develop a preliminary preset schedule shown in Table 12.2.
Image ©Kevin Beswick

FCC1d and 1e/Z17-GC
CFL reverse cove. All lamps on one non-dim zone.

FCD3/Z10-GC and Z11-GC
CFL downlights. Half on one non-dim zone and half on second non-dim zone.

MPW1/Z15-GC
CMH wallwashers opposite ballroom dropoff on one non-dim zone.

MPD1b/Z9-GC
CMH spot downlights at door thresholds on one non-dim zone.

FTQ1/Z5-GC
Linear fluorescent sconces all on one non-dim zone.

MPW1/Z4-GC
CMH wallwashers here on same non-dim zone as MPW1 lights in corner.

MPW1/Z4-GC
CMH wallwashers in corner on same non-dim zone as MPW1 lights in foreground.

MPD1c/Z16-GC
CMH spot downlights in floating ceiling on non-dim zone.

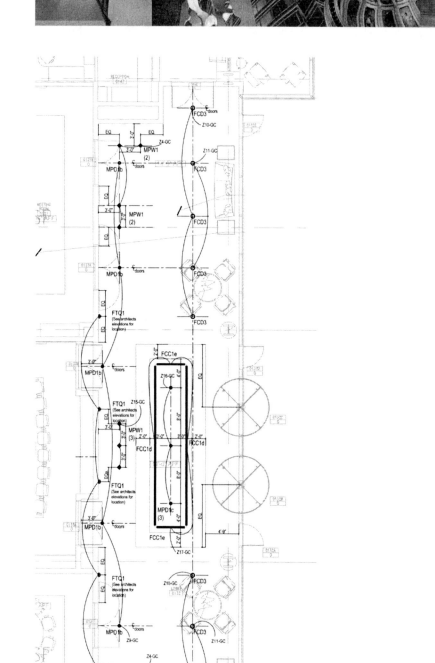

Camera View for Figure 12.6

Figure 12.7

A reflected ceiling plan showing luminaire locations, their type designations, and their control zone looping. This is sometimes referred to as a looping diagram. Lights are grouped based on function and a preconceived plan on how they can be switched or dimmed on/off to create various scenes. Here, the scenes are used solely for night setback so that sufficient light remains for basic circulation.

Reflected ceiling lighting plan ©GarySteffyLightingDesign Courtesy JW Marriott Grand Rapids and BETA Design Group

Table 12.2 Preset Schedule Example/Grand Concourse

This is the schedule of lighting zones and preset events used to program the preset lighting system used on the project shown in Figures 12.5 and 12.6. The "OffOdd/OnE" and "OffE/OnOdd" functions will help extend in-service lamp life by alternating between days which luminaires are energized for the late night lighting scenes.
©GarySteffyLightingDesign

PRELIMINARY PRESET SCHEDULE
Grand Concourse Example
Location
©Gary Steffy Lighting Design Inc., 4/22/2008
file 10206.Pool2007092801 for 11606 grand concourse example.xls

Customer Zone	What	Load Type	3:00 AM [5] (AKA Night)	4:30 AM	10:00 AM	
Grand Concourse [automated]						
Z1-GC	FCD3	FL switched	OffOdd/OnE	ON	ON	
Z2-GC	FCD3	FL switched	OffE/OnOdd	ON	ON	
Z3-GC	FCD1	FL switched	ON	ON	ON	
Z4-GC	MPW1	CMH switched	OFF	ON	ON	
Z5-GC	FTQ2	FL switched	ON	ON	ON	
Z6-GC	FTS4	FL switched	ON	ON	ON	
Z7-GC	FCD3	FL switched	ON	ON	ON	
Z8-GC	MPD1a	CMH switched	OFF	ON	ON	
Z9-GC	MPD1d	CMH switched	OFF	ON	ON	
Z10-GC	FCD3	FL switched	OffOdd/OnE	ON	ON	
Z11-GC	FCD3	FL switched	OffE/OnOdd	ON	ON	
Z12-GC	MPW1	CMH switched	OffOdd/OnE	ON	ON	
Z13-GC	FCD3	FL switched	OffE/OnOdd	ON	ON	
Z14-GC	FCD3	FL switched	OffOdd/OnE	ON	ON	
Z15-GC	MPW1	CMH switched	OFF	ON	ON	
Z16-GC	MPD1c	CMH switched	OFF	ON	ON	
Z17-GC	FCC1d,1e	FL switched	ON	ON	ON	

Table 12.3 Preset Schedule Example/Restaurant

Here is an example schedule of lighting zones and preset events for the restaurant discussed in the text. The "CS1-R" parenthetical reference beside the "Restaurant" title indicates that these are the scenes to be assigned to and accessible from Control Station #1 in space R (the restaurant in this case). The "GENERAL NOTE" indicates how fast the lights are to respond to each scene toggle. In some establishments, scene changes are expected to occur over extended time periods to be imperceptible. If all lights are dimmable, this works well. However, as is the case here, where some lights are non-dim (switching on/off), then a quick fade is best.
©GarySteffyLightingDesign

PRELIMINARY PRESET SCHEDULE
Restaurant Example
Location
©Gary Steffy Lighting Design Inc., 5/5/2008
file 10206.Pool2007092801 for 11606 restaurant example in text.xls

Customer Zone	What	Load Type	Breakfast	Lunch	Cocktails	
Restaurant [CS1–R]						
Z1-R	CFL sconces	CFL dimmable	85	65	50	
Z2-R	CFL pendents (3 lamps)	FL switched	OFF	OFF	ON	
Z3-R	CFL pendents (2 lamps)	FL switched	ON	ON	OFF	
Z4-R	LMD3	EMAG 12V INC dim	90	90	75	
Z5-R	Maitre d' (floral pinspot)	ELTRONIC 12V INC dim	90	95	75	
Z6-R	Wine cooler (pinspots)	ELTRONIC 12V INC dim	0	85	75	
Z7-R	Wine cooler (LED)	non-dim LED	ON	ON	ON	

Architectural Lighting Design

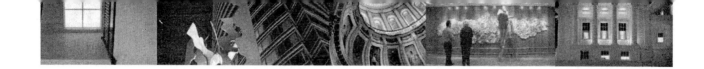

	2:00 PM	5:00 PM	7:00 PM (AKA ALL ON)	1:00 AM [5]					
	ON	ON	ON	OffOdd/OnE					
	ON	ON	ON	OffE/OnOdd					
	ON	ON	ON	ON					
	ON	ON	ON	OFF					
	ON	ON	ON	ON					
	ON	ON	ON	ON					
	ON	ON	ON	ON					
	ON	ON	ON	ON					
	ON	ON	ON	OFF					
	ON	ON	ON	OffOdd/OnE					
	ON	ON	ON	OffE/OnOdd					
	ON	ON	ON	OffOdd/OnE					
	ON	ON	ON	OffE/OnOdd					
	ON	ON	ON	OffOdd/OnE					
	ON	ON	ON	ON					
	ON	ON	ON	OFF					
	ON	ON	ON	ON					
					GENERAL NOTE: All fade rates shall be 2 seconds.				

	Dinner	Late Night	Cleanup	Closed					
	35	35	100	0					
	ON	ON	ON	OffOdd/OnE					
	OFF	OFF	ON	OffE/OnOdd					
	75	50	0	0					
	85	60	0	0					
	75	50	0	0					
	ON	ON	ON	OFF					
					GENERAL NOTE: All fade rates shall be 2 seconds.				

Figure 12.8

Five of the eight presets for this chapel outlined in Table 12.4 are illustrated here. 12.8a is day mass scene, 12.8b shows night mass scene, 12.8c shows night peace scene, 12.8d is music scene (cross is not accented, house (congregation) is dark, music "stage" to right is focus along with altar and tabernacle), 12.8e is night peace scene for meditation throughout the night.

Systems integration issues prevented installation of the wallslot in a 2-foot section of the slot about halfway along the wall. This creates the shadow pattern. The wallslot was determined an important way to accentuate the wall/ceiling juncture and introduce ambient brightness with a minimum of hardware.

Uplighting on the wood ceiling was determined an important concept to accentuate the beauty of the ceiling, help balance the window daylighting with interior surfaces, and introduce ambient brightness with a minimum of hardware.

The CMH light slots were determined to be the best way to introduce the fair number of accents required for the varying focals throughout the day and night with a minimum amount of hardware. Accent luminaires are arrayed in a relatively tight zone but spaced for appropriate aiming angles to the various focals. See Figures 7.8 and 9.13 also.

Figure 12.9 shows the linear accent lights integrated with the wood ceiling.

Images ©Gene Meadows

Figure 12.9

Although each linear slot contains 1, 2, or 4 lamps, the multilamp units exhibit two control zones so that at least two focals can be highlighted from one linear slot. The single-lamp units are used as downlights over the congregation.
Slot accent luminaires by RSA Lighting (www.rsalighting.com).
Image ©Gene Meadows

12.5 Timeclocks

Timeclocks can be used to automatically sequence lighting at predetermined times. These devices range from the very simple electromechanical types to electronic devices with many functions. Timeclock selection is based on the extent of the required function and the number and types of lighting equipment being controlled. For example, a few exterior lights at a residence could be timed "on" and "off" with a simple electromechanical timeclock. However, if the front lawn is to be controlled separately from the back lawn, and if some interior security lights are also to be controlled at yet another time, then either three simple timeclocks are required or an electronic timeclock that can handle the multiple functions should be specified. As noted earlier, astronomical timeclocks are convenient since they also keep track of the solar time (actual sunrise and sunset times throughout the year, as well as tracking daylight savings and standard times). Timeclocks can also be specified with battery backup in case of power failure. Generally, the most convenient timeclock and the one consistently yield-

Table 12.4   Preset Schedule Example/Chapel

The lighting in the chapel illustrated in Figure 12.8 is operated on these presets. With the exception of a few linear fluorescent pendent lights and three MR16/IR low voltage accents, all lights are non-dim CMH. The chapel is used in such a way that each scene can be static for the duration of a particular celebration or function.

©GarySteffyLightingDesign

Chapel Project
Project Location
©Gary Steffy Lighting Design Inc., January 11, 2008
file name

Customer Zone		What	Load Type	Day Peace	Day Pray
Lower Level					
Z1	Tabernacle Focal	MPA1	CMH switched	ON	ON
Z2	Music Focal	MPA3a, 3b (floods)	CMH switched	OFF	OFF
Z3	Cantor Focal	MPA3b (spot and flood)	CMH switched	OFF	ON
Z4	Ambo Focal	MPA3b (spots), 3c (spot)	CMH switched	OFF	ON
Z5	Altar Focal	MPA3c (spots and flood)	CMH switched	ON	ON
Z6	Altar Ambient	MPA3a, 3c (select lamps)	CMH switched	OFF	OFF
Z7	Altar Accent	MPA3c (select lamps)	CMH switched	OFF	ON
Z8	Celebrants Focal	MPA3c (select lamps)	CMH switched	OFF	ON
Z9	Tapestry Focal	MPA2a	CMH switched	ON	ON
Z10	Floor Focal	MPA3c (select lamps)	CMH switched	OFF	OFF
Z11	Font Screen	MPA1	CMH switched	ON	ON
Z12	Font Focal	MPA1	CMH switched	ON	ON
Z13	Ambient Uplight	FCP1	ECO10	OFF	50%
Z14	Ambient Downlights	MPD1	CMH switched	ON	ON
Z15	Upper Slots	FCS1a, 1b	ECO10	75%	95%
Z16	Lower Downlights	FCD1	FL switched	ON	ON
Z17	Accents Lower Focals	LMA1	MagLV INC dim	OFF	75%
Z18	Lower Slots	FCS2c, 2d	ECO10	75%	75%
Z19	Entry Downlights	FCD1	FL switched	ON	ON
Z20	Ambry	FCL1	ECO10	75%	75%
Z21	Door/Title Accents	MTA1, MTD1	CMH switched	ON	ON
Z22	Cross Accent	MPA1	CMH switched	ON	ON
Z23	Dominican Saints Focal	MPA2b	CMH switched	ON	ON
Z24	Accents Upper Focals	MPA1	CMH switched	OFF	ON

ing the best tailored energy use and sustainability timeclock arrangement is an electronic, astronomical timeclock with battery backup; however, these are also the most expensive timeclocks.

more online @
www.cooperwiringdevices.com/index.cfm
www.geindustrial.com/cwc/Dispatcher?REQUEST=PRODUCTS&famid=18&lang=en_US
www.homeselect.net/Catalog2.htm
www.intermatic.com/
www.leviton.com/OA_HTML/ibeCZzpHome.jsp?minisite=10026&respid=22372
www.lithonia.com/controls/SynergyOnlineBrochure/Default.htm
www.lolcontrols.com/
www.lutron.com/
www.passandseymour.com/
www.pcilightingcontrols.com
www.tork.com/
www.wattstopper.com/

Day Mass	Nite Peace	Nite Pray	Nite Mass	Music	Wake	'Off' Scene
ON	ON	ON	ON	OFF	ON	OFF
ON	OFF	OFF	ON	ON	ON	OFF
ON	OFF	ON	ON	ON	ON	OFF
ON	OFF	ON	ON	OFF	ON	OFF
OFF	ON	ON	ON	ON	OFF	OFF
ON	OFF	ON	ON	OFF	ON	OFF
ON	OFF	ON	ON	OFF	ON	OFF
ON	OFF	ON	ON	OFF	ON	OFF
ON	ON	ON	ON	ON	ON	OFF
OFF	OFF	OFF	OFF	OFF	ON	OFF
ON	OFF	ON	ON	ON	ON	OFF
ON	ON	ON	ON	OFF	ON	OFF
85%	50%	95%	95%	65%	95%	OFF
ON	OFF	ON	ON	ON	ON	OFF
95%	50%	75%	95%	100%	ON	75%
ON	ON	ON	ON	ON	ON	OFF
95%	65%	75%	95%	OFF	95%	OFF
95%	85%	85%	95%	75%	95%	OFF
ON	ON	ON	ON	ON	ON	ON
95%	85%	85%	95%	OFF	95%	OFF
ON	ON	ON	ON	ON	ON	OFF
ON	ON	ON	ON	OFF	ON	OFF
ON	ON	ON	ON	OFF	ON	OFF
ON	ON	ON	ON	OFF	ON	OFF

12.6 Motion Sensors

Motion sensors can be integrated into switches or can be independently mounted devices—typically mounted on the ceiling. Motion sensors offer the promise of, and usually deliver energy savings by, switching lights off when lighted areas are unoccupied for a predetermined period. Placement of motion sensors is important to their successful function. If sensors are located out of the line of sight of occupants, then it is likely the sensors won't sense occupants and may inadvertently switch lights off. Additionally, sensor technology influences how well it detects occupants. Some sensors use infrared technology, others use ultrasonic technology, some use a combination, and still others have exquisite electronic filters to sort out "work noise" from background noise. The dual technology and the electronic filter sensors appear to offer the best coverage and sensitivity for a variety of occupancy situations. Motion sensors aren't appropriate if spaces are always occupied or if occupancy isn't likely to be down for more than 10 or 15

minutes at a time. CMH lights generally should not be motion-sensed as these have warm-up times. Filament lamps are good candidates for motion sensors, but hopefully there are few, if any, filament lamps on any given project.

Where motion sensors control fluorescent lights, it is important to determine the likely frequency of on/off switching. Fluorescent lamps have a shortened life if they are switched off and on frequently. Programmed start ballasts offer the softest and smoothest lamp start and are intended to improve lamp life even if frequent on and off switching occurs. If it is suspected that the motion sensor(s) will only activate fluorescent lights up to four times each day, then instant start and rapid start ballasting would be reasonable. If more frequent activation is expected, programmed ballasts should be used. Although the lamps may not last their full rated life, their actual time in service (in place until relamping is required) is likely to be quite long since the sensor will keep them off much of the day.

more online @
www.cooperwiringdevices.com/index.cfm
www.geindustrial.com/cwc/Dispatcher?REQUEST=PRODUCTS&famid=18&lang=en_US
www.homeselect.net/Catalog2.htm
www.leviton.com/OA_HTML/ibeCZzpHome.jsp?minisite=10026&respid=22372
www.lithonia.com/controls/SynergyOnlineBrochure/Default.htm
www.lolcontrols.com/
www.lutron.com/
www.novitas.com/
www.passandseymour.com/
www.sensorswitch.com/
www.tork.com/
www.wattstopper.com/

12.7 Photocells

Where daylighting is available, consider dimming or switching off electric lights when the daylight intensities are sufficient to accommodate the task(s). This is only practical when automated and activated by a photocell. Photocells are available for indoor use and for exterior use. Location of photocells should relate quite directly to their intent (e.g., if lighting along a north window wall is to be photocell controlled, the photocell should not be located on the south wall unless sophisticated algorithms and very careful commissioning are employed). Typically, in large applications, more than one photocell is necessary to relate directly to the locale and architectural conditions of each area to be controlled. Photocells must be kept cleaned and should be kept away from the influence of electric light. See also Section 9.6.

more online @
www.leviton.com/sections/prodinfo/newprod/npleadin.htm
www.lithonia.com/
www.lolcontrols.com/products/default.asp
www.lutron.com/
www.passandseymour.com/
www.tork.com/
www.wattstopper.com/webc/home.htm!

Where rooms are small and/or lighting layouts are simple, then individual switches to each light or group of lights is a reasonable approach to switching. Always plan for a switch at the entry to a space or area so that people can light a path immediately upon entering and extinguish the lighted path immediately upon exiting. Where daylight is available, switch the lights nearest the daylight zone separately from others or, alternatively, switch half the lamps in the lights nearest the daylight zone separately from the other half of the lamps. The remainder of the lights in the area that are not within the daylight zone are then switched separately.

Where lighting layouts are more complicated and/or include distinct light groupings intended to operate independently, consideration might be given to preset switching. Where such complicated lighting persists in other rooms or areas of a facility, then networked switching and/or networking of the preset switches is desirable so that lighting can be centrally controlled. Alternatively, where an area or group of areas simply have lots of luminaires, centralized control offered by networked switching is desirable. These centralized systems are automated and can be easily orchestrated by computer.

Combine photocell and astronomical timeclock functions with computer-controlled networked switching for the most efficient and, therefore, the most sustainable lighting approach. With each upgrade in switching technique and technology, initial costs increase. Further, maintenance requirements become more sophisticated. Finally, few complete systems can be easily specified and integrated with all technologies combined. This puts greater burden on the designer, the registered professionals, and the installation contractor.

12.8 Strategies

For any control devices, recognize there will be decisions and/or issues regarding color, finish, mechanical attachment, ganging, button type consistency, and backlighting, if any. Most control devices are plastic, although some metal devices are available. Colors are typically limited to white (a certainty), ivory (a near certainty), brown (a possibility), and black (a possibility). If mixing one vendor's devices with another's, count on the colors not matching. Additionally, the finish itself is likely to be glossy, satin, or matte. Again, this is likely to be inconsistent from vendor to vendor.

Many control devices screw to switchboxes in the wall. Two screws are ever-present on the faceplate. However, several manufacturers have developed screwless (at least in appearance) options. These faceplates have a clean, architectural appearance and are considered aesthetically preferable in many residential and commercial applications.

Ganging of controls is desired if two or more devices are in or near one location. This becomes increasingly difficult when the devices are from different manufacturers and will be difficult if each device has significantly different functions

12.9 Styles/Layouts

(e.g., a preset switch with four buttons is difficult to gang with a single on/off switch since the buttons and switch do not have similar appearances).

Some switches are available with an internal, soft light source. This is more easily identifiable in the dark upon entering a space or when wakening in the middle of the night. However, some of these "nightlights," particularly those with the "new blue" LEDs are annoying and actually can disturb the circadian rhythm (see Section 2.9). Some switches are available in an engraved, backlighted configuration that makes it easy to identify preset switch functions in the dark. Finally, some switch devices are themselves internally illuminated miniature computer screens that can have a nightlight presence or are light-activated upon the touch of the screen.

To assist in any of these selection criteria and to ease integration of various switch functions, it is best to standardize on a family of vendor-specific control products most appropriate for each project. Further, control operations should be carefully reviewed with the client and/or users. Where infrared (IR) or radio frequency (RF) are to be used as remote control devices, users must be comfortable with such issues as keeping remotes consistently available (they may easily be lost or inadvertently left in other spaces or areas); the use of such devices around other IR or RF devices in the same room, area, or building; and, for IR devices, maintaining a line of sight between the remote device and the IR receiver (the advantage of RF over IR is its ability to work "around corners" and in "blind" setups where the receiver is not visible from the point where the remote control is actually being used); and if more than one IR or RF device is in use, the potential for cross-talk and cancellation between the devices (e.g., if Joe is using the remote to change lights in his office or workstation, can he inadvertently change the lights in Sue's office?).

12.10 References

The American National Standards Committee on Graphic Symbols and Designations, Y32, 1972. *American National Standard Graphic Symbols for Electrical Wiring and Layout Diagrams Used in Architecture and Building Construction.* New York: Institute of Electrical and Electronics Engineers.

Department of Justice, 1994. *Excerpt from 28 CFR Part 36: ADA Standards for Accessible Design, Appendix A.* Washington, DC: Department of Justice.

National Electrical Contractors Association, 1999. *American National Standard NECA 100-1999 Symbols for Electrical Construction Drawings.* Bethesda: National Electrical Contractors Association.

A project's design effort cannot be considered complete until it is known that the proposed solution(s) will work. To know this, however, requires considerable experience and/or quantifiable documentation. Because considerable experience can be gained only over a significant period of time, this text deals with the quantifiable documentation aspects. There comes a time on a project when the designer, other team members, and the client want some degree of confidence that the proposed lighting solution will, indeed, meet most or all of the needs most or all of the time. The best way to determine a proposed solution's success is to build it. This is, however, an extremely costly method of testing a solution. Many design tools are available that will help build a level of confidence with the proposed solution(s)—or not, in which case the solution(s) needs to be reevaluated and revised accordingly.

Most design tools are part of an iterative process. A design is established, however tentative, and some "test" of that design is made. As the design is finessed, so are the tests. Indeed, the tests will likely help finesse the design. Design, then test, then redesign based on test results, then test again, and so on. Design tools can be classified into qualitative tools and quantitative tools. Qualitative tools allow the designer to assess the lighting quality aspects of the design. For example, will a particular design really result in an impression of spaciousness when compared against other possible designs? On the other hand, quantitative tools allow the designer to assess the lighting quantities—luminances, luminance ratios, illuminances, and illuminance ratios to name a few.

13.1 Qualitative Tools

Before getting bogged down on a project in the technical data and predictive techniques, it is desirable to have some degree of confidence if the lighting design will meet the softer, more subjective, or psychological criteria. After all, it is relatively easy to achieve certain luminances and illuminances—this is done by revising final luminaire selections, spacings, and lamping after lighting concepts and techniques have been established. However, establishing those lighting techniques in the first place is the difficult part. Techniques will depend on how the space is to look and feel, which areas and surfaces are to be relatively light, which are to be relatively dark, and which are to be somewhere in between. Two- and/or 3-dimensional visualizing provides the most appropriate qualitative design tools. This includes mood shots, field trips, lighting renderings, models, and mockups.

Mood Shots

Sometimes clients and/or users are only comfortable after having seen examples of installations that are similar to the design work being proposed for their specific project. Photos and magazine images can serve this purpose, but this technique must be used with great care. Often professional photos include photographer's fill light, which makes the scene especially attractive as photo art. Indeed, a fine exercise in art is to take the latest architectural and interior design magazines and attempt to determine where fill light was applied (few of these shots are done without fill light). Look for odd shadows (e.g., chair leg shadows raked across the floor for more than a foot or two mean that fill light is likely located off to one side [the side away from which the shadows are directed] at a few feet above the floor). Look for vivid detail (e.g., if floor covering,

seating upholstery, wall coverings, and the like are dark in tone, but subtle patterning is visible, then fill light is likely used to overlight the pattern). Look for odd luminance patterns (e.g., odd wall scallops [although these may be from poorly aimed architectural lighting], or odd floor scallops or ceiling scallops [a dead giveaway that fill was used]). Look for image washout (if the entire photo appears to be effusively lighted to the point of looking as if the installation would be glary or uncomfortable, then banks and banks of fill light were likely used). So, if a client is shown a mood shot that has been filled by the photographer and this isn't appreciated or explained by the lighting designer, it is likely the client will be disappointed with the end result (because it won't look like the picture looked!). To avoid such disappointment, use photos that are believed to present a reasonable facsimile of the actual installed lighting effects; use photos of similar space, style, taste, and budget as the project under consideration; and/or clearly state that the image is being shown for the lighting effects (as opposed to the furnishing's/finishes' styles and character).

Some photographers have taken the time and patience to learn and apply techniques that avoid harsh and unrealistic fill light, yielding photography that is itself an art, while portraying space and light realistically. Many images throughout this text were so taken and prepared. Finally, remember that there is no substitute for seeing an installation firsthand to appreciate actual light characteristics.

Field Trips

Viewing an actual lighting installation (rather than looking at photos of it) is best. Field trips to the installation(s) should be considered. On larger projects, it is very reasonable to take a one- or two-day trip to a distant locale to view projects of similar lighting scale and scope. Even though several thousands of dollars may be expended, this is no more costly than the time/fee involved in developing models or computer analyses. Of course, this technique is appropriate only when the project being viewed has a close character and lighting solution(s) as the proposed project. Field trips also allow the client to review in situ conditions with workers in place and the comings and goings of visitors, and to experience the importance of maintenance (or lack thereof).

Hand Renderings

Expressing a sense of light and dark, and shade and shadow to a client will be necessary if the client is uninitiated in lighting or if new techniques or modified applications are to be used on a project. Although some expression can be conveyed in written form, being "there" (through virtual reality or mockups) or seeing a picture or light rendering of "there" will be the most expeditious means of convincing a client of your intentions. Lighting renderings are also excellent learning tools. Hand renderings, at least the early ones and certainly the complicated ones (architecturally), may be time-intensive. This time investment helps the designer better visualize the space or area and allow for exploration of more appropriate solutions. This time also helps the designer actually study and better understand lighting effects, better understand how light interacts with surface configurations, and better sort effective lighting techniques.

Light renderings can take many forms. Relatively simple pencil sketches can address spatial form, shade, shadow, and highlighting. Figure 10.1 shows such a sketch and the finished project. The architect established the perspective wireform and the lighting

Figure 13.1

The pencil sketch was based on a wire perspective diagram supplied by the architect. After a lighting concept was discussed with team members, the sketch was then made by developing shade, shadow, and brightness patterns that were both desired for the environment and anticipated from the lighting. This is an interactive process. The sketch attempts to illustrate the desired light patterns, and then the lighting equipment and exact placement are established.

The sketch was used to convince the team, including the client, that the proposed lighting approach would be an appropriate method of lighting the linear atrium. The actual installation has a remarkable resemblance to the pencil sketch. This photo was taken from a second-floor bridge over the linear atrium space, hence the different perspective and the view of the second-floor interior wall. Of course, extensive lighting calculations were done to convince the team that appropriate luminances and illuminances could be achieved. Calculations also helped finalize surface finishes.

Image courtesy and ©GE

designer shaded the wireform to illustrate the anticipated effect of a particular lighting concept. Here, the structural ceiling coffer is proposed to be uplighted to accentuate the height of the space, maintain an "open" or "airy" feeling, and to articulate the coffer structure. Luminaires were proposed along the interior-side upper bulkhead running the length of the atrium circulation space. The luminaires were proposed as asymmetric throw—to throw light out across the ceiling toward the window wall. The sketch convinced the design team and the client that the aesthetic was appropriate. Quantitative calculations were performed to ascertain the luminance and illuminance components.

Pencil and charcoal sketches can be quick and effective. The key, of course, is understanding what light will do—how it will shade, shadow, highlight, sparkle, wash, streak, and so on. This can be learned only through observation. The Observation Journal in Section 1.7 is a convenient if not necessary reference for such work. Pencil and charcoal are limited to monochromatic renderings, but can be used quite effectively to illustrate the effect of lighting. Learn to establish which kinds of lights are in a given space and then attribute various lighting effects to them. Airbrushing with marker is another technique that can be used to show not only shade, shadow, and highlight, but can also show the subtle gradations between these and can illustrate the effect of color. Figure 10.2 shows an airbrush rendering, and the finished project. As presentations are made to upper management on the larger projects, and as the criticality of the decision tends to increase, it may be necessary to develop more refined presentation renderings.

If a professional renderer is retained as a consultant to the design team, then careful explanation of both the lighting hardware and its likely effects will need to be made to the renderer. Otherwise, lighting patterns are likely to be wrong (as the renderer may simply render in a "high contrast" mode for dramatic effect of the image) or lighting patterns may even be nonexistent (as the renderer may simply render in "100 percent" daylight) or they may be entirely false (the north façade is rendered in sunlight).

Figure 13.2

During the conceptual design phase for the exterior lighting of the Michigan State Capitol, an airbrushed elevation was developed to convey the key components of the structure for which lighting was proposed. This helped convince the design team that an overall façade wash was unnecessary. Indeed, it was agreed that even the flatness expressed on the rendering was undesirable and that additional enhancement of the architectural character of the structure was desired.

The finished result shows more dramatic lighting than initially proposed in the airbrushed rendering. The architectural lintels and details are dramatized by shadows they create on upper façade areas, yet some accenting of the upper pediments is used to help define the overall structure. The dome, while completely lighted, exhibits a strong flood from the lower colonnade, with soft, fading light grazing the dome, and then strong accenting of the cupola.

Rendering ©GarySteffyLightingDesign
Image ©Balthazar Korab

Light renderings can be convenient, requiring a relatively small investment of time and money to illustrate lighting concepts for the design team's edification and the client's comprehension. A variety of techniques are available that lend themselves to black/white/gray value studies or to color renderings. Although light renderings can be a good way to capture the look of a space, a good sense of how a space may feel and function cannot be acquired through renderings.

Digital Renderings

Lighting software offers fairly quick and rough visualizations or fairly lengthy and detailed renderings. The beauty of this approach, of course, is that once the computer model is established, it is quite convenient to review various lighting schemes' effects on the architecture. The US Department of Energy (DOE) has a listing of available lighting software (see "more online@ www.eere.energy" below). The IESNA's monthly magazine, *LD+A*, periodically lists available lighting software and its proclaimed capabilities based on voluntary response to an industry survey.[1] While there is little doubt that these software programs are accurate in their ability to calculate illuminance and luminance data, many are fraught with quirks of input style and recitation, presentation format, and output style and capabilities. Some programs include such oddities as no input mirror on the output, pagination errors, wasted paper, import/export dyslexia, and goofy presentation scales and tables. But if all you need is an answer, and an accurate one, then this software will be fine. If additional time is put into reworking formatting and output details, the resulting printouts can be useful for review with other team members and even as presentations to clients. Many luminaire manufacturers have packaged lighting software as a loss-leader item to engineers and architects. Typically for some amount less than US$200 (some even free), decent, if not excellent, computer programs are made available to practitioners. Some manufacturers even offer training sessions. Tools independent of manufacturers, some quite robust, are also available. AGi32 (by Lighting Analysts, Inc.) is one such program and was used in generating output illustrated in Figures 13.3, 13.4, 13.5, and 13.11. For those with great patience and computer aptitude, finessed input with AGi32 or such programs as Radiance (by Lawrence Berkeley National Laboratory) can provide excellent imagery. These are extraordinarily time-consuming, even for the computer literate and software-savvy; however, the gain is usually worth the pain. Results are stunning—and typically sufficient to help convince a client of a particular solution. If educational facilities and talent are available for tutorial on AGi32, Radiance, and/or other lighting software recognized in IESNA and US DOE listings, take advantage of this—this skill for lighting design work is very valuable. Beware the "light rendering" utilities built into architectural design and sketch software packages. These may not have the lamp/source accuracy or the calculation-engine accuracy to develop "truthful" renderings. If teaser graphics look too good to be true (and/or highlight and shadow appear seductively unreal) and/or if rigorous photometric input and/or luminance or illuminance data output aren't options, then the software's imagery won't convey practical reality.

```
more online @
www.agi32.com/
www.eere.energy.gov/buildings/tools_directory/subjects.cfm/
    pagename=subjects/pagename_menu=materials_components/
    pagename_submenu=lighting_systems
radsite.lbl.gov/
```

Physical Models

Rough physical models have long been used to establish basic architectural form and in the study of daylight. Scale models are particularly effective in review of fenestration and/or shading techniques on daylight distribution and intensities. Photographs, and especially slides or video, of models can be used for team review and perhaps for the client. Physical models do not necessarily require much time or money and yet can be helpful in establishing team consensus on an approach. However, the time invested in

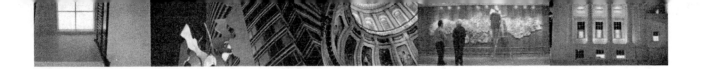

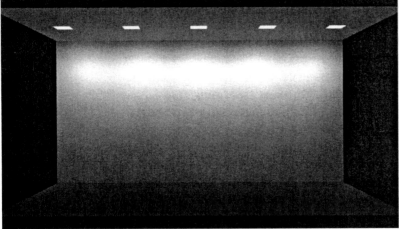

```
7.5  11.6 12.4 11.2 11.3 13.5 13.8 11.5 11.8 13.8 13.8 11.9 11.5 13.8 13.5 11.3 11.1 12.4 11.6 7.4
14.2 20.6 22.8 21.2 21.9 24.8 25.1 22.7 22.7 25.3 25.4 22.9 22.5 25.1 25.0 21.9 21.2 22.7 20.7 14.2
13.5 18.2 20.3 20.4 21.1 22.8 23.3 22.1 22.0 23.4 23.8 22.2 21.8 23.1 22.9 21.3 20.3 20.4 18.2 13.5
9.8  12.5 14.0 14.8 15.4 16.5 16.9 16.5 16.5 17.1 16.9 16.5 16.4 16.8 16.4 15.4 14.8 14.4 12.6 9.8
7.0  8.5  9.8  10.5 11.1 11.5 11.7 11.8 11.8 12.0 12.2 11.9 11.8 11.7 11.5 11.0 10.3 9.6  8.6  7.0
5.0  6.1  6.9  7.5  8.0  8.3  8.4  8.6  8.7  8.9  8.8  8.8  8.6  8.6  8.3  8.0  7.4  6.9  6.0  5.1
3.7  4.3  4.9  5.4  5.7  6.0  6.1  6.3  6.3  6.5  6.4  6.3  6.3  6.2  6.0  5.7  5.3  4.9  4.3  3.7
2.6  3.1  3.5  3.9  4.0  4.4  4.4  4.5  4.6  4.7  4.7  4.6  4.5  4.5  4.3  4.0  3.7  3.5  3.1  2.6
2.0  2.3  2.6  2.8  3.0  3.2  3.3  3.4  3.4  3.5  3.5  3.4  3.3  3.4  3.2  3.1  2.8  2.6  2.3  2.0
```

Illuminance on the wall

Numeric Summary Label	CalcType	Units	Avg	Max	Min	Avg/Min	Max/Min
Room_Wall_1	Illuminance	Fc	11.15	25.4	2.0	5.58	12.70

Columbia Parawash 81 1-F18BX w/Kicker
3 feet from wall, 4 feet on center

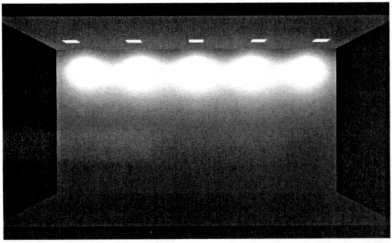

Render Image - View Name : Render

```
1.5  1.7  2.0  2.1  2.2  2.4  2.5  2.6  2.6  2.7  2.7  2.6  2.5  2.5  2.4  2.3  2.2  2.0  1.7  1.5
1.1  1.3  1.4  1.6  1.8  1.8  1.9  1.9  2.0  2.0  2.0  2.0  1.9  1.9  1.8  1.7  1.6  1.5  1.4  1.2
```

Illuminance on the wall

Numeric Summary Label	CalcType	Units	Avg	Max	Min	Avg/Min	Max/Min
Room_Wall_1	Illuminance	Fc	12.33	40.5	1.1	11.21	36.82

Columbia Parawash 81 1-F18BX w/Kicker
2 feet from wall, 4 feet on center

Render Image - View Name : Render

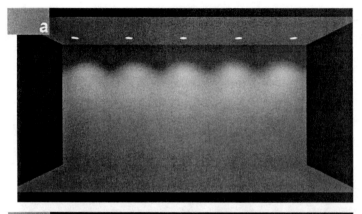

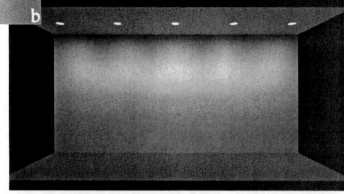

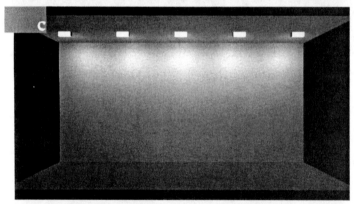

Figure 13.3

Some quick computer simulations can help determine which wallwash approach is most appropriate for a particular ceiling height and wall length. AGi32 software was used for the evaluation. This series was made for a wall 9' to 9' 6" in height by about 20' in length. Unless otherwise noted all are with FT32/830/4P CFLs. 13.3a shows the effect of a recessed open bottom 6" diameter downlight spaced 2' from the wall and 4' on center. 13.3b is a 6" diameter recessed spreadlens wallwash located 3' from the wall and 4' on center. 13.3c is a semi-recessed rectilinear lensed wallwasher using an FD26/830/4P CFL and located 3' from the wall and 4' on center. 13.3d shows a 5" diameter recessed spreadlens wallwash using a 39CMH/PAR20/FL25 lamp located 3' from the wall and 4' on center.

On the far left, two simulation reports are shown. Both use a recessed rectilinear open wallwasher (see example and cutsheet in Figure 1.13), but the top graphic spaces the lights 3' from the wall and 4' on center, while the bottom graphic spaces lights 2' from the wall and 4' on center. These lights use an FL18/830/4P CFL lamp.

Figure 13.4

During the early design phases for the lighting of a large historic reading room (untouched project shown in 13.4a), a series of views were made in AGi32 of various lighting options. One option included uplights in the historic chandeliers (Figure 13.4b). Another option included uplights *and* cleaning of the ceiling (Figure 13.4c).

After testing schemes in AGi32, a mockup was undertaken. Figure 13.4d shows the effect of a channel (mounted at the window sill—circled) containing CMH 39W/PAR20/SP uplights aimed onto the central portion of the decorative ceiling bay. The luminance of the ceiling better balances with the window luminances—making the windows less glary, the space less cave-like and, more importantly, better balancing luminance ratios with the work surfaces (reading tables) to minimize tired eyes and headaches that can be a result of extreme luminance contrasts. Figures 13.4e and f show the effect of the uplights both day and night. This mockup was then used to develop a lighting specification during the Construction Document Phase.
Images©GarySteffyLightingDesign
Renderings ©GarySteffyLightingDesign

even a quick physical model study is likely as much or more as might be invested in a computer model study—with the computer's benefit of relatively easy modification to the architecture and/or to the daylighting techniques. Additionally, the computer model expands review to include electric lighting techniques and the interaction of daylight and electric light.

Mockups

Mockups are very effective qualitative techniques that can, in some instances, also be used for quantitative purposes. Mockups need not be full-scale or highly refined or detailed, and they sometimes can be done with just a few hundred dollars' worth of materials. Indeed, mockups can be made of FomeCor® and sheets (these materials are then painted or dyed for reasonably close hue and value).

Many mockups are done for aesthetic reasons, but sometimes mockups are necessary for quantitative reasons. If the mockup is sufficiently large (so that edge effects due to proximity of tight walls can be ignored) or is sufficiently accurate (with fenestration and architectural surface colors and finishes as planned), lighting measurements can be made to confirm that the proposed lighting resolutions will meet criteria or redesign accordingly.

FomeCor® is a registered trademark of Alcan Composites USA, Inc.

Architectural Lighting Design

Although full-scale mockups may sound expensive and time-consuming, in the context of a building worth tens or hundreds of millions of dollars, a US$250,000 mockup may be very well worth the cost.

Finally, mockups need not be grand, full-scale efforts. It is quite reasonable to request a few sample luminaires and then to mockup these few lights in your studio space to ascertain quantity and quality of light aspects and the effects from the subject luminaire(s) when energized. This also allows assessment of the manufacturer's quality control on the assembly and quality of the base luminaire materials. Other times, somewhat more extensive mockups can be purchased at cost. Figure 13.4d illustrates the use of four customized luminaires purchased at cost to make a relatively quick and effective mockup.

13.2 Quantitative Tools

There comes a time when the designer and the client need to know if the proposed design will meet the project's luminance and illuminance criteria. It is necessary to assess average, maximum, and minimum luminances; luminance ratios; maximum, minimum, and average vertical illuminances; and maximum, minimum, and average horizontal illuminances. The designer need not be a calculus or computer whiz, but does need to know which criteria are important for a given project and which specific target values should be achieved. Lighting designers and engineers should be capable of performing these calculations. Interior designers and architects can, for a fee, have calcula-

Figure 13.5

Fractional daylighting was an aspect of this chapel project—siting and architectural form were determined with fenestration consisting primarily of west-facing windows. To assist in transmittance selection of glazing and window treatment, a series of daylighting studies were made with AGi32. These images represent relative daylight on the equinox at 8 a.m. (top), 11 a.m. (second from top), 2 p.m. (third from top), and 5 p.m. (bottom) solar time. Since all are possible times of chapel use (and represent sun conditions at other times for other days of the year). Glazing transmittance and window treatment were selected based on sun patterns and on actual luminance data (which were available from these AGi32 calculations). Figures 9.13 and 12.8 illustrate the as-built condition.
Renderings ©GarySteffyLightingDesign

Architectural Lighting Design

tions made by engineering consultants or by manufacturers' representatives if necessary. Of course, manufacturers' representatives may do these calculations at "no cost," providing the designer is willing to use those brands that the representative represents.

Some basic calculations can assist designers in early budgeting phases and help start layouts. These include templates, the zonal cavity (or lumen) method, the inverse square method, and computer simulations. Initial attempts at any one of these will be somewhat dubious. The designer needs to try any or all of these techniques several times and test actual results against predicted results in order to establish the method(s) that are both convenient and reasonably reliable.

initial values

All lighting literally loses its luster over time. As lamps burn, electrodes, filaments, gases, phosphors, and the like decompose. As luminaires age, they get dirty and their metal finish deteriorates. Further, architectural surfaces also deteriorate and reflect slightly less light. These factors yield maintained levels of light over time. Hence, at system start-up, initial levels or values of light are available that are higher than will be available after some time of operation—typically a year or so.

Templates

Templates can be useful in establishing a preliminary equipment layout. Primarily used for site lighting or path lighting, templates are commonly available for postlights and steplights. These templates consist of isocontour plots or lines of lux/footcandle values printed on white paper. By overlaying tracing paper or vellum onto the white-paper template, the designer can establish luminaire spacings based on horizontal illuminance criteria. The illuminance values provided with the contours should be considered as **initial values** without any **interreflection.** Although templates are a quick technique, they may not be sufficiently accurate to qualify as a final design—especially if the effect of bounce light from neighboring walls and/or ceilings is desired for efficiency. Figure 13.6 shows a luminaire cutsheet with dimensional specifics along with a template illustrating illuminance isocontour plots.

Lumen Method

The lumen, or zonal cavity, method, of calculation is based on luminaire or lamp lumens and is no doubt the simplest method of determining a uniform luminaire layout based on horizontal illuminance criteria (typically at floor height for corridors and circulation spaces or desk height for work spaces). Although lots of factors, coefficients, lamp lumen data, and other values must be sought from a variety of references, the calculation itself entails nothing more than simple addition, multiplication, and division. Because this technique does require some research time to collect the appropriate data, and because the calculation formula has a cumbersome appearance (an appearance of scientific accuracy), many people believe that this is the extent of lighting design. *The lumen method is only a single-criterion compliance technique and only for establishing uniform luminaire layouts.* Figure 13.7 illustrates the layout uniformity concept of the lumen method.

The single greatest benefit of the lumen method is its general ease of use in establishing preliminary lighting layouts for initial budget projections and initial layout development and preliminary architectural design integration. With some calculational and room geometry tricks, the lumen method can serve as a fairly accurate design layout tool, even for somewhat nonuniform lighting. However, this does require a good understanding of the lumen method technique.[2] Generally, more accurate, final calculations by one of the computer methods using flux transfer or ray tracing techniques are suggested to better meet illuminance, luminance, and energy criteria.

The lumen method is so named for the axiom that illuminance on a large surface is equal to the total lumens falling onto that surface divided by the area of the surface. In its simplest form, then, the lumen method is the total number of lumens available in a room divided by the area of the room. The lumen method can be used in a number

Interreflection

Except in totally black rooms, light strikes surfaces and reflects to other surfaces and so on, until finally reaching the surface (task area) of interest. This is called interreflection. With relatively light surface finishes, interreflections can add a significant amount of light to a setting. So, to design the most efficient lighting layout, interreflection must be considered. This is typically achieved with the aid of the computer—which can either account directly for all of these interreflections by ray diagramming (time intensive even for a computer) or perform difficult mathematical analyses to mimic the effect of interreflections (complicated for humans, but more expedient for the computer).

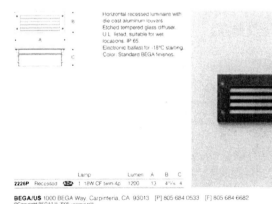

Figure 13.6

This FS18/4P (18W CFL) steplight is louvered to limit light spill. An iso-contour template (top image) can be used to establish a layout necessary to meet project illuminance criteria. Cutsheets ©BEGA-US (available at www.bega-us.com)

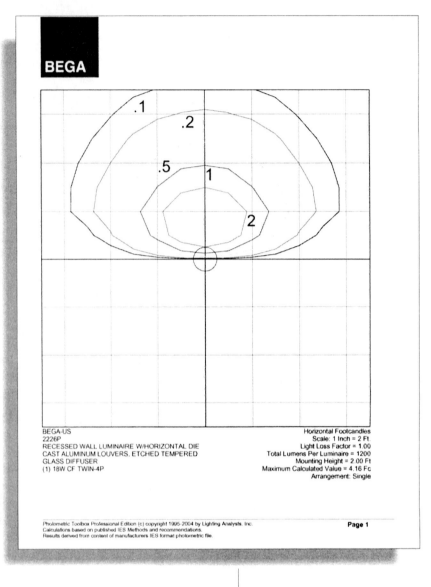

BEGA

.1
.2
.5
1
2

BEGA-US
2226P
RECESSED WALL LUMINAIRE W/HORIZONTAL DIE
CAST ALUMINUM LOUVERS, ETCHED TEMPERED
GLASS DIFFUSER
(1) 18W CF TWIN-4P

Horizontal Footcandles
Scale: 1 Inch = 2 Ft.
Light Loss Factor = 1.00
Total Lumens Per Luminaire = 1200
Mounting Height = 2.00 Ft
Maximum Calculated Value = 4.16 Fc
Arrangement: Single

Photometric Toolbox Professional Edition (c) copyright 1995-2004 by Lighting Analysts, Inc.
Calculations based on published IES Methods and recommendations.
Results derived from content of manufacturers IES format photometric file.

Page 1

Recessed wall luminaires

Housing: Constructed of die cast and extruded aluminum with integral wiring compartment. Mounting tabs provided.

Enclosure: One piece die cast aluminum faceplate. Clear glass, .157" thick etched. Faceplate is secured by four head, stainless steel captive screws threaded into stainless the housing casting. Continuous high temperature, molded gasket for weather tight operation.

Electrical: Compact fluorescent lampholder: 2G11, 4-pin. 75W, 600V. Ballast: Electronic, HPF for -18°C starting (120V through 277V). Use only 9.0" MOL lamps.

Through Wiring: Maximum four (4) No. 12 AWG conductors suitable for 75°C. Two ½" knockouts provided for ½" conduit.

Finish: These luminaires are available in five standard colors: Black (BLK), White (WHT), Bronze (BRZ), Silver (SLV), Gold. To specify, add appropriate suffix to catalog number. For description of BEGA finishing process, refer to technical section at end of catalog. Custom colors supplied on request.

U.L. listed, suitable for wet locations and for installation in ground. Suitable for all types of construction, including Type non-IC. Protection class: IP 65.

Horizontal recessed luminaire with die cast aluminum louvers.
Etched tempered glass diffuser.
U.L. listed, suitable for wet locations. IP 65.
Electronic ballast for -18°C starting.
Color: Standard BEGA finishes.

	Lamp		Lumen	A	B	C
2226P	Recessed	ADA	1 18W CF twin-4p	1200	13	4⅞	4

BEGA/US 1000 BEGA Way, Carpinteria, CA 93013 [P] 805-684-0533 [F] 805-684-6682
©Copyright BEGA/US 2005 updated 4/05

of ways, to find: the initial average illuminance on a horizontal surface to be expected from a proposed layout; the maintained average illuminance (average illuminance to be expected over time, compensating for dirt buildup and lamp depreciation factors) to be expected from a proposed layout; or the quantity of specific luminaires required in a given space in order to achieve a specific average maintained illuminance on a horizontal surface. These three lumen method variations are formulated in Table 13.1 with variables outlined in Table 13.2. Table 13.3 outlines references for the variables needed to undertake a lumen method calculation: maintained illuminance criterion; area of the space; initial lamp lumens; recoverable light loss factors; nonrecoverable light loss factors; and the luminaire's coefficient of utilization (CU).

The maintained illuminance criterion is established in programming. See Table 8.6, the latest IESNA Handbook, the latest CIE guidelines, the latest CIBSE guidelines, and/or for the experienced designer, consider past experiences. This criterion is intended to be a target value maintained over time. Note the distinction. Unless otherwise cited in IESNA literature, illuminance criteria are not to be considered initial, nor maximums nor minimums, but rather the target maintained over time toward which a designer should aim. It is well understood that lighting is dependent on so many variables, and that precise prediction is impractical. Indeed, illuminance meters and the accuracy of calculations, even with computer programs, along with factors out of the designer's control may lead to a good 20 to 25 percent variance from design targets. Nevertheless, the designer is to do his/her best.

The area of the space is simply the entire free area from wall to wall. This is why the lumen method is not to be used as a "final design" tool. If an office has a single occupant and is 300 ft^2 (about 27 m^2) and the horizontal illuminance criterion on the desk is 50 fc (about 500 lx), then using the lumen method as a design tool will result in 50 fc average over the entire room area. This will waste energy if the desk and return work surfaces compose only 30 ft^2 (about 2.7 m^2). Indeed, it may be more appropriate to establish an ambient or general illuminance of perhaps 20 or 30 fc (about 200 or 300 lx) throughout the room, and then research a desk light that can provide the remaining 20 to 30 fc on the work surface to achieve the 50 fc criterion target.

Initial lamp lumens are reported in lamp manufacturers' literature. Depending on the lamp type, manufacturers might list mean lumens and center beam candlepower also. Make certain to use initial lamp lumens for all lumen method calculations. Recognize that the intensity of focused lamps with center beam candlepower data may not be properly accounted in the lumen method. All the more reason to use the lumen method as a "first cut" tool for establishing order-of-magnitude luminaire counts for preliminary budgeting and very early layouts.

Recoverable light loss factors (RLLF—see Tables 13.2 and 13.3) include all of the light loss factors (LLFs) that can be "recovered" over the course of an installation's lifetime. As discussed in Chapter 10, lamps lose some light output over time. This is barely perceptible with halogen lamps and deluxe triphosphor fluorescent lamps, but is noticeable with ceramic metal halide lamps. This particular recoverable light loss is known as lamp lumen depreciation (LLD). By group relamping at 70 to 80 percent of rated lamp life, LLD can be recovered on a regular, ongoing basis. This is typically more cost-effective and is more sustainable (because of the energy efficiency gains after each group relamping) than purchasing and installing more luminaires and lamps initially. The key, of course, is to recycle the spent lamps. Further, this reduces ongoing

Design Tools

Figure 13.7

The lumen method is intended for development of uniform lighting layouts. This is not lighting design, but lighting layout. The lumen method is used to determine how many luminaires are needed to generate a certain illuminance level at the floor or workplane. Once the number of luminaires is determined, the layout then needs to establish center-to-center spacings and spacings from room edges. Typical spacing guidance is shown for ambient recessed lighting (CIE direct lights) such as downlights shown in 13.7a and parabolic luminaires shown in 13.7b) and ambient pendent lighting (CIE indirect, semi-indirect, or direct/indirect) as shown in 13.7c.

Note 1: Spacing distance S should not exceed the manufacturers' reported spacing criteria or SC (a few examples of **SC** for downlights are Figures 11.7, 11.8, and 11.9).

Note 2: The perimeter or edge distance should range between 0.3S and 0.5S, but not less than 1' and not more than 3' (about 300 mm and 900 mm respectively).

Note 3: With ambient pendents, the perimeter distance at the ends of the luminaires should be about 0.3S, but not less than 1' and not more than 4' (about 300 mm to 1200 mm respectively).

SC

Spacing criteria are reported on manufacturers' photometric reports. SC is the ratio of the maximum allowable spacing distance divided by height above the workplane.

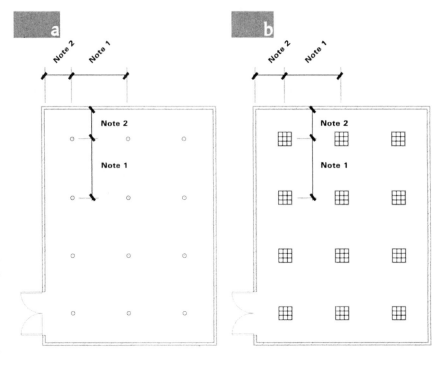

maintenance costs since group relamping is less expensive per lamp than spot relamping (which requires retrieval of the ladder every time a lamp burns out). A second RLLF is luminaire dirt depreciation (LDD). As a building is operated over time, dust collects on luminaire reflectors, lenses, louvers, and lamps. These losses might amount to a few percent decrease in light output over time in buildings with newer HVAC systems. Higher losses have been reported and may be experienced; however, this suggests more frequent cleaning cycles for lamps/luminaires (which might typically be annually or every two years). Otherwise, more lamps/luminaires are required during initial installation—which is not considered an efficient nor sustainable approach.

Finally, room surface dirt depreciation (RSDD) is also a recoverable factor. As room surfaces age, they collect dirt; and although this is certainly a secondary factor compared to LLD or LDD, it can have some impact on reducing reflected light. Through the repainting and/or refinishing of walls, floors, and ceilings from time to time, this factor is minimized. These surface losses might amount to a few percent decrease in light output over time. Higher losses have been reported and may be experienced, but just as with LDD, this suggests more frequent cleaning or refinishing of room surfaces rather than the more costly and less sustainable approach of installing more lamps and luminaires to account for a greater RSDD loss.

Nonrecoverable light loss factors (NRLLF—see Tables 13.2 and 13.3) include all those factors that negatively affect the lighting system and are permanent. These are factors that account for the varying conditions of the real world, but that are laboratory constants when manufacturers report test results on lamps and luminaires. During photometric tests, for example, very exacting voltage and temperature conditions are established in the laboratory. Reference transformers or ballasts are used so that all lamps and luminaires are operated under similar situations, and, therefore, their ratings and data are all relative to each other. This allows the designer to compare one manufacturer's lamp or luminaire performance against another's and know that any performance differences are due to lamp or luminaire design and engineering rather than to differing test conditions.

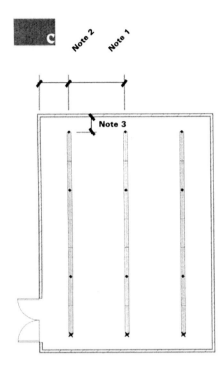

Voltage factor is an NRLLF and is a result of the nominal voltage to the lamp, ballast, or transformer not being delivered. Voltage drop because of long wiring runs and/or incorrect wire sizes, voltage surges, and primary voltages above or below nominal conditions from the utility can reduce light output.

Another NRLLF is ballast factor (BF). BF accounts for the differences experienced when operating a fluorescent lamp on a ballast having characteristics that vary from the test reference ballast used in measuring lamp performance in the test lab. BF can result in significant under performance of a lighting system. Unfortunately, this situation is exacerbated by ballast manufacturers with nearly all "standard electronic" ballasts for T8 fluorescent lamps exhibiting BFs of 0.88. To achieve a lamp manufacturers' rated light output, a BF of 1.0 is required. Thus, designers may find themselves accidentally short of the illuminance target by 12 percent, or conversely may find that their clients need to purchase 13 percent more lamps and luminaires for the initial installation. This is not very energy efficient or sustainable.

Ballast factors can help the designer finely "tune" a design. Think of BFs as permanent dimmers. There may be a need to maintain a certain luminaire spacing for uniformity, yet the lowest wattage lamp is already in place but the illuminance value is predicted to be too high. Using ballasts with a BF of 0.88 or 0.78 could help in this situation. Other times, however, it is more sustainably appropriate to stick with a specific layout, and rather than add luminaires and lamps, look for a ballast with a BF of 0.98 or 1.18 to achieve the illuminance target. This BF range of 0.78 to 1.18 seems to define the limits within which the lamp manufacturers would prefer lamps to operate in order to achieve rated life.

Another NRLLF is the thermal factor. This accounts for the difference in luminaire ambient temperature between that experienced in the lamp/luminaire testing lab and the real environment. A reasonable thermal loss is perhaps 3 to 5 percent, although this does vary from lamp type to lamp type and luminaire to luminaire. For example, the newer T5 triphosphor fluorescent lamps are designed to operate optimally in a higher ambient temperature—more appropriate for the smaller, more confining luminaires anticipated with T5 lamps. Only if the luminaire manufacturer has very carefully designed the luminaire reflector and housing around a specific lamp will thermal factor be a nonissue. Even then, if the room or plenum ambient temperature is hotter or colder than what the luminaire manufacturer used as a reference, then some light loss will occur.

Perhaps the most problematic and frequently overlooked NRLLF is the partition factor. A partition factor is considered in those spaces where partial height partitions are used to subdivide space into office cubicles or workstations. Generally, the lower

Table 13.1   Lumen Method Formulae

Variable	Intent		Formula
E_i	Predicts *initial* average illuminance from a given layout	$=$	$$\frac{\text{(Lumens per lamp)} * \text{(Number of lamps per luminaire)} * \text{(Number of luminaires)} * \text{(CU)} * \text{(NRLLF)}}{\text{Area of room [e.g., (Length of room)} * \text{(Width of room) for rectilinear space]}}$$
E_M	Predicts *maintained* average illuminance from a given layout	$=$	$$\frac{\text{(Lumens per lamp)} * \text{(Number of lamps per luminaire)} * \text{(Number of luminaires)} * \text{(CU)} * \text{(NRLLF)} * \text{(RLLF)}}{\text{Area of room [e.g., (Length of room)} * \text{(Width of room) for rectilinear space]}}$$
# of Luminaires	Number of luminaires required for a given room and a given illuminance target	$=$	$$\frac{E_m * \text{Area of room [e.g., (Length of room)} * \text{(Width of room) for rectilinear space]}}{\text{(Lumens per lamp)} * \text{(Number of lamps per luminaire)} * \text{(CU)} * \text{(NRLLF)} * \text{(RLLF)}}$$

the ceiling and the higher or taller the partitions, the worse the partition factor. Partition factors are usually worse for direct, well-controlled luminaires (e.g., parabolic luminaires) and usually better for indirect, widespread distribution luminaires. Table 13.4 outlines some estimated partition factors for various ceiling heights and partition heights. Accommodating this effect typically results in the use of smaller luminaires, each with fewer lamps, but uses more total luminaires (since they need to be spaced closer together to overcome the losses attributable to the partitions). Here, clerestories and sidelights in partition systems help significantly. For example, if a partition is 80" (about 2000 mm) in height, but the top 18" (about 450 mm) is a clerestory, then for lighting purposes the partition will act more like a 72" (about 1800 mm) high partition in the way light is blocked, absorbed, or redirected.

It is conceivable to have total LLFs (adding the RLLFs and NRLLFs) approaching 0.60 for some commercial lighting applications—where ballast factors are 0.88 and moderately tall open office partitions in low-ceiling spaces. For typical commercial settings, however, total LLFs might range from a low of 0.80, to perhaps 0.90.

Coefficients of utilization (CUs) are an expression of the lighting system's efficiency in producing lumens on the work surface in the given room geometry, reported in decimal form. Some light output (lumens) from the lamps is absorbed by the luminaire, walls, and ceiling. The CU depends on: efficiency of the luminaire; distribution of light from the luminaire (narrow, medium, or widespread); room surface reflectances; and geometry (size and proportions) of the room. CU values are found in manufacturers' data. Reported in tabular form, CUs are determined by the designer, on the basis of given room proportions and room surface reflectances. Figures 11.7, 11.8, and 11.9 offer CU tables.

Room proportions for CU data are identified by a single number, known as the room cavity ratio (RCR). Figure 13.8 illustrates the variables that affect the RCR. This ratio, the formula for which may look complicated, is actually quite simply determined. The information needed to establish the RCR is: the mathematical constant of 2.5; the room perimeter (for rectangular spaces this is simply the length and the width); and

Lumen Method Variables Table 13.2

Variable	Intent	Description
E_i	Predicts initial average illuminance	• With a given number of luminaires (e.g., existing room condition, or confirmation is desired of a preliminary guess of how many luminaires might be needed in a given situation), the lumen method enables you to predict the *initial* average illuminance on the floor or workplane throughout the entire room.
		• *Initial* means this is the light level predicted just after the lights are installed and the room finished.
E_M	Predicts maintained average illuminance	• With a given number of luminaires (e.g., existing room condition, or confirmation is desired of a preliminary guess of how many luminaires might be needed in a given situation), the lumen method enables you to predict the *maintained* average illuminance on the floor or workplane throughout the entire room.
		• *Maintained* means this is the light level predicted after several years of operation, accounting for dirt buildup in luminaires and on room surfaces and accounting for lamp lumen depreciation.
CU	Coefficient of utilization	• CU is a representation of how efficient or effective the luminaire of interest will be in lighting the workplane or floor of a given room size.
RLLF	Recoverable light loss factor	• For purposes of predicting maintained illuminance, light losses must be accounted. Some of these light losses are *recoverable* because maintenance action can be taken to reset or reclaim the losses. There are three RLLFs: LLD, LDD, and RSDD.
		• LLD = lamp lumen depreciation. Over the time that lamps are energized, they lose light output. This usually amounts to between 5% and 10% depending on the type of lamp. However, this loss is recovered as soon as the lamps are replaced with new lamps.
		• LDD = luminaire dirt depreciation. As time progresses, regardless whether lights are energized, dirt builds up on luminaire reflectors and lenses and on the lamp envelopes. This might amount to 2% to 5% over a few years depending on the cleanliness of the environment. This loss is recovered as soon as luminaires and lamps are cleaned. Note the energy implication of keeping equipment clean.
		• RSDD = room surface dirt depreciation. As time progresses, dirt builds up on room surfaces. This might amount to 1% or 2% over a few years depending on the cleanliness of the environment. Note the energy implication of keeping equipment clean.
NRLLF	Nonrecoverable light loss factor	• For purposes of predicting maintained illuminance, light losses must be accounted. Some of these light losses are *nonrecoverable* because these are permanent and no manner of maintenance or relamping can recover them. There are four NRLLFs: voltage factor, thermal factor, partition factor and, maybe ballast factor.
		• Voltage factor. Fluctuations from nominal design voltage may result in light losses. This depends on lamp and ballast/transformer/driver combination, utility voltage consistency, wire sizes, and run distances. This could amount to a loss between 0% and 10%.
		• Thermal factor. Fluctuations from nominal lamp and ballast/transformer/driver design temperatures may result in light losses. This depends on lamp and ballast/transformer/driver combination, ambient temperature, luminaire characteristics. This could amount to a loss between 0% and 20%.
		• Partition factor. This is an issue in open offices. Furniture partitions block and absorb light. Depending on their height, density, and color and the ceiling height of the room, this could amount to a loss between 0% and 20%.
		• Ballast factor. Fluorescent ballasts are responsible for how many lumens the fluorescent lamps actually produce. Fluorescent lamp lumen ratings by the lamp manufacturers are based on ballast factors (BFs) of 1.0. However, many T8 ballasts have ballast factors of 0.88—meaning the lamps will produce 88% of their rated lumens. If this reduction isn't addressed in calculations, this could amount to a 12% error.

Table 13.3 Lumen Method Data Resources

Variable	Factor	Reference	Defaults
E_M	Illuminance criterion	• Table 8.6 • Codes and/or ordinances	NA
Area	Area of room	• Floor plan takeoff • Field measurements	NA NA
Lumens	Lamp lumens	• Lamp manufacturers	NA
RLLF	• LLD	• Lamp manufacturers	NA
	• LDD	• IESNA/NALMCO RP-36-03[3] • Experience	0.97 to 0.95—a 3% to 5% loss for a typical modern clean commercial building if cleaned annually
	• RSDD	• IESNA Handbook[4] • Experience	0.97 to 0.95—a 3% to 5% loss for a typical modern clean commercial building if cleaned every two years
NRLLF	• Voltage factor	• Electrical Engineer • Utility • Electrical Contractor	1.0—no loss based on perfect voltage rating and/or electronic ballasts/transformers/drivers that tolerate some fluctuation
	• Thermal factor	• Luminaire manufacturers • Lamp manufacturers	0.97 to 0.95—a 3% to 5% loss for typical modern lamp/ballast/luminaire assemblies
	• Partition factor	• Table 13.4	0.95 to 0.90—a 5% to 10% loss for typical modern open plan situations where ceilings are 9′ to 10′ in height and partitions are 43″ to 65″ in height in moderate density
	• Ballast factor	• Ballast manufacturers • Luminaire manufacturers	0.88 common for T5 and 1.0 common for T5 fluorescent
CU		• Luminaire manufacturers • IESNA Handbook[5]	NA

the height of the cavity from the workplane or floor to the bottom of the luminaires. See Figure 13.7 for the formula that is used.

After the RCR is established, the room surface reflectances must be estimated. For purposes of using the lumen method as an early estimator, and because the floor reflectance has little impact on the illuminance level on the workplane or floor, the floor reflectance can be presumed to be 20 percent. Again, for purposes of this lumen method estimator tool, wall and ceiling reflectance values need not be finalized, but rather can be categorized as light, medium, or dark. Tables 8.4 and 8.5 offer guidance and estimates on surface reflectances.

Now the CU can be determined from the manufacturer's data. Find the CU table, and locate the appropriate ceiling reflectance zone, and then the appropriate wall reflectance column. Then locate the RCR column (generally the left-most column), and read down to the RCR for the room in question. Read across from the appropriate RCR and down the appropriate ceiling/wall reflectance to find the CU. The CU must be in decimal form to be used in the lumen method formula.

Refinements can be made for more accurate calculations based on specific wall, floor, and ceiling reflectances, and based on floor cavities (a floor cavity is the cavity

Partition Factor Estimates Table 13.4

Ceiling Height	Partition Height	Partition Factor Estimate
Between 8′ 6″ and 9′ (about 2.6 m to 2.75 m)	• Less than 42″ (about 1100 mm)	1.00
	• 43 to 54″ (about 1100 to 1400 mm)	0.95
	• 55 to 65″ (about 1400 to 1650 mm)	0.85
	• 66 to 80″ (about 1650 to 2050 mm)	0.75
Between 9′ and 9′ 6″	• Less than 42″ (about 1100 mm)	1.00
	• 43 to 54″ (about 1100 to 1400 mm)	0.97
	• 55 to 65″ (about 1400 to 1650 mm)	0.90
	• 66 to 80″ (about 1650 to 2050 mm)	0.80
Between 9′ 6″ and 10′	• Less than 42″ (about 1100 mm)	1.00
	• 43 to 54″ (about 1100 to 1400 mm)	0.97
	• 55 to 65″ (about 1400 to 1650 mm)	0.95
	• 66 to 80″ (about 1650 to 2050 mm)	0.85

between the workplane and the floor plane if they are not one and the same) and ceiling cavities (a ceiling cavity is the cavity between the plane defined by the bottom of the luminaires and the ceiling if they are not one and the same). Typically, however, these are tedious and cumbersome calculations that result in mathematically insignificant changes—and time that would be better spent using computer simulations to determine more precisely and more quickly lighting layouts and light intensities and patterns.

Point Method

The point method, or inverse square method, is based on luminaire or lamp candlepower and determines illuminance at a specific point or series of points that are intended to be lighted by more directional point sources (e.g., CMH PAR, HIR PAR, and HIR MR lamps); or to get an idea of the appropriateness of a focused downlight prior to setting up computer calculations. Figure 13.9 illustrates the point method relative to predicting maintained illuminance at a point on a horizontal surface (workplane or floor) and Figure 13.10 illustrates the method relative to a point on a vertical plane (e.g., piece of artwork on a wall).

Interreflection is not taken into account in the point method as it is in the lumen method. Although the reflection from the artwork, for example, onto the floor surface might result in a relatively small amount of light reaching the floor, counting on this interreflection can reduce initial hardware purchases and, thus, reduce lamp replacement and energy use over time. So, the point method should be used to get an idea of a lamp/luminaire's likelihood of meeting criteria, but final layouts should be based on computer software that includes the effects of interreflections.

The point method is particularly accurate for exterior lighting and for interiors with walls and ceilings finished in very low reflectances.

Digital Predictions

As noted previously in 13.1/Digital Renderings, quite a few software programs are available for the analysis of design solutions. These programs not only offer the visualization tools discussed previously, but also include methods for calculating quantitative values. Quick prediction programs are available online at several manufacturers' websites to help the designer establish preliminary layouts and quantities. Confirm that the programs distributed for use on your computer are using accurate flux transfer or ray tracing techniques (which are more accurate and do require a fair amount of computer running

Design Tools

Figure 13.8

These room sections illustrate the dimensions that must be known in order to determine a room cavity ratio.

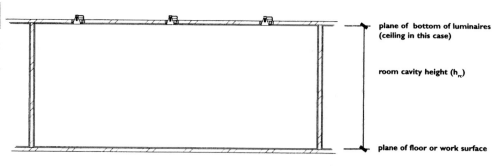

- plane of bottom of luminaires (ceiling in this case)
- room cavity height (h_{rc})
- plane of floor or work surface

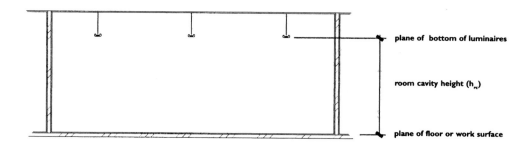

- plane of bottom of luminaires
- room cavity height (h_{rc})
- plane of floor or work surface

$$\text{the basic formula is} \quad RCR = \frac{2.5 * h_{rc} * \text{Room perimeter}}{\text{Room area}}$$

$$\text{for a rectangular room then} \quad RCR = \frac{2.5 * h_{rc} * (\text{length} + \text{width} + \text{length} + \text{width})}{\text{length} * \text{width}}$$

$$\text{which simplifies to} \quad RCR = \frac{5 * h_{rc} * (\text{length} + \text{width})}{\text{length} * \text{width}}$$

time) and not just computerized lumen method or point method techniques (which are less accurate). These programs should allow the designer to develop nonuniform, task- or area-specific lighting solutions that are more energy efficient and sustainable than uniform lighting systems stretching from room corner to room corner.

Because the computer spews forth reams of printed input and output data, computer calculations can easily eat trees. Attempt to be judicious in determining the calculations that should be printed out for review. Further, these reams of information give the false impression of flawless finality and degree of accuracy. First and foremost, the accuracy of computer calculations is limited by the accuracy of the input data—the luminaire photometry, the lamp lumen data, all of the RLLFs and NRLLFs, room surface reflectances, room geometry, partition factors, and the like need to be as accurate as is known at the time of the assessment. Second, as mentioned previously, the computer software may not be much more than simple hand calculation techniques put on a machine—this doesn't make the answer any more accurate. Third, the accuracy of any calculation technique is difficult to ascertain because measured light levels usually are, at best, within 10 to 20 percent, sometimes more, of calculated values. This is a result of light meter inaccuracies, voltage fluctuations on the lighting system, room surface reflectance variations, and so on.

Whenever computer calculations are made, the RLLF and NRLLF values discussed previously are applicable and need to be used. This is especially important when a third party (manufacturer or engineer, for example) runs computer calculations for the designer. Such

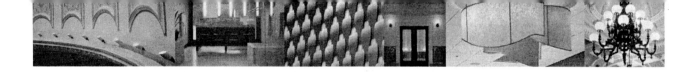

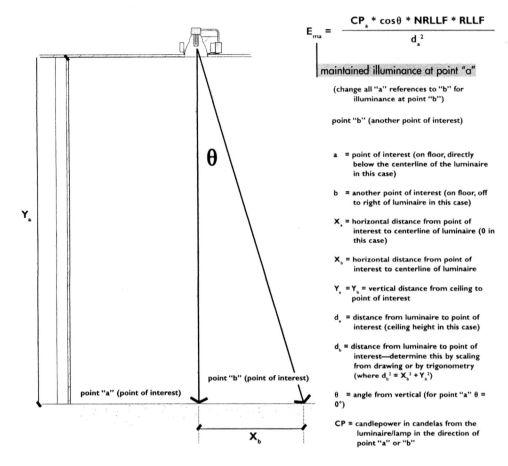

$$E_{ma} = \frac{CP_a * \cos\theta * NRLLF * RLLF}{d_a^2}$$

maintained illuminance at point "a"

(change all "a" references to "b" for illuminance at point "b")

point "b" (another point of interest)

a = point of interest (on floor, directly below the centerline of the luminaire in this case)

b = another point of interest (on floor, off to right of luminaire in this case)

X_a = horizontal distance from point of interest to centerline of luminaire (0 in this case)

X_b = horizontal distance from point of interest to centerline of luminaire

Y_a = Y_b = vertical distance from ceiling to point of interest

d_a = distance from luminaire to point of interest (ceiling height in this case)

d_b = distance from luminaire to point of interest—determine this by scaling from drawing or by trigonometry (where $d_b^2 = X_b^2 + Y_b^2$)

θ = angle from vertical (for point "a" θ = 0°)

CP = candlepower in candelas from the luminaire/lamp in the direction of point "a" or "b"

Figure 13.9

Illuminance at a point on a horizontal plane: Using the point method, also known as the inverse square method. Predicting illuminance at a point on a horizontal surface from a single luminaire.

third parties may use LLFs different from those reported in Table 13.3, may elect to use no LLFs or may only use selected LLFs. Room surface reflectance assumptions can significantly alter calculations. Many manufacturers and engineers have standardized on reflectances of 80 percent for ceilings, 50 percent for walls, and 20 percent for floors. These may not relate to actual design conditions and, therefore, calculations may be off by as much as 30 percent.

Computer calculations permit more detailed analyses more quickly of various lighting layouts, which can result in more efficient lighting applications. Lighting layouts need not be in a regular array of consistent spacing for computer analysis. Lighting can then be oriented according to task locations, according to subjective aspect requirements, or both.

Figure 13.11 illustrates some output examples of a hotel lobby lighting concept. AGi32 was used to look at the subtleties of uplighting exterior columns or not. Although the dynamic range of luminances is better perceived on the computer monitor, this printed copy expresses the difference between uplighting the exterior columns just outside the lobby window wall and not uplighting the columns. These techniques are helpful in convincing the designer and team members of the validity of proposed lighting concepts. Without the graphics, it is much too easy to have these lighting concepts dismissed because of cost.

Spreadsheets

Quantitative data extend beyond illuminance and luminances. Power budgets are another criterion that must be assessed. Some of the lighting software programs will also attempt to address power budgeting; however, these may not correctly track lamp wattage and BF (and, therefore, ballast wattage). As such, the designer must pull together a spreadsheet either by hand or by computer (e.g., Excel, Quattro Pro, Lotus 1•2•3, etc.)

Figure 13.10

Illuminance at a point on a vertical plane: Using the point method, also known as the inverse square method. Predicting illuminance at a point on a vertical surface from a single luminaire.

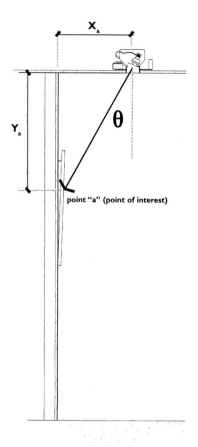

$$E_{ma} = \frac{CP_a * \sin\theta * NRLLF * RLLF}{d_a^2}$$

| maintained illuminance at point "a"

a = point of interest (at or just above centerline of artwork in this case)

X_a = horizontal distance from wall to centerline of luminaire

Y_a = vertical distance from ceiling to point of interest

d_a = distance from luminaire to point of interest—determine this by scaling from drawing or by trigonometry (where $d_a^2 = X_a^2 + Y_a^2$)

θ = aiming angle from vertical (straight down would be 0° while angle shown here is about 30°)

CP_a = candlepower in candelas from the luminaire/lamp in the direction of point "a"
Note: In this case, lamp is actually aimed in the correct orientation; hence be certain when interpreting candlepower data from manufacturer that the correct candlepower value is used.

outlining luminaire type, lamp, lamp wattage, transformer (for low voltage luminaires) wattage or ballast (for fluorescent and metal halide) wattage, number of lamps/ballasts per luminaire, and luminaire count in order to eventually tally total lighting wattage on a per room basis. Further, tracking the net square footage of each room is necessary in order to establish the power load (watts per square foot [per square meter]) that the design imposes on the building. This is then used to determine if the power budget criterion has been met. When the designed lighting load is equal to or less than the power budget criterion, then compliance is achieved. When the lighting load is greater than the power budget criterion, the design must be reworked to reach compliance. Figure 13.12 shows a spreadsheet outlining a series of indirect lighting systems analyzed for a specific open office project. This review covered several luminaire manufacturers and various indirect options from each manufacturer. Lamps and ballasts were also reviewed. Highlighted options were considered most promising relative to illuminance predictions versus illuminance criteria and relative to power budget and cost.

13.3 Endnotes

[1] IESNA Computer Committee, "2006 Lighting Software Directory," *Lighting Design + Application*, November 2006, 59–69.

[2] Mark S. Rea, ed., *The IESNA Lighting Handbook: Reference and Application*, Ninth Edition (New York: Illuminating Engineering Society of North America, 2000), pp. 9-28 to 9-46.

[3] IESNA Maintenance Committee, *IESNA/NALMCO Recommended Practice for Planned Indoor Lighting Maintenance* (New York: Illuminating Engineering Society of North America, 2003).

[4] Mark S. Rea, ed., *The IESNA Lighting Handbook: Reference and Application*, Ninth Edition (New York: Illuminating Engineering Society of North America, 2000), pp. 9-21 to 9-23.

[5] Mark S. Rea, ed., *The IESNA Lighting Handbook: Reference and Application*, Ninth Edition (New York: Illuminating Engineering Society of North America, 2000), pp. 9-35 to 9-44.

Figure 13.11

AGi32 was used to explore the differences, if any, in the view from a lobby to its exterior. Although these are relatively simple graphics, they helped the design team recommend uplights on the exterior columns. The top graphic shows columns lighted with CMH 39W/T6/G12 uplights along the left side of the interior "rendering." The bottom graphic shows the effect of no column lights. The uplights present a more inviting and visually interesting scene. Even though the columns are located physically outside of the lobby, they help define the outer edge of the lobby space.

Graphics ©GarySteffyLightingDesign

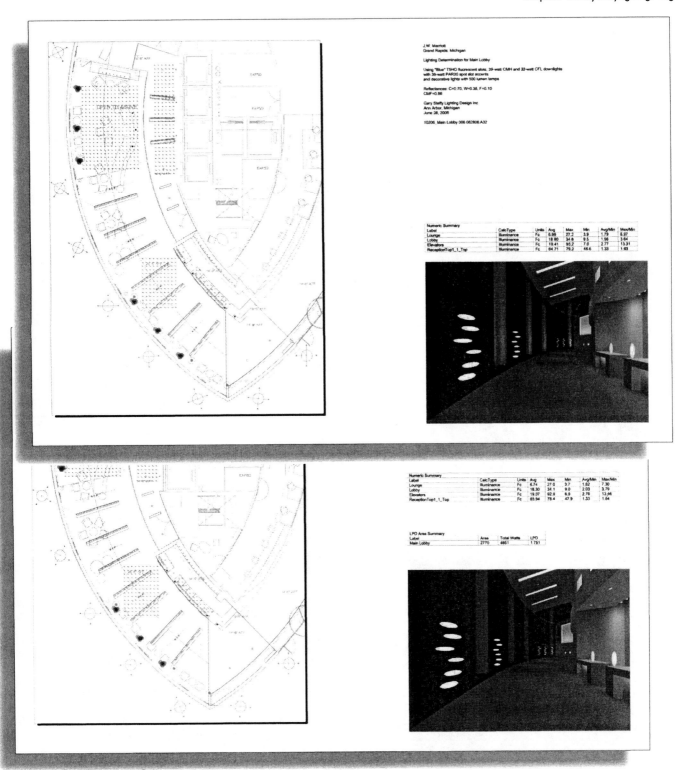

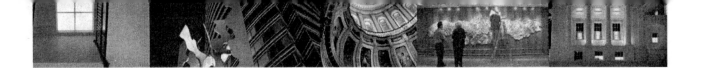

Figure 13.12

Indirect Lighting Systems Comparison: A spreadsheet is used to present various aspects on a number of indirect lighting systems. The highlighted luminaires were considered promising with the darker highlights recommended as best in meeting the criteria reviewed here.

Open Plan Lighting Review

Gary Steffy Lighting Design Inc.
Date inserted here
Filename inserted here

		Layout	Luminaire (FA)	Lamp	BF	Lamp Spec
1		Layout	Luminaire (FA)	Lamp	BF	Lamp Spec
2			(9' C.H./7' 4" to bottom of light)			
3			(2007 CMF ~ 0.86			
4						
5		Status Quo				
6	018	8 ft O.C.	1992 Peerless LD7 w/new lamp	1-T8	0.88	GE F32T8/XL
7						
8	017		2007 Peerless ENVISION	1-T8	0.88	GE F32T8/XL
9			ENM1-1-32-[FT]-[R4/R8/R12]-120-GEB10-[1SE/2SE/XSE]-[EL/EC]-[SCT/DCT]-LPGE¡			
10						
11	019		2007 Corelite Class A Indirect	1-T8	0.88	GE F32T8/XL
12			AI-S-N-1-T8-1-[C/E/B]-120-A-C-48-[T1/T9/TS]-[4/8/12]			
13						
14		More Light	(change ceiling reflectance)			
15	extrapolated	8 ft O.C.	2007 Peerless ENVISION	1-T8	0.88	GE F32T8/XL
16	from 017		ENM1-1-32-[FT]-[R4/R8/R12]-120-GEB10-[1SE/2SE/XSE]-[EL/EC]-[SCT/DCT]-LPGE¡			
17						
18	extrapolated		2007 Corelite Class A Indirect	1-T8	0.88	GE F32T8/XL
19	from 019		AI-S-N-1-T8-1-[C/E/B]-120-A-C-48-[T1/T9/TS]-[4/8/12]			
20						
21		More Light	(use high ballast factor ballast and high–light lamp)			
22	extrapolated	8 ft O.C.	2007 Peerless ENVISION	1-T8HL	1.15	GE F32T8/XL
23	from 017		ENM1-1-32-[FT]-[R4/R8/R12]-120-GE#49776-[1SE/2SE/XSE]-[EL/EC]-[SCT/DCT]-LP			
24						
25	extrapolated		2007 Corelite Class A Indirect	1-T8HL	1.15	GE F32T8/XL
26	from 019		AI-S-N-1-T8-1-[C/E/B]-120GE#49776-A-C-48-[T1/T9/TS]-[4/8/12]			
27						
28	031	10 ft O.C.	2007 Corelite as–designed w/new lamp and 7'-4" MH	2-T8	0.88	GE F32T8/XL
29			AB-W-E-2-T8-1-C-UNV-A-C-48-4			
30						
31	025		2007 Peerless ENVISION w/high BF and HL lamp	1-T8HL	1.15	GE F32T8/XL
32			ENM1-1-32-[FT]-[R4/R8/R12]-120-GE#49776-[1SE/2SE/XSE]-[EL/EC]-[SCT/DCT]-LP			
33						
34	extrapolated		2007 Peerless ENVISION w/high BF and HL lamp	1-T8HL	1.15	GE F32T8/XL
35	from 025		ENM1-1-32-[FT]-[R4/R8/R12]-120-GE#49776-[1SE/2SE/XSE]-[EL/EC]-[SCT/DCT]-LP			
36						
37	extrapolated		2007 Peerless ENVISION	1-T8	0.88	GE F32T8/XL
38	from 025		ENM1-1-32-[FT]-[R4/R8/R12]-120-GEB10-[1SE/2SE/XSE]-[EL/EC]-[SCT/DCT]-LPGE¡			
39						
40	extrapolated		2007 Peerless ENVISION w/1.0 BF	1-T8	1	GE F32T8/XL
41	from 025		ENM1-1-32-[FT]-[R4/R8/R12]-120-1.0BF-[1SE/2SE/XSE]-[EL/EC]-[SCT/DCT]-LPGE#:			
42						
43	028		2007 Corelite Class A Indirect	1-T8HL	1.15	GE F32T8/XL
44			AI-S-N-1-T8-1-[C/E/B]-120GE#49776-A-C-48-[T1/T9/TS]-[4/8/12]			
45						
46	extrapolated		2007 Corelite Class A Indirect	1-T8HL	1.15	GE F32T8/XL
47	from 028		AI-S-N-1-T8-1-[C/E/B]-120GE#49776-A-C-48-[T1/T9/TS]-[4/8/12]			
48						
49	024		2007 Peerless LDM	1-T5HE	1	GE F28W/T5/
50			LDM1-1-28T5-[FT]-[R4/R8/R12]-120-GEB10-[1SE/2SE/XSE]-[EL/EC]-[SCT/DCT]-LPG			
51						
52	026		2007 Peerless ENZO	1-T5HE	1	GE F28W/T5/
53			EZM1-1-28T5-SPR-[FT]-[R4/R8/R12]-120-GEB10-[1SE/2SE/XSE]-[EL/EC/EN]-[SCT/[			
54						
55	029		2007 Peerless Prima w/high BF and HL lamp	1-T8HL	1.15	GE F32T8/XL
56			PRM1-1-32-WHR-[FT]-[R4/R8/R12]-120-GE#49776-[1SE/2SE/XSE]-[EL/EC/EN]-[SCT			
57						
58	extrapolated		2007 Peerless Prima w/high BF and HL lamp	1-T8	1	GE F32T8/XL
59	from 029		PRM1-1-32-WHR-[FT]-[R4/R8/R12]-120-1.0BF-[1SE/2SE/XSE]-[EL/EC/EN]-[SCT/DC1			

	Rated Lamp Life (hours) (12 hours per start)	Reflectances Clg/Walls/Flr	Ills (fc) (PF ~ 0.65)	Ceiling Ratio (avg:min/max:min)	W/SF	Budget USD/linear ft	Leadtime (from approval)
B/XL/SPX35ECO (#27620)	29,000	80/40/20	36	1.8:1/3:1	0.85		not available
B/XL/SPX35ECO (#27620) PGE#27620-F1-24-C200-ACG-[Fuse]	29,000	80/40/20	36	1.9:1/3:1	0.85	35 (w/lamp)	3 to 5 weeks
B/XL/SPX35ECO (#27620)	29,000	80/40/20	39	1.9:1/2.7:1	0.85		
B/XL/SPX35ECO (#27620) PGE#27620-F1-24-C200-ACG-[Fuse]	29,000	90/40/20	39	1.9:1/3:1	0.85	35 (w/lamp)	3 to 5 weeks
B/XL/SPX35ECO (#27620)	29,000	90/40/20	42	1.9:1/2.7:1	0.85		
B/XL/SPX35/HLEC (#10326)]-LPGE#10326-F1-24-C200-ACG-[Fuse]	29,000	90/40/20	54	1.9:1/3:1	1.07	38 (w/lamp)	3 to 5 weeks
B/XL/SPX35/HLEC (#10326)	29,000	90/40/20	58	1.9:1/2.7:1	1.07		
B/XL/SPX35ECO (#27620)	29,000	80/40/20	70	2.5:1/5.8:1	1.44		
B/XL/SPX35/HLEC (#10326)]-LPGE#10326-F1-24-C200-ACG-[Fuse]	29,000	90/40/20	45	2:1/3.7:1	0.86	38 (w/lamp)	3 to 5 weeks
B/XL/SPX35/HLEC (#10326)]-LPGE#10326-F1-24-C200-ACG-[Fuse]	29,000	80/40/20	41	2:1/3.7:1	0.86	38 (w/lamp)	3 to 5 weeks
B/XL/SPX35ECO (#27620) PGE#27620-F1-24-C200-ACG-[Fuse]	29,000	90/40/20	33	2:1/3.7:1	0.71	35 (w/lamp)	3 to 5 weeks
B/XL/SPX35ECO (#27620) GE#27620-F1-24-C200-ACG-[Fuse]	29,000	90/40/20	37	2:1/3.7:1	0.73	36 (w/lamp)	3 to 5 weeks
B/XL/SPX35/HLEC (#10326)	29,000	90/40/20	47	2.1:1/3.4:1	0.86		
B/XL/SPX35/HLEC (#10326)	29,000	80/40/20	43	2.1:1/3.4:1	0.86		
/T5/835/ECO (#46705) -LPGE#46705-F1-24-C200-ACG-[Fuse]	36,000	90/40/20	36	1.5:1/2.2:1	0.73	45 w/lamp	3 to 5 weeks
/T5/835/ECO (#46705) CT/DCT]-LPGE#46705-F1-24-ACG-[Fuse]	36,000	90/40/20	35	1.9:1/3.8:1	0.73	33 w/lamp	3 to 5 weeks
B/XL/SPX35/HLEC (#10326) [SCT/DCT]-LPGE#10326-F1-24-ACG-[Fuse]	29,000	90/40/20	47	1.9:1/3.9:1	0.86	36 (w/lamp)	3 to 5 weeks
B/XL/SPX35ECO (#27620) /DCT]-LPGE#27620-F1-24-ACG-[Fuse]	29,000	90/40/20	39	1.9:1/3.9:1	0.73	34 (w/lamp)	3 to 5 weeks

Design Tools

As design progresses, designers prepare concept sketches of proposed lighting details and develop reflected ceiling plans (RCPs) showing lighting layouts. From this and other information, contract documents are prepared by the registered design professionals. Contract documents typically contain detailed, dimensioned, and accurate architectural reflected ceiling plans, elevations, sections, details, specifications, and cutsheets needed to convey design information to a contractor(s). During the construction administration process, contract documents will also include shop drawings. Any particular project is only as good as its contract documents. Typically, the reflected ceiling plans contain information indicating the luminaire type or designation, the luminaire location and/or spacing, and, if necessary, the luminaire orientation or direction of light throw. See Figure 12.7 for an example.

Elevations and sections are shown for lighting purposes when luminaires are floor- or wall-mounted or have a unique profile or inner optical characteristic that must be illustrated. These elevations and sections can be particularly useful in conveying ADA-compliance aspects.

Details are used to convey the exact architectural dimensions and construction parameters necessary for a particular luminaire or lighting effect.

Specifications are, perhaps, the most critical aspect of any lighting design because they outline some of the expected duties of the contractor; indicate specific lamp, ballast, transformer, and luminaire requirements; and cite applicable industry standards and code references.

14.1 RCPs

Reflected ceiling plans are so named because they are a mirror-image (reflected) view of the ceiling. Imagine that you are looking down onto a mirror inserted as a plane about 4' (about 1.2 m) above the floor, and the luminaires and various ceiling elements are all visible in this mirror. This view constitutes a reflected ceiling plan.

Figure 12.7 shows a reflected ceiling plan for a hotel project. Figures 14.1 and 14.2 illustrate a full lighting plan drawing which uses the architectural reflected ceiling plan as background. Note that luminaires are tagged or typed for easy cross reference to the specification. This type designation is usually located adjacent to each luminaire or series of luminaires (whichever is clearest). Where luminaires are intended to be centered in ceiling tile, it is not necessary to give luminaire dimensions, although notational references periodically throughout the plan may help avoid any misunderstanding since grid backgrounds (particularly in CAD) might move during final design documentation. For drywall ceilings, dimensions to all luminaires are usually necessary. Where luminaire dimensions from walls and/or other luminaires are quite repetitive, such can be noted without showing all dimensions repetitively. In any event, the contractor should be directed not to scale dimensions from drawings since drawing reproduction may have actually shrunk or expanded the actual inked plan somewhat. The lighting designer should be given an opportunity to review the final reflected ceiling plans that the registered professionals developed to confirm that the lighting intent remains intact.

To develop reflected ceiling plans, the designer needs to know equipment locations, spacings, and focus or aiming directions (if applicable). Symbols are needed to provide a cohesive indication of specific luminaires throughout a project.

CAD

CAD, or computer-aided design, refers to the method of recording a design in plan, elevation, and, perhaps, 3-D electronic files. These electronic files can then be transmitted easily to other team members and/or can be plotted to paper for distribution.

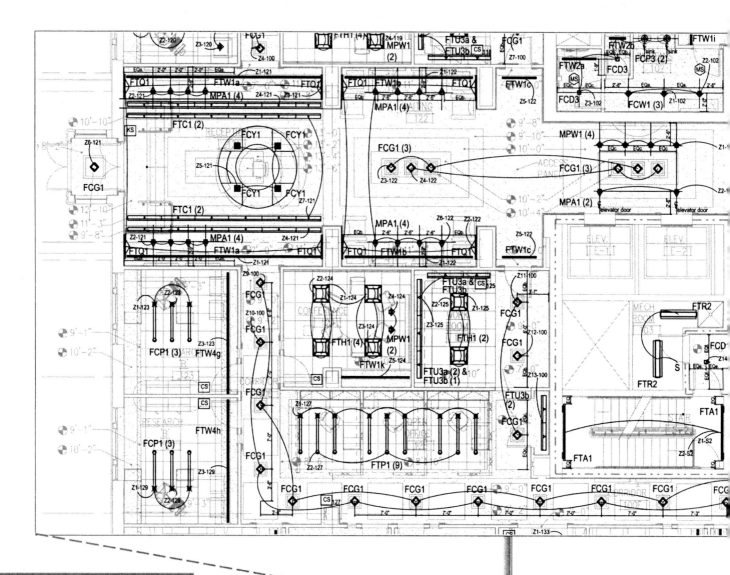

Figure 14.1

The lighting plan for a financial services firm was overlaid on the reflected ceiling plan on a 24″ by 36″ sheet and issued as a lighting design plan. A close-up excerpt is shown here and with annotations in Figure 14.2. These plans show luminaire types and specific locations. Control zone information is also shown along with control keypads. Lights are grouped based on function, appearance, lighting effects, and a preconceived plan on how they can be switched or dimmed on/off to create various scenes. Here, the scenes are used for visual task requirements as well as after-hours setback.

Reflected ceiling lighting plan ©GarySteffyLightingDesign courtesy Catalyst Development and Eckert Wordell.

Architectural Lighting Design

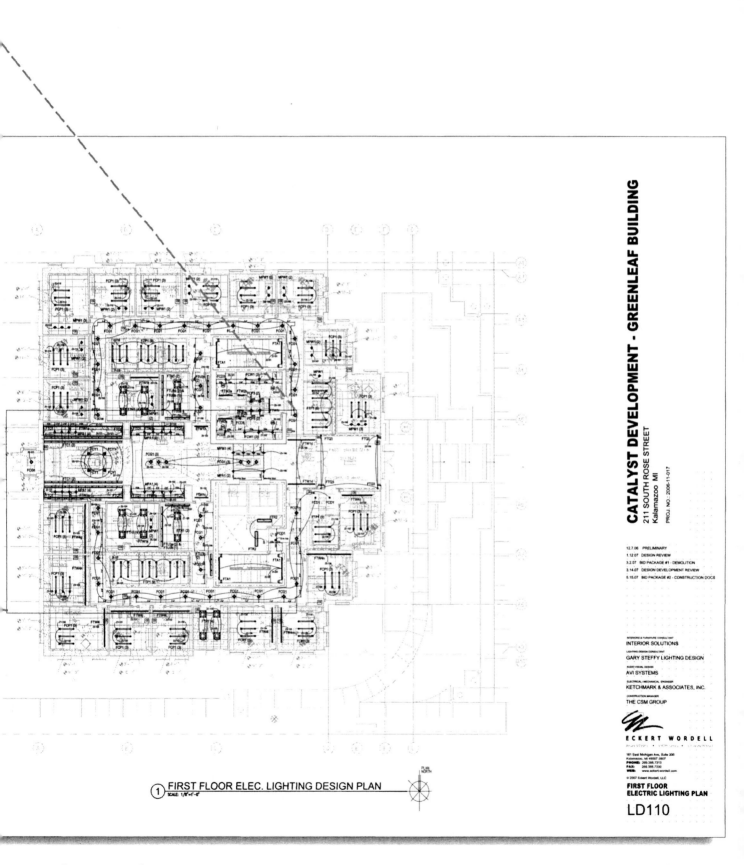

CATALYST DEVELOPMENT - GREENLEAF BUILDING

211 SOUTH ROSE STREET
Kalamazoo MI

PROJ. NO.: 2006-11-017

12.7.06   PRELIMINARY
1.12.07   DESIGN REVIEW
3.2.07   BID PACKAGE #1 - DEMOLITION
3.14.07   DESIGN DEVELOPMENT REVIEW
5.15.07   BID PACKAGE #2 - CONSTRUCTION DOCS

INTERIORS & FURNITURE CONSULTANT
INTERIOR SOLUTIONS

LIGHTING DESIGN CONSULTANT
GARY STEFFY LIGHTING DESIGN

AUDIO VISUAL DESIGN
AVI SYSTEMS

ELECTRICAL / MECHANICAL ENGINEER
KETCHMARK & ASSOCIATES, INC.

CONSTRUCTION MANAGER
THE CSM GROUP

ECKERT WORDELL

161 East Michigan Ave, Suite 200
Kalamazoo, MI 49007-3907
PHONE: 269.388.7313
FAX: 269.388.7330
WEB: www.eckert-wordell.com

© 2007 Eckert Wordell, LLC

FIRST FLOOR
ELECTRIC LIGHTING PLAN

LD110

1 FIRST FLOOR ELEC. LIGHTING DESIGN PLAN
SCALE: 1/8"=1'-0"

PLAN
NORTH

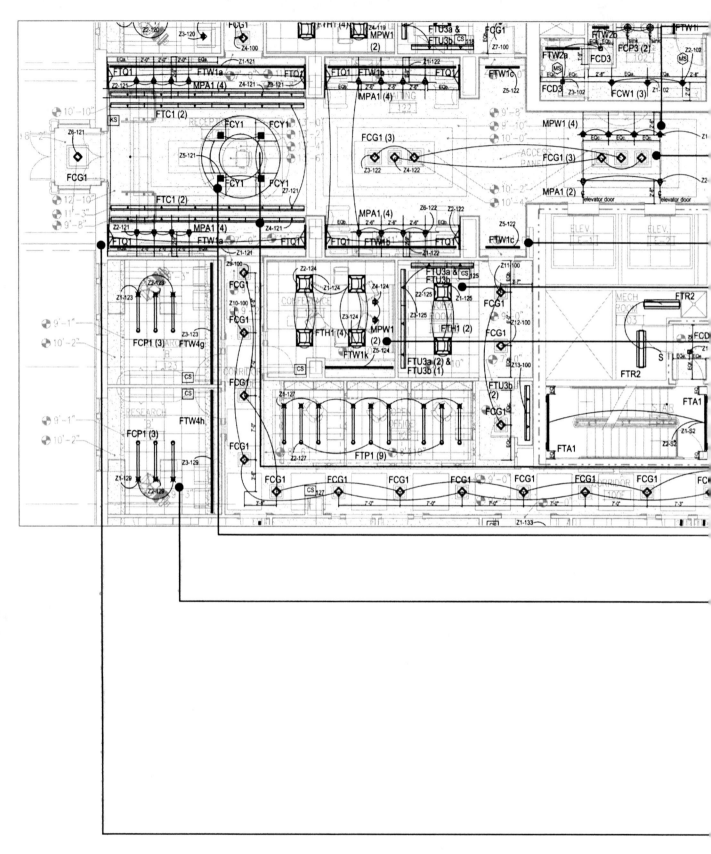

Figure 14.2

MPW1 = CMH wallwashers placed in stepped drywall ceiling detail and speced equally about the centerline of elevator doors. Show distance from wall and indicate on-center spacing. "EQc" tells installer to establish 3 equal spacings. So, if elevator doors are 9' (about 2.75 m) on center, the MPW1 lights will be placed 3' (about 1 m) on center. Since exact locations and dimensions of major architectural features (in this case centerline of elevator door to centerline of elevator door) may shift during construction or may be an inconvenient measure (e.g., 8' 10¾"), it is best to allow the spacing of the MPW1 lights to simply be defined as 3 equal spaces centered on the elevator doors. Kurt Versen H8452-SC-CG-LPFR-277-F.

FCG1 = Custom CFL luminaire inset in drywall detailing. Architect develops drywall detail and exact positioning of custom luminaire within the detailing. Baldinger Lighting.

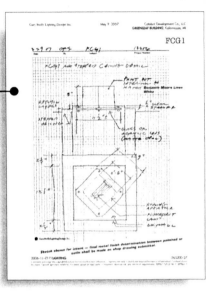

FTW1c = Linear fluorescent wall slot luminaire drawn to show length of lamp and approximate position of lamp relative to wall. Neoray 790S series.

FTH1 = 2' by 2' (600 mm by 600 mm) recessed fluorescent 4-sided "basket" luminaire in 2' by 2' modular lay-in ceiling. Focal Point FSK-22-B-T5-UNVB228PUNV115D-277-G-PS-FU-2SC/opposinglamps-WH. No dimensions shown because grid defines luminaire locations. Designer establishes grid layout (e.g., center grid in room leaving partial tiles around perimeter).

Or place grid to achieve optimal wallwash or accent luminaire positions. Here, MPW1 luminaires are centered in ceiling tile for best look, but also should be positioned about 2' 6" (750 mm) from wall being lighted for this particular luminaire to provide best wallwash effect in this room with a ceiling height of 8' 10" (about 2.7 m).

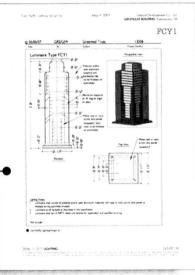

FTC1 = Linear fluorescent cove detail (see Figure 11.28 for similar detail). LiteControl CC-AI-25-1-23ft-T5-CWM-LPD/ELB/LutronECO10-1CWQ-F-277

FCY1 = Custom fluorescent columnaire (columnlike light on reception desk) shown relative to circular reception desk. These permanent luminaires are shown on the lighting plan. The Architect's final detailing of the reception desk will provide spacing dimensions. Baldinger Lighting.

FCP1 = Linear CFL slim indirect pendent luminaire shown relative to ceiling grid. Typically dimensions unnecessary unless suspension points are not to be centered in ceiling tile. Ceiling grid is laid out to position lights over desk zone to achieve an increased ambient illuminance at desk. Task lights (shown on a different plan) are specified for each desk to achieve criteria illuminance on work surface. Note how the lighting plan shows all architectural luminaires—reference to the specification is necessary to understand if lights are surface mounted, recessed, pendent mounted, millwork mounted, etc. Litecontrol P-1-02-14-T5-RAL9006-LP/ELB-1CWQ-F-WhiteStraightCord-FAI/ACC-277. Cutsheet ©Litecontrol.

FTQ1 = Custom fluorescent sconce centered on millwork detail developed by Architect (because dimensions are shown on Architect's detail they are not shown here on the lighting plan). Baldinger Lighting.

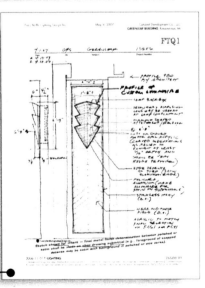

Figure 14.3

These are some lighting symbols (plan-view graphic representations) for a variety of ceiling recessed, small aperture luminaires. A wall (in plan) is represented to the near left for reference orientation on wallwash luminaires and adjustable accents. Where adjustable accents are shown, if the aiming orientation is known, the arrow should be directed in that specific direction.

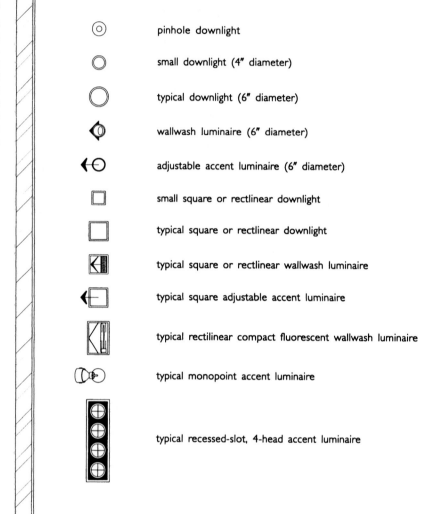

⊙	pinhole downlight
○	small downlight (4″ diameter)
○	typical downlight (6″ diameter)
◖	wallwash luminaire (6″ diameter)
◀○	adjustable accent luminaire (6″ diameter)
□	small square or rectlinear downlight
□	typical square or rectlinear downlight
◁	typical square or rectlinear wallwash luminaire
◀	typical square adjustable accent luminaire
	typical rectilinear compact fluorescent wallwash luminaire
	typical monopoint accent luminaire
	typical recessed-slot, 4-head accent luminaire

The ANSI standards for lighting symbols are devoid of "visual content"—with a very limited palette of lighting options. To make drawings more meaningful at initial glance to both designers and contractors, a more diverse and realistic representation of luminaires is suggested. Figures 12.7, 14.1, 14.2 14.3, 14.4, and 14.5 illustrate various possible luminaire symbols. Such symbols are appropriate for the architectural and electrical reflected ceiling plans that typically are used to show lighting, and/or can be used on separate lighting plans that are referenced by the architectural and electrical reflected ceiling plans. These symbols are entered in CAD databases as templates and then drawn to scale on reflected ceiling plans.

14.2 Details

The concept details developed during design development (discussed in Section 11.8) now must be finalized. The lighting designer should confirm exact dimensions required of the detail. The registered professionals then need to identify appropriate supports, connections, integration details, materials, and finishes and finalize the de-

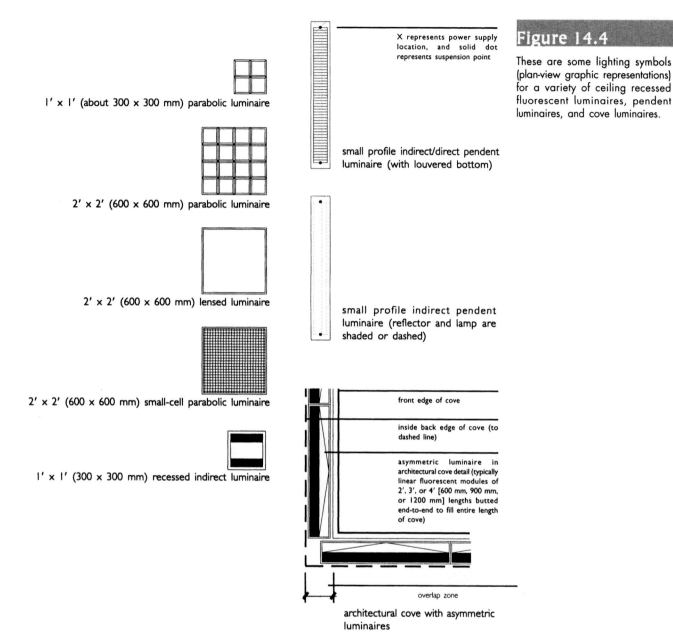

1' x 1' (about 300 x 300 mm) parabolic luminaire

2' x 2' (600 x 600 mm) parabolic luminaire

2' x 2' (600 x 600 mm) lensed luminaire

2' x 2' (600 x 600 mm) small-cell parabolic luminaire

1' x 1' (300 x 300 mm) recessed indirect luminaire

X represents power supply location, and solid dot represents suspension point

small profile indirect/direct pendent luminaire (with louvered bottom)

small profile indirect pendent luminaire (reflector and lamp are shaded or dashed)

front edge of cove

inside back edge of cove (to dashed line)

asymmetric luminaire in architectural cove detail (typically linear fluorescent modules of 2', 3', or 4' [600 mm, 900 mm, or 1200 mm] lengths butted end-to-end to fill entire length of cove)

overlap zone

architectural cove with asymmetric luminaires

Figure 14.4

These are some lighting symbols (plan-view graphic representations) for a variety of ceiling recessed fluorescent luminaires, pendent luminaires, and cove luminaires.

tails accordingly. The lighting designer should be given an opportunity to review these final details to confirm that the lighting intent remains intact given the actual construction detail requirements developed by the registered professionals.

14.3 Specifications

Lighting specifications are the backbone of any successful lighting project. Specifications should be just that—specific, detailed descriptions of the work to be done and citation of a specific manufacturer's or several specific manufacturers' hardware that the lighting designer/specifier has deemed capable of meeting the project lighting criteria. The designer has an implicit, if not explicit, understanding with the client to assimilate the client's criteria, prioritize that criteria (since it is very unlikely that all

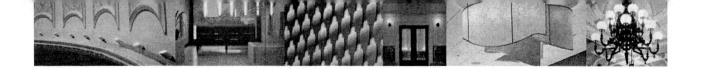

Figure 14.5

These are some lighting symbols (plan-view graphic representations) for a variety of wall sconce and wallslot luminaires. A wall (in plan) is represented to the far left for reference orientation.

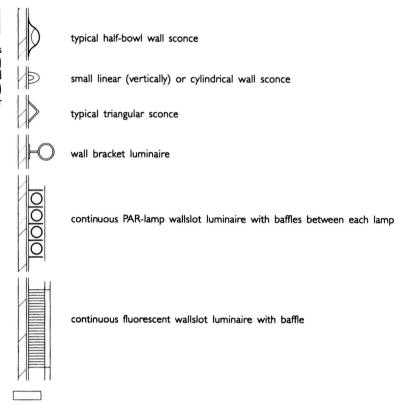

typical half-bowl wall sconce

small linear (vertically) or cylindrical wall sconce

typical triangular sconce

wall bracket luminaire

continuous PAR-lamp wallslot luminaire with baffles between each lamp

continuous fluorescent wallslot luminaire with baffle

criteria can always be met), analyze solutions to best meet that criteria, and lay out and specify those solutions. As such, the specification, along with drawings, becomes a legal document. Therefore, it must be drafted carefully, reviewed with the project team, presented to the registered professionals (if the lighting designer is not also the architect or electrical engineer on the project), released to the contractors, and used as a resource during bidding, shop drawing review, and construction.

The seed for a good specification is not how well one writes or how many details are outlined in lamp and luminaire descriptions. The integrity of the lighting design solution sets the stage for the integrity of the specification. Extensive review of hardware alternatives, and review of interior and/or exterior architectural and task requirements, energy and other building code requirements, lighting calculations and analyses of various solutions, and integration of the lighting with other building systems constitute the lighting design—a task demanding the entire design team's attention. If any one or several of these aspects are not addressed or are only briefly considered, then the lighting specification will represent a weak design—one that can be called to question with little or no rebuttal and enabling contractors, distributors, lighting reps, and even the client to make substitutions with no substantiation of their own and, more importantly, with little or no refutation by the lighting designer. After all, if little design preparation went into the lighting layout and specification, then little rationale will exist for that layout and specification. As such, little defense can be made when others challenge that layout and specification.

Before writing a specification then, a solid design must be developed. During a robust design process, sufficient information becomes available regarding the lamp, ballast, and luminaire requirements necessary to meet project criteria. This information should be documented clearly and in detail in the specification so that others may understand what equipment needs to be purchased and installed in order to achieve the anticipated results. Table 8.1 (in Chapter 8) outlines a checklist of issues or elements that should be considered for inclusion in the specification of luminaires.

A good specification outlines the expected duties of the contractor, sometimes above and beyond the general standard of care and practice expected from a licensed electrician. Further, a good specification outlines all of the lighting equipment required for a complete project that is expected to meet lighting criteria developed and agreed upon by the design team. A good specification never cedes equipment selection to contractors or distributors unless it has been determined that *any* selection will meet criteria. This is an important point and a key distinction between specifications and design guidelines. In final specifications, using such terms as "or equal" or simply listing five, ten, or fifteen manufacturers with no catalog numbers for various luminaire designations (unless custom equipment is involved, in which case no catalogic exists) is simply shirking design responsibility. No client should accept such work as that of professionals—indeed, such work should be viewed skeptically since it will be unclear how much, if any, design work the designer performed to substantiate layouts and hardware selections.

Specification snippets are interspersed throughout the text—in rather great detail at the ends of Chapters 5 and 10. Specifications should include only those requirements with which the designer is comfortable, familiar, and willing to uphold, and may be as long or as short as desired and/or necessary to convey the designer's requirements. Ultimately, however, a project's success depends on the integrity of the design and of the specification of that design.

more online @
www.csinet.org/s_csi/index.asp

14.4 Cutsheets

The lighting specification should also include cutsheets of the various luminaires specified (many such examples are shown throughout this text). This allows the other team members, the client, and the contractor(s) to understand appearance, size, and photometric characteristics of the luminaires. Cutsheets also help the contractor better understand the lighting equipment that will be purchased and installed. This is an effort to limit misunderstanding or confusion on the luminaires and their attributes.

Cutsheets are copyrighted documents. Reproduction is restricted. Most manufacturers have come to realize that in order for other team members, contractors, lighting reps, and distributors to clearly understand what is being specified on any given project, cutsheets need to accompany the specification. Nevertheless, the specification, as well as tags on the cutsheets, should clearly indicate this material is for purposes of understanding and quoting the specified product—it is not to be copied or circulated for purposes of seeking substitutions or knockoffs.

14.5 Review

The lighting designer may be asked to review the architect's and/or electrical engineer's lighting plans to confirm that lights were not erroneously moved around, deleted, or types changed. Sometimes components, such as structure, sprinklers, HVAC ducts, and the like, require lights to be rearranged. The designer should confirm that these rearrangements do not significantly alter the lighting intent. The registered professionals then issues a complete set of construction documents to contractors for bidding. Once a contractor is awarded the bid, construction gets underway. Throughout this process of issuing construction documents, awarding the bid, and commencing construction, the lighting designer may be called upon for assistance. For purposes of this text, these activities make up the Construction Administration Phase, or simply Construction.

14.6 Bids

During the bidding process, questions may arise from contractors and/or electrical distributors about lighting hardware, lamping, and potential substitutions. At or near the end of bidding, the lighting designer may be asked to review the lighting bids or may be asked to defend the cost of the lighting bids. This is when the process can get dicey. Knowledge and/or expectations are important here. To understand the steps involved in pricing, a review of team member responsibilities and some backtracking to how lighting design gets done are necessary.

14.7 Client

The client has the ultimate authority on how any project is specified. Indeed, the client quite likely will direct the team to specify certain products, develop certain details, and/or provide certain layouts based on the client's own experiences or desires. However, design aspects affecting life safety or compliance with codes or ordinances are the responsibility of the registered professionals on the team and/or of the building authorities that have jurisdiction in the municipality of the project. The client has a responsibility to know and understand the lighting purchasing chain, an example of which is shown in Figure 14.6. The client also has the ultimate authority on decisions regarding bid awards, substitutions, and what ultimately gets done on a project.

14.8 Knowledge

Some designers are also buyers and sellers of lighting equipment. Manufacturers' representatives may have design support. Electrical distributors may have design departments. Luminaire manufacturers may have design or application groups. Construction managers and contractors may have in-house design consultants. Apparently value engineers like to portray themselves as lighting experts. In each case and for most projects, these potential construction team members may, therefore, bring some or a lot of lighting knowledge to the party, but many times with a specific angle of interest. Any team member, regardless of affiliation or independence, can offer the client some degree of lighting knowledge integrity by subscribing to the NCQLP *Standard of Conduct*. The *Standard* outlines standards of performance, education, confidentiality, disclosure, courtesy, and professional representation aspects that encourage professional conduct and continuing education. NCQLP-certified individuals are expected to conduct themselves according to these standards. Clients would be well advised to use Lighting Certified (LC) individuals. Students are encouraged to pursue this certifica-

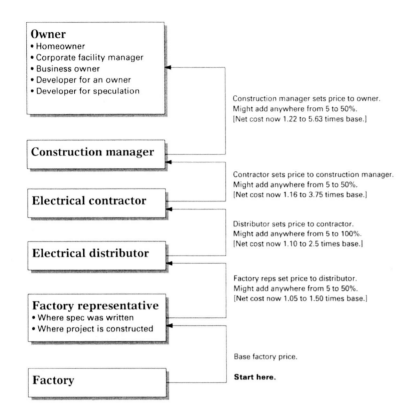

Owner
- Homeowner
- Corporate facility manager
- Business owner
- Developer for an owner
- Developer for speculation

Construction manager

Construction manager sets price to owner.
Might add anywhere from 5 to 50%.
[Net cost now 1.22 to 5.63 times base.]

Electrical contractor

Contractor sets price to construction manager.
Might add anywhere from 5 to 50%.
[Net cost now 1.16 to 3.75 times base.]

Electrical distributor

Distributor sets price to contractor.
Might add anywhere from 5 to 100%.
[Net cost now 1.10 to 2.5 times base.]

Factory representative
- Where spec was written
- Where project is constructed

Factory reps set price to distributor.
Might add anywhere from 5 to 50%.
[Net cost now 1.05 to 1.50 times base.]

Base factory price.

Start here.

Factory

Figure 14.6

A flow chart illustrating the possible, and for most projects the likely, purchasing chain for lighting equipment. Start at the "Factory" (bottom). Each link in the chain results in a cost markup on the original base price. Clients should endeavor to select a construction team that agrees to a reasonable markup in each link. This is a paradigm shift in dealing with costs. Most projects elect to cheapen the originally specified equipment to get a lower base factory price. However, this is not where the greatest markup in cost occurs. Hence, even cheap products might continue to cost the owner quite a bit more than the base factory price.

tion—one that identifies an individual's level of lighting knowledge. Note the distinction. LC relates to one's knowledge level, not to one's practice level or to one's design capabilities. Since so many people are involved in the chain of lighting specification, purchasing, distribution, and installation, and since lighting so significantly influences energy use and users' comfort and productivity, the lighting community established the NCQLP and the LC certification to set a required level of knowledge for all involved in lighting. Hence, the public's better interests are served by lighting designers, representatives, distributors, installers, and maintainers who are certified to this common level of lighting knowledge, and who therefore are more likely to operate in unison to deliver and maintain efficient, comfortable lighting installations to the public.

more online a
www.ncqlp.org/

14.9 Designer's Role

It is incumbent upon the lighting designer to diligently address lighting criteria, including understanding and reviewing budget information. The designer must be in a position to help the client fully appreciate the lighting criteria at stake and the attendant costs. Leading the charge on the users' issues—ergonomics (physiology of lighting) and psychology of lighting while simultaneously monitoring costs (both initial and operational). Further, reminding others of the purpose for the building project can yield greater appreciation for the need to adhere to original lighting criteria and original lighting design recommendations. To these ends, the designer must develop a good lighting specification and uphold it throughout the project duration.

14.10 Lighting Reps

The lighting representative can be the lighting designer's best friend or worst enemy. Good reps will keep the designer informed of new products, product technical or leadtime problems, and product updates. Good reps will have or be able to get, in short order, answers to technical, pricing, and leadtime questions, and be able to provide working samples. The lighting designer should view working samples of luminaires intended to be used in a specification. Graphic representations can be very misleading.

Lighting reps can be instrumental in helping the designer hold a specification. Alternatively, lighting reps can substitute a specification quite readily. Know the reps. Copy the reps with specifications for projects prior to any bidding. Include cover notes indicating that the rep is being copied with the specification as a courtesy (reps make commission only on those projects for which they "register" with the factory—a copy of the designer's specification facilitates this registration process). Further, ask the rep to review the specification and confirm catalog numbers (perhaps you've transposed some numbers or letters, catalog numbers have changed recently, or the product has been discontinued, etc.), and to provide DN pricing and leadtime for the specified equipment for which he/she is a rep. Advise the rep that you are not seeking any alternatives or substitutions (unless, of course, you are). Finally, advise the rep of the actual project location. Since reps have territories of coverage, your project may be outside of his/her territory. In this event, the rep must notify the rep responsible for the particular locale in which the project is located. Hopefully, your local rep will advise the distant rep that no substitutions are being sought. It is very easy for folks to get greedy. The distant rep may elect to try to get the whole lighting order! In this situation, he/she would have to substitute all of his/her products wherever you have specified other manufacturers' products. Clearly, the rep is now making design decisions and, ultimately, changing the legal aspects of the project's chain of responsible parties. This easily escalates into a situation where every other rep whose products are in the specification will also likely attempt to substitute the entire project with his/her specific brands. Ultimately, the client ends up "holding the bag," with lighting equipment that doesn't precisely meet the original design intent—perhaps missing some key programming requirements and/ or design aspects that the team labored over for months.

This aspect of substitutions has become rampant over the past decade. Consolidation in the lighting industry has led to three or four conglomerates. Each conglomerate has commodified most lighting equipment and, thereby, believes that its products are as good or bad as those of the competition. To boost the bottom line, each conglomerate encourages its reps and distributors to "package" lighting projects—pull together a complete package of products that are what the conglomerate believes to be equal to the originally specified equipment. In reality, each conglomerate has strong products and weak products. By mixing and matching on any given project, the designer can put together a complete design specification that will meet most, if not all, of the client's needs most, if not all, of the time. Allowing substitutions will simply mean most of the criteria won't be met most of the time. The user ultimately suffers.

14.11 DN Budget

DN budget pricing should be sought for lighting on all projects. This is the budget pricing the manufacturers' lighting representatives propose for their respectively specified lighting equipment. Various scenarios have been proposed, most notably by lighting designer

Randy Burkett.[1] The designer provides the various lighting representatives of the specified manufacturers with a copy of the specification and a request that the manufacturers' representatives review the specification of their respective products for accuracy and to establish DN budget pricing. The reference to accuracy is important to ensure that the catalog numbering has not changed recently and/or that the designer has properly and accurately interpreted the catalog information. DN budget pricing is the price that the representative will likely quote to a creditworthy electrical distributor for the kinds and quantities of equipment specified. Nevertheless, this "DN budget price" is typically 10 to 15 percent higher than actual pricing—confirm with your lighting representatives what kinds of markups they have included in their budgeting. Remember, inflation and/or simple raw material price costs may fluctuate by at least that much between now and the time the contractor actually purchases the lighting hardware (which may be months away). **Advisory:** It is imperative to ask for and receive DN pricing. Contractor pricing, distributor list pricing, and consumer list pricing (also known as "list pricing") may be grossly inflated to cover the vagaries of industry markups and purchasing chain agents. Even the difference between the DN budget pricing and the final bid DN pricing can confound the designers and clients. It is crucial to seek clarity from reps about what quotes they are providing (DN pricing or DN budget pricing). For DN budget pricing, it is imperative to understand the percentage of "slop" involved.

14.12 VE

Value engineering was introduced to the building design and construction process in the early 1970s. Initially, its noble goal was to offer the client a project with measurable value. At the time, a series of magazine articles on lighting warned of consequences if value engineering failed to account also for the more subjective (and immeasurable) qualitative aspects of building design.[2] Today, value engineering (VE) simply means cost cutting. There will be fancy arguments and spins on VE and "what it can do for the client." Since some VE arrangements offer the value engineer a percentage of the costs saved, there is extraordinary pressure to save costs at most any cost! Initial cost is reduced at the sacrifice of qualitative aspects and/or at the sacrifice of future operations' costs. Qualitative aspects include aesthetics, but more critically include subjective aspects, such as occupant attitude, well-being, and motivation. All of these elements drive productivity (in a work environment) and comfort (in a living environment) and, ultimately, should establish life cycle payback. Ironically, as energy criteria and talks of sustainability (building projects for the "long haul" that stand the test of time and make great living and working environments) require finely honed solutions, VE simply overlooks these aspects in an effort to drive initial cost budgets downward. Clients often will be left with little more than vapid, uniformly and dimly lighted drywall boxes—not much of a value! The question is this: How can a partial team (value engineers) enter a project; spend little, if any, time on understanding the programming; have little, if any, interaction with the design team and client/owner and/or users during the design process; and propose effective solutions that will meet all of the same criteria and design issues as the proposed design? The answer: It can't!

14.13 Shop Drawings

Shop drawings are issued during construction by the contractor if he/she wants the design team to confirm that he/she is procuring the correct equipment. It is also an opportunity to ensure that all of the specification information has been correctly interpreted by the contractor, distributor, and manufacturer. Finally, it is one last check to confirm that the specification was originally submitted with correct catalog designations.

It is the contractor's responsibility to determine if shop drawings will even be a part of the process and, if so, how, when, and to which team members they will be distributed. The contractor should distribute shop drawings to the registered professionals who, in turn, must decide if any of the project consultants will be asked to offer review comments. These review comments must then be considered by the registered professionals and either ignored or addressed accordingly.

Reputable contractors will use the shop drawing process to be certain that the specification was interpreted correctly, and that no technology, manufacturing, or cataloging changes have taken place since the original specification was written. Shop drawings also may help the contractor better understand installation or identify installation issues.

Less reputable contractors will "sit on the shop drawings" as a tactic to force the design team to accept substitutions. To minimize the unnecessary hassle of incompetently made substitutions, the designer should qualify the specification to indicate that the contractor shall incur the cost of fees required for the design team to review, calculate, assess, and, if accepted as a substitute, revise plans. After all, the client hired a professional team for its professional expertise and opinions, and hired the contractor to execute those opinions.

The lighting designer, if given the opportunity and part of the work scope, must review shop drawings carefully and quickly to assure correct and timely procurement. However, it is the contractor's responsibility to secure shop drawings from the manufacturers through the electrical distributor and then to submit these shop drawings to the registered professional architect or engineer on the project. The registered professional is responsible for final authority on shop drawing approval. The lighting designer's role is to confirm that the lighting equipment represented by the shop drawings will meet the lighting design intent—aesthetic appearance of the luminaire, aesthetic effect of the light from the luminaire, and light intensity from the luminaire. Typical disposition of shop drawings by the lighting designer includes: approved; approved as noted; approved as changed; not approved for reasons noted; or no substitutions accepted. Having indicated the recommended disposition of the shop drawings, the lighting designer should then sign and date them, and forward them to the registered professional(s).

A note of "approved" indicates that the lighting hardware shown on the shop drawing appears to meet the aesthetic qualities of the luminaire as specified, the aesthetic qualities of the lighting effect anticipated from the luminaire as specified, and the intensity requirements of the luminaire as specified. A note of "approved as noted" indicates that some notations have been made by the lighting designer. For example, if the luminaire was originally specified as "Polar White" in color, but the shop drawing indicates the color is "Winter White," a notation that the "Painted finish shall be Polar White as originally specified"

would be appropriate. Another example, if a fluorescent striplight was specified with one lamp but the shop drawing shows two lamps, it would be noted that the "Luminaire shall use one (1) lamp in cross-section as originally specified."

Sometimes some subtle (and hopefully simple) changes to lighting equipment are desired. For example, as construction progresses, the team may decide that the reflector cones on downlights will look better with other building hardware finishes if the cones are diffuse aluminum rather than specular aluminum. After confirming with the lighting rep that such a change would not affect the cost or leadtime of the luminaire, or that any additional cost and/or leadtime is acceptable with the client and contractor, then an "approved as changed" note like, "Luminaire reflector shall be diffuse aluminum, with a catalog designation of XXX-XX" is appropriate (where XXX-XX is the actual catalog number for the now-desired diffuse aluminum reflector).

Where the shop drawing has significant errors, these errors should be cited along with a note of "not approved for reasons noted." This will typically result in resubmittal of lighting shop drawings so noted in order to confirm that the errors have been corrected.

If a shop drawing illustrates the wrong luminaire entirely or is a substitution attempt, then noting that "no substitutions accepted" will suffice. Shop drawing resubmittal will then occur with, hopefully, the as-specified luminaire shown.

14.14 Assistance

The designer should be prepared to assist the team as questions arise from the field. This may even necessitate a few visits to the project site. There will be times when, regardless of the effort that went into the systems' integration and planning, one trade's work will interfere with another trade's work. Lighting is bound to be one of those trades. So, a luminaire may have to be moved 6" (about 150 mm) to avoid interference with a duct, sprinkler, structural element, or water line, etc. that's already installed and is presumably immovable. Conversely, lighting may need to influence the location of a duct, beam, or pipe, etc., if the luminaire's location is important for either the correct lighting effect, the correct symmetry of ceiling layout, or both. Clearly, this sort of effort must be team-based, because registered professionals need to assess the impact of any such interferences and resulting moves.

14.15 Review

The designer is not a qualified inspector of installation, but the project, near its completion, should be reviewed for lighting effects and luminaire finishes, fit, and alignment as they relate to the visual aesthetics of the lighting effects and the lighting hardware that is exposed to view. This constitutes a lighting review. Where luminaire finishes are marred or incorrect, these need to be corrected by the electrical and/or general contractor. Until the project is turned over to and accepted by the owner, the project is itself the contractors' responsibility. Excuses of "it was damaged in shipment" or "no one knows how it got that way" do not release the contractor from providing a complete and satisfactory project to the owner. Any lighting effects or luminaire finishes or layouts that are incorrect and/ or damaged should be noted by the lighting designer and passed along to the

registered professional(s) for his/her (their) consideration as a punchlist item (a formal record of final work and adjustments that the contractor needs to make prior to final owner acceptance of the installation). It is important to note that inspection of the physical installation aspects (e.g., how are lights mechanically secured, how are electrical connections made, is the circuit of sufficient size to handle the lighting loads, etc.) are not the responsibility of the lighting designer, but rather are part of the contractor's work, the registered professional(s) work, and the work of municipal building inspectors.

Wherever adjustable lights are specified, it is the contractor's responsibility to aim such lights under the design team's observation. This may necessitate the architect, engineer, and/or designer visiting the project site very near the time that the project is turned over to the client or owner and observing the contractor during aiming sessions. Where aiming is rather consistent, aiming observation may only require a few sample setups that the contractor then replicates. Other projects, with extensive accents aimed onto varying sized elements and details, may take days (and/or nights) of aiming observation. In any event, the contractor has the responsibility of providing all of the necessary equipment (lifts, ladders, and scaffolds), tools (for locking lights once aimed), and crews for the aiming.

14.16 Commissioning

Depending on the fee structure and scope of work agreed upon, as well as the degree of complexity of the lighting system and controls, commissioning of the installation may be appropriate. This might involve a commissioning consultant or agent and/or the respective manufacturer's commissioning or technical representative and/or may involve all or some of the team members, including the registered professional(s), the lighting designer, possibly the lighting representatives, the client, and perhaps the users and/or the client's maintenance personnel. Commissioning is a "first run" of the lighting. Final aiming tweaks and/or control tweaks may be made at this stage. If motion sensors, photocells, timers, and/or other control mechanisms are used, this is the time to finalize their respective sensitive settings, output/input settings, and instruction to the client's authorized personnel on their operation and programming.

14.17 Post Occupancy

This is a much-discussed, little-implemented phase of the work. It must be the last phase because it occurs after some period of facility occupancy. The intent, of course, is to understand how successful the project was at meeting the program criteria and how successful the program criteria were in establishing a comfortable, productive, and satisfactory environment. While some small, informal evaluation can be done by the design team, so many variables are involved in actual environments that a professional team of experts (typically researchers) need to be retained for meaningful results.

14.18 Endnotes

[1] Randy Burkett, "Building Quality Lighting Specifications," *Architectural Lighting*, April/May, 1999, 74–78.
[2] John Flynn, "The Psychology of Light, Article 8, The Scope of 'Value Engineering' in Lighting Design," *Electrical Consultant*, August, 1973, 20–25.